The Law of Business Organizations

THIRD EDITION

The Law of Business Organizations

John E. Moye

WEST PUBLISHING COMPANY
St. Paul   New York   Los Angeles   San Francisco

Text Design: Lucy Lesiak Design
Copyediting: Cheryl Drivdahl
Composition: Carlisle Communications, Ltd.

COPYRIGHT ©1974, 1982   By WEST PUBLISHING COMPANY
COPYRIGHT ©1989   By WEST PUBLISHING COMPANY
                        50 W. Kellogg Boulevard
                        P.O. Box 64526
                        St. Paul, MN 55164-1003

All rights reserved

Printed in the United States of America

96 95 94 93 92 91   8 7 6 5 4 3

Library of Congress Cataloging-in-Publication Data

Moye, John E.
    The law of business organizations / John E. Moye.—3rd ed.
       p.   cm.
    Includes index.
    ISBN 0-314-47359-9
    1. Corporation law—United States.   2. Partnership—United States.
I. Title.
KF1366.M68   1989
346.73'066—dc19
[347.30666]
                                              88-37303
                                                  CIP

To Fern

"*And, finally, to my wife, my love and appreciation for her understanding and critical insights, without whom this project would never have been accomplished.*"

• •

Drawing by Koren; © 1988
The New Yorker Magazine, Inc.

CONTENTS

Preface xi
Acknowledgments xv

1 SOLE PROPRIETORSHIP 1
Characteristics of a Sole Proprietorship 1
Liability of the Sole Proprietor 2
Termination upon Death of the Proprietor 2
Taxation of a Sole Proprietorship 3
Formation and Operation of a Sole Proprietorship 3

2 GENERAL PARTNERSHIP 5
Characteristics of a Partnership 5
Partnership Property 6
Partner's Interest in a Partnership 9
Management of a Partnership 10
Profits and Losses 12
Liability of Partners 15
Dissolution and Termination of a Partnership 16
Tax Considerations of a General Partnership 21
Formation and Operation of a General Partnership 23

3 LIMITED PARTNERSHIP 46
Characteristics of a Limited Partnership 46
General Partners of a Limited Partnership 47
Limited Liability and Contributions 48
Management and Control 49
Admission, Substitution, and Withdrawal of a Limited Partner 50
Dissolution of a Limited Partnership 51
Taxation of a Limited Partnership 53
Formation and Operation of a Limited Partnership 54

4 BUSINESS CORPORATION 68
Entity Characteristics of a Corporation 68
Statutory Powers of a Corporation 70
Ownership and Management of a Corporation 74
Limited Liability 87
Continuity of Existence and Dissolution 89
Taxation of a Corporation 89

5 SPECIAL CORPORATE FORMS 98
Close Corporations 98
Professional Corporations 102

6 FORMATION OF A CORPORATION 109
Preincorporation Responsibility 109
Preincorporation Share Subscriptions 110
Selection of Jurisdiction 112
Selection and Reservation of Corporate Name 113
The Articles of Incorporation 116
Filing and Other Formalities 134
Corporate Existence 134
Formalities after Formation of a Corporation 135
By-laws 136

7 CORPORATE FINANCIAL STRUCTURE 153
Generally 153
Types of Corporate Securities 153
Equity Securities 155
Stages of Equity Securities 155
Par Value or No Par Value 156
Certificates for Shares 158
Classifications of Shares 159
Fractions of Shares or Scrip 163
Consideration for Shares 163
Common Stock Rights 165
Preferred Stock Rights 166
Transfer Agents 176
Debt Securities 177
Types of Corporate Debt Securities 178
Trust Indenture 181
Common Provisions in Debt Securities 181
Important Considerations Regarding Debt and Equity 183

8 CORPORATE MEETINGS 188
Types of Purposes of Meetings 188
Requirement for Organizational Meetings 188

Directors' Organizational Meeting   *189*
Incorporators' Organizational Meeting   *190*
Business Conducted at Organizational Meetings   *190*
Directors' Regular and Special Meetings   *205*
Shareholder Meetings   *208*
Shareholder Business and Vote Required   *216*
Action without a Meeting   *223*
Minutes   *225*

9 CORPORATE DIVIDENDS AND OTHER DISTRIBUTIONS   *229*
Types of Corporate Distributions   *229*
Sources of Funds for Distribution   *230*
Cash and Property Dividends   *233*
Share Dividends   *237*
Stock Splits   *239*
Corporation's Purchase of Its Own Shares   *241*
Partial Liquidations   *244*
Dissolution and Liquidation   *245*

10 AGENTS, EMPLOYMENT, AND COMPENSATION   *247*
Agency   *247*
Employment Agreements   *254*
Restrictive and Proprietary Covenants   *263*
Employer's Right to Employee Work Product   *264*
Trade Secret Protection   *267*
Covenants Not to Compete   *268*
Incentive Compensation Plans   *272*
Deferred Compensation   *273*
Pension and Profit Sharing Plans   *276*
Incentive Stock Options   *282*
Insurance Programs   *289*
Employee Expense Reimbursement Plans   *290*

11 AGREEMENTS REGARDING SHARE OWNERSHIP   *298*
Purposes and Legal Support   *298*
Concentration of Voting Power   *299*
Share Transfer Restrictions and Buy-out Agreements   *304*

12 CORPORATIONS IN FOREIGN JURISDICTIONS   *327*
Selection of Jurisdiction   *327*
Constititional Basis for Qualification   *327*
Authorization to Qualify as a Foreign Corporation   *328*
Statutory Prohibition from Doing Business without Qualification   *328*

Transacting Business *329*
Sanctions for Not Qualifying *331*
Application for Certificate of Authority *331*
Certificate of Authority *335*
Effect of Qualification *335*
Structural Changes of a Foreign Corporation *337*
Withdrawal of Authority *339*
Revocation of Certificate of Authority *340*

13 CHANGES IN CORPORATE STRUCTURE AND DISSOLUTION *342*

Amendment of the Articles of Incorporation *342*
Merger, Consolidation, and Exchange *346*
Sale, Mortgage, or Other Disposition of Assets *354*
Rights of Dissenting Shareholders *357*
Voluntary Dissolution *361*
Involuntary Dissolution *364*
Liquidation *366*

APPENDICES

A THE UNIFORM PARTNERSHIP ACT *371*
B UNIFORM LIMITED PARTNERSHIP ACT *381*
C REVISED UNIFORM LIMITED PARTNERSHIP ACT, 1976, WITH 1985 AMENDMENTS *387*
D REVISED MODEL BUSINESS CORPORATION ACT *399*
E MODEL STATUTORY CLOSE CORPORATION SUPPLEMENT *447*
F MODEL PROFESSIONAL CORPORATION SUPPLEMENT (1984) *455*
G FORMS *463*

INDEX *657*

PREFACE

I have had the pleasure of practicing corporate law and of teaching various law school classes and practice seminars for lawyers on the subject of business organizations. I also taught one of the pioneer paralegal courses in business organizations under the auspices of the Continuing Legal Education Program of the University of Denver College of Law. This book orginally began as a paralegal textbook and was used in paralegal training courses. It was also used in several law schools and by practitioners who taught other lawyers in continuing legal education courses. This third edition is a greatly expanded version of the materials developed for all of those courses, improved through the helpful comments and suggestions of the now-experienced paralegals and lawyers who attended or taught those classes and through my own experiences in counseling clients since the second edition was completed. These materials are directed toward the training and practice of paralegals and lawyers in organizing, drafting, operating, and providing service to business organizations.

The book is designed to be used in two environments. In the first place it is intended to be used as a classroom teaching source for the training of paralegals and lawyers in the practical aspects of the law of business organizations. It also qualifies as a reference work to be used by paraprofessionals and attorneys in the practice of this field. It is probably best described as a how-to-do-it approach to the law, with an explanation of the legal principles that must be observed in counseling an enterprise. Numerous sample clauses and forms are sprinkled throughout the text to illustrate the legal rules described; procedural checklists are included for study and client contact; and sample forms from various states and reference form books are used. The textual treatment of the law is designed to introduce or review the important legal topics to be considered in the drafting techniques, organization, development, and operation of an enterprise. A student reading this text should study the explanation of the law, compare the wording in the sample clauses and forms, suggest drafting variations based upon the law or upon different facts, and observe the application of the law in its practical setting. A practicing paralegal or lawyer should apply the explanations of the law and the drafting examples to client variations in practice. To facilitate the use of sample forms and clauses in the preparation of assignments and documents, separate indexes are included for these materials.

With the exception of the sole proprietorship, business organizations are founded upon statutory authority. To ensure national application of this book, the textual explanation of the law is based upon the Uniform Partnership Act, the Revised Uniform Limited Partnership Act, and the Model Business Corporation Act.

The new Close Corporation Supplement and the Model Professional Corporation Act are now discussed in this third edition. Both the Uniform Limited Partnership Act and the Model Business Corporation Act have been extensively revised during the past fourteen years (since the first edition of this book), and the text discusses both the revisions and the former approaches of the statutes, since most states' laws continue to be based upon the prerevision statutes. The revised organization and modern corporate concepts of the new Model Business Corporation Act are included as the basis of the corporate statutory rules. Important jurisdictional variations from these statutes are noted in footnotes in many cases, but you are continually cautioned to analyze the appropriate state law in practice.

The uniform and model acts are set forth in Appendixes A to E. A student should refer to the acts to become acquainted with statutory authority underlying the law as explained in the text. A practicing paraprofessional or lawyer may compare these acts with local statutes to highlight variations and to recognize additional local requirements.

The breadth of the law of business organizations necessarily results in cursory treatment of some complex principles in a book of this size. I have attempted to refer you to more detailed texts, particularly in matters of taxation and certain tangential matters such as estate planning for the sole proprietor. The laws of the registration and regulation of securities under the federal securities acts and state blue-sky laws are certainly intimately connected with these materials, but they constitute a separate subject which deserves its own book. Accordingly, I have merely mentioned them in the appropriate places, with references to other treatises for further explanation.

The book begins with the most simple form of business enterprise, the sole proprietorship; progresses through general partnership and limited partnership; and dwells upon the most complex business organization, the corporation. Chapter 5 separately considers problems of special corporate variations—the close corporation and professional corporations. Other hybrid forms of business enterprise, such as joint ventures and joint stock associations, are not covered, partly because of space limitations, partly because of their infrequent appearance in practice, and partly because they may be explained in classroom discussion and are so identifiable with the described organizations that they may be easily comprehended.

Chapters 1, 2 and 3 contain discussions of frequently encountered problems in the organization and operation of sole proprietorships and partnerships, including procedures for the formation and operation of the business, characteristics of the enterprise, liabilities of the associated parties, taxation, dissolution, and termination. The materials on limited partnerships are based on the Revised Uniform Limited Partnership Act, as amended in 1985, with references to differences contained in the prior uniform acts, which are still the sources of most states' laws. Since most jurisdictions are considering the revisions for adoption, the law of limited partnerships will soon be consistent with the approach described in this text.

The corporate materials are arranged somewhat chronologically as they usually will be met in practice. Following the identification of the intracorporate parties and a general discussion of the characteristics, powers, continuity, and taxation of the corporation (including the latest tax revision), the remaining chapters consider formation procedures, development of the corporate financial structure, corporate meetings, dividends and corporate distributions, agreements affecting employment and share ownership, qualification and operation as a foreign corporation, modifications to the corporate structure, and dissolution. Of course, matters involving shareholder agreements may arise in the formation stages, and some may assert that a discussion of liquidation distributions belongs with the discussion of dissolution. The material is all cross-referenced by footnotes for easy organization and understanding among the chapters.

The materials covering formation of the corporation, corporate meetings, and shareholder agreements have been considerably expanded in this edition to illustrate variations in corporate practice and to provide more forms and checklists to use in preparing corporate documents for the client.

The placement and content of Chapter 10 on employment and compensation deserve special comment. Serveral users of the second edition suggested that it would be helpful to have a general discussion of the law of agency as a backdrop to explain the relationship of the people who operate business organizations. The first section of the chapter now provides an overview of the relationships of principals and agents. The chapter appears in the corporate section of the book because it involves agreements that will be executed with key employees in corporate practice, and the discussions on pension and profit sharing plans, stock options, and insurance programs are almost exclusively corporate in nature. However, the remaining sections, and particularly the discussion of agency law in the first section, are equally applicable to sole proprietorships and partnerships. In class discussion, it may be appropriate to study some or all of the interchangeable sections when discussing proprietorships and partnerships, and to remind students of their applicability to corporations when the unique corporate compensation schemes are considered.

Chapter 13 contains a brief discussion of new statutes and concepts relating to hostile takeovers and the special protection of minority shareholders in corporate dissolutions. The general background and terms that are becoming popular in these areas of corporate practice are discussed in the text; classroom discussion could expand on these areas for advanced students.

Having incorporated suggestions from the various teachers, practitioners, and students who have used the first and second editions of this book, I am confident that this third edition covers the important areas of enterprise practice. I commend it to you with the hope that I have created a usable manual for the practice of the law of business organizations.

John E. Moye
Denver, Colorado

ACKNOWLEDGMENTS

I wish to express gratitude to some very special people who contributed significantly to the preparation of this work.

First I thank my partners at Moye, Giles, O'Keefe, Vermeire and Gorrell for giving me the professional support and encouragement I needed to take the time to work on this book. I also thank Jackie Goetchius, our corporate paralegal at the firm, for her excellence and proficiency in the practice of business organizations, much of which she will recognize in some of the forms and checklists used in the book.

I gratefully acknowledge the contributions of other authors, government officials, and corporate personnel for the forms and checklists used as examples. I thank West Publishing Company for the use of its Modern Legal Forms volumes to illustrate sample clauses and agreements throughout the book. The secretaries of state for California, Colorado, Delaware, Iowa, Massachusetts, Mississippi, New Jersey, New York, North Dakota, Oregon, Pennsylvania, South Carolina, South Dakota, and Texas permitted the use of official forms for their respective states. Professor Harry G. Henn of the Cornell Law School allowed the reprint of his Preincorporation Checklist from his unexcelled works on corporations, which I studied at Cornell to learn the law of business organizations. The Committee on Economics of Law Practice of the American Bar Association permitted the reproduction of an excellent sample partnership agreement from a previous publication. I thank Prentice-Hall, Inc., Bradford-Robinson Printing Company, the University of Florida Law Review, and author Sidney A. Ward for granting permission to use their corporate materials as examples. Special thanks are due to Louis S. Kelley of the Black Hills Power and Light Company; Mr. Richard F. Atwood, general counsel for the Coca-Cola Company; Mr. William Lee Phyfe of American Telephone and Telegraph Company; and Mr. Thomas F. Macan of General Motors Corporation for their assistance in obtaining sample corporate agreements, share certificates, and bonds for publication.

I am indebted and grateful to Glenna McKelvy, my secretary, and Dee Zenz and Sharon Sevedge of my law firm's word processing staff for their dedication in the preparation and typing of the manuscript.

Last, but certainly not least, I thank my many friends and associates who appear as characters in the sample clauses throughout the book. Their assent to join the cast of business personalities in the various transactions adds a flavor of realism and is sincerely appreciated.

1 SOLE PROPRIETORSHIP

CHARACTERISTICS OF A SOLE PROPRIETORSHIP

The sole proprietorship or individual proprietorship is the simplest and most common form of business enterprise. In the sole proprietorship organization, the individual proprietor owns all business properties and carries on business as sole owner. The typical individual proprietor is a merchant in a small retail store or corner grocery, but even a youngster who mows lawns during summer vacation is an individual proprietor. The distinguishing characteristic of the sole proprietorship is that it is owned and managed by one person, and thereby exists as an extension of the personal life of that person. The single owner operating the business as an individual activity is a key element. If the business is conducted by co-owners, it is most likely a partnership. Unlike the corporation, a sole proprietorship requires no grant or charter from the state to exist as a going concern.

The greatest advantages to a sole proprietorship are the ease by which it may be formed and the degree of flexibility in managing the business. As sole owner, the individual proprietor may operate the business as he or she chooses. While the owner may hire employees and agents to assist in the operation of the business, he or she is vested with ultimate responsibility for all decisions affecting the business. Consequently, management is usually flexible and informal.

The disadvantages of the sole proprietorship all flow from the fact that the business has complete identity with the proprietor. As a practical matter, this individual's personal strengths and weaknesses are, necessarily, superimposed upon the business operations. Since management functions are vested in the proprietor, the proprietor's management ability will have a direct effect on the success or failure of the business. That alone may explain why sole proprietorships are most frequently used for small limited businesses. The larger the scope of a business, the more that organization requires specialized business talent that few individuals could supply alone. Similarly, the identity of the individual with the business limits available business capital, and may thereby limit the size of the business. Unlike a corporation, the sole proprietorship has no shares which can be sold to outside investors. The only available methods of obtaining funds for this form of business are personal contributions of the individual proprietor and loans from financial institutions or other private sources. Further, the proprietor's ability to borrow money is limited by the potential of the business and the extent of the proprietor's personal assets, which may have to be pledged as collateral to secure a loan.

LIABILITY OF THE SOLE PROPRIETOR

The law also imposes certain disadvantages on the sole proprietorship, again equating the identity of the proprietor with the business. The proprietor is personally responsible for all business losses and must bear them to the full extent of available personal resources. The proprietor is personally liable for all business liabilities. In contrast with a corporate shareholder or a limited partner, a proprietor carries a financial risk that is not limited to his or her investment in the enterprise but extends to all personal assets, including the proprietor's home, car, furniture, and similar property. This risk of unlimited liability may be diminished to some extent by insurance, but it may be impossible, and is at least impracticable, to insure against every conceivable business hazard. In matters involving contracts with the sole proprietorship, it is possible to provide by agreement that any liability on the contract shall be limited to the business assets and shall not extend to the personal assets of the proprietor. Such an agreement will provide little advantage, however, if the proprietor has contributed personal assets for use in the business or as collateral to secure business loans.

The unlimited liability of a sole proprietorship may be a severe disadvantage to an entrepreneur with extensive personal wealth which would preferably not be subjected to the risks of the business, since absent insurance or agreement to the contrary, all personal assets must be made available to satisfy business liabilities. The problem is further compounded if the business is unusually speculative or hazardous.

On the other hand, the individual proprietor has full control over the extent of the business liability by virtue of his or her individual right to manage the business. While the law permits all partners to obligate a partnership and the officers to obligate a corporation, only the proprietor, or individuals personally selected by the proprietor, may obligate the sole proprietorship.

TERMINATION UPON DEATH OF THE PROPRIETOR

With very few exceptions specifically authorized by state statutes,[1] the sole proprietorship terminates by law upon the death of the proprietor. The owner is entitled to will the business to relatives or to an employee, but there is no assurance of continuity of the business after death. If the owner managed the business, and there are no relatives or associates willing to continue, the business will probably be liquidated. Liquidation must be accomplished by a legal representative of the deceased owner, such as a trustee or an executor, and cannot be done by agents appointed by the owner during the owner's lifetime since, with the exception of a few ministerial acts authorized by specific statutes,[2] agents are powerless to act after the death of their principal. Because the business will be included in the personal estate of the deceased owner, a number of estate-planning considerations for the sole proprietor become essential. Generally, some authority must be granted to the proprietor's personal representatives to permit them to continue the business as necessary until it may be conveniently and profitably liquidated, to employ persons to assist in liquidation, and to execute all necessary documents incident to liquidation.[3] If the beneficiary of the deceased owner is willing to continue the business, a new sole proprietorship is created and it will be governed by these same rules.

TAXATION OF A SOLE PROPRIETORSHIP

The federal and state laws regarding taxation of a sole proprietorship may constitute an advantage in some cases. The law provides that all business income or loss will be treated as individual income or loss and taxed accordingly. The sole proprietor declares the business income on a separate schedule of an individual tax return. Once total income, including business income or loss, is computed, the individual income tax rates are applied. If the business is small and the owner has little income from other sources, the individual tax rates as applied to income from a sole proprietorship may be significantly lower than corporate tax rates. Similarly, if the business operates at a loss, the loss will be applied directly to offset other active personal income of the sole proprietor, and will thereby result in direct tax savings.

Federal and state taxing authorities frequently change their tax rates for individuals and corporations to place greater burdens on or produce more desirable tax advantages for various business enterprises. For many years, certain individual tax rates were lower than corporate rates for small amounts of income. Recently, the federal government has increased the corporate rates so an individual's taxable income is taxed at a lower rate than is a corporation's taxable income. Selection of a particular business entity requires careful tax planning to ensure that the income earned by the business will be taxed at rates that are not surprising to the owners. Effective business managers use the tax on income as a planning tool for determining both the sources of cash and the availability of deductions for predictable business expenses.

As a matter of tax planning, when individual rates are on a graduated basis so that they eventually reach or exceed corporate tax rates, it is possible to commence a business as a sole proprietorship to enjoy the lower tax rates or other tax benefits in the early stages of development, and to subsequently incorporate the business for more favorable tax rates as profits increase and as the graduated individual tax rates surpass the corporate rate. So long as the individual tax rates are less than the corporate rate, the tax incurred in a sole proprietorship will be less than the tax incurred in a corporation. Furthermore, corporate income may be subjected to *double taxation:* once as corporate income, and, if distributed as dividends to the shareholders, a second time as income to the shareholder.[4]

In addition to tax benefits, which are a major consideration, many other factors can be considered in selecting a form of business enterprise.

FORMATION AND OPERATION OF A SOLE PROPRIETORSHIP

Virtually no formalities are required in the formation and operation of a sole proprietorship, and this is a distinct advantage of this form of business over other forms. The sole proprietor may simply commence business by the exercise of initiative.

If the proprietor intends to sell goods, a sales tax license will be required in most jurisdictions. Any other license peculiar to the particular business must also be obtained. For example, doctors must be licensed to practice medicine, a liquor license is required to sell alcoholic beverages, and so forth.

If employees are contemplated, the sole proprietor must apply for a tax identification number from the Internal Revenue Service office and make arrangements to contribute to Social Security and unemployment compensation on behalf of the employees.

A sole proprietor may conduct business under a name other than his or her own, and state statutes usually require registration of an assumed name by the filing of an affidavit or certificate for that purpose with a public official. These statutes usually also provide that the name used cannot be the same as, or deceptively similar to, another registered or well-known name. The circumstances under which a particular name must be filed are subject to some fine distinctions. Generally, a firm name that contains the proprietor's surname and does not imply that other owners are associated with the business need not be registered. For example, Smith Auto Parts or Lyons Retail Goods should not require filing. On the other hand, the use of the word *Company* or *Associates* implies other owners and should be registered. In any questionable case, it is a good practice to register the name and avoid the problems associated with failure to file. Various penalties are prescribed for failure to register an assumed or trade name, but the usual sanction is refusal to allow the proprietor to pursue any litigation in state courts until filing has been accomplished. The filing procedure may vary by jurisdiction. Some states require a single filing with a county or state official. Others, such as California, require filing plus publication once a week for four weeks in a local newspaper. The appropriate statute should be consulted for guidance on local procedure.

Sole proprietorships are permitted to do business in more than one state without additional formalities for qualification to do business. Of course, local licensing and assumed name statutes must be observed.

The operation of a sole proprietorship is extremely flexible and personal to the individual. Governmental regulation of such a business is found only in licensing requirements and periodic reports that may be required for certain types of business. The individual proprietor will personally determine the complexity or simplicity of the business records, the need for expansion and capital improvements, salaries, and other matters affecting the policy and daily operations of the business. Compared with owners in other forms of business, the sole proprietor has considerable freedom in these matters.

NOTES

1. Some states provide statutory authority for the continuity of a sole proprietorship by a proper testamentary distribution. E.g., McKinney Consol. Laws of N.Y.S.C.P.A. § 2108.
2. E.g., a bank is authorized to continue to pay checks of a deceased sole proprietor after death under U.C.C. § 4–405 until the bank learns about the death and has a reasonable opportunity to act on it.
3. See C. Rohrlich, Organizing Corporate and Other Business Enterprises, § 13.02 (1967).
4. See Taxation of Corporation.

individual partners may be vulnerable to partnership obligations, the property should be clearly divided for operating purposes.

Partnership property is first acquired from contributions by the individual partners. Partners may contribute specific assets to the firm, such as land, buildings, furniture, or patents, and upon contribution the assets become partnership property. A partner may also contribute cash, which is used to purchase specific assets. The cash and the assets so purchased also become firm property. The Uniform Partnership Act provides that "unless the contrary intention appears, property acquired with partnership funds is partnership property."[7] It should also follow that property purchased on credit by the firm will be partnership property. For the most part, it is not difficult to ascertain which property has been purchased with firm funds, but it may be difficult to identify property that has been contributed to the partnership unless the partnership agreement accurately reflects the intention of the parties. If a court were asked to decide whether certain property belongs to the firm or to the individual partner, it would test the intention of the parties, as found in their agreement and other overt acts.

The best guide to the intention of the partners is their written agreement. Thus, a complete description and agreed value of the property partners contribute is essential to good drafting. It is normal practice to describe the property contributed in a separate schedule, which is attached to the partnership agreement and incorporated by reference.

> **EXAMPLE: Contribution of Property**
> Glenna McKelvy shall contribute certain property valued at Five thousand dollars ($5,000.00). Such property is described in Schedule A attached hereto.[8]

The contribution of property to the partnership may have certain tax consequences, which are explored in detail later.[9]

Just as it is important to accurately and thoroughly describe the property contributed to the partnership, it is also important to specify which property is merely "loaned" to the partnership for its use, with the intention of retaining title in the individual partner's name. A clause covering this point should also include the period of time the firm shall be permitted to use the property, unless indefinite; any restrictions on the owner that are desirable or necessary to ensure the use of the asset by the firm; and any compensation to be paid to the partner for the use of the asset.

> **EXAMPLE: Property Loaned to Partnership**
> Craig Carver, as the owner of one 1989 Chevrolet pick-up truck, agrees to contribute to the partnership the use of such truck, with the understanding that it shall remain his separate property, and not in any event become an asset of the partnership. It is agreed that until the termination of the partnership, or until the death of retirement of Craig Carver, he will not, without the consent of all other partners, sell, assign or pledge or mortgage such property. Craig Carver further agrees that any money or rights occurring from the sale or assignment of the truck shall belong to the partnership during the term of the operation of the partnership. For the purpose of computation of profits, and not for participation in the distribution of the assets, the sum of ten thousand dollars ($10,000.00) shall be included in Craig Carver's capital account to represent the value of the truck.[10]

Thus, for property contributed at the commencement of the partnership, the intent of the parties with respect to ownership may be clearly expressed in the agreement.

The Uniform Partnership Act assists in determining the partners' intentions with respect to property subsequently acquired by the firm. It was previously noted that the act creates a presumption that property purchased with partnership funds is firm property. Moreover, the firm may hold property in its own name. Nevertheless, it is common to title partnership property in the names of the individual partners. In such a case, the agreement should provide for this arrangement and indicate that the assets so titled are held as partnership property.

> **EXAMPLE: Title to Property**
> Partnership property (including real estate) may, by unanimous consent of the partners, be acquired and conveyed in the name of any partner or other person as nominee for the partnership. Such property shall be recorded as partnership property in the partnership accounts.[11]

In addition to the specific provisions in the agreement, with respect to partnership property, legal counsel should be sensitive to the need to provide other indicia of intent to determine ownership of the property. Partnership property should be identified in the firm's books, and all expenses, including repairs, insurance, taxes, interest on a mortgage, and so forth, should be paid by the firm. To be consistent, the firm should deduct these payments as expenses on its income tax return. Careful drafting and planning will avoid confusion regarding ownership of partnership property.

Assuming that a particular asset is partnership property and not individual property, the Uniform Partnership Act has adopted a peculiar method of legal title for such assets.

Historically, partners joined together as co-owners of a business, and most jurisdictions considered all assets to be owned jointly in an ownership classification known as *tenancy in common*. In the pure sense, tenancy in common, as its name indicates, stands for common ownership, with each owner entitled to a fraction of full title, and with each owner entitled to *partition,* or to sever his or her fractional ownership and assign or sell it to another. As the law of partnership developed, it modified this right of partition and imposed a limitation to the extent that partnership assets should first be used for partnership purposes (including satisfying obligations of the firm) and no partner should be able to otherwise alienate any fractional ownership until partnership purposes are satisfied.

The Uniform Partnership Act continues the theory that partners are co-owners of partnership property, but it creates a new ownership classification called *tenancy in partnership,*[12] which better conforms to the reality that a partnership is a commercial entity using its own property for business purposes. All partnership assets are held under this form of title, and while partners are said to be co-owners, they have very limited ownership rights. In general, a partner may not possess firm property for other than partnership purposes without the consent of the other partners; a partner may not sell firm property (or any fractional interest in such property) without the consent of the other partners; a partner's individual creditors cannot apply their claims against the partner to firm assets; and a partner's heirs have no interest in the partnership assets when the partner dies.

On the last point, note that the *surviving partners* are vested with the deceased partner's fractional ownership upon the partner's death. To be specific, suppose a three-person partnership owns a delivery truck that is used in the partnership's appliance business. No partner may use the truck to transport his or her family to a picnic without the other partners' consent. Similarly, all partners must agree to sell the truck; no single partner could sell his or her one-third interest in it. If one partner is being sued for a personal bill and refuses to pay, the creditor cannot use the truck to satisfy the judgment. Finally, if one partner dies, the truck belongs to the other two partners, and the deceased partner's heirs do not acquire the deceased partner's fractional ownership rights.

PARTNER'S INTEREST IN A PARTNERSHIP

It should be obvious that specific assets really belong to the firm, and not to the individual partners. However, each individual partner is entitled to an "interest in the partnership," which is best described as an intangible interest that includes a partner's proportionate share of the assets and that partner's proportionate share of the liabilities together with an interest in profits and rights to management. With respect to assets and liabilities, for example, if the hypothetical appliance partnership owned $100,000 in assets and owed $40,000 in liabilities, the total partnership interests would equal $60,000. If the partnership agreement provided that each partner shared equally, each partner's interest in the firm would be valued at $20,000. Thus, upon the death of one partner, the deceased partner's heirs would be entitled to that partner's interest in the firm, meaning they would have the right to be paid $20,000 from the two surviving partners. Similarly, any partner could assign his or her right to the $20,000 equity to any person outside the partnership who would be willing to purchase it.

The partner's interest in the partnership is initially determined by the partner's capital contribution to the firm. This is one reason a value must be assigned to the contributions in the agreement. Thereafter, additional capital contributions will increase the contributing partner's interest, and subsequent profits will also increase the partner's interests as they are distributed in the proportions specified in the agreement. Conversely, if a partner withdraws funds from the partnership, the interest will be reduced. To illustrate, suppose the partners in the appliance business began as follows: Smith contributed his delivery truck, valued at $5,000; Jones contributed $10,000 in cash to buy inventory and to lease a store; and Williams did not contribute tangible property but agreed to manage the store. The agreement provided that the partners will share equally in profits and losses. At that point, each partner's interest was equal to his or her contribution. Williams had no interest since she had yet to contribute anything. During the year, Smith contributed a cash register valued at $400 and Jones withdrew $500 in cash for personal reasons. At the end of the year, the business showed a profit of $3,000. The partners' respective interests in the partnership are now as follows: Smith's interest is $6,400, including the value of the truck and cash register, plus his share of profit; Jones's interest is $10,500, including his initial cash contribution, plus his profit, less his withdrawal; and Williams's interest is $1,000, all of which came from profit.

This intangible interest in the partnership is the partner's personal property right in the firm. It is considered to be a personal asset, which the partner owns just as one owns a home or other personal possessions. Consequently, this property interest will pass to the partner's heirs upon death, and may be reached by the partner's individual creditors for unpaid obligations. Similarly, a partner may assign this interest to an outsider and thereby confer his or her proportionate rights to profits and the value of the assets on the assignee.[13] Note that an assignment of a partner's interest in the firm does not make the assignee a partner, since no person may become a partner without the consent of all other partners.[14] Nor does the assignee acquire any right to interfere with the management of the business. The assignee's sole right is to receive the profits and assets to which the assigning partner is entitled.[15]

MANAGEMENT OF A PARTNERSHIP

Right to Manage

The right to manage and control the affairs of the partnership is governed by the Uniform Partnership Act and by the agreement of the partners. In the absence of an agreement to the contrary, all general partners have equal rights in the management and conduct of partnership business.[16] It is also possible (and perhaps desirable) to specify by agreement the specific management responsibilities and limitations for each partner.

Since each partner is an agent for the partnership, every act a partner performs on behalf of the firm must be an authorized act. Authority may come from specific provisions in the agreement itself, or from the vote of the partners in the manner specified in the agreement or by law. The Uniform Partnership Act provides that decisions regarding ordinary matters of partnership business are to be made by a majority vote of the partners.[17] Each partner, regardless of that partner's contribution or share of profits, will have one vote on such matters. Thus, under the statute, even though one partner has contributed 95% of the capital and is entitled to 95% of the profits, that partner will have an equal voice with the other partners in management matters.

If the statutory management scheme—that is, equal rights in management and rule by majority vote—is deemed desirable by the partners, a clause reciting this scheme should be included in the agreement.

> **EXAMPLE: Management**
> All partners shall have equal rights in the management of the partnership business. Decisions shall be by majority vote, each partner having one vote, except as otherwise provided in this Agreement.[18]

On the other hand, if not all partners will be actively engaged in the management of the business, it may be appropriate to appoint a managing partner or managing partners to control business affairs. In drafting such an appointment, it is good practice to specify the authority of the managing partners with reasonable detail and to provide a method for the resolution of disagreement between multiple managing partners.

> **EXAMPLE: Managing Partners**
> The management and control of the partnership business shall be vested in Fern Portnoy, James Lyons and Scott Charlton. Such managing partners shall have and are hereby given the sole power and authority:
> a) To contract and incur liabilities for and on behalf of the partnership.
> b) To borrow for and on behalf of the partnership from time to time such sum or sums of money which in their sole discretion is necessary to the conduct of the

business of the partnership, and to mortgage, pledge or otherwise encumber its assets to secure the repayment of such monies so borrowed.

c) To make all contracts for and on behalf of the partnership generally in the conduct of its business.

d) To employ and discharge all employees, including any of the other partners who may be so employed in respect to the transaction of the partnership business.

e) To otherwise carry on and transact or cause to be carried on and transacted, under their sole supervision and control, all of the other business of the partnership.

f) To determine whether or not at any accounting period the profits, if any, of the partnership shall be apportioned and distributed, in whole or in part, to the partners, or retained and continued in use in the business of the partnership.

In the event of disagreement among the managing partners a decision by the majority of them shall be binding upon the partnership. If any one or two of the managing partners shall die or retire from the partnership business or become unwilling or unable to act as a managing partner, the management and control of the partnership business shall be vested in the remaining partner or partners.

It is understood and agreed that the managing partners shall consult and confer with the other partners before taking any steps resulting in any substantial change in the operation or policies of the partnership affairs, or the sale of any portion of the partnership assets other than in the usual course of business, or in any manner affecting the partnership business unusually as judged by the ordinary operation of the partnership business.[19]

With reference to the last paragraph of the example, note that the Uniform Partnership Act prohibits certain acts outside of the ordinary course of business unless all partners consent. These acts include assignment of partnership property in trust for creditors, sale of the goodwill of the business, confession of judgment against the firm, submission of a partnership claim to arbitration, and any other act that would make it impossible to carry on the partnership business.[20] Managing partners could not accomplish these acts unless all partners approved. In any case, it is advisable to require the managing partners to refer unusual matters affecting the business to a committee of the whole for resolution rather than granting the managers unfettered discretion in these matters.

In a negative sense, it is possible to provide by agreement what partners may *not* do without the unanimous consent of the other partners. Such a provision will usually include acts specifically prohibited by the Uniform Partnership Act, in addition to other specific acts deemed appropriate by the partners.

EXAMPLE: Limitations on Authority

Unless authorized by the other partners one or more but less than all the partners have no authority to:

a) Assign the partnership property in trust for creditors or on the assignee's promise to pay the debts of the partnership.

b) Dispose of the goodwill of the business.

c) Do any other act which would make it impossible to carry on the ordinary business of a partnership.

d) Confess a judgment.

e) Submit a partnership claim or liability to arbitration or reference.

f) Make, execute or deliver for the partnership any bond, mortgage, deed of trust, guarantee, indemnity bond, surety bond or accommodation paper or accommodation endorsement.

g) Borrow money in the partnership name or use partnership property as collateral.

h) Assign, transfer, pledge, compromise or release any claim of or debt owning to the partnership except upon payment in full.

i) Convey any partnership real property.

j) Pledge or transfer in any manner his or her interest in the partnership except to another partner.

k) Do any of the acts for which unanimity is required by other paragraphs of this Agreement.[21]

Duties and Compensation

Partners are expected to devote their full time and attention to the activities of the partnership. This duty flows from a traditional reality that partners customarily participated in the conduct of the business, and it may have limited justification in modern practice. Moreover, the law denies partners the right to remuneration for services performed on behalf of the firm,[22] since their compensation is supposed to come from profits generated by their services and shared in a manner provided by the agreement.

If the parties desire a modification of the legal rule, matters such as salary and devotion to duty should be addressed in the partnership agreement.

> **EXAMPLE: Salaries and Duties**
> There shall be paid to each partner the following monthly salaries: To Anne Berardini, Two thousand dollars; to Michael Corrigan, One thousand five hundred dollars; etc. No increase in salaries shall be made without unanimous agreement. The payment of salaries to partners shall be an obligation of the partnership only to the extent that partnership assets are available therefor, and shall not be an obligation of the partners individually. Salaries shall, to this extent, be treated as an expense of the partnership in determining profits or losses.[23]

> **EXAMPLE: Expense Allowance**
> An expense account, not to exceed Two hundred dollars ($200.00) per month, shall be provided for each partner for his or her actual, reasonable and necessary expenses, in engaging in the business and pursuits of the partnership. Each partner shall be required to keep an itemized record of such expenses and shall be paid once each month upon the submission of such statements of records.[24]

Devotion to duty may be covered by specifying the responsibilities of each partner.

> **EXAMPLE: Devotion to Duty**
> Each partner shall devote his or her entire time and attention to the partnership business, except that each may devote reasonable time to civic, family and personal affairs; and except that Peter McLaughlin shall be permitted to pursue the business of selling magazine subscriptions during his own time and at hours other than the business hours of the partnership business.

PROFITS AND LOSSES

Sharing of profit is an important element of co-ownership, the crux of the partnership. Previous discussion considered that a partner is not entitled to expect compensation for services performed for the partnership. It is hoped that the partner's reward is a rich share of profits from a successful business. Unfortunately, the right to enjoy profits carries with it the obligation to bear losses—perhaps the only distressing characteristic of co-ownership.

The agreement between partners usually states the proportion in which profits and losses will be shared, and these provisions may be as simple or as complex as the parties desire. If the partners have not specified any provision for profit sharing, the Uniform Partnership Act provides that losses shall be divided equally, regardless of the contributions of the parties. The act further provides that losses shall be shared in the same proportion as profits.[25] Stated another way, if the agreement is silent, profits and losses are shared equally. If the agreement provides that profits shall be shared in a 75%/25% proportion between two partners, losses will be shared in the same proportion. Note that there is no requirement that profit-loss sharing have any relationship to the respective capital contributions of the partners. For example, one partner may contribute all of the cash and property to the firm while the other contributes only services, but the partners may share profits and losses in any agreed proportion.

Unusual profit distribution formulas may be used in special cases. For example, the parties may agree that one partner should have a preference to profits for some compelling reason.

> **EXAMPLE: Preferential Distribution of Profit**
> As part of the consideration for Keith Burn joining the firm, it is understood that for a period of two years, in the annual distribution of profits, he shall receive a cumulative preference of ten per cent on his share; that is, out of the annual profits there shall first be a distribution to him up to ten per cent on his share of the capital, and also to cover any deficiency from said ten per cent in any previous years, and then a distribution pro rata to the other partners up to ten per cent on their shares of the capital, and any surplus profits shall then be distributed among the partners according to their respective shares of the capital.[26]

This example not only establishes a profit preference, but also requires that profit be distributed in the same proportions as capital contributions. Lest the point be lost for being too obvious, although the partners are not required to distribute profits in the same proportion as they have contributed capital, they are certainly permitted to do so.

It is also good practice to include provisions for computing *net distributable profit,* so as to avoid any later dispute among the partners. These provisions are particularly appropriate when the partnership is likely to incur unusual obligations, which otherwise may not be included as expense items for profit computation.

> **EXAMPLE: Division of Profits and Losses and Computation**
> The net profits of the partnership shall be divided and the net losses of the partnership shall be borne in the following proportions: Fern Portnoy, 25%; Michael Corrigan, 10%; etc. Net profits of the partnership for any period shall be made by deducting from the gross profits disbursements made by or on behalf of the partnership for the usual and customary expenses of conducting the business, taxes chargeable to and paid by the partnership, reserves for taxes accrued but not payable, interest on all interest-bearing loans of the partnership, salaries paid to employees and partners, reserves for depreciation of partnership property and contingencies, including bad debts, allowance for accruing liabilities, and any and all other disbursements made by the partnership during such period incidental to the conduct of the business, excepting, however, payments to the partners on account of partnership profits.[27]

In drafting the partnership agreement, a distinction may be made between profits, losses, deductions, credits, and cash. All of these items may be allocated the same way among partners, but a disproportionate allocation may be appropriate among partners in some cases. First, it should be understood that although these allocable items are related to each other, they are also quite separate and distinct and will have varying importance in the eyes of the various partners. A business may operate "profitably" but because of certain deductions (such as depreciation on buildings owned by the business) may incur losses for tax purposes, which are shared equally unless allocated differently in the agreement. Nevertheless, because revenues have exceeded expenses for which expenditures were required (depreciation not being such an expense), there may be a surplus of cash in the business, which is available for distribution to partners. In addition, various tax credits might be available to the business, which are to be allocated and passed through to the partners.[28]

Add to these variations the preferences of the partners. Partner A may have contributed all or most of the capital of the partnership and may prefer to receive the constributed cash back as soon as possible with a disproportionately high allocation of distributable cash. Partner B may have a very low income and a high cash need, while Partner C may have a very high income and a low need for cash. Between them, it may be appropriate to give B more cash and profits and to give C more losses and credits, to maximize B's enjoyment of life and minimize the tax C suffers because of C's high income. You may recognize correctly that these disproportionate allocations are a method by which tax can be avoided. Do not think that the Internal Revenue Service is in the dark about them. The service will not allow a disproportionate allocation without significant economic justification.[29]

For example, if Partner A contributed all of the cash to start the business, it may be justifiable economically to give A a preference to cash. If Partner B does most of the work managing the business, it may be justifiable economically to give B profits and cash in higher proportion than for the others. But what can you say Partner C did to justify the receipt of losses? There's the rub. You must be able to justify *all* allocations, or the Internal Revenue Service may reallocate items of profit, loss, deductions, and credits in a way that will produce additional tax to the partners.

Examples of a disproportionate allocation of some of the items follow.

> **EXAMPLE: Allocations of Profits, Losses, Deductions, and Credits**
> Except as otherwise provided herein (dealing with the allocation of the proceeds upon sale or other disposition of the assets of the Partnership), ninety-five percent (95%) of the net profits, and losses of the Partnership and each item of income, gain, loss, deduction or credit entering into the computation thereof, shall be allocated to the partners other than the managing General Partner in accordance with their respective capital contributions. Five percent (5%) of such net profits, and losses and items of income, gain, loss, deduction or credit entering into the computation thereof, shall be allocated to the Managing General Partner.

> **EXAMPLE: Distribution of Cash**
> One hundred percent (100%) of net cash, including amounts required to be retained by the Partnership pursuant to this Agreement, shall be allocated to the partners other than the Managing General Partner and no cash shall be allocated to the Managing General Partner until the partners other than the Managing General Partner have received cash distributions totaling $1,925,000. Thereafter, ninety-five per cent (95%) of net cash shall be allocated to the partners other than

the Managing General Partner and five percent (5%) of net cash shall be allocated to the Managing General Partner throughout the term of the Partnership. The Managing General Partner shall determine the net cash available for distribution after establishing a reasonable reserve for replacements, contingencies and operating capital, and after satisfying other obligations of the Partnership then due and payable. The Managing General Partner shall distribute the net cash available for distribution no less frequently than quarterly.

LIABILITY OF PARTNERS

Like sole proprietorships, general partnerships suffer the disadvantage of unlimited liability for each partner. If the assets of the partnership are inadequate to pay partnership creditors, the personal assets of the individual partners may be reached to satisfy these obligations.[30] In one sense, there is an advantage to a partnership over a sole proprietorship since liabilities will be apportioned to the partners pro rata and no one person is required to bear the full responsibility. On the other hand, since each partner has the capacity to bind the partnership, the potential risk of liability is proportionately increased.

The element of unlimited liability is a substantial disadvantage to hazardous and speculative enterprises, and it further imposes an unwelcome burden on a partner who enjoys substantially greater personal wealth than the other partners. It is possible, as with a sole proprietorship, to insure against potential liability whenever it may be anticipated. Moreover, the partnership may negotiate agreements with outsiders which provide that liability on the contract shall be limited to the partnership assets and will not extend to the individual assets of the partners. Additional protection for the partner's individual assets is provided by a rule called *marshaling of assets,* which requires that firm creditors must first look to firm property for satisfaction of their obligations, and that only if partnership assets are inadequate may they pursue the individual assets of the partners. Nevertheless, a partnership's potential unlimited liability, which can never be completely circumscribed by insurance, agreement, or rule for priority of assets, limits the desirability of the partnership form of business enterprise.

The Uniform Partnership Act creates an obligation of the partnership to indemnify a partner who has paid expenses or incurred liability in the ordinary course of partnership business.[31] Thus, if a particular partner used individual assets to pay firm creditors, that partner is entitled to be reimbursed for the appropriate share of the other partners. Although the law grants this right of indemnification, the specific authority for indemnification should be specified in the agreement.

EXAMPLE: Indemnification
The partnership shall promptly indemnify each partner in respect of payments reasonably made and personal liabilities reasonably incurred by him or her in the ordinary conduct of its business, or for the preservation of its business or property.[32]

A partner who leaves the firm, by retirement, withdrawal, or for some other reason, remains individually liable for debts incurred while that partner participated in the firm.[33] As discussed in detail later, whenever a partner leaves the firm, a technical dissolution of the partnership occurs.[34] If the remaining partners are to continue the business, certain notice is necessary to persons who transacted business with the former firm in order to relieve the withdrawn partner from future liability. Personal notice must be given to persons or companies who extended credit to the firm while the retiring partner was a member. Notice by publication will suffice for other persons who dealt with the firm.[35] Usually the remaining partners will agree to indemnify the withdrawing partner from any further liability for firm obligations. An indemnification clause as provided in the preceding example will create the obligation to indemnify if included in the original partnership agreement.

New partners to the firm are individually liable for obligations existing when they join only if they specifically agree to be. Absent an assumption of these obligations, their individual assets may not be reached to satisfy existing obligations. They are, however, individually liable for any obligations incurred after they become partners.[36]

DISSOLUTION AND TERMINATION OF A PARTNERSHIP

The law provides that the partnership enterprise is dissolved whenever any partner ceases to be associated with the partnership business. In this respect, a partnership is very much like a sole proprietorship, where the business entity expires when the proprietor retires, dies, or is otherwise disassociated from the business. However, the partnership is an association of two of more persons, which adds an element of continuity to the partnership business, since dissolution does not necessarily require termination of the business. In fact, the partnership may be technically dissolved, yet the remaining partners may continue the business without the partner who has been disassociated from the business. By a strict interpretation of partnership law, a new partnership is created immediately and is governed essentially by the terms of the original agreement. In many cases, however, dissolution of the partnership requires termination and "winding-up" of the business.

This section explores the circumstances that cause dissolution and the specific statutory authority to continue the partnership business without winding it up. The partnership agreement plays an important role in these matters, and thus specific clauses are discussed.

Causes of Dissolution

Dissolution of partnership may result from a variety of causes. Since a partnership is created by agreement of the partners, it may also be dissolved by agreement. This agreement may state a specific date for termination of the business, or may provide that the business should be dissolved upon the happening of a contingent event.[37] For example, the parties may agree that the partnership will be dissolved on July 1, 1999, or if the business sustains operating losses for five consecutive months, whichever occurs first. The latter contingency may be a realistic agreement insofar as the parties usually seek to avoid operating a business at a loss. The former provision, specifying a date for dissolution, is unrealistic and uncommon, since most partnerships hope to generate profits from a continuing business and the abrupt termination because of a specific provision in the original agreement could result in considerable loss of "going concern" values.

> **EXAMPLE: Dissolution Contingent upon Results of Operations**
> If the operation of the business over a period of five consecutive months or more discloses an average net monthly profit of less than $500.00, the managing partner is hereby authorized and empowered to negotiate a sale, exchange or other disposition of the entire partnership business upon the best possible terms available at such time, and in the event of such disposition of the partnership business the proceeds derived therefrom after the payment of the necessary costs and expenses of such disposition of the business shall be applied first to the payment of the debts of the business according to their respective legal priority, and if any balance of such proceeds shall remain after the payment and satisfaction of the debts, obligations and liabilities of the business, the same shall be divided equally between the partners. Either partner may become a purchaser of the business at any such sale.[38]

Whether or not the original agreement contains any provision for dissolution, all partners may unanimously agree to dissolve the firm at any time.[39] Better practice requires that a subsequent agreement of the partners to dissolve the firm should be reduced to writing.

> **EXAMPLE: Agreement to Dissolve**
> The partnership heretofore subsisting between us, the undersigned Michael Corrigan, Karen Burn, and Anne Berardini, under and pursuant to the within articles of partnership, is hereby dissolved, except so far as may be necessary to continue the same for the liquidation and settlement of the business thereof. The said Michael Corrigan [*or* each of the undersigned] is authorized to sign in liquidation.
>   Dated _____, 19 ___.   *Signatures*[40]

Since a primary element of a partnership is that it be a "voluntary association" of persons, any partner who no longer desires to be associated with the firm may withdraw at will, and thereby cause a dissolution.[41] If the original agreement provided that the partnership would continue for a specified term, the willful withdrawal of a partner may result in liability to the other partners for breach of the agreement, but the partnership is nevertheless dissolved. However, if the original agreement between the partners was indefinite regarding the duration of the partnership, this right or power to withdraw at will may be fully exercised, without regard to the harm it may cause to the business or the other partners. Of course, the law requires that the withdrawing partner must act in good faith to escape a surprise dissolution with impunity.

A partner may not have the choice of leaving the firm if the agreement provides that he or she may be expelled by the other partners. Such provisions may be drafted in the original agreement and usually will be conditioned upon some misconduct by a party, such as neglecting the business, refusing to pay an assessment, and so on. The expulsion provision may be as general and broad as the parties desire, but provisions permitting expulsion "without cause" or "in the best interests" of the partnership are rare. If an expulsion provision is included in the agreement, the "innocent" partners may cause a dissolution of the firm by exercising their right to expel a partner.[42]

Dissolution may be required by operation of law. The partnership business may be declared unlawful, as was the case for liquor stores operated as partnerships when prohibition was imposed. More frequently, the partnership is dissolved whenever a partner dies or becomes individually bankrupt.[43] Both of these events cause dissolution because the partner's interest in the firm, which was once the partner's personal property, becomes the property of the partner's heirs or a trustee in bankruptcy, none of whom are partners. In both cases, the partner has withdrawn from the firm in a sense.

Finally, dissolutions may be decreed by a court whenever any partner becomes insane or incapable of furthering the partnership business, or if a partner acts in a manner so that it is impracticable to carry on the business, or in any other case that renders a dissolution equitable under the circumstances.[44] Thus, when partners simply cannot agree on the proper operation of the business and their constant disagreement is detrimental to the success of the business, a court may, on application by a partner, dissolve the partnership. In some cases of disagreement between partners, dissolution by a court may be the only available remedy since, although a partner may terminate the partnership at will, that partner may be risking liability for breach of the partnership agreement by causing dissolution.

Continuation of a Partnership Despite Dissolution

As a general rule, the dissolution of a partnership requires the winding-up and termination of the business and the liquidation of the firm's assets. There are two major exceptions to this rule: The business may be continued by the remaining partners if the dissolution was wrongful or if the partners' original agreement so provided.[45]

A *wrongful dissolution* results whenever a partner has caused a dissolution without having the right to do so. If a partner has been expelled from the firm for misconduct or a violation of the partnership agreement, the resulting dissolution is wrongful and the remaining partners are permitted to continue the business without liquidation. Similarly, a partner who causes a dissolution by withdrawing from the firm in violation of the agreement has caused a wrongful dissolution. Remember that whether or not withdrawal is wrongful depends upon whether the agreement specifies the duration of the partnership.

Whenever the business is continued by the remaining partners following a wrongful dissolution, the remaining partners are required to compensate or to ensure compensation to the disassociated partner for that partner's interest in the firm and to indemnify the disassociated partner from partnership liabilities.[46]

Even when the dissolution is innocent, it may be desirable to continue the partnership business. Particularly in the case of the untimely death of a partner, liquidation following dissolution could result in unnecessary economic loss to the remaining partners. Continuation following an innocent dissolution requires an agreement to that effect between the parties, and while the agreement may be concluded legally after dissolution has actually occurred, it is far better to provide for continuation in the detached negotiations of the original agreement of the parties.

First, the agreement should contain a continuation provision authorizing the remaining partners to proceed with the business.

> **EXAMPLE: Right to Continue the Business**
> In the event of a dissolution caused by the retirement, death, withdrawal, permanent disability, or bankruptcy of a partner, the remaining partners shall have the right to continue the partnership business under the same name by themselves

or with any other person or persons they may select, but they shall pay to the other partner or his or her legal representatives the value of his or her interest in the partnership as of the date of dissolution.

Second, a method for computing the outgoing partner's interest and a method of payment should be specified. The various methods of providing for payment of outgoing interests, be they the result of death, withdrawal, or other act dissolving the partnership, have different tax consequences, which are sufficiently complex to be avoided here. An enterprising student may explore these various methods in detail by referring to other sources.[47] Frequently used methods of settling the outgoing interest include (1) the purchase of the interest of the outgoing partner by the continuing partners and (2) liquidating distributions from the partnership to the outgoing partner, which, in effect, result in the sale of the partner's interest to the firm itself. The second may provide for guaranteed periodic payments or payments out of partnership profits or partnership property.

> **EXAMPLE: Payments for Partnership Interest**
> For the interest of a retiring or deceased partner in the partnership property, including goodwill, the partnership shall pay to the retiring partner, or to the successor in interest of the deceased partner, $20,000.00 in each of the five years following the retirement or death of a partner, which amount may not be prepaid except with the consent of the payee. It is the intention of the partners that the payments provided under this paragraph shall qualify under 26 U.S.C.A. § 736(a), and shall constitute ordinary income to the recipient and reduce the taxable income of the continuing partners.[48]

The agreement will specify the method of disposing of the partner's interest, and the method of computing the compensation to the partner. An example of a provision permitting the purchase of the outgoing partner's interest by the remaining partners follows.

> **EXAMPLE: Purchase of a Partner's Interest**
> Upon the death, withdrawal, or insolvency of either of the partners during the existence of the partnership, the surviving or remaining partner shall purchase all the right, share and interest of the deceased, withdrawn, or insolvent partner in all the partnership business and property, and shall assume all the then existing liabilities of the partnership. The price to be paid for such purchase is hereby fixed and agreed upon as follows: It shall be the amount stated as the net value of the share in the partnership of the deceased, withdrawn or insolvent partner in the balance sheet of the first of January next preceding his or her death or withdrawal or insolvency, together with interest thereon from the date of said balance sheet at the rate of ten per cent per annum until paid. Such purchase price shall be paid as follows: fifty per cent thereof within six months from the date of such death, withdrawal or insolvency and the remainder at such times and in such amounts as may suit the convenience of the surviving or remaining partner; provided, that the whole thereof shall be paid within two years. The estate of the deceased partner, or the withdrawing or insolvent partner shall not be entitled to share in any increase or profits gained, nor be liable for any losses incurred, in the business after the first of January next preceding his or her death, withdrawal or insolvency but all such profits shall belong to, and such losses be borne by, the purchasing partner.[49]

One other item must be considered for purchase of a deceased partner's interest: life insurance. If the partnership agreement provides for the purchase of a deceased partner's interest, life insurance *funding* will ensure that money will be available to consummate the intention of the parties when a partner dies. The partnership may apply for and purchase life insurance on the lives of the partners, or the partners may individually apply for and purchase insurance on each other. The former is commonly called an *entity purchase plan,* and the latter is referred to as a *cross-purchase plan.* Such insurance agreements usually are executed separately and are not a part of the partnership agreement. However, since they are intended to fund the purchase of the deceased partner's interest, the provisions of the insurance agreement and the insurance acquired thereby should be consistent with the buy-out arrangements specified in the partnership agreement.[50]

In addition to permitting the continuation of the business and the disposition of the withdrawing or deceased partner's interest, a properly drafted agreement should also require the continuing partners to assume and pay all existing partnership obligations. Moreover, since creditors will likely have extended credit to the firm before withdrawal, and the withdrawing partner may remain liable for future obligations unless proper notice is given, the agreement should specifically require such notice.

> **EXAMPLE: Notice of Dissolution**
> Actual notice of dissolution shall be given to all persons who have had dealings with the partnership during the two years prior to dissolution.[51]

Finally, it may be desirable to include an anticompetition clause, to prevent, as much as possible, the withdrawing partner from competing against the firm or divulging the firm's trade secrets.

> **EXAMPLE: Noncompete Agreement**
> The retiring partner shall not for a period of two years from the date of his or her retirement, either alone, or jointly with, or as agent for, any person, directly or indirectly, set up, exercise or carry on the trade or business of metal processing and plating within 500 miles from Denver, Colorado, and shall not set up, make or encourage any opposition to the said trade or business hereafter to be carried on by the other party or his or her representatives or assigns, nor do anything to the prejudice thereof, and shall not divulge to any person any of the secrets, accounts or transactions of or relating to the partnership. For any violation of this stipulation the parties bind themselves to each other in the sum of Five thousand dollars, to be deemed liquidated damages, and total extinction of this convenant, and not in the nature of a penalty.[52]

Termination and Winding-up

In the event that the remaining partners do not desire to continue the business, a dissolution requires that the partnership be terminated and wound up. For these purposes, the remaining partners have the right to complete all pending partnership business and thereafter collect and dispose of the assets, pay the firm's creditors, and enjoy whatever is left. Depending upon the size of the partnership, it may be desirable to appoint one partner to liquidate the business. Any remaining partner is eligible. If a liquidating partner is named in the original agreement, a successor should also be named in the event of that person's death. In any case, following a dissolution, a partner's authority to act for the partnership is limited to acts necessary to wind up the firm's affairs.[53]

The Uniform Partnership Act provides that in the event of winding-up, the assets of the firm must be distributed against the claims of

1. creditors other than partners;
2. partners other than for capital and profits;
3. partners in respect of capital; and
4. partners in respect of profits.[54]

The partners may agree to vary this distribution priority in any manner, except that partnership creditors, who are not bound by the terms of the partnership agreement, must always be completely satisfied before the partners are entitled to share the assets among themselves.

TAX CONSIDERATIONS OF A GENERAL PARTNERSHIP

A major consideration in the selection of the partnership as the appropriate form for a business enterprise is income taxation. The partnership itself pays no federal income tax. Instead, each partner is required to declare a share of the partnership income on his or her individual tax return. The partnership is thus treated very much like the sole proprietorship for tax purposes. The only difference is that the business income will be divided among the partners in their respective proportions, rather than being applied completely to one person.

The partnership files an information tax return with the federal government, and the return is used to ascertain whether the partners have declared and paid tax on their proportionate shares of income. It does not matter whether the profits have actually been distributed to the partners during the year. Even if profits are retained in the business, the partners must declare as though all profit had been distributed. When losses are considered, this rule could operate as an advantage of partnership taxation; all losses from the business are attributed personally to the partners and may be offset against other personal income produced from other similar sources.

Because of the similarity of a partnership to a sole proprietorship for tax purposes, the sole proprietorship is not a viable alternative for tax advantage. A corporation, however, is taxed as an entity at special corporate rates, and a choice between a partnership and a corporation may depend on the tax differences. The comparison of corporate tax rates with individual tax rates is complicated because two or more persons are involved in the partnership. The business form that may be most desirable for one person may work a disadvantage to the others. Various partners may have various incidents of taxation that are important to them, such as significant amounts of income from other sources that are subject to minimum alternative taxes, or one partner may have substantial passive income that can be offset by passive losses from the partnership while the other partners do not have similar income that would allow for similar deductions. Consequently, the only general statement that may be safely advanced regarding partnership tax considerations is that each case must be evaluated separately, based upon the potential profit or loss, the expected distributions from the business, and the individual financial positions and sources of income of the parties.

The sale of a partner's interest in the partnership results in a capital gain or loss much the same as does a shareholder's sale of corporate stock. When partnership property is sold, the capital gain or loss is attributable to the individual partner in the same proportion as are profits, unless altered by agreement. Since contributed property is partnership property, a special problem may arise with respect to its valuation for determining gain or loss. To illustrate the problem, consider the following case.

Murlin and Short formed a partnership with equal rights to profits. Murlin contributed $5,000 in cash and Short contributed a machine that had a fair market value of $5,000, but an adjusted basis (the cost to Short plus improvements by him) of $4,000. The basis of that machine to the partnership, for computing gain or loss, is the same as the basis to the individual: $4,000. If, during the year, the machine is sold at its fair market value of $5,000, the partnership will receive a capital gain of $1,000, which is attributable to the partners in their respective proportions. Thus, both partners must claim a $500 capital gain that year. This should concern Murlin, who has now paid half the tax on Short's contributed asset. If Short had sold the machine when he owned it as an individual, and contributed cash to the partnership, Short would have been individually responsible for the $1,000 gain.

Similarly, the rule may work a hardship on Short. Suppose the adjusted basis of the asset were $7,000, and Short contributed the machine when its fair market value was $5,000. When the machine is sold, the capital loss of $2,000 is shared between the partners. Murlin thereby acquires a tax benefit that Short really deserves.

In a case such as this, complicated matters arise in determining the fair allocation of depreciation on the asset between the parties. The Internal Revenue Code formerly offered a solution to the problem by permitting the parties to agree to the manner in which depreciation, depletion, gain, or loss of contributed property would be allocated between the partners to account for variations of this sort.[55] However, current tax law requires that all income, gain, loss, and deductions from property contributed to the partnership will be shared among partners so as to account for variations between the basis of the property to the partnership and the property's fair market value at the time of contribution, regardless of the partners' desires as specified in the partnership agreement.[56] A clause in the agreement should address this issue so that partners are not surprised about the tax consequences that may result from contributed property.

> **EXAMPLE: Allocation of Tax-related Items**
> The partners understand that for income tax purposes the partnership's adjusted basis of property contributed by Maynard Short differs from the fair market value at which such property was accepted by the partnership at the time of its contribution. The partners recognize and understand that in determining the taxable income or loss of the partnership and the distributive share of each partner's depreciation or gain or loss with respect to such contributed property, the Internal Revenue Code requires that such items shall be shared among the partners so as to take account of the variation between the basis of the property to the partnership and its fair market value at the time of contribution.

Many other tax considerations apply to the partnership form, most of which are complicated because the partnership operates as an entity, acquiring property and earning money as an apparently separate legal unit, but is treated merely as an aggregation of individuals for tax purposes. Thus, the distributions of current assets or in liquidation, determination of partnership taxable year, and transfer of partnership interests all pose unique tax problems, which are ably covered by other authors.[57]

FORMATION AND OPERATION OF A GENERAL PARTNERSHIP

In many respects, the formation of a general partnership parallels the formation of a sole proprietorship. The obvious difference is the most important formality for the partnership: the agreement. In the true spirit of procrastination, the drafting of the agreement is saved until last.

Selection of a Name

A partnership may operate under any name it chooses, provided the name is not deceptively similar to that of another well-known company so as to constitute a deceptive trade practice. As with sole proprietorships, any fictitious partnership name must be registered in most states under the assumed name statutes.[58]

If all of the partners' surnames are used in the firm name, the name is not considered to be fictitious; if fewer than all of the partners' names are used in the firm title, the name is fictitious. Thus, a partnership formed by Levine, Conviser, and Chess may use all names without registration, but if the firm name is Levine and Chess, registration is required. Similarly, the name Levine & Co. would require registration.

The sanctions imposed on a partnership for failure to file the assumed name information are the same as those imposed upon sole proprietors.[59]

Governmental Formalities

Partnerships may conduct any legal business just as a natural person may do, and where state law imposes particular licensing requirements, the partnership must conform. Consequently, sales tax licenses must be obtained where appropriate, and the partnership must obtain any necessary licenses peculiar to the particular business conducted.

Tax identification numbers are necessary for partnerships since informational returns are filed annually with federal and state authorities. If employees are to be hired, social security and unemployment compensation laws must be considered.

Interstate Business

Partnerships are not usually subjected to any peculiar formalities for doing business in states other than the state where the firm is formed. They must, however, comply with local licensing requirements, and the name of the firm must be registered appropriately with the foreign state. A few states, including California and New Hampshire, have required *qualification* of a foreign partnership by insisting on a registered office and agent within the state and the payment of a fee for the privilege of doing business.[60] This qualification procedure is not popular and is clearly a minority approach to interstate general partnership business.

The Agreement

Without the partnership agreement, the simple organizational formalities for the partnership would be extremely attractive. So far, organizing the partnership has been essentially the same as organizing the sole proprietorship. It is even possible to form a partnership with nothing more than a gentleman's agreement to do business together. However, it should be apparent from the previous discussions of the nature of the partnership that informality is usually a fatal oversight.

An old axiom states that one should never be a partner with a friend, recognizing the common tendency of human nature toward disagreement in business transactions. Eventually there will be some discord (or at least a friendly disagreement) between the parties, and an informal agreement offers no guidance whatever in the resolution of such disputes. Thus, the only proper practice requires the drafting of a comprehensive agreement between the parties, carefully specifying their purposes, contributions, management authority, voting powers, duties, rights, and responsibilities.

The partnership agreement, which is also frequently called the *articles of partnership,* must be tailored to the specific desires of the future partners. The following checklist with examples and references to the detailed discussions in this chapter may be used as a guide for preparing the agreement.[61]

1. Names and addresses of the partners

> **EXAMPLE: Agreement**
> Agreement made this ___ day of _____, 19___, between James A. Murlin, whose address is 526 Park Avenue, New York, New York, and Maynard P. Short, whose address is 1901 K Street, N.W., Washington, D.C., (hereinafter referred to as individuals or collectively as "Partners").

2. Recitals—The background of the partners' business relationship may be stated in order to explain the agreement. Recitals of such information are inserted at the beginning of the agreement. The recitals further serve to state the intent to form a partnership and may explain the business objectives of the enterprise.

> **EXAMPLE: Recitals**
> WHEREAS, Murlin has acquired certain business expertise in the manufacturing and marketing of rubber bicycle tires; and
> WHEREAS, Short has the financial ability to contribute certain sums of money for the manufacturing and marketing of rubber bicycle tires; and
> WHEREAS the parties intend to operate a business for the manufacture and marketing of rubber bicycle tires and desire to do so under the form of a partnership;
> NOW, THEREFORE, it is agreed:

3. Name of the partnership—If the firm name does not contain the surnames of the individual partners, a trade name affidavit is required (see "Selection of a Name" earlier in this section).

> **EXAMPLE: Name**
> The name of the Partnership shall be Shoylin Associates.

4. Place of business—The proposed offices of the firm should be stated, with permission for the partners to establish other offices as appropriate. If the firm will operate branch offices and their locations are known, those locations should be specified. If a multistate business is contemplated, the partners should have authority to establish offices in other states.

> **EXAMPLE: Place of Business**
> The principal place of business of the firm shall be located at 526 Park Avenue, New York, New York, or such other place as shall be designated by the partners from time to time. Branch offices may be located at 156 Cayuga Street, Ithaca, New York, and at a street address to be determined by agreement of the partners in Albany, New York. The partnership shall be authorized to conduct business and to establish offices in locations to be selected by agreement of the partners in the states of Connecticut, Rhode Island, and Pennsylvania.

5. Purposes—The description of the partnership business should be included in general terms, unless restrictive language is dictated by the partners' objectives. Any intended restrictions upon the scope of the partnership's business should be detailed, or, following a specific description of the contemplated purposes, the agreement may provide that the partnership will operate "no other business." Be certain to include a provision that allows the partners to *agree* to enter into other ventures so the agreement will not be unduly restrictive.

> **EXAMPLE: Nature of Business**
> The partnership shall engage in the business of manufacturing and marketing rubber bicycle tires, and in such other lawful business as is permitted in the jurisdiction of formation and as may be agreed upon from time to time by the partners.[62]
>
> [or]
>
> The partnership shall engage in the business of manufacturing and marketing rubber bicycle tires, and shall not engage in any other business or activity except as shall be directly related and incident to such business or except as shall be agreed upon from time to time by the partners.

6. Duration
   (a) The partnership may be formed for a definite term.
   (b) The partnership may be subject to termination by mutual agreement.
   (b) The partnership may be terminable at will when one partner gives the specified notice to the other partners.
   (d) The partnership may be terminated upon the completion of its purposes (e.g., the sale of a parcel of real estate).
   (e) The partnership may be terminated upon the happening of a contingent event (e.g., continuous losses for a specified period).
   (f) The partnership may be terminated under any combination of the preceding conditions.

> **EXAMPLE: Duration**
> The partnership shall begin on May 1, 1989, and shall continue for the term of ten years thereafter.[63]
>
> [or]

> The partnership shall continue for the full term of five years from the date of this agreement, and thereafter until thirty days' written notice is given by any of the partners to the others.[64]

7. Capital—The capital contributions of the partners should be described in detail. There are many possible variations of contributions (see "Partnership Property" and "Tax Considerations of a General Partnership" earlier in this chapter), but the following situations are most typical.

(a) The partners' contributions will be cash. The agreement should specify the amount of the contribution and the time of payment.

> **EXAMPLE: Capital**
> The capital of the partnership shall be contributed in cash by the partners as follows:
>
> | | |
> |---|---|
> | James A. Murlin | $5,000.00 |
> | Maynard P. Short | $3,000.00 |
>
> Such contribution shall be paid in full on or before May 10, 1989.[65]

(b) One or more of the partners will contribute services. The value of the services and the treatment of the respective capital accounts should be discussed.

> **EXAMPLE: Contribution of Services**
> James A. Murlin shall not be required to make a cash or property contribution to the partnership but shall devote his entire time to the partnership, and for such he shall be entitled to twenty per cent (20%) of the profits to be divided [*term for division*] among the partners. In the event that his monthly share of the profits shall exceed Three thousand dollars ($3,000.00), he shall contribute the excess to his capital account of business until the total amount of such contributions shall equal the capital contributions made by each of the other partners.[66]

(c) One or more of the partners will contribute tangible property. The agreed value of the property should be specified. Further, if the cost of the property to the contributing partner and the agreed value of the contribution are different, it is appropriate to consider and describe the tax consequences of the precontribution gain or loss in the agreement (see "Tax Considerations of a General Partnership" earlier in this chapter).

> **EXAMPLE: Contribution of Property**
> Maynard P. Short shall contribute property which the partners agree will be valued at Ten thousand dollars ($10,000.00). Such property is described in Schedule A attached hereto.[67]

(d) The partners may be required to furnish additional capital. The agreement should specify the circumstances under which additional contributions may be assessed (e.g., in the event of continuous losses for a specified period, or upon the vote of the majority of the partners). The partners' respective proportions for additional contributions and the procedure by which the partners will be notified of the contributions should be specified.

> **EXAMPLE: Additional Capital Contributions**
> In the event that the cash funds of the partnership are insufficient to meet its operating expenses, the partners shall make additional capital contributions, in the same proportions in which they share the net profits of the firm.[68]
>
> The managing partner, after determining a cash deficit, shall notify the other partners in writing at least ten (10) days prior to the date upon which such cash funds are needed and each partner shall be required to make such additional contributions on the date specified in the notice, or, if none, on the tenth day after the date of the notice.

(e) Excess contributions may be construed as advances, and may be treated as loans to the firm. The authority to make such loans comes from the agreement, which should specify the need for the consent of the other partners, the amount of the loan, and any desired restriction on the frequency of such advances.

> **EXAMPLE: Loans and Advances**
> Any of the partners may, from time to time, with the consent of all of the other partners, advance sums of money to the partnership by way of loan, and each such advance shall bear interest at the rate of twelve per cent (12%) per annum.[69]

(f) Profits may be accumulated as capital.

> **EXAMPLE: Accumulated Profits**
> Each of the partners shall be required to allow to remain in the business each year as a contribution to net worth of the partnership capital, an amount equal to thirty per cent (30%) of the partnership profits which would otherwise be distributed to him or her. Such contributions shall be allocated to or reserved in accounts for each of the partners, and shall remain in the business and be employed as capital for the business subject to further direction and order of the partners.[70]

(g) Capital may accumulate interest if the agreement so provides. If the partners agree that capital contributions should not accumulate interest, a statement to that effect should be included.

> **EXAMPLE: Interest on Capital**
> No interest shall be paid to the partners on any contributions to capital.
> [or]
> Each of the partners shall be entitled to interest at the rate of ten per cent (10%) per annum on the amount of his or her respective contributions, payable semiannually, on June 1 and December 1, of each calendar year.[71]

(h) If withdrawal of capital contributions is to be permitted, the agreement should detail the circumstances of withdrawal, limitations upon the amount of the withdrawal, if any, and any requirements for replenishing the capital account at specified times.

> **EXAMPLE: Withdrawal of Capital**
> Each of the partners may withdraw from the partnership, for his or her own use, a sum not exceeding Seven hundred dollars ($700.00) per month. If, at the close of each fiscal year, it is found that any of the partner's share withdrawn by him or her is in excess of his or her distributive share for that fiscal year, he or she shall

forthwith refund the difference within a period not exceeding five days from the time of such determination.[72]

(i) If one partner allows profits to accumulate in a greater proportion than do the others, the excess may be described as a debt to that partner, and the agreement may provide an interest rate to be applied to the excess amount.

> **EXAMPLE: Individual Accumulation of Profit**
> All profits of the partnership during the year shall be allocated to the partners in their respective proportions in an income account which shall be subject to withdrawal by any partner from time to time. If a partner does not withdraw all of his or her income account during the year, the excess amount, not withdrawn, shall be treated as a loan to the partnership by the partner, and shall accumulate interest at the rate of ten percent (10%) per annum on the amount of the income account not withdrawn at the close of each calendar year, so long as such amount shall remain in the income account and is not withdrawn by the partner.

8. Salaries and expenses

(a) Since partners are not ordinarily entitled to remuneration for their services (see "Management of a Partnership"), the authority to pay salaries must be established by the agreement. Salaries may be contingent upon profits, or may be fixed by the agreement.

> **EXAMPLE: Salaries**
> There shall be paid to each partner the following monthly salaries: To James A. Murlin, three thousand dollars; to Maynard P. Short two thousand dollars; *etc.* No increase in salaries shall be made without unanimous agreement. The payment of salaries to partners shall be an obligation of the partnership only to the extent that partnership assets are available therefor, and shall not be an obligation of the partners individually. Salaries shall, to this extent, be treated as an expense of the partnership in determining profits or losses.[73]

(b) Expense accounts are common in business partnerships. The agreement should establish a maximum periodic amount, a procedure for submitting expenses, and a procedure for reimbursement. The agreement also should specify that only expenses incurred in furtherance of the partnership business will be reimbursed.

> **EXAMPLE: Expenses**
> An expense account, not to exceed One hundred dollars ($100.00) per month, shall be provided for each partner for his or her actual, reasonable and necessary expenses, in engaging in the business and pursuits of the partnership. Each partner shall be required to keep an itemized record of such expenses and shall be paid once each month upon the submission of such statements of records.[74]

9. Profits, losses, deductions, and credits—The agreement should establish a method for determining profit and loss. Simply providing for a determination of profit or loss by the partnership's accountant (or bookkeeper) using generally accepted accounting principles will create an objective standard for the determination which should avoid most disputes. However, the phrase "generally accepted accounting principles" frequently baffles even the accountant who uses it, if it is

necessary for that accountant to justify the method upon which he or she has determined financial information. It may be preferable to select a method of accounting, such as cash or accrual, and to specify that method as the partnership accounting procedure. Frequently, partnership agreements provide that income and loss will be determined on the same basis as that required for federal income tax purposes, so that accountants do not have to create separate financial statements for a partnership's internal use and for federal income tax reporting purposes. It may be desirable to allow for any partner to question a profit and loss determination by permitting another accountant (at the challenging partner's expense) to determine, independently, profits or losses, and then permitting arbitration (or some other objective determination) if the results vary more than a stated percentage from the original amount.

In some cases, extraordinary expenses are involved, such as legal fees for litigation or unusual travel and entertainment in the start-up period of the business. These expenses may be detailed in the agreement and excluded from the normal profit and loss computation so that they may be shared in some other agreed proportion. Profits, losses, deductions, and credits are usually shared in the same proportions, but not necessarily.[75] This clause is especially tailored to the desires of the partners. Some common schemes are as follows:

(a) Sharing profits, losses, deductions, and credits equally
(b) Sharing profits, losses, deductions, and credits according to proportion of capital contributions
(c) Allocating all items primarily to the partner who provides financial backing until he or she receives profits (or tax benefits) equal to the capital contributed, then making a primary allocation to the managing partner who is producing those profits
(d) Requiring that losses caused by the willful neglect or default of a partner be borne by that partner
(e) Guaranteeing profits for certain partners, which usually requires the other partners to contribute any deficiency if the annual profit distribution does not exceed a certain amount

> **EXAMPLE: Allocations of Profits, Losses, Deductions, and Credits**
> Seventy per cent (70%) of the net profits and losses of the partnership and each item of income, gain, loss, deduction or credit entering into the computation thereof, shall be allocated to the partners other than the Managing General Partner in accordance with their respective capital contributions. Thirty per cent (30%) of such net profits and losses, and items of income, gain, loss, deduction or credit entering into the computation thereof, shall be allocated to the Managing General Partner.

10. Cash distributions—A partnership is a unique entity that allows for accumulations of cash when the business is actually producing a "paper" loss. For example, if the partnership operates an apartment building, depreciation and interest may reduce the profits of the partnership (and may actually produce a loss) even when rental receipts exceed operating expenses. The agreement should provide for distributions of cash to the partners in certain proportions, and this determination could be made separately from the distribution of profits, losses, deductions, and credits. Again, the specific desires of the partners should be observed. Some common methods of cash distribution include the following:

(a) In the same proportion as profits, losses, deductions, and credits are shared
(b) To the partners who contributed cash or property as capital contributions, to the exclusion of any partner who is contributing only services, until a certain proportion of the contributed amount has been recovered
(c) To the partner who needs it the most, at least for a period of time
(d) To the partner who will be required to pay the most taxes as a result of partnership operations, thereby permitting that partner to pay the taxes from the cash distributed

> **EXAMPLE: Cash Distributions**
> One hundred per cent (100%) of the net cash of the partnership shall be allocated to the partners other than the Managing General Partner in accordance with their respective capital contributions for the first three years of the operation of the business, and no cash shall be allocated to the Managing General Partner during that time. Thereafter, twenty per cent (20%) of the net cash of the partnership shall be allocated to the partners other than the Managing General Partner and eighty per cent (80%) of the net cash shall be allocated to the Managing General Partner.

11. Books and records
(a) The fiscal year of the partnership must be established. The taxable year of the partnership is determined, for tax purposes, as though the partnership were a taxpayer. Normally this means that the taxable year must be the same for the partnership as for the partners who have an interest in the partnership profits and capital of greater than 50%. If the partners are individuals, that means the partnership's taxable year is the calendar year. The partnership can have a different taxable year only if it establishes a legitimate business purpose for a fiscal year different from the calendar year.

> **EXAMPLE: Fiscal Year**
> The fiscal year of the partnership shall be from November 1 until October 31.
> [or]
> The fiscal year of the partnership shall be the calendar year.[76]

(b) The method of accounting for the firm (accrual or cash) should be established. The agreement should further provide that generally accepted accounting principles will govern any matters not specifically covered by its terms.

> **EXAMPLE: Method of Accounting**
> The partnership shall keep accounts on the accrual [or cash] basis. The accounts shall readily disclose items which the partners take into account separately for income tax purposes. As to matters of accounting not provided for in this agreement, generally accepted accounting principles shall govern.[77]

(c) The location of the firm's books and records must be established, and the partners' access to the books should be considered. Any restrictions upon a partner's right to inspect or copy books and records will be included here.

> **EXAMPLE: Location of Books**
> The partnership books shall be kept at the principal place of business of the partnership, and every partner shall at all times have access to and may inspect and

copy any of them.[78] [*Or,* all partners shall have access to such books and records only upon 72 hours prior written notice to the managing partner and during normal business hours.]

(d) The bank accounts and other banking arrangements are stated in the agreement, including the persons authorized to sign checks, to borrow funds, and otherwise to conduct banking transactions on behalf of the firm.

> **EXAMPLE: Banking Arrangements**
> The partnership shall maintain such bank accounts as the partners shall determine. Checks shall be drawn for partnership purposes only and may be signed by any person or persons designated by the partners. All moneys received by the partnership shall be deposited in such account or accounts.[79]

(e) Provisions should be included for the rendering of periodic reports to partners (e.g., monthly, quarterly, semiannually, or annually). The partners may be required to sign and verify the reports, subject to objection for manifest errors within a specified period of time.

> **EXAMPLE: Reports of Operations**
> The managing partner shall provide reports of cash activity, profit or loss, and the current balance sheet of the partnership to each partner at least quarterly, within 15 days following the close of the calendar quarter of the partnership. Each partner shall be required to signify his or her receipt of such reports by signing a duplicate copy of the reports and returning the same to the managing partner within ten days following receipt of such reports. Any objections or questions concerning such reports must be addressed to the managing partner within 30 days following the receipt of the reports by each partner or the reports shall be deemed to be correct as to the matters presented therein.

(f) The person responsible for keeping the partnership books should be named.

> **EXAMPLE: Responsibility for Records**
> The managing partner shall be responsible for the partnership books and records and shall maintain the same at the principal place of business of the partnership. The managing partner may, upon notice to the other partners, delegate such persons who may assume the obligations of keeping the partnership records.

(g) An audit by independent certified public accountants may be appropriate for some businesses, and the agreement will authorize such an audit.

> **EXAMPLE: Audit of Books and Records**
> As soon as practical after the close of the partnership's calendar year, the managing partner shall engage an independent certified public accountant to audit the partnership books and records, and shall provide copies of the audit report furnished by such accountant to each of the partners.
>
> [*or*]
>
> Each partner shall be entitled to engage the services of an independent certified public accountant to audit the books and records of the partnership following the close of the partnership's calendar year. The partner so desiring such audit shall pay all expenses and fees of the accountant, and no such expenses shall be assessed against the partnership, unless the results of the audit indicate a variance of over

or under ten percent of the profit and loss reported to the partners by the managing partner in any calendar year, in which event the expenses of the audit shall be borne by the partnership as a partnership expense.

12. Meetings—Partners' meetings may be established on a regular basis by the agreement, specifying the time and place for such meetings. Special meetings may be called in accordance with the agreement. A clause authorizing special meetings should consider the parties who are entitled to call special meetings, the notice required, and whether the notice must specify the purpose of the meeting.

> **EXAMPLE: Meetings**
> Partners meetings will be held on the second Tuesday of each month at 5:00 p.m. at the principal place of business of the partnership. No notice shall be required for the regular meetings of the partnership. A special meeting may be called by any partner upon giving three days written notice to the other partners, specifying a time and place for the meeting and the purpose of the meeting.

13. Management

(a) Method of management (see "Management of a Partnership" earlier in this chapter)—The management of the business affairs of the firm must be decided in accordance with the agreement. One or more of the partners may have a specialized business skill, and this should not be overlooked. Many variations are possible for management activities, including the following:

(1) Each partner has an equal voice in management.

(2) Some partners (usually those with larger capital contributions) will have a greater vote than others.

(3) A committee of partners will be established to make certain decisions.

(4) A managing partner (or partners) will be appointed to control the daily business affairs of the firm.

(5) Some partners may have no management activities under the agreement. These persons are usually called *dormant* or *silent* partners.

> **EXAMPLE: Equal Management**
> Management and the conduct of the business of the partnership shall be vested in all partners, and no partner shall be solely responsible for management functions. The partners shall have an equal vote on all partnership matters and all issues to be resolved in the partnership shall be determined by a majority vote.

> **EXAMPLE: Other-than-Equal Management**
> Management and the conduct of the business shall be vested in all Partners, and no Partner shall be solely responsible for management functions. The Partners shall have the following votes on Partnership matters:
>
> | | |
> |---|---|
> | Peter J. McLaughlin | 11 |
> | James T. Johnston | 33 |
> | Steve Forness | 11 |
> | David A. French | 11 |
> | Thomas Stubbs | 33 |
> | Michael Theisen | 1 |
>
> A quorum shall be the presence at a meeting of 50 votes. No Partnership matter may be approved except at a meeting in which a quorum of votes is represented in the manner provided in this Paragraph, or as otherwise provided in this agreement.

(b) Management duties
   (1) If a managing partner is used, the managing partner's duties should be specified in the agreement. Moreover, any management decisions that are to be referred to all of the partners should be described.

   > **EXAMPLE: Duties of a Managing Partner**
   > a) The affairs of the Partnership shall be managed and conducted by the Managing General Partner in accordance with the provisions of the Colorado Uniform Partnership Act, as amended, and subject to the terms and provisions of this Agreement.
   > b) The Managing General Partner shall devote such of his or her time as may be necessary to select, at his or her sole discretion, and to acquire master recordings for the Partnership; to retain a distributor for the recordings owned by the Partnership; to supervise the activities of the distributor and to hire replacement or additional distributors if deemed necessary by the Managing General Partner; to make inspections of any physical assets owned by the Partnership and to see to it that such assets are being properly maintained; to prepare or cause to be prepared all reports of operations which are to be furnished to the Partners or which are required by any government agencies; and to do all other things which may be necessary to supervise the affairs and businesses of the Partnership in a prudent and businesslike manner in the best interest of the Partners.
   > c) The Managing General Partner is hereby authorized, on behalf of the Partnership, to execute any contracts, notes, or other documents which may be required in connection with the acquisition, financing and operation of the assets and business described in this Agreement.
   > d) The Managing General Partner, in addition to the other powers and rights granted to him or her and subject to the specific limitations imposed by this Agreement, shall have the right, upon such terms and conditions as he or she may deem proper, to (1) borrow money on the general credit of the Partnership for use in the Partnership business, including the right to borrow money from himself or herself and to charge the Partnership interest on funds so borrowed, provided the interest rate to be charged by the Managing General Partner for such borrowed funds shall not exceed the rate available from commercial lenders, and provided the Managing General Partner shall not further encumber any master recordings acquired by the Partnership after their initial acquisition, other than in the ordinarycourse of business, without the approval of the Partners; (2) purchase personal property for use in connection with the business of the Partnership and finance such purchases, in whole or in part, by giving the seller or any other person a security interest in the property purchased; (3) make reasonable and necessary capital expenditures and improvements with respect to the assets of the Partnership and take all action reasonably necessary in connection with the management thereof; (4) establish a reasonable reserve for contingencies and operating capital from available cash flow of the Partnership; (5) contract with himself or herself and affiliated persons on terms competitive with those which may be obtained in the open market for property or services required by the Partnership, provided, however, that the Managing General Partner shall not receive from himself or herself, or affiliated persons, or grant to himself or herself, or affiliated persons, any rebates, kickbacks, or give-ups, directly or indirectly, in such transactions or agreements; (6) make reasonable and necessary expenditures for the maintenance and operation of the assets of the Partnership; and (7) enter into agreements for the management of the assets of the Partnership.
   > e) The Managing General Partner shall assume a fiduciary responsibility for the safekeeping and use of all Partnership funds and assets, whether or not in his or her immediate possession or control, and shall not employ, or permit another to

employ, such funds or assets in any manner except for the exclusive benefit of the Partnership. Partnership funds shall not be commingled with the funds of any other person or entity.

f) The Managing General Partner shall not cause the Partnership to purchase interests in other business organizations, underwrite the securities of any other businesses, offer Partnership interests in exchange for anything other than cash or notes, or make loans to other persons or entities.

g) Except where power or duties are reserved to the Managing General Partner, other Partnership matters shall be determined by the unanimous vote of the Partners.

EXAMPLE: Limitations on Powers of the Managing General Partner

The Managing General Partner shall have full, exclusive and complete discretion in the management of and control over the affairs of the Partnership; provided, however, the Managing General Partner shall not take any of the following actions without the consent of all Partners:

a) Sale, exchange, or other disposition of all or substantially all of the Partnership's assets other than in the ordinary course of business;

b) Refinancing, recasting, increasing, modifying or extending any loans secured in whole or in part by master recordings owned by the Partnership, other than in the ordinary course of business;

c) Sale, assignment or encumbrance of the Managing General Partner's interest in the Partnership;

d) Admission of a Successor Managing General Partner to the Partnership;

e) Admission of additional Partners to the Partnership;

f) Engagement of the Partnership in a business other than that specified in this Agreement; and

g) Amendment or modification of this Agreement unless that amendment or modification is otherwise permitted under this Agreement without action of all Partners.

(2) All partners are expected to devote their time and energies to the partnership business.[80] Any deviation from this rule must be detailed in the agreement.

EXAMPLE: Outside Activities

No partner shall engage in, or invest or deal in the securities of, any business that in any wise competes with that of this firm, nor shall he or she give any time or attention to any outside business, except that of bank director, without the written consent of his or her copartners.[81]

(3) Each partner should be required, upon request, to account to the other partners regarding all transactions relating to the partnership business of which that partner has knowledge.

EXAMPLE: Reports of Activities

The managing partner shall, at least ten days prior to the regular meeting of the partnership, specify which of the partners are to report on areas of the partnership business within their control and responsibility. Such reports may be furnished orally at the meeting, unless the managing partner requires a written report in the notice, in which case a copy of the report shall be distributed to the partners at the meeting and appended to the minutes of the partnership meeting.

(4) The agreement may require certain partners to provide a bond for faithful performance of their management duties.

> **EXAMPLE: Fidelity Bond**
> The managing partner shall, at the expense of the partnership, acquire and maintain a fidelity bond in the amount of $100,000.00 with an insurance company acceptable to a majority of the partners. The bond shall provide for the payment upon such bond for any willful failure or neglect of the managing partner to perform his or her duties hereunder, upon defalcation or embezzlement by the managing partner, upon the loss to the partnership of any asset as a result of the negligence of the managing partner, and upon such other terms and conditions as may be required by the majority of the partners.

(c) Management formula—Depending upon the management method selected (e.g., equal voice, managing partner, etc.), the agreement will state a formula for determining partnership action. For example, if all partners have an equal voice, the formula may require a majority, two-thirds, or unanimous vote to carry action on behalf of the firm. The decision of a managing partner is usually final on matters within his or her control. In certain cases, unanimity of partners will be required by law.[82]

(d) Disputes—In case of a deadlocked dispute on management matters, the agreement usually requires submission of the dispute to an independent third party or to arbitration.

> **EXAMPLE: Arbitration**
> All disputes and questions whatsoever which shall, either during the partnership or afterwards, arise between the partners or their respective representatives, or between any partners or between a partner and the representative of any other or others, touching these articles, or the construction or application thereof, or any clause or thing herein contained, or any account, valuation or division of assets, debts, or liabilities to be made hereunder, or as to any act, deed or omission of any partner, or as to any other matter in any way relating to the partnership business or the affairs thereof, or the rights, duties or liabilities of any person under these articles, shall be referred to a single arbitrator in case the parties agree upon one; otherwise to two arbitrators, one to be appointed by each party to the difference, or, in case of their disagreement to an umpire, to be appointed by said arbitrators.[83]

(e) Prohibited activities[84]

(1) Certain matters affecting the partnership must be decided by all partners, including assignment of the partnership property in trust for creditors, sale of the goodwill of the business, confession of judgment against the firm, submission of a partnership claim to arbitration, and other acts that would make it impossible to carry out the partnership business.

> **EXAMPLE: Limitation on a Partner's Authority**
> No partner, shall, without the unanimous consent of the other partners, do any of the following acts:
>
> a) Assignment of the partnership property in trust for creditors;
> b) Sale of the goodwill of the business or substantially all of the assets of the business;

c) Confess a judgment against the partnership or its assets;
d) Submit a partnership claim to arbitration;
e) Commit any other act which would make it impossible to carry out the partnership business.

(2) Partners may be further restricted in their power to bind the firm. An individual partner is usually not permitted to extend credit, pledge the partnership property, hire and fire employees, cause an attachment of firm property, or release debts without the appropriate consensus of the other partners.

EXAMPLE: Further Limitations on a Partner's Authority
No partner shall, without the consent of the others, borrow or lend money on behalf of the partnership; sell, assign, or pledge his or her interest in the partnership; or execute any lease, mortgage, security agreement, or endorsement on behalf of the partnership.[85] No purchase or other contract, involving a liability of more than Five thousand dollars, nor any importation from abroad, shall be made, nor any transaction out of the usual course of the retail business shall be undertaken, by either of the partners without the previous consent and approval of the other partner.[86]

(3) It may be desirable to govern the private lives of the partners in certain respects. For example, the agreement may forbid any partner from going into debt except for living necessaries; may restrict a partner's ability to deal in securities on margin; may demand that a partner discharge any filed liens within a thirty-day period; and so on.

EXAMPLE: Limitation on Extraordinary Debts
In order to protect the property and assets of the Partnership from any claim against any Partner for personal debts owed by such Partner, each Partner shall promptly pay all debts owing by him or her and shall indemnify the Partnership from any claim that might be made to the detriment of the Partnership by any personal creditor of such Partner.

(4) The partners may be restricted in their sale or assignment of any or all of their interests in the partnership.[87] Common restrictions include the requirement of consent by the other partners, or a right of first refusal for the other partners, permitting them to purchase the interest at the offered price.

EXAMPLE: Sale of a Partner's Interest
In the event that a Partner desires to sell, assign, or otherwise transfer his or her share of interest in the Partnership hereby created and has obtained a bona fide offer for the sale thereof made by some person not a member of this Partnership, he or she shall first offer to sell, assign or otherwise transfer the said interest to the other Partners at the price and on the same terms as previously offered him or her, and each other Partner shall have the right to purchase his or her proportionate share of the selling Partner's interest. If any Partner does not desire to purchase the said interest on such terms or at such price, no other Partner may purchase any part of the interest, and the selling Partner may then sell, assign, or otherwise transfer his or her entire interest in the Partnership to the person making the said offer at the price offered. The intent of this provision is to require that the entire interest of a Partner be sold intact, without fractionalization. A purchaser of an interest of

the Partnership shall not become a Partner without the unanimous consent of the non-selling Partners.

14. Partnership property
    (a) The name in which partnership property will be titled is established by the agreement.

> **EXAMPLE: Title to Property**
> All assets of the partnership shall be titled in the name of the partnership, Shoylin Associates.

(b) If any property is loaned to the firm by a partner, it should be separately described and the agreement should detail the duration of the loan, any restrictions upon the disposition of the property by the partner, and any compensation to be paid to the partner for the use of the asset.[88]

> **EXAMPLE: Loans of Property by a Partner**
> Maynard P. Short has loaned to the partnership, and by this agreement, agrees to the exclusive use of the partnership, all of the property listed and described on Exhibit B, attached to this agreement and incorporated herein by reference. The partnership shall have exclusive use and enjoyment of the property for a period of one year from the date of this agreement, and for successive annual periods, unless, prior to the expiration of an annual term, Mr. Short gives written notice of at least 30 days to the partnership of his intention to reacquire the possession and use of the property. So long as the partnership shall be in possession of the property, Mr. Short shall not assign, sell, encumber, or otherwise deal with such property, and any such action by Mr. Short shall be deemed to be a breach of this agreement. The partnership shall pay Mr. Short the sum of $10,000.00 per year in equal quarterly installments for the use of the property described on Exhibit B.

(c) Accounting procedures for partnership property, including the treatment of depreciation, repairs, insurance, taxes, interest, and other expenses, should be considered.

> **EXAMPLE: Method of Accounting for Assets**
> All accounting for partnership assets shall be done according to generally accepted accounting procedures, using the most conservative methods of accounting for depreciation, investment tax credits, etc. The managing partner shall be directed to provide for depreciation, repairs, insurance, taxes, interest and other reserves as necessary for partnership operations in order to meet such operating and capital expenses when they are incurred.

15. Causes of dissolution[89]
    (a) Retirement or withdrawal
        (1) The agreement may describe the circumstances under which a partner may retire. Most agreements permit the partner to retire and withdraw at any time after a certain date or after the partner has reached a certain age.
        (2) Notice of retirement or withdrawal is usually required to be given to the other partners.
        (3) A noncompetition clause may be appropriate to restrict the business activities of a retiring or withdrawing partner.[90]

(4) The agreement should provide for indemnification of the retiring or withdrawing partner for all existing liabilities if the remaining partners elect to continue the business.

(5) If the withdrawal of a partner is wrongful, any penalties to be imposed as a result of wrongful withdrawal should be specified in the agreement.

> **EXAMPLE: Retirement or Withdrawal**
> A Partner shall have the right, at any time during the continuance of this agreement and of the Partnership created hereby, to withdraw or retire from the said Partnership by giving three (3) months notice to the other Partners at the Partnership's place of business.
>
> Upon giving notice, the withdrawing or retiring Partner shall be entitled to payment of his or her interest in the Partnership, the amount of which and method of payment is determined by this agreement with reference to purchase of an expelled Partner's interest. Upon the receipt of such payment, the interest of the withdrawing or retiring Partner in the Partnership shall cease and terminate.
>
> Notwithstanding the provisions above, if the remaining Partners shall decide not to continue the business upon withdrawal or retirement of a Partner, the remaining Partners may elect to terminate and dissolve the Partnership, in which case the withdrawing or retiring Partner shall only be entitled to his or her interest in liquidation, as stated in this agreement with reference to voluntary termination.

(b) Expulsion of a partner

(1) The circumstances justifying expulsion of a partner must be specifically detailed.

(2) A method for deciding upon expulsion and a procedure for notifying the expelled partner should be established. If a hearing will be permitted, the procedure for conducting the hearing should be described.

(3) The agreement should provide for indemnification of the expelled partner for all existing liabilities if the remaining partners elect to continue the business.

> **EXAMPLE: Expulsion**
> A partner of this partnership may, upon the affirmative vote of the other partners, be expelled for the following acts:
>
> a) Committing a felony under the laws of the state in which this partnership is organized;
> b) Failing to cure any default or breach of this agreement after receipt of a notice of such default or breach from the other partners in writing;
> c) Committing an act which is deemed to be detrimental to the business or reputation of the partnership;
> d) Adjudication of insanity of the partner;
> e) Competing with the business of the partnership for his or her personal account.
>
> The partners so voting for expulsion shall give notice of expulsion, specifying the reasons therefor, to the expelled partner, who, upon receipt of such notice, shall have ten (10) days to request in writing a hearing on the matters specified in the notice. If a hearing is requested, the partner subject to expulsion shall appoint an impartial third party, and the other partners shall appoint an impartial third party, and each such third party shall appoint another impartial third party to hear such evidence or other matters as the expelled partner wishes to present on his or her behalf. Following such hearing, this panel shall determine whether the partner shall be expelled, and their decision shall be final.

The remaining partners may continue the business without the expelled partner and without liquidation of the partnership by paying the expelled partner his or her capital account, and by furnishing such indemnification and hold harmless documents as may be reasonably requested by the expelled partner for obligations of the partnership which come due following an expulsion.

(c) Bankruptcy of a partner

(1) Provisions should be included for the continuance of the business in case of the bankruptcy of an individual partner.

(2) The purchase of the individual partner's interest in the partnership must be authorized.

EXAMPLE: Bankruptcy of a Partner
Upon the adjudication of bankruptcy of a partner, or the assignment by a partner for the benefit of his or her creditors, or the appointment of a receiver or conservator for the disposition of a partner's debts, the other partners shall have the right either to purchase the bankrupt partner's interest in the partnership or to terminate and liquidate the partnership business. If the remaining partners elect to purchase the bankrupt partner's interest, they shall serve notice of such election upon the trustee in bankruptcy, receiver, conservator or assignees of the bankrupt partner within twenty (20) days following such event, and shall pay to such person or persons the value of the bankrupt partner's interest in the partnership determined as of the day before such event occurred. If the remaining partners do not elect to purchase the bankrupt partner's interest, and instead elect to terminate the business, they shall appoint a managing partner who shall proceed with reasonable promptness to sell the property of the partnership and to liquidate the business of the partnership. The bankrupt partner's estate shall thereafter share in the proceeds of liquidation in accordance with his or her pro rata share of the proceeds thereof.

(d) Death of a partner

(1) Provisions should be included for the continuance of the business when one partner dies.

(2) If the deceased partner's estate is to participate in profits of the business, the agreement should describe the extent of participation. This clause should discuss the amount of profits to be distributed to the estate, the period during which such distributions are to be made, and whether profit distributions are guaranteed.

(3) The agreement will establish the authority for the purchase of life insurance on the partners. The partners may purchase life insurance on each other (cross-purchase plan) or the firm may purchase the insurance (entity purchase plan). The amount of the insurance to be maintained and the type of plan should be described in the agreement.

(4) If the life insurance plan is to be administered by a trustee, the trustee is named and his or her power and duties should be defined in the agreement.

EXAMPLE: Death of a Partner
Upon the death of any Partner, the surviving Partners shall have the right either to purchase the decedent's interest in the Partnership or to terminate and liquidate the Partnership business. If the surviving Partners elect to purchase the decedent's interest, they shall serve notice in writing of such election, within three (3) months after the death of the decedent, upon the executor or administrator of the

decedent, or, if at the time of such election no legal representative has been appointed, upon any one of the known legal heirs of the decedent at the last known address of such heir. The closing of such purchase shall be within thirty (30) days of the notice of such election.

If the surviving Partners elect to purchase the decendent's interest, the purchase price and method of payment shall be as stated in this agreement with reference to purchase of an expelled Partner's interest, except in the event insurance is in effect with respect to decedent the method of payment is provided in this section. The period from the beginning of the fiscal year in which decedent's death occurred until the end of the calendar month in which his or her death occurred shall be the period used for purposes of calculating his or her share of Partnership profits and losses in the year of death. The decedent's share of profits and losses shall also include his or her share of profits and losses of the Partnership during the period between the end of the calendar month in which death occurred and the end of the calendar month preceding the closing of purchase.

If the surviving Partners do not elect to purchase the decedent's interest, and instead elect to terminate the business, they shall appoint a managing partner who shall proceed with reasonable promptness to sell the real and personal property owned by the Partnership and to liquidate the business of the Partnership. The surviving Partners and the estate of the deceased Partner shall share in their respective proportions stated during the period of liquidation, except that the decedent's estate shall not be liable for losses in excess of the decedent's interest in the Partnership at the time of his or her death. The managing Partner shall be entitled to reasonable compensation for services performed in liquidation. Except as otherwise stated herein, the procedure as to liquidation and distribution of the Partnership assets shall be the same as stated in this agreement with reference to voluntary termination.

The Partnership may contract for life insurance protection on the lives of each of the Partners, in any amount not disproportionate to the value of each Partner's interest. Each Partner may designate the beneficiary for such life insurance. In the event of death of a Partner, insurance proceeds paid to the Partnership will be used to purchase the decedent's interest, at the purchase price determined above, except that the payment of such price to the decedent's representatives or heirs shall be made within thirty (30) days following receipt of the insurance proceeds. Any surplus in insurance proceeds not required to purchase the decedent's interest shall be retained in the Partnership and proportionately added to the capital account of the surviving Partners. If the surviving Partners elect to liquidate the business in lieu of purchasing the decedent's interest, the proceeds of any life insurance shall be treated as an asset of the Partnership for liquidation.

(e) Other disabilities—The partnership may be dissolved when an individual partner becomes disabled, insane, or otherwise incapable of continuing in the business relationship. These special incidents of dissolution should be considered in the agreement, with provisions for continuation of the business and purchase of the former partner's interest.

> **EXAMPLE: Disability of a Partner**
> In the event a partner becomes disabled, is adjudicated insane, or is otherwise unable to perform the duties required by this agreement, the remaining partners shall have the right either to purchase the disabled partner's interest in the partnership or to terminate and liquidate the disabled partner's interest in the partnership. If the surviving partners elect to purchase the disabled partner's

interest, then the procedure described in this agreement for the purchase of a deceased partner's interest in the partnership shall apply. If the remaining partners elect to terminate and liquidate the business, they shall appoint a managing partner who shall proceed with reasonable promptness to terminate the business, sell the property of the partnership, and distribute the proceeds of such liquidation, after payment to creditors, in the manner provided for dissolution and liquidation in this agreement.

16. Continuation of the business—Following a dissolution, the remaining partners will have the authority to continue the business if the dissolution was wrongful. In other cases of dissolution, the business may be continued only if the agreement so provides. A specific clause granting the remaining partners the right to continue business is appropriate. Notice of the intent to continue the business may be required to be given to the former partner or to the former partner's estate. In all cases, the withdrawing, retiring, or disabled partner or the estate of the deceased partner should be indemnified from business liabilities.

17. Purchase of the partner's interest—If a partner has caused a dissolution and the remaining partners intend to continue the business, the interest of the withdrawing, disabled, or deceased partner will be purchased by the firm or by the other partners.[91]

(a) The agreement may provide that the former partner's interest will be purchased by the other partners jointly or individually in an established proportion.

(b) The agreement may provide for liquidating distributions to the former partner, resulting in a purchase of that partner's interest by the firm.

(c) The value of the partner's interest should be ascertained in accordance with a formula specified in the agreement. Independent public accountants may be necessary to make the computations under the formula. The following typical alternatives are available:

   (1) A return of the capital contribution plus interest
   (2) A stipulated value as described in the agreement
   (3) A formula based upon historical earnings of the partnership (earnings multiple formula)
   (4) A formula based upon the value of the assets of the partnership (book value formula)
   (5) An appraisal by an independent third party[92]

(d) The extent to which goodwill is to be used to compute the value of the former partner's interest is established by the agreement. Goodwill may be ignored, or it may be considered an asset and appraised in determining the value of the interest.

(e) Payment terms should be established in the agreement. The period of time for installment payments, whether a promissory note is to be executed, and whether the obligation will be secured by assets of the partnership are appropriate topics for this provision.

(f) A fund may be withheld for a period of time for contingent claims arising before the dissolution.

(g) The treatment of the purchased interest should be discussed. The interest may be divided among partners in their remaining proportion of capital contributions, equally, or by some other formula.

> **EXAMPLE: Continuation of Business and Purchase of Partner's Interest**
> The Partners may elect to continue the business despite a dissolution of the partnership, by purchasing the deceased, disabled, expelled or bankrupt Partner's interest, and in such case the purchase price shall be equal to the deceased, disabled, expelled or bankrupt Partner's capital account as of the date of the notice required by this agreement, plus his or her income account as of the end of the prior fiscal year, increased by his or her share of Partnership profits, or decreased by his or her share of Partnership losses, computed to the date of the notice, and decreased by withdrawals such as would have been charged to his or her income account during the present year to the date of the purchase of his or her interest. The purchase price is subject to set-off for any damages incurred as the result of the expelled or bankrupt Partner's actions, and nothing in this paragraph is intended to impair the Partnership's right to recover damages for such reasons.
>
> The date of the notice, referred to above, shall be the date personal notice is received, or the date the certified mail is postmarked, in the case of a breach of this agreement.

18. Liquidation and winding-up (see "Dissolution and Termination of a Partnership" earlier in this chapter)—If the business will not be continued following dissolution, liquidation and winding-up must follow in accordance with the agreement.

(a) A full and general account of the firm's assets, liabilities, and transactions should be authorized. An independent certified public accountant may be necessary for this purpose.

(b) A liquidating partner or committee of partners should be named. Since partners may receive remuneration for services in liquidation, the value of such services should be fixed by agreement.

(c) If the assets are capable of distribution to the partners, this may be authorized in the agreement, following the payment of business debts. Otherwise, the agreement should authorize the sale of the assets (usually in the discretion and good judgment of the liquidating partner) and the distribution of the cash received.

(d) The order of distribution of the assets is set by law.[93] If the order of distribution is to be altered, the agreement must specifically describe the new order of distribution.

(e) If the partnership has sustained a loss, so that one or more of the partners will be required to make additional capital contributions to facilitate distribution of assets, a period of time in which such payments are to be made and the manner of payment (cash, promissory note, etc.) should be specified.

> **EXAMPLE: Distribution on Termination**
> Upon termination of the Partnership, its affairs shall be concluded in the following manner:
>
> a) The Managing General Partner shall proceed to the liquidation of the Partnership and the proceeds of such liquidation shall be applied and distributed in the following order of priority:
>
> 1) To the payment of all debts and liabilities of the Partnership;
>
> 2) To the setting up of any reserve which the Managing General Partner shall deem reasonably necessary to provide for any contingent or unforeseen liabilities or obligations of the Partnership; provided, however, that at the expiration of such period of time as the Managing General Partnership shall

deem advisable, the balance of such reserve remaining after the payment of such contingency shall be distributed in the manner set forth in this section;

3) To the payment to the partners other than the Managing General Partner of an amount which, when added to any amount previously distributed to the partners other than the Managing General Partner pursuant to this agreement hereof, will equal their aggregate capital contributions to the Partnership;

4) Any balance then remaining shall be distributed as follows:

  i) Ninety percent (90%) of such balance to the partners other than the Managing General Partner;

  ii) Ten percent (10%) of such balance of the Managing General Partner;

b) A reasonable time shall be allowed for the orderly liquidation of the assets of the Partnership and the discharge of liabilities to creditors;

c) Each Partner shall be furnished with a statement certified by the Partnership's independent accountants which shall set forth the assets and liabilities of the Partnership as of the date of the complete liquidation.

NOTES

1. For general discussions of the law of agency and partnership, see J. Crane and A. Bromberg, Law of Partnership § § 2, 49–56, 68–72 (1968); and W. Seavey, Agency § § 10A, 14A, 59 (1964).
2. 6 U.L.A. 1 (1969) and Supp. (1980). The Uniform Partnership Act (hereafter cited as U.P.A.) has not been adopted in Georgia and Louisiana.
3. U.P.A. § 6(1).
4. Model Business Corporation Act (hereafter cited as M.B.C.A.) § 3.02(9).
5. U.P.A. § 18(a), (e).
6. U.P.A. § 2.
7. U.P.A. § 8(2).
8. West's Modern Legal Forms § 6332.
9. See "Tax Considerations of a General Partnership" later in this chapter.
10. West's Modern Legal Forms § 6342.
11. West's Modern Legal Forms § 6343.
12. U.P.A. § 25.
13. U.P.A. § 27.
14. U.P.A. § 18(g).
15. A sample assignment by a partner of his or her interest in the partnership appears as Form 2A in Appendix G.
16. U.P.A. § 18(e).
17. U.P.A. § 18(h).
18. West's Modern Legal Forms § 6366.
19. West's Modern Legal Forms § 6368.
20. U.P.A. § 9(3).
21. West's Modern Legal Forms § 6360.
22. U.P.A. § 18(f).
23. West's Modern Legal Forms § 6347.
24. West's Modern Legal Forms § 6348.
25. U.P.A. § 18(a).
26. West's Modern Legal Forms § 6354.
27. West's Modern Legal Forms § 6353.
28. Partnership taxation is *pass-through* taxation, which means that each individual partner is taxed on the partner's pro rata share of each item of profit, loss, deductions, and credits. See "Tax Considerations of a General Partnership" later in this chapter.
29. Internal Revenue Code of 1986, 26 U.S.C.A. § 704(b). The regulations under Section 704(b) of the Code (adopted before the Tax Reform Act of 1976) outline several relevant considerations in making a determination as to whether a special allocation will be recognized for federal income tax purposes. Among these are (1) the presence of a business purpose for the allocation; (2)

whether related items of income, gain, loss, deduction, or credit from the same source are subject to the same allocation; (3) whether the allocation was made without recognition of normal business factors; (4) whether it was made only after the amount of the specially allocated items could reasonably be estimated; (5) the duration of the allocation; and (6) the overall tax consequences of the allocation.

30. General partners are jointly and severally liable for damages caused by any tort or breach of trust committed by a partner within the scope of the partnership business. They are jointly liable for all other partnership obligations. U.P.A. § 15.
31. U.P.A. § 18(b).
32. West's Modern Legal Forms § 6350.
33. U.P.A. § 36(1).
34. See "Dissolution and Termination of a Partnership" later in this chapter.
35. U.P.A. § 35(1)(b). Examples of the necessary notice appear as Forms 2B and 2C in Appendix G.
36. U.P.A. § 17.
37. U.P.A. § 31(1)(a).
38. West's Modern Legal Forms § 6381.
39. U.P.A. § 31(1)(c).
40. West's Modern Legal Forms § 6421.
41. U.P.A. § 31(1)(b), (2).
42. Examples of preliminary notice and final notice of expulsion appear as Forms 2D and 2E in Appendix G.
43. U.P.A. § 31(3), (4), (5).
44. U.P.A. §§ 31(6), 32.
45. U.P.A. § 38(1).
46. U.P.A. § 38(2)(b).
47. See J. Crane and A. Bromberg, Law of Partnership §§ 86, 90A (1968).
48. West's Modern Legal Forms § 6303. Other examples of liquidating distributions may be found in §§ 6302 and 6304, and in Article V, Sections C and D of the Complex Partnership Agreement, Form 2F in Appendix G.
49. See West's Modern Legal Forms § 6307.
50. Examples of cross-purchase and entity purchase insurance agreements may be found in West's Modern Legal Forms §§ 6402–04.
51. West's Modern Legal Forms § 6379.
52. West's Modern Legal Forms § 6375. See also "Trade Secret Protection" and "Covenants Not to Compete" in Chapter 10.
53. U.P.A. § 33.
54. U.P.A. § 40.
55. Internal Revenue Code of 1986, 26 U.S.C.A. § 704(c)(2).
56. Internal Revenue Code of 1986, 26 U.S.C.A. § 704(c).
57. See, e.g., 1 Z. Cavitch, Business Organizations §§ 7.01–8.03 (1973).
58. Examples of the trade name affidavits and certificates appear as Forms 1A–1E in Appendix G.
59. See "Formation and Operation of a Sole Proprietorship" in Chapter 1.
60. The qualification of a *foreign partnership* is patterned after the requirements for qualification of foreign corporations, discussed in Chapter 12.
61. Other helpful references include M. Volz, C. Trower, and D. Reiss, The Drafting of Partnership Agreements, American Law Institute (1986); R. Rowley and D. Sive, Rowley on Partnership, Vol. II, Chapter 59 (1960); and J. M. Barrett and E. Seago, Partners and Partnerships Law and Taxation, Vol. II, Appendixes 1 and 10 (1956).
62. West's Modern Legal Forms § 6325.
63. West's Modern Legal Forms § 6328.
64. West's Modern Legal Forms § 6329.
65. West's Modern Legal Forms § 6331.
66. West's Modern Legal Forms § 6336.
67. West's Modern Legal Forms § 6332.
68. West's Modern Legal Forms § 6337.
69. West's Modern Legal Forms § 6340.
70. West's Modern Legal Forms § 6338.
71. West's Modern Legal Forms § 6339.
72. West's Modern Legal Forms § 6344.

73. West's Modern Legal Forms § 6348.
74. West's Modern Legal Forms § 6347.
75. See "Profits and Losses" earlier in this chapter.
76. West's Modern Legal Forms § 6357.
77. West's Modern Legal Forms § 6355.
78. West's Modern Legal Forms § 6358.
79. West's Modern Legal Forms § 6359.
80. See "Management of a Partnership" earlier in this chapter.
81. West's Modern Legal Forms § 6365.
82. See "Management of a Partnership" earlier in this chapter.
83. West's Modern Legal Forms § 6376.
84. See "Management of a Partnership" earlier in this chapter.
85. West's Modern Legal Forms § 6361.
86. West's Modern Legal Forms § 6364.
87. See "Partner's Interest in a Partnership" earlier in this chapter.
88. See "Partnership Property" earlier in this chapter.
89. See "Dissolution and Termination of a Partnership" earlier in this chapter.
90. See "Covenants Not to Compete" in Chapter 10.
91. See "Dissolution and Termination of a Partnership" earlier in this chapter.
92. See also "Share Transfer Restrictions and Buy-Out Agreements" in Chapter 11.
93. See "Dissolution and Termination of a Partnership" earlier in this chapter.

3 LIMITED PARTNERSHIP

CHARACTERISTICS OF A LIMITED PARTNERSHIP

In many important particulars of partnership law, the limited partnership is the same as a general partnership. It is an association of two or more persons carrying on business as co-owners for profit with one or more general partners and one or more limited partners.[1] The limited partnership enjoys certain characteristics of a corporation insofar as the limited partners are concerned, since their investment and limited liability resemble those of a shareholder of a corporation. The general partners in a limited partnership are governed by all the rules of a general partnership as discussed in Chapter 2. It may be said that a limited partnership is a bifurcated business form, and the rights and responsibilities of the limited and general partners must be distinguished.

Most states have adopted the Uniform Limited Partnership Act[2] to regulate the formation and operation of limited partnerships. The first Uniform Limited Partnership Act was approved by the Commissioners on Uniform State Laws in 1916, and is still being used in its original form in many states. In 1976, the commissioners approved a revised Uniform Limited Partnership Act, which significantly modified the original act and has been accepted in many states.[3] In 1985, the commissioners approved several amendments to the Revised Uniform Limited Partnership Act, and a few states have adopted the amendments as well. Therefore, nationally, three different approaches may be found in any local law concerning the statutory basis of limited partnerships. Since the purpose of the revisions and the amendments was to modernize the prior uniform law concerning limited partnerships, it is likely that most states will eventually adopt the revised act with the amendments. Consequently, this chapter refers primarily to the rules from the revised act with amendments, although it also discusses unique issues that exist under the original act (for those who insist on knowing everything about limited partnership law throughout the country).

The most important statutory requirement under both the original and revised acts, the filing of a limited partnership certificate, is discussed in detail at a later point in this chapter. However, it is important to note at the outset that the limited partnership may be formed only with the formality prescribed in the statute, and may not be born of a simple private agreement between the parties. Like a corporation, this form of business is imbued with quasi-public characteristics, which pose additional problems for the person drafting the documents and may operate as a trap for the unwary.

GENERAL PARTNERS OF A LIMITED PARTNERSHIP

Each limited partnership must have at least one general partner, who faces all of the same risks and responsibilities as a partner in a general partnership. The liability exposure of limited partners is confined to their contributions, but the general partner suffers unlimited liability, meaning that his or her individual assets are vulnerable to firm creditors. Similarly, the general partner has full responsibility for management and control of the partnership affairs, since limited partners are generally forbidden to participate in the control of the business if they are to maintain their limited liability status.[4]

One person may be a general partner and a limited partner at the same time,[5] and the authority to do this produces some benefits. In a person's status as general partner, he or she is fully liable for firm obligations and has no limited liability. However, that person's contribution as a limited partner will rank with the priorities of other limited partners for dissolution purposes,[6] and his or her limited partnership interest is freely transferable without causing a dissolution of the partnership.[7]

If the limited partnership has two or more general partners, the rights and responsibilities between those general partners are the same as in any general partnership.

A partner's status is determined to be that of a general partner if that partner has been identified as a general partner in the partnership agreement and named as a general partner in the certificate of limited partnership.[8] Once the original certificate of limited partnership has been filed, additional general partners may be admitted in the manner provided in the partnership agreement, or, if the agreement is silent, with the written consent of all partners, both general and limited.[9]

There are several ways a general partner can withdraw from the limited partnership, either intentionally or accidentally. The general partner "ceases to be a general partner of the partnership" whenever one or more of the following situations occur.

1. The general partner withdraws by giving notice to the other partners (this may violate the partnership agreement and cause the general partner to be liable for damages).[10]
2. The general partner assigns the interest he or she owns in the partnership to another person who is not a partner. This does not make the other person a partner in the partnership, and only entitles that person to receive the distributions to which the general partner would be entitled. Nevertheless, the assignment causes the general partner to cease being a partner of the partnership.[11]
3. The general partner is removed as a general partner in accordance with the procedure described in the partnership agreement.[12]
4. The general partner admits personal insolvency (such as by filing a petition in bankruptcy or by agreeing to reorganization of a general partner's debts), but the general partner may continue being a partner if the partnership agreement excuses such an act.[13]
5. The general partner dies or is incompetent or, in the case of a general partner that is an association (such as a corporation, a trust, or another partnership), the association is terminated or dissolved.[14]

Recall that the withdrawal of a general partner has the effect of dissolving the partnership under general partnership law.[15] The same effect occurs under limited partnership law, with three major exceptions: (1) All of the partners may consent to the continued service of a general partner who has been subject to the foregoing events of withdrawal.[16] (2) Another general partner may be permitted under the partnership agreement to continue the business even though a fellow general partner has withdrawn. Or (3), all of the partners may agree in writing within ninety days after the withdrawal of the general partner to continue the business by the appointment of one or more additional general partners.[17]

If the partnership agreement permits it, general partners will have a right to vote (on a per capita or any other basis prescribed in the agreement) separately as general partners or together with the limited partners on any matter affecting partnership business.[18]

The remaining sections in this chapter deal with the limited partnership's unique variations from a general partnership. In all respects except those specifically set forth in the following sections, a limited partnership is governed by the same rules as a general partnership.[19]

LIMITED LIABILITY AND CONTRIBUTIONS

The most significant characteristic of the limited partnership is that limited partners are protected from full individual liability. The liability of the limited partner is limited to the amount of that partner's investment as stated in the partnership agreement.[20] In this respect, the limited partner is almost exactly like a shareholder of a corporation. This feature makes the limited partnership particularly attractive for persons with substantial private resources that they prefer not to risk in the business enterprise. The only potential loss is the investment.

The original Uniform Limited Partnership Act significantly limited the limited partner's available source of contributions. That statute permitted contributions by a limited partner in cash or other property only. No contribution of services was permitted.[21] This rule was based, in part, on the prohibition against a limited partner's participation in management. Under the revised act, partners may contribute cash, property, or services rendered, or may simply promise through a promissory note or other agreement to contribute cash or property or perform services in the future.[22] These expanded contribution rules reflect the attitude of the drafters of the revised act that persons who participate as limited partners in modern limited partnerships should be able to participate in some aspects of the management of the business without losing their limited liability protection. The management rights of the limited partner under the new statutory provisions are discussed in the next section of this chapter.

Partnership creditors are entitled to rely upon a limited partner's contribution as a source for payment of their obligations. Consequently, the limited partner's written promise in the partnership agreement to contribute assets or services to the partnership can be enforced by the creditors of the partnership. If a partner is unable to perform (because he or she has disposed of the asset promised to be contributed or is dead or disabled), that partner (or his or her estate) will be obligated to contribute cash equal to the value of the defaulted contribution.[23] The other partners of the partnership may be forgiving, however, and may, by a unanimous consent, agree to forgo any contribution not made by a limited partner. Nevertheless, any creditors who extended credit to the partnership before the other partners forgave the obligation may still be able to enforce the original obligation for the contribution against the limited partner.[24]

Limited liability will be observed provided the limited partner does not actively participate in the control of the business and does not knowingly permit the use of his or her name in the firm name (with some exceptions that are discussed later). However, even under these circumstances, the limited partner would be liable to a person who reasonably believed, based upon the limited partner's conduct, that the limited partner is a general partner of the partnership. The limited partner could also be liable to creditors who extend credit to the partnership without actual knowledge that the limited partner is not a general partner.[25]

Whenever a limited partner discovers that there is a possibility of personal liability, and erroneously and in good faith believes that he or she was a limited partner in the partnership, that partner may avoid individual liability by filing the appropriate certificate or amendment to the certificate (if a creditor is asserting that the limited partnership was improperly formed or maintained). The limited partner may withdraw from future equity participation in the partnership by filing a certificate of withdrawal. By taking these actions, a limited partner would be liable only to a creditor who believed in good faith that the limited partner was a general partner of the partnership at the time of the transaction for which liability is claimed.[26]

MANAGEMENT AND CONTROL

The general partners of a limited partnership manage the business, and their management responsibilities and rights are the same in a limited partnership as they are in a general partnership.[27] Normally, the partnership agreement provides for the specific authority of the general partner and for any desired limitations on the general partner's authority. There are certain activities a general partner may never do without the consent of the limited partners, including acting in contravention of the agreement or interfering with the ordinary business of the partnership, possessing partnership property for other than business purposes, admitting another general partner, and confessing a judgment against the firm.[28]

To preserve the limited partner's limited liability status, all management and control over partnership affairs should be vested in the general partner. Historically, this prohibition against management participation caused some uncomfortable uncertainty in the limited partnership organization because it was difficult to predict the extent of participation that would defeat a partner's limited status.

Under the Revised Uniform Limited Partnership Act, limited partners are told that they cannot participate in the control of the business but that they do not participate in the control of the business simply because they are involved in one or more of the following situations.

1. Being a contractor for or agent or employee of the limited partnership or the general partner, or being an officer, director, or shareholder of the corporate general partner
2. Consulting with and advising the general partner regarding the business of the partnership
3. Acting as a surety for the partnership to guarantee or assume its specific obligations
4. Bringing a derivative action on behalf of the partnership

5. Requesting or attending a meeting of partners
6. Proposing or voting on the firm's dissolution, a sale of substantially all of the firm's assets, the incurrence of debt outside the ordinary course of business, a change in the nature of the business, the admission or removal of a general or limited partner, amendments to the partnership agreement, transactions having a conflict of interest, or anything else that the partnership agreement permits the limited partners to decide by vote.

The statute even recognizes that this is not a complete list of activities a limited partner may undertake. So long as the limited partner does not participate in the control of the business, limited liability will be preserved.[29]

Limited partners are always entitled to inspect and copy the books and to have an accounting of partnership affairs. They also have the right to be informed on all matters respecting the business of the firm, and may demand any information from the general partners as is just and reasonable.[30]

ADMISSION, SUBSTITUTION, AND WITHDRAWAL OF A LIMITED PARTNER

Unlike general partners, limited partners may freely come and go, with very few restrictions. If provisions are made in the partnership agreement and the certificate of limited partnership, additional limited partners may be admitted without the consent of the existing limited partners by complying with the procedures in the partnership agreement, and, if necessary under local law, by filing an amendment to the certificate.[31] Similarly, a limited partner may withdraw from the partnership and receive a return of his or her capital contribution without causing a dissolution of the firm.[32] Of course, if the limited partner's contribution is essential to the continued operation of business, this right to withdraw may be restricted or denied by the agreement.

Both the original and revised Uniform Limited Partnership Acts permit a limited partner to withdraw and demand the return of his or her contribution on the date specified for return of the contribution in the partnership agreement or upon giving six months' notice in writing.[33] The contribution may also be returned at any time if all partners, general and limited, consent to its return. However, the investment will be returned only if the firm's creditors have been paid or sufficient assets remain to pay them.[34] Unless the partnership agreement provides otherwise, or all members consent, the limited partner has the right to demand only cash in withdrawal, even if other property was contributed to the partnership.[35] In many states, an amendment of the certificate must also be filed to reflect the withdrawal.

The partnership agreement or certificate may grant to a limited partner authority to substitute a new limited partner in his or her place without the consent of the other partners. If the agreement does not contain such express authority, the assignment of a limited partner's interest has an effect similar to that of the assignment of a general partnership interest. The assignment grants the assignee the right to receive all profits and other distributions to which the limited partner is entitled, but it does not make the assignee a new partner, unless all the partners consent.[36] Any substitution of limited partners, by the power of agreement or by consent, may require an amendment to the certificate to reflect the change.[37]

DISSOLUTION OF A LIMITED PARTNERSHIP

Causes of Dissolution

Dissolution of limited partnerships is very similar to dissolution of general partnerships (discussed in Chapter 2). The major distinctions stem from the limited partner's position outside of the management of the business. A limited partner is a passive investor, like a shareholder of a corporation, and although the limited partner's demise, insanity, bankruptcy, or withdrawal may be a sad event, none of those things should affect the continuation of the business. Consequently, the incapacity of a limited partner does not cause dissolution. Similarly, the limited partner may withdraw his or her capital contribution (investment) and demand its distribution, and the partnership may continue without that partner. Most authorities agree, however, that misconduct by a limited partner, including any act that would adversely affect the business of the firm, would be grounds for dissolution by the other partners.

The limited partnership will be dissolved at the times for termination of the partnership specified in the certificate of limited partnership or in the partnership agreement. Furthermore, as with general partnerships, all members of the limited partnership may consent to a dissolution at any time.[38]

Limited partners have only limited rights to ask for dissolution of the partnership if all other members are not willing to dissolve the firm. A limited partner may have the right to request a dissolution by decree of court whenever it is not reasonably practical to carry on the business under the partnership agreement.[39] This is a very broad standard, and probably incorporates most of the causes justifying dissolution under the original laws of limited partnership, such as incapacity of a general partner, misconduct or breach of the partnership agreement by a partner, or other business or legal reasons that would justify termination of the business based upon changed circumstances.[40] On the other hand, the limited partner may not be able to require a dissolution of the partnership for purely selfish reasons under the Revised Uniform Limited Partnership Act. For example, under the original act, it was possible for a limited partner to request a dissolution of the firm if the limited partner had rightfully demanded a return of a capital contribution but the demand had been ignored.[41] Under the revised act, the demanding limited partner is simply treated as an ordinary creditor of the partnership and may obtain a judgment against the partnership for the amount of the unreturned contribution.[42] Nevertheless, if, in the formation of the partnership, it is considered appropriate to grant limited partners the power to request dissolution under such circumstances, it is still possible to incorporate that right into the original partnership agreement.

The general partner is still an integral member of the firm in the law of limited partnerships. A general partner will be deemed to have withdrawn from the limited partnership by resigning (through written notice); assigning his or her interest in the partnership to a third person; being removed in accordance with the agreement; becoming bankrupt (or taking action similar to bankruptcy); dying; becoming incompetent; or, in the case of a general partner that is another business organization, ceasing to be a valid entity under law.[43] These *events of withdrawal* will result in a dissolution of the partnership unless there is at least one other general partner and the partnership agreement permits the business to be carried on by the remaining general partner, or if, within ninety days after the withdrawal, all partners agree in writing to continue the business and to the appointment of a new or additional general partner.[44] Although the revised act does not explicitly so state, acts of misconduct by the general partner that violate the partnership agreement but which have not resulted in removal of the partner probably still qualify as grounds for dissolution through court action on the request of either general or limited partners.[45]

Continuation of a Limited Partnership Following Dissolution

A disadvantage of a general partnership is the possibility that an accidental dissolution would trigger the obligation to wind up and liquidate the assets of the business at an inopportune time. The antiquated rules of general partnership permit a continuation of the business by the remaining partners only if the agreement anticipated the dissolution or if the dissolution was wrongfully caused.[46] Since the limited partnership is considered to be a useful business organization for modern transactions, and since limited partnership law has been revised twice to be responsive to modern practices, the consequences of dissolution are much less drastic under limited partnership law than they are under general partnership law. As previously mentioned, the mere inability of the general partner to continue in that capacity does not eliminate the continuation of the partnership business. The partnership agreement may anticipate such an event and provide for the continuation of the business by another named general partner. Even if the partnership agreement is silent on this issue, the limited partners may, within ninety days after an event of withdrawal, agree in writing to continue the business without interruption.[47] Nevertheless, it is preferable to anticipate all potential events of dissolution and to provide in the partnership agreement for the procedure to continue the business. It is also best to name the person who will serve as a general partner if the original general partner is unable to do so.

Termination and Winding-Up

If a cause for dissolution occurs and the business is not continued, the limited partnership must be liquidated. Again, the partnership agreement may (and should) anticipate the procedure for winding-up by designating appropriate liquidators and giving them specific instructions concerning the procedure for liquidation. Limited partners were formerly prohibited from participating in the winding-up of a limited partnership unless they obtained court permission.[48] Under the Revised Uniform Limited Partnership Act, unless the partnership agreement provides otherwise, limited partners may serve as liquidators, as may general partners who have not wrongfully dissolved the limited partnership.[49]

The original act prescribed for the distribution of assets of a limited partnership a scheme of priorities that created a substantial incentive for capital investment by limited partners. The effect of the original act was to prefer limited partners in the distribution of assets, so the general partners could be paid only after the limited partners were fully satisfied. The statute required that assets be distributed as follows:

1. To outside creditors of the partnership
2. To limited partners in respect to their share of profits and income such as interest on their contributions

3. To limited partners in respect to their contributions
4. To general partners for claims against the partnership other than capital or profits
5. To general partners in respect to profits
6. To general partners in respect to capital[50]

As with general partnerships, this scheme of distribution could be altered by the agreement of the members as long as business creditors were fully paid.

Under the revised act, the assets are to be distributed as follows:

1. To creditors, including partners who are creditors, in satisfaction of liabilities of limited partnership, other than liabilities for distributions provided to the partners in the partnership agreement
2. To all partners and former partners in satisfaction of any liabilities for distributions agreed under the partnership agreement
3. To all partners for the return of their contributions and, then, for their proportionate share of the excess assets (which constitute their share of profit)[51]

Notice that general and limited partners rank at the same level for receipt of partnership distributions under the new statutory provisions, but it is still possible to provide for a different scheme of distributions in the partnership agreement. Thus, if a preference to distributions is an incentive to obtain the capital contributions of limited partners, the partnership agreement may adopt any desired distribution procedure to accomplish that result.

TAXATION OF A LIMITED PARTNERSHIP

For the most part, a limited partnership will be treated like a general partnership for tax purposes. Recall that the general partnership acts only as a conduit through which income is deemed to be distributed to each partner in the proportions specified in the agreement. The normal limited partnership has the same treatment, and this may be an advantage to the limited partner seeking to declare losses to offset similar passive income from other sources. This tax advantage from offsetting losses is one reason limited partnerships became favored forms of organization for developing real estate and operating rental property. The accelerated depreciation allowances available for these enterprises produced paper losses, which were passed directly to the partners and sheltered other income from taxation. Modern tax laws have significantly reduced this advantage, requiring that losses from partnership investments (where a partner is not actively involved in the business of the partnership) can be offset only against income from other passive investment sources. Federal law has developed a hostile attitude toward tax-sheltered investments of any type and has imposed significant restrictions on a partner's ability to offset income with losses and severe penalties for tax-motivated deductions that are not clearly authorized by the law. Consequently, the perception of a limited partnership as a tax-advantaged business enterprise has been considerably blurred. Most limited partnerships now promise significant real economic benefits to attract limited partners, rather than promising paper deductions and losses for tax-motivated investors.

Under certain circumstances, however, a limited partnership will be considered a corporation for tax purposes. This means that the tax advantages gained through depreciation, depletion, or other losses will not be passed directly to the investor. Instead, the partnership will be considered a separate tax-paying entity and will be taxed at corporate rates. What is worse is the possibility that higher corporate tax rates will apply to all income of the partnership and will be applied as the first level of taxation, only to have the individual rates apply to all distributions made to the partner from the business. Such "restructuring" by taxing authorities occurs when the operation of a limited partnership closely resembles the operation of a corporation. For example, the partnership agreement may authorize a limited partner to assign his or her interest and substitute the assignee as a limited partner in his or her place. This, of course, is a characteristic of corporate share ownership. Similarly, the agreement may provide for continuity of the business despite the death, incapacity, or withdrawal of the general partner. Continuity of existence is a primary corporate element. Further, if management is centralized in a few general partners, the operation of the partnership resembles the acts of a board of directors of a corporation. As previously discussed, limited partners enjoy limited liability, which is another corporate attribute for shareholders. When the structure of the limited partnership includes more corporate characteristics than partnership characteristics, the partnership may be taxed as a corporation.[52]

FORMATION AND OPERATION OF A LIMITED PARTNERSHIP

With the singular, but extremely important, exception of the limited partnership certificate, the formation of a limited partnership is the same as the formation of a general partnership. Thus, licensing requirements would have identical application to this form of business, and other state formalities must be observed. The agreement plays an even more important role in a limited partnership, and it should give special attention to the idiosyncrasies of the limited partnership.

Name

The revised statute governing the name of the limited partnership is very similar to statutes regulating corporate names. The name of the limited partnership must be stated in the limited partnership certificate, and the name of the limited partnership must contain, without abbreviation, the words *limited partnership,* which should give notice to the world of the limited liability of certain of the firm's members.[53] Some states permit the use of abbreviations, such as *L.P.* or *Ltd.,* although at least the latter may cause some confusion with corporate organizations, which are also permitted to use the words *Limited* and *Ltd.*

The name may usually not contain any word or phrase indicating or implying that the partnership is organized other than for a purpose stated in its agreement or certificate, and it may not be the same as or deceptively similar to the name of any corporation or other limited partnership organized or qualified under the laws of the local jurisdiction.

The name of the limited partnership may be reserved by anyone attempting to organize the limited partnership or intending to qualify a foreign limited partnership in the state. The normal period for the reservation of a name is 120 days, and the reservation may usually be extended for an additional 60 days. Moreover, similar to corporate law, limited partnership law allows the reserved limited partnership name to be transferred by an appropriate notice of transfer.[54]

Both the old and new laws contain a provision designed to avoid confusion of persons doing business with a partnership as to the identity of the general and limited partners. The use of a limited partner's surname in the name of the limited partnership is prohibited if the limited liability of that partner is to be maintained, unless (1) the partnership has a general partner with the same name, or (2) the business had been carried on under a name including the limited partner's surname before that person became a limited partner. Thus, a limited partnership composed of Ron Williams and Charlie Langhoff as general partners and Mary Williams, Scott Charlton, and Bob Thompson as limited partners could use the name "Williams and Langhoff, Limited Partnership", even though Mary Williams is a limited partner. Similarly, if Charlie Langhoff subsequently becomes a limited partner, the firm may continue under the name "Williams and Langhoff, Limited Partnership", under the second exception.

The Partnership Agreement

The *partnership agreement* is defined in the Revised Uniform Limited Partnership Act as any valid agreement, written or oral, of the partners as to the affairs of the limited partnership and the conduct of business. (The agreement should be written, but the definition permits the use of an oral agreement.) The original act did not refer to the partnership agreement at all, and appeared to assume that all important matters would be set forth in the certificate of limited partnership. Under modern practice, however, it is common for partners to enter into a comprehensive partnership agreement, only part of which is included in the certificate, which is filed as a matter of public notice. The revised act was originally written to provide that the certificate would furnish public notice concerning the addition and withdrawal of partners and capital, and that other important issues among the partners would be addressed in the partnership agreement. The 1985 amendments to the revised act substantially reduced the significance of the certificate, confining it principally to identifying the partnership and general partners. All other issues are now left to be included in the partnership agreement.[55]

Preparation of the limited partnership agreement usually will be based upon the expressed desires of the proposed general partners, since limited partners play a passive role in the formation and operation of the business. The basic form of the agreement resembles a general partnership agreement, since the limited partnership includes at least one general partner. Especially when more than one general partner will manage the business, all considerations specified in the checklist proposed for general partnerships (see "Formation and Operation of a General Partnership" in Chapter 2) should be considered in the drafting of the limited partnership agreement.

Several special matters, raised by the specific statutory rules that govern limited partnerships, should be addressed in the agreement. The following checklist is designed to be used in addition to the matters covered in Chapter 2 to draft a complete limited partnership agreement.

1. Provide for the recording of a certificate of limited partnership and other necessary documents in the appropriate filing places.

> **EXAMPLE: Certificate of Limited Partnership, Trade Name Affidavit, and So Forth**
> A Certificate of Limited Partnership created hereby shall be recorded in accordance with the Limited Partnership Act in each state in which the Partnership may establish a place of business. In addition, the General Partner shall file and publish a Trade Name Affidavit and any other notices, certificates, statements or other instruments required by any provision of any law of the state in which the partnership is organized or is qualified to do business.

2. State such provisions as are agreed upon or the admission of additional limited partners.

> **EXAMPLE: Admission of Additional Limited Partners**
> Subject to any other provision of this Agreement, after the formation of the Partnership, a person may be admitted as an additional Limited Partner with the written consent of the General Partner and the execution by the additional Limited Partner of a counterpart of this Agreement.

3. State such provisions as are agreed upon for the admission of assignees of limited partners.

> **EXAMPLE: Admission of Assignees of Limited Partners**
> Subject to the other provisions of this Agreement, a person who has received a valid written assignment of a partnership interest in this Partnership, including an assignee of a General Partner, may become a Limited Partner in the Partnership by a specific grant of authority from the assignor to the assignee of the right to become a Limited Partner in the Partnership. In addition, prior to admission of the assignee as a Limited Partner in the Partnership, the General Partner may require such opinions of counsel as are necessary or desired in the sole discretion of the General Partner, to determine that the transfer of the interest in the Partnership from the assignor to the assignee does not violate any federal or state securities law, or affect the tax consequences of the Partnership. The assignee shall also be required to execute a counterpart of this Agreement prior to admission as a Limited Partner.

4. Provide that any new partners must agree to be bound by the terms of the partnership agreement.

> **EXAMPLE: Additional Partners Bound by Agreement**
> Notwithstanding any other provisions of this Agreement, before any person is admitted or substituted as a Limited Partner, he or she shall agree in writing to be bound by all of the provisions of this Agreement.

5. Provide for additional capital contributions by limited partners if desired, and describe any restrictions or limitations on additional capital contributions.

> **EXAMPLE: Limitation on Additional Capital Contributions**
> After the initial capital contributions have been paid, Limited Partners may be required to contribute their proportionate share of the capital of this Partnership or such additional sums of money or property as shall be determined to be necessary by the General Partner to meet operating expenses of the Partnership when funds generated from Partnership operations are insufficient to meet such expenses. However, Limited Partners shall not be required to contribute more than twenty percent (20%) of their initial capital contributions as additional capital.

6. Describe the rights of limited partners to withdraw or reduce their capital contributions to the partnership. In addition, if limited partners will have the right to demand or receive property other than cash in return for a contribution, describe the circumstances under which such property would be distributed.

> **EXAMPLE: Withdrawal and Return of Capital**
> No Limited Partner shall have the right to withdraw or reduce his or her contribution to the capital of the Partnership without the consent of the General Partner. No Limited Partner shall have the right to bring an action for partition against the Partnership. No Limited Partner shall have the right to demand or receive property other than cash in return for his or her contribution. No Limited Partner shall have priority over any other Limited Partner, either as to the return of his or her contribution of capital or as to profits, losses or distributions.

7. Ensure that the agreement prevents the limited partner from participating in the control of the business.

> **EXAMPLE: Role of Limited Partner**
> Except as otherwise provided in the Agreement, a Limited Partner shall have no part in or interfere in any manner with the conduct or control of the business of the Partnership, and shall have no right or authority to act for or by the Partnership. The Limited Partner of this Partnership will be permitted, if agreed by the General Partner, to perform the following acts on behalf of the Partnership:
> 1) Acting as a contractor for or agent or employee of the Limited Partnership or of the General Partner or being an officer, director, or shareholder of the Corporate General Partner;
> 2) Consulting with and advising the General Partner with respect to the business of the Limited Partnership;
> 3) Acting as a surety for the Limited Partnership or guaranteeing or assuming one or more specific obligations of the Limited Partnership;
> 4) Taking any action required or permitted by the laws of the state under which the Partnership was organized or qualified to bring or pursue a derivative action in the right of the Limited Partnership;
> 5) Requesting or attending a meeting of partners;
> 6) Proposing, approving, or disapproving, by voting or otherwise, one or more of the following matters:
>   i) the dissolution and winding up of the Partnership;
>   ii) the sale, exchange, lease, mortgage, pledge, or other transfer of all or substantially all of the assets of the Limited Partnership;
>   iii) the incurrence of indebtedness by the Limited Partnership other than the ordinary course of its business;
>   iv) a change in the nature of the business;
>   v) the admission or removal of a General Partner;
>   vi) the admission or removal of a Limited Partner;
>   vii) a transaction involving an actual or potential conflict of interest between the General Partner and the Partnership or the Limited Partners;
>   viii) an amendment to the Partnership Agreement or Certificate of Limited Partnership;
>   ix) the approval of capital contributions in excess of $100,000;
>   x) the location of the Partnership's offices within this state.

8. Describe in some detail the rights, powers, and obligations of the general partner, and the extent to which management may be delegated.

EXAMPLE: Rights, Powers, and Obligations of the General Partner

The management and control of the Partnership and its business and affairs shall rest exclusively with the General Partner who shall have all the rights and powers which may be possessed by a general partner by law, and such rights and powers as are otherwise conferred by law or are necessary, advisable or convenient to the discharge of its duties under this Agreement and to the management of the business and affairs of the Partnership. Without limiting the generality of the foregoing, the General Partner shall have the following rights and powers which it may exercise.

a) To spend the capital and net income of the Partnership in the exercise of any rights or powers possessed by the General Partner hereunder.

b) To acquire, purchase, hold and sell real estate and lease the same to third parties and to enter into agreements with others with respect to such activities, which agreements may contain such terms, provisions and conditions as the General Partner in its sole and absolute discretion shall approve.

c) To borrow money to discharge the Partnership's obligations, or to protect and preserve the assets of the Partnership, or to incur any other indebtedness in the ordinary course of business and to pledge all or any of the Partnership's assets or income to secure such loans.

d) To employ a business manager or managers to manage the Partnership's affairs.

e) To execute leases, licenses, rental agreements, and use agreements, on behalf of the Partnership, of and with respect to all or any portion of the real property.

f) To delegate all or any of its duties hereunder, and in furtherance of any such delegation to appoint, employ or contract with any person it may in its sole discretion deem necessary or desirable for the transaction of the business of the Partnership, which persons may, under the supervision of the General Partner: administer the day-to-day operations of the Partnership; serve as the Partnership's advisers and consultants in connection with policy decisions made by the General Partner; act as consultants, accountants, correspondents, attorneys, brokers, escrow agents, or in any other capacity deemed by the General Partner necessary or desirable; investigate, select, and on behalf of the Partnership, conduct relations with persons acting in such capacities, and enter into appropriate contracts with, or employ, or retain services performed or to be performed by, all or any of them in connection with the real estate; perform or assist in the performance of such administrative or managerial functions necessary in the management of the Partnership and its business as may be agreed upon with the General Partner; and perform such other acts or services for the Partnership as the General Partner, in its sole and absolute discretion, may approve.

9. Describe any limitations or restrictions on the general partner's powers.

EXAMPLE: Limitations on General Partner's Powers

The General Partner shall not, without the written consent or ratification of the specific act by the Limited Partners:

a) Make, execute, or deliver any assignment for the benefit of creditors, or sign any confession of judgment on behalf of the Partnership.

b) Possess partnership property or assign its rights in specific partnership property for other than a Partnership purpose.

c) Act in contravention of the Agreement.

d) Conduct any act which would make it impossible to carry on the ordinary business of the Partnership.

e) Admit a person as a general partner.

f) Permit a creditor who makes a nonrecourse loan to the Partnership to acquire any interest in profits, capital or property of the Partnership other than as a secured creditor.

10. Describe the agreed rights of limited partners, consistent with the limited partners' passive role in the partnership.

> **EXAMPLE: Rights of the Limited Partners**
> Limited Partners shall have the right to:
>
> a) Have the Partnership books kept at the principal place of business of the Partnership or such other place as designated by the General Partner, and to inspect and copy any of them in accordance with this Agreement.
> b) Obtain from the General Partner any information concerning the financial condition of the Partnership by requesting the same with 72 hours' written notice and meeting with the General Partner to obtain such information during normal business hours of the Partnership.
> c) Receive a copy of the Limited Partnership's federal, state and local income tax returns for each year within 120 days after the close of the Partnership's fiscal year.

11. Describe any rights that will be granted to the limited partners to remove and replace the general partner. Since the limited partners cannot take active part in management without losing limited liability, their failure to designate a new general partner should require a liquidation of the partnership.

> **EXAMPLE: Removal of General Partner**
> Limited Partners shall have the right to remove the General Partner, by written vote or written consent signed and acknowledged by at least ninety percent (90%) of the then outstanding limited partnership interests, and given to the General Partner within thirty (30) days prior to the effective date of removal.
>
> a) Removal of the General Partner shall be effective upon the substitution of the new General Partner;
> b) Concurrently with such notice of removal or within thirty (30) days thereafter by notice similarly given, the Limited Partners shall, in addition, designate a new General Partner.
> c) Substitution of a new General Partner shall be effective upon written acceptance of the duties and the responsibilities of General Partner hereunder. Upon effective substitution of a new General Partner, this Agreement shall be and remain in full force and effect except for the change in General Partner and the business of the Partnership shall be continued by the new General Partner. The new General Partner shall thereupon execute, acknowledge, file and publish, as appropriate, amendments to the Certificate of Limited Partnership and Trade Name Affidavit.
> d) Failure of the Limited Partners to designate a General Partner within the time specified herein or failure of a new General Partner so designated to execute written acceptance of the duties and responsibilities of General Partner hereunder within ten (10) days after such designation shall require the liquidation of the Partnership as provided in this Agreement.

12. For ease of management of the partnership, it is good practice to provide that each limited partner grants a power of attorney to the general partner to execute documents to maintain limited partnership status in his or her name. This avoids the nuisance of attempting to locate all limited partners to obtain their signatures for documents that need to be filed to properly maintain the partnership. Under the recent amendments to the Revised Uniform Limited Partnership Act, only general partners are required to sign the limited partnership certificate. However, most local laws are still based upon the original act and the unamended revised act, so administrative requirements such as these should be considered.

EXAMPLE: Power of Attorney
Each of the Limited Partners hereby irrevocably constitutes and appoints the General Partner as true and lawful attorney-in-fact for such Limited Partner with power and authority to act in his or her name and on his or her behalf in the execution, acknowledgment, filing and recording of documents, which shall include the following:

a) A Certificate of Limited Partnership and any amendment thereto, under the laws of the State of Colorado or the laws of any other state or other jurisdiction in which such certificate or any other amendment is required to be filed.

b) Any other instrument which may be required to be filed or recorded by the Partnership under the laws of any state or by any governmental agency, or which, in the General Partner's discretion, it is advisable to file or record.

c) Any document which may be required to effect the continuation of the Partnership, the admission of an additional or substituted Limited Partner to the Partnership or the dissolution and termination of the Partnership, provided that such documents are in accordance with the terms of the Partnership Agreement.

Such Power of Attorney (i) shall be a special power of attorney coupled with an interest, shall be irrevocable and shall survive the death of such Limited Partner; (ii) may be exercised by the General Partner for each Limited Partner by a facsimile signature of the General Partner or by listing all of the Limited Partners executing any instrument with a single signature of the General Partner acting as attorney-in-fact for all of them; and (iii) shall survive the delivery of any assignment by such Limited Partner of the whole or any portions of his or her interest except that where the assignee of the whole thereof has been approved by the General Partner for admission to the Partnership as a substituted Limited Partner, the Power of Attorney shall survive the delivery of such assignment for the sole purpose of enabling the General Partner to execute, acknowledge and file any instrument necessary to effect such substitution.

13. Describe any limitations to be placed on the transfer of limited partnership interests.

EXAMPLE: Transfer of Limited Partnership Interests
No heir, successor, donee, assignee, or other transferee (including a partner's spouse) of the whole or any interest in a Limited Partner's interest in the Partnership shall have the right to become a substituted Limited Partner in place of his or her assignor unless all of the following conditions are satisfied:

a) Upon receipt of a bona fide offer to purchase a limited partnership interest in an amount at least equal to or greater than the minimum subscription amount required by the securities laws in the respective states where the transferor and transferee reside, the holder of such interest shall communicate such offer to the General Partner. The General Partner shall have a right of first refusal to purchase such interest according to the price and terms of the bona fide offer which option must be exercised within thirty (30) days from the date of first receipt of the notice of said bona fide offer. In the event that the General Partner fails to exercise its option hereunder, the Limited Partner may transfer his or her interest upon the same terms as the offer and upon satisfaction of all other requirements of this Article.

b) The written instrument of assignment which has been filed with the Partnership is fully executed and acknowledged and sets forth the intention of the assignor that the assignee become a substituted Limited Partner in his or her place.

c) The assignor and assignee execute and acknowledge such other instruments as the General Partner may deem necessary or desirable to effect such substitution,

including the written acceptance and adoption by the assignee of the provisions of this Agreement.
d) Recordation of an amendment to the Certificate of Limited Partnership in accordance with the Colorado Limited Partnership Act.
e) Payment by the transferor of all reasonable expenses of the Partnership connected with such transfer, including, but not limited to, legal fees and costs (which costs may include, for example, the cost of obtaining opinion of counsel as to the transferability of such interest or of filing any amendment to the Certificate of Limited Partnership).
f) The consent to such transfer in writing by the General Partner.

14. Describe any limitations to be placed upon partnership loans or other transactions of business with a limited partnership.

> **EXAMPLE: Limitations on Partnership Loans**
> No Partner, General or Limited, may lend money to the Partnership on a basis which is less favorable than the Partnership may obtain from independent financial institutions. All Partnership loans shall bear interest at a rate not to exceed the prime lending rate of the Partnership's principal financial institution, and shall provide for repayment no earlier than six months after the date of the loan.

15. Describe any voting procedures and rights that are desired for the various partners.

> **EXAMPLE: Voting Rights of Partners**
> The General Partners shall be permitted to vote on all matters respecting the business of the Partnership. The Limited Partners shall be entitled to vote on all matters which are referred to them by the General Partners for their approval. In any vote of the Partnership, the matters submitted to the vote of the Partners shall be approved by a majority of the vote of the General Partners, with the General Partners voting as a class, and a majority of the Limited Partners, with the Limited Partners voting as a class.

16. Provide for the admission of additional general partners, if desired, with a procedure that is different from the consent of all members of the partnership.

> **EXAMPLE: Admission of General Partners**
> Additional General Partners may be admitted to the Partnership by the majority vote of the Limited Partners.

17. Provide for any limitations of the general partner's liability to the partnership or to the limited partners. It is not possible to limit the liability of the general partner to outsiders, but the partnership agreement may regulate claims among the partners.

> **EXAMPLE: Limitations on Liability of General Partner**
> The General Partner in this Partnership shall not be liable to the Partnership or to the Limited Partners except for acts of gross negligence and willful misconduct.

The Limited Partnership Certificate

A traditionally troublesome formality associated with the limited partnership was the certificate, which had to be properly filed and maintained to ensure limited liability for the limited partners. Failure to properly file and amend the certificate when necessary would prevent recognition of the limited partnership, and all members would be treated as though they belonged to a general partnership. Recognizing that the failure to maintain the certificate of limited partnership could accidentally cause a change in the status of the partners, the drafters of the Revised Uniform Limited Partnership Act substantially minimized the importance of the certificate in their most recent amendments. The policy of the revised act is to place greater emphasis on the terms of the partnership agreement, and to permit the certificate to be simply public notice of matters the general partners desire to make known and the public needs to know.

Content. Under the original Uniform Limited Partnership Act, the certificate of limited partnership roughly resembled a corporation's articles of incorporation. (In some respects, it was more specific and revealing.) The requirements for the content of the certificate were specified in the act, and the limited partnership agreement could be filed as the certificate if all the appropriate information was contained in the agreement. The certificate had to contain all of the following information.

1. Name of the partnership
2. Character of the business
3. Location of the principal place of business
4. Name and place of residence of each member, general and limited partners being respectively designated
5. Term for which the partnership was to exist
6. Amount of cash, and description and agreed value of other property contributed by each limited partner
7. Additional contributions, if any, agreed to be made by each limited partner, and times at which or events on the happening of which they shall be made
8. Time, if agreed upon, when the contribution of each limited partner is to be returned
9. Share of the profits or other compensation by way of income to be received by each limited partner by reason of his or her contribution
10. Right, if given, of a limited partner to substitute an assignee as contributor in his or her place, and terms and conditions of the substitutions
11. Right, if given, of the partners to admit additional limited partners
12. Right, if given, of one or more limited partners to priority over other limited partners, as to contributions or as compensation by way of income, and the nature of such priority
13. Right, if given, of the remaining general partner or partners to continue the business on the death, retirement, or insanity of a general partner
14. Right, if given, of a limited partner to demand and receive property other than cash in return for his or her contribution[56]

Under the amended revised act, the information contained in the certificate of limited partnership is substantially simplified, requiring only the following:

1. Name of the limited partnership
2. Address of the office and name and address of the agent for service of process (discussed later in this section)
3. Name and business address of each general partner
4. Latest date upon which the limited partnership is to dissolve

5. Any other matters the general partner has determined to include in the certificate of limited partnership[57]

All states have some combination of the original act or the amended revised act as the local requirements for certificates of limited partnership. In each case, local law must be carefully reviewed to ensure that the certificate contains the required information.

Registered Office and Agent. The benefit to the public and to local government agencies of a designated office for business records and an agent for service of process has long been recognized for corporations. An agent for service of process on the limited partnership must be an individual resident of the state and must be continuously maintained by the limited partnership. The limited partnership must also specify an office, which need not be its place of business in the state, where records of the partnership will be maintained.[58] At this office, the partnership is required to keep a current list of all partners in alphabetical order; a copy of the certificate of limited partnership and all amendments; copies of the partnership's financial statements and federal, state, and local income tax returns for three years; and copies of any effective written partnership agreement. The records maintained at the registered office must also include a description of the capital contributions of each partner, the times where additional capital contributions will be required, the right of a partner to receive a distribution that may include part of the contributions, and any events upon which the partnership will be dissolved. If these items are contained in the written partnership agreement, separate records do not have to be maintained for such matters. These records are all subject to inspection and copying by any partner upon reasonable request during normal business hours.

Filing. Most states (and the Revised Uniform Limited Partnership Act) designate the office of the secretary of state as the repository for the certificate. A few states still require a single filing of the certificate in the office of the county clerk in the county where the partnership's principal place of business is situated. Even fewer require filing in both places. New York requires publication once a week for six weeks in two newspapers of general circulation in the county, one of which should be in the city where the partnership is located. The appropriate state statute should be carefully reviewed in any case. Moreover, if the partnership intends to do business in more than one location, appropriate multiple filings should be made to avoid any question of compliance with these important provisions.

Amendments. During the course of operating a limited partnership, several situations may require an amendment to the certificate. So much information is required in the certificate of limited partnership filed under the original act that amendments will frequently be required under local laws following that statute. They will be required whenever there is a change in the name, amount, or character of the limited partners' contributions; the character of the business; or the time for dissolution or return of contribution. Amendments will also be required on the admission of any partner; on the substitution of a limited partner; for the continuation of the business after withdrawal, death, or insanity of a general partner; or in any case where there is a need to correct an erroneous statement in the certificate or to represent accurately the agreement between members.[59]

Under the new law, the certificate may be amended at any time that the general partners decide to add or delete information that is optionally included, and must be amended whenever a general partner is aware that a statement in a certificate is false or that circumstances have changed to make a statement inaccurate. An amendment must be filed within thirty days after a new general partner is admitted, an old general partner withdraws, or the business has been continued after a general partner has withdrawn.[60]

The amending statement must state the name of the limited partnership, the filing date of the certificate, and the contents of the amendment. It must be signed by at least one general partner and by any new general partner. In jurisdictions that still operate under the original act, signatures of limited partners will be required on the amendment. To avoid the nuisance of locating and obtaining the signature of each limited partner (or of a new general partner if he or she is not available), a power of attorney to permit an existing general partner to sign the amendment on behalf of other partners may be appropriately contained in the partnership agreement.[61]

It should be apparent that even under the revised act, the amendment procedure is cumbersome and may be annoying. The details for which a limited partnership amendment is required are even more specific, especially under the original statute, than the details for which a corporate amendment is required. For example, a corporation does not have to amend its articles of incorporation every time it acquires a new shareholder or loses a director, but the limited partnership may be required to amend for analogous changes in personnel.

Cancellation of the Certificate. When the limited partnership is dissolved and winding-up has commenced, or when there are no more limited partners, the certificate of limited partnership must be cancelled. Since the limited partnership was formed in a public manner, by filing the certificate, it should be dissolved with the same formality. A certificate of cancellation is provided for this purpose, and it must be signed by all general partners.[62]

The certificate of cancellation is required when there is a dissolution of the partnership, but only if the partnership has commenced a procedure to wind up its affairs. As discussed earlier, a technical dissolution may occur under a number of situations, such as the death of a general partner. However, such a situation does not necessarily require that the partnership be liquidated, and the agreement may allow the business to continue with an existing additional general partner or with the limited partners' appointment of another general partner. Consequently, only the commencement of the winding-up of the partnership will require a certificate of cancellation, so that if the business is to be continued following a dissolution, a certificate of cancellation need not be filed.

Foreign Limited Partnerships

The Revised Uniform Limited Partnership Act borrowed a number of corporate rules providing for the qualification and registration of foreign limited partnerships in other states. Any foreign limited partnership (defined as a partnership formed under the laws of some other state) must register with the secretary of state before transacting business in a new state.[63]

An application for registration as a foreign limited partnership must contain the following items:

1. Name of the foreign limited partnership and, if different, name under which that partnership proposes to register and transact business in the new state (including the words *Limited Partnership* as part of the name)
2. State and date of the partnership's formation
3. Name and address of any agent for service of process who is either a resident of the new state or an entity formed under the laws of and or qualified to do business in the new state
4. Appointment of the secretary of state of the new state as the agent of the foreign limited partnership if the otherwise appointed agent can no longer be found
5. Address of the partnership's office
6. Name and business address of each general partner
7. Address of the office at which the list of names and addresses of the limited partners and their capital contributions may be found—The foreign limited partnership must commit to keep those records available until its registration in the foreign state is withdrawn.[64]

There are requirements for amendments to the registration certificate and for cancellation of registration when the partnership ceases to do business in the foreign state.[65]

A foreign limited partnership that transacts business without registration in a state operating under the revised act is prohibited from maintaining any action, suit, or other proceeding in a court of that state until registration has occurred. However, merely failing to register does not affect any contract or act that the foreign limited partnership may have conducted in the new state, nor will it affect the limited liability of limited partners in the new state.[66]

Derivative Actions

Stockholders of a corporation may, under certain circumstances, maintain a derivative action to enforce the rights of their corporation. A limited partner never expressly had such a right under the original Uniform Limited Partnership Act, and many cases considered whether limited partners were entitled to bring derivative actions, with diverse results. The revised act expressly permits a limited partner to bring an action in the right of the limited partnership to recover a judgment in its favor if the general partners with authority to do so have refused to bring the action or if an effort to cause the general partners to bring such an action is not likely to succeed.[67]

The provisions for derivative actions under the revised act are very similar to those under state corporate laws. The partner bringing the action must have been a partner at the time of the transaction that is the subject of the lawsuit, and must be a partner at the time of bringing the action. The partner must also attempt to have the general partners bring the action on behalf of the partnership, and must state with particularity in a complaint what actions were taken in that regard. If a partner is successful in prosecuting a claim on behalf of the partnership and obtains a judgment, compromise, or settlement of the claim, that partner may be awarded reasonable expenses, including attorneys' fees for bringing the action.[68]

NOTES

1. Uniform Limited Partnership Act (hereafter cited as U.L.P.A. § 1, and Revised Uniform Limited Partnership Act (hereafter cited as R.U.L.P.A.) § 101(7).

2. 6 U.L.A. 561 (1969). The Uniform Limited Partnership Act has not been adopted in Louisiana.
3. Connecticut and Wyoming adopted the Revised Uniform Limited Partnership Act in 1979.
4. U.L.P.A. § 7 and R.U.L.P.A. § 303(a).
5. U.L.P.A. § 12 and R.U.L.P.A. § 404.
6. See "Dissolution of a Limited Partnership" later in this chapter.
7. U.L.P.A. § 19(1) and R.U.L.P.A. § 702.
8. R.U.L.P.A. § 101(5).
9. U.L.P.A. § 9(1)(e) and R.U.L.P.A. § 401.
10. R.U.L.P.A. §§ 402(1) and 602.
11. R.U.L.P.A. §§ 402(2) and 702.
12. R.U.L.P.A. § 402(3).
13. R.U.L.P.A. § 402(4).
14. R.U.L.P.A. § 402(6)–(10).
15. See "Dissolution and Termination of a Partnership" in Chapter 2.
16. R.U.L.P.A. § 402.
17. R.U.L.P.A. § 801(4).
18. R.U.L.P.A. § 405.
19. U.P.A. § 6(2) and R.U.L.P.A. § 1105.
20. U.L.P.A. § 7 and R.U.L.P.A. § 303(a).
21. U.L.P.A. § 4.
22. R.U.L.P.A. §501.
23. R.U.L.P.A. § 502(b).
24. R.U.L.P.A. § 502(c).
25. R.U.L.P.A. § 303.
26. R.U.L.P.A. § 304.
27. R.U.L.P.A. § 403.
28. U.L.P.A. § 9 and R.U.L.P.A. § 403.
29. R.U.L.P.A. § 303.
30. U.L.P.A. § 10 and R.U.L.P.A. § 303.
31. U.L.P.A. § 8 and R.U.L.P.A. § 301(a).
32. U.L.P.A. § 16 and R.U.L.P.A. § 603.
33. U.L.P.A. § 16 and R.U.L.P.A. § 603. Under the original act, notice must be given to "all members"; under the revised act, notice is given to "each general partner."
34. U.L.P.A. § 16 and R.U.L.P.A. § 607.
35. U.L.P.A. § 16(3) and R.U.L.P.A. § 605.
36. U.L.P.A. § 19(4) and R.U.L.P.A. §§ 301(2) and 704.
37. U.L.P.A. § 19 and R.U.L.P.A. § 301(b). Forms for the assignment and consent to substitution by a limited partner appear as Forms 3A and 3B in Appendix G. The revised act abandons the terminology of a "substituted" limited partner. Instead, the revised act refers to an assignee who has been granted the right to become a limited partner. Amendment of the certificate is discussed in "Formation and Operation of a Limited Partnership" later in this chapter.
38. R.U.L.P.A. § 801 and U.L.P.A. §§ 9(1)(g) and 20.
39. R.U.L.P.A. § 802.
40. See U.L.P.A. § 10(c) and U.P.A. § 32.
41. U.L.P.A. § 16(4)(a).
42. R.U.L.P.A. § 606.
43. R.U.L.P.A. § 402 and see "General Partners of a Limited Partnership" earlier in this chapter.
44. R.U.L.P.A. § 801(3).
45. The misconduct of a general partner would cause dissolution to be "equitable and proper" under U.L.P.A. § 10(c) and presumably would be an event that makes it reasonably impracticable "to carry on the business in conformity with the partnership agreement" under R.U.L.P.A. § 802.
46. See "Dissolution and Termination of a Partnership" in Chapter 2.
47. R.U.L.P.A. § 801(4). An example of an agreement to continue the business appears in clause 26 of the sample limited partnership agreement, Form 3C, in Appendix G.
48. U.L.P.A. § 10(c).
49. R.U.L.P.A. § 803.
50. U.L.P.A. § 23.
51. R.U.L.P.A. § 804.
52. See Treas. Reg. § 3–1.7701–2 (1960, as amended 1983) for an enumeration of corporate characteristics that may affect the tax status of limited partnerships.

53. R.U.L.P.A. § 102.
54. R.U.L.P.A. § 103.
55. R.U.L.P.A. § 101(9).
56. U.L.P.A. § 2.
57. R.U.L.P.A. § 201.
58. R.U.L.P.A. § 104.
59. U.L.P.A. § 24.
60. R.U.L.P.A. § 202. A sample amendment to a certificate of limited partnership appears as Form 3F in Appendix G.
61. R.U.L.P.A. § 204.
62. R.U.L.P.A. § 203. A sample cancellation certificate appears as Form 3G in Appendix G.
63. R.U.L.P.A. §§ 101(4) and 902.
64. R.U.L.P.A. § 902.
65. R.U.L.P.A. §§ 905 and 906.
66. R.U.L.P.A. § 907.
67. R.U.L.P.A. § 1001.
68. R.U.L.P.A. §§ 1002–1004.

4 | BUSINESS CORPORATION

The business corporation is the most interesting and most complex form of business enterprise, and the remainder of these materials are concerned primarily with the joys and sorrows of doing business as a corporation. To begin, this chapter defines the legal characteristics of the corporation, the interaction of the corporation's members in the management of its business, and some recognized advantages and disadvantages of the corporate business form. Later chapters discuss problems of formation and organization, corporate finance, internal agreements, distributions of cash and property, qualification of foreign corporations, corporate structural changes, and dissolution.

The term *business corporation* excludes the many other types of corporations that may be formed under federal or state law. For example, most states authorize the formation and operation of nonprofit corporations, religious and charitable corporations, and municipal corporations, all of which have peculiar characteristics that are not discussed in this work. The *professional corporation,* formed for the purpose of practicing the learned professions, such as law, medicine, accounting, and so forth, is considered in the next chapter.

ENTITY CHARACTERISTICS OF A CORPORATION

The characteristic that distinguishes a corporation from other forms of business enterprise is that the corporation is considered by the law to be a separate legal entity, a separate "person." The business therefore exists quite apart from its aggregate membership. It should be clear that a sole proprietorship is no more than an extension of the personal life of the proprietor, its owner. Moreover, a partnership is treated as an association of individuals, and, for the most part, is also an extension of their personalities, as evidenced by rules that prohibit the addition of a partner without the unanimous consent of the other partners and rules that require dissolution whenever a partner leaves the firm. A corporation, however, exists alone and detached, so that shareholders (its owners) may come and go without affecting its legal status. Continuing this theme, the corporation is liable for its own obligations, and the individual assets of its owners usually may not be reached for satisfaction of those obligations. The remaining discussion of corporate characteristics shows that this concept of separateness creates special advantages (and occasionally causes special disadvantages) for the corporation as compared with other business organizations.

Since the corporation is treated as a legal entity, it should be recognized that the corporation is a creature of statute. It obtains life from the applicable state law, which authorizes certain corporate powers, prescribes certain rules and requirements for the regulation of the corporation's business affairs, and controls the internal relationships between shareholders and management. State statutes vary considerably on their approach to corporations, and thus the corporate structure in one state is often quite different from the corporate structure in another state. For example, a Delaware corporation may have a one-person board of directors, while many states still require at least three members on the board.[1] Similarly, in some states the initial by-laws of the corporation are adopted by the board of directors, while a few states permit the shareholders to adopt by-laws.[2] These details are dictated by local corporate statutes, which authorize the formation and operation of a corporation as a business form. Consequently, the analysis of these statutory requirements and strict compliance with them are the touchstones of a successful corporate practice. A few words about the statutory variations and their history follow.

The law of corporations was developed by each state to regulate the internal affairs of the corporations that state had chartered to do business within its boundaries. As American businesses expanded, interstate operations became commonplace, and it was possible for the organizers of a corporation to shop around for a state whose corporation laws were the most permissive, so that the formation and operation of the corporation would be an easy exercise. The more strict and complex a state's regulation, the less attractive that state became for establishing a corporation within its boundaries. Since it is possible to do business in one state and be incorporated in another, and since a state acquires certain benefits by having businesses incorporated under its laws (not the least of which is the authority to levy taxes), state legislatures began to recognize that they could attract corporate businesses by adopting flexible and permissive statutory provisions. New Jersey was the first state to liberalize its laws for this purpose, and Delaware followed closely. Delaware has remained the consistent leader in "mothering" corporations, and its statute is considered by many to be the most modern, most permissive, and most sympathetic to the problems of corporate organization and operation.[3]

In 1950, the American Bar Association Committee on Corporate Laws prepared a Model Business Corporation Act, which was initially patterned after Illinois law. The act has since been revised extensively, also with a view toward permissiveness and flexibility, and has been used as a model by many states in their own revisions of corporate statutes. The discussion of corporate law in this book concentrates on the provisions of the Model Business Corporation Act, but unusual variations from important states are separately noted and discussed. No state has adopted the Model Business Corporation Act in its most current form verbatim, and, consequently, there is no substitute for full and complete analysis and understanding of the particular requirements of the state statute under which incorporation is contemplated.

In addition to the statutory regulation of corporate affairs, corporate operations are also governed by certain rules and regulations adopted by the persons forming the business. The articles of incorporation and the by-laws (both discussed in detail later) are adopted by the corporate membership and will govern the corporation's activities throughout its operation.[4] Note that most state statutes are very broad in their descriptions of corporate powers, because each statute is designed to cover every conceivable corporate form and every type of business. The articles of incorporation may contain only the essential information required by statute, or they may elaborate on specific matters to govern internal corporate affairs. If the articles are general, then the by-laws should provide specific rules for regulation of corporate activities. Of course, a properly formed corporation will have no conflict between the by-laws, the articles, and the appropriate state law. Rather, the by-laws and articles will refine and elaborate upon the concepts embodied in the state statute, and thereby provide a comprehensive and workable scheme for the regulation of the corporation. It is also important to recognize that the by-laws are adopted and modified by internal action of the corporation, and, consequently, the rules contained therein are easily changed. The articles of incorporation, which are filed with the secretary of state as public notice of the existence and structure of the corporation, may be amended only by a cumbersome amendment procedure. The most flexible regulation of internal affairs will result from drafting the rules for these corporate activities in the easily amendable by-laws.

In summary, a properly formed corporation exists as a legal entity and is treated for all practical purposes as an individual person, separate and distinct from the persons who own and manage it. Its formation and operation are governed by specific state statutes and by its own articles of incorporation and by-laws, as adopted to suit the particular needs of its business.

STATUTORY POWERS OF A CORPORATION

Each state's law grants a corporation the necessary powers to conduct business, and to conduct any other activities necessary to the business in which it is engaged. Most statutes granting corporate powers permit the corporation to do almost everything a private individual could do. Section 3.02 of the Model Business Corporation Act enumerates corporate powers as follows: Unless its articles of incorporation provide otherwise, every corporation has perpetual duration and succession in its corporate name and has the same powers as an individual to do all things necessary or convenient to carry out its business and affairs, including without limitation, power:

(1) to sue and be sued, complain and defend in its corporate name;
(2) to have a corporate seal, which may be altered at will, and to use it, or a facsimile of it, by impressing or affixing it or in any other manner reproducing it;
(3) to make and amend by-laws, not inconsistent with its articles of incorporation or with the laws of this state, for managing the business and regulating the affairs of the corporation;
(4) to purchase, receive, lease, or otherwise acquire, and own, hold, improve, use, and otherwise deal with, real or personal property, or any legal or equitable interest in property, wherever located;
(5) to sell, convey, mortgage, pledge, lease, exchange, and otherwise dispose of all or any part of its property;
(6) to purchase, receive, subscribe for, or otherwise acquire; own, hold, vote, use, sell, mortgage, lend, pledge, or otherwise dispose of, and deal in and with shares or other interests in, or obligations of, any other entity;
(7) to make contracts and guarantees, incur liabilities, borrow money, issue its notes, bonds and other obligations (which may be convertible into or include the option to purchase other securities of the corporation), and secure any of its obligations by mortgage or pledge of any of its property, franchises, or income;

(8) to lend money, invest and reinvest its funds, and receive and hold real and personal property as security for repayment;

(9) to be a promoter, partner, member, associate, or manager of any partnership, joint venture, trust, or other entity;

(10) to conduct its business, locate offices, and exercise the powers granted by this Act within or without this state;

(11) to elect directors and appoint officers, employees, and agents of the corporation, define their duties, fix their compensation, and lend them money and credit;

(12) to pay pensions and establish pension plans, pension trusts, profit sharing plans, share bonus plans, share option plans, and benefit or incentive plans for any or all of its current or former directors, officers, employees, and agents;

(13) to make donations for the public welfare or for charitable, scientific, or educational purposes;

(14) to transact any lawful business that will aid governmental policy;

(15) to make payments or donations, or do any other act, not inconsistent with law, that furthers the business and affairs of the corporation.

Remember that the foregoing powers are conferred by statute, and a corporation is permitted to do all things authorized therein. The attorney may, in his or her discretion, deem it appropriate to grant broad powers or restrict powers in the articles of incorporation.

> **EXAMPLE: Powers**
> To do everything necessary and proper for the accomplishment of any of the purposes, or the attainment of any of the objects, or the furtherance of any of the powers hereinbefore set forth, either alone or in association with other corporations, firms, or individuals, and to do every other act or acts, thing or things, incidental to or growing out of or connected with the aforesaid business or powers, or any part or parts thereof; provided, the same is not inconsistent with the laws under which this corporation is organized.[5]

In most cases, however, the articles of incorporation and the by-laws of the corporation will refine the statutory powers to tailor the corporate structure to the incorporators' needs.

Notice that some statutory powers suggest that elaboration is necessary in the articles of incorporation or by-laws. For example, the articles of incorporation or by-laws must define the duties of officers,[6] and they may predetermine the maximum interest rate at which the corporation may borrow funds.[7]

> **EXAMPLE: Power to Borrow**
> To borrow money, and to make and issue notes, bonds, debentures, obligations, and evidences of indebtedness of all kinds, whether secured by mortgage, pledge, or otherwise, without limit as to amount, but with interest not to exceed 12 per cent per annum, and to secure the same by mortgage, pledge, or otherwise, and generally to make and perform agreements and contracts of every kind and description.[8]

It is also good practice to elaborate upon the corporation's power to conduct business in other states and countries.

> **EXAMPLE: Power to Qualify in Foreign Jurisdictions**
> The company shall have power to conduct and carry on its business, or any part thereof, and to have one or more offices, and to exercise all or any of its corporate

powers and rights, in the State of New York, and in the various other states, territories, colonies, and dependencies of the United States, in the District of Columbia, and in all or any foreign countries.[9]

Thus, the general grant of power under the state statute represents the maximum limits of corporate power. If incorporators or organizers intend to restrict this power, the modifications are drafted into the articles of incorporation and by-laws.

Also note that Subsection (15) of Section 3.02 of the Model Business Corporation Act grants power to do any act that is not inconsistent with law and that furthers the business and affairs of the corporation. The extent of the business and affairs of the corporation are defined in the articles of incorporation as the corporate purposes. The corporate *purposes* are the particular business objectives that the incorporators direct their corporation to pursue, such as operating a restaurant, owning and leasing real estate, and so forth. These purposes are specified in the articles of incorporation, are drafted in accordance with the objectives of the incorporators, and guide corporate management in the type of business to be conducted.[10] The permitted purposes are also regulated by statute, but this is one place where permissiveness is rampant. The Model Business Corporation Act and most states permit business corporations to be organized for "any lawful business," subject to other state statutes that may regulate certain industries, such as banking and insurance. Consequently, if the incorporators adopt very broad corporate purposes, and authorize the corporation to transact any lawful business, the statutory corporate powers, permitting all power to do any act that furthers the business and affairs of the corporation, will grant the corporation as much power as any individual would have in conducting a business.

The corporate powers enumerated and described in the Model Business Corporation Act are typical of the powers contained in most state statutes. There are, however, some important variations and details pertaining to certain powers, which are discussed here.

Power to Exist Perpetually

A vast majority of states allow a corporation to exist indefinitely, and also permit the existence of a corporation to be limited to a specific period of time, if such a restriction is deemed important by the incorporators. Most statutes require that the articles of incorporation recite the period of corporate existence, and if none is stated, the corporation will be deemed to exist perpetually. A very few states do not permit perpetual existence and specifically limit the duration of a corporation. For example, Mississippi limits the duration of a corporation to ninety-nine years.

Power to Own and Deal with Real Property

Every state permits a corporation to acquire and hold real property in the corporate name. In several jurisdictions, however, this power is limited to such property necessary to further corporate purposes.[11] Thus, if a restaurant corporation were to acquire a larger building than it actually needed for its restaurant business, there would be a question about its power to do so. However, if the corporation could show that the larger building was purchased with a view to future expansion of the restaurant business or is otherwise convenient and appropriate to its specified corporate purposes, its ownership of that building would be authorized. A specific power clause on this point in the articles of incorporation may help.

> **EXAMPLE: Power to Deal in Property**
> To the same extent as natural persons might or could do, to purchase or otherwise acquire, and to hold, own, maintain, work, develop, sell, lease, exchange, hire, convey, mortgage, or otherwise dispose of and deal in lands and leaseholds, and any interest, estate, and rights in real property, and any personal or mixed property, and any franchises, rights, licenses, or privileges necessary, convenient, or appropriate for any of the purposes herein expressed.[12]

Power to Lend Money to Assist Employees

These provisions vary considerably among the states. Most states have no statutory power for corporate loans to employees, directors, or officers. Some completely prohibit loans to officers and directors. Those that do grant such power usually impose certain restrictions on it. Shareholder approval of a loan is frequently required, and in some cases the directors must be able to show that the transaction will be of some benefit to the corporation.[13]

Power to Make Donations

Statutes authorizing corporate power to make donations specify various purposes for which donations may be made, different procedures for internal authorization of donations, and certain limitations on the amount. Usually donations may be made for charitable, educational, religious, public welfare, and scientific purposes.[14] In most states, the decision to donate would be made by the board of directors, but shareholder approval could be required in the articles of incorporation or by-laws to restrict the authority. Some states permit charitable donations "irrespective of benefit to the corporation,"[15] and several states impose limitations on the amount donated. Limitations on donated amounts may be somewhat flexible, such as a "reasonable sum" in New Jersey, or they may be firm, such as 5% of net income before taxes in Virginia.

Power to be a Partner or Member of Another Enterprise

Early law prohibited a corporation from having the power to become a partner in a separate enterprise. Nearly all states have finally adopted statutory authority granting this power. (The judicial attitude toward the power had become increasingly favorable even without statutory support.) In most cases and in some statutes, this power is limited to permit a corporation to become a partner or member of another enterprise conducting a business that would be authorized in the corporate purposes—that is, a business the corporation could lawfully conduct on its own.[16]

Power to Engage in Transactions to Aid Government Policy

The Model Business Corporation Act has always permitted the corporation to engage in transactions that would aid government policy. Theoretically, this power could be broadly interpreted to include the making of a profit, since that will cause taxes to be collected, which certainly is an important government policy. Theoretically, this power may also allow the corporation to sell arms privately to foreign governments, provided that would be consistent with the policy of the administration. This power is treated differently in various states. In some jurisdictions, the corporation will have this power only in a time of war or national emergency.

Other jurisdictions require that the government must first request the corporation's aid before the corporation is authorized to assist.

Power to Establish Pension Plans

Almost all states permit the corporation to establish pension, profit sharing, and other benefit plans for certain employees. The Model Business Corporation Act permits these plans to benefit any current or former directors, officers, employees, and agents of the corporation. A few states permit these benefits to extend to such persons serving a subsidiary corporation.[17] Not all states grant the power to adopt such benefit plans for all persons who service the corporation. Only a very few states permit the payment of pensions to agents such as the new Model Business Corporation Act provides.[18]

Emergency Powers

Although the corporation is a separate legal entity, it can act only through its directors and officers. As explained later, directors are required to function at a properly called meeting or by written consent with an appropriate number of directors present for that purpose. If, because of some catastrophic event, the directors were unable to assemble according to the regular rules of the corporation, the corporation could not function. Accordingly, the Model Business Corporation Act and nearly half the states have provided separate emergency powers in case of a disaster or other event that would otherwise prevent the corporation from taking action.

Originally, the Model Business Corporation Act limited the use of emergency powers to situations involving an attack on the United States or a nuclear or atomic disaster. Now those powers may be exercised whenever there is a "catastrophic event." In such situations, the board of directors of the corporation may modify lines of succession to accommodate incapacitated corporate employees; relocate the principal office (presumably to get it out of the way); have a meeting with directors who can be reached by any practical manner; and promote officers into directors, if necessary, to achieve a quorum of the board. Since it is likely that corporate action will be taken quickly and furiously under these circumstances, the statute further provides that any action taken in good faith will bind the corporation, but may not be used to impose liability on corporate employees who had to make the decisions. It is typical, even in states that provide the enabling statutory rules for this power, to include appropriate provisions in the by-laws of the corporation so that some guidance is available under these circumstances, assuming that the corporate employees will have the time, and the inclination, to locate those by-laws.

OWNERSHIP AND MANAGEMENT OF A CORPORATION

The corporation departs significantly from the sole proprietorship and the partnership in the areas of ownership and management of the business enterprise. Recall that the sole proprietor is the owner and manager of his or her own business. In the general partnership, each partner is an owner and each partner is vested with the responsibilities of management. More analogous to a corporation, a limited partnership has investors with restrictions on their management control who merely contribute cash or property to the capital of the business while the general partners are responsible for management. Corporate business is managed by a board of directors and by officers that the board has appointed. The owners of the business are the shareholders, who contribute cash, property, or services in exchange for their ownership rights, evidenced by share certificates. It is possible for a shareholder to also be a director and an officer, but the rights and responsibilities of each intracorporate group are clearly segregated in corporate law, and each capacity must be separately considered and observed.

Incorporators

The incorporators are responsible for filing the articles of incorporation and securing preincorporation agreements and share subscriptions. The incorporators are usually the "promoters" of the corporation who work closely with counsel in drafting the appropriate documents to comply with the statutory requirements. The main tasks of the incorporators are to prepare and execute the articles of incorporation and to file those articles with the secretary of state. Attorneys or their staff who are forming the corporation may act as the incorporators (sometimes referred to as "dummy" incorporators), since the act of incorporation is primarily a technical legal function.

The necessary number of incorporators and their qualifications are specified by statute. The original provision of the Model Business Corporation Act required that three or more incorporators were needed to incorporate properly and that such persons must be over the age of twenty-one. In keeping with the trend toward "permissive" corporate statutes, the act has recently been amended to require one or more incorporators without mention of age or other qualifications.[19] Most states require adult natural persons to incorporate, and only a small minority of states have state residency requirements for the incorporators.[20] Some states, such as Pennsylvania, require that the incorporators subscribe for shares. The modern trend is to permit any one person to act as an incorporator; nearly all states have adopted statutes permitting a single incorporator.

Directors

General Powers. Section 8.01 of the Model Business Corporation Act states that the business and affairs of a corporation shall be managed by a board of directors, which shall exercise all powers of the corporation unless otherwise provided in the statute or in the articles of incorporation. Thus, the board of directors is the autocratic governing body of the corporation and the directors are responsible for managing the shareholder's enterprise. The directors are usually charged with the responsibility of determining corporate policies, managing the affairs of the business, and selecting and supervising the officers who handle the detailed business matters.

The Model Business Corporation Act vests all corporate power in the directors "subject to any limitation set forth in the articles of incorporation." In addition, Section 8.01(c) provides that a corporation having fifty or fewer shareholders may dispense with or limit the authority of a board of directors by describing in the articles of incorporation the persons who will perform some or all of the duties of the board. Therefore, in any corporation, the incorporators (or shareholders at a later date) may limit the authority of the board of directors by placing restrictions on the board's authority in the articles of incorporation. Similarly, a corporation with only a few shareholders may eliminate or minimize the authority of the board, and provide that the shareholders will have the management power. Such provisions are found most frequently in close corporations, which are discussed in detail in the next chapter.

Election and Term. Since directors act as the primary governing body for a shareholder-owned business, it is only fair that the shareholders be entitled to elect the directors. The first directors of the corporation must be named in the articles of incorporation in most states, and this initial board serves until the shareholders meet to elect their successors. If the initial directors are not named in the articles of incorporation, an organizational meeting of the shareholders is necessary to elect a board. After the initial board is elected, subsequent elections should occur at each annual shareholder's meeting, and the directors so elected usually serve until the next directors are elected. While the directors' terms expire at the next annual shareholders' meeting following their election, a director will continue to serve until a successor is elected and qualified or until the number of directors is decreased by official corporate action.

It is possible to *stagger* or *classify* the board of directors to ensure continuity of corporate management. This procedure avoids the election of a complete new board every year by varying the term of office for each director. Section 8.06 of the Model Business Corporation Act authorizes as many as three classes if the board has more than nine members. Thus, if the board has twelve members and is classified to three classes, four directors would serve until the first annual meeting, four would serve until the second annual meeting, and four would serve until the third annual meeting. When the four new directors are elected at the first annual meeting, they serve for three years, until the fourth annual meeting, and the process repeats itself. Thus, shareholders will elect four new directors every year and those new directors will join a board of eight old directors, who are presumably familiar with existing corporate policy and will ensure continuity in management principles. The classification procedure is treated differently in state statutes, but most states permit it. The number of classes and the necessary size of the board before classification is permitted are the major variants.

In another classification technique permitted by Section 8.04 of the Model Business Corporation Act, if the shares of stock of a corporation are divided into classes, the articles of incorporation may authorize the election of certain directors by the holders of certain classes of shares. This feature will permit certain shareholders to elect a representative to the board of directors even if those shareholders hold only a minority of the total outstanding shares of stock. For example, if a corporation has a board of directors consisting of three members, it can classify its board of directors, by an amendment to the articles of incorporation, to designate one director position for a new class of stock it hopes to sell to investors. Those investors could purchase only a small number of shares of the new class, but would always be assured of electing a representative to the board of directors, because one director position has been designated to be elected by that class alone.

Qualifications. Any person may be a director of a corporation, and only a few states require that a director be of "full" or "legal age."[21] The Model Business Corporation Act specifically provides that directors do not have to be shareholders of the corporation or residents of the state unless the articles of incorporation or the by-laws so require.[22] No state requires share ownership by a director, but a few impose residency requirements on at least a fraction of the board.[23] The articles of incorporation or the by-laws may impose residency or share ownership requirements as necessary qualifications to hold the office of director. Moreover, these documents may also prescribe any other reasonable qualifications for directors, such as a minimum or maximum age or United States citizenship.

Number of Directors. In most states, the board of directors must consist of at least three members, and the exact number is fixed in the articles of incorporation or the by-laws. The Model Business Corporation Act was amended in 1969 to require only one director, if the incorporators or shareholders felt that was appropriate.[24] The "one director" provision is also found in approximately half of all states, including Delaware. In some states, three directors will be required unless there are fewer than three shareholders, in which case the corporation may have the same number of directors as shareholders. Thus, if a corporation has only one shareholder, only one director will be required; if it has two shareholders, two directors will be required and if it has three or more shareholders, at least three directors will be required.

A corporation may usually have an unlimited number of directors, but the greater the number of persons on the board, the more difficult it becomes to make corporate decisions. The number of directors, as fixed in the articles of incorporation or by-laws, may be increased or decreased by an appropriate amendment thereto, but the amendment may never authorize less than the minimum number of persons required by the state statute.

Vacancies. If any vacancy occurs in the board, either by death, removal, or retirement of a director or by an amendment increasing the number of directors, the vacancy may be filled under the Model Business Corporation Act either by the shareholders or by the affirmative vote of a majority of the remaining directors.[25] This is the only time a director is not elected by the shareholders, and some states expressly reserve to shareholders the power to fill the vacancy, especially if the vacancy has been created by the shareholders' removal of a director.[26] A director selected to fill a vacancy serves for the remaining term of the previous director, and a new director will be elected at the next meeting of shareholders.

A director may resign at any time by delivering written notice to the other members of the board or to the corporation. The resignation will be effective when the notice is delivered unless a later effective date is specified in the notice. During the period before the effective date of the resignation, a replacement director may be selected, but the new director may not take office until the resignation is effective and the vacancy occurs.[27]

Removal. Directors serve at the pleasure of the shareholders. As owners of the corporate business, the shareholders probably have their most important power in their control over the positions of corporate directors. Section 8.08 of the Model Business Corporation Act amplifies this power by permitting the shareholders to remove a director with or without cause, unless the articles restrict that power to removal for cause only. Therefore, according to the act, whether or not a director is guilty of misconduct, the shareholders may remove the director at will and for whatever reason. Further, the shareholders' purge is not limited to one director at a time; the shareholders may vote to remove the entire board if that is deemed appropriate.

The required vote for removal of a director is usually a majority of the shares that were entitled to vote for the election of the same director. Consequently, if a director was elected by a special voting group of shareholders, such as where the director position was classified, only the shareholders of that voting group may vote to remove the director. A recent revision to the act at least removes the element of surprise from this decision. If a director is to be removed by the shareholders, the notice of the meeting must state that the purpose of the meeting is to consider the removal of that director.

Duties. The board of directors takes action on behalf of the corporation at regular or special meetings where the directors consider and adopt resolutions of corporate policy. These meetings are called in accordance with the corporate by-laws and are discussed in greater detail in Chapter 8.

Generally, the board of directors is empowered to make all corporate decisions, but realistically its actions are concerned with certain special important matters, and the day-to-day activities of the corporation are left to the officers. Directors are considered by the law to be *fiduciaries,* which means that all of their actions should be directed to further and protect the interests of those they serve. Their fiduciary capacity requires that they act independently, however, and they are not bound by the will of the shareholders who elect them. Of course, a director who ignores the desires of his or her constituents, the shareholders, runs the risk of being removed from office or losing reelection at the next shareholder meeting. Apart from this realistic possibility of losing his or her job by acting too independently, a director is only required to act in the best interests of the corporation by using independent discretion. More specifically, a director is required to use his or her best judgment in determining corporate policy and in authorizing corporate action, and to avoid any act that is in conflict with the director position or that will cause a personal profit to the director to the detriment of the corporation.

Because of the substantial increase in shareholder litigation against directors in recent years, most state statutes now specify guidelines for directors to follow in making corporate decisions. Section 8.30 of the Model Business Corporation Act instructs a director to perform the duties "in good faith," "with the care an ordinarily prudent person would exercise under similar circumstances," and "in a manner he reasonably believes to be in the best interests of the corporation." The director is also entitled to rely upon information, opinions, reports, or statements prepared by officers believed to be reliable and competent in such matters, professional advisers in their expert capacities, and committees of the board if their recommendations merit confidence. A director will not be liable for corporate action taken so long as the director complies with these standards. Some states are even more protective of their directors. Indiana will permit a director to be liable only if breach of the director's duty "constitutes willful misconduct or recklessness,"[29] and Delaware permits the articles of incorporation to eliminate or limit the personal liability of a director for monetary damages for breach of a fiduciary duty.[30]

Any transaction with the corporation in which a director has a personal interest will be tainted by a potential conflict of interest. If the director personally owns a piece of real estate that the corporation desires to acquire, the director is obviously in a superior bargaining position, knowing of the corporation's interest in the property and being a part of the decision-making body that will eventually approve the transaction. Consequently, shareholders or creditors of the corporation may object to transactions in which a director has a personal interest unless those transactions have been approved by independent persons. Section 8.31 of the Model Business Corporation Act provides that a director will have a personal interest in such a transaction if the director is personally involved in the transaction (such as the purchase of the director's own property) or if another entity that the director has a material financial interest in or manages is involved in the transaction (such as when another corporation sells the property, but the director of the buyer is also a director of the seller). In such cases, the statute provides a scheme by which the transaction may be approved so that it will not be voidable as a result of the conflict of interest. Approval may be obtained by doing one of the following:

1. Disclosing all material facts of the transaction to other members of the board who independently approve it. For this purpose, the interested director's vote cannot count for approval, and a majority of the disinterested directors will constitute a quorum (even though they otherwise may not be sufficient for a quorum of the directors at a meeting). If only one director is not interested in the transaction, that person alone may not approve the transaction.

2. Disclosing all material facts of the transaction to the shareholders, who approve the transaction by a majority vote. Similarly, if the director is also a shareholder, the director's vote may not count to approve the transaction. A majority of the shares held by shareholders who are not interested in the transaction may be a quorum for this purpose, although this majority may not otherwise qualify as a quorum of shareholders in a normal meeting. It is common to address these issues in the articles of incorporation to warn prospective directors and shareholders about the standards to be applied in approving transactions in which a director or officer may have a potential conflict of interest.

> **EXAMPLE: Transactions with an Interested Director or Officer**
> No contract or other transaction between this corporation and one or more of its directors, officers or stockholders or between this corporation and any other corporation, firm or association in which one or more of its officers, directors or stockholders are officers, directors or stockholders shall be either void or voidable (1) if at a meeting of the board of directors or committee authorizing or ratifying the contract or transaction there is a quorum of persons not so interested and the contract or other transaction is approved by a majority of such quorum, or (2) if the contract or other transaction is ratified at an annual or special meeting of stockholders, or (3) if the contract or other transaction is just and reasonable to the corporation at the time it is made, authorized or ratified.

A director could also have a conflict of interest in approving a loan from the corporation to the director. Section 8.32 of the Model Business Corporation Act permits such a transaction to be approved by a majority vote of the shareholders (not counting the votes of the benefited director-shareholder) or if the corporation's board of directors determines that the loan benefits the corporation. Remember that the other directors must make an independent determination, using their best judgment, that the corporation would be benefited by a loan to a director, so any resolution authorizing such a transaction should specifically state all of the reasons why such a benefit will result.

Delegation of Duties. While directors are generally vested with primary responsibility for management decisions, their powers may be delegated to officers or to an executive committee unless such a delegation is prohibited by the articles of incorporation or by-laws.

> **EXAMPLE: Executive Committee**
> The Board of Directors may, by resolution or resolutions passed by a majority of the whole Board, designate one or more committees, each committee to consist of two or more of the directors of the Corporation, which, to the extent provided in said resolution or resolutions, shall have and may exercise the powers of the Board of Directors in the management of the business and affairs of the Corporation, and may have power to authorize the seal of the Corporation to be affixed to all papers which may require it. Such committee or committees shall have such name or names as may be determined from time to time by resolution adopted by the Board of Directors.

The articles of incorporation or by-laws may restrict the authority of any committee created by the board of directors to consider certain corporate matters. However, even if the articles or by-laws are silent on this subject, there are some specific matters upon which the directors are required to act as a board and not through committees.

Selection of Officers. Section 8.40 of the Model Business Corporation Act provides that the officers shall be described in the by-laws or appointed by the board of directors as prescribed by the by-laws. Many important jurisdictions, including Massachusetts, have adopted statutes permitting the articles of incorporation or by-laws to allow for the election of certain officers by the shareholders. Since the officers are selected by the directors in most cases, and are required to be appointed by the directors in jurisdictions following the Model Business Corporation Act, the directors are under a duty to supervise the officers. The directors may be liable for failure to use due care in the appointment or supervision of an officer.

Determination of Management Compensation. The board of directors fixes executive compensation, including that of the officers and that of the directors themselves, but the articles of incorporation or by-laws may require shareholder approval.

> **EXAMPLE: Management Compensation**
> No salary or other compensation for services shall be paid to any director or officer of the corporation unless and until the same shall have been approved in writing or at a duly held stockholders' meeting by stockholders owning at least seventy-five per cent in amount of the capital stock of the corporation then outstanding.[31]

By-laws. In most states and under the Model Business Corporation Act, the initial by-laws of the corporation are adopted by the board of directors if the incorporators have not already prepared and adopted by-laws.[32] The directors also retain, concurrently with the shareholders, the power to alter, amend, or repeal the by-laws or to adopt new by-laws, but the articles of incorporation may reserve these rights exclusively to the shareholders. In either case, the articles should be specific on the authority desired.

> **EXAMPLE: Adoption, Amendment, or Repeal of By-laws.**
> The directors shall also have power, without the assent or vote of the stockholders, to adopt, amend or repeal bylaws relating to the business of the corporation, the conduct of its affairs and the rights or powers of its shareholders, directors or officers.[33]

Initiation of Extraordinary Corporate Matters. Extraordinary corporate matters, such as amendments of the articles of incorporation, sale or lease of all the corporate assets not in the regular course of business, merger, consolidation, and so forth, are usually initiated by the board of directors, and approved by the shareholders. These matters are obviously beyond the scope of day-to-day management, and may have considerable ramifications on the ownership rights of the shareholders. Consequently, the shareholders must approve such action by an appropriate vote after the action has been initiated by the board of directors.[34] The articles of incorporation should contain provisions respecting the directors' powers in such cases.

> **EXAMPLE: Disposition of Assets**
> The directors shall also have power, with the consent in writing of a majority of the holders of the voting stock issued and outstanding, or upon the affirmative vote of the holders of a majority of the stock issued and outstanding having voting power, to sell, lease, or exchange all of its property and assets, including its good will and its corporate franchises, upon such terms and conditions as the Board of Directors deem expedient and for the best interests of the corporation.[35]

Declaration of Distributions. Distributions are paid to shareholders from time to time as a return on their investment. The determination of whether distributions are to be paid is a decision for the board of directors, and broad discretion is reserved to directors in this area.[36]

Issuance of Stock and Determination of Value. The articles of incorporation must state the number of shares of stock the corporation is authorized to issue. It is most unusual for a corporation to issue all of the authorized stock at the beginning of its corporate existence. Consequently, the subsequent determination to issue stock is a decision for the board of directors. The articles of incorporation may also reserve to the board of directors the right to set preferences, limitations, and relative rights of classes of shares so that the corporation has the flexibility to fix the rights to accommodate the particular needs of a potential investor.[37] A committee of the board of directors may not assume this responsibility, except within limits specifically prescribed by the board of directors.[38]

Reacquisition of Shares The corporation has the power to repurchase its own shares, and the board of directors must make the decision to do so.[39] A committee of the board may not undertake this responsibility, except according to a formula or method prescribed by the board of directors.[40]

Officers

As indicated earlier, officers usually are appointed by and receive their power from the board of directors. Traditionally, corporations were required to have a president, a secretary, and a treasurer, and many states still require these offices. However, modern corporate law is beginning to recognize that there is little advantage to specifying certain particular offices in a statute. In fact, such statutes may create problems of implied or apparent authority and cause confusion with other offices that are created by corporations and are not specifically authorized by statute. For example, long before the offices of chief executive officer and chief financial officer started creeping into state statutes as authorized positions, many corporations used the titles anyway, and asked lawyers to draft specific descriptions of the authority of those offices in the articles or by-laws. Many states that require certain offices in the statute also prohibit one person's holding certain different offices, such as the offices of president and secretary.

The new Model Business Corporation Act does not require any specific officers, and permits the corporation to describe in its by-laws the officers it desires, or to grant to the board of directors the authority to appoint officers in accordance with the procedure described in the by-laws. The same individual may simultaneously hold more than one office in any corporation, and officers are permitted to appoint additional officers if they are authorized to do so by the by-laws or the board of directors. The only statutory duty the officers must perform is to prepare minutes of the directors' and shareholders' meetings and to authenticate records of the corporation.[41]

The authority and responsibility of the officers is a very broad topic. Generally, officers perform whatever duties have been delegated to them by the board of directors or the by-laws,[42] and the officers are responsible for managing the day-to-day affairs of the corporation. In addition, state statutes frequently require officers to perform certain administrative tasks. These typically include the execution of articles of merger, articles of consolidation, articles of amendment, and articles of dissolution[43] by appropriate officers of the corporation. Similarly, the officers usually must sign the certificates representing the shares of the corporation.

Officers are subject to removal at the pleasure of the board of directors, but in some states the directors may have to establish that the best interests of the corporation will be served by removing an officer. The revised Model Business Corporation Act permits the board of directors to remove any officer at any time with or without cause.[44] However, if the officer negotiated an employment contract with the corporation, removing that officer before the term of the contract expires may subject the corporation to a lawsuit for breach of contract.[45] Considering the potential liability of the corporation, the removal of an officer under an employment contract must be supported by a very good reason, even if the directors have an opportunity to remove an officer without cause.

An officer may resign at any time by delivering a notice to the corporation. The resignation will be effective when the notice is delivered, unless the notice specifies a later effective date. The board of directors may fill a vacancy before the effective date, but the successor may not take office until the effective date.[46]

Officers are generally subject to the same standard of conduct as are directors, and are entitled to rely on information, reports, or statements that justify reliance or are based upon professional competence. While this standard appears to be the same for officers and directors, keep in mind that officers are much more familiar than directors with the daily activities of the corporation. Consequently, an officer's reliance on reports and information prepared or submitted by others may be less justified under the circumstances.[47]

Shareholders

The shareholders are the owners of the corporation. They contribute capital for investment in the business, and receive in exchange stock certificates representing their ownership interest. For purposes of most state statutes, shareholders are defined as "holders of record of shares in a corporation." The words *holder of record* deserve some explanation. A corporation maintains a stock transfer ledger, in which the names of the owners of shares of the corporation are registered. The persons listed in the ledger are the holders of record. Whenever shares are transferred, the new owner's name is entered on the stock transfer ledger and that person becomes the holder of record. The holder of record is entitled to vote the shares, to receive distributions, and to receive a proportionate share of assets in dissolution, depending on the voting, distribution, and dissolution characteristics of the stock.[48]

Corporations and stock transfer agents have long worried that someday the proliferation of shareholders and the number of certificates transferred on stock exchanges would result in an unbreakable logjam of paperwork, which would eventually cause the system of delivering stock certificates to collapse. Accordingly, the Uniform Commercial Code has been amended in many states to permit shares in a corporation to be represented by "uncertificated securities," meaning that the corporation records the ownership of shares on its books and records, but does not issue to the shareholder a certificate representing the shares. To accommodate this modern approach to stock ownership, the revised Model Business Corporation Act recognizes that a shareholder could be "a person in whose name shares are registered in the records of the corporation or the beneficial owner of shares to the extent of the rights granted by a nominee certificate on file with the corporation."[49] Consequently, the recognition of shareholder status depends upon whether the records of the corporation reflect the shareholder as an owner. Shareholders may be "beneficial owners" of shares subject to voting trust agreements (discussed in detail later), and a "nominee certificate" is a certificate held by a stockbroker or other financial institution to represent shares held by many shareholders. These nominee arrangements may allow for individual owners to be considered shareholders for corporate purposes, even though shares are not actually registered in their names.[50]

As owners of the corporation, shareholders enjoy certain ownership rights, but not in the same sense as a sole proprietor owns a proprietorship, or even as a general partner has ownership rights in a partnership. Rather, the shareholder's rights as an owner are strictly limited by the state corporation statute. Generally, the shareholders' ownership rights include only their right to vote, their right to a return on their investment by way of distributions if the directors declare such distributions, and their right to share in the assets if the business is liquidated. From the previous discussion about directors and officers it should be apparent that shareholders have little or no voice in the day-to-day management of the corporation. However, they do have the power to elect the directors, who are responsible for the appointment and supervision of the officers, who are in turn responsible for the daily corporate activities. Thus, shareholders indirectly control corporate policy and activity by electing directors who are sympathetic to their desires. Moreover, the law requires that shareholders be consulted whenever the governing body, the board of directors, intends to modify or transform the character of the business in any manner that will materially affect the shareholders' ownership interests. These "fundamental" corporate changes are described in this book as extraordinary changes in corporate structure, and they include such matters as amendments to the articles, merger, consolidation, exchange of stock, sale or exchange of assets not in the ordinary course of business, and dissolution. Shareholder control is limited, therefore, to the shareholders' rights to vote in the selection of the corporate management and to be consulted in matters that may modify the character of their investment in the business. These indirect ownership rights are explored here in some detail.

Right to Elect and Remove Directors. The initial directors of the corporation may be named in the articles of incorporation, and those directors usually serve until the first shareholders' meeting. Shareholders then elect new directors at the first annual meeting, and those directors serve for the prescribed term, usually, until the next annual shareholders' meeting. As previously discussed, directors are also subject to removal with or without cause by an appropriate vote of the shareholders, as prescribed by state statute. If the statute does not specifically provide for removal without cause, a clause to that effect in the articles of incorporation or by-laws is necessary if that right is deemed important.

> **EXAMPLE: Removal of Directors**
> The stockholders of the Corporation may, at any meeting called for the purpose, remove any director from office, with or without cause, by a vote of a majority of the outstanding shares of the class of stock which elected the director or directors to be removed; provided, however, that no director shall be removed in case the votes of a sufficient number of shares are cast against his or her removal, which if cumulatively voted at an election of the entire board of directors would be sufficient to elect him or her.[51]

In corporate law, there is a special procedure for the election of directors, called cumulative voting. This procedure may or may not be in effect in a particular corporation, depending upon the appropriate state law and the articles of incorporation. Some states guarantee cumulative voting by constitutional provision.[52] Other states have statutes that require cumulative voting to be used unless the procedure is specifically denied in the articles of incorporation.[53] Yet other states, including Delaware, do not grant cumulative voting unless the articles of incorporation specifically authorize it.[54] The Model Business Corporation Act offers still another variation on this issue. Under the revised act, shareholders do not have a right to cumulate their votes unless the articles of incorporation so provide, and cumulative voting may not be used unless:

1. the notice for the meeting to elect directors says that cumulative voting will be permitted; or
2. a shareholder who has the right to cumulate votes gives notice to the corporation within forty-eight hours before the time set at the meeting of an intention to cumulate votes at the election. In the second case, if one shareholder gives proper notice, all other shareholders will have the right to cumulate their votes without further notice.[55]

As with most specific points of corporate law, it is very important to review the appropriate state statute to determine the manner by which cumulative voting is authorized, and to state the desired procedure in the articles of incorporation.

> **EXAMPLE: Cumulative Voting**
> At all elections for directors each stockholder shall be entitled to as many votes as shall equal the number of his or her shares of stock multiplied by the number of directors to be elected, as he or she may cast all of such votes for a single director, or may distribute them among the number to be voted for, or any two or more of them, as he or she may see fit.[56]

Right to Amend the Articles of Incorporation. The articles of incorporation may be amended upon the suggestion of the board of directors and, in some states, upon the suggestion of a certain percentage of shareholders. In any case, the proposed amendment must be submitted to a vote of the shareholders, either at an annual meeting or at a special meeting called for that purpose. Shareholders' approval of such amendments to the basic "charter" of their corporation is consistent with their rights as owners.[57]

Right to Take Other Extraordinary Corporation Action. Shareholder approval is also required for certain other extraordinary corporate matters, such as merger, consolidation, exchange of shares, sale or exchange of assets out of the ordinary course of business, and dissolution of the corporation. Since these actions may significantly alter the character of the investment, a shareholder objecting to such action may have his or her stock appraised and purchased. As a simple rule of thumb, any matter that may have a substantial impact on the operation of the business or the ownership rights of the shareholders requires shareholder approval. Even without a statutory mandate for shareholder approval, a sensible board of directors will request shareholder approval of major corporate decisions, perhaps for no other reason than to gauge shareholder sentiment regarding the directors' activities.

Right to Inspect. A corollary to the shareholders' voting right is the right to check up periodically on management and inspect corporate records. Most states have statutes that permit the shareholder to inspect and copy books and records, including minutes of shareholders' meetings and other shareholder records. To avoid recalcitrant persons who simply buy shares to harass corporate management, these statutes also establish certain criteria as a condition to the shareholders' right to inspect. The original Model Business Corporation Act and most states, for example, require the demanding shareholder to have share ownership for at least six months preceding a demand of inspection or to be a holder of record of at least 5% of all the outstanding shares of the corporation. Thus, the demanding shareholder must be established as a shareholder or must purchase a significant block of stock in order to have the right to inspect. Moreover, in all of these statutes, the demand for inspection must state the purpose of the inspection and the stated purpose must be "proper," and not for a reason conflicting with the best interests of the corporation. In states following these procedures, it may also be a good idea to grant the directors power to control inspection times and procedures in the by-laws.

> **EXAMPLE: Inspection by Shareholders**
> The directors from time to time may determine at what times and places, and under what conditions and regulations, the accounts and books of the Corporation shall be open to the inspection of the stockholders.[58]

The modern trend in corporate statutes is to permit any shareholder of a corporation to inspect the corporation's books and records under certain conditions. The shareholder must give written notice of an intention to inspect at least five business days before the date of inspection. The shareholder must also state the purpose of the inspection, and the records the shareholder desires to inspect must be directly connected with that purpose. Upon meeting these requirements, a shareholder will be entitled to inspect and copy minutes of meetings, accounting records, and the record of shareholders.[59] Unlike most current state statutes, the Model Business Corporation Act does not permit the articles or by-laws to abolish or limit the shareholders' inspection rights.

Preemptive Rights. The shareholders' preemptive rights are their rights to purchase newly issued shares of the corporation in the same proportions as their present share ownerships before outsiders may purchase them. For example, suppose XYZ Corporation has three shareholders—Judi Wagner, who owns 100 shares; Gail Schoettler, who owns 200 shares; and Fern Portnoy, who owns 300 shares—and the corporation determines that it will issue 1,500 new shares of stock. If the shareholders have preemptive rights, Wagner has the right to buy 250 shares (one-sixth) of the new issue, Schoettler has the right to buy 500 shares (one-third) of the new issue, and Portnoy has the right to buy 750 shares (one-half) of the new issue. If the shareholders fail to buy their allocated number of shares, the shares may then be sold to outsiders.

Preemptive rights began as a common law theory designed to protect shareholders' proportionate interests and to preserve their proportionate control over the corporation. In the previous example, Wagner, Schoettler, and Portnoy would suffer complete loss of control if the 1,500 shares were sold to a single outsider. Of course, if control is not important, the shareholders do not have to purchase their proportionate amount of the new issue, in which case the shares will be sold to other investors.

Most states now specifically treat preemptive rights in their corporate statutes. Some states provide that preemptive rights are granted automatically by law unless the articles of incorporation specifically deny them.[60] Other states, including Delaware, provide that the articles of incorporation must specifically grant preemptive rights or those rights do not exist.[61] The new Model Business Corporation Act has adopted the latter position.[62]

It is generally recognized that preemptive rights are important to shareholders of close corporations and a nuisance to shareholders of large, publicly held corporations. If American Telephone & Telegraph Company had to offer a proportionate right to purchase to each of its millions of shareholders, for example, the procedural problems and expense would be overwhelming. To assist in the flexibility of incentive compensation programs, it is also a good idea to exclude employee stock option plans from preemptive rights. In any case, the articles of incorporation should specify the corporate policy with respect to preemptive rights.

> **EXAMPLE: Preemptive Rights**
> No holder of any stock of the Corporation shall be entitled, as a matter of right, to purchase, subscribe for or otherwise acquire any new or additional shares of stock of the Corporation of any class, or any options or warrants to purchase, subscribe for or otherwise acquire any such new or additional shares, or any shares, bonds, notes, debentures or other securities convertible into or carrying options or warrants to purchase, subscribe for or otherwise acquire any such new or additional shares.[63]

Distributions. In addition to voting, inspection, and preemptive rights, shareholders are entitled to a return on their investment by way of dividend distributions if the corporation makes a profit, and if the directors in their discretion and good judgment deem such a distribution desirable. The objectives of the shareholders' investment are to receive dividend distributions and to realize capital appreciation when the value of the stock increases.

As owners of the corporation, shareholders may share in the assets of the corporation when the business is dissolved and the corporate creditors have been paid. The remaining assets will be divided among the shareholders proportionately according to the terms of their stock.[64]

LIMITED LIABILITY

An attractive characteristic of the corporation is that the investors risk only the amount of their investment and are not individually responsible for corporate obligations. This limited liability advantage flows from the recognition by the law that a corporation is a separate legal person, and its debts and liabilities are personal to it.

Limited liability for the corporation can be contrasted with the full individual liability of a partner in a partnership or an owner in a sole proprietorship. The limited partnership borrows this characteristic of limited liability from the corporation in protecting limited partners. The shareholder, who is the owner of the corporation, risks only the amount contributed for shares of the corporation. While the shareholder may lose the amount of money he or she paid for the shares, personal assets of the shareholder are not exposed if the corporation should incur excessive liability. Similarly, the persons who manage the corporation—the directors, officers, and other corporate executives—are not personally liable for corporate obligations unless they have exceeded their authority or breached their fiduciary duties of using good judgment and due care in incurring such obligations.

The protection of limited liability offered by corporations is a principal reason for choosing the corporate form over others, and the theory of limited liability is well established in judicial decisions. There are, however, two limitations on the principle, one practical and the other legal.

When a new corporation has been formed, it usually has not matured to an established business, and, while it may own certain assets and have good prospects for future profit, its ability to generate profits is untested. Consequently, potential creditors are understandably wary of extending credit to a new corporation. If the business is not as good as predicted, or if the managers are not as capable as they think they are, the corporation may not prosper, and a creditor may be forced to look only to the corporate assets for satisfaction of the obligation. Anticipating this problem, sophisticated creditors of the corporation will attempt to obligate all available parties for the repayment of the obligation—just in case something goes wrong. In such a case, the shareholders and directors may personally agree to pay corporate obligations in order to persuade outsiders to advance credit to their corporation, and they then become individually responsible for the obligation. Practical realities may thus cause the limited liability protection to be diminished by agreement.

The legal problem associated with limited liability is a theory called "piercing the corporate veil." The courts that have imposed personal liability on shareholders under the theory have recognized the corporate organization as offering a "shield" of limited liability for shareholder protection. Having found an abuse of this protection, courts are perfectly willing to pierce the shield, disregard the corporate entity, and hold shareholders responsible for the acts of the corporation. Implicit in the finding of abuse of this protection is a finding that the shareholders have neglected to comply with the statutory requirements for proper operation of a corporation. It is possible, therefore, to advise a client in advance of ways to avoid this problem.

Typical abuses of the corporate form that reappear consistently in piercing cases are a failure by the shareholders to supply the corporation with adequate financial resources to support its operations; and a failure to observe corporate formalities, such as holding meetings for shareholders and directors, keeping separate books of the corporation, distinguishing personal assets from corporate assets, and issuing stock. Notwithstanding these typical unoffensive abuses, if the corporation is used to perpetrate fraud or for other illegal purpose, a court will have no trouble looking behind the corporate veil to hold the individual shareholders responsible, whether or not the corporation was properly funded or the formalities were observed.

It should be apparent that these problems are most likely to arise in a closely held corporation rather than in one of our industrial giants. The entrepreneur who has formed a corporation for its limited liability benefits is most vulnerable to piercing the veil. If this person uses the family typewriter for business letters, uses excess family furniture in the office, commingles personal funds with corporate funds, and ignores formal meetings in making corporate decisions, the corporate protection is weak. Recognize, however, that if the entrepreneur's corporate assets are substantial, this piercing problem may never arise, even with the suggested transgressions. The piercing doctrine is a judicial theory used to resolve litigation if necessary. If the corporation is sued by a business creditor or a victim who slipped on its snow-covered sidewalk, and if the corporate assets are adequate to pay the claim, there is no need to pierce the corporate veil to reach the shareholders' personal resources. On the other hand, if the creditor or victim will suffer because of an inadequately financed corporation, a court will tend to reach behind the corporate shield to require the shareholders to pay.

As a precautionary measure, it has been suggested that all corporate clients should be advised to observe four principal objectives:

(1) The formalities of corporate procedure, including the holding of shareholders' and directors' meetings and the keeping of minute books, should be observed.
(2) The corporation should be operated as a really separate business and financial unit, with separate books and accounts, and without any intermingling or confusing of its funds, affairs, and transactions with those of the shareholders (whether individuals or corporations), officers, directors, or affiliated corporations in disregard of the corporate entity.
(3) No representation or other holding out should be made which would lead outsiders to believe that the business is being conducted as a sole proprietorship or as a partnership (with the assurance of the personal liability of those forms).
(4) The corporation should have adequate capital to meet its obligations and such contingencies as are reasonably to be expected in its business.[65]

One final observation on the theory of piercing the corporate veil: This is also a frequent problem with parent-subsidiary corporations. If a large, profitable corporation is seeking to enter a risky enterprise, it may be imprudent to risk all of the corporation's profit and other assets for one questionable venture. The solution is to form a separate corporation (called a subsidiary), whose stock is primarily or wholly owned by the large corporation (called a parent corporation), and the only risk, if the subsidiary corporation's shield of liability is observed, is the subsidiary's assets. The questions here are substantially the same as those detailed earlier. If the subsidiary is undercapitalized, and there is a loose separation between the parent and subsidiary, the parent may be required to respond to all liabilities and obligations of the subsidiary.

CONTINUITY OF EXISTENCE AND DISSOLUTION

A corporation has the power to exist perpetually under most state statutes, and will therefore be unaffected by the death of an owner or manager or by the transfer of ownership interests. The definitive term of a sole proprietorship, which ends when the proprietor dies, and of a partnership, which is technically dissolved upon the death, withdrawal, or other incapacity of a partner, was deemed to be a disadvantage to those forms of business. The corporation does not suffer from this infirmity. It is assured indefinite life by statute, and its ownership interests (shares) can be freely transferred without impairing its continuity.

Continuity of existence is an extremely important characteristic for a large corporation, since any abrupt termination of existence could result in financial tragedy. On the other hand, the continuity of a corporation may work a hardship on a minority shareholder who is dissatisfied with the investment and can find no market for his or her shares. This shareholder will be unable to terminate the corporate entity in order to withdraw investment, and may simply be forced to continue in shareholder status at the mercy of the majority shareholders and management.

Dissolution of a corporation may be accomplished by agreement of the appropriate intracorporate group (incorporators or shareholders) as provided by statute. These voluntary dissolutions are cumbersome and require the consensus of at least a majority of the appropriate intracorporate group to carry a resolution for dissolution.[66] A corporation may also be dissolved by a court upon request of the attorney general whenever the corporation has failed to comply with statutory requirements, has procured its articles by fraud, or has otherwise abused its authority. In addition, many modern corporate statutes have provisions for involuntary dissolution for the benefit of minority shareholders who are being unfairly prejudiced by those in control of the corporation,[67] and the Model Business Corporation Act permits a judicial dissolution if the directors or those in control are acting in a manner that is illegal, oppressive, or fraudulent.[68] It is hoped that these court-ordered dissolutions will remain rare

TAXATION OF A CORPORATION

Corporations, like natural persons, are subject to taxation by the federal, state, and local governments based on the amount of income they earn each year. Consistent with the separate corporate personality, the corporation is regarded as a separate taxable entity for most federal and state tax purposes and is taxed on separate corporate tax rates. This separate entity taxation is a significant distinguishing characteristic of the corporation from the sole proprietorship and partnership, where income is merely funneled to the individuals who make up the business organization and is declared as individual income for tax purposes.[69] Taxation of corporations has some advantages and some disadvantages, all of which must be carefully considered by the attorney in advising the client that the corporate form is the proper organization for a proposed business.

Double Taxation

The greatest disadvantage of corporate taxation is the concept of *double taxation*. Income received by the corporation is taxed at the corporate level according to the corporate rates then in effect. The profit remaining after taxes is available to be distributed to shareholders as dividends. If dividends are distributed, the distribution is taxed again as personal income to the shareholder.

Recall that federal and state governments set different individual and corporate tax rates. For years, individual tax rates were graduated from a low of approximately 14% to a high of approximately 50% on ordinary income. Corporate tax rates have also been adjusted regularly to accomplish various tax policies. For many years, corporate tax rates were also set on graduated rates, from a low of approximately 15% to a high of approximately 46%, depending on total taxable income. Regardless of the level of tax rates now in effect, certain tax planning principles will be relevant to the taxation of a corporation. Some hypothetical situations are reviewed here to illustrate how double taxation is a significant disadvantage to the corporate business form.

Whenever corporate tax rates are higher than individual tax rates, no tax advantage can be achieved for ordinary income in the corporate form, since every dollar earned by the corporation will be taxed at a higher rate than any dollar earned by the individual. Consequently, since sole proprietorships and partnerships are taxed based on individual rates, fewer after-tax dollars will be available for any business that is operating under the corporate form.

Even when the corporate tax rates for ordinary income are lower than individual tax rates, the concept of double taxation places the corporation at a disadvantage. For example, suppose the corporate tax rate is 20% and the individual tax rate is 30%. At first glance, it would appear that the business profit produced by the corporation will result in less tax than the same business profit produced by an individual proprietor or a partnership. However, if the only way the corporation can distribute cash to its shareholders is through distributions of dividends, those distributions must be paid from after-tax corporate dollars. (Dividends distributed to shareholders are not deductible by the corporation as an expense.) Consequently, when the corporation earns $1.00 of profit, that profit is immediately reduced to $0.80 through the corporate tax rate. Thus, when the dividend is paid to the shareholder, the shareholder must pay ordinary income tax on dividends received. The $0.80 is thus reduced by an additional $0.24, leaving $0.56 as the net after-tax available cash. If the same business were conducted as a partnership or sole proprietorship, only the individual tax rate would be applied to each dollar of profit, leaving $0.70 available after taxes were paid.

When tax rates are graduated (when they increase as the level of income increases) for both corporations and individuals, the double taxation problem can be considerably worse for successful corporations owned by successful shareholders. For example, if the highest corporation tax rate is 40% for all corporate profit over $100,000, and the highest individual tax rate is 50% for all income earned over $100,000, almost all profit that is earned by the corporation and distributed to the shareholder will be paid to the federal and state taxing authorities. Every corporate dollar earned over $100,000 will be reduced $0.40 at the corporate taxation level. If the remaining $0.60 is distributed to a shareholder who is taxed in the 50% bracket, it is taxed an additional $0.30. Thus, the corporate dollar is reduced a total of $0.70 in taxes, leaving the shareholder with $0.30 cash to spend!

With parent-subsidiary corporations, there may even be triple taxation—when the subsidiary pays its corporate tax and distributes remaining profits to the parent as dividends, which are taxed as the parent's corporate income, and the dividends are then distributed to the parent corporation's shareholder, who is taxed at individual tax rates.

Double taxation is recognized as a distinct disadvantage for the corporation as compared with other business forms, especially if a significant portion of the corporate income will be paid to the shareholders as dividend distributions. Large corporations with many stockholders simply accept the disadvantage, since the corporate form offers many advantages that are essential to the operation of a large business. In small, closely held corporations, double taxation may be minimized by several options. Whenever shareholders are officers or employees of the corporation, as is frequently the case in small organizations, they may be paid salaries, which are deductible as a corporate expense. The shareholder-employee is thereby compensated, and since the corporate tax is not imposed on the salary, double taxation is avoided. Furthermore, anticipating this problem, a small corporation may be structured so that much of its capital comes from loans to the business, rather than from shareholder investment. Having established sufficient equity capital (money paid through shareholder investment), the corporation may raise the remaining funds needed for the business through interest-bearing loans, and the interest is deductible to the corporation as an expense. The interest paid to the creditor (investor) is income, which substitutes for dividends and is not subject to double taxation. Similarly, shareholders of closely held corporations may purchase property and equipment and lease it to their corporation, receiving rental payments, which are treated as expenses to the corporation and are taxed only as rental income to the shareholder-lessors.

Another practical approach to double taxation is to leave the corporate profits in the business and not distribute dividends. Then only corporate tax rates are applied, and while the retained profits will increase the value of the stock, resulting in a capital gains tax when the stock is sold, no individual income tax is applied to the profits themselves. This solution is too simple to be effective, however, since the taxing authorities have devised a penalty that encourages corporations to distribute earnings to the shareholders rather than accumulate them. The accumulated earnings tax is applied to income unreasonably retained by the corporation. The company must pay a penalty tax of 27.5% on the first $100,000 of accumulated earnings (for which no adjustments are available) and 38.5% of the accumulated taxable income in excess of $100,000.[70] The corporation has the burden of establishing adjustments to the accumulated earnings tax for certain transactions that might qualify for adjustments, or the corporation must prove that income has been accumulated for the reasonable needs of the business in order to avoid the penalty.

Subchapter S Election

The Internal Revenue Code of 1986 provides that a "small business corporation" may elect not to be taxed at the corporate level but to have its income (whether distributed or not) passed through and taxed pro rata to its shareholders as ordinary income.[71] This election effectively treats the corporation as a sole proprietorship or partnership for tax purposes, and all profits are attributed proportionately to the persons who own the business. Similarly, corporate losses may be offset against other personal income of the shareholders. The election is particularly beneficial to shareholders whose tax rates are significantly lower than the corporate tax rate, or when it is expected that most of the corporate profits will be distributed to the shareholders. The election avoids two disadvantages of corporate taxation: the profits are not double taxed, and when a shareholder actively participates in the business, corporate losses may be taken as ordinary losses, thereby reducing the personal income of the shareholder.

To be classified as a small-business corporation for the Subchapter S election, a corporation must meet the following requirements:

1. There may be no more than thirty-five shareholders (spouses are treated as one shareholder, regardless of how the stock is held).
2. Shareholders must be natural persons, and cannot be another corporation or partnership, but may be an estate of a natural person or certain trusts.
3. The corporation may have only one class of stock (although different classes are permitted provided the only difference among them is voting rights).
4. The corporation cannot have a nonresident alien as a shareholder.

The election of a small-business corporation refers to the number of shareholders, as indicated in the listed requirements for qualification, and has nothing to do with the size of the corporation in terms of its assets, revenue, or earnings. These requirements effectively limit the Subchapter S election to close corporations.[72]

Under the Subchapter S election, corporate profits, whether distributed or not, must be claimed as taxable income by each shareholder in the proportion of ownership interest held, and, consequently, shareholders must consent to the election. Each shareholder should sign a separate statement of consent acknowledging the effect of the election. The statement is submitted with the form electing taxation under Subchapter S.[73]

The election to be taxed under Subchapter S is made on Form 2553 of the Internal Revenue Service,[74] and it may be made for any taxable year at any time during the previous taxable year or at any time before the fifteenth day of the third month of the taxable year (March 15 for calendar year corporations).[75] Thus, if the corporation determined to elect Subchapter S taxation, and had adopted September 1 to August 31 as its taxable year, the election may be made anytime during the preceding fiscal year for the following year or before November 15 for the present year.

The election may be terminated in one of several ways. The most common termination results from the corporation ceasing to qualify as a small-business corporation under the requirements listed earlier, as, for example, when it acquires a thirty-sixth shareholder. It may also be terminated if the majority of the shareholders consent to revocation of the election.

Finally, the Subchapter S election may be terminated whenever the corporation has received more than 25% of its gross income during three consecutive taxable years from passive sources, such as royalties, rents, dividends, interest, annuities, and sales or exchanges of stock or securities.[76] The election cannot be terminated by a new shareholder who does not affirmatively consent to tax treatment under Subchapter S, unless the new shareholder is the thirty-sixth shareholder of the corporation, or unless the new shareholder purchases a majority of the stock and then affirmatively revokes the election.

As a practical matter, Subchapter S is particularly desirable when the corporation is expected to incur losses during the first few years of operation, when shareholders' individual tax rates are lower than the corporate rates, or when corporate profits are expected to be distributed to shareholders as dividends. Note that the election and maintenance of Subchapter S treatment increase the burdensome formalities required for corporate existence, and will increase the legal and accounting costs incident to corporate operation.

State Income Tax

Corporations operating within any given state are also subject to state income tax. The general rule is that a state may tax a corporation operating within its borders in a reasonable relation to the business activity conducted within the state. Thus, a corporation incorporated in Colorado will automatically be subject to the Colorado state tax if it does business there or has Colorado source income, because it was originally formed in that state. If the corporation then does business in Wyoming and Nebraska, those states may also tax its income in relation to the business conducted within their borders. The domestic or domicile state, in this case Colorado, usually allows a tax credit for taxes paid to other states.

Various formulas are employed by the states to determine a proper allocation of tax on local business activity. As a practical matter, states attempt to devise formulas that will maximize tax revenue from business activity. For example, a state with very little localized industry usually has a formula based on sales made within the state rather then on corporate assets located within the state. On the other hand, a state with a heavy industrial population will probably tax on a percentage of total assets located within the state.

In addition to state and federal income taxes, corporations are frequently subject to other special taxes, which may result in the corporation bearing a greater tax burden than other forms of business enterprise. Franchise taxes, organization and capital taxes, original issue taxes for the issuance of shares of stock, and taxes on transfers of shares and other corporate securities are the most common. Proper planning in the selection of a business organization requires an analysis of the myriad charges imposed by various states on the corporations operating within their boundaries.

Section 1244 Stock

The foregoing discussion has been primarily concerned with income taxes assessed against a corporation and its shareholders. The other tax ramifications of a corporation include capital gains and losses associated with the purchase of sale of stock. Each share of stock is a capital asset, and if it is sold after appreciating in value, a taxable gain is realized. Similarly, when stock is sold after depreciating in value, a capital loss is claimed. Capital losses for individuals may be used only to offset capital gains, if there are any, or deducted from ordinary income up to a maximum limitation. For example, suppose a shareholder invested $5,000 in the stock of a corporation, which then became bankrupt, thus making the stock worthless and resulting in a capital loss of $5,000. If the stockholder had no other capital gains that year, the stockholder may not be able to deduct the loss. While there are certain carry-forward provisions for individual losses, it would be preferable to be able to claim the full $5,000 against ordinary income for that taxable year. Section 1244 of the Internal Revenue Code provides this effect for stock that qualifies as small business stock.[77]

The definition of a small-business is different for Section 1244 stock than for a Subchapter S election. In this case, the qualification of a corporation as a small business depends upon the amount of money to be raised by a plan to sell Section 1244 stock and the existing equity capital of the corporation. The amount of stock that is offered under the plan and intended to qualify under Section 1244, and the amounts received by the corporation as contributions to capital or paid in surplus, cannot exceed $1,000,000. Any property contributed for stock (other than money) is valued at the adjusted basis of the property to the corporation, less any liability against the property assumed by the corporation.

For example, suppose the Lyons Corporation adopts a Section 1244 plan to offer stock for an amount not in excess of $500,000. If its equity capital were $600,000 at the time the plan was adopted, $100,000 of the stock would not qualify under Section 1244 because the equity capital plus the aggregate amount offered would exceed $1,000,000. In such a case, the maximum amount that would qualify under the plan would be $400,000. The corporation has a right to designate which stock shall qualify. However, suppose the Lyons Corporation was newly formed when it adopted the plan. In its first year, it sold $400,000 in stock, and business successes deposited $800,000 into equity capital. This does not destroy the qualification of the stock because the equity capital test includes only amounts paid for contributions to capital, not revenues from operations.

To qualify for Section 1244 stock, the corporation must acquire most of its income (more then 50%) from sources other than other than royalties, rents, dividends, interest, annuities, and transactions in stock for five years preceding the loss.[78] The effect of the plan will be lost if the business does not comply with this source-of-income provision after the stock is issued and for five years before the investor sustains a loss.

For taxable years beginning after 1979, the former requirement that the Section 1244 stock be issued pursuant to a written plan has been repealed. Nevertheless, it is good practice to prepare a plan or a written corporate resolution to indicate clearly that the shares are being sold pursuant to Section 1244.[79] If all requirements of the statute are met, all stock issued pursuant to the plan will receive ordinary loss treatment if a loss is incurred when the stock is sold. This means that the selling shareholders may use any loss on the stock to offset ordinary income during the taxable year, rather than treating the loss as a capital loss with its limited and deferred tax treatment.

Other Tax Advantages of a Corporation

Tax authorities allow a corporation to deduct certain "necessary" expenses incurred in providing fringe benefits to employees to encourage their continuous faithful performance. There are also tax advantages to the employee under "qualified" incentive plans. If these employees are also shareholders, the deductibility of such expenses is unaffected. Incentive benefits with tax advantages include share options; medical and dental reimbursement plans; qualified pension and profit-sharing plans; and life, health, and accident insurance programs.[80]

Incentive compensation programs give the employee a right to participate in the success of the business, while enjoying significant tax breaks on the compensation received under the plan. For example, a qualified profit sharing plan permits a corporate deduction of profits accumulated for employees under the plan, but the employee is not taxed until he or she recieves payment. Qualified pension plans are similarly treated for tax purposes.

Insurance plans may provide a direct economic benefit to employees, who may also be shareholders, without tax on the proceeds of the insurance. The corporation may deduct the expense of paying insurance premiums for employees as an ordinary business expense. Hospital, accident, health, and disability insurance plans may be maintained by the corporation with very few limitations. Group life insurance, with maximum dollar limitations per employee, may be maintained by the corporation, with the premiums treated as an expense of the corporation but not taxable to the employee.

These special insurance and incentive compensation plans, with their attendant tax advantages, are unique to the corporation, with its separate legal personality. Partnerships and sole proprietorships do not enjoy the separate entity characteristic, and therefore do not obtain tax advantages through these devices.

NOTES

1. See "Ownership and Management of a Corporation" later in this chapter.
2. "Ownership and Management of a Corporation" later in this chapter.
3. Many states advertise the advantages of incorporation under their laws. Delaware sends the following synopsis of its permissive corporate laws to persons requesting information regarding incorporation:

    The Outstanding advantages of incorporating in Delaware are as follows:
    The fees payable to the State of Delaware are based upon the number of shares of authorized capital stock, with the no par shares fee one-half the par shares fee.
    The franchise tax compares favorably with that of any other State.
    Shares of stock owned by persons outside of the State are not subject to taxation.
    Shares of stock which are part of the estate of a non-resident decedent are exempt from the State Inheritance Tax Law.
    The policy of Delaware courts has always been to construe the Corporation law liberally, to interpret any ambiguities or uncertainties in the wording of the Statutes so as to reach a reasonable and fair construction. This causes the careful investor to have confidence in the security of the investment.
    The corporation service companies throughout the nation consider the Delaware corporation Law among the most attractive for organization purposes and the State of Delaware a valuable jurisdiction in which to organize new companies.

4. See "The Articles of Incorporation" and "By-laws" in Chapter 6.
5. West's Modern Legal Forms §2692.
6. M.B.C.A. § 3.02(11) , and see "By-laws" in Chapter 6. Also see Article VI, clauses 6–10, of sample By-Laws, Form 6Q in Appendix G.
7. M.B.C.A. § 3.02(7).
8. West's Modern Legal Forms § 2693.
9. West's Modern Legal Forms § 2698.
10. Examples of specific corporate purposes appear in the discussion of the articles of incorporation in Chapter 6.
11. This restriction may appear in the state constitution, as in Oklahoma (Okla.Const.Art. XXII, § 2), or in the state corporation statutes (e.g., New Hampshire, N.H.Rev.Stat.Ann. § 293–A:4(V)).
12. West's Modern Legal Forms § 2695.
13. M.B.C.A. §§ 3.02(8) and 8.32.
14. See M.B.C.A. § 3.02(13).
15. E.g., New Jersey, N.J.State.Ann. § 14A:3–4.
16. E.g., Delaware, 8 Del.Code Ann. § 122(11).
17. E.g., Tennessee, Tenn.Code § 48–13–102(12).
18. E.g., New Jersey, N.J.Stat.Ann. § 14A:3–1(1)(1).

19. M.B.C.A. § 2.01.
20. E.g., South Dakota, S.D.Comp.Laws Ann. § 47-2-4.
21. E.g., Pennsylvania, 15 Pa.Stat. §§ 1401 and 1402.
22. M.B.C.A. § 8.02.
23. E.g., Hawaii requires that at least one member of the board must be a resident of the state, Hawaii Rev.Stat. § 415-35.
24. M.B.C.A. § 8.03(a).
25. M.B.C.A. § 8.10.
26. E.g., Wisconsin, Wis.Stat.Ann. § 180.34.
27. M.B.C.A. §§ 8.07 and 8.10.
28. E.g., 8.08 However, if cumulative voting is in effect for the election of directors, the same procedure must be followed in the removal of a director. See "Shareholder Business and Vote Required" in Chapter 8.
29. Ind.Code Ann. § 23-1-35-1.
30. 8 Del.Code Ann. § 102(b)(7).
31. West's Modern Legal Forms §2718.
32. M.B.C.A. § 2.06.
33. West's Modern Legal Forms § 2713.
34. See "Amendment of the Articles of Incorporation," "Merger, Consolidation, and Exchange," and "Sale, Mortgage, or Other Disposition of Assets" in Chapter 13.
35. West's Modern Legal Forms § 2714.
36. M.B.C.A. § 6.40. Corporate distributions and dividends are fully discussed in Chapter 9.
37. M.B.C.A. § 6.02. Characteristics of corporate stock are discussed fully in Chapter 7.
38. M.B.C.A. § 8.25(e)(8).
39. M.B.C.A. § 6.31.
40. M.B.C.A. § 8.25(e)(7).
41. M.B.C.A. § 8.40.
42. See Article VI, clauses 6-10 of the sample by-laws, Form 6Q in Appendix G.
43. These documents are required to accomplish extraordinary corporate actions and are discussed in Chapter 13.
44. M.B.C.A. § 8.43(b).
45. See "Employment Agreements" in Chapter 10 and M.B.C.A. § 8.44.
46. M.B.C.A. § 8.43(a).
47. M.B.C.A. § 8.42
48. These characteristics are discussed in "Common Stock Rights" and "Preferred Stock Rights" in Chapter 7.
49. M.B.C.A. § 1.40(22).
50. See M.B.C.A. § 7.23.
51. West's Modern Legal Forms § 2720.
52. E.g., Illinois, Ill.Const. Transition Schedule § 8.
53. E.g., Texas, Texas Stat.Ann. § 2.29.
54. E.g., 8 Del.Code Ann. § 214.
55. M.B.C.A. § 7.28. Cumulative voting is discussed in detail in "Shareholder Business and Vote Required" in Chapter 8.
56. West's Modern Legal Forms § 2712.
57. The procedure for accomplishing amendments to the articles is more fully explored in "Amendment of the Articles of Incorporation" in Chapter 13.
58. West's Modern Legal Forms § 2731.
59. M.B.C.A. § 16.02.
60. E.g., Colorado, Colo.Rev.Stat. § 7-4-110.
61. E.g., Delaware, 8 Del.Code Ann. § 102(b)(3).
62. M.B.C.A. § 6.30.
63. West's Modern Legal Forms § 2735.
64. Dividend distributions are discussed in Chapter 9; distributions in dissolution are considered in Chapter 13.
65. R. Deer, The Lawyers Basic Corporate Practice Manual § 1.02 (1971).
66. Precise elements and the procedure for dissolution are discussed in Chapter 13.
67. E.g., Minnesota, Minn.Stat.Ann. § 302A-751.
68. M.B.C.A. § 14.30.

69. See "Taxation of a Sole Proprietor" in Chapter 1 and "Tax Considerations of a General Partnership" in Chapter 2.
70. Int.Rev.Code of 1986, 26 U.S.C.A. § 531.
71. Int.Rev.Code of 1986, 26 U.S.C.A. § 1361–1379.
72. Close corporations are specifically discussed in "Close Corporations" in Chapter 5.
73. A sample statement of consent appears as Form 4A in Appendix G.
74. Form 2553 is Form 4B in Appendix G.
75. Int.Rev.Code of 1986, 26 U.S.C.A. § 1362(b).
76. Int.Rev.Code of 1986, 26 U.S.C.A. § 1362(d).
77. Int.Rev.Code of 1986, 26 U.S.C.A. § 1244(c)(3).
78. Int.Rev.Code of 1986, 26 U.S.C.A. § 1244(c)(1)(C).
79. A sample plan and resolution to issue stock under Section 1244 appear as Forms 4C and 4D in Appendix G.
80. See Chapter 10 for a full discussion of incentive benefit plans.

5 SPECIAL CORPORATE FORMS

The corporate model described in the last chapter is typical of most American business corporations. In some corporations, however, special variations modify the general corporate characteristics in certain particulars.

CLOSE CORPORATIONS

Corporations whose shares are not traded on an exchange and are owned by a small group of shareholders are called close corporations. The shareholders of a close corporation are frequently closely related by blood or at least by friendship. In most jurisdictions, these corporations are distinguishable from other business corporations only in that their share ownership is restricted to a select few persons who are intimately involved with the business and who operate the corporation with substantial shareholder participation. A significant characteristic of the close corporation is that the shareholders actively participate in the management of the business. Thus, unlike a large, publicly held corporation, the close corporation has a mixture of management and ownership and this unique relationship between the shareholders usually results in a guarded interest in maintaining ownership control through internal shareholder agreements and restrictions on the transfer of equity securities. These corporate objectives accurately suggest that the operation of a close corporation resembles the operation of a partnership. An examination of any close corporation should reveal a group of persons who might as well have been partners, but instead selected the corporate form for its limited liability and tax consequences.

The attorney's greatest challenges in the formation and operation of a close corporation are the various agreements among shareholders that are designed to perpetuate management and ownership control through voting power and share transfer restrictions. These intricate agreements are separately considered in a later chapter.[1] For now, the primary concern is the manner in which the structure and operation of close corporations differ from those of other corporations.

Many jurisdictions have no separate "close corporation statute" and require that close corporations be formed and operated under the normal corporation code. In these states, any desired informality and owner management must be achieved by procedures or agreements that comply with the normal statutory requirements. However, the trend toward permissiveness in modern corporate statutes has provided the close corporation with statutory authority for the desired flexibility and informality. For example, formal shareholder meetings may be avoided under Section 7.04 of the Model Business Corporation Act. Instead, action by shareholders may be taken without a meeting if all shareholders entitled to vote at the meeting sign a written consent to the action. To enable the shareholders of a close corporation to maintain tight personal control over corporate activities, Section 7.25 of the act permits greater-than-normal voting requirements for shareholder action to be drafted into the articles of incorporation. If the statute normally permitted shareholder action by the vote of the majority, the articles could specify a two-thirds, three-fourths, or even unanimous voting requirement to increase individual control. The act further authorizes an important adjustment in management functions for the close corporation by providing that a corporation having fifty or fewer shareholders may provide in its articles of incorporation the persons who will perform the duties of a board of directors, and may thereby limit the authority of a board of directors or even dispense with the board of directors completely.[2] Shareholder management authority may, therefore, be specified in the articles of incorporation to the extent desired by corporate personnel. Some states, notably New York and North Carolina, allow shareholder agreements to impinge on management functions that are usually reserved to the board of directors. Thus, persons seeking close corporation status may be accommodated under several modern corporate statutes that permit sufficient flexibility in operation and control to use close corporation procedures.

A few jurisdictions have adopted more sophisticated statutory authority for close corporations by adding in the regular corporation statute separate sections specifically directed to the unique operations of close corporations.[3]

The Model Business Corporation Act has adopted a close corporation supplement to provide for flexible and certain rules for the operation of a close corporation. The purpose of these statutory provisions is to avoid the expense of drafting an elaborate set of specially tailored close corporation documents. The statutory provisions would be particularly useful for a small business that is likely to remain a closely held business, all or most of whose shareholders are active in the business; a professional corporation whose shareholders wish to be taxed as a corporation but would prefer to operate internally as a partnership; or a wholly owned subsidiary corporation, which may be created and operated with a very simple corporate structure.

Definition

A statutory close corporation is a corporation whose articles of incorporation contain a statement that the corporation is intended to be a "statutory close corporation." A corporation having fifty or fewer shareholders may become a statutory close corporation by amending its articles to say that it is a statutory close corporation.[4] Some states define their close corporations as those whose shares are not "publicly traded." This provision is concerned with a public offering, which requires registration under state and federal securities laws. Any corporation whose shares are not publicly traded is usually permitted to elect close corporation status under those statutes.[5]

Usually, a warning that the corporation is a close corporation must be placed on each share certificate. For example, the Model Business Corporation Act requires a legend on the stock certificate stating the following:

The rights of shareholders in a statutory close corporation may differ materially from the rights of shareholders in other corporations. Copies of the articles of incorporation and bylaws, shareholder agreements, and other documents, any of which may restrict transfers and affect voting and other rights, may be obtained by a shareholder on written request to the corporation.[6]

Provisions Relating to Shares

One traditional feature of a close corporation is that the stock issued to shareholders is subject to certain restrictions on transfer. Restrictions can be established by a shareholder agreement (under the regular corporation law), or they may be automatic (as in a statutory close corporation). The Model Business Corporation Act provides that shareholders of a close corporation may transfer their shares to other shareholders, members of their immediate families, and persons who have been approved in writing by all the holders of the corporation's shares having general voting rights. In addition, transfers are permitted to executors and administrators when a shareholder dies, to trustees (as in the case of bankruptcy of a shareholder), in mergers or other business combinations where shares are normally exchanged, or as collateral for a loan.[7] Otherwise, any person who wishes to transfer shares in a close corporation must offer them first to the corporation. The corporation then has an opportunity to purchase the shares if the shareholders authorize the purchase. If the corporation purchases the shares, it may allocate some or all of those shares to the other shareholders. If the corporation and the selling shareholder cannot agree upon the price or terms of purchase, the shareholder is free to sell the shares to an outsider.[8] The outsider must be eligible to become a shareholder without affecting the corporation's tax status.[9] If a shareholder attempts to transfer shares in violation of these restrictions, the transfer is ineffective.[10]

If the articles of incorporation of a close corporation provide, the corporation is required to purchase shares of a deceased shareholder.[11] The procedure in case of death is similar to the procedure for voluntary transfer. After receiving notice of the shareholder's death and a request for the corporation to purchase the shares, the corporation, if authorized to do so by its shareholders, will make a purchase offer for the shares, accompanied by recent financial statements. The price and other terms may be fixed in advance by provisions in the articles of incorporation, by-laws, or a written agreement. If the corporation fails to make an offer for a compulsory purchase, a court may order the corporation to purchase the shares at a fair value.[12]

Shareholder Management

Recall that the owner-manager characteristics of a business are usually found in partnerships. In a close corporation, it is possible to adopt shareholder management provisions that effectively structure the operation of the business to be like that of a partnership. Under the Model Business Corporation Act, in any corporation with fifty or fewer shareholders, provisions may be adopted that dispense with or limit the authority of a board of directors and permit shareholders to perform those duties.[13] All shareholders may agree in writing concerning the management of the affairs of the corporation, and the agreement could eliminate a board of directors, restrict the power of the board of directors, cause the corporation to be treated as a partnership, and permit partner-type relationships among shareholders.[14] For example, a shareholder agreement could state when distributions are to be made from the corporation and who the corporate officers will be. An agreement could also provide that the corporation would be dissolved whenever a shareholder dies or is bankrupt. These are typical partnership characteristics, but shareholders of a close corporation may also have legitimate reasons for such rules to operate their business.

If the corporation has a board of directors, it would be unfair to permit a shareholder agreement to reserve management power to the shareholders and still expose the board of directors to liability for shareholders' decisions. Consequently, any agreement that restricts the discretion of the board of directors also relieves the directors from liability for such matters, and places the liability on the people who are making the decisions.[15] It is also possible to completely eliminate the board of directors if the articles of incorporation say so.[16] When this happens, the powers of the corporation are exercised by the shareholders, and the rules that normally apply to the directors apply to and are carried out by the shareholders. If an official demands evidence of director action, it is possible for the shareholders of a close corporation without directors to appoint a shareholder (or several shareholders) to sign documents as a "designated director."[17] As with a designated hitter in baseball, this person ought to be someone who is particularly talented at pretending to be entitled to this privileged capacity.

Anticipating that the shareholders of a close corporation will address management issues in their agreement, certain formalities are relaxed in the statute. For example, it is not necessary to have by-laws (if the normal provisions are contained in the articles or a shareholder agreement),[18] and an annual meeting need not be held unless a shareholder demands it.[19]

Fundamental Changes

Statutory close corporations may participate in mergers and share exchanges, and may transfer all of their assets of the corporation with shareholder approval, just as regular corporations do. However, these transactions must be approved by at least a two-thirds vote of the shares, based upon the policy that shareholders will more actively participate in such decisions in a close corporation.[20] Another major departure from typical corporate law is the authority for any shareholder to dissolve the corporation at will or upon the occurrence of a specified event or contingency.[21] This provision acknowledges the integral position played by each shareholder in a close corporation. It is very similar to the right of a partner to terminate the partnership enterprise at will, a right that is particularly important in a close corporation, where a deadlock may easily occur if the shareholders cannot agree on the operation of the business.

Judicial Supervision

A corporation organized under the Model Business Corporation Act is usually managed by a board of directors composed of sophisticated, intelligent, and judicious individuals. These directors usually seek legal advice to be certain they are exercising their judgment and management duties correctly, and they are willing to compromise and make reasonable business judgments in order to make the business successful. In a close corporation, where the owners-shareholders are entitled to manage the business, petty disputes and selfish decisions are more likely to occur. Consequently, a close corporation may be subject to extensive judicial review if the shareholders begin to squabble among themselves.

Any shareholder may ask for judicial relief if the persons in control of the corporation are acting in an illegal, oppressive, fraudulent, or unfairly prejudicial manner toward the shareholder. Similarly, a court may be asked to break a deadlock that injures the business affairs of the corporation.[22] Upon finding that such allegations are justified, a court may order practically anything to remedy the situation, including changing the action adopted by management, cancelling articles or by-laws, removing officers or directors, or appointing a custodian to manage the business. The court also has very broad power if it finds that a shareholder asked for court help to harass the other members of the corporation. The court may award all attorneys' fees and expenses against the shareholder if it finds the action was brought arbitrarily, vexatiously, or not in good faith.[23] If the court believes the situation cannot be reconciled, it may order the corporation to be dissolved or to purchase the shares of the complaining shareholder at fair value.[24]

Protection from Piercing the Corporate Veil

Remember that a classic remedy of creditors who are unable to satisfy their claims against the corporation is the right to pierce the corporate veil when corporate formalities have not been properly observed.[25] A close corporation may be operated without much formality at all, and thus would seem always to be vulnerable to a claim that the corporation was merely operating as the alter ego of the shareholders without observing normal statutory formalities. To avoid that result, the Model Business Corporation Act provides that the failure of the close corporation to observe the usual corporate formalities will not be a basis for imposing personal liability on the shareholders for liabilities of the corporation.[26]

PROFESSIONAL CORPORATIONS

The "learned" professions, such as law, medicine, accounting, and others, have traditionally been prohibited from operating as corporations. The policy reasons behind this interdiction have never been clearly defined, but they probably grew out of the desire to limit the association of persons engaged in such professions to duly licensed practitioners and out of the concern that professional persons should not be allowed to shield themselves from liability through the use of the corporate form. The obvious disadvantage to professionals who were required to practice as sole proprietors or partners is that they could not use favorable corporate tax rates and fringe benefit plans unique to corporations. Some states recognized this disadvantage and enacted professional corporation statutes in 1961, but it was not until 1969 that the Internal Revenue Service conceded that a professional organization should be treated like any other corporation for income tax purposes. In 1979, the Model Business Corporation Act finally adopted the Model Professional Corporation Supplement,[27] referred to in this text as the Model Professional Corporation Act.

Some states now permit professionals to form professional associations, which are really partnerships with a sufficient number of corporate characteristics, such as continuity of life, centralized management, and transferability of ownership interests, so they will be taxed like corporations.[28] Other states permit the formation of either an association or a corporation for professionals.[29] This section is primarily concerned with the professional corporation.[30]

The statutory authority for professional corporations varies widely from state to state. Several states include the authority to incorporate with other statutes regulating the particular profession (such as licensing and qualification statutes). These states have no single professional corporation law, and the Model Professional Corporation Act has not yet been adopted in its entirety in any state. In a few jurisdictions, the authority for professional legal corporations for attorneys is contained in a Supreme Court rule rather than in a statute.[31] In states where the professional corporation has been added as an adjunct to the business corporation statutes, the business corporation statutes control except for the specific provisions of the professional corporation section.

All states now allow the creation of professional corporations, and all include attorneys, doctors, and dentists. Accountants, veterinarians, psychologists, engineers, and architects are also usually included, and a few states permit corporate practice by registered nurses, physical therapists, pharmacists, and marriage counselors.

The structural variations of the professional corporation from the business corporation are also treated differently in the individual state statutes, but most states have adopted certain general modifications that are the same as the provisions of the Model Professional Corporation Act.

Scope

Under the Model Professional Corporation Act, organizations in professions in which a service is rendered lawfully only by persons licensed under provisions of a licensing law of a state may become "Professional Corporations". Some existing state statutes under which professional persons are permitted to incorporate cover all licensed services and are not restricted to persons who are otherwise prohibited from incorporating under the business corporation law. Other existing state statutes limit those who may incorporate to members of a specific profession or professions described in a single statute or in a series of similar statutes each applicable to one profession. The definition in the Model Professional Corporation Act has the effect of restricting the use of the act to the practice of the professions. However, rather than listing designated professions, the act follows the precedents set by many existing state statutes of defining professional services as licensed services that may not be rendered by a corporation organized under the business corporation law.[32]

Purposes, Powers, and Prohibited Activities

Most state statutes have limited the purposes of a professional corporation to the practice of a single profession because of the ethical proscriptions placed upon joint practice of various professions. The Model Professional Corporation Act permits the practice of various professional services and ancillary services within a single profession, but will also permit a joint practice of various professions if this combination of professional purposes is permitted by the licensing laws of the local state.[33]

A professional corporation formed under the Model Professional Corporation Act would be permitted all of the powers enumerated in the Model Business Corporation Act, except that the professional corporation may not be a promoter, general partner or entity associated with a partnership, joint venture, trust, or other enterprise unless it is engaged only in rendering professional services or carrying on a business permitted by the corporation's articles of incorporation. Similarly, the professional corporation can engage only in the profession or professions and businesses permitted by its articles of incorporation. The professional corporation act permits, however, the investment of funds in real estate, mortgages, stock, and bonds, or any other type of investment, as part of the activities of a professional corporation.[34]

Name

Existing state statutes vary in the selection of terms required in the corporate name as corporate designations for a professional corporation. The Model Professional Corporation Act permits the designations *professional corporation, professional association,* or *service corporation,* or an abbreviation *P.C., P.A.,* or *S.C.*[35] As with other corporate statutes, the name of a professional corporation should not be the same as or deceptively similar to the name of any other corporation. However, the act makes a special exception if similarity results from the use in the corporate name of personal names of shareholders who are or were associated with the organization or if written consent of the other corporation who uses a similar name if filed with the secretary of state.[36] These special provisions are intended to provide for the similarity of personal names used by professional practitioners in their practice and the likelihood that the public will not be confused significantly if professional corporations have similar names that are personal to those who practice as members of the corporation.

Share Ownership

Shares in professional corporations may be owned only by persons who are authorized to render professional services permitted by the articles of incorporation. The Model Professional Corporation Act and only a few states permit shares to be owned by partnerships and other professional corporations that are authorized to render the professional services permitted by the articles of the corporation and by persons licensed outside of the state of incorporation.[37]

No shares of a professional corporation can be transferred or otherwise disposed of except to persons who are qualified to hold shares issued by the professional corporation. The intent of these provisions is to require that the shares of a professional corporation be held only by persons who are licensed to practice the particular profession, so that any transfer of the shares to persons who are not so licensed would be void, against public policy, and in violation of the statute.[38] To accomplish this objective, each certificate representing shares of a professional corporation should state conspicuously on its face that the shares are subject to restrictions upon transfer imposed by the statute and by the licensing authority that supervises the profession.

If a shareholder dies or becomes disqualified (for example, by losing his or her license to practice the profession), the shares should be transferred to a qualified shareholder or purchased by the corporation within a specified period of time following the shareholder's death or disqualification. The Model Professional Corporation Act requires payment of fair value for such shares if the corporation does not establish an alternative method, and the procedure for determining fair value is analogous to the procedure of the Model Business Corporation Act with respect to the determination of rights of dissenting shareholders.[39] If shares of a deceased or disqualified shareholder have not been transferred or purchased within ten months after the death or five months after disqualification or transfer, the shares are cancelled and the shareholder's interest becomes a creditor's claim against the corporation.[40]

Liability for Professional Activities

The principal excuse for refusing corporate status to professional service organizations was that each practitioner should be individually responsible for all professional acts, and that no professional person should be able to hide behind the corporate shield of limited liability when professional services were improperly rendered. All existing state statues concerning professional corporations include some provision about professional liability or professional responsibility. Most enabling statutes specifically provide that the professional person shall be personally liable for improper acts performed by that person or under that person's supervision. In some cases, limited liability will be allowed when the corporation maintains a minimum amount of liability insurance.

Most states are silent as to the vicarious liability of shareholders of a professional corporation, although some statutes clearly provide that shareholder liability is limited as it would be in a business corporation. In other words, if one doctor committed malpractice in a professional corporation, that doctor may be personally liable for his or her own malpractice, but fellow shareholders of the professional corporation would not be liable individually for their colleague's malpractice. A few other states expressly state that the shareholders are jointly and severally liable for obligations of the corporation. Most states simply provide that the statute does not modify any law applicable to the relationship between a person furnishing professional services and a person receiving such services, including liability arising out of professional services. The Model Professional Corporation Act affirmatively states rules for liability of the professional corporation, its employees, and its shareholders resulting from negligence in the performance of professional services. A professional employee is responsible for only his or her personal negligence, and the corporation may be liable for the conduct of professional employees within the scope of their employment or within their apparent authority.[41]

The Model Professional Corporation Act proposes three alternative provisions as to the liability of shareholders of professional corporations:

1. Limited liability as in a business corporation
2. Vicarious personal liability as in a partnership
3. Personal liability limited in amount and conditioned upon financial responsibility in the form of malpractice or negligence insurance or a surety bond.[42]

Most state statutes and the Model Professional Corporation Act specifically provide that any relationship of confidence that exists between a professional person and a client or patient is preserved notwithstanding the use of the corporate form. In fact, any privilege applicable to communications with a professional person extends to the professional corporation and is preserved.[43]

Directors and Officers

Most states express a preference that all directors and officers be licensed to practice the particular profession involved. Where lay directors are permitted, they usually are not allowed to exercise any authority over professional matters. The Model Professional Corporation Act requires that not less than one-half the directors of a professional corporation and all the officers other than the secretary and the treasurer should be qualified persons (licensed to practice the particular profession) with respect to the corporation.[44]

Fundamental Changes

Professional corporations are capable of normal fundamental corporate acts, such as amendment of the articles of incorporation, merger, consolidation, and dissolution. Most state statutes and the Model Professional Corporation Act provide enabling legislation to permit such activities by professional corporations, provided the professional status and purposes of the corporation and the qualifications of shareholders are observed always. For example, Section 40 of the Model Professional Corporation Act permits mergers and consolidations among professional corporations and business corporations only if every shareholder of each corporation is qualified to be a shareholder of the surviving or new corporation.

If a professional corporation ceases to render professional services, the Model Professional Corporation Act permits the corporation to amend its articles to delete the rendering of professional services from its purposes and to conform to the requirements of the Model Business Corporation Act regarding its corporate name. The corporation may then continue in existence as a corporation under the Model Business Corporation Act.[45] This section would avoid the forced dissolution of a professional corporation whose shareholders have died or become disqualified. Rather, the corporation could continue in business under the Model Business Corporation Act to invest its funds or conduct any other business that may be lawfully permitted under the local law.

Foreign Professional Corporations

Many professional practices are conducted in more than one state by individuals licensed to practice in more than one state or by partnerships whose members are licensed to practice in various states. Few state statutes contain any provisions concerning foreign professional corporations, but the Model Professional Corporation Act has specifically provided for the admission, qualification, and authority to do business of professional corporations among states.

The professional corporation that seeks to practice the profession in a new state will not be entitled to avoid the professional corporation laws of the state in which it carries on its practice by incorporating in a state with more lenient professional corporation requirements. Foreign corporations must comply with the domestic state law requirements concerning corporate purposes and the qualifications of shareholders, directors, and officers.[46] A foreign corporation may render professional services only through persons permitted to render such services in the state.[47] Responsibility for professional services and security for professional responsibility is made applicable to foreign corporations as well as domestic corporations, and foreign corporations are also subject to regulation by the local licensing authority to the same extent as are domestic corporations.[48]

A professional corporation must obtain a certificate of authority if the corporation maintains an office in a state.[49] The application for a certificate of authority of a foreign professional corporation would include information required for normal business corporations, and a statement that all the shareholders, not less than one-half the directors, and all the officers other than the secretary and treasurer are licensed to render a professional service described in the statement of purposes of the corporation.[50]

Under the state statutes that permit a professional corporation and under the Model Professional Corporation Act, professional persons will be entitled to the advantage of the corporate business form. Although one important advantage of corporateness—limited liability—is lost to the professions, and although the statutory requirements for shareholder-director-officer qualification and operation are strict and rigidly observed, the tax consequences and operating flexibility of the corporate organization make the professional corporation an attractive business form.

NOTES

1. See Chapter 11. An agreement between shareholders organizing a close corporation appears as Form 5A in Appendix G.
2. M.B.C.A. § 8.01(c).
3. E.g., Delaware, 8 Del.Code Ann. §§ 341–56.
4. Model Statutory Close Corporation Supplement (M.S.C.C.S.) § 3. The text of the M.S.C.C.S. is reproduced in Appendix E.
5. E.g., Delaware, 8 Del.Code Ann. §§ 342 and 343.
6. M.S.C.C.S. § 10(a).
7. M.S.C.C.S. § 11.
8. M.S.C.C.S. § 12.
9. M.S.C.C.S. § 12(b).
10. M.S.C.C.S. § 13.
11. M.S.C.C.S. § 14.
12. M.S.C.C.S. §§ 15–17.
13. M.B.C.A. § 8.01(c).
14. M.S.C.C.S. § 20(b).
15. M.S.C.C.S. § 20(c).
16. M.S.C.C.S. § 21(a).
17. M.S.C.C.S. § 21(c)(5).
18. M.S.C.C.S. § 22.
19. M.S.C.C.S. § 23.
20. M.S.C.C.S. § 30.
21. M.S.C.C.S. § 33.
22. M.S.C.C.S. § 40.
23. M.S.C.C.S. § 41.
24. M.S.C.C.S. §§ 43 and 44.
25. See "Limited Liability" in Chapter 4.
26. M.S.C.C.S. § 25.
27. The text of the Model Professional Corporation Supplement (1984) to the Model Business Corporation Act is reproduced in Appendix F.
28. E.g., Pennsylvania, 15 Pa.Stat. §§ 12601–19. Forms for the formation of a professional association may be found in West's Modern Legal Forms §§ 6461–66.
29. E.g., Texas, Vernon's Ann.Tex.Civ.Stat. arts. 1528(e) and 1528(f).
30. Articles of incorporation of a professional medical corporation and its application for registration appear as Forms 5B and 5C in Appendix G.
31. E.g., Colorado, 7A C.R.S. Chapter 22, Rule 265.
32. Model Professional Corporation Supplement to the Model Business Corporation Act (hereinafter cited M.P.C.A.) § 3(7).

33. M.P.C.A. § 11(b).
34. M.P.C.A. §§ 12(b) and 14(b).
35. M.P.C.A. § 15(a).
36. M.P.C.A. § 15(b).
37. M.P.C.A. § 20.
38. See M.P.C.A. § 22.
39. See M.P.C.A. §§ 23–26 and M.B.C.A. §§ 13.01–13.28.
40. M.P.C.A. § 27.
41. M.P.C.A. § 34(a) and (b).
42. M.P.C.A. § 34(c).
43. M.P.C.A. § 33.
44. M.P.C.A. § 30.
45. M.P.C.A. § 41.
46. M.P.C.A. § 50(b)(2).
47. M.P.C.A. § 50(b)(3).
48. M.P.C.A. § 64.
49. M.P.C.A. § 50(a).
50. M.P.C.A. § 51.

6 FORMATION OF A CORPORATION

PREINCORPORATION RESPONSIBILITY

The embryo of a corporation is the business idea conceived by an individual or group of individuals. The idea may be fresh, as with entrepreneurs who simply decide to begin a business, or it may evolve from an established commercial enterprise that will continue under the corporate form. Regardless of the genesis of the idea, the attorney is consulted for the purpose of forming the appropriate structure for operation of the business. If limited liability, flexible capital structure, and tax advantages are desired, the corporate organization may be most desirable. The organizers rely upon the attorney to properly consider the advantages and disadvantages of the various business forms and to advise them of the most beneficial organization.[1]

At this point, the organizers are private individuals with a business idea, and good practice suggests that they agree among themselves in writing as to certain important matters regarding the corporation to be formed. The relationship between these organizers or promoters resembles a joint venture, which is like a partnership. Even without a written agreement, the law imposes certain rights and responsibilities upon the relationship, including duties to disclose important information to each other and to avoid any conflict of interest that might interfere with their participation in the project. However, to avoid disputes and to facilitate the smooth incorporation of their business, a written agreement between the organizers is appropriate.[2]

The organizers or promoters are responsible for investigating the particular business opportunity and assembling the property, cash, and personnel to accomplish the business objectives. Generally, the promoters will look for a suitable business establishment; negotiate a lease or purchase of that establishment; and contract for necessary furniture, fixtures, and so forth. They will search for capable employees, if needed, and may negotiate employment contracts with them. If the business opportunity is unique, patents, copyrights, or trademarks must be obtained. A common denominator to each of these activities is that the promoters are acting as individuals in a joint venture relationship on behalf of a corporation yet to be formed. They cannot bind the corporation to the contracts they are negotiating because the corporation does not exist. This means that the promoters will usually be required to obligate themselves individually on those contracts. After the corporation is formed, it may adopt the contracts through appropriate action by the board of directors, but the promoters who have signed the contracts in their individual capacities will usually remain obligated for performance of the contracts. Promoters considering the corporate form should always be advised of these ramifications of preincorporation agreements. The advice should not deter them from a corporation, however, since they would not escape individual liability by using an alternative business form.

When soliciting capital for the corporation, the promoters' activities are governed by a different set of rules. Operating capital may be obtained through loans or by the sale of stock in the corporation to be formed. Loans negotiated before the formation of the corporation are treated as ordinary preincorporation agreements, with the promoters risking individual liability for repayment. Sales of stock are accomplished by a preincorporation share subscription.

PREINCORPORATION SHARE SUBSCRIPTIONS

Share subscriptions are offers from interested investors to purchase shares of a corporation. Preincorporation subscriptions are, as the name indicates, offers to purchase shares when the corporation is subsequently formed. These may be necessary to the proper formation of a corporation for several reasons.

In a practical sense, every corporation needs capital to commence business, and investors must be identified and promises to purchase shares must be secured before the new enterprise is launched. In addition, from a strictly legal standpoint, some state statutes require the use of preincorporation share subscriptions in various stages of the formation procedure. One such provision, not found in the Model Business Corporation Act, is that the incorporators must also be subscribers.[3] In states with this provision, a prospective incorporator must tender a preincorporation share subscription in order to qualify as an incorporator. Several other states require that a corporation must have a minimum amount of paid-in capital before it may commence business. The Model Business Corporation Act formerly required that $1,000 must be collected as capital as a condition to doing business, but this requirement was eliminated in 1969. Several states have retained the minimum paid-in capital requirement,[4] and in these jurisdictions preincorporation share subscriptions will be used to solidify promises to contribute the amount required by statute. The corporation will not be allowed to commence business without the requisite capital. Thus, preincorporation share subscriptions will be used in most cases for practical or legal reasons to secure promises to purchase shares once the corporation is formed.

A preincorporation share subscription may be executed by anyone who has decided to invest in the company. The terms of the subscription describe an offer to purchase shares. If the corporation accepts the offer, a binding contract is created. A few states require written, signed subscriptions, and it is good practice to obtain a written offer in any case. A single subscription may be executed by several subscribers, or each subscriber may execute his or her own subscription.

> **EXAMPLE: Share Subscription for Several Subscribers**
> We, the undersigned, hereby severally subscribe for the number of shares of the capital stock of Trouble, Inc., set opposite our respective names. The Corporation is to be organized under the laws of the State of Delaware, with an authorized capital stock of $50,000.00 consisting of 5,000 shares of common stock, $10.00 par value. We further agree to pay the amount subscribed in cash on demand of the treasurer of the said Corporation as soon as it is organized [*or* at such times and

in such amounts as may be prescribed by the Board of Directors of the Corporation].

Dated July 1, 1990.

Names	Addresses	Shares Subscribed	Amount Subscribed
_____	_____	_____	_____ [5]
_____	_____	_____	_____

_____

EXAMPLE: Share Subscription for a Single Subscriber

The Dillon Manufacturing Company to be incorporated under the laws of the State of Michigan.

Capital Stock $1,000,000.00   Shares $100.00 par value

I, the undersigned, hereby subscribe for 100 shares of the capital stock of the Dillon Manufacturing Company to be incorporated and agree to pay in cash for said stock the sum of $10,000.00 on demand of the Board of Directors of the Corporation.

This agreement is made upon the condition that eighty per cent of the capital stock of the Corporation is subscribed in good faith by solvent persons on or before the 1st day of July, 1990, and the Corporation is incorporated within 30 days thereafter.

Dated May 1, 1990.

_____ [6]

These subscriptions are also assignable. Therefore, in jurisdictions where incorporators are required to be subscribers by law, the incorporators must subscribe, but if they do not intend to invest, they may assign their preincorporation share subscriptions to outsiders who have acknowledged a desire to invest.

The law presumes that the corporation is formed in reliance upon the offers of subscribers to purchase shares, especially when the statute requires minimum paid-in capital as a condition to commencing business. Under common law, share subscriptions were revocable until the corporation had been formed and had accepted them by agreeing to issue shares for the amount of the subscriptions. Modern statutes now provide that the preincorporation share subscriptions are irrevocable for a period of time. Section 6.20 of the Model Business Corporation Act states that a preincorporation subscription of shares of a corporation is irrevocable for a period of six months unless otherwise provided in the terms of the subscription agreement or unless all of the subscribers consent to the revocation. The period of irrevocability varies among the state statutes from three months to one year.[7] A few states specify the period to be a stated time after the certificate of incorporation is issued.[8] If a corporation is formed during the period of irrevocability, it may accept the subscription and require the subscriber to purchase the shares for the amount stated therein. In most jurisdictions, acceptance occurs by action of the board of directors after the corporation is formed,[9] but Pennsylvania makes acceptance automatic upon the filing of articles of incorporation,[10] and a few states make acceptance automatic upon the issuance of a certificate of incorporation.[11] When the subscription is accepted by the corporation or automatically under the statute, the subscriber is usually required to pay the amount in full, but the board of directors may permit payment in installments.

> **EXAMPLE: Call of Subscription**
>
> August 1, 1990
>
> To: James Lyons
> [Address]
> Dear Sir:
>
> At a regular meeting of the Board of Directors of Trouble, Inc., held on July 30, 1990 a resolution was duly adopted fixing the amount of calls on stock issued as partly paid and the date of payment of each call.
>
> You are hereby notified that the first call on your subscription for partly paid stock amounts to $500.00, which sum is due and payable at the office of the Corporation on August 15, 1990.
>
> Trouble, Inc
> By _____ Secretary[12]

If a subscriber defaults on the subscription contract and refuses to pay any installment when due, the corporation may sell the shares to another investor, and the defaulting subscriber may be liable for breach of contract. Moreover, under the Model Business Corporation Act, a subscriber may forfeit any right to the shares if the amount due is not paid within twenty days after a written demand has been made.[13]

> **EXAMPLE: Demand for Payment and Notice of Forfeiture**
>
> September 1, 1990
>
> To: James Lyons
> [*Address*]
>
> You are hereby notified that at a regular meeting of the Board of Directors of Trouble, Inc., the following resolution was duly adopted:
>
> "Resolved, that the entire [or _____ percent of the] unpaid balance on all subscriptions to the common stock of this Corporation is hereby called for payment forthwith, and the Secretary is hereby directed to demand payment from each subscriber having an unpaid balance, by mailing to him, at his last known address, a written demand requiring payment within 20 days from receipt of such notice, in default of which his shares and all previous payments thereon will be forfeited."
>
> Demand is hereby made upon you for payment in accordance with the provisions of the above resolution, and you are hereby notified that, in default of payment within 20 days from receipt of this notice and demand, your shares and previous payments thereon will be forfeited.
>
> Trouble, Inc.
> By _____ Secretary[14]

Most statutes further permit the by-laws to prescribe other penalties for failure to pay in accordance with the subscription.

SELECTION OF JURISDICTION

Preceding sections have discussed the variations in corporate statutes and the trend toward permissiveness and flexibility in the jurisdictional approach to corporate problems. Moreover, states approach corporate taxation differently, and they subject corporations doing business outside the boundaries of their domestic or home states to special procedures when qualifying them to do business.[15] These factors play an important role in the selection of the jurisdiction in which to incorporate.

A corporation formed within the state is known as a domestic corporation, and one formed in some other state is called a foreign corporation. Each state's statute has provisions regulating domestic corporations and special provisions for foreign corporations. If a particular state's statute contains flexible and advantageous provisions for its domestic corporations, and restrictive and cumbersome procedures for foreign corporations, that state should be considered a good candidate for incorporation (domestication). Of course, the converse is also true. There are also other considerations, such as whether the state corporation law has been well tested by court decisions so as to be capable of accurate interpretation; whether the state's taxation structure is acceptable; and whether the state laws will permit all desired corporate features. This last consideration requires an analysis of all important points of corporate law in each jurisdiction to be considered. A 108-question checklist for jurisdiction selection appears as Form 6D in Appendix G.

Having perused the checklist, you may be reeling at the thought of the monumental task of comparing all of those points for each of fifty states, and also wondering how a corporation is ever formed if that much research is required as a preface. A couple of observations may decrease your anxiety.

First, a corporation should not consider incorporating in a state where it does not intend to do business. The exceptional case may arise when a permissive jurisdiction, such as Delaware, is particularly attractive for some special reason.[16] Thus, incorporators of a restaurant business in Santa Fe, New Mexico, would not consider incorporating outside the state unless an extremely attractive feature of another state is deemed particularly important for their corporate structure. To domesticate the corporation in a state where no business activity will be conducted without compelling reasons only complicates the corporate structure, increases the cost of organizational expenses, and may result in double taxation. Consequently, the first predisposition in the selection of jurisdiction is to incorporate in the state where the corporation will conduct most of its business. If business is to be conducted in only one state, that state should be the prime candidate for incorporation.

Second, when a corporation intends to conduct relatively equal amounts of business in several jurisdictions, a state-by-state comparison of all of the checklist items will yield a net result of advantages and disadvantages for each state, and a coin-toss decision may be appropriate. The permissive jurisdictions will stand out in relative advantages and flexibility, and they should always be considered when extensive interstate business is contemplated. Remember, however, that flexibility and ease of formation and operation are frequently costly. Most states with permissive corporate laws are seeking to attract corporate business—so they can impose taxes. Make certain that the choice of a permissive state is worth the cost.

Other than the foregoing rules, perhaps the most accurate statement that can be made regarding jurisdiction selection is that the choice depends upon the circumstances of each case. The particular needs and desires of the client on each of the enumerated points in the checklist must be considered, and the decision will depend upon the weight assigned to each element of the corporate structure.

SELECTION AND RESERVATION OF CORPORATE NAME

Every corporation must have a name that indicates it is a corporation, and the selection and determination of the availability of the name should come at an early stage in the incorporation procedure. The Model Business Corporation Act specifically requires that all names of corporations contain the words Corporation, Company, Incorporated, or Limited, or some abbreviation of one of those words, or an abbreviation of similar meaning in another language.[17] This requirement is common to most jurisdictions. A few states will not permit Limited or Company, and other statutory restrictions specify certain names and titles that may not be used in a corporate name.[18] Many state statutes also prohibit a corporate name that contains any word or phrase indicating that the corporation is organized for any purpose other than the purposes stated in its articles of incorporation. Moreover, every jurisdiction forbids a corporate name that is the same as, or deceptively similar to, the name of any other domestic corporation existing under the laws of the state or any foreign corporation authorized to transact business in the state.[19] This last requirement is a response to unfair competition, and is designed to avoid the use of one organization's name and reputation by another in order to induce public patronage. For example, the Great Atlantic and Pacific Tea Company, which operates A & P Food Stores, prevented a separate corporation from using the name A & P Trucking Corporation because of the possible public confusion in the names. It may not even be necessary for the name to belong to another corporation; for example, television entertainer Ed Sullivan once prevented another Edward J. Sullivan from using Ed Sullivan Radio & TV, Inc., as his corporate name.

The prohibition against deceptive similarity has several ramifications. On the negative side, care must be taken to avoid the selection of a name that is dangerously close to that of another well-known company or individual. Moreover, if the new corporation intends to do business in several states, the name cannot approximate a well-known name in any of those states, even if the similar name is recognized only regionally and would be unknown in all the other states. On the positive side, the selected corporate name should be one the state courts will protect against infringement by others. For example, descriptive names, such as Janitorial Service, Inc., or Builders Supply Company are very vulnerable to infringement because of their general application. Similarly, Jones and Smith, Inc., could not expect complete protection because of the courts' reluctance to prohibit other Joneses and Smiths from using their own names. On the other hand, coined names that are selected arbitrarily, such as Gazorninplat Corporation, Jello, Inc., or Sunkist Fruit Co., will receive the greatest protection from infringement by a competitor.

The selection of the name is another of those individual matters for the client to decide. However, the problems of similarity, overstating corporate purposes, and statutory requirements must be considered in making that decision.

Availability of Name

To determine whether the proposed corporate name is available for use in a particular state, counsel should consult the state agency designated as the repository of corporate names, which is usually the secretary of state. That office will review the records to determine if the name has been used or if it is deceptively similar to the name of another corporation. The decision regarding availability is usually discretionary with the state authorities, and those authorities will refuse to accept a reservation of name or the articles of incorporation if they feel the name is too similar to another in use. Sometimes this issue may be negotiated if the name is important to the client, and the addition of an extra word to the name may be enough to obtain permission to use the desired name. According to legend, the Colorado secretary of state once refused the use of the name Westwind Corporation because another corporation was using it, but permitted the new corporation to be formed under the name Westwind Corporation Jr. The addition of one word—Jr.—was enough to distinguish the names. Both corporations (apparently operating different types of businesses) lived happily ever after.

Since the name will appear on all corporate documents, the choice of the name and its reservation must come early in the incorporation procedure.

Reservation of Name

If the proposed corporate name is available, it should be reserved while the corporate papers are being prepared. Nothing can be more frustrating and embarrassing than to learn that a name is available, and to prepare all corporate documents using that name, only to learn upon filing that the name has just been taken by another organization. Most states permit reservation of a corporate name for a limited period of time (from 30 days to 12 months) for a small fee,[20] and a few states allow extension of the reservation for another limited period. Reservation holds the particular name for the exclusive use of the corporation for the specified period.

Under the Model Business Corporation Act, a corporate name may be reserved by any person intending to organize a corporation, domestic or foreign; any foreign corporation intending to qualify to do business within the state; or any organized domestic or foreign corporation intending to change its name. The period of reservation provided by the act is 120 days.[21]

It is usually possible to transfer the reserved name to any person by filing a notice of transfer with the same state officer. This procedure allows an attorney or a member of the attorney's staff to reserve the name for the client, and to transfer the name to the corporation when the articles of incorporation are filed.[22]

The Model Business Corporation Act and jurisdictions that follow it have an additional statutory provision that allows a corporation to *register* the corporate name for periods of one year at a time. Registration of the corporate name has the same effect as reservation of the name, but registration is permitted only for a corporation already organized and existing and would, therefore, be used only by foreign corporations interested in qualifying to do business within the state. (An organized and existing domestic corporation would have no use for the registration procedure since incorporation reserves its name as long as the corporation remains in good standing.) The registered name may not be the same as or deceptively similar to the name of a domestic or qualified foreign corporation. The initial registration is effective until the close of the calendar year in which the application for registration is filed, and the fee is prorated for the portion of the year remaining when filed. Thereafter, a corporation may continue to renew such registration from year to year by filing an application for renewal.[23]

States without this registration procedure pose problems for a multistate corporation that wants to be certain its name is protected nationwide. Reservation of the name is not a viable alternative, since the reservation is good only for a limited period, and actual qualification to do business in every state will subject the corporation to additional regulation and taxation.[24] Consequently, many corporations use "name-saver" subsidiaries to protect their corporate names. A domestic subsidiary corporation that uses the corporate name is formed within each state, and the name is thereby permanently reserved. Since the subsidiary usually has no major assets and conducts no business, the taxation and regulation imposed on the name-saver corporation are minimal.

Operation under an Assumed Name

The corporation may be formed under one name but may desire to operate under another, especially when it operates several different types of businesses and wants its various divisions to conduct business under separate names. An assumed name is also frequently used to satisfy the statutory restriction that the name may not contain any word or phrase that indicates or implies that the corporation is organized for any purpose other than the purposes stated in its articles of incorporation.

The procedure for the use of an assumed or trade name by a corporation is very similar to that followed by a sole proprietorship or partnership. Several state statutes allow the use of assumed names by corporations, and they usually require the filing of a statement with the secretary of state.[25] The corporation also may have to file with county officials where business is conducted. The statutes specify whether an assumed name must contain the special corporate words (Company, Incorporated, Limited, Corporation), and the assumed name may not be deceptively similar to any other well-known or reserved name.[26]

THE ARTICLES OF INCORPORATION

The document that initiates the creation of the corporate existence and defines the corporate structure is the articles of incorporation, or corporate charter. The document is also variously called certificate of incorporation, articles of association, or articles of agreement.[27] Recall that corporate existence is regulated first by state statute. The articles of incorporation then flesh out the statutory provisions to tailor a particular corporate structure to the needs of its incorporators.

The articles of incorporation may be thorough and detailed or they may contain only the bare essentials required by statute. The content of the articles is not arbitrarily determined, however; certain matters are required by the state statute, and these must always be included. Thereafter, any aspect of corporate existence may be regulated by the articles if desired—but remember that the articles, once filed, are difficult to change. The amendment procedure requires the approval of the shareholders and filing with the designated public officials.[28] Thus, if the incorporators want certain rules that will have some degree of permanence, these rules should be included in the articles of incorporation. On the other hand, if certain rules for regulation of corporate affairs are expected to change in the future, they are best reserved to the by-laws of the corporation, where the amendment procedure is considerably more convenient. These matters should be determined in an early conference with the incorporators when all statutory requirements and other drafting possibilities for the articles of incorporation are discussed. A checklist for this conference is Form 6N in Appendix G.

Statutory Requirements

The Model Business Corporation Act requires that the articles of incorporation set forth the following information:

(1) a corporate name for the corporation that satisfies the requirements of section 4.01;
(2) the number of shares the corporation is authorized to issue;
(3) the street address of the corporation's initial registered office and the name of its initial registered agent at that office; and
(4) the name and address of each incorporator.

The articles of incorporation may set forth:

(1) the names and addresses of the individuals who are to serve as the initial directors;
(2) provisions not inconsistent with law regarding:
    (i) the purpose or purposes for which the corporation is organized;
    (ii) managing the business and regulating the affairs of the corporation;
    (iii) defining, limiting, and regulating the powers of the corporation, its board of directors, and shareholders;
    (iv) a par value for authorized shares or classes of shares;
    (v) the imposition of personal liability on shareholders for the debts of the corporation to a specified extent and upon specified conditions; and
(3) any provision that under this Act is required or permitted to be set forth in the bylaws.

The articles of incorporation need not set forth any of the corporate powers enumerated in the Act.[29]

Over the years, the Model Business Corporation Act and various state statutes have substantially relaxed the requirements of the articles of incorporation. The act's provisions, quoted here, require very little information to meet the minimum statutory requirements. Most states require that the following additional issues be addressed.

(1) The period of duration, which may be perpetual
(2) The designation of each class of shares, and the statements concerning the preferences, limitations, and relative rights of the shares of each class
(3) The question of whether the corporation will allow preemptive rights to the shareholders and
(4) The question of whether the corporation will allow cumulative voting for the shareholders

The specific demands of each state statute should be carefully studied and scrupulously followed. It is usually unnecessary for the articles of incorporation to repeat the corporate powers enumerated in the statute,[30] but the articles should specify the corporate purposes. Most states print and distribute "official" forms, which may be used for the articles of incorporation and contain the bare essentials necessary for compliance with the statute. The incorporators or counsel will usually prefer more elaboration in the articles that is permitted on the official forms.[31]

Many of the items specified as necessary ingredients to the articles of incorporation have been previously discussed or will be discussed in detail later. Nevertheless, let us wander through the typical requirements briefly here.

Name of the Corporation. The articles of incorporation must contain the corporate name selected by the incorporators and approved by the secretary of state or other designated public official. If the name has not previously been reserved, the articles of incorporation will reserve the name for the use of the corporation during its existence.[32]

> **EXAMPLE: Name**
> The name of the corporation shall be Five Points Land and Cattle Company.

Shares. The corporation's *equity securities,* or shares, must be accurately described in the articles of incorporation. The articles of incorporation establish the number of shares that the corporation has authority to issue, and the corporation is limited to the number of shares so authorized, unless an amendment to the articles is adopted permitting the issuance of additional shares. The articles should also detail and describe the classes of equity securities, such as common stock, preferred stock, and so forth, but they generally do not contain any information about the corporation's *debt securities,* or bonds.

Every corporation must have at least one class of stock, and if only one class is authorized, it is usually called *common stock.* The financial structure of a corporation has infinite flexibility—it may be as simple or as complex as desired, depending upon the projected financial needs of the businesses and, probably, the imagination of the drafter.[33] Details of the financial structure that must be described in the articles of incorporation in order to authorize the issuance of equity securities typically include the following:

1. The number of shares the corporation will have authority to issue
2. The par value of the shares to be issued or a statement that the shares are without par value (although the Model Business Corporation Act no longer requires such a distinction)
3. If the shares are to be divided into classes,
   (a) the designation of each class;
   (b) a statement of the preferences, limitations, and relative rights of the shares of each class;
   (c) the par value of each class, or a statement that the shares are to be without par value;
   (d) the authority, if any, of the board of directors to establish a class or series and determine variations in the rights and preferences between series[34]

The articles of incorporation must authorize one or more classes of shares that have unlimited voting rights and one or more classes of shares that are entitled to receive the net assets of the corporation upon dissolution.[35] In addition, the revised Model Business Corporation Act provides certain guidance concerning the permissible variations of shares among classes. They are as follows:

1. Shares that have special, conditional, or limited voting rights, or no right to vote
2. Shares that are redeemable or convertible at the option of the corporation, the shareholder, or another person, or upon the occurrence of a designated event; for cash, indebtedness, securities, or other properties; in a designated amount or in an amount determined in accordance with the designated formula
3. Shares that entitle the holders to distributions calculated in any manner, including dividends that may be cumulative, noncumulative, or partially cumulative
4. Shares that have a preference over other shares with respect to distributions, including dividends and distributions upon dissolution of the corporation[36]

The share authorization clause in the articles of incorporation may be very simple, as when the corporation intends to issue only one class of common stock, or quite complex, as when multiple classes of stock are to be issued with varying rights and preferences among the classes.

> **EXAMPLE: Capital Stock**
> The amount of the total authorized capital stock of the Corporation shall be 50,000 shares of common stock of the par value of $1.00 per share.[37]

> **EXAMPLE: Capital Stock**
> a) The total authorized capital stock of this Corporation shall be divided into one thousand (1000) shares of which five hundred (500) shares shall be preferred stock and shall be issued at a par value of One Hundred Dollars ($100) each; and five hundred (500) shares shall be common stock which shall be issued without par value and shall be sold at $1 per share.
> b) The holders of the shares of preferred stock shall be and are entitled to receive and shall so receive dividends on the value of such stock at the rate of six per cent (6%) per annum, which shall be cumulative and which shall be set aside and paid before any dividend shall be set aside or paid upon the shares of common capital stock.
> c) The voting power of the shares of capital stock in this Corporation shall be vested wholly in the holders of the shares of common capital stock. The preferred capital stock shall have no voting power whatever.
> d) In the event of the liquidation or dissolution, or the winding up of the business affairs of the Corporation, the holders of the preferred shares of capital stock shall be and they are entitled to be paid first for the full and determined value of their shares, together with unpaid dividends up to the time of the payment; after the payment to the preferred stockholders, the remaining assets of the Corporation shall be distributed among the holders of the common capital stock to the extent of their respective shares.
> e) This Corporation shall have the right at its option to retire the preferred stock upon ten (10) days notice, by a resolution of its Board of Directors, by paying for each share of preferred stock One Hundred Two Dollars ($102) in cash, and in addition thereto all unpaid dividends accrued thereon to the date fixed for such redemption.[38]

The capital stock structure is developed after studying many financial and practical matters, all of which are discussed in detail later.[39] Briefly, the decision to issue par value or no par value shares depends upon the consideration (money, property, or services) expected to be given in exchange for the shares, the organizational taxes imposed by the state, and the accounting ramifications of each value approach. Par value shares may not be sold for less than par value,[40] which means that a share of $100 par value stock can be issued only in exchange for cash, property, or services valued at $100 or more. No par value shares may be sold at their *stated value,* which is determined from time to time by the board of directors.[41] The no par feature adds some flexibility to the sale of shares since the board of directors may exert control over the going price of the shares.

Organizational taxes are imposed in some jurisdictions on the total aggregate value of the authorized capital stock structure, and the distinction between par value and no par value shares is also important for tax computation. To compute the total aggregate value, state statutes usually place a value on no par shares. For example, suppose the state imposes a $10 tax for each $10,000 aggregate authorized capital stock, and places a $100 value on each no par share. A corporation could authorize 100 shares with no par value for a tax of $10; it could also set par value of $1 per share and authorize 10,000 shares for the same tax. A few jurisdictions with organization taxes based upon the capital stock structure try to discourage no par shares by placing a high valuation on them for tax computation purposes.[42]

Finally, accounting principles require that the par value of issued shares must be placed in an account called *stated capital,* and that account is restricted so that no dividends may be paid from it. However, the consideration for no par shares may be allocated to an account called *capital surplus,* and those funds may be available in special circumstances for distribution to shareholders or for repurchase of corporate shares.[43] Thus, if the corporation issued $100 par value shares for $100 cash, all of the funds must go to the restricted stated capital account; however, if it issued no par shares for the same amount, some or all of the $100 could be placed in capital surplus, a more flexible account. These accounting ramifications may be important to a corporation that requires the flexibility to be able to distribute its equity accounts before it has accumulated profits to distribute.

The decision to issue several classes of equity securities is usually based upon the attractiveness of the securities to potential investors. If shares of common stock will sell well enough to raise the needed capital, there is usually no reason to authorize other classes of stock. However, if some investors insist that their stock must have special preferences to dividends, voting, or liquidation, then separate classes of securities will be necessary.

All special features of equity securities should be described in the articles of incorporation. Conversion privileges, redemption provisions, and restrictions on the sale of stock should also be specifically described in the articles of incorporation as part of the capital stock structure.[44]

Registered Office and Agent. The corporation must maintain a registered office and a registered agent within the state so that all legal or official matters pertaining to its corporate existence may be addressed there. The registered office does not have to be the principal place of business of the corporation, although it frequently is. The registered agent may be any person who is located at that office.

The registered office serves many functions, and is referred to throughout state corporate laws. For example, most statutes require notices to the corporation to be addressed to the registered office, and many states require the corporation to keep the stock transfer record at the registered office.

The registered agent has the primary responsibility for receiving notices of litigation (service of process) for the corporation. If the corporation has no available registered agent, the secretary of state receives process on behalf of the corporation, and, under the Model Business Corporation Act, the failure to maintain a registered agent for sixty days is grounds for an administrative dissolution of the corporation.[45]

Every state, except California and Connecticut, requires a registered office, but several, including New York, Pennsylvania, and Minnesota, do not require a registered agent. Again, the corporate statute of the jurisdiction where incorporation is contemplated should be carefully studied for this purpose.

> **EXAMPLE: Registered Office and Agent**
> The registered office of the corporation shall be at 730 Seventeenth Street, Suite 600, Denver, Colorado, 80202 and the name of the initial registered agent at such address is Nancy A. Stober. Either registered office or the registered agent may be changed in a manner provided by law.

Incorporators. The incorporators are also named in the articles of incorporation, and they sign the articles. Usually the incorporators must be adults of "legal age," and they may have to meet other qualifications, such as citizenship, residency, or share subscription requirements.[46]

Permissive Provisions

The preceding material considered certain provisions that are required to be enumerated in the articles of incorporation under the Model Business Corporation Act. Many other provisions must be included in the articles of incorporation under many state statutes and *may* be included under the Model Business Corporation Act.

Initial Directors. The Model Business Corporation Act permits the articles of incorporation to name the initial board of directors and to give their addresses.[47] Regarding the structure of the board of directors, the articles of incorporation may do one of three things: (1) specify the number of directors who will constitute the board; (2) specify a formula or procedure to determine the desired number; or (3) delegate this determination to the by-laws.

> **EXAMPLE: Initial Board of Directors**
> The initial board of directors of the corporation shall consist of three directors and the names and addresses of the persons who shall service as directors until the first annual meeting of shareholders or until their successors are elected and shall qualify are as follows:
>
> *Name*   *Address*
> _____   _____
> _____   _____
> _____   _____

> **EXAMPLE: Number of Directors**
> The number of directors of the corporation shall be fixed and may be altered from time to time as may be provided in the bylaws. In case of any increase in the number of directors, the additional directors may be elected by the directors or by the stockholders at an annual or special meeting, as shall be provided in the bylaws.[48]

No particular qualifications are required for directors under the Model Business Corporation Act, although some states require legal age, share ownership, or state citizenship.[49] Moreover, the act permits a single director, but many states require three or more. If specified in the articles of incorporation, the initial directors hold office until the shareholders meet to elect their successors. The written consent of the initial board of directors to serve as directors may be necessary under state law, and may be a desirable procedure in any case.

Period of Duration. If the issue of duration is addressed in the articles of incorporation (as it must be in many states), the articles usually state that the corporation shall exist perpetually. It is possible to establish a specified period after which the corporate existence will automatically terminate, but this may cause an unnecessary burden in that an amendment to the articles of incorporation would be required if the owners should subsequently decide to continue the business. If perpetual existence is specified in the articles of incorporation, the corporation will terminate only if dissolved according to the statutory procedure.[50]

> **EXAMPLE: Period of Duration**
> This corporation shall exist perpetually [or shall terminate on December 31, 2010], unless dissolved according to law.

Corporate Purposes. The corporation may engage in any lawful business, unless the articles of incorporation restrict the corporate purposes, and then the corporation may do only acts that are within the scope of its stated authorized purposes. Corporate purposes should be distinguished from corporate powers, which were discussed in "Statutory Powers of a Corporation" in Chapter 4. The purposes are the business objectives of the corporation, and the powers are the means by which those objectives are achieved. For example, the incorporators may form a corporation to purchase and rent apartment buildings. Their corporate *purposes* would specify real estate investment, management, operation, lease, and so on. Their statutory *powers* would provide that the corporation has the power to purchase and hold property, make contracts, borrow money, and so on. The powers are, therefore, the enabling authority for the corporation to pursue its purposes.

The modern trend of corporate law is to either eliminate the need to even address purposes in the articles of incorporation, or to permit the incorporators to adopt broad corporate purposes and thereby authorize the corporation to do any legal act. Most states allow the formation of a corporation for any lawful purposes, except banking and insurance. Several states, including Delaware and Pennsylvania, permit the articles of incorporation to authorize "any lawful activity."

In the drafting stages, the incorporators will have described the general nature of the contemplated business, such as operating a bookstore, manufacturing bicycles, conducting environmental services, and so forth. After formation, however, the management of the corporation may decide to invest in real estate with its merchandising profits, or to open a cafeteria next to its bookstore, and the scope of the designated purposes in the articles of incorporation then becomes a critical consideration.

The purpose clauses of the corporation usually specify a particular type of business, as shown in the following examples.

> **EXAMPLE: Purposes for a Cherry Fruit Business**
> To buy and sell, and otherwise deal in, at both wholesale and retail, all kinds and brands of cherries; to brine and preserve maraschino cherries of every nature and character; to engage in the canning and pitting of cherries and to prepare cherries for every possible purpose and use; to engage in the buying, selling, and otherwise dealing with and in the canning, preservation and preparation of all kinds of fruits of every nature, character and description; and generally to do all acts reasonable and necessary for the furtherance of the foregoing business.[51]

> **EXAMPLE: Purposes for a Jewelry Store**
> To carry on business as jewelers, gold and silver smiths; as dealers in china, curiosities, coins, medals, bullion and precious stones; as manufacturers of and dealers in gold and silver plate, plated articles, watches, clocks, chronometers, and optical and scientific instruments and appliances of every description; and as bankers, commission agents and general merchants.[52]

These limited purposes would not allow the corporations to operate a restaurant, or to manufacture bicycles, or to invest in real estate. When the incorporators anticipate such additional activities and specified purposes are desired in the articles of incorporation, additional purpose clauses must be added.

If the state statute is sufficiently permissive to allow the articles of incorporation to authorize "any lawful activity" without further specification and the incorporators want broad purposes, the drafting of the purpose clause is simple.

However, if the state requires specificity of corporate purposes, or if the incorporators desire to restrict the corporate purposes, the drafter's job becomes more difficult. Counsel must pay close attention to detail to ensure that the drafted purpose clauses in the articles of incorporation will permit the corporation to do everything necessary to operate the intended business. The purpose clauses must also anticipate expansion and give the corporation room to do everything it might be expected to do in the near future. Finally, the corporate purposes must not be overbroad, so management has no business guidance. The incorporators may restrict the corporate purposes to direct management toward specific business objectives.

Remember that the law provides implied power for the corporation to conduct any necessary act that is consistent with its stated purposes, but the law will not allow the corporation to exceed its purposes if those purposes are restricted in the articles of incorporation. Admittedly, this is a delicate distinction. Consider the cherry fruit business described in the preceding example purpose clause. The corporate *powers* would permit the corporation to buy a cannery to conduct its canning and pitting operations, and they may allow it to also buy an adjacent building if expansion was contemplated. However, the corporate *purposes* would not allow it to buy the adjacent building for investment purposes. Consequently, under modern statutes it is best to state the corporate purposes as broadly as possible. In any case, the drafter should attempt to prepare a statement of corporate purposes that is sufficiently specific to avoid excursions into unauthorized areas of business while being sufficiently broad to allow expansion of the contemplated business without amendment of the articles of incorporation.

A word about the dangers lurking in the statement of corporate purposes: A corporation is not permitted to exceed its stated corporate purposes; if it does, it is said to have committed an *ultra vires* act. The law protects the shareholders from such abuses of corporate authority by allowing their application to a court to have the unauthorized act stopped. The attorney general may protect the interests of the state by suing to stop the act, or by dissolving the corporation for committing unauthorized acts. Moreover, directors and officers who have caused the corporation to venture forth into the unauthorized business activities may be held personally liable for any loss occasioned by such transactions.[53]

Preemptive Rights. The articles of incorporation may contain a statement regarding shareholders' preemptive rights. Recall that a shareholder's preemptive right is the common law right to maintain a proportionate ownership interest in the corporation. If the corporation intends to issue additional shares of stock, the existing shareholders have the right to buy their proportionate shares of the new stock. Some states require preemptive rights for the shareholders unless they are specifically denied in the articles of incorporation.[54] Other statutes provide that preemptive rights will not exist unless specifically granted in the articles of incorporation.[55] In any case, it is good practice to always specify the desires of the incorporators on this point.

The articles of incorporation may simply deny or grant preemptive rights without further elaboration.

> **EXAMPLE: Preemptive Rights**
> No holder of any stock of the Corporation shall be entitled, as a matter of right, to purchase, subscribe for or otherwise acquire any new or additional shares of stock

of the corporation of any class, or any options or warrants to purchase, subscribe for or otherwise acquire any such new or additional shares, or any shares, bonds, notes, debentures or other securities convertible into or carrying options or warrants to purchase, subscribe for or otherwise acquire any such new or additional shares.[56]

They may also distinguish preemptive rights among specified classes of equity securities.

> **EXAMPLE: Preemptive Rights among Classes**
> Holders of preferred stock shall have the right to subscribe for and purchase their pro rata shares of any new preferred stock which may be issued by the Corporation, but shall have no such preemptive rights with respect to new shares of common stock which may be issued. Holders of common stock shall have the right to subscribe for and purchase their pro rata shares of any new common stock which may be issued, but shall have no such preemptive rights with respect to new shares of preferred stock which may be issued.[57]

In addition, it is possible to otherwise limit, define, or expand preemptive rights in the articles of incorporation. For example, preemptive rights may be limited to stock issued only for cash and maybe excluded from employee stock option plans. It is also good practice to specify the scope of preemptive rights with respect to treasury shares (stock that is repurchased by the company and may subsequently be resold).

Cumulative Voting. If shareholders are to be permitted to cumulate their shares in elections of directors, a statement to that effect in the articles of incorporation is appropriate and may be required. Cumulative voting is treated like preemptive rights in the various state statutes; that is, some states grant the right unless it is specifically denied, and others deny it unless specifically granted.[59] The articles should always reflect the corporate policy either way.

> **EXAMPLE: Cumulative Voting**
> At all elections for directors each stockholder shall be entitled to as many votes as shall equal the number of his or her shares of stock multiplied by the number of directors to be elected, and each stockholder may cast all of such votes for a single director, or may distribute them among the number to be voted for, or any two or more of them, as he or she may see fit.[60]

Optional Provisions

The Model Business Corporation Act allows the articles of incorporation to contain any provision for the regulation of internal affairs of the corporation that might ordinarily be set forth in the by-laws, as long as those provisions are not inconsistent with the statute.[61] By virtue of this broad statutory authority, the articles of incorporation may contain any number of various rules and regulations pertaining to the operation of the company. However, remember that provisions in the articles are more permanent than are by-law provisions, since the amendment procedure for articles of incorporation is considerably more difficult.[62] The drafter should begin with this inflexibility in mind when considering miscellaneous optional provisions for the articles of incorporation.

Generally, the articles of incorporation may contain any regulation of internal affairs that is not inconsistent with the law. If the incorporators have devised a procedure for distributing keys to the corporate restrooms, for example, the procedure could be posted on a bulletin board, written into the by-laws, or given special dignity (and public notice) by being drafted into the articles of incorporation. In this case, the inflexibility of the articles could become painfully obvious if it were later discovered that the specified procedure did not cover certain corporate executives, and those executives had to wait for keys to the restroom until an amendment could be adopted.

There are, however, several instances in the Model Business Corporation Act and other corporate statutes where the articles of incorporation may modify the statutory rules, but a by-law provision is ineffective for that purpose. Therefore, if the incorporators desire a modified approach to their corporate structure, certain additional optional provisions must be included in the articles of incorporation. The following statutory rules of the act and other corporation codes may be modified or amplified only by a special provision in the articles of incorporation.

Directors. Several procedures regulating the conduct of directors must be addressed in the articles of incorporation for those procedures to be changed from the normal statutory scheme. The Model Business Corporation Act permits the board of directors to be dispensed with entirely under certain circumstances, and the directors' activities may be limited or restricted by provisions in the articles of incorporation.[63] Limitations may be placed on the directors' ability to fix their own compensation.[64] Several provisions may be included concerning the election and terms of the directors, requiring a vote greater than a plurality,[65] providing for directors to be elected by specific classes of shares,[66] and staggering directors' terms so that all directors are not elected in the same year.[67] Shareholder's power over the removal of directors may be restricted or eliminated,[68] and the power to fill vacancies on the board of directors may be limited to a decision by the shareholders.[69]

All of these provisions should be discussed in detail with the incorporators to determine the specific corporate structure that will best suit their needs. If these issues are not addressed in the articles of incorporation, the statutory provision concerning the resolution of these matters will govern the issue.

Indemnification of Officers and Directors. The corporation has the power to indemnify its management personnel from any liability or expenses incurred by reason of litigation against them in their capacities as directors, officers, or employees of the corporation. The Model Business Corporation Act specifically confers this power in Sections 8.50 through 8.58. These complex provisions generally grant the right to indemnification if the individual was not negligent in the performance of his or her duties to the corporation and if the director was acting in good faith and in a manner he or she reasonably believed to be in the best interests of the corporation. In addition, if a director is acting outside of the directors' "official capacity" (which would include service for any other corporation or any partnership, joint venture, trust, employee benefit plan, or other enterprise), the director may be indemnified if the director's conduct was not opposed to the best interest of the corporation. In jurisdictions adopting the act's provision, the statutory authority for indemnification obviates any need to grant such power in the articles of incorporation, but in most jurisdictions the statutory right to indemnification is considerably more limited. Many persons would not agree to serve as a director, officer, or employee unless they knew that the corporation would stand behind them for litigation fees, expenses, and liability incurred as a result of their employment. Consequently, the articles of incorporation should establish the scope of indemnification for corporate personnel.

> **EXAMPLE: Indemnification**
> The Corporation shall indemnify any director, officer, or employee, or former director, officer, or employee of the Corporation, or any person who may have served at its request as a director, officer, or employee of another corporation in which it owns shares of capital stock, or of which it is a creditor, against expenses actually and necessarily incurred by him or her in connection with the defense of any action, suit or proceeding in which he or she is made a party by reason of being or having been such director, officer, or employee, except in relation to matters as to which he or she shall be adjudged in such action, suit, or proceeding to be liable for negligence or misconduct in the performance of duty. The Corporation may also reimburse to any director, officer, or employee the reasonable costs of settlement of any such action, suit, or proceeding, if it shall be found by a majority of a committee composed of the directors not involved in the matter in controversy (whether or not a quorum) that it was to the interests of the corporation that such settlement be made and that such director, officer, or employee was not guilty of negligence or misconduct. Such rights of indemnification and reimbursement shall not be deemed exclusive of any other rights to which such director, officer, or employee maybe entitled under any bylaws, agreement, vote of shareholders, or otherwise.[70]
>
> [or]
>
> (1) *Definitions*. The following definitions shall apply to the terms as used in this Article:
>
> (a) "Corporation" includes this corporation and any domestic or foreign predecessor entity of the corporation in a merger, consolidation, or other transaction in which the predecessor's existence ceased upon consummation of the transaction.
>
> (b) "Director" means an individual who is or was a director of the corporation and an individual who, while a director of the corporation, is or was serving at the corporation's request as a director, officer, partner, trustee, employee, or agent of any other foreign or domestic corporation or of any partnership, joint venture, trust, other enterprise, or employee benefit plan. A director shall be considered to be serving an employee benefit plan at the corporation's request if his or her duties to the corporation also impose duties on or otherwise involve services by him or her to the plan or to participants in or beneficiaries of the plan. "Director" includes, unless the context otherwise requires, the estate or personal representation of a director.
>
> (c) "Expenses" includes attorney fees.
>
> (d) "Liability" means the obligation to pay a judgment, settlement, penalty, fine (including an excise tax assessed with respect to an employee benefit plan), or reasonable expense incurred with respect to a proceeding.
>
> (e) "Official capacity," when used with respect to a director, means the office of director in the corporation, and, when used with respect to a person other than a director, means the office in the corporation held by the officer or the employment or agency relationship undertaken by the employee or agent on behalf of the corporation. "Official capacity" does not include service for any other foreign or domestic corporation or for any partnership, joint venture, trust, other enterprise, or employee benefit plan.

(f) "Party" includes an individual who was, is, or is threatened to be made a named defendant or respondent in a proceeding.

(g) "Proceeding" means any threatened, pending, or completed action, suit, or proceeding, whether civil, criminal, administrative, or investigative and whether formal or informal.

(2) *Indemnification for Liability.*

(a) Except as provided in paragraph (d) of this section (2), the corporation shall indemnify against liability incurred in any proceeding any individual made a party to the proceeding because he or she is or was a director or officer if:

(I) He or she conducted himself or herself in good faith;

(II) He or she reasonably believed:

(A) In the case of conduct in his or her official capacity with the corporation, that his or her conduct was in the corporation's best interests; or

(B) In all other cases, that his or her conduct was at least not opposed to the corporation's best interests; and

(III) In the case of any criminal proceeding, he or she had no reasonable cause to believe his or her conduct was unlawful.

(b) A director's or officer's conduct with respect to an employee benefit plan for a purpose he or she reasonably believed to be in the interests of the participants in or beneficiaries of the plan is conduct that satisfies the requirements of this Section (2). A director's or officer's conduct with respect to an employee benefit plan for a purpose that he or she did not reasonably believe to be in the interests of the participants in or beneficiaries of the plan shall be deemed not to satisfy the requirements of this Section (2).

(c) The termination of any proceeding by judgment, order, settlement, or conviction, or upon a plea of nolo contendere or its equivalent, is not of itself determinative that the individual did not meet the standard of conduct set forth in paragraph (a) of this Section (2).

(d) The corporation may not indemnify a director or officer under this Section (2) either:

(I) In connection with a proceeding by or in the right of the corporation in which the director or officer was adjudged liable to the corporation; or

(II) In connection with any proceeding charging improper personal benefit to the director or officer, whether or not involving action in his or her official capacity, in which he or she was adjudged liable on the basis that personal benefit was improperly received by him or her.

(e) Indemnification permitted under this Section (2) in connection with a proceeding by or in the right of the corporation is limited to reasonable expenses incurred in connection with the proceeding.

(3) *Mandatory Indemnification.*

(a) Except as limited by these Articles of Incorporation, the corporation shall be required to indemnify a director or officer of the corporation who was wholly successful, on the merits or otherwise, in defense of any proceeding to which he or she was a party against reasonable expenses incurred by him or her in connection with the proceeding.

(b) Except as otherwise limited by these Articles of Incorporation, a director or officer who in or was a party to a proceeding may apply for indemnification to the court conducting the proceeding or to another court of competent jurisdiction. On receipt of an application, the court, after giving any notice the court considers necessary, may order indemnification in the following manner:

(I) If it determines the director or officer is entitled to mandatory indemnification, the court shall order indemnification under paragraph (a) of this Section (3), in which case the court shall also order the corporation to pay the director's or officer's reasonable expenses incurred to obtain court-ordered indemnification.

(II) If it determines that the director or officer is fairly and reasonably entitled to indemnification in view of all the relevant circumstances, whether or not he or she met the standard of conduct set forth in paragraph (a) of Section (2) of this Article or was adjudged liable in the circumstances described in paragraph (d) of Section (2) of this Article, the court may order such indemnification as the court deems proper; except that the indemnification with respect to any proceeding in which liability shall have been adjudged in the circumstances described in paragraph (d) of Section (2) of this Article is limited to reasonable expenses incurred.

(4) *Limitation on Indemnification.*

(a) The corporation may not indemnify a director or officer under Section (2) of this Article unless authorized in the specific case after a determination has been made that indemnification of the director or officer is permissible in the circumstances because he or she has met the standard of conduct set forth in paragraph (a) of Section (2) of this Article.

(b) The determination required to be made by paragraph (a) of this Section (4) shall be made:

(I) By the board of directors by a majority vote of a quorum, which quorum shall consist of directors not parties to the proceeding; or

(II) If a quorum cannot be obtained, by a majority vote of a committee of the board designated by the board, which committee shall consist of two or more directors not parties to the proceeding; except that directors who are parties to the proceeding may participate in the designation of directors for the committee.

(c) If the quorum cannot be obtained or the committee cannot be established under paragraph (b) of this Section (4), or even if a quorum is obtained or a committee designated if such quorum or committee so directs, the determination required to be made by paragraph (a) of this Section (4) shall be made:

(I) By independent legal counsel selected by a vote of the board of directors or the committee in the manner specified in subparagraph (I) or (II) of paragraph (b) of this Section (4) or, if a quorum of the full board cannot be obtained and a committee cannot be established, by independent legal counsel selected by a majority vote of the full board; or

(II) By the shareholders.

(d) Authorization of indemnification and evaluation as to reasonableness of expenses shall be made in the same manner as the determination that indemnification is permissible; except that, if the determination that indemnification is permissible is made by independent legal counsel, authorization of indemnification and evaluation as to reasonableness of expenses shall be made by the body that selected said counsel.

(5) *Advance Payment of Expenses.*

(a) The corporation shall pay for or reimburse the reasonable expenses incurred by a director, officer, employee or agent who is a party to a proceeding in advance of the final disposition of the proceeding if:

(I) Th director, officer, employee or agent furnishes the corporation a written affirmation of his or her good-faith belief that he or she has met the standard of conduct described in subparagraph (I) of paragraph (a) of Section (2) of this Article;

(II) The director, officer, employee or agent furnishes the corporation a written undertaking, executed personally or on his or her behalf, to repay the advance if it is determined that he or she did not meet such standard of conduct; and

(III) A determination is made that the facts then known to those making the determination would not preclude indemnification under this Section (5).

(b) The undertaking required by subparagraph (II) of paragraph (a) of this Section (5) shall be an unlimited general obligation of the director, officer, employee or agent, but need not be secured and may be accepted without reference to financial ability to make repayment.

(c) Determinations and authorizations of payments under this Section shall be made in the manner specified under Section (4) hereof.

(6) *Reimbursement of Witness Expenses.* The corporation shall pay or reimburse expenses incurred by a director in connection with his or her appearance as a witness in a proceeding at a time when he or she has not been made a named defendant or respondent in the proceeding.

(7) *Insurance for Indemnification.* The corporation may purchase and maintain insurance on behalf of a person who is or was a director, officer, employee, fiduciary, or agent of the corporation or who, while a director, officer, employee, fiduciary, or agent of the corporation, is or was serving at the request of the corporation as a director, officer, partner, trustee, employee, fiduciary, or agent of any other foreign or domestic corporation or of any partnership, joint venture, trust, other enterprise, or employee benefit plan against any liability asserted against or incurred by him or her in any such capacity or arising out of his or her status as such, whether or not the corporation would have the power to indemnify him or her against such liability under the provisions of this Article. Any such insurance may be procured from any insurance company designated by the Board of Directors of the corporation, whether such insurance company is formed under the laws of Colorado or any other jurisdiction of the United States of America, including any insurance company in which the corporation has equity or any other interest, through stock or otherwise.

(8) *Notice of Indemnification.* Any indemnification of or advance of expenses to a director in accordance with this Article, if arising out of a proceeding by or on behalf of the corporation, shall be reported in writing to the shareholders with or before the notice of the next shareholder's meeting.

(9) *Indemnification of Officers, Employees and Agents of the Corporation.* The Board of Directors may indemnify and advance expenses to an officer, employee or agent of the corporation who is not a director of the corporation to the same or greater extent as to a director if such indemnification and advance expense payment is provided for in these Articles of Incorporation, the Bylaws, by resolution of the shareholders or directors or by contract, in a manner consistent with the Colorado Corporation Code.

Purchase of Corporate Shares. Although the Model Business Corporation Act has been amended to eliminate statutory restrictions on purchases of corporate shares,[71] most state statutes permit the corporation to repurchase its own shares from investors, thereby creating *treasury shares,* but these statutes limit the source of funds for such purchases to unreserved and unrestricted earned surplus. This means that the corporation may repurchase its own shares from investors only with accumulated profits that have not been designated for any other purpose. Under the statute, if no profits have accumulated, the corporation may not repurchase its own stock. However, the articles of incorporation may provide that capital surplus (the excess amount collected over par value, or the amount collected and designated capital surplus for no par value shares) may be used in addition to earned surplus for this purpose. There are many reasons supporting this flexibility. For example, management may desire to reduce the number of shares outstanding so as to increase the earnings-per-share figures, or it may wish to reacquire outstanding shares to hold for employee stock purchase plans. Counsel should remember that an appropriate clause in the articles of incorporation is necessary to open the capital surplus account for the repurchase of shares.

The provisions of the articles of incorporation may also have a negative impact on the corporation's purchase of its own securities. The articles may restrict management by requiring that all corporate shares repurchased by the corporation must be cancelled, and cannot be resold or reissued. Management would not be bound to cancel such shares without an express provision to that effect in the articles of incorporation.

> **EXAMPLE: Repurchase of Corporate Shares**
> The corporation shall have the power to repurchase its shares of cumulative preferred stock with any surplus then in existence which has not been otherwise reserved or restricted. [Check statutory authority for the type of surplus which may be permitted for repurchase of shares]
>
> [and]
>
> Upon repurchase of shares of the corporation the corporation shall cancel and retire the same, and such shares shall not be held as treasury shares or reissued to shareholders under any circumstances.

Reservation of the Right to Fix Consideration for Shares to the Shareholders. Many matters that are ordinarily determined by the directors may be reserved to the shareholders by an appropriate clause in the articles of incorporation. This is one of them. Section 6.21 of the Model Business Corporation Act vests in directors the power to determine the price of shares and proper consideration for the issuance of those shares, but the shareholders may exercise this power if the articles of incorporation so provide.

> **EXAMPLE: Right to Fix Consideration for Shares**
> The shareholders of the corporation at a meeting duly called for such purpose shall fix and determine the stated value of the shares of the corporation.

Stock Rights and Options. The corporation may create stock options or stock rights that entitle the holder of the option or right to buy shares at a designated price. The articles of incorporation may restrict management in creating such options or rights and may also elaborate upon the terms of those options or rights, including time of exercise and price. A restrictive provision in the articles of incorporation would be necessary only if the incorporators wanted to narrow management's broad statutory authority to create such options, as is contained in Section 6.24 of the Model Business Corporation Act.

> **EXAMPLE: Restrictions on the Issuance of Stock Rights and Options**
> The board of directors may not, without the express approval of at least the majority of the then outstanding shares of the corporation at a meeting duly called for such purpose, create or issue rights or options entitling the holders thereof to purchase from the corporation shares of any class or classes. Further, even upon such approval by the shareholders, the board of directors shall not create and issue such rights or options which shall provide for a price less than 50% of the then market value of such shares, determined by an independent certified public accountant of the corporation, or upon terms which would permit the holder of such options or rights to pay the purchase price of such shares over a period longer than six months.

Quorum and Vote of Shareholders and Directors. A majority of the shares entitled to vote is a quorum for shareholder meetings, and the affirmative vote of the majority of the quorum carries action on behalf of the shareholders under Section 7.25 of the Model Business Corporation Act. The articles of incorporation may vary these requirements in any manner, but most states still provide that a quorum may never be less than one-third of the shares entitled to vote. Thus, the articles of incorporation could provide that a quorum shall be 40% of the shares entitled to vote and shareholder action requires an affirmative vote of 75% of the shares represented, or that a quorum requires 80% of the shares entitled to vote and shareholder action requires 80% of the shares represented, and so forth.

The articles of incorporation may similarly modify the quorum and vote necessary for director action under Section 8.24. However, a quorum or vote of directors usually may not be reduced below a majority, and the voting or quorum requirements may only be increased by the articles of incorporation. The new Model Business Corporation Act permits the quorum of a board of directors to be reduced to as low as one-third of the directors in office.[72]

> **EXAMPLE: Quorum and Vote of Shareholders**
> The quorum of the shareholders of this corporation for each annual or special meeting of the shareholders shall be one-third of the shares then outstanding and entitled to vote. No resolution of the corporation at any meeting of the shareholders shall be adopted except by the vote of at least seventy-five percent (75%) of the shares represented in a properly called meeting at which a quorum of the shares is present.

> **EXAMPLE: Vote of Directors**
> No resolution of the Corporation at any meeting whether regular or special, shall be adopted except by the unanimous vote of the three directors duly elected as provided herein.[73]

Directors are also permitted by statute to take action without a meeting by signing a consent to action in writing.[74] The articles of incorporation may deny this power, however, if the incorporators want their directors to act only in formal session.

Shareholder Control of By-laws. The initial by-laws of the corporation are adopted by the incorporators of the board of directors at their organizational meeting, and the normal statutory rule is that the board of directors has the power to alter, amend, or repeal the by-laws.[75] This power may be reserved to the shareholders in the articles of incorporation.

> **EXAMPLE: Amendments to the By-laws**
> The bylaws of this corporation shall not be amended, modified or altered except by the vote of the shareholders of the corporation at a meeting of the shareholders, duly called, at which a quorum is present.

The articles of incorporation may also reserve to the shareholders the right to adopt or amend a by-law that provides for greater quorum or voting requirements for the shareholders than are required by statute.[76] With this authority placed in the articles of incorporation, the shareholders may, from time to time, amend and modify their own quorum and voting requirements by simply changing the by-laws.

Distribution Provisions. The board of directors has full discretion under the Model Business Corporation Act for the payment of distributions to shareholders.[77] The articles of incorporation may restrict this discretion, and may establish certain conditions that must be satisfied before dividends may be declared. Conversely, in most states the articles of incorporation may expand the corporation's ability to distribute cash or property to shareholders by expressly authorizing such distributions out of capital surplus.[78] Moreover, the articles of incorporation for a corporation whose principal business is the exploitation of natural resources, as in timber operations, oil wells, and mines, may authorize the payment of dividends from depletion reserves, an account that reflects the reduction of the natural resources available to the corporation.[79]

> **EXAMPLE: Restriction on Payment of Dividends**
> The board of directors of the corporation may not pay or declare a dividend during the first two years of the corporation's operation of its business. Thereafter, the board of directors may, from time to time, declare and pay dividends in accordance with the law provided that the corporation has adequate cash reserves at all times to meet six-months projected operating expenses.
>
> **EXAMPLE: Distributions from Capital Surplus**
> The board of directors of the corporation may, from time to time, distribute to the shareholders out of capital surplus of the corporation a portion of the assets of the corporation, in cash or property, provided:
>
> a) No such distribution shall be made at a time when the corporation is insolvent or when such distribution would render the corporation insolvent.
> b) No such distribution shall be made to the holders of any class of shares unless all cumulative dividends accrued on all preferred classes of shares entitled to preferential dividends shall have been fully paid.
> c) No such distribution shall be made to the holders of any class of shares which would reduce the remaining net assets of the corporation below the aggregate preferential amount payable in the event of an involuntary liquidation to the holders of shares having preferential rights to the assets of the corporation in the event of liquidation.
> d) Even such distribution, when made, shall be identified as a distribution from capital surplus and the amount per share disclosed to shareholders receiving the same concurrently with the distribution thereof.
>
> **EXAMPLE: Payment of Dividends from Depletion Reserves**
> The board of directors may, from time to time, declare and the corporation may pay dividends in cash of the depletion reserves earned by the corporation through its business of exploiting natural resources, but such reserves and the amount per share paid from such reserves shall be disclosed to the shareholders receiving the same concurrently with the distribution thereof.

Transactions with Interested Directors. A director owes a most strict duty of loyalty to the corporation, and, in exercising his or her responsibilities must strive to represent the corporation without any conflict of interest. The common law looked askance at any contract formed between a director's corporation and the director in a personal capacity or between the director's corporation and another corporation for which the same person also served as a director. When the same director appeared in the negotiations for both sides of the transaction, either personally or as a director to another corporation, the transaction was always vulnerable to a court test and would be upheld only upon a showing that it was eminently fair despite the apparent conflict.

In modern corporations, common or *interlocking* directors appear frequently, and it is good practice to include in the articles of incorporation a clause that describes the corporation's position on transactions where a conflict of interest may be implied. The clause should provide that such transactions will not be considered automatically invalid, but also should not completely exculpate the directors involved. The conflict of interest protection should be preserved for the rare cases where a director has compromised the corporation for personal gain.

> **EXAMPLE: Transactions with Interested Directors**
> No contract or other transaction between the corporation and any other corporation, whether or not a majority of the shares of the capital stock of such other corporation is owned by the corporation, and no act of the corporation shall in any way be affected or invalidated by the fact that any of the directors of the corporation are pecuniarily or otherwise interested in, or are directors or officers of, such other corporation; any director individually, or any firm of which such director may be a member, may be a party to, or may be pecuniarily or otherwise interested in, any contract or transaction of the corporation, provided that the fact that the director or such firm is so interested shall be disclosed or shall have been known to the Board of Directors, or a majority thereof; and any director of the corporation who is also a director or officer of such other corporation, or who is so interested, may be counted in determining the existence of a quorum at any meeting of the Board of Directors of the corporation which shall authorize such contract or transaction, and may vote thereat to authorize such contract or transaction, with like force and effect as if he or she were not such director or officer of such other corporation or not so interested.[80]

Classification, Compensation, and Qualifications of Directors. The articles of incorporation may provide for staggered terms for directors to ensure continuity of management policies. A staggered board of directors will always have some "seasoned" members.[81] Section 8.06 of the Model Business Corporation Act permits classification of directors only if the entire board consists of nine or more members. A sample classification clause for the articles of incorporation follows.

> **EXAMPLE: Classification of Directors**
> At the first annual meeting of the shareholders, the members of the Board of Directors shall be divided into three classes of three members each. The members of the first class shall hold office for a term of one year; the members of the second class shall hold office for a term of two years; the members of the third class shall hold office for a term of three years. At all annual elections thereafter three directors shall be elected by the shareholders for a term of three years to succeed the three directors whose term then expires; provided that nothing herein shall be construed to prevent the election of a director to succeed himself or herself.[82]

As long as the articles of incorporation are touching upon some matters relating to directors, qualifications may also be covered. Under the Model Business Corporation Act, directors need not have any particular qualifications to serve as such,[83] but the articles of incorporation or the by-laws may impose any reasonable qualifications for directors. It may be desirable to require that directors be shareholders, for example, or over thirty-five years of age, or perhaps under thirty-five years of age. Director qualifications should be tailored to the desires of the incorporators.

FILING AND OTHER FORMALITIES

Filing Procedure

The articles of incorporation are filed with the secretary of state or other designated public official, and the Model Business Corporation Act requires an original and an exact or conformed copy to be filed.[84] Several states also require that the articles be filed with certain designated county offices in which the corporation has its registered office, and the corporation is not properly formed unless the articles of incorporation are filed in all places required by statute.[85] After determining that the articles of incorporation are in proper form and that all fees have been paid, the secretary of state will return the duplicate copy of the articles of incorporation with the certificate of incorporation.

Miscellaneous Formalities

Each state statute treats the execution and filing of the articles of incorporation differently. All jurisdictions require that the articles of incorporation must be signed by the incorporators. The Model Business Corporation Act states simply that the incorporators sign the document, but acknowledgment (a procedure whereby the signatures of the incorporators must be notarized) is required in the New York statute and in several other states.[86] As previously stated, county recording of the articles of incorporation is a common formality. Some states require approval of the state corporation commission,[87] filing with a probate judge,[88] or publication of the articles of incorporation in a newspaper of general circulation in the county where the corporation has its registered office.[89] Finally, a state may require certain other documents to be filed with the articles of incorporation. For example, California requires the filing of an application for a permit to issue stock with the commissioner of corporations, and many states that require payment of a minimum amount of paid-in capital also require an affidavit of subscription or payment to accompany the articles of incorporation.

Careful analysis of the particular state statute under which the corporation is to be formed is absolutely necessary to ensure strict compliance with its provisions.[90]

Payment of Capital

The Model Business Corporation Act formerly required that a certain amount of capital must be collected before a corporation may commence business, and many states have preserved this rule. In those states, the payment of the preincorporation share subscriptions in the prescribed amount is a formality that must be satisfied before the corporation may commence business.

CORPORATE EXISTENCE

Modern statutes have adopted simple incorporation procedures, the principal features of which are the preparation and filing of the articles of incorporation and, in most cases, the subsequent issuance of the certificate of incorporation. In most states, corporate existence begins when the secretary of state, after reviewing the articles of incorporation, issues a certificate of incorporation.[91] The Model Business Corporation Act and several other jurisdictions, including Michigan, New York, Delaware, and California, provide that corporate existence begins when the articles of incorporation are *filed* with or endorsed by the appropriate state official.[92]

The point at which the corporation is born is used to circumscribe shareholder and promoter liabilities for corporate obligations and to establish the beginning of corporate characteristics, such as taxation as a separate entity. When the certificate of incorporation is issued, or, in the appropriate case, when the articles are filed, the corporation is said to be a *de jure* corporation, or a corporation by law, and it acquires all power to act in accordance with the statute under which it is organized.

FORMALITIES AFTER FORMATION OF A CORPORATION

Although the corporation is formed when the articles of incorporation are filed or when a certificate of incorporation is issued, several other matters should precede commencement of the corporate business.

Organizational Meetings

Organizational meetings of the incorporators and the initial directors are usually required as one of the first matters of corporate business. Because organizational meetings are quite routine, counsel may draft the minutes in advance and use the predrafted minutes as an agenda for the meetings. The particular statute of each state should be consulted to determine which of the corporate groups (incorporators, directors, or shareholders) are required to hold an organizational meeting. The Model Business Corporation Act requires an organizational meeting of the incorporators if initial directors are not named in the articles of incorporation. If initial directors are named in the articles of incorporation, the initial directors are to hold the organizational meeting.[93] Several states require only an organizational meeting of the incorporators.[94] Florida, Hawaii, New Jersey, and most other states require only an organizational meeting of the directors. In Delaware, either the incorporators or the directors must have an organizational meeting, and in Illinois shareholders and directors must have an organizational meeting. In addition, there is nothing wrong with holding an organizational meeting for a corporate group that is not required to meet by statute.

Organizational meetings assist in establishing the air of formality that must be continually observed in corporate operations. The important point, however, is the corporation's need to hold the statutory organizational meetings so as to be considered a properly formed corporation. Even if corporate existence begins when the certificate of incorporation is issued or the articles are filed, a failure to observe the statutory formalities following these events may destroy the protection and special privileges of the corporation.

An organizational meeting of the incorporators may consider acceptance of the certificate of incorporation or articles of incorporation and acknowledgment of the payment of taxes; election of initial directors (if they are not named in the articles of incorporation) and resignation of any accommodation (dummy) directors; authorization of the board of directors to issue shares; adoption of by-laws;

transfers of any subscriptions from accommodation (dummy) incorporators; and transaction of any other business appropriate for incorporators to consider.

An organizational meeting of the board of directors will consider many of the same matters, and, if an organizational meeting of incorporators has been held, the board usually reviews and approves the business conducted there. In addition, the board of directors will decide other matters relating to the issuance and transfer of shares, preincorporation agreements, banking arrangements, the election of officers, qualification as a foreign corporation, and tax plans.[95]

Corporate Supplies

The attorney's office usually orders the corporation's supplies for the newly formed business. The corporation must maintain a minute book and a stock transfer ledger, and it must have share certificates and a corporate seal. Corporation supply kits are available from many local printers and those who advertise in legal periodicals.

BY-LAWS

By-laws complement the state statute and the articles of incorporation by prescribing rules to regulate the internal affairs of the corporation. Rules that are for the internal management and are intended to be flexible are best described in the by-laws, since they are most easily amended. On the other hand, rules that require permanence should be placed in the articles of incorporation. Interchangeability between the articles and by-laws is facilitated by the statutory rule that any provision that is required or permitted to be set forth in the by-laws may also be included in the articles of incorporation.[96] The converse is not true.

The authority to adopt by-laws is contained in the state statute, which may also suggest certain matters that should be contained in the by-laws.[97] Most states and the Model Business Corporation Act simply provide that the by-laws may contain any provision for the regulation and management of the corporation's affairs that is not inconsistent with the statute or the articles of incorporation.[98] In these jurisdictions, the by-laws may be as simple or as complicated as is desired. Certain provisions usually appear in the by-laws, such as the place of holding meetings of shareholders and the time of the annual meeting of shareholders; the number of directors, except the first board of directors; the notice to be given for directors' meetings; the procedure for the election and appointment of officers; and a description of the officers' duties.

The by-laws should not be complicated with intricate procedures for corporate operation, because a complicated by-law provision may become a trap for the unwary, rather than a useful guide to corporate management. However, the by-laws should be as extensive and thorough as necessary to ensure that the procedures for internal management of the corporation are fully described in writing for the officers and directors.

Initial By-laws

The adoption of the initial by-laws is the responsibility of the incorporators, the shareholders, or the board of directors, depending upon the jurisdiction involved. In New York, the incorporators adopt the initial by-laws. The by-laws are then approved by the board of directors at its organizational meeting. In a few jurisdictions, the shareholders adopt the initial by-laws.[99] The Model Business Corporation Act provides that the incorporators or the board of directors (if the initial board is named in the articles of incorporation) will adopt the initial by-laws of the corporation.[100] Most jurisdictions and the act provide for the adoption of the initial by-laws by the board of directors, but the articles of incorporation may reserve this power to the shareholders.[101]

The by-laws are prepared by counsel, with guidance from the incorporators and the initial directors, and they are presented at the organizational meeting for the approval of the appropriate intracorporate group.

Content of By-laws

Standard by-law provisions deal with the following matters:

1. Offices
   (a) Location of the principal office of the corporation
   (b) Location of the registered office of the corporation
   (c) Authority to change the address of the registered office by the board of directors

> **EXAMPLE: Offices**
> The principal office of the Corporation in the State of South Dakota shall be located in the City of Deadwood, County of Lawrence. The Corporation may have such other offices, either within or without the State of South Dakota, as the Board of Directors may designate or as the business of the Corporation may require from time to time.
>
> The registered office of the Corporation required by The South Dakota Business Corporation Act to be maintained in the State of South Dakota may be, but need not be, identical with the principal office in the State of South Dakota, and the address of the registered office may be changed from time to time by the Board of Directors.

2. Shareholders[102]
   (a) Time of the annual meeting

> **EXAMPLE: Annual Meeting**
> The annual meeting of the shareholders shall be held on the first Tuesday in the month of May in each year, beginning with the year 1990, at the hour of 9:00 o'clock A.M., for the purpose of electing directors and for the transaction of such other business as may come before the meeting. If the day fixed for the annual meeting shall be a legal holiday in the State of South Dakota, such meeting shall be held on the next succeeding business day. If the election of directors shall not be held on the day designated herein for any annual meeting of the shareholders, or at any adjournment thereof, the Board of Directors shall cause the election to be held at a special meeting of the shareholders as soon thereafter as conveniently may be.

   (b) Procedure for calling special meetings of shareholders

> **EXAMPLE: Special Meetings**
> Special meetings of the shareholders, for any purpose or purposes, unless otherwise prescribed by statute, may be called by the President or by the Board of

Directors, and shall be called by the President at the request of the holders of not less than one-tenth of all the outstanding shares of the corporation entitled to vote at the meeting.

(c) Place of the shareholder meetings

(d) Authority for waiver of notice to be signed by shareholders entitled to vote at the meeting—This procedure permits a cure of defective notice or failure to give notice by obtaining written waivers from shareholders entitled to notice.

> **EXAMPLE: Place of Meeting and Waiver of Notice**
>
> The Board of Directors may designate any place, either within or without the State of South Dakota, as the place of meeting for any annual meeting or for any special meeting called by the Board of Directors. A waiver of notice signed by all shareholders entitled to vote at a meeting may designate any place, either within or without the State of South Dakota, as the place for the holding of such meeting. If no designation is made, or if a special meeting be otherwise called, the place of meeting shall be the principal office of the Corporation in the State of South Dakota.

(e) Procedure for sending notice of meeting and time period for which notice is appropriate

> **EXAMPLE: Notice of Meeting**
>
> Written notice stating the place, day and hour of the meeting and, in case of a special meeting, the purpose or purposes for which the meeting is called, shall be delivered not less than ten or more than fifty days before the date of the meeting, either personally or by mail, by or at the direction of the President, or the Secretary, or the persons calling the meeting, to each shareholder or record entitled to vote at such meeting. If mailed, such notice shall be deemed to be delivered when deposited in the United States mail, addressed to the shareholder at his or her address as it appears on the stock transfer books of the corporation, with postage thereon prepaid.

(f) Procedure for determining the shareholders entitled to notice or entitled to vote or entitled to receive dividends—This procedure states a particular time that the stock transfer books will be closed in order to determine the holders of record.

> **EXAMPLE: Determination of Shareholders Entitled to Notice or Vote**
>
> For the purpose of determining shareholders entitled to notice of or to vote at any meeting of shareholders or any adjournment thereof, or shareholders entitled to receive payment of any dividend, or in order to make a determination of shareholders for any other proper purpose, the Board of Directors of the Corporation may provide that the stock transfer books shall be closed for a stated period but not to exceed, in any case, fifty days. If the stock transfer books shall be closed for the purpose of determining shareholders entitled to notice of or to vote at a meeting of shareholders, such books shall be closed for at least ten days immediately preceding such meeting. In lieu of closing the stock transfer books, the Board of Directors may fix in advance a date as the record date for any such determination of shareholders, such date in any case to be not more than fifty days and, in case of a meeting of shareholders, not less than ten days prior to the date on which the particular action, requiring such determination of shareholders, is to

be taken. If the stock transfer books are not closed and no record date is fixed for the determination of shareholders entitled to notice of or to vote at a meeting of shareholders, or shareholders entitled to receive payment of a dividend, the date on which notice of the meeting is mailed or the date on which the resolution of the Board of Directors declaring such dividend is adopted, as the case may be, shall be the record date for such determination of shareholders. When a determination of shareholders entitled to vote at any meeting of shareholders has been made as provided in this section, such determination shall apply to any adjournment thereof except where the determination has been made through the closing of the stock transfer books and the stated period of closing has expired.

(g) Procedure for preparation of a voting list

(h) Provision for examination of voting lists

> **EXAMPLE: Voting Lists**
> The officer or agent having charge of the stock transfer books for shares of the Corporation shall make a complete list of the shareholders entitled to vote at each meeting of shareholders or any adjournment thereof, arranged in alphabetical order, with the address of and the number of shares held by each. Such list shall be produced and kept open at the time and place of the meeting and shall be subject to the inspection of any shareholder during the whole time of the meeting for the purposes thereof.

(i) Number of shares required to constitute a quorum, and number of shares required to adjourn the meeting of shareholders

> **EXAMPLE: Quorum**
> A majority of the outstanding shares of the Corporation entitled to vote, represented in person or by proxy, shall constitute a quorum at a meeting of shareholders. If less than a majority of the outstanding shares are represented at a meeting, a majority of the shares so represented may adjourn the meeting from time to time without further notice. At such adjourned meeting at which a quorum shall be present or represented, any business may be transacted which might have been transacted at the meeting as originally notified. The shareholders present at a duly organized meeting may continue to transact business until adjournment, notwithstanding the withdrawal of enough shareholders to leave less than a quorum.

(j) Authorization for voting by proxy

> **EXAMPLE: Proxies**
> At all meetings of shareholders, a shareholder may vote in person or by proxy executed in writing by the shareholder or by his or her duly authorized attorney in fact. Such proxy shall be filed with the secretary of the Corporation before or at the time of the meeting. No proxy shall be valid after eleven months from the date of its execution, unless otherwise provided in the proxy.

(k) Voting entitlements of each class of stock

> **EXAMPLE: Voting of Shares**
> Each outstanding share entitled to vote shall be entitled to one vote upon each matter submitted to a vote at a meeting of shareholders.

(l) Authorization to vote by representatives of the holder of record (e.g., administrator, executor, agent of another corporation, etc.)

> **EXAMPLE: Voting of Shares by Certain Holders**
> Shares standing in the name of another corporation may be voted by such officer, agent or proxy as the bylaws of such corporation may prescribe, or, in the absence of such provision, as the board of directors of such corporation may determine.
> Shares held by an administrator, executor, guardian or conservator may be voted by that person, either in person or by proxy, without a transfer of such shares into his or her name. Shares standing in the name of a trustee may be voted by him or her, either in person or by proxy, but no trustee shall be entitled to vote shares held by that trustee without a transfer of such shares into his or her name.
> Shares standing in the name of a receiver may be voted by such receiver, and shares held by or under the control of a receiver may be voted by such receiver without the transfer thereof into his or her name if authority so to do be contained in an appropriate order of the court by which such receiver was appointed.
> A shareholder whose shares are pledged shall be entitled to vote such shares until the shares have been transferred into the name of the pledgee, and thereafter the pledgee shall be entitled to vote the shares so transferred.
> Neither shares of its own stock held by the Corporation, nor those held by another corporation if a majority of the shares entitled to vote for the election of directors of such other corporation are held by the Corporation, shall be voted at any meeting or counted in determining the total number of outstanding shares at any given time for purposes of any meeting.

(m) Informal action by the shareholders

> **EXAMPLE: Informal Action by Shareholders**
> Any action required to be taken at a meeting of the shareholders, or any action which may be taken at a meeting of the shareholders, may be taken without a meeting if a consent in writing, setting forth the action so taken, shall be signed by all of the shareholders entitled to vote with respect to the subject matter thereof.

(n) Cumulative voting rights

> **EXAMPLE: Cumulative Voting**
> At each election for directors every shareholder entitled to vote at such election shall have the right to vote, in person or by proxy, the number of shares owned by that shareholder for as many persons as there are directors to be elected and for whose election that shareholder has a right to vote, or to cumulate his or her votes by giving one candidate as many votes as the number of such directors multiplied by the number of his or her shares shall equal, or by distributing such votes on the same principles among any number of candidates.

3. Board of directors
   (a) Authorization for the board of directors to manage the business[103]

   > **EXAMPLE: General Powers**
   > The business and affairs of the Corporation shall be managed by its Board of Directors.

   (b) The number, tenure, and qualifications of directors

> **EXAMPLE: Number, Tenure, and Qualifications**
> The number of directors of the Corporation shall be nine. Each director shall hold office until the next annual meeting of shareholders and until his or her successor shall have been elected and qualified. Directors need not be residents of the State of South Dakota or shareholders of the Corporation.

(c) Classification of directors (if desired)

> **EXAMPLE: Classification of Directors**
> At the first annual meeting of the shareholders, the members of the Board of Directors shall be divided into three classes of three members each. The members of the first class shall hold office for a term of one year; the members of the second class shall hold office for a term of two years; the members of the third class shall hold office for a term of three years. At all annual elections thereafter three directors shall be elected by the shareholders for a term of three years to succeed the three directors whose term then expires; provided that nothing herein shall be construed to prevent the election of a director to succeed himself or herself.[104]

(d) Time and place for regular meetings[105]

> **EXAMPLE: Regular Meetings**
> A regular meeting of the Board of Directors shall be held without other notice than this By-law immediately after, and at the same place as, the annual meeting of shareholders. The Board of Directors may provide, by resolution, the time and place, either within or without the State of South Dakota, for the holding of additional regular meetings without other notice than such resolution.

(e) Procedure for calling special meetings

> **EXAMPLE: Special Meetings**
> Special meetings of the Board of Directors maybe called by or at the request of the President or any two directors. The person or persons authorized to call special meetings of the Board of Directors may fix any place, either within or without the State of South Dakota, as the place for holding any special meeting of the Board of Directors called by them.

(f) Procedure for giving notice of special meetings
(g) Authorization to waive notice of any meeting

> **EXAMPLE: Notice and Authorization to Waive Notice**
> Notice of any special meeting shall be given at least two days previously thereto by written notice delivered personally or mailed to each director at his or her business address, or by telegram. If mailed, such notice shall be deemed to be delivered when deposited in the United States mail so addressed, with postage thereon prepaid. If notice be given by telegram, such notice shall be deemed to be delivered when the telegram is delivered to the telegraph company. Any director may waive notice of any meeting. The attendance of a director at a meeting shall constitute a waiver of notice of such meeting, except where a director attends a meeting for the express purpose of objecting to the transaction of any business because the meeting is not lawfully called or convened. Neither the business to be transacted at, nor the purpose of, any regular or special meeting of the Board of Directors need be specified in the notice or waiver of notice of such meeting.

(h) The number of directors for a quorum and to adjourn the meeting

> **EXAMPLE: Quorum**
> A majority of the number of directors fixed by these By-laws shall constitute a quorum for the transaction of business at any meeting of the Board of Directors, but if less than such majority is present at a meeting, a majority of the directors present may adjourn the meeting from time to time without further notice.

(i) The number of directors required to approve a certain matter

> **EXAMPLE: Manner of Acting**
> The act of the majority of the directors present at a meeting at which a quorum is present shall be the act of the Board of Directors.
> [or]
> No resolution of the Corporation at any meeting whether regular or special, shall be adopted except by the unanimous vote of the directors duly elected as provided herein.[106]

(j) Informal action by the board of directors

> **EXAMPLE: Action without a Meeting**
> Any action that may be taken by the Board of Directors at a meeting may be taken without a meeting if a consent in writing, setting forth the action so to be taken, shall be signed before such action by all of the directors.

(k) Procedure for filling vacancies and removing directors[107]

> **EXAMPLE: Vacancies**
> Any vacancy occurring in the Board of Directors may be filled by the affirmative vote of a majority of the remaining directors though less than a quorum of the Board of Directors. A director elected to fill a vacancy shall be elected for the unexpired term of his or her predecessor in office. Any directorship to be filled by reason of an increase in the number of directors may be filled by election by the Board of Directors for a term of office continuing only until the next election of directors by the shareholders.

> **EXAMPLE: Removal**
> The stockholders of the Corporation may, at any meeting called for the purpose, remove any director from office, with or without cause, by a vote of a majority of the outstanding shares of the class of stock which elected the director or directors to be removed; provided, however, that no director shall be removed in case the votes of a sufficient number of shares are cast against that director's removal, which if cumulatively voted at an election of the entire board of directors would be sufficient to elect that director.[108]

(l) Compensation and payment of expenses

> **EXAMPLE: Compensation**
> By resolution of the Board of Directors, each director may be paid his or her expenses, if any, of attendance at each meeting of the Board of Directors, and may be paid a stated salary as a director or a fixed sum for attendance at each meeting of the Board of Directors or both. No such payment shall preclude any director from serving the Corporation in any other capacity and receiving compensation therefor.

(m) Presumption of assent when the director is present at a meeting

> **EXAMPLE: Presumption of Assent**
> A director of the Corporation who is present at a meeting of the Board of Directors at which action on any corporate matter is taken shall be presumed to have assented to the action taken unless that director's dissent shall be entered in the minutes of the meeting or unless that director shall file his or her written dissent to such action with the person acting as the secretary of the meeting before the adjournment thereof or shall forward such dissent by registered mail to the Secretary of the Corporation immediately after the adjournment of the meeting. Such right to dissent shall not apply to a director who voted in favor of such action.

4. Executive committees[109]

    (a) Authority for the appointment of executive committees and the delegation of authority

    > **EXAMPLE: Appointment**
    > The Board of Directors, by resolution adopted by a majority of the full board, may designate two or more of its members to constitute an Executive Committee. The designation of such committee and the delegation thereto of authority shall not operate to relieve the Board of Directors, or any member thereof, of any responsibility imposed by law.

    > **EXAMPLE: Authority**
    > The Executive Committee, when the Board of Directors is not in session, shall have and may exercise all of the authority of the Board of Directors except to the extent, if any, that such authority shall be limited by the resolution appointing the Executive Committee and except also that the Executive Committee shall not have the authority of the Board of Directors in reference to amending the Articles of Incorporation, adopting a plan of merger or consolidation, recommending to the shareholders the sale, lease or other disposition of all or substantially all of the property and assets of the Corporation otherwise than in the usual and regular course of its business, recommending to the shareholders a voluntary dissolution of the Corporation or a revocation thereof, or amending the By-laws of the Corporation.

    (b) Tenure and qualifications of members of the executive committee

    > **EXAMPLE: Tenure and Qualifications**
    > Each member of the Executive Committee shall hold office until the next regular annual meeting of the Board of Directors following his or her designation and until his or her successor is designated as a member of the Executive Committee and is elected and qualified.

    (c) Time and place for regular meetings of the executive committee
    (d) Procedure for calling special meetings of the executive committee
    (e) Procedure for giving notice of a meeting to the executive committee

    > **EXAMPLE: Meetings**
    > Regular meetings of the Executive Committee may be held without notice at such times and places as the Executive Committee may fix from time to time by resolution. Special meetings of the Executive Committee may be called by any member thereof upon not less than one day's notice stating the place, date and hour of the meeting, which notice may be written or oral, and if mailed, shall be

deemed to be delivered when deposited in the United States mail addressed to the member of the Executive Committee at his or her business address. Any member of the Executive Committee may waive notice of any meeting and no notice of any meeting need be given to any member thereof who attends in person. The notice of a meeting of the Executive Committee need not state the business proposed to be transacted at the meeting.

(f) Number of the members of the committee necessary to constitute a quorum, and vote required of the committee to authorize certain acts

EXAMPLE: Quorum
A majority of the members of the Executive Committee shall constitute a quorum for the transaction of business at any meeting thereof and action of the Executive Committee must be authorized by the affirmative vote of a majority of the members present at a meeting at which a quorum is present.

(g) Informal action by the executive committee

EXAMPLE: Action without a Meeting
Any action that may be taken by the Executive Committee at a meeting may be taken without a meeting if a consent in writing, setting forth the action so to be taken, shall be signed before such action by all of the members of the Executive Committee.

(h) Procedure for filling vacancies, accepting resignations, and removing members of the executive committee

EXAMPLE: Vacancies
Any vacancy in the Executive Committee may be filled by a resolution adopted by a majority of the full Board of Directors.

EXAMPLE: Resignation and Removal
Any member of the Executive Committee may be removed at any time with or without cause by resolution adopted by a majority of the full Board of Directors. Any member of the Executive Committee may resign from the Executive Committee at any time by giving written notice to the President or Secretary of the corporation, and unless otherwise specified therein, the acceptance of such resignation shall not be necessary to make it effective.

(i) Procedure for conducting executive committee meetings

EXAMPLE: Procedure
The Executive Committee shall elect a presiding officer from its members and may fix its own rules of procedure which shall not be inconsistent with these By-laws. It shall keep regular minutes of its proceedings and report the same to the Board of Directors for its information at the meeting thereof held next after the proceedings shall have been taken.

5. Officers[110]
   (a) Number of officers

   EXAMPLE: Number
   The officers of the Corporation shall be a President, one or more Vice Presidents (the number thereof to be determined by the Board of Directors), a Secretary, and

a Treasurer, each of whom shall be elected by the Board of Directors. Such other officers and assistant officers as may be deemed necessary may be elected or appointed by the Board of Directors. Any two or more offices may be held by the same person, except the offices of President and Secretary.

(b) Procedure for election and term of office

EXAMPLE: Election and Term of Office
The officers of the Corporation to be elected by the Board of Directors shall be elected annually by the Board of Directors at the first meeting of the Board of Directors held after each annual meeting of the shareholders. If the election of officers shall not be held at such meeting, such election shall be held as soon thereafter as conveniently may be. Each officer shall hold office until that officer's successor shall have been duly elected and shall have qualified or until that officer's death or until that officer shall resign or shall have been removed in the manner hereinafter provided.

(c) Removal and the filling of vacancies

EXAMPLE: Removal
Any officer or agent may be removed by the Board of Directors whenever in its judgment the best interests of the Corporation will be served thereby, but such removal shall be without prejudice to the contract rights, if any, of the person so removed. Election or appointment of an officer or agent shall not of itself create contract rights.

EXAMPLE: Vacancies
A vacancy in any office because of death, resignation, removal, disqualification or otherwise, may be filled by the Board of Directors for the unexpired portion of the term.

(d) Responsibilities of the officers

EXAMPLE: Officers
President. The President shall be the principal executive officer of the Corporation and, subject to the control of the Board of Directors, shall in general supervise and control all of the business and affairs of the Corporation. The President shall, when present, preside at all meetings of the shareholders and of the Board of Directors. The President may sign, with the Secretary or any other proper officer of the corporation thereunto authorized by the Board of Directors, certificates for shares of the corporation, any deeds, mortgages, bonds, contracts, or other instruments which the Board of Directors has authorized to be executed, except in cases where the signing and execution thereof shall be expressly delegated by the Board of Directors or by these By-laws to some other officer or agent of the corporation, or shall be required by law to be otherwise signed or executed; and in general shall perform all duties incident to the office of President and such other duties as may be prescribed by the Board of Directors from time to time.
The Vice Presidents. In the absence of the President or in the event of his or her death, inability or refusal to act, the Vice President (or in the event there be more than one Vice President, the Vice Presidents in the order designated at the time of their election, or in the absence of any designation, then in the order of their election) shall perform the duties of the President, and when so acting, shall have all the powers of and be subject to all of the restrictions upon the President. Any Vice President may sign, with the Secretary or an assistant Secretary, certificates for

shares of the Corporation; and shall perform such other duties as from time to time may be assigned to him or her by the President or by the Board of Directors.

The Secretary. The Secretary shall: (a) keep the minutes of the proceedings of the shareholders and of the Board of Directors in one or more books provided for that purpose; (b) see that all notices are duly given in accordance with the provisions of these By-laws or as required by law; (c) be custodian of the corporate records and of the seal of the Corporation and see that the seal of the Corporation is affixed to all documents the execution of which on behalf of the Corporation under its seal is duly authorized; (d) keep a register of the post office address of each shareholder which shall be furnished to the Secretary by such shareholder; (e) sign with the President, or a Vice President, certificates for shares of the Corporation, the issuance of which shall have been authorized by resolution of the Board of Directors; (f) have general charge of the stock transfer books of the Corporation; and (g) in general perform all duties incident to the office of Secretary and such other duties as from time to time may be assigned to him or her by the President or by the Board of Directors.

The Treasurer. The Treasurer shall: (a) have charge and custody of and be responsible for all funds and securities of the Corporation; (b) receive and give receipts for moneys due and payable to the Corporation from any source whatsoever, and deposit all such moneys in the name of the Corporation in such banks, trust companies or other depositories as shall be selected in accordance with the provisions of these By-laws; and (c) in general perform all of the duties incident to the office of Treasurer and such other duties as from time to time may be assigned to the Treasurer by the President or by the Board of Directors. If required by the Board of Directors, the Treasurer shall give a bond for the faithful discharge of his or her duties in such sum and such surety or sureties as the Board of Directors shall determine.

Assistant Secretaries and Assistant Treasurers. The Assistant Secretaries, when authorized by the Board of Directors, may sign with the President or a Vice President certificates for shares of the Corporation the issuance of which shall have been authorized by a resolution of the Board of Directors. The Assistant Treasurers shall respectively, if required by the Board of Directors, give bonds for the faithful discharge of their duties in such sums and with such sureties as the Board of Directors shall determine. The Assistant Secretaries and Assistant Treasurers, in general, shall perform such duties as shall be assigned to them by the Secretary or the Treasurer, respectively, or by the President or the Board of Directors.

(e) Salaries

EXAMPLE: Salaries
The salaries of the officers shall be fixed from time to time by the Board of Directors and no officer shall be prevented from receiving such salary by reason of the fact that he or she is also a director of the Corporation.

[*or*]

No salary or other compensation for services shall be paid to any director or officer of the corporation unless and until the same shall have been approved in writing or at a duly held stockholders' meeting by stockholders owning at least seventy-five per cent in amount of the capital stock of the corporation then outstanding.[111]

6. Authorization for executing contracts and other written matters on behalf of the corporation—These provisions permit the board of directors to authorize any officer to contract on behalf of the corporation, and they may further restrict the ability of management to contract loans or other indebtedness. It is also common

to specify here which persons must sign checks, drafts, and other evidences of indebtedness issued in the name of the corporation, and where the funds of the corporation will be deposited.

> **EXAMPLE: Authorization**
> *Contracts.* The Board of Directors may authorize any officer or officers, agent or agents, to enter into any contract or execute and deliver any instrument in the name of and on behalf of the Corporation, and such authority may be general or confined to specific instances.
> *Loans.* No loans shall be contracted on behalf of the Corporation and no evidences of indebtedness shall be issued in its name unless authorized by a resolution of the Board of Directors. Such authority may be general or confined to specific instances.
> *Checks, Drafts, etc.* All checks, drafts or other orders for the payment of money, notes or other evidences of indebtedness issued in the name of the corporation, shall be signed by such officer or officers, agent or agents of the Corporation and in such manner as shall from time to time be determined by resolution of the Board of Directors.
> *Deposits.* All funds of the Corporation not otherwise employed shall be deposited from time to time to the credit of the Corporation in such banks, trust companies or other depositories as the Board of Directors may select.

7. Matters involving the certificates of shares and their transfer[112]—These provisions usually permit the board of directors to determine the form of the share certificates and prescribe which of the corporate officers will be required to sign them. Section 6.25 of the Model Business Corporation Act requires that if certificates are used by the corporation, each certificate representing shares shall set forth on its face that the corporation is organized under the laws of the particular state; the name of the person to whom issued; and the number and class of shares represented. In addition, if the corporation is authorized to issue different classes of shares, the certificates should specify the designations, preferences, limitations, and relative rights of the shares of each class. These statutory requirements need not be restated in the by-laws. If the incorporators wish to restrict the board of directors' use of uncertificated shares, a prohibitive provision to that effect should be stated in the by-laws. Any other special provisions respecting the transfer of shares and the method of keeping the stock transfer ledger should also be included under this by-law section.

> **EXAMPLE: Certificates for Shares**
> Certificates representing shares of the Corporation shall be in such form as shall be determined by the Board of Directors. Such certificates shall be signed by the President or a Vice President and by the Secretary or an Assistant Secretary and sealed with the corporate seal or a facsimile thereof. The signatures of such officers upon a certificate may be facsimiles if the certificate is countersigned by a transfer agent, or registered by a registrar, other than the Corporation itself or one of its employees. All certificates for shares shall be consecutively numbered or otherwise identified. The name and address of the person to whom the shares represented thereby are issued, with the number of shares and date of issue, shall be entered on the stock transfer books of the Corporation. All certificates surrendered to the Corporation for transfer shall be cancelled and no new certificate shall be issued until the former certificate for a like number of shares shall have been surrendered and cancelled, except that in case of a lost, destroyed

or mutilated certificate a new one may be issued therefor upon such terms and indemnity to the Corporation as the Board of Directors may prescribe.

The board of directors shall not be permitted to issue "uncertificated" shares without the express approval of at least two-thirds of the then outstanding stock entitled to vote.

> **EXAMPLE: Transfer of Shares**
> Transfer of shares of the Corporation shall be made only on the stock transfer books of the Corporation by the holder of record thereof or by his or her legal representative, who shall furnish proper evidence of authority to transfer, or by his or her attorney thereunto authorized by power of attorney duly executed and filed with the Secretary of the Corporation, and on surrender for cancellation of the certificate for such shares. The person in whose name shares stand on the books of the corporation shall be deemed by the Corporation to be the owner thereof for all purposes.

> **EXAMPLE: Transfer Agent**
> The Secretary of the Corporation shall act as Transfer Agent of the certificates representing the shares of common stock and preferred stock of the Corporation. That person shall maintain a Stock Transfer Book, the stubs in which shall set forth, among other things, the names and addresses of the holders of all issued shares of the Corporation, the number of shares held by each, the certificate numbers representing such shares, the date of issue of the certificates representing such shares, and whether or not such shares originate from original issue or from transfer. The names and addresses of the stockholders as they appear on the stubs of the Stock Transfer Book shall be conclusive evidence as to who are the stockholders of record and as such entitled to receive notice of the meetings of stockholders; to vote at such meetings; to examine the list of the stockholders entitled to vote at meetings; to receive dividends; and to own, enjoy and exercise any other property or rights deriving from such shares against the Corporation. Each stockholder shall be responsible for notifying the Secretary in writing any change in his or her name or address and failure to do so will relieve the Corporation, its directors, officers and agents, from liability for failure to direct notices or other documents, or pay over or transfer dividends or other property or rights, to a name or address other than the name and address appearing on the stub of the Stock Transfer Book.[113]

8. The fiscal year of the corporation

> **EXAMPLE: Fiscal Year**
> The fiscal year of the Corporation shall begin on the first day of January and end on the thirty-first day of December in each year.

9. Authority of the board of directors to declare and pay distributions on the outstanding shares of the corporation[114]

> **EXAMPLE: Distributions**
> The Board of Directors may from time to time declare, and the Corporation may pay, dividends on its outstanding shares in the manner and upon the terms and conditions provided by law and its Articles of Incorporation.

10. Description of the corporate seal

> **EXAMPLE: Seal**
> The Board of Directors shall provide a corporate seal which shall be circular in form and shall have inscribed thereon the name of the Corporation and the state of incorporation and the words, "Corporate Seal."

11. Provisions for adopting emergency by-laws and the term for which those by-laws will be in effect

> **EXAMPLE: Emergency By-laws**
> The Emergency By-laws provided in this Article shall be operative during any emergency in the conduct of the business of the Corporation resulting from a catastrophic event, notwithstanding any different provision in the preceding Articles of the By-laws or in the Articles of Incorporation of the Corporation or in the Business Corporation Act. To the extent not inconsistent with the provisions of this Article, the By-laws provided in the preceding Articles shall remain in effect during such emergency and upon its termination the Emergency By-laws shall cease to be operative.
> During any such emergency:
> (a) A meeting of the Board of Directors may be called by any officer or Director of the Corporation. Notice of the time and place of the meeting shall be given by the person calling the meeting to such of the Directors as it may be feasible to reach by any available means of communication. Such notice shall be given at such time in advance of the meeting as circumstances permit in the judgment of the person calling the meeting.
> (b) At any such meeting of the Board of Directors, a quorum shall consist of [*here insert the particular provision desired*].
> (c) The Board of Directors, either before or during any such emergency, may provide, and from time to time modify, lines of succession in the event that during such an emergency any or all officers or agents of the Corporation shall for any reason be rendered incapable of discharging their duties.
> (d) The Board of Directors, either before or during any such emergency, may, effective in the emergency, change the head office or designate several alternative head offices or regional offices, or authorize the officers so to do.
>
> No officer, Director or employee acting in accordance with these Emergency By-laws, shall be liable except for willful misconduct.
> These Emergency By-laws shall be subject to repeal or change by further action of the Board of Directors or by action of the shareholders, but no such repeal or change shall modify the provisions of the next preceding paragraph with regard to action taken prior to the time of such repeal or change. Any amendment of these Emergency By-laws may make any further or different provision that may be practical and necessary for the circumstances of the emergency.

12. Provisions for amending, altering, or repealing the by-laws or adopting new by-laws

> **EXAMPLE: Amendment**
> These By-laws may be altered, amended or repealed and new By-laws may be adopted by the Board of Directors at any regular or special meeting of the Board of Directors.

Sample by-laws for a Delaware corporation appear as Form 6Q in Appendix G.

NOTES

1. The advice must consider the particular needs of the business, including ownership rights, management responsibilities, duration, need for capital, potential liability, and taxation. If a corporation is selected as the appropriate business form, certain special information must be obtained from the organizers. A preincorporation checklist appears as Form 6A in Appendix G.
2. An example of a preincorporation agreement between promoters appears as Form 6B in Appendix G.
3. E.g., Pennsylvania, 15 Pa.Stat. §§ 1201 and 1204(8).
4. Several states require $1,000 minimum paid-in capital [e.g., Texas, Tex.Bus.Corp.Act. Ann. § 3.02(7)]. A few states require that if an initial amount of capital is desired, it must be stated in the Articles of incorporation (e.g., Ohio, Ohio Rev.Code § 1701.04). A certificate of payment of capital stock is Form 6C in Appendix G.
5. West's Modern Legal Forms § 2452.
6. West's Modern Legal Forms § 2455.
7. E.g., New York, three months, McKinney Consol.Laws of N.Y.Bus.Corp. Law § 503; and Louisiana, one year, La.Rev.Stat.Ann. § 12:71.
8. E.g., New Jersey, six months or sixty days after filing certificate of incorporation, N.J.Stat.Ann. § 14A:7-3.
9. See M.B.C.A. § 6.20.
10. 15 Pa.Stat. § 1207.
11. Oklahoma, Okla.Stat.Ann. tit. 18§ 1.31.
12. West's Modern Legal Forms § 2468.
13. M.B.C.A. § 6.20(d).
14. West's Modern Legal Forms § 2471.
15. See Chapter 12.
16. For example, it may be particularly important for management to be able to declare dividends out of current profits even though the corporation has no "earned surplus." This would be permitted in Delaware, 8 Del.Code Ann. § 170, but would not be permitted in Colorado, Colo.Rev.Stat. 1973 § 7-5-110.
17. M.B.C.A. § 4.01.
18. See 1 Prentice-Hall, Corporation Reporter, Corporation Checklists ¶ 9002, subparagraph 14 under each state.
19. See, e.g., M.B.C.A. § 4.01(b). Some jurisdictions, and the Model Business Corporation Act, allow the use of a similar corporate name, provided the written consent of the holder of the name is obtained, and a distinguishing word is added to the name.
20. Many states use a thirty-day period for reservation of corporate names [e.g., Maryland, Md.Ann.Code art. 23 § 6; and Massachusetts, Mass.Gen. Laws Ann. c. 155 § 9(a)].
21. M.B.C.A. § 4.02.
22. An application for reserved name, a certificate of reserved name, a notice of transfer of reserved name, and a certificate of transfer of reserved name are forms 6E, 6F, 6G, and 6H, respectively, in Appendix G.
23. M.B.C.A. § 4.03. Examples of an application for registration, a certificate of registration, an application for renewal, and a certificate of renewal appear as Forms 6I, 6J, 6K, and 6L, respectively, in Appendix G.
24. See Chapter 12 on the qualification of foreign corporations.
25. E.g., Colorado, Colo.Rev.Stat. § 7-71-101.
26. A statement of assumed name is Form 6M in Appendix G.
27. The Model Business Corporation Act and most jurisdictions use the term *articles of incorporation*. M.B.C.A. §§1.40(1) and 2.02.
28. See "Amendment of the Articles of Incorporation" in Chapter 13.
29. M.B.C.A. § 2.02.
30. See "Statutory Powers of a Corporation" in Chapter 4.
31. Examples of articles of incorporation appear as Forms 6O and 6P in Appendix G.
32. See "Selection and Reservation of Corporate Name" earlier in this chapter.
33. The details and flexibility of the corporate financial structure are discussed more fully in Chapter 7.
34. This summary paraphrases the requirements of M.B.C.A. § 6.01, except that the act does not require any statement concerning par value of shares. Most states still require this designation for shares.
35. M.B.C.A. § 6.01(b).

FORMATION OF A CORPORATION **151**

36. M.B.C.A. § 6.01(c).
37. West's Modern Legal Forms § 2752.
38. West's Modern Legal Forms §2755.1.
39. See Chapter 7.
40. See "Par Value or No Par Value" and "Consideration for Shares" in Chapter 7.
41. M.B.C.A. § 6.21 permits shares to be issued at a price set by the board of directors, and the price set would be entirely at the directors' discretion if par value were not required in the articles of incorporation. See M.B.C.A. § 2.02.
42. E.g., Alabama places a value of $50 on each no par share for computation of the initial taxes. In this state, a corporation could authorize fifty times as many $1 par value shares as no par shares for the same tax.
43. See "Sources of Funds for Distribution" in Chapter 9.
44. See "Preferred Stock Rights" in Chapter 7 and "Share Transfer Restrictions and Buy-out Agreements" in Chapter 11.
45. See M.B.C.A. § 14.20 and "Involuntary Dissolution" in Chapter 13.
46. See "Ownership and Management of a Corporation" in Chapter 4.
47. M.B.C.A. § 2.02(b)(1).
48. West's Modern LegalForms § 2711.
49. See "Ownership and Management of a Corporation" in Chapter 4.
50. See "Voluntary Dissolution" and "Involuntary Dissolution" in Chapter 13.
51. West's Modern Legal Forms § 2562.
52. West's Modern Legal Forms § 2613.
53. M.B.C.A. § 3.04.
54. E.g., New York, McKinney Consol.Laws of N.Y.Bus.Corp.Law § 622.
55. E.g., Delaware, 8 Del.Code Ann. § 102(b)(3).
56. West's Modern Legal Forms § 2735.
57. West's Modern Legal Forms § 2736.
58. Treasury shares are defined in most corporation statutes. On preemptive rights and treasury shares, see clause 9 in the Delaware articles of incorporation, Form 60 in Appendix G.
59. See "Ownership and Management of a Corporation" in Chapter 4 and "Shareholder Business and Vote Required" in Chapter 8.
60. West's Modern Legal Forms § 2712.
61. M.B.C.A. §2.02(b)(3).
62. See "Amendment of the Articles of Incorporation" in Chapter 13.
63. M.B.C.A. § 8.01.
64. M.B.C.A. §8.11.
65. M.B.C.A. § 7.28.
66. M.B.C.A. §8.04.
67. M.B.C.A. §8.06.
68. M.B.C.A. § 8.08.
69. M.B.C.A. § 8.10.
70. E.g., California, West's Ann.Calif.Corp.Code § 317.
71. M.B.C.A. § 6.31.
72. M.B.C.A. § 8.24.
73. West's Modern Legal Forms § 2803.
74. M.B.C.A. § 8.21.
75. M.B.C.A. § 10.20.
76. M.B.C.A. § 10.21.
77. M.B.C.A. § 6.40, and see "Sources of Funds for Distribution" and "Cash and Property Dividends" in Chapter 9.
78. See, e.g., Delaware, 8 Del.Code. Ann. § 170.
79. See, e.g., Delaware, 8 Del.Code. Ann. § 170(b).
80. West's Modern Legal Forms § 2719.1.
81. See "Ownership and Management of a Corporation" in Chapter 4.
82. West's Modern Legal Forms § 2802.
83. M.B.C.A. § 8.02.
84. M.B.C.A. § 55.
85. E.g., Delaware,8 Del.Code Ann. § 103(c)(5).
86. McKinney Consol.Laws of N.Y.Bus.Corp.Law § 402(a).
87. E.g.,Arizona, Ariz.Rev.Stat. § 10–055.

88. Alabama, Ala.Bus.Corp.Act § 65.
89. E.g., Pennsylvania, 15 Pa.Stat. § 205.
90. The myriad variations of filing requirements may be easily reviewed by consulting 1 Prentice-Hall, Corporation Reporter, Corporation Checklists, ¶ 9002 *et seq.*
91. E.g., Nevada, Nev. Stat. § 78.050.
92. M.B.C.A. § 2.03.
93. M.B.C.A. § 2.05.
94. E.g., New York, McKinney Consol.Laws of N.Y.Bus.Corp.Law § 404.
95. Checklists and a full discussion of organizational meetings are contained in Chapter 8.
96. See M.B.C.A. § 2.02(b)(3).
97. Some state statutes prescribe certain specific matters that must be contained in the by-laws. E.g., California, West's Ann.Calif.Corp. Code § 212.
98. See M.B.C.A. § 2.06.
99. E.g., Nebraska, Neb.Rev.Stat. § 21–2026.
100. M.B.C.A. § 205.
101. E.g., Kentucky, Ky.Rev.Stat.Ann. § 271A.145.
102. See "Shareholder Meetings" in Chapter 8.
103. See "Ownership and Management of a Corporation" in Chapter 4.
104. West's Modern Legal Forms § 2802. The Model Business Corporation Act requires that a classification provision appear in the articles of incorporation, and a by-law provision would be ineffective. See M.B.C.A. § 2.01 and "Filing and Other Formalities" earlier in this chapter. However, several states permit classification of the board of directors to be accomplished in the by-laws. E.g., New York, McKinney Consol. Laws of N.Y.Bus.Corp.Law § 704; Pennsylvania, 15 Pa.Stat. § 403.
105. See "Directors' Regular and Special Meetings" in Chapter 8.
106. West's Modern Legal Forms § 2803.
107. See "Taxation of a Corporation" in Chapter 4.
108. West's Modern Legal Forms § 2720.
109. See M.B.C.A. § 2.15.
110. See "Ownership and Management of a Corporation" in Chapter 4.
111. West's Modern Legal Forms § 2718.
112. See "Certificate for Shares" earlier in this chapter and "Share Transfer Restrictions and Buy-out Agreements" in Chapter 11.
113. West's Modern Legal Forms § 2806.01.
114. See "Cash and Property Dividends" and "Share Dividends" in Chapter 9.

7 CORPORATE FINANCIAL STRUCTURE

GENERALLY

Corporate capital is obtained principally from investors, creditors, and shareholders, who exchange money, property, or services for securities issued by the corporation. The attractiveness of shares as an investment is an important advantage to the corporate form of business enterprise. In addition to corporate equity securities, or shares, a corporation may contract for many varied types of debt financing, transactions whereby the corporation borrows money from outsiders who are willing to lend funds to the corporation. Unlike shareholders, these creditors are not owners of the company, but their loans are generally considered to be a more conservative investment. The corporation is obligated to repay a loan from a debt investor, but there is no obligation to repay the funds invested by shareholders, who risk the loss of some or all of their funds.

The corporate financial structure has great flexibility, and corporate securities may have any number of various features that increase the quality and attractiveness of the investment. The capitalization may be limited only to common stock, or may be some combination of equity securities, including separate classes and series, and debt securities.

TYPES OF CORPORATE SECURITIES

The term *securities* has a special meaning in the law. It generally refers to a contractual-proprietary obligation that exists between a business enterprise and an investor. For purposes of the federal and state securities acts, the term may include any one of several different forms of investment obligations. In the corporate sense, securities fall into two classes:

1. *Debt securities,* which evidence a corporate obligation to repay money borrowed from a creditor and are also typically called *bonds*
2. *Equity securities,* which evidence a shareholder's ownership interest in the corporation and are usually referred to as *shares*

When a corporation borrows money, it executes a document or bond that represents the obligation of the corporation to repay the borrowed funds. Bonds may be unsecured or secured for payment with property of the corporation. An unsecured obligation, the corporate equivalent of a personal signature loan, is called a *debenture*. Secured bonds may be called *mortgage bonds*.

Bonds always state a principal amount owed by the corporation, a date when repayment of the principal amount is due, and a provision for interest, which is usually paid periodically. Debt securities may be marketed at a higher price than the principal amount if the attractiveness of the investment creates a demand, in which case it is said that they are sold at *a premium*, or if the investment is not all that attractive, at a lower price than the principal amount, in which case they are sold at a *discount*. Debt securities usually do not have voting rights in the corporate affairs. Instead, they represent a loan obligation in the strict business sense and the holders are merely creditors. As a practical matter, debt securities are often issued under an agreement executed by the corporation, the outside lender, and a trustee who is usually a financial institution. The agreement is called an *indenture*, and it includes the terms of the obligation, the rights of the security holders and the trustee, and any conditions upon which the bonds are issued. Debt securities issued by large corporations are freely sold on an open market, and the price of a bond depends upon the quality of the investment. Bonds frequently have several advantageous features that make them a very desirable investment, such as a high interest rate, a provision allowing conversion into common shares at a specified price, and redemption features.

Equity securities are distinguished from debt securities by the relationship between the investor and the corporation. A purchaser of equity securities, a shareholder, becomes a part owner of the corporation. The proportion that the shareholder's shares bear to the total number of shares outstanding represents the shareholder's fractional ownership interest. When shares are issued, the corporation, instead of creating a liability, creates a capital account, which represents the equity of the corporation. Unlike a debt security, the corporation is under no obligation to repay a shareholder, and the return of the investment is usually strictly dependent upon the shareholder's ability to sell his or her shares to another investor. The income paid on equity securities is usually a distribution of the profit of the corporation and is called a *dividend*. The frequency and amount of these distributions are determined within the discretion of the board of directors. An equity investment is attractive if it appears that the corporation's business will expand and be profitable, thereby increasing the value of the equity security and likely resulting in dividend distributions to the shareholders. Shareholders usually have the right to vote, and they also have the right to a proportionate distribution of corporate assets upon dissolution of the corporation.

Imaginative entrepreneurs have developed all sorts of variations on these two basic types of corporate securities, and most state corporation statutes encourage inspired financial configurations by imposing very few restrictions upon the corporate financial structure. However, since some unscrupulous entrepreneurs have duped investors with worthless securities, it should be noted that the issuance and sale of corporate securities is strictly regulated by federal and state securities laws. Any public sale of corporate shares or bonds is subject to the disclosure requirements of the Securities Act of 1933[1] or the applicable state blue-sky laws. These acts and the Securities Exchange Act of 1934[2] are generally designed to fully inform a potential investor of the character and quality of the investment, and to avoid untrue statements of fact and misleading omissions about the security, which may affect a decision to purchase or sell. The detailed requirements of the securities acts are beyond the scope of this work, but counsel should explore their provisions and should examine helpful research sources[3] before advising the corporate client to sell any securities.

EQUITY SECURITIES

Equitiy securities grant the shareholder a three-pronged ownership interest in the corporation. A shareholder is entitled to a proportionate share of earnings, distributed as dividends at the discretion of the board of directors; a proportionate share of assets in corporate dissolution; and a vote on all shareholder matters, which gives indirect control over management activities. Ignoring special classes of equity securities for a moment, a common stock shareholder is entitled to share in the earnings and assets of the corporation in the proportion of the number of shares owned compared against the total number of shares outstanding. Each common shareholder is also entitled to one vote for each share. Every corporate statute authorizes the issuance of a certain number of shares, and the division of those shares into classes, allowing preferences, limitations, and other special rights as specified in the articles of incorporation. The Model Business Corporation Act grants this general authority in Section 6.01.

STAGES OF EQUITY SECURITIES

The articles of incorporation must state the number of shares the corporation will have the authority to issue.[4] This number will be determined by the incorporators and counsel, considering the anticipated capital requirements of the corporation. Having established the authority, the corporation may issue up to the specified number of shares without any requirement for an amendment to the articles of incorporation. Thus, the first step in the issuance of corporate equity securities is the creation of the authority to issue them by describing the characteristics of the securities and specifying the number of shares in the articles of incorporation. The shares described in the articles of incorporation are the *authorized shares* of the corporation.

It is not necessary to issue all of the authorized shares of the corporation, and it is sometimes undesirable to do so. Of course, it will be necessary to issue the number of shares required for the minimum paid-in capital, if that is a requirement under the applicable state statute,[5] and to issue enough shares for sufficient capital to commence business even if no minimum capital requirements exist. Other authorized shares should be saved to allow for additional capital financing in future corporate operations. Shares that have been authorized and sold are issued to the holders, and are then described as *issued and outstanding shares*. Thus, a shareholder holds authorized, issued, and outstanding shares of the company.

Shares that have been sold to investors may be reacquired by the corporation by one of several methods. The shareholder could donate or resell them to the company, or the corporation may, if so authorized in the articles of incorporation, redeem the shares or convert them to other shares. When shares are reacquired by the corporation, they are called *treasury shares*.[6] Treasury shares are authorized and issued, but not "outstanding," since they are held by the corporation and not by investors.

The issuance and sale of shares is initiated by the decision of the board of directors to obtain additional capital for the corporation. The board of directors may not issue more shares than have been authorized in the articles of incorporation. It must also observe the present shareholders' preemptive rights, if they exist, by offering newly issued shares to existing shareholders in their respective proportions of share ownership before selling the shares to other investors.[7]

The distinction between the stages of equity securities is important for several reasons. For equity securities to be fully active (including entitlement to vote, receipt of a proportionate share of earnings, and receipt of a proportionate share of assets upon dissolution), shares must be authorized, issued, and outstanding. Treasury shares are usually not counted for determining a quorum and are not entitled to a vote.[8] They also may not be entitled to any dividend distributions.[9]

Another distinguishing feature involves the consideration for shares. If shares are authorized and are being issued and sold, they usually must be sold for an amount no less than the par value if they have par value, or for the stated value if they are no par value shares. Thus, if shares bear a $10 par value, the corporation may not sell them for less than $10 per share. If the corporation should sell shares for less than that amount, the consideration is inadequate and the shares become *watered* or *discount shares*. Shareholders who purchase watered shares can be assessed for the full amount of unpaid consideration. On the other hand, shares that have been authorized, issued, and outstanding and have been reacquired and held by the corporation as treasury shares may be sold again for any consideration fixed by the board of directors, whether or not the consideration is equal to or less than par value.

PAR VALUE OR NO PAR VALUE

Most jurisdictions still require a statement in the articles of incorporation indicating whether shares are to be issued for a stated par value or for no par value. The Model Business Corporation Act has recently taken the modern position first propounded by California that it is not necessary to state whether shares have a par value or not.[10] The corporation always has a choice between no par or par value shares, except in Nebraska, where all shares must have a par value.[11] The distinction between these provisions relates to the value required to be given for the purchase of shares and to the rates of capital franchise fees that must be paid in some states upon incorporation. In addition, shares with no par value permit greater flexibility in allocating the amount received in exchange for the shares to certain surplus accounts in the corporate books.

Shares with a par value may be issued only for such consideration expressed in dollars, not less than the par value, as may be fixed from time to time by the board of directors. This provision is common in most state statutes. It means that shares with a $10 par value may be issued for $20 if someone is willing to pay that amount, but in no case may they be issued for less than $10. A handful of states make exceptions to this rule if the board of directors can justify the reason for selling below par value.

Shares without par value may be issued for whatever consideration may be fixed from time to time by the board of directors,[12] although many states provide that the articles of incorporation may reserve the right to fix the consideration for no par value shares to the shareholders.[13] A few jurisdictions reverse this authority—they grant it to the shareholders unless it is reserved to the directors in the articles of incorporation. Thus, shares without par value may be issued for any amount set by the board of directors or shareholders in their good judgment. The only limitation on this authority to fix the amount of no par shares is that the shares must be issued for approximately the same amount of consideration at approximately the same time.

Major variations in prices of no par shares within a short time period raise a question of breach of the director's duty of due care in dealing with shareholders. For example, suppose a corporation intended to sell no par value shares to three investors: Burn, Bush, and Bradford. In private discussions with the three investors, it was determined that Burn and Bush would pay approximately $10 per share, but Bradford could be persuaded to pay $15 per share. If 100 shares were simultaneously issued to each investor at those prices, Bradford would have immediate grounds for complaint. Bradford's shares were immediately "diluted" with the sales to the other two investors because the board of directors effectively reduced the stated value by $5 per share. However, if Burn and Bush purchased their shares in January, and Bradford's purchase at $15 per share occurred in September, it may be said that the shares increased in value enough to warrant the increase in price. The dilution problem results when no par value shares are sold at substantially lower prices at about the same time as other no par shares, so as to undercut the contribution of an investor. Notwithstanding the foregoing, if the board of directors can establish that the varying prices were set for a good business reason, they will be permitted to rapidly adjust the prices on shares without par value.

The par value–no par value distinctions have other ramifications in states that exact annual franchise fees based upon the aggregate authorized capital of the corporation. In some states, the franchise fee is computed upon the amount stated in the articles of incorporation as the total aggregate value of authorized shares. To compute this fee, shares without par value are assigned an arbitrary value. For example, if an arbitrary value of $1 per share were placed on each no par share to compute the franchise fee for a state, the franchise fee would be the same for a corporation authorized to issue 10,000 shares at $5 par value as it would be for a corporation authorized to issue 50,000 shares at no par value in that state. States that discourage the use of no par shares impose a high statutory valuation on those shares to compute the fee. It then becomes more advantageous to set a lower par value and to authorize more shares.[14]

Certain accounting classifications also depend upon the distinction between par value and no par value shares. In some cases it may be desirable to create a capital surplus account for the corporation in the early stages of corporate existence—assuming, for example, that the incorporators predict the desirability of repurchasing some of the shares issued by the corporation. Many statutes, and formerly the Model Business Corporation Act, permit the corporation to repurchase its own shares only if it has a surplus account from which it may make the purchase.[15]

The creation of a surplus account occurs in different ways. The typical surplus accounts are *earned surplus* and *capital surplus*. Earned surplus is created when the corporation accumulates profits from operations. Capital surplus is an account created for surplus funds received from the sale of stock. If the corporation issues $10 par value stock for $30 per share, $10 must be placed in stated capital, and $20 may be placed in capital surplus. Any consideration in excess of par value may be placed in capital surplus, and with no par stock, any part of the consideration may be placed in capital surplus.[16]

If there is a need for a surplus account in the early stages of the corporate operations, the par value or no par value characteristic of the stock is important. These principles may be illustrated as follows. If the corporation has issued shares with $10 par value, and those shares are sold for exactly $10 each, that amount of money must be placed in an account called *stated capital*. In that event there would be no capital surplus, and if the corporation has not yet earned profits to hold as retained earnings, there would be no earned surplus. In such a case, the corporation would not be able to repurchase its own shares, since there is no surplus account. On the other hand, if the corporation had sold shares with no par value for $10 a share, it would be possible to divert any portion of that consideration to a capital surplus account. The board of directors may, usually within sixty days after no par shares have been issued, allocate a portion of the consideration to capital surplus. For example, capital surplus could receive $9 per share and stated capital would receive the other $1 per share. The corporation could then use the amount of capital surplus to repurchase its own shares, provided the articles of incorporation authorize the use of capital surplus for this purpose.

Dividends and other distributions to shareholders are subject to similar rules. Most states limit the payment of distributions to funds available from earned surplus, with a few exceptions. The corporation is permitted to distribute cash or property to its shareholders out of capital surplus under certain circumstances.[17] If management intends to make a distribution to shareholders before there is sufficient earned surplus to declare a dividend, the creation of a capital surplus account is essential. No par stock will assure the ability of the board of directors to create the account immediately upon issuance of the first shares.

CERTIFICATES FOR SHARES

The shares of the corporation are generally represented by certificates, examples of which appear in Appendix G. Recently, the Model Business Corporation Act was amended to permit uncertificated shares. This amendment, together with amendments to the Uniform Commercial Code, permit a corporation to provide by resolution that some or all of the classes and series of shares shall be *uncertificated*, which means that the ownership of the shares is recorded in the corporate records, but the shares are not represented by a certificate, which is generally regarded to be negotiable. The rights and obligations of the holders of uncertificated shares and the rights and obligations of the holders of certificates representing shares of the same class and series are identical under corporate law. The only purpose of the uncertificated provision is to avoid the paper crunch anticipated as more and more corporations issue certificates for shares and those certificates are rapidly traded on over-the-counter and national stock exchanges. The new system is intended to simplify the transfer of ownership in a corporation by not requiring the transfer of a piece of negotiable paper as part of that transaction. It is also intended to guard against the loss or theft of the negotiable piece of paper (the certificate) representing ownership in the corporation.

When certificates are used, all states prescribe the content of the certificate representing shares, and the requirements of the Model Business Corporation Act are typical:

Each share certificate (1) must be signed (either manually or in facsimile) by two officers designated in the bylaws or by the board of directors and (2) may bear the corporate seal or its facsimile.[18]

The statute further provides that the signature of any person who was an officer and ceased to be such before the certificate is issued will have the same effect as if that person were still an officer as of the date of the issuance.[19] Each certificate representing shares must state upon its face

1. the name of the corporation and that the corporation is organized under the laws of the particular state;
2. the name of the person to whom the shares are issued; and
3. the number and class of shares and the designation of the series, if any, represented by such certificate.

The major variations among the state statutes with respect to requirements for share certificates are what officers are required to sign the certificates; the circumstances under which facsimile signatures may be used; the need for a corporate seal; and whether the certificate must state that the shares are fully paid. In all states, if the shares have a par value, the amount of the par value must be stated on the certificate.

A corporation may choose to issue shares in various classes or in series, and in such a case each certificate must describe the particular elements of each class or series. Section 6.25 of the Model Business Corporation Act requires that every share certificate of a corporation authorized to issue shares of more than one class shall set forth (or state conspicuously that the corporation will furnish to any shareholder upon request and without charge) a full statement of the designations, preferences, limitations, and relative rights of the shares of each class authorized to be issued. Further, if the corporation is authorized to issue preferred or special classes in series, the variations between the shares so far as they have been determined and the authority of the board of directors to fix the relative rights of the shares must be stated on the certificate. The classes and series of shares are explored in detail in the next section of this chapter.

If the corporation is authorized to issue only one class of stock, therefore, its share certificates need contain only the bare statutory requirements. If the corporation has adopted a complex financial structure, including classes of common stock, preferred stock, or special classes and series of either, the certificate is more complex. The certificate may describe in detail the relative variations of each class of securities, or, as is more common, it may merely state that the corporation will furnish a full statement of these variations to any shareholder of the corporation upon request and without charge. Such a statement should also describe the authority of the board of directors to determine the rights and preferences of each class and series of shares. If the latter procedure is used, it is not necessary to amend or otherwise modify the certificates representing shares whenever the corporate financial structure is changed.

CLASSIFICATIONS OF SHARES

The articles of incorporation may authorize the issuance of only one class of shares (i.e., common stock), in which case the shareholders of the common stock are entitled to all of the voting rights, all of the dividends, and all of the net assets in a dissolution distribution. However, the corporate financial structure may be more complicated.

Classes of Shares

The equity securities of the corporation may be divided into several classes of shares. Common stock is the basic class, and additional classes may be authorized to grant certain shareholders a preferred right to dividends or a preferred right to assets in case of corporate dissolution. Various classes of securities may also have different voting rights, such as no vote, or two votes per share, or any other formula. When more than one class is to be authorized, the articles of incorporation must set forth the designations, preferences, limitations, and relative rights of each class.

> **EXAMPLE: Classes of Stock**
> The total number of shares of all classes of stock which the Corporation shall have authority to issue is 500,000, of which 100,000 shares shall be Class A common stock without par value and 400,000 shares shall be Class B common stock without par value. There shall be no distinction between the two classes, except that the holders of the Class B common stock shall have no voting power for any purpose whatsoever and the holders of the Class A common stock shall, to the exclusion of the holders of the Class B common stock, have full voting power for all purposes.

As mentioned in the preceding section, the share certificate must also contain this information, or contain conspicuous statement that the corporation will provide the information without charge to any shareholder requesting it.

It may be helpful to pause and consider the circumstances under which the authority to issue preferred shares will be used. The general principle to be observed is that certain investors may insist upon a superior ownership position in the corporation, and, to obtain necessary financing, it may be necessary to *prefer* those investors over others. For example, suppose Phil Hopkins and Terrence Conner plan to form a corporation for the operation of a restaurant. Hopkins intends to run the business and to invest his available personal capital of $25,000, and Conner is capable of investing $100,000. Assume further that no other shareholders are contemplated at this point. Conner may be willing to take a greater proportion of common stock for his $100,000 investment, but that will give him 80% of the common stock to Hopkins' 20%. Conner clearly would have shareholder control in such a case, and Hopkins' may be thereby hampered in his efforts to run the business. Hopkins will be aware of Conner's potential control, and may object to this posture.

It is possible, however, to issue each investor $25,000 in common stock (with voting rights) and to issue nonvoting preferred shares, with dividend and liquidation preferences, to Conner for his $75,000 excess investment. With this arrangement, Conner and Hopkins have equal voting rights and an equal investment in the basic equity of the corporation. Conner's excess investment is protected by his preferred status, ensuring that Conner will receive the first distributions of profit through his dividend preference, and the first distribution of assets in dissolution through the liquidation preference. Thereafter, Conner and Hopkins share equally, just as though each had invested only $25,000.

Similar problems arise when a third investor is considered. Suppose Craig Carver has offered to invest $50,000, but has no expertise in the restaurant business, and no interest in management and control. However, Carver is concerned about two things: a high return on his investment and a right to assert a vote if the business is being managed improperly. A separate class of securities can be created for Carver's investment. He may receive first dividend preference, even over Conner's preferred status, and his preference may be at a higher rate and cumulative to ensure an accumulated high return on his investment every year. His securities would have no voting rights until the happening of a contingent event, such as when the gross receipts from the business drop below a certain amount for several consecutive months.

The possibilities for variations in preferred shares are endless, and each class can be structured to fit the peculiar needs of each class of investors.

The statutory authority for issuance of shares in classes usually specifies the manner in which those shares may differ from common shares. For example, Section 6.01 of the Model Business Corporation Act provides that a corporation may issue shares of preferred or special classes that

1. have special, conditional, or limited voting rights, or no right to vote, except to the extent provided by the statute;
2. are redeemable or convertible as specified in the articles of incorporation at the option of either the shareholder, the corporation, or other persons, or on the occurrence of a designated event; for cash, indebtedness, securities, or other property; in a designated amount or in any amount determined in accordance with a designated formula or by reference to other events;
3. entitle the holders to distributions calculated in any manner, including dividends that may be cumulative, noncumulative, or partially cumulative; and
4. have preference over any other class of shares with respect to distributions, including dividends and distributions upon the dissolution of the corporation.

These variations among the shares are not considered to be exhaustive; the Model Business Corporation Act permits additional variations, so long as they do not conflict with other statutory rules.[20] In any case, one or more classes of shares, together, must have unlimited voting rights, and one or more classes of shares, together, must be entitled to receive the net assets of the corporation upon dissolution. These rules are designed to require that someone will also be entitled to exercise the shareholders' voting rights (even if that entitlement shifts among classes from time to time or on certain events) and that someone will be entitled to receive the assets of the corporation if the corporation is dissolved and liquidated.[21] However, the articles of incorporation may limit or deny the voting rights or provide special voting rights for certain classes under the authority of Section 7.21. The individual variations in these rights are explored in detail in "Preferred Stock Rights" later in this chapter.

Shares in Series

The articles of incorporation may authorize the division and issuance of any class of shares in series.[22] The principle behind series shares is a refinement of the theory behind preferred shares. As previously discussed, classes of preferred shares are created to meet the particular needs and demands of certain investors. Series shares do the same thing. However, recall that all authority to issue shares eminates from the articles of incorporation. Thus, for a special class of shares to be issued, the articles of incorporation must authorize that class and define its designations, preferences, limitations, and relative rights. If the articles of incorporation do not specifically authorize the issuance of a particular class of shares, the articles must be amended to grant this authority, and an amendment requires a board of directors' resolution, the approval of the shareholders, and the appropriate filing with the secretary of state.[23] The corporate officals attempting to raise capital may thus be hindered by a cumbersome, time-consuming amendment procedure in tailoring the corporate securities to the requirements of potential investors. This procedure may be particularly frustrating when prompt action is essential, such as when the corporation is negotiating to acquire desirable property in exchange for its preferred shares.

Series shares are designed to avoid this problem. The board of directors may be authorized (by the articles of incorporation) to fix the terms of a series of preferred shares, without requiring a formal amendment to the articles or shareholder approval. This broad authority to vary the terms of the stock is the source of the common name, blank stock, for series shares. With this authority, the Model Business Corporation Act permits directors to issue shares that vary from other shares of the same class so long as the board of directors determines the preferences, limitations, and relative rights before the issuance of any shares of that class. The board of directors may thus set any rights for any series of shares within the boundaries of the various rights provided by the statute.[24]

Most states permit the creation of series shares, but are more specific than the Model Business Corporation Act in identifying the types of rights that may be varied among the series. In most states, the series shares may differ in the following particulars: (1) the rate of dividend; (2) the price at and the terms and conditions upon which shares may be redeemed; (3) the amount payable upon shares in the event of voluntary or involuntary liquidation; (4) sinking fund provisions, if any, for the redemption or purchase of shares; (5) the terms and conditions upon which shares may be converted. (6) voting rights. In all other respects, the shares of the series must be the same as other shares of the same class.

The scope of the directors' authority to establish series shares is defined by the articles of incorporation. The articles could state that the board of directors has full authority to divide classes of shares into series and to determine the variations in the relative rights.

> **EXAMPLE: Shares in Series**
> The preferred stock of the Corporation shall be issued in one or more series as may be determined from time to time by the board of Directors. In establishing a series the Board of Directors shall give to it a distinctive designation so as to distinguish it from the shares of all other series and classes, shall fix the number of shares in such series, and the preferences, rights and restrictions thereof. All shares of any one series shall be alike in every particular. All series shall be alike except that there may be variation as to the following: (1) the rate of dividend, (2) the price at and the terms and conditions on which shares shall be redeemed, (3) the amount payable upon shares in the event of involuntary liquidation, (4) the amount payable upon shares in the event of voluntary liquidation, (5) sinking fund provisions for the redemption of shares, and (6) the terms and conditions on which shares may be converted if the shares of any series are issued with the privilege of conversion.[25]

The articles could also limit the authority to vary series shares to certain characteristics, such as conversion privileges or dividend preferences.

The procedure for establishing a series is considerably less formal than that for establishing a formal amendment to the articles of incorporation. The directors adopt a resolution stating the designation of the series and fixing the rights of the series shares. A statement, which the Model Act refers to as the articles of amendment, is filed with the secretary of state. This statement is effective without shareholder action. It quotes the resolution and acknowledges that the resolution was adopted by the board of directors on a certain date. In some states, franchise taxes and fees will be due upon the establishment of the series shares. The resolution, as filed, must contain the following information:

1. The name of the corporation
2. The text of the resolution determining the terms of the class or series of shares
3. The date the resolution was adopted
4. A statement that the amendment was duly adopted by the board of directors[26]

FRACTIONS OF SHARES OR SCRIP

In some cases the corporation may need to issue fractions of shares of stock, and the authority for the issuance of a fractional share must come from the appropriate state statute. For example, fractional shares may be required when a corporation has declared a stock dividend entitling the holders of 100 shares of stock to receive one additional share as a dividend. In that case, the holder of 150 shares of stock would be entitled to one and one-half shares. If the state statute permits fractional shares, the corporation may issue a certificate for one-half share. Alternatively, many statutes authorize the issuance of scrip, in lieu of fractional shares. *Scrip* is a separate certificate representing a percentage of a full share. It entitles a shareholder to receive a certificate for one full share when the shareholder has accumulated scrip aggregating a full share.

The Model Business Corporation Act provides that a corporation may, but is not obligated to, issue a certificate for fractional share, or it may issue scrip in lieu thereof. Its other alternatives are to arrange for the disposition of fractional interests, as by finding two shareholders who are each entitled to one-half share and arranging for a sale from one to the other so a whole share will be issued, or to pay the shareholder cash equal to the fair value of the fractional interest.[27] If a certificate for a fractional share is issued, the holder is entitled to exercise a fractional voting right, to receive a fractional share of dividends, and to participate accordingly in the corporate assets in the event of liquidation.[28] Unless otherwise provided by the board of directors, a holder of scrip is not usually entitled to these rights. The board of directors may further provide that the scrip will become void if not exchanged for full certificates before a specified date.

State statues take divergent positions with respect to fractional shares and scrip, and the individual statutes should be consulted. Most states authorize one or more of the options specified in the Model Business Corporation Act.

CONSIDERATION FOR SHARES

As previously indicated, the consideration required for shares depends in part upon whether the shares have a par value or are without par value.[29] Shares with a par value usually may be issued for no less than the par value, and shares with no par value receive a stated value as fixed from time to time by the board of directors or the shareholders, as provided by statute and the articles of incorporation. Thus, in the quantitative sense, the consideration given in exchange for shares must at least equal the par value or the stated value for no par shares, whichever the case may be.

When the consideration for shares is cash, the quantity valuation is obvious. When property is transferred or services are performed in exchange for shares, the law has developed at least three rules for appraising the consideration. The first rule, the *true value rule,* requires that the property or services have, at the time of the issuance of shares, an actual value that is no less than par value or no less than the stated value for no par shares. This means that the property or services must be appraised and the actual value compared with the minimum requirements for the particular type of stock. Most jursidictions follow the second rule, the *absence of fraud rule,* which requires that the property or services be evaluated and deemed adequate by the board of directors, who must determine in good faith that the consideration received has a value at least equal to the minimum requirements and whose determination of value will be conclusive in the absence of fraud. The third, and most flexible, rule is contained in the new Model Business Corporation Act, and simply provides that "the board of directors must determine that the consideration received or to be received for shares to be issued is adequate."[30] The determination by the board of directors will be conclusive in determining the adequacy of the consideration. These rules are used to determine whether the consideration received for shares is legally adequate in quantity. When the second or third rule is used, the board of directors, in determining the value of the offered consideration, should go on record with their evaluation.

Statutes also dictate which types of consideration may be given in exchange for stock. This is a question of the quality of the consideration. Most states still limit the permissible consideration to money; other property, tangible or intangible; or labor or services actually performed for the corporation.[31] A handful of state statutes permit promissory notes to be given in exchange for shares,[32] and future services are rarely included as proper consideration.[33] There is some authority to the effect that preincorporation services—the services performed by the promoters and incorporators—are not really performed for the corporation because the corporation does not yet exist. Consequently, preincorporation services are not generally considered adequate consideration for stock.[34]

The new Model Business Corporation Act is developing a trend toward greater permissiveness in the financial provision for the issuance of shares. Acceptable consideration for shares now includes any tangible or intangible property (including benefits the corporation may receive from a contract or other instrument), cash, promissory notes, services already performed for the corporation and contracts for services to be performed, or other securities of the corporation that may be exchanged for newly issued shares. These new rules give the board of directors greater flexibility in accepting items of value in exchange for shares, and place the corporation on a much more equal footing with the limited partnership in accepting almost anything that is offered by an investor in exchange for ownership interest. Notice that a potential shareholder may not be obligated to give any current value in exchange for shares. The promise to pay money in the future through a promissory note or the promise to perform services at a later time under a contract are both recognized as valuable consideration, and a shareholder may receive shares immediately upon the issuance of the note or the execution of the contract. To be certain the shareholder will perform these promises, the corporation may place the issued shares in escrow or otherwise restrict their transfer until the services are performed or the money has been contributed. If the promises are never performed, the shares that are escrowed or restricted may be cancelled.[35]

When the corporation receives the consideration for which the board of directors authorized the issuance of shares, the shares are considered fully paid and nonassessable. If shares that are not fully paid are issued, the shareholders may be liable to the creditors of the corporation for the deficiency, and the shares are assessable. In such a case, the directors who vote to issue shares that are not fully paid and fail to place those shares in escrow or to restrict their transfer have probably violated their fiduciary duty to the corporation and other shareholders, and may be personally liable.

COMMON STOCK RIGHTS

The corporation organized with only one class of stock has only common stock, which is best described as shares of the corporation without any special features. To authorize the issuance of common stock, the articles of incorporation need only describe the number of shares authorized and, if desired or required by statute, their par value, or contain a statement that the shares have no par value. Common stock has the following rights under most state statutes.

Distribution Rights

Distributions may be declared from time to time at the discretion of the board of directors, and may be paid in cash, property, or other shares of the corporation, provided the corporation is solvent. Common stockholders receive distributions in the same proportion that their individual shares bear to the total number of common shares outstanding. The common stockholder's right to declared distributions is limited only by the solvency of the corporation (so creditors cannot be harmed by a distribution of assets as a dividend from an insolvent corporation) and by preferred stockholders' rights to distributions, which must be paid before the common shares are entitled to distributions. The rules relating to these distributions are expanded in a later chapter.[36]

Voting Rights

The one-vote-per-share rule is codified by statute in Section 7.21 of the Model Business Corporation Act. Each outstanding share regardless of class is entitled to one vote, and each fractional share is entitled to a corresponding fractional vote on each matter submitted to a vote at the meeting of the shareholders. The statute further provides, however, that the voting rights of any class may be limited or denied by the articles of incorporation. These voting rules are common to most jurisdictions. If the corporation has only one class of stock, which is not divided into series, the single class must have full voting rights. If the corporation's financial structure includes several classes or series of securities, one or more of those classes or series may have limited or greater voting rights.

The voting right of a shareholder may be the most important right in the corporation, since it permits the shareholder to express his or her views concerning the performance of management. If several corporations have *circular holdings,* where one corporation owns a majority of the stock in a subsidiary, and the subsidiary also owns a majority of the stock in the parent, the minority stockholders of both corporations would always be outvoted, since the same board of directors may be voting the majority shares in both corporations. For example, if X Corporation owns 60% of the stock of Y Corporation, and thereby elects all of the members of Y Corporation's board, and if Y Corporation also owns 60% of the stock of X Corporation, and thereby elects all of the members of X Corporation's board, the minority stockholders of both corporations will have nothing to say in the election of directors. To counter that problem, the Model Business Corporation Act provides that unless there are "special circumstances," the shares of a corporation may not be entitled to vote if they are owned by a second corporation and the first corporation owns a majority of the shares entitled to vote for the directors of the second corporation. If a court decided that there was no abuse as a result of this circular ownership, it could allow the shares owned by the respective corporations to be voted for the election of directors. Otherwise, those shares must be silent and the minority stockholders will be entitled to control the vote for the respective corporations.[37]

Depending upon the statutory requirements and the provisions in the articles of incorporation, cumulative voting may be authorized for shares of common stock.[38]

Liquidation Rights

After a decision has been made to dissolve the corporation, corporate officials are required by law to collect and dispose of the assets, and to satisfy all liabilities and obligations. Thereafter, the remaining assets in cash or property are distributed to the shareholders according to their respective interests. If the corporation has a single class of common stock, those shareholders will receive a proportionate interest in all of the net assets following dissolution and liquidation. The liquidation rights of common stock may be subordinated by the issuance of additional classes of securities that have a preference to the assets in dissolution.

Preemptive Rights

Depending upon the state statute, preemptive rights may exist unless denied, or may not exist unless granted in the articles of incorporation. The Model Business Corporation Act uses the latter approach in Section 6.30. The preemptive right of a shareholder is the right to purchase a pro rata share of newly issued stock before that share may be offered to outsiders.[39]

PREFERRED STOCK RIGHTS

Preferred stock is a common term for a class of stock that has been granted a preference to one or more of the normal shareholder rights. That is, a preferred stock usually has a preference to distributions, or a preference to assets in liquidation, or both. Issuance of preferred stock must be authorized by the articles of incorporation, and the terms of the articles must contain a distinguishing designation of each class and a statement of the preferences, limitations, and relative rights of the shares issued in each class. Moreover, if management intends to issue the shares of a preferred class in series, the designation of each series and a statement of the variations in the rights and preferences between series must be contained in the articles of incorporation. The articles also must describe any authority to be vested in the board of directors to establish the series and to determine the variations in the relative rights of the series.

Preferred stock is customarily preferred in the following ways.

Distribution Preference

A common attraction to preferred stock is a distribution preference, if and when the board of directors declares a distribution. Preferred shareholders may have a mandatory priority to distributions, in a predetermined amount, before the corporation may pay any distributions to the holders of any other class of stock. A distribution preference may be cumulative, noncumulative, or a compromise of the two, and may also include a participation provision.

Cumulative. A cumulative distribution preference means that preferred stockholders will accrue an entitlement to distributions each year, whether or not the distributions are declared and paid. If the distributions are not paid during a certain year, they accumulate in the prescribed amount, and when the board of directors finally declares a distribution, all accumulated distributions on the preferred stock must be paid before distributions may be paid on any other stock. For example, suppose preferred stock is entitled to a cumulative distribution of $4 per share and Alexis Levine owns 100 shares. In the first and second years the corporation pays no distributions, so that Alexis' stock accumulates distributions in the amount of $800. In the third year management declares a distribution on all classes of stock. The corporation must first pay Alexis $1200 on her shares ($800 accumulated plus $400 for the present year) before it may pay any distributions to any other class of stock.

A statement of a cumulative distribution preference follows:

> **EXAMPLE: Cumulative Preferred Distributions**
> The holders of the preferred stock shall be entitled to receive, when and as declared by the Board of Directors, out of the assets of the Corporation legally available therefor, cash distributions at the rate of $8.40 per share per year, and no more, payable quarter-annually on the first days of January, April, July and October in each year, prior to the payment of any distributions of the common stock. Such distributions shall be cumulative from the date of original issue.

Noncumulative. Noncumulative preferred stock is entitled to receive a distribution preference in any given year, but if distributions are not paid during that year, the preferred shareholders lose right to those distributions (just as common shareholders have no right to undeclared distributions). Using the same example of Alexis, if the preferred stock is entitled to a $4 per share noncumulative distribution, when the corporation fails to pay in the first and second year, Alexis loses the right to the $800 preference she would have had during those years. In the third year, if management decides to pay distributions, it must pay her $400 (that year's preferred amount) before it can pay other shareholders.

> **EXAMPLE: Noncumulative Preferred Distributions**
> The holders of the preferred stock shall be entitled to receive out of the surplus or net profits of the Corporation, in each fiscal year, distributions at such rate or rates, not exceeding 8.4 percent per annum, as shall be determined by the Board of Directors in connection with the issue of the respective series of said stock and expressed in the stock certificates therefor, before any distributions shall be paid upon the common stock, but such distributions shall be noncumulative. No distributions shall be paid, declared, or set apart for payment on the common stock of the Corporation, in any fiscal year, unless the full distribution on the preferred stock for such year shall have been paid or provided for. However, if the Directors in the exercise of their discretion fail to declare distributions on the preferred stock in a particular fiscal year the right of such stock to distributions for that year shall be lost even though there was available surplus or net profits out of which distributions might have been lawfully declared.

Other Provisions for Distribution Preferences. Preferred stock may have a "cumulative to the extent earned" preference to distributions, permitting distributions to accumulate on preferred stock if the corporation earned money and could have declared distributions in a given year, but the board of directors decided not to declare distributions that year. On the other hand, if the corporation had not earned or accumulated enough profit to declare a distribution that year, the distribution is lost and does not carry forward.

Another common provision is the right of the preferred stockholder to participate in other distributions declared, in addition to the preference. For example, if Alexis' stock provided for a $4 per year preference, noncumulative but participating, then in the third year when the corporation determined to pay distributions, Alexis would be entitled to $400 as a preference. She would also be entitled to share on a pro rata basis with all other securities in the remaining distributions that are declared and paid.

Liquidation Preference

Holders of preferred stock are also frequently granted a preference upon dissolution and liquidation of the corporation. The terms of the stock usually recite the right for the preferred stockholder to be paid a specified amount, plus any accrued distributions that have not been paid, before any other security holder is entitled to share in the assets upon liquidation. The preferred shareholder is thus placed in a position analogous to that of a priority creditor. A liquidation preference is as good a guarantee as can be made that shareholders will recoup their investment in case of liquidation. Although the preferred shareholders are subordinate to corporate creditors, they are paid before any other investor, and are entitled to be fully satisfied before any other shareholder receives a distribution in liquidation.

Liquidation preferences may be determined at a fixed percentage of par value.

> **EXAMPLE: Liquidation Preference at a Fixed Percentage of Par Value**
> In the event of any liquidation, dissolution or winding up of the Corporation, either voluntary or involuntary, or in the event of any reduction of capital of the Corporation resulting in a distribution of assets to its stockholders, the holders of preferred shares shall be entitled to receive out of the assets of the Corporation, without regard to capital or the existence of a surplus of any nature, an amount

equal to one hundred per cent (100%) of the par value of such preferred shares, and, in addition to such amount, a further amount equal to the distributions unpaid and accumulated thereon to the date of such distribution, whether or not earned or declared, and more, before any payment shall be made or any assets distributed to the holders of the common shares. After the making of such payments to the holders of the preferred stock, the remaining assets of the Corporation shall be distributed among the holders of the common stock alone, according to the number of shares held by each. If the assets of the Corporation distributable as aforesaid among the holders of the preferred stock shall be insufficient to permit of the payment to them of said amounts, the entire assets shall be distributed ratably among the holders of the preferred stock.

These liquidation rights may also be based on a fixed sum, with participation rights.

EXAMPLE: Liquidation Preference Based on a Fixed Sum, with Participation Rights
In the event of any liquidation, dissolution or winding up of the corporation, whether voluntary or involuntary, the holders of the preferred stock of the Corporation shall be entitled, before any assets of the Corporation shall be distributed among or paid over to the holders of the common stock, to be paid in full $100.00 per share of preferred stock, together with all accrued and unpaid distributions and with interest on said distributions at the rate of fifteen per cent (15%) per annum. After payment in full of the above preferential rights of the holders of the preferred stock, then the holders of the preferred stock and common stock shall participate equally in the division of the remaining assets of the Corporation, so that from such remaining assets the amount per share of preferred stock distributed to the holders of the preferred stock shall equal the amount per share of common stock distributed to the holders of the common stock.

Voting Rights

Each corporation must have one or more classes of shares that together have full voting rights, so at least some shareholder will be entitled to vote on all matters submitted to the shareholders.[40] A corporation with multiple classes of stock may have one class with full voting rights in shareholder matters, and another class with no voting rights at all. It is also permissible to grant more than one vote per share to one class while retaining the single vote per share for another class. These provisions are designed to establish voting control in one of the classes of securities. A typical application of these machinations may involve shareholders of a corporation who wish to retain their control, but need to issue additional shares to secure new capital. With the establishment of a new class of nonvoting shares, the issuance of new shares will not dilute present voting control.

Modifications to voting rights are described in the articles of incorporation, and they may be expanded, denied or granted subject to a contingency. For example, preferred shares may have no voting rights unless they have not received distributions for a specified period of time, in which case they will be entitled to vote.

EXAMPLE: Modifications to Voting Rights
The holders of the preferred stock shall not have any voting power whatsoever, except upon the question of selling, conveying, transferring or otherwise disposing of the property and assets of the Corporation as an entirety, provided, however:

> In the event that the Corporation shall fail to pay any distribution upon the preferred stock when it regularly becomes due, and such distribution shall remain in arrears for a period of six (6) months, the holders of the preferred stock shall have the right to vote on all matters in like manner as the holders of the common stock, during the year next ensuing, and during each year thereafter during the continuance of said default until the Corporation shall have paid all accrued distributions upon the preferred stock. The holders of the common stock shall have the right to vote on all questions to the exclusion of all other stockholders, except as herein otherwise provided.

The articles of incorporation may also reconfirm the statutory voting scheme.

> **EXAMPLE: Reconfirmation of Statutory Voting Rights**
> The preferred stock and common stock shall have equal voting powers and the holders thereof shall be entitled to one vote in person or by proxy for each share of stock held. The common stock, however, to the exclusion of the preferred stock, shall have the sole voting power with respect to the determination as to whether or not the preferred stock shall be redeemed, as hereinafter provided.[41]

If no modifications of voting rights appear in the articles, the Model Business Corporation Act and most states grant each outstanding share (including preferred shares) one vote on each matter submitted to a vote at the meeting of the shareholders.[42]

If voting rights are denied to a particular class of shares, the holders of that class are not entitled to vote on typical shareholder business. A potential problem lurks in this rule. Consider that the structure (including distribution and liquidation entitlements) of the nonvoting securities is specified in the articles of incorporation and this structure may be changed by an amendment to the articles that has been approved by the shareholders. If the holders of the nonvoting classes were never entitled to vote, even on such matters, they would be at the mercy of the voting shareholders, who could vote to amend away the advantageous features of their stock. Consequently, corporate statutes uniformly provide for class voting on matters that may affect the rights of the class.

Section 7.25 of the Model Business Corporation Act permits shares to vote as a "separate voting group" and to take action in a meeting when a quorum of the separate voting group is present. The separate voting group may be one or more classes of stock that are entitled to vote on certain matters, either because the articles of incorporation provide for a vote of the separate group, or the statute requires such a vote.

Section 10.04 of the act provides that a class will be entitled to vote as a separate voting group on any proposed amendment that would

1. increase or decrease the aggregate number of authorized shares of such class;
2. effect an exchange, reclassification, or cancellation of all or part of the shares of such class;
3. effect an exchange, or create a right of exchange, of all or any part of the shares of another class into the shares of such class;
4. change the designations, preferences, limitations, or relative rights of the shares of such class;
5. change the shares of such class into the same or a different number of shares of the same class;

6. create a new class of shares having rights and preferences prior, superior, or substantially equal to the shares of such class;
7. increase the rights and preferences or the number of authorized shares of any class having rights and preferences prior, superior, or substantially equal to the shares of such class;
8. limit or deny any existing preemptive rights of the shares of such class; or
9. cancel or otherwise affect distributions or dividends on the shares of such class that have accrued but have not been declared.

Redemption Rights

The terms of preferred stock may include provisions for the redemption of the shares. A corporation may have the right to redeem or reacquire its shares if redemption terms are included in the description of the class. The redemption feature is a greater advantage to the corporation than to the shareholders. For example, suppose the corporation issued 20% cumulative redeemable preferred stock to acquire needed capital. The distribution percentage would make this stock very attractive, but management would prefer not to continue paying a high cumulative distribution any longer than necessary. The redemption feature would permit the corporation to retire the securities when it has generated enough capital from operations to do so.

A proper redemption provision should spell out the terms of the "forced" sale from the preferred shareholders to the corporation and the procedure that must be followed to accomplish the sale. A redemption clause must appear on the articles of incorporation and on the share certificate, and it typically includes

1. a date upon which the stock will be redeemable by the corporation;
2. a price at which the stock is redeemable, usually including a provision to the effect that an amount equal to accrued and unpaid distrubutions will be added to the price;
3. a period of notice preceding the date of redemption and the persons to whom notice must be given;
4. a place at which payment is to be made, and the person who will make payment;
5. a time at which payment is to be made and whether the board of directors has a right to accelerate the payment date;
6. provisions regarding the surrender of share certificates and the cancellation of all rights of the shareholder upon redemption; and
7. provisions covering the possibility that a shareholder will not surrender shares for cancellation in accordance with the redemption right.

> **EXAMPLE: Redemption of Shares**
> The preferred stock may be redeemed in whole or in part on any quarterly dividend payment date, at the option of the Board of Directors, upon not less than sixty (60) days prior notice to the holders of record of the preferred stock, published, mailed and given in such manner and form and on such other terms and conditions as may be prescribed by the bylaws or by resolution of the Board of Directors by payment in cash for each share of the preferred stock to be redeemed of one hundred two per cent (102%) of the par amount thereof and in addition thereto all unpaid dividends accrued on such share.
>
> From and after May 1, 1991, the Board of Directors shall retire not less than 1,000 shares of preferred stock per annum; but the Board of Directors shall first set

aside a reserve to provide full dividends for the current year on all preferred stock which shall be outstanding after such purchase or retirement, and provided further that no such purchase or retirement shall be made if the capital of the Corporation would thereby be impaired.

If less than all the outstanding shares are to be redeemed, such redemption may be made by a lot or pro-rata as may be prescribed by resolution of the Board of Directors; provided, however, that the Board of Directors may alternatively invite from shareholders offers to the Corporation of preferred stock at less than One hundred two dollars ($102.00), and when such offers are invited, the Board of Directors shall then be required to buy at the lowest price or prices offered, up to the amount to be purchased.

From and after the date fixed in any such notice as the date of redemption (unless default shall be made by the Corporation in the payment of the redemption price), all dividends on the preferred stock thereby called for redemption shall cease to accrue and all rights of the holders hereof as stockholders of the Corporation, except the right to receive the redemption price, shall cease and determine.

Any purchase by the corporation of shares of its preferred stock shall not be made at prices in excess of said redemption price.[43]

[or]

By a unanimous vote of a full board of directors of the number fixed by the stockholders at their last annual meeting, all or any shares of common stock of the Corporation held by such holder or holders as may be designated in such vote may be called an any time for purchase, or for retirement or cancellation in connection with any reduction of capital stock, at the book value of such shares as determined by the Board of Directors as of the close of the month next preceding such vote. Such determination, including the method thereof and the matters considered therein, shall be final and conclusive.

Not less than 30 days prior to the day for which a call of common stock for purchase or for retirement or cancellation is made, notice of such call shall be mailed to each holder of shares of stock called at his or her address as it appears upon the books of the Corporation. The Corporation shall, not later than said day, deposit with a bank to be designated in such notice, for the account of such holder, the amount of the purchase price of the shares so called. After such notice and deposit all shares so called shall be deemed to have been transferred to the Corporation, or retired or cancelled as the case may be, and the holder shall cease to have, in respect thereof, any claim to future dividends or other rights as stockholder, and shall be entitled only to the sums so deposited for his or her account. Any shares so acquired by the Corporation may be held and may be disposed of at such times, in such manner and for such consideration as the Board of Directors shall determine.[44]

The redemption of corporate securities requires large disbursements of cash which may not be absorbed in normal corporate operations. To plan for eventual redemption, therefore, management should consider a *sinking fund* for the payment of the purchase price. The objective of the sinking fund is the same as that of a Christmas savings plan. By faithfully depositing a certain amount at periodic intervals, depositors can ensure that a lump sum will be available at the projected date of need. A clause establishing redemption of preferred stock with a sinking fund might look like this:

EXAMPLE: Sinking Fund

a) There shall be a sinking fund for the benefit of the shares of the preferred stock. So long as there shall remain outstanding any preferred stock, the Corporation shall set aside annually, on or before October 15, 1991, and on or before October 15th in each year thereafter, as and for such sinking fund for the then current year, an amount in cash equal to the lesser of $25,000, or 2.7% of the Consolidated Net Earnings of the Corporation and its subsidiaries for the preceding calendar year (computed as hereinafter provided). So long as dividends on the preferred stock for any past quarterly dividend payment date shall not have been fully paid or declared and a sum sufficient for the payment thereof set apart, the date for the setting aside of any amounts for the sinking fund shall be postponed until all such dividends in arrears shall have been paid or declared and a sum sufficient for the payment thereof set aside, and no amounts shall be set aside for the sinking fund while such arrears shall exist. In addition to the aforesaid sinking fund payments, the Corporation shall pay out of its general funds all amounts paid in excess of $103 per share (for commissions or as, or based upon, accrued dividends) upon any purchase or redemption of preferred stock through the sinking fund, as hereinafter provided.

b) The moneys set aside for any annual installment for the sinking fund (with any amounts remaining unexpended from previous sinking fund installments), may, at the option of the Corporation, be immediately applied (but not earlier than the October 15th on or before which such installment is required to be set aside), as nearly as possible, to the redemption of shares of preferred stock at the redemption price of $103 per share plus dividends accrued thereon to the date of redemption, in the manner provided herein for the redemption of preferred stock; provided, however, that if at the time any such annual installment is set aside (but not earlier than the October 15th on or before which such installment is required to be set aside), any holder of preferred stock shall hold 5% or more of the then outstanding shares of preferred stock, then there shall promptly be redeemed from such holder the number of whole shares of preferred stock (and no more) that shall bear, as nearly as practicable, the same ratio to the total number of shares which could be redeemed pursuant to this subdivision with such moneys, as the number of shares of preferred stock then owned by such holder shall bear to the total number of shares of preferred stock then outstanding.

c) Any moneys set aside for the sinking fund, as hereinabove required, and not applied to the redemption of preferred stock as provided in the preceding clause (b) (with any amounts remaining unexpended from previous sinking fund payments) shall be applied from time to time by the Corporation to the purchase, directly or through agents, of preferred stock in the open market or at public or private sale, with or without advertisement or notice, as the Board of Directors shall in its discretion determine, at prices not exceeding $103 per share plus accrued dividends and plus the usual customary brokerage commissions payable in connection with such purchases. If at the expiration of a full period of 90 days following the date each such amount is set apart during which the Corporation shall have been entitled hereunder to purchase shares of preferred stock with such funds, there shall remain in the sinking fund amounts exceeding $5,000 in the aggregate which shall not have been expended during such periods, then the Corporation shall promptly select and call for redemption at $103 per share plus dividends accrued thereon to the date of redemption, in the manner herein provided for the redemption of preferred stock such number of shares of preferred stock as is necessary to exhaust as nearly as may be all of said moneys, except that no shares shall then be allocated for redemption from any holder if the pro rata share of the then current sinking fund payment shall have been applied to the redemption of shares of such holder as hereinabove in paragraph (b) of this subdivision provided. Anything herein to the contrary notwithstanding, no purchase or redemption of shares of preferred stock with any moneys set aside for the sinking fund shall be made or ordered unless full cumulative dividends for all past quarterly dividend payment dates have been paid or declared and a sum sufficient for the payment thereof set aside upon all shares of preferred stock then outstanding. When no shares of preferred stock shall remain outstanding any balance remaining in the sinking fund shall be and become part of the general funds of the Corporation.[45]

The Model Business Corporation Act repealed its statutory restrictions on redemption of shares in 1979. Most state statutes are still based on the former act provisions, however, and they continue to address the redemption right in two important areas. Redemption or purchase of shares is prohibited when the corporation is insolvent or would be rendered insolvent by the redemption. Redemption is also forbidden if the transaction would reduce the net assets below the aggregate amount payable to the holders of shares having prior or equal rights to the assets of the corporation upon involuntary dissolution.

The last provision deserves an illustration. Suppose the corporation has $1,000,000 in assets, $700,000 in liabilities, and three classes of stock outstanding (1,000 shares of 8% noncumulative preferred stock with a $105 liquidation preference; 2,000 shares of 10% noncumulative preferred stock redeemable at $100 per share; and 100,000 shares of common stock). The net assets of the corporation (assets minus liabilities) total $300,000. The corporation could not redeem all 2,000 shares of the 10% preferred, since that would require $200,000 and payment of that amount would reduce net assets to $100,000. The remainder is insufficient to pay the 8% preferred shareholders' liquidation preference of $105,000.

Redeemed shares are usually cancelled and restored to authorized-but-unissued status. Under the amended Model Business Corporation Act, the restoration of the shares to this status is automatic unless the articles of incorporation provide that the shares shall not be reissued. In such a case, the redeemed shares are eradicated by reducing the total authorized shares. A statement of cancellation must be filed upon redemption, describing the name of the corporation; the reduction in the number of authorized shares, itemized by class and series; and the total number of authorized shares remaining after the reduction. The act regards this statement as an amendment to the articles of incorporation without shareholder action.[46]

Conversion Privileges

Certain classes of stock may be entitled to a conversion privilege whereby a holder of those shares may convert the shares of one class for shares of another class at a specified rate and time. A conversion feature enhances the marketability of conservative classes of stock, because the holder has the best of both worlds. A holder of preferred shares with a conversion privilege, for example, enjoys the preferences and conservative investment protection of the preferred stock while also maintaining the option to convert to common stock if its growth rate is attractive. The shareholder who owns convertible preferred stock, therefore, receives the security of preferred shares plus the right to elect an interest in the basic equity growth of the company.

A conversion clause should appear in the articles of incorporation and on the share certificates. A conversion privilege provision should include

1. a conversion rate specifying the number of shares of common stock (or another class) into which each share of preferred stock is convertible;
2. provisions respecting the issuance of fractional shares, since the conversion may result in a fractional share problem;[47]
3. a procedure for the method of conversion, detailing the written notice required to convert the shares and a period of time following the election that the conversion will become effective;
4. provisions for the adjustment of conversion rates, in cases of a stock dividend, stock split, or other corporate action that changes the character of the shares into which the preferred is convertible;
5. requirement of notice to preferred shareholders when the conversion rate is adjusted; and
6. reservation of an adequate number of shares of common stock, in case all conversion privileges are exercised.

Remember that a corporation must have authority to issue common stock in its articles of incorporation, and the common shares must be reserved if they are to be issued to preferred shareholders.

> **EXAMPLE: Conversion of Shares**
> The preferred stock of this Corporation of $100 par value may, at the option of the holder thereof, at any time on or before January 10, 2000, be converted into common stock of this Corporation of $100 par value upon the following terms:
>
> a) Any holder of such preferred stock desiring to avail himself or herself of the option for conversion of that stock shall, on or before January 10, 2000, deliver, duly endorsed in blank, the certificates representing the stock to be converted to the Secretary of the Corporation at its office, and at the same time notify the Secretary in writing over the holder's signature that the holder desires to convert his or her stock into common stock of $100 par value pursuant to these provisions.
>
> b) Upon receipt by the Secretary of a certificate or certificates representing such preferred stock and a notice that the holder desires to convert the same, the Corporation shall forthwith cause to be issued to the holder one share of common stock for each share of preferred stock surrendered, and shall deliver to such holder a certificate in due form for such common stock.
>
> c) One hundred thousand shares of common stock of this Corporation shall be set aside and such shares shall be issued only in conversion of preferred stock as herein provided.
>
> d) Shares of preferred stock which have been converted shall revert to the status of unissued shares and shall not be reissued. Such shares may be eliminated as provided by law.
>
> e) If, at any time the convertible preferred stock of this Corporation is outstanding, the Corporation increases the number of common shares outstanding without adjusting the stated capital of the corporation, the conversion rate shall be adjusted accordingly, so as to make each share of preferred stock convertible into the same proportionate amount of common stock as it would have been convertible without such adjustment to the common stock. Each preferred shareholder shall be notified in writing of the adjusted conversion rate within thirty (30) days of such action by the Corporation.
>
> f) These provisions for conversion of preferred stock of this Corporation shall be subject to the limitations and restrictions contained in section 57.100 of the Business Corporation Law of the State of Oregon.[48]

TRANSFER AGENTS

Many corporations employ transfer agents and registrars to keep track of the record holders of the corporate securities. By statute, a stock transfer ledger must be maintained either at the place of business of the corporation or at the office of its transfer agent or registrar,[49] which is normally a bank or other financial institution that has a separate division for the explicit purpose of maintaining such records for corporations. The transfer agent is responsible for issuing new stock certificates. Blank certificates are usually kept in bulk at the agent's office and the statutory signatures are usually printed on the certificates, since the Model Business Corporation Act permits a facsimile signature of the officers.[50] If a registrar is used separately, the transfer agent delivers newly prepared certificates to the registrar for registration and countersignature. The registrar then returns the registered and signed certificate to the transfer agent who issues it. The registrar's responsibilities include recording all certificates representing shares of stock in the corporation. If the transfer agent and registrar are separate individuals, all entries made in the stock transfer ledger are made by the registrar, and the ledger is kept at the registrar's office. Transfer agents and registrars receive corporate authority by resolution of the board of directors.

EXAMPLE: Appointment of Transfer Agent and Registrar

Appointment of   TRANSFER AGENT
                        REGISTRAR

_____
(Name of Corporation)

"Resolved, that The _____ Bank _____
is hereby appointed [sole] [Transfer Agent] [Registrar] for all of the shares

of the _____ Preferred stock, and

_____ shares
all of the shares

of the _____ Common stock

of this Company, to act in accordance with its general practice and with the regulations set forth in the pamphlet submitted to this meeting entitled 'Regulations of The _____ Bank _____
for the Transfer and Registration of Stock', which pamphlet the Secretary is directed to mark for identification and file with the records of the Company."

I, the undersigned, Secretary of the above named Corporation, do hereby certify that the foregoing is a true and correct copy of a resolution duly adopted by the Board of Directors of said Corporation at a meeting thereof duly called and held on _____, 19__, at which a quorum were present, and that said resolution has not been in any wise rescinded, annulled or revoked but the same is still in full force and effect.

And I do further certify to the following facts:
The authorized and outstanding stock of the Corporation is as follows:

Class	*Par Value*	*Authorized*	*Outstanding*
_____	_____	_____	_____
_____	_____	_____	_____

The address of the Corporation to which notices may be sent is
_____

The below named persons have been duly elected, have duly qualified, and this day are, officers of the Corporation, holding the respective offices below set opposite their names, and the signatures below set opposite their names are their genuine signatures.

_____ President _____
_____ Vice-President _____
_____ Vice-President _____
_____ Treasurer _____
_____ Assistant Treasurer _____
_____ Secretary _____
_____ Assistant Secretary _____

The name and address of legal counsel for the Corporation is

The names and addresses of all of the Transfer Agents and Registrars of the stock of the Corporation are as follows:

Class of Stock	Transfer Agent(s)	Registrar(s)
_____	_____	_____
_____	_____	_____

Witness my hand and the seal of the Corporation this_____ day of _____, 19 ___ .

_____ 51
Secretary

[Corporate Seal]

In addition to a specification of authority to act as transfer agent or registrar, such a resolution may also include a statement that the officers of the company are authorized and empowered to give instructions to the transfer agent and to the registrar and to take any other action they deem necessary to effect the issuance of the common stock.

DEBT SECURITIES

Every state empowers a corporation to borrow funds for corporate purposes. Debt securities represent loans to the corporation, and a debt security holder is a creditor of the corporation. A debt holder usually enjoys no right to participate in management and also has no right to receive profits. A debt security holder is, however, entitled to the repayment of the loan with the prescribed interest, and if the debt remains unpaid at the time of dissolution, repayment of the debt may be obtained from the available assets. Furthermore, debt security holders enjoy greater security for their investment than do equity security holders, since debt holders are creditors and are entitled to be satisfied from the available assets first.

Debt securities state a principal amount, a maturity date, and a periodic interest rate. The interest is the return on the investment, and usually determines the attractiveness of a debt security. State statutes do not strictly regulate debt obligations, and as a matter of law these securities are considered to be individual agreements between the debt security holder and the corporation, containing negotiated terms. The terms of debt securities (bonds) issued by large corporations are fixed and not subject to negotiation or modification. However, in smaller corporations, debt securities may contain a variety of terms that are negotiated between the creditor-investor and the corporation. Nevertheless, it is possible to generalize some typical features of debt securities.

TYPES OF CORPORATE DEBT SECURITIES

Unsecured Debt

A corporate debt obligation may be as simple as a promissory note, the terms of which include the amount of the debt, a promise to pay the principal at a certain time, and a promise to pay interest:

> **EXAMPLE: Promissory Note**
>
> _____$50,000.00_____   _____November 1_____, _1991_
>
> _____One year_____ after date, for value received, Happiness, Inc. promises to pay to _____Pamela A. Ray_____ or order, payable at _____1216 Charlotte Avenue, Austin, Texas,_____
>
> the sum of _____Fifty thousand_____ DOLLARS, with interest thereon at the rate of <u>15</u> per cent, per <u>annum</u> from date, payable <u>monthly</u> until paid.
>
>   Failure to pay any installment of principal or interest when due shall cause the whole note to become due and payable at once, or the interest to be counted as principal, at the option of the holder of this note, and it shall not be necessary for the holder to declare the same due, but she may proceed to collect the same as if the whole was due and payable by its terms.
>
>   Presentment for payment, notice of dishonor, and protest are hereby waived by the maker or makers, and endorser or endorsers, and each endorser for himself or herself guarantees the payment of this note according to its terms. No extension of payment shall release any signer or be paid by the parties liable for the payment of this note.
>
> _____   _____

or it may be a lengthy, complex debenture obligation:

> **EXAMPLE: 18% Twenty-Year Debenture Due August 1, 2010**
> $1,000   No. _____
> Trouble, Inc., a Colorado corporation (hereinafter called the "Company", which term includes any successor corporation under the Indenture hereinafter referred to), for value received, hereby promises to pay to the bearer, or, if this Debenture be registered as to principal, to the registered holder hereof, on August 1, 2010, the sum of One Thousand Dollars and to pay interest thereon, from the date hereof, semi-annually on June 1 and December 1 in each year, at the rate of Eighteen (18) per cent per annum. Payment of the principal of (and premium, if any) and interest on this Debenture will be made at the office or agency of the Company maintained for that purpose in Denver, Colorado, in such coin or currency of the United States of America as at the time of payment is legal tender for payment of public and private debts.

This Debenture is one of a duly authorized issue of Debentures of the Company designated as its 18% Twenty-Year Debentures Due August 1, 2010, (hereinafter called the "Debentures"), limited in aggregate principal amount to $1,500,000.00, issued and to be issued under an indenture dated August 1, 1990 (hereinafter called the "Indenture"), between the Company and Glorious Trust Company as Trustee (hereinafter called the "Trustee", which term includes any successor trustee under the Indenture), to which Indenture and all indentures supplemental thereto reference is hereby made for a statement of the respective rights thereunder of the Company, the Trustee and the holders of the Debentures and coupons, and the terms upon which the Debentures are, and are to be, authenticated and delivered.

If an Event of Default, as defined in the Indenture, shall occur, the principal of all the Debentures may be declared due and payable in the manner and with the effect provided in the Indenture.

The Indenture permits, with certain exceptions as therein provided, the amendment thereof and the modification of the rights and obligations of the Company and the rights of the holders of the Debentures under the Indenture at any time by the Company with the consent of the holders of 66⅔% in aggregate principal amount of the Debentures at the time outstanding, as defined in the Indenture. The Indenture also contains provisions permitting the holders of specified percentages in aggregate principal amount of the Debentures at the time outstanding, as defined in the Indenture, on behalf of the holders of all the Debentures, by written consent to waive compliance by the Company with certain provisions of the Indenture and certain past defaults under the Indenture and their consequences. Any such consent or waiver by the holder of this Debenture shall be conclusive and binding upon such holder and upon all future holders of this Debenture and of any Debenture issued in exchange herefor or in lieu hereof whether or not notation of such consent or waiver is made upon this Debenture.

No reference herein to the Indenture and no provision of this Debenture or of the Indenture shall alter or impair the obligation of the Company, which is absolute and unconditional, to pay the principal of (and premium, if any) and interest on this Debenture at the times, place and rate, and in the coin or currency, herein prescribed.

This Debenture is transferable by delivery, unless registered as to principal in the name of the holder in the Debenture Register of the Company. This Debenture may be so registered upon presentation hereof at the office or agency of the Company in any place where the principal hereof and interest hereon are payable, such registration being noted hereon. While registered as aforesaid, this Debenture shall be transferable on the Debenture Register of the Company by the registered holder hereof, upon like presentation of this Debenture for notation of such transfer hereon, accompanied by a written instrument of transfer in form satisfactory to the Company and the Debenture Registrar duly executed by the registered holder hereof or his or her attorney duly authorized in writing, all as provided in the Indenture and subject to certain limitations therein set forth; but this Debenture may be discharged from registration by being in like manner transferred to bearer, and thereupon transferability by delivery shall be restored. This Debenture shall continue to be subject to successive registrations and transfers to bearer at the option of the bearer or registered holder, as the case may be. Such registration, however, shall not affect the transferability by delivery of the coupons appertaining hereto, which shall continue to be payable to bearer and transferable by delivery. No service charge shall be made for any such registration, transfer or discharge from registration, but the Company may require payment of a sum sufficient to cover any tax or other governmental charge payable in connection therewith.

> The Company, the Trustee and any agent of the Company may treat the bearer of this Debenture, or, if this Debenture is registered as herein authorized, the person in whose name the same is registered, and the bearer of any coupon appertaining hereto, as the absolute owner hereof for all purposes, whether or not this Debenture or such coupon be overdue, and neither the Company, the Trustee nor any such agent shall be affected by notice to the contrary.
>
> The Debentures are issuable as coupon Debentures, registrable as to principal, in the denomination of $1,000 and as registered Debentures without coupons in denominations of $1,000 and any multiple thereof. As provided in the Indenture and subject to certain limitations therein set forth, Debentures are exchangeable for a like aggregate principal amount of Debentures of a different authorized kind or denomination, as requested by the holder surrendering the same, upon payment of taxes and other governmental charges.
>
> Unless the certificate of authentication hereon has been executed by the Trustee by the manual signature of one of its authorized officers, neither this Debenture, nor any coupon appertaining hereto, shall be entitled to any benefit under the Indenture, or be valid or obligatory for any purpose.
>
> In witness whereof, the Company has caused this Debenture to be duly executed under its corporate seal, and coupons bearing the facsimile signature of its Treasurer to be hereto annexed.
>
> Date: December 15, 1990
>
> By_____ [52]
>
> Attest:
> _____

In any case, these are unsecured obligations, meaning that the corporation simply borrows money on the strength of its own ability to repay. The characteristic common to the simple promissory note and the debenture bond is that there is no specific corporate property to which the creditor will be entitled if the corporation defaults.

Secured Debt

The unsecured debenture or promissory note should be contrasted with a mortgage bond or secured note in which the corporation pledges certain property as collateral to secure repayment of the obligation. If there is a default, the creditor may reach the collateral to satisfy the debt. Mortgage bonds usually have corporate land as collateral. The obligation between the creditor and the corporation is represented by a mortgage bond, or note, and a mortgage agreement, which specifies the terms under which the property will be held for the benefit of the creditor. A mortgage agreement usually requires the mortgagor (corporation) to insure the property, maintain it in good order, and keep it free from other liens or obligations so that the creditor will have its full benefit, if necessary. Secured debt obligations may also involve personal property collateral, including equipment, inventory, accounts, and so on. Personal property security interests are governed by the Uniform Commercial Code, which has been adopted in every state. The code requires a security agreement between the creditor and the debtor and creditor.[53] Further, a financing statement, which meets the statutory requirements,[54] must be recorded in the appropriate state or county offices.[55]

TRUST INDENTURE

When numerous bonds are issued at once, a trustee is usually appointed to act on behalf of the holders of the security in case of default by the corporation. The appointment of a trustee is particularly desirable for secured debt obligations. If the corporation defaults, the trustee will act on behalf of the creditors to recover the property securing the obligations. The trustee is usually a financial institution, and is appointed by the execution of a trust indenture, an agreement that specifies the rights and responsibilities of the corporation, the rights and responsibilties of the trustees, and the rights of the security holders. If the bonds are to be sold to the public, the indenture must comply with the requirements of the Trust Indenture Act of 1939, the federal Securities Act of 1933,[56] and perhaps state securities statutes. The document that evidences the obligation, the bond itself, merely refers to the trust indenture for all details of the obligation. Trust indentures are unconscionably lengthy documents, and most experienced financial institutions have standard indentures for the use of their corporate customers.[57]

COMMON PROVISIONS IN DEBT SECURITIES

As with stock, it is possible to introduce into debt securities various privileges that make the investment more attractive. Debt securities may also accommodate redemption or conversion provisions, and the terms of the obligation may contain a *subordination feature,* which establishes a priority of one debt security over another. The investment objectives of a debt security holder are twofold: repayment of the principal and receipt of the periodic interest. The security may become more or less attractive depending upon the circumstances under which it may be redeemed (terminating the interest); converted (altering the character of the investment); or subordinated (endangering repayment of the principal).

Redemption

Bonds may be redeemable at the option of the board of directors at a specified time and a specified price. The redemption price for bonds is usually stated in terms of a percentage of the principal amount, and it may be determined by a declining percentage from the date of issue to maturity or a fixed percentage figure throughout. For example, a bond may be redeemable during the first year at 110% of the principal amount, during the second year at 109.5%, during the third year at 109%, and so forth. As the bond nears maturity, the redemption price will approach 100%. The declining percentage is designed to protect the bondholder by discouraging early redemption by the corporation.

The terms of bond redemption provisions are similar to the redemption clauses for shares enumerated in earlier in the "Preferred Stock Rights" section of this chapter, including the authority to create a sinking fund for redemption. An example of a fixed percentage redemption provision follows.

> **EXAMPLE: Redemption Provisions**
> The Company may at its option redeem this debenture at any time hereafter upon payment of the principal amount hereof, plus a premium of five per cent (5%) of

such principal amount, plus any unpaid interest payable for any fiscal year ended prior to the date of redemption, plus interest at the rate of five per cent (5%) per annum upon such principal amount for the period from the first day of the fiscal year in which redemption is so made to the date of redemption, provided that notice of such redemption, stating the time and place of redemption, shall be published at least once each week for four (4) successive weeks prior to the redemption date in a daily newspaper of general circulation published in Cook County, Illinois. Thereupon this debenture shall become due and payable at the time and place designated for redemption in such notice, and payment of the redemption price shall be paid to the bearer of this debenture upon presentation and surrender thereof and of all unpaid interest coupons annexed hereto. Unless default shall be made in the redemption of this debenture upon such presentation, interest on this debenture shall cease from and after the date of redemption so designated. If the amount necessary to redeem this debenture shall have been deposited with the Abraham Lincoln Trust Company and if the notice of redemption shall have been duly published as aforesaid, this debenture shall be conclusively deemed to have been redeemed on the date specified for redemption, and all liability of the Company hereon shall cease on such date and all rights of the holder of this debenture, except the right to receive the redemption price out of the moneys so deposited, shall cease and terminate on such date.[58]

The notice required by the redemption provision could be worded as follows:

EXAMPLE: Notice of Redemption
Notice is hereby given that the Ten Year Convertible Income Debentures due November 30, 1999 of The Nobles Corporation have been called for redemption at 110% of the principal amount thereof and will be redeemed at the office of the Abraham Lincoln Trust Company, 1198 West Adams Street, Chicago, Illinois, on May 15, 1991. From and after May 15, 1991, the holders of said Debentures will have no conversion rights or any other rights, except to receive the redemption price.[59]

Conversion

Debt securities may be convertible into equity securities, and this convertibility further enhances the value of a bond. The bond conversion feature will specify the number of shares of stock into which the bond is convertible, the procedure for conversion, a reservation of an appropriate number of common shares, and adjustments and other matters that concern the conversion privilege.

EXAMPLE: Conversion Provisions
As provided in the indenture with Abraham Lincoln Trust Company this bond is convertible at the option of the holder thereof, at any time prior to maturity (or, if this bond is at any time called for redemption, then at any time before the date fixed for redemption), upon surrender of this bond for that purpose at the office of the Nobles Corporation, Chicago, Illinois. Conversion shall be made into common shares of the Nobles Corporation upon the basis of one common share for each $100 of principal sum of this bond, subject to the provision of the indenture as to interest on bonds converted and dividends on shares received therefor, and as to change in the conversion basis or substitution of other shares, securities, or property in the event of consolidation, merger, conveyance of assets, recapitalization, or the issuance of additional shares.

Priority and Subordination

Management of the corporation may desire to subordinate the existing debt securities in order to secure additional financing at a later time. If the bondholders agree to accept second or third place to other creditors for certain purposes, the subordination of their debt should assist in obtaining the maximum borrowing capacity for the corporation. The subordination feature would apply only if the bonds are not paid. If the corporation defaults on the obligation, the subordination clause will determine which creditors have prior rights to corporate assets to enforce their respective obligations against the corporation.

When a bond issue is already outstanding and management is attempting to obtain additional financing, subordination may be an afterthought. Corporate officials may approach existing bondholders and solicit their agreement to subordinate their debt. On the other hand, subordination may be a condition precedent to the bond obligation. For example, an investor may be willing to invest in the corporation and purchase a bond, or lend the money, provided the corporation will subordinate any future borrowing to this debt security. Subordination provisions always include the amounts that will be subordinated (principal only, principal and interest, interest only, etc.), and they always describe the senior obligations to which the bond is subordinated.

> **EXAMPLE: Subordination Provisions**
> The rights of the holder hereof to the principal sum or any part thereof, and the interest due thereon, are and shall remain subject and subordinate to the claims as to principal and interest of the holders of 7¾% First Mortgage Bonds of the corporation, and upon dissolution or liquidation of the corporation no payment shall be due or payable upon this debenture until all claims of the holders of said bonds shall have been paid in full.

Voting Rights

A rare privilege accorded to bondholders in a minority of jurisdictions is the right to vote on corporate matters, if so authorized in the articles of incorporation.[60] If holders of debt securities are permitted to vote in corporate elections, they are treated like a separate class of voting shareholders.

IMPORTANT CONSIDERATIONS REGARDING DEBT AND EQUITY

In planning the capitalization of the corporation, the drafter has tremendous flexibility. The necessary capital may be raised any number of ways and represented by any of the myriad debt or equity securities depending upon the expectations of the investors and the selected corporate capitalization structure. However, certain practical matters should be considered in choosing between debt and various classes of equity securities.

Anticipation of Later Financing

If the capital structure of the corporation is simple in the beginning, management will have greater flexibility to raise money in the future. If the initial corporate structure has several classes of stock and various debt securities, it will be considerably more difficult to create new classes of stock later, since new classes will probably affect the rights of the existing shareholders, whose approval must be acquired for any such amendments to the articles of incorporation. It is important, therefore, to consider the future capital needs of the business at the outset, and to plan the initial capital structure with those predictions in mind.

Advantages to Common Shareholders through the Use of Senior Securities

Preferred stock and bonds are commonly called *senior securities* because of their special preferential rights. Preferred shareholders are usually entitled to a dividend preference and liquidation preference, ensuring a return on and a return of their investment. Similarly, holders of debt securities have a right to interest and a right to repayment of their obligation upon maturity. Recall that the common shareholders have no special rights to distributions, and are entitled to share in the assets in liquidation, but only after the holders of debt securities and the holders of preferred stock have been satisfied. However, the common shareholders may gain an advantage through the use of senior securities when the expected profit return on capital each year exceeds the payments that must be made, either in distributions or in interest, to the holders of senior securities. The converse is also true. If the expected profit return on capital each year is less than the payments that must be made to the holders of senior securities, the common shareholders are at a disadvantage.

These principles may be illustrated by considering the following example. Suppose Trouble Incorporated needs $100,000 capital for the operation of its business and can reasonably predict profits after taxes of $20,000 or more each year. Assuming a hypothetical federal income tax rate of 30% the profit before taxes must be $28,572 or better. The securities that will be issued in exchange for the $100,000 capital may be any combination of common stock, preferred stock, and debt. The profit return on capital after taxes is now estimated to be 20% or more each year. If 1,000 shares of common stock are issued to raise the $100,000 capital, the earnings per share are computed as follows, assuming the estimated profit is realized.

Profit before tax	$28,572
Federal income tax (30%)	8,572
Profit after tax	$20,000
Earnings per share of common stock (1,000 shares)	$ 20.00

Now assume that investors are found who are willing to take preferred stock with $100 par value and a preferred dividend rate of 16%. The $100,000 capital may be raised by issuing 500 shares of 16% preferred stock for $50,000, and 500 shares of common stock for $50,000. The common stock earnings per share are computed as follows:

Profit before taxes	$28,572
Federal income tax (30%)	8,572
Profit after taxes	$20,000

Preferred dividends (16% of $50,000)	8,000
Profit after preferred dividends	$12,000
Earnings per share of common stock (500 shares)	$ 24.00

Next assume that instead of preferred stock, debt securities with the same interest rate (16%) are issued for the $50,000 capital. The interest paid on debt securities is deductible as an expense before taxes, and this further improves the common shareholder's earnings. The statement looks like this:

Profit before interest	$28,572
Interest (16% of $50,000)	8,000
Profit before taxes	$20,572
Federal income tax (30%)	6,172
Profit after taxes	$14,400
Earnings per share of common stock (500 shares)	$ 28.80

A combination of all three securities will be even better for the common shareholders. Suppose $40,000 capital is raised by the sale of 400 common shares, $30,000 by the sale of 300 shares of 16% preferred stock, and $30,000 by 16% debt securities. The result is as follows:

Profit before interest	$28,572
Interest (16% of $30,000)	4,800
Profit before taxes	23,772
Federal income tax (30%)	7,132
Profit after taxes	$16,640
Dividends for preferred stock (16% of $30,000)	$ 4,800
Profit after preferred dividends	$11,840
Earnings per share of common stock (400 shares)	$ 29.60

Of course, the common stock takes the full risk that profits will reach or exceed expectations. The illustrated advantage depends upon the profits after taxes being a greater percentage of capital than the percentage return required to be paid to the senior securities. Watch what happens to the last example if profits dip to $15,000 (before deducting interest) rather than the predicted $28,572 or better. The statement looks like this:

Profit before interest	$15,000
Interest (16% of $30,000)	4,800
Profit before taxes	$11,200
Federal income tax (30%)	3,360
Profit after taxes	$ 7,840
Dividends on preferred stock (16% of $30,000)	4,800
	$ 3,040

Earnings per share of common stock (400 shares)	$7.60

Contrast this earnings figure with the one on the following statement from the original capital structure, where all $100,000 had been raised by the sale of $1,000 shares of common stock.

Profit before taxes	$15,000
Federal income tax (30%)	4,500
Profit after taxes	$11,500
Earnings per share of common stock (1000 shares)	$11.50

In the last case, the common shareholders benefit more from complete common stock capitalization than from combinations of common stock, preferred stock, and debt.

Taxes

The concepts of double taxation and its erosion of corporate profits were discussed in "Taxation of a Corporation" in Chapter 4. Debt securities avoid double taxation since the interest paid on the debt is deductible as an expense to the corporation, rather than being taxed as corporate profit. In this respect, debt securities enjoy a tax advantage over equity securities, since distributions to shareholders in the form of dividends are taxed first as corporate profit and again as individual income.

The solution, you might propose, would be to issue as many debt securities and as few equity securities as possible. The tax authorities of the federal government have thought of this. A disproportionate debt-to-equity ratio is called *thin incorporation*. When thin incorporation exists, the tax authorities may characterize interest payments on debt securities as dividends on equity securities for tax purposes, disallowing the interest expense deduction and requiring tax to be paid on the resulting increased profits. This restructuring has been upheld in severe cases, such as where the majority shareholder loaned considerable sums to the corporation in return for separate debt securities, and where all shareholders loaned disproportionately large amounts to a corporation with very little investment represented in common stock. It has been suggested that a good debt-to-equity ratio should not exceed 4:1 to avoid problems of thin incorporation.[61]

NOTES

1. Securities Act of 1933, 15 U.S.C.A. §§ 77a–77aa.
2. Securities Exchange Act of 1934, 15 U.S.C.A. §§ 78a–78m.
3. See H. Henn and J. Alexander, Corporations, §§ 292–308 (3d ed. 1983); R. Deer, The Lawyer's Basic Corporate Practice Manual, §§ 6.01–6.08 (1970).
4. See M.B.C.A. § 6.01 and "The Articles of Incorporation" in Chapter 6.
5. See "Filing and Other Formalities" in Chapter 6.
6. See 8 Del.Stat.Ann. § 160.
7. See "Ownership and Management of a Corporation" in Chapter 4.
8. See, e.g., Colorado, Col.Rev.Stat. § 7–4–116.

9. E. G., Wyoming, Wyo.Stat. § 17–1–139.
10. See M.B.C.A. § 2.02(b) and "The Articles of Incorporation" in Chapter 6.
11. Neb.Rev.Stat. § 21–2014.
12. See M.B.C.A. § 6.21(b).
13. E. g., Georgia, Ga.Code Ann. § 14–2–84.
14. "The Articles of Incorporation" in Chapter 6.
15. E. g., Idaho, Idaho Code § 30–1–6.
16. See, e.g., Colorado, Colo.Rev.Stat. § 7–6–101(2).
17. Dividends and other distributions are discussed in detail in Chapter 9.
18. M.B.C.A. § 6.25(d).
19. M.B.C.A. § 6.25(e).
20. M.B.C.A. § 6.01.
21. M.B.C.A. § 6.01(b).
22. See M.B.C.A. § 6.02.
23. See "Amendment of the Articles of Incorporation" in Chapter 13.
24. M.B.C.A. § 6.02.
25. West's Modern Legal Forms § 2755.10.
26. M.B.C.A. § 6.02(d), and see Form 7B in Appendix G.
27. M.B.C.A. § 6.04(a).
28. M.B.C.A. § 6.04(c).
29. See "Par Value or No Par Value" earlier in this chapter.
30. M.B.C.A. § 6.21(c).
31. E. g., Missouri, Mo.Ann.Stat. § 351.160 (Vernon).
32. E.g., Oregon, Ore.Rev.Stat. § 57.106; and Florida, Fla.Stat.Ann. § 607.054.
33. E.g., Michigan, Mich.Comp.Laws Ann. § 21.200(315).
34. Compare New Mexico's corporation statute, which specifically allows shares to be issued for preincorporation services. N.Mex.Stat.Ann. § 53–11–19.
35. M.B.C.A. § 6.21.
36. See Chapter 9.
37. M.B.C.A. § 7.21(b).
38. See "The Articles of Incorporation" in Chapter 6.
39. See "Ownership and Management of a Corporation," in Chapter 4 and "The Articles of Incorporation" in Chapter 6.
40. M.B.C.A. § 6.01(b).
41. West's Modern Legal Forms § 2759.
42. M.B.C.A. § 7.21(a).
43. West's Modern Legal Forms § 2757.1.
44. West's Modern Legal Forms § 2757.2.
45. West's Modern Legal Forms § 2762.
46. M.B.C.A. § 6.31. A sample statement of cancellation appears as Form 7C in Appendix G.
47. See "Fractions of Shares or Scrip" earlier in this chapter.
48. See West's Modern Legal Forms § 2758.
49. See M.B.C.A. § 16.01.
50. See M.B.C.A. § 23.
51. West's Modern Legal Forms § 2957. See also § 2957.1.
52. West's Modern Legal Forms § 2979.1.
53. Uniform Commercial Code (hereinafter cited U.C.C.) § 9–203. An example of a security agreement under the U.C.C. appears as Form 7D in Appendix G.
54. U.C.C. § 9–402.
55. U.C.C. § 9–401. A sample financing statement in Form 7E in Appendix G.
56. Securities Act of 1933, 15 U.S.C.A. §§ 77a–77aa; Trust Indenture Act of 1939, 15 U.S.C.A. §§ 77aaa–77bbbb.
57. A skeletal trust indenture, including articles, section, and subsection headings, is Form 7F in Appendix G.
58. West's Modern Legal Forms § 2972.1.
59. West's Modern Legal Forms § 2972.2.
60. E.g., Delaware, 8 Del.Code Ann. § 221; Pennsylvania, 15 Pa.Stat. § 309.1.
61. See H. Henn and J. Alexander, The Law of Corporations, § 166 n.15 (3d ed. 1983).

8 CORPORATE MEETINGS

TYPES AND PURPOSES OF MEETINGS

Corporate activity is conducted through meetings of the internal corporate groups: the incorporators, the directors, and the shareholders. Under the common law of corporations, the directors of a corporation do not act individually, but may act only as a board collectively convened. Shareholder and incorporator activities are somewhat more individual, but the democratic rule that the majority will control the minority is applied to both groups. Traditionally, corporate action may not be taken unless it has been approved by one of these groups duly convened at a meeting. In theory, then, any action taken by the corporation requires an approving resolution by the appropriate intracorporate group. In reality, however, it would be much too cumbersome to hold a meeting of one of these groups for daily business decisions. Instead, the board of directors delegates authority for the everyday business affairs of the corporation to the officers, and the board is responsible for the supervision of officer activities. Nevertheless, a corporate decision of any magnitude should be made at a directors' meeting with an appropriate resolution set forth in the minutes, and some major corporate decisions require shareholder approval.[1]

Three types of corporate meetings may be held by the intracorporate groups described here: organizational meetings, regular meetings, and special meetings. State statutes variously detail the need for such meetings, authority to call the meetings, notice required for the meetings, and time and place for the meetings.

REQUIREMENT FOR ORGANIZATIONAL MEETINGS

As previously discussed, the corporation is formed by the filing of articles of incorporation or the issuance of a certificate of incorporation, depending upon the law of the particular jurisdiction.[2] Thereafter, certain organizational meetings must be held, and each state statute should be consulted to determine the parties to the meeting and the business that must be conducted. The organizational meetings are, by most statutes, a required condition that should be satisfied before the corporation commences business operations.[3] Some states require only an organizational meeting of the incorporators; others require only an organizational meeting of the directors. Still other states permit either group to hold an organizational meeting, and a few also require the shareholders to have an organizational meeting.[4] Section 2.05(a) of the Model Business Corporation Act provides as follows:

> After incorporation:
>> (1) if initial directors are named in the articles of incorporation, the initial directors shall hold an organizational meeting, at the call of a majority of the directors, to complete the organization of the corporation by appointing officers, adopting bylaws, and carrying on any other business brought before the meeting;
>> (2) if initial directors are not named in the articles, the incorporator or incorporators shall hold an organizational meeting at the call of a majority of the incorporators:
>>> (i) to elect directors and complete the organization of the corporation; or
>>> (ii) to elect a board of directors who shall complete the organization of the corporation.

DIRECTORS' ORGANIZATIONAL MEETING

The Model Business Corporation Act formerly provided that the directors' organizational meeting was to be called by the incorporators. The act was amended to provide that the meeting may be called by a majority of the directors named in the articles of incorporation, or a majority of the incorporators if no initial directors were named in the articles. Several states have adopted this rule.

Notice

In many states, at least three days' notice must be given to the directors by mail. Some states and the Model Business Corporation Act require no notice, and Pennsylvania prescribes five days' notice.[5] It is common practice, however, to secure a waiver of notice from the initial directors to avoid the observance of the notice period.

> **EXAMPLE: Waiver of Notice of Organizational Meeting**
> We, the undersigned, constituting all of the directors of Happiness, Inc., a corporation organized under the laws of the State of Colorado, do hereby severally waive notice of the time, place and purpose of the first meeting of directors of said corporation, and consent that the meeting be held at the corporate offices, and on the 10th day of June, 1990, at 8:30 o'clock A.M., and we do further consent to the transaction of any and all business that may property come before the meeting.
> Dated June 10, 1990
>
> _____
> _____
> _____ [6]

Nominal Directors

If initial directors are named, the articles of incorporation need only contain the names of the persons who will serve as directors until the first meeting of shareholders and until their successors have been elected and qualified. If the persons named are the actual directors of the corporation, they may transact all necessary director business at their organizational meeting. On the other hand, if the directors named in the articles of incorporation are only *nominal* or dummy directors, they should not be expected to conduct any more than the formal statutory business, such as adopting by-laws and electing officers. Other corporate business should be reserved for the consideration of the actual directors elected by the shareholders. If multiple meetings are undesirable, it is possible to have the nominal directors submit their resignations one by one at the organizational meeting, with the board of directors adopting by resolution the resignation of each dummy director and electing the actual director to fill the vacancy. The actual director will then serve for the period of the predecessor dummy director, or until the next shareholder meeting when a successor will be elected.

> **EXAMPLE: Resignation of a Dummy Director**
> To the Board of Happiness, Inc.
> I regret that, owing to other business commitments, I am no longer able to act as a director, and I hereby tender my resignation as a director of Happiness, Inc. to take effect as and from the 10th day of June, 1990.
>
> [*Signature*][7]

> **EXAMPLE: Acceptance of the Resignation of a Director**
> RESOLVED, that the resignation of Edward O'Keefe as director of this Corporation be accepted to take effect on June 10, 1990, and that the secretary be and he hereby is directed to notify Edward O'Keefe of such acceptance.[8]

If the directors are not named in the articles of incorporation, they are elected at an organizational meeting of the incorporators. The elected directors then hold an organizational meeting after their election.

INCORPORATORS' ORGANIZATIONAL MEETING

If the state statute requires an organizational meeting of the incorporators, it may also require a period of notice preceding the meeting and will usually specify the business to be conducted at the meeting. Of course, the statutory requirements must be strictly followed. Even if the statute does not specify the business that must be conducted, certain matters are normally considered at all organizational meetings.

BUSINESS CONDUCTED AT ORGANIZATIONAL MEETINGS

Most state statutes describe specific matters that must be on the agenda of an organizational meeting. In the Model Business Corporation Act, the organizational meeting must consider the adoption of the by-laws and the election of officers. The statute further provides that the organizers should consider "carrying on any other business brought before the meeting."[9] The following discussion considers the chronological order of business at an organization meeting and includes examples of how the minutes should reflect the actions taken.

Determination of a Quorum and Election of a Chair and Secretary

Counsel (or whoever is initially presiding) should be certain to determine the presence of a quorum according to the rules stated in the articles of incorporation or the statute. If a quorum is present, the fact should be noted in the minutes, and the persons present and absent should be named in the minutes.

A chair and a secretary should be elected as the first order of business of an organizational meeting. The secretary is responsible for the minutes of the meeting. The minutes are frequently prepared in advance by counsel and may serve as an agenda for the meeting, but the secretary should review them for accuracy and add any necessary new material. The chair is responsible for an orderly meeting.

> **EXAMPLE: Recital of Quorum, and Election of Chair and Secretary**
> The following directors named in the articles of incorporation were present: Edward Giles, Gary Nakarado, and Terryl Gorrell. The following directors named in the articles of incorporation were absent: Richard Vermeire and Karen Burn.
>
> The presence of the foregoing directors constituted a quorum. By unanimous vote of the directors, Edward Giles was elected Chairman of the meeting and Gary Nakarado was elected Secretary of the meeting.

Notice or Waivers of Notice

If the appropriate notice has been given to the members of the group, a copy of the notices should be presented to the meeting and attached to the minutes. If waivers of notice of the meeting have been obtained from those present, the waivers should be presented to the meeting and affixed to the minutes as an attachment.

> **EXAMPLE: Recognition of Notice**
> The Secretary presented the waiver of the notice of the meeting signed by all of the directors, which was ordered filed with the minutes of the meeting.

Determination of Actual Directors

If the directors named in the articles of incorporation are the actual directors of the corporation, no further action regarding their status is required at the organizational meeting. Some states do not require the naming of the initial directors, and all states would permit dummy directors to be named in the articles of incorporation.

Election of the actual directors will occur at the incorporators' organizational meeting if no directors are named in the articles of incorporation. If the directors are named, but are only nominal directors, the incorporators may obtain the resignations of the nominal directors and replace those directors with actual directors at the incorporators' organizational meeting.

The directors' organizational meeting should be conducted by actual directors. Therefore, if nominal directors are named in the articles of incorporation, and there is no meeting of incorporators to elect actual directors, the nominal directors may be replaced by the procedure suggested earlier in this chapter under "Directors' Organizational Meeting."

The resignations of nominal directors should be affixed to the minutes of the meeting wherein they were replaced.

> **EXAMPLE: Determining Actual Directors**
> The Secretary announced that resignations had been received from Richard Vermeire and Karen Burn, who were nominal directors of the corporation named in the articles of incorporation.

Thereupon, upon motion duly made, seconded and unanimously adopted it was
> RESOLVED, that the resignations of Richard Vermeire and Karen Burn as directors of this corporation be accepted to take effect on the date of this meeting, and that the Secretary be and he hereby is directed to notify Mr. Vermeire and Ms. Burn of such acceptance, and to affix to the minutes of this meeting the original written resignations of these directors.
> FURTHER RESOLVED, that Edward Naylor and James Burghardt shall be appointed to fill the vacancies created by the resignations of these directors, and shall be directors of this corporation to serve until the first annual meeting of the shareholders or until their successors are otherwise elected and qualified.

Presentation of Articles of Incorporation

The articles of incorporation, returned by the secretary of state with the certificate of incorporation (if one has been issued under local law), should be presented to the meeting and affixed as an attachment to the minutes of the meeting. It is not necessary to have a resolution approving the articles of incorporation, but the minutes should reflect that the articles were presented to the meeting and the secretary should be instructed to insert the articles and the certificate of incorporation in the minute book.

> **EXAMPLE: Presentation of the Articles of Incorporation**
> The Chairman submitted to the meeting a copy of the Articles of Incorporation of the corporation and an original receipt showing payment of the statutory organization taxes and filing fees. The Chairman reported that the original of these Articles of Incorporation had been filed in the office of the Secretary of State, State of Nebraska, on November 1, 1990. Thereupon, upon motion duly made, seconded and unanimously adopted, it was:
>> RESOLVED, that the Articles of Incorporation as presented be, and they hereby are, accepted and approved and that said Articles of Incorporation, together with the original receipt showing payment of the statutory organization taxes and filing fees, be placed in the minute book of the corporation.

Approval of Action Taken at Previous Meetings

When the incorporators have held an organizational meeting and the board of directors subsequently conducts an organizational meeting, it is customary for the board to approve, ratify, and confirm all of the actions taken at the incorporators' meeting. This has the effect of making the action of the incorporators the action of the board of directors. For example, if the incorporators have adopted the by-laws, this resolution grants the same approval by the board of directors. The minutes of the board of directors' meeting may be abbreviated in this fashion:

> **EXAMPLE: Acceptance of Incorporator's Action**
> The Secretary presented to the meeting the minutes of the first meeting of incorporators of the Corporation together with a copy of the By-laws adopted by the incorporators at their meeting held November 10, 1990.
> On motion duly made and seconded, it was unanimously
>> RESOLVED, that the minutes of the first meeting of the incorporators of the

Corporation held on November 10, 1990 be and they hereby are in all respects ratified, approved and confirmed.

FURTHER RESOLVED, that the By-laws adopted by the incorporators at such first meeting hereby are adopted by this Board as and for the By-laws of this Corporation.

Approval of By-laws

Counsel should have drafted the by-laws pursuant to the instructions of the incorporators before the organizational meeting. The by-laws are presented to the organizational meeting of the appropriate group for approval. The minutes must contain a resolution that the by-laws have been approved, and the secretary should be instructed to insert a copy of the by-laws in the minutes.

> **EXAMPLE: Acceptance of By-laws**
>
> RESOLVED, that the By-laws submitted to the meeting be and are adopted as the By-laws of the Corporation, and that the Secretary is instructed to insert a copy of such By-laws, certified by the Secretary, in the minute book immediately following the Certificate of Incorporation with affixed duplicate original of the Articles of Incorporation.

Approval of Corporate Seal

As a part of the corporation supplies, counsel should have obtained a corporate seal designed to the specifications of the incorporators. It is customary to adopt a resolution to the effect that the seal is accepted as the corporate seal, and to affix the seal to the margin in the minute book page. If any regulation of the use of the seal is comtemplated, the regulation should be specified in the resolution.

> **EXAMPLE: Acceptance of the Seal**
>
> RESOLVED, that the seal now produced by the secretary, an impression whereof is now made in the minute book of the Company, be adopted as the seal of the Company, and that such seal shall not be affixed to any deed or instrument of any description, except in the presence of an officer, or director, and the secretary of the Company, who shall respectively sign said deed or instrument.[10]

Approval of Share Certificates

Share certificates are also obtained as part of the corporate supplies, and a specimen certificate should be presented to the meeting. The share certificate should contain all appropriate legends if share transfer restrictions are contemplated, and it will also contain other matters unique to the particular corporation or the particular class of stock.[11] The share certificate is accepted by resolution at the organizational meeting, and the secretary should insert the specimen in the minute book.

> **EXAMPLE: Acceptance of Share Certificate**
>
> RESOLVED, that the form of share certificate presented at this meeting is adopted as the form of share certificate for this Corporation; and the Secretary of the meeting is instructed to append a sample of such certificate to the minutes of this meeting.

Authorization to Issue Shares

At their organizational meeting, the incorporators authorize the board of directors to issue the shares of the company. The incorporators' authorizing resolution should be contained in the minutes of their meeting. The directors may adopt such a resolution at their organizational meeting authorizing the appropriate officers (as specified by statute) to issue the certificates.

> **EXAMPLE: Authority to Issue Shares**
> RESOLVED, that the President and Secretary of this Corporation be, and they are hereby authorized to issue certificates for shares in the form as submitted to this meeting and ordered attached to these minutes.

Acceptance of Transfers of Share Subscriptions from Dummy Incorporators

As previously indicated, some states require that an incorporator subscribe for shares as a condition to qualification as an incorporator.[12] To satisfy this rule, incorporators frequently subscribe for shares they do not intend to purchase. In such cases, the incorporators may assign their preincorporation share subscriptions to actual investors in the company, and these subscription transfers are presented to the organizational meeting of the board of directors for the directors' approval. A resolution reflecting the directors' approval should be included in the minutes.

> **EXAMPLE: Transfer of Subscription**
> Dated, Kearney, Nebraska, October 31, 1990
> FOR VALUE RECEIVED, I, Charles Luce, hereby sell, assign and transfer unto William Callison all my right, title and interest as subscriber to the shares of common stock of Happiness, Inc., which subscription was executed by me on the 3rd day of October 1990, and, when accepted, entitles me to receive 500 shares of the common stock of Happiness, Inc., and I hereby direct said corporation to issue certificates for said shares of stock to and in the name of the aforesaid assignee, or his nominees or assigns.
>
> [*Signature*]

> **EXAMPLE: Adoption of Assignment**
> RESOLVED, that the assignment and transfer of a stock subscription from Charles Luce to William Callison, dated October 31, 1990, is hereby approved and accepted on behalf of the Corporation.

Acceptance of Share Subscriptions

The preincorporation share subscriptions are offers to the corporation to buy shares when the corporation is formed.[13] Once formation has been accomplished, the board of directors should accept the offers on behalf of the corporation and thereby obligate the subscribers to pay for the shares they have offered to purchase. The acceptance of the share subscriptions is accomplished by a resolution, and each subscription should be listed therein, specifying the number of shares the subscriber has offered to purchase, the class of the security, the par value, and the price at which the offer was tendered.

If cash has been offered for share purchases, the resolution accepting the offer need only state the amount offered when describing the consideration.

> **EXAMPLE: Acceptance of Cash Subscriptions**
> RESOLVED, that the written offers dated March 23, 1990, pertaining to the issuance of shares of the Corporation, to wit:
>
> | Name | Number of Shares | Consideration |
> |---|---|---|
> | John O'Brien | 100 | $100 |
> | Adam Golodner | 1000 | $1000 |
> | Margo Stevenson | 750 | $750 |
>
> be, and the same hereby are, in all respects accepted for and on behalf of the Corporation.

If property or services are offered to the corporation in exchange for shares, the board of directors must evaluate the property and services consistently with the valuation rule of the particular jurisdiction. Some states require that an actual market value be determined and used by the board in appraising property or services, but most states permit the board of directors to determine the value of the property or services in good faith considering the best interests of the corporation. The directors' determination of value is then conclusive in the absence of fraud. The Model Business Corporation Act requires a directors' determination of adequacy of consideration in Section 6.21. This determination of value is critical to the issuance of par value securities, since those securities cannot be sold for less than par value. Thus, if a corporation receives an offer to transfer certain land in exchange for 1,000 shares that each have a $10 par value, the board of directors must appraise the land, by the appropriate valuation rule, at an amount equal to or greater than $10,000. The resolution in the minutes should state the valuation determination.

> **EXAMPLE: Acceptance of Property Subscription**
> RESOLVED, that this Corporation hereby accepts the offer of Marcia Kearney and Stephen Roark, as joint owners, to sell and convey to it good and marketable title to the fee of the premises known as 3590 E. Nobles Road, Littleton, Colorado, 80122, together with the buildings thereon, and all personal property belonging to them used in connection with the premises free and clear of all liens and encumbrances, in consideration of this Corporation's issuing and delivering to Stephen Roark, or his nominee, certificates for 150 of its fully paid and nonassessable shares of its 5½% preferred shares, $100 par value, and of its issuing and delivering to Marcia Kearney, or her nominee, certificates for 150 of its fully paid and nonassessable 5½% preferred shares, $100 par value. The Board of Directors does hereby adjudge and declare that said property is of the fair value of $30,000, and that the same is necessary for the business of the corporation.

If the cash or property is not immediately tendered with the offer, it is appropriate for the directors to adopt a resolution to assess or *call* the consideration due. Unless otherwise stated in the subscription agreement, the offer is payable in full upon acceptance, but the board of directors may permit payment by installments.[14]

> **EXAMPLE: Partial Call of Subscriptions**
> RESOLVED, that a call of fifty per cent is hereby made upon each and every share of the capital stock of the Company subscribed for, and same is to be paid by each subscriber to the treasurer of the Company, on or before the 30th day of November, 1990, (and that the president and secretary issue certificates of fully-paid stock therefor).[15]

> **EXAMPLE: Full Call of Subscriptions**
> RESOLVED, that a full call is hereby made upon each and every share of the capital stock of the Company subscribed for, and the same is to be paid by each subscriber to the treasurer of the Company, on or before the 30th day of November, 1990, (and that the president and secretary issue certificates of fully-paid stock therefor).

Authorization to Issue Shares

The board of directors should authorize the officers of the company to issue the shares represented by the accepted share subscriptions. The resolution generally states that the company will issue and deliver the prescribed number of shares to the subscriber when full consideration has been received for the shares. The resolution should further state that the officers are authorized to execute common stock certificates and to register the shares in the names of the subscribers.

> **EXAMPLE: Authorization to Issue Shares**
> RESOLVED, that the Corporation issue and deliver to those persons upon receipt of the consideration therefor, pursuant to the terms of the aforesaid offer, certificates representing the subscribed shares of the Corporation, no par value, each such shares to include the shares originally subscribed for by the subscribers to the capital stock of the Corporation, and subsequently assigned to the officers; and
> FURTHER RESOLVED, that the officers of the Corporation be, and they hereby are, authorized, empowered and directed to take any and all steps, and to execute and deliver any and all instruments in connection with consummating the transaction contemplated by the aforesaid offer and in connection with carrying the foregoing resolutions into effect; and
> FURTHER RESOLVED, that upon the delivery to this Corporation of proper instruments of conveyance, assignment, and transfer, in such form as counsel for this Corporation may approve and the proper officers of this Corporation may approve, the proper officers of this Corporation be and they hereby are authorized and directed to issue to Ms. Kearney an appropriate certificate for 150 of its 5½% preferred shares, $100 par value, which when issued as provided in the foregoing resolutions shall be fully paid and nonassessable.

If the shares are being issued in excess of par value, or if no par value shares are being sold in excess of stated value, the board of directors should resolve to allocate the excess consideration to the capital surplus account.

> **EXAMPLE: Allocation to Capital Surplus**
> RESOLVED, that since the corporation's common stock has a par value of $.50 per share, and the same is being sold for $1.00 per share, the excess amount over par value shall be allocated to the capital surplus account of the corporation;
> AND FURTHER RESOLVED, that seventy-five percent (75%) of the consideration received for the company's no par value stock shall be allocated and applied to the capital surplus account of the corporation.

Since the Model Business Corporation Act now permits shares to be issued for promissory notes and services to be performed, the board of directors may authorize the issuance of shares in such cases, but should take steps to protect the corporation in the event the promissory note is not paid or the contract is not performed. Section 6.21(e) of the act suggests that the corporation may place shares in escrow or otherwise restrict the transfer of shares until the entire purchase price has been received. Provisions concerning the disposition of the shares, in the event that the payment or performance does not occur, should also be included.

> **EXAMPLE:** *Escrow of Shares*
> RESOLVED, that the corporation issue and deliver in escrow to the First Interstate Bank certificates representing the subscribed shares of the corporation, no par value, in exchange for the subscriptions by the subscribers to the capital stock of the corporation which have not been fully performed, including promissory notes and contracts to perform future services; and
> FURTHER RESOLVED, that the officers of the corporation be, and they hereby are, authorized, empowered and directed to collect all promissory notes and require the performance of all contracts for services, and to notify the First Interstate Bank as escrow agent of the collection of the promissory note or the performance of the contracts for services; and
> FURTHER RESOLVED, that upon the payment of the promissory note or the performance of contracts for services, that the officers of the corporation shall release the escrow of shares with First Interstate Bank, and cause the share certificates to be delivered to the subscribers; and
> FURTHER RESOLVED, that in the event that the promissory notes are not fully paid or the contracts for services are not fully performed that the officers of the corporation shall notify First Interstate Bank as escrow agent of the default on such notes and contracts, and to take any and all steps, and to execute and deliver any and all instruments or documents necessary to cancel those shares which have not been paid.

Reimbursement of Fees

The authority to pay expenses in connection with the formation of the corporation emanates from the board of directors in its organizational meeting. The treasurer is authorized to pay all taxes, fees, and other expenses incurred and to be incurred in connection with the organization of the company and to reimburse any persons who have made expenditures on behalf of the company during the formation procedure. Legal fees are included herein, and that usually makes this a very important resolution.

> **EXAMPLE: Authorization to Pay Expenses**
> FURTHER RESOLVED that the President of this Corporation be and she hereby is authorized to pay all charges and expenses incident to or arising out of the organization of this Corporation, including the bill of Gail Klapper, Esq., for legal services in connection therewith in the sum of $500, and to reimburse any person who has made any disbursement therefor.

Adoption of Preincorporation Agreements

Before formation of the corporation, the incorporators may have entered contracts on behalf of the corporation to ensure that the necessary resources for conducting business would be available when the corporation was formed. For example, they may have leased office space or they may have purchased equipment on credit. An earlier section discussed the general resolution by which the board of directors adopts the acts of the incorporators,[16] but any prior agreements that were intended to benefit the corporation should be adopted by a separate, specific resolution during the board of directors' organizational meeting. The resolution should summarize the terms of the agreement and clearly express the directors' approval of the transaction.

> **EXAMPLE: Adoption of Preincorporation Agreements**
> RESOLVED, the board of directors has reviewed and considered an agreement on behalf of the corporation, a copy of which is attached to these minutes as Exhibit A and incorporated herein by reference. This agreement was entered into prior to the existence and formation of the corporation, and the board of directors, having considered the agreement on behalf of the corporation, does hereby adopt and accept the agreement according to its terms, and agrees that the corporation shall perform all of its obligations and be entitled to all of its rights as specified therein.

Election of Corporate Officers

The officers of the corporation are elected by the board of directors, and this is one of the prescribed matters to be considered at the directors' organizational meeting. The resolution for the election usually states that the officers will serve for a stated period of time or at the discretion of the board of directors, and fixes the officers' compensation.

> **EXAMPLE: Election and Compensation of Officers**
> The meeting then proceeded to the election of officers to serve until the next annual meeting of stockholders or until their successors are elected and qualified. The following nominations were made and seconded:
>
> | | |
> |---|---|
> | President | Glenna McKelvy |
> | Vice President | Bill Bradford |
> | Secretary | Amy Jo Ellis |
> | Treasurer | Dave Herrenbruck |
>
> There being no further nominations the foregoing persons were unanimously elected to the office set opposite their respective names.
>   RESOLVED, that until further action by the Board of Directors, the annual salaries of the officers are fixed in the following amounts, effective as of January 1, 1991, and payable in twelve equal monthly installments:
>
> | | |
> |---|---|
> | President | $50,000.00 |
> | Vice President | $45,000.00 |
> | Secretary | $25,000.00 |
> | Treasurer | $20,000.00 |

Bank Resolution

The bank resolution prescribes the authority for the maintenance of a bank account and names the persons who have authority to obligate the corporation in banking matters. Every bank supplies a form for a banking resolution, which should be completed and attached to the minutes of the meeting. The minutes contain a directors' resolution that authorizes the opening of the bank account, and adopts by reference the provisions in the attached bank form. The directors' resolution looks like this:

> **EXAMPLE:** **Acceptance of Bank Resolutions**
> RESOLVED that the funds of the Corporation be deposited in the Central City Bank of Kearney, 6th Avenue Branch, and that the printed resolutions supplied by that bank, as filed in at this meeting, be attached to the minutes of this meeting and be deemed resolutions of this Corporation duly adopted by the Board of Directors.

The bank resolution looks like this:

> **EXAMPLE:** **Bank Resolution**
>
> ....
> *(Name of Corporation)*
> I HEREBY CERTIFY TO ....,
> that at a meeting of the Board of Directors of ...., a corporation organized under the laws of the State of .... duly called (a quorum being present) and held at the office of said corporation, No .... in the city of .... State of .... on the .... day of ...., 19 ., the following resolutions were duly adopted and are now in full force and effect:
>
> Depositary and Signing Resolution
>
> RESOLVED, that the above bank be designated as a depositary of this corporation and that funds of this corporation deposited in said Bank be subject to withdrawal upon checks, notes, drafts, bills of exchange, acceptances, undertakings of other orders for the payment of money when signed on behalf of this corporation by any .... of its following officers to wit:
> *(Number)*
> RESOLVED, that the above bank, is hereby authorized to pay any such orders and also to receive the same for credit of or in payment from the payee or any other holder without inquiry as to the officer or tendered in payment of his individual obligation.
>
> Borrowing Resolution
>
> RESOLVED, that ....
> ....
> be and they hereby are authorized to borrow from time to time on behalf of this corporation from the above bank sums of money for such period or periods of time, and upon such terms, rates of interest and amounts as may to them in their discretion seem advisable, and to execute notes or agreements in the forms required by said Bank in the name of the corporation for the payment of any sums so borrowed.
>
> That said officers are hereby authorized to pledge or mortgage any of the bonds, stocks or other securities, bills receivable, warehouse receipts or other property real or personal of the corporation, for the purpose of securing the payment of any moneys so borrowed; to endorse said securities and/or to issue the necessary powers of attorney and to execute loan, pledge or liability agreements in the forms required by the said bank in connection with the same.
>
> That said officers are hereby authorized to discount with the above bank any bills receivable held by this corporation upon such terms as they may deem proper.
>
> That the foregoing powers and authority will continue until written notice of revocation has been delivered to the above bank.
>
> RESOLVED, that the secretary of this corporation be and he or she hereby is authorized to certify to the above bank, the foregoing resolutions and that the provisions thereof are in conformity with the charter and by-laws of this corporation.
>
> I FURTHER CERTIFY that there is no provision in the charter or by-laws of said corporation limiting the power of the board of directors to pass the foregoing resolutions and that the same are in conformity with the provisions of said charter and by-laws.
>
> I further certify that the following are the genuine signatures of the persons now holding office in said company as indicated opposite their respective signatures.
>
> .... (Title)
> .... (Title)
> .... (Title)

................................(Title)
................................(Title)

IN WITNESS WHEREOF, I have hereunto set my hand as secretary of said corporation and affixed the corporate seal this ......day of ......, 19 ......

(CORPORATE SEAL) Secretary of the Corporation

NOTE: *In case the secretary or other recording officer is authorized to sign checks, notes, etc., by the above resolutions, this certificate must also be signed by a second officer of the corporation.*[17]

Application for Qualification as a Foreign Corporation

If management contemplates doing business in another jurisdiction, the board of directors must adopt an appropriate resolution authorizing the officers of the corporation to apply for admission and qualification of the corporation as a foreign corporation in any other jurisdiction where it plans to do business.

EXAMPLE: Authorization of Foreign Qualification
RESOLVED, that the officers of the Corporation be authorized and directed to qualify the Corporation as a foreign corporation authorized to conduct business in the State of Kansas, and in connection therewith to appoint all necessary agents or attorneys for service of process and to take all other action which may be deemed necessary or advisable.

Appointment of Resident Agents and Office

The articles of incorporation name the resident agents, but the appointment of those agents should be *ratified* by a resolution of the board of directors. Similarly, the establishment of a principal office of the corporation may be resolved at the organizational meeting.

EXAMPLE: Principal Office and Agent
RESOLVED, that the Articles of Incorporation correctly state the principal office of the corporation and that the person named therein as registered agent shall remain registered agent until subsequently changed by a resolution of the board of directors.

Designation of Counsel and Accountant

The board of directors may designate a certain attorney to act as the general counsel of the company, if appropriate, and also may specify the persons to be retained as the corporation's accountants.

EXAMPLE: Appointment of Counsel and Auditors
RESOLVED, that Charles Passaglia be hereby appointed to act as attorney for the Company, and that he be paid the ordinary professional charges for his services as attorney.
RESOLVED, that Bert Bondi & Co. be hereby appointed auditors of the Company for the ensuing year, and that the remuneration for their services as such auditors be the sum of $2,000.00.[18]

Authority to Use Assumed Name

Some states permit the corporation to conduct business under an assumed name as long as that name is not deceptively similar to another reserved or registered name. Usually the corporation must file a statement of assumed name with the appropriate state official.[19] The authority to use such a name and to file the statement comes from a resolution of the directors.

> **EXAMPLE: Adoption of an Assumed Name**
> RESOLVED, that the corporation may use the name "Black, Inc." as an assumed business name to carry out its purposes and objects in the state of Oregon, and that the officers of the corporation as required by the statute are authorized to execute such documents as are necessary to accomplish the registration of the corporation's assumed business name.

Adoption of Section 1244 Plan

The Small Business Tax Revision Act added Section 1244 of the Internal Revenue Code to offer special loss protection for shareholders of a small corporation. Losses on Section 1244 stock are fully deductible as business losses up to certain dollar limits per year, instead of being treated as capital losses. (The substantive rules of Section 1244 stock are explained in detail in "Taxation of a Corporation" in Chapter 4.) To qualify to issue Section 1244 stock, a corporation must be a small-business corporation, as defined by the statute.[20]

This discussion is concerned with the adoption of a Section 1244 plan. If a new corporation qualifies as a small-business corporation and issues Section 1244 stock, shareholder losses from the sale of the shares will be treated as ordinary losses and not capital losses, so the shareholder may offset the lost value against ordinary income, such as the shareholder's wages, interest, dividends, and so on. Unless the shares qualify under Section 1244, any such losses offset only capital gains and, to a very limited extent, ordinary income.

In 1978, Section 1244 was amended to eliminate the requirement of a *written* plan to issue stock under Section 1244. Nevertheless, it is good practice to clearly indicate the intention to qualify for this special protection by adopting a resolution and plan in the minutes of the organizational meeting. A proper resolution adopting a Section 1244 plan should restate the statutory requirements. Thus, it should recite that the payment of the shares will be in cash or other property but not securities or services, and it should provide that the stock will be offered for sale at a price not lower than the par value of the shares and not higher than an aggregate of $1,000,000.

> **EXAMPLE: Section 1244 Plan**
> A plan was read and (unanimously) adopted for the issuance of common stock of the corporation to qualify the same as "small business corporation" stock under the provisions of Section 1244 of the Internal Revenue Code of 1986. The Secretary was directed to place a copy of the Plan immediately following these minutes.
>
> Plan for Issuance of Stock
>
> 1. The corporation shall offer and issue under this Plan, a maximum of 50,000 shares of its common stock at a maximum price of ten dollars ($10.00) per share.
> 2. This offer shall terminate by:
>   (a) Complete issuance of all shares offered hereunder, or
>   (b) Appropriate action terminating the same by the Board of Directors and the Stockholders, or
>   (c) By the adoption of a new Plan by the Stockholders for the issuance of additional stock under Section 1244, Internal Revenue Code.

3. No increase in the basis of outstanding stock shall result from a contribution to capital hereunder.
4. No stock offered hereunder shall be issued on the exercise of a stock right, stock warrant, or stock option, unless such right, warrant, or option is applicable solely to unissued stock offered under the Plan and is exercised during the period of the Plan.
5. Stock subscribed for prior to the adoption of the Plan, including stock subscribed for prior to the date the corporation comes into existence, may be issued hereunder, provided, however, that the said stock is not in fact issued prior to the adoption of such Plan.
6. No stock shall be issued hereunder for a payment which, along or together with prior payments, exceeds the maximum amount that may be received under the plan.
7. Any offering or portion of an offer outstanding which is unissued at the time of the adoption of this Plan is herewith withdrawn. Stock rights, stock warrants, stock options or securities convertible into stock, which are outstanding at the time this Plan is adopted, are likewise herewith withdrawn.
8. Stock issued hereunder shall be in exchange for money or other property except for stock or securities. Stock issued hereunder shall not be in return for services rendered or to be rendered to, or for the benefit of, the corporation. Stock may be issued hereunder however, in consideration for cancellation of indebtedness of the corporation unless such indebtedness is evidenced by a security, or arises out of the performance of personal services.
9. Any matters pertaining to this issue not covered under the provisions of this Plan shall be resolved in favor of the applicable law and regulations in order to qualify such issue under Section 1244 of the Internal Revenue Code. If any shares issued hereunder are finally determined not to be so qualified, such shares, and only such shares shall be deemed not to be in the Plan, and such other shares issued hereunder shall not be affected thereby.
10. The sum of the aggregate amount offered hereunder plus the equity capital of the corporation amounts to $500,000.00.
11. The date of adoption of this Plan is November 15, 1990.[21]

This plan should be copied directly into the minutes.

Subchapter S Election

To elect taxation under Subchapter S, the corporation must again qualify as a small-business corporation, but the Subchapter S definition of a small-business corporation is different than the Section 1244 definition.[22] Under a Subchapter S election, the income of the corporation is treated as ordinary income of the shareholders and thus the problem of double taxation of corporation income is avoided.[23] If the shareholders desire to be taxed under Subchapter S, the board of directors should adopt a resolution that provides that the corporation has elected to be taxed as a small-business corporation. The resolution should also state that the corporation meets the statutory requirements.

> **EXAMPLE: Subchapter S Election**
> WHEREAS, the corporation qualifies as a small business corporation under Section 1361(b) of the Internal Revenue Code of 1986, as amended; and
> WHEREAS, the board of directors deems it to be in the best interests of the corporation and the shareholders to elect to be taxed as a small business corporation under the Internal Revenue Code of 1986, as amended, it is

> RESOLVED, that the election to be so taxed be submitted to the shareholders for their consent, and that, upon obtaining said consent, the officers of the corporation shall prepare and submit the necessary documents and forms to accomplish said election under Section 1362 of the Internal Revenue Code of 1986, as amended.

The shareholder consent, duly executed, should be attached to the minutes.

> **EXAMPLE: Shareholder Consent to Subchapter S**
>
> _____, 19__
>
> We, the undersigned, being all of the stockholders in Happiness, Inc., a Nebraska corporation, hereby consent to the election under Section 1361 of the Internal Revenue Code of 1986 as amended, to be treated as a small business corporation for income tax purposes, and submit the following information:
>
> Name and Address of Corporation: Happiness, Inc., 200 West 14th Avenue, Kearney, Nebraska
>
> | *Name and Address of Stockholders* | *No. of Shares* | *Date Acquired* |
> | --- | --- | --- |
> | _____ | _____ | _____ |
> | _____ | _____ | _____ |
>
> [24]

Dates of Meetings

The by-laws usually permit the directors to establish regular meetings for their board, and a resolution establishing dates and times is appropriate at the organizational meeting. The resolution usually also identifies the place for the meeting.

> **EXAMPLE: Place of Regular Meetings**
>
> RESOLVED, that regular meetings of the Board of Directors be held at the office of the Corporation at 200 West 14th Avenue, Kearney, Nebraska, on the third Wednesday of the months of February, May, September, and December, and that a regular meeting also be held in April immediately following the annual meeting of shareholders. No notice shall be required to be given of any of these regular meetings.

Delegation of Authority to the Officers

The board of directors may adopt a resolution defining the authority of the officers. These resolutions are usually drafted broadly, and they are not necessary. They may be useful, however, as a written record that the directors have delegated the authority. The typical rubric of the resolution includes grants of authority to the president and vice-president to conduct all business on behalf of the corporation, to sign all documents necessary in the ordinary course of business in the corporate name, and to perform other necessary managerial acts on behalf of the corporation. The secretary is authorized to procure and maintain necessary corporate books and records, and to open and maintain a stock transfer ledger in accordance with the statute and by-laws. The treasurer is always authorized to pay and discharge any obligations of the corporation, and to perform all other acts necessary and proper within the financial structure of the corporation. The authority of the officers is also specified in the by-laws,[25] and by approving the by-laws, the directors accomplish the same delegation of authority.

EXAMPLE: Delegation of Authority to Officers

The authority of the officers of the corporation was discussed, and upon motion made and unanimously approved, the following authority is granted to the officers of the corporation, until subsequently modified by appropriate resolution of the Board of Directors:

President. The President shall be the principal executive officer of the Corporation and, subject to the control of the Board of Directors, shall in general supervise and control all of the business and affairs of the Corporation. The President shall, when present, preside at all meetings of the shareholders and of the Board of Directors. The president may sign, with the Secretary or any other proper officer of the corporation thereunto authorized by the Board of Directors, certificates for shares of the corporation, any deeds, mortgages, bonds, contracts, or other instruments which the Board of Directors has authorized to be executed, except in cases where the signing and execution thereof shall be expressly delegated by the Board of Directors or by the By-laws to some other officer or agent of the corporation, or shall be required by law to be otherwise signed or executed; and in general shall perform all duties incident to the office of President and such other duties as may be prescribed by the Board of Directors from time to time.

The Vice Presidents. In the absence of the President or in the event of the President's death, inability or refusal to act, the Vice President (or in the event there be more than one Vice President, the Vice Presidents in the order designated at the time of their election, or in the absence of any designation, then in the order of their election) shall perform the duties of the President, and when so acting, shall have all the powers of and be subject to all the restrictions upon the President. Any Vice President may sign, with the Secretary or an Assistant Secretary, certificates for shares of the Corporation; and shall perform such other duties as from time to time may be assigned to him or her by the President or by the Board of Directors.

The Secretary. The Secretary shall; (a) keep the minutes of the proceedings of the shareholders and of the Board of Directors in one or more books provided for that purpose: (b) see that all notices are duly given in accordance with the provisions of the By-laws or as required by law; (c) be custodian of the corporate records and of the seal of the Corporation and see that the seal of the Corporation is affixed to all documents the execution of which on behalf of the Corporation under its seal is duly authorized; (d) keep a register of the post office address of each shareholder which shall be furnished to the Secretary by such shareholder; (e) sign with the President, or a Vice President, certificates for shares of the Corporation, the issuance of which shall have been authorized by resolution of the Board of Directors; (f) have general charge of the stock transfer books of the Corporation; and (g) in general perform all duties incident to the office of Secretary and such other duties as from time to time may be assigned to him or her by the President or by the Board of Directors.

The Treasurer. The Treasurer shall; (a) have charge and custody of and be responsible for all funds and securities of the Corporation; (b) receive and give receipts for moneys due and payable to the Corporation from any source whatsoever, and deposit all such moneys in the name of the Corporation in such banks, trust companies, or other depositaries as shall be selected in accordance with the provisions of the By-laws; and (c) in general perform all of the duties incident to the office of Treasurer and such other duties as from time to time may be assigned to him or her by the President or by the Board of Directors. If required by the Board of Directors, the Treasurer shall give a bond for the faithful discharge of his or her duties in such sum and with surety or sureties as the Board of Directors shall determine.

Assistant Secretaries and Assistant Treasurers. The Assistant Secretaries, when authorized by the Board of Directors, may sign with the President or a Vice

President certificates for shares of the Corporation the issuance of which shall have been authorized by a resolution of the Board of Directors. The Assistant Treasurers shall respectively, if required by the Board of Directors, give bonds for the faithful discharge of their duties in such sums and with such sureties as the Board of Directors shall determine. The Assistant Secretaries and Assistant Treasurers, in general, shall perform such duties as shall be assigned to them by the Secretary or the Treasurer, respectively, or by the President or the Board of Directors.

Adjournment, Signatures, and Attachments

After all the business has been conducted, the minutes should close with the statement, "There being no further business the meeting is adjourned."

Normally, the secretary, who is in charge of complete and accurate minutes, will sign the minutes of the organizational meeting. It is also permissible to have all the directors, after their review, sign the minutes of the meeting, signifying their approval.

Remember the attachments to the minutes of the meeting. A typical organizational meeting will have at least the following attachments:

1. Notice or waiver of notice of the meeting
2. Articles of incorporation and certificate of incorporation
3. Minutes and attachments of incorporators' meeting, if appropriate
4. By-laws
5. All promoter or incorporator contracts approved by the board of directors
6. Specimen share certificates
7. Written stock subscriptions
8. Bills for organizational expenses
9. Bank resolution
10. (If Subchapter S has been elected) Internal Revenue Service form 2553 Election of a Small Business Corporation by the Shareholders

DIRECTORS' REGULAR AND SPECIAL MEETINGS

Directors' meetings are not strictly regulated by statute. The Model Business Corporation Act merely states that the directors may meet at regular or special meetings, either within or without the state, and defers to the by-laws most details such as notice and frequency of the meetings.[26] Since the statutes contain little guidance for directors' meetings, the by-law provisions should be carefully drafted to specify any desired procedures or notice for these meetings.[27] Even in states where the statutes specify certain rules regulating directors' meetings, the rules may usually be changed in the by-laws.

Matters Provided by Statute

The quorum of directors required for action by the board is specified in Section 8.24 of the Model Business Corporation Act to be the majority of the number of directors fixed by the by-laws or stated in the articles of incorporation, but either of these documents may provide that a greater number than a majority is required for a quorum.

The articles of incorporation or by-laws may also reduce the quorum of the board of directors to as low as one-third of the directors. If the corporation has a variable-size board (such as when a provision in the articles states that the board of directors shall be between nine and fifteen members), a quorum is a majority of the directors in office immediately before the meeting begins. Section 8.24 further provides that a board of director action will be approved by a majority vote of the directors present, unless the articles of incorporation or by-laws state that a greater-than-majority vote is required.

These director quorum and voting provisions are common to most jurisdictions. To observe how they work, suppose the corporation has a nine-member board of directors. If five members are present, they constitute a quorum and may conduct business. The affirmative vote of three members will carry action for the board, since the three members are the majority of those present even though they represent only one-third of the total board.

Most state statutes and the Model Business Corporation Act provide that the attendance of a director at a meeting shall constitute a waiver of notice of the meeting unless the director attends for the express purpose of objecting to the transaction of any business because the meeting is not lawfully convened. To perfect such an objection, the director must object at the beginning of the meeting (or promptly upon arrival) and may not vote on or assent to any action taken at the meeting.[28] The procedures for sending notice and the content of the notice are left for determination by the by-laws.

Section 8.20 of the Model Business Corporation Act authorizes directors to participate in any meeting by conference telephone or by other communication devices by which all directors may simultaneously hear each other during the meeting. Most modern corporate statutes are now including this meeting technique to take advantage of modern electronic technology so that not all directors have to travel to a single meeting place. Whether or not communication devices are used, directors must have an interchange of ideas, as if they were in a single room discussing the issues, so it is necessary that the directors be able to participate in the meeting by hearing all comments of all directors and communicating their comments to all others.

Matters Contained in By-laws or Resolutions

Place of Regular Meetings. The place for the regular directors' meeting may be specified in the by-laws or may be left to the determination of the board of directors from time to time. If the by-laws leave the decision to the board members, a resolution should be adopted at each meeting of the board of directors specifying where the next regular meeting will be held.[29]

Call and Procedure for Special Meetings. Certain rules for special meetings of the board of directors should be detailed in the by-laws, such as the persons authorized to call such a meeting and the notice that must be given. The place for special meetings of the board may also be established in the by-laws, but it is preferable to defer the selection of a meeting place to the person calling the meeting.

> **EXAMPLE: Notice of a Directors' Special Meeting**
> To Jerry Jones, Stephen Hess, and Randall Wilson, Directors:
> Pursuant to the power given me by the By-laws of Happiness, Inc., I hereby call a special meeting of its Board of Directors to be held at the corporate offices, on

the 20th day of July, 1992, at 4:00 o'clock P.M., for the purpose of considering the advisability of authorizing the officers of the Company to renew the lease on the offices now occupied by them, and for such other action in regard thereto as the Board may deem advisable.

_____, President

The undersigned hereby admit receipt of a copy of the foregoing notice and consent that the meeting may be held as called.

_____
_____
_____
Directors[30]

Notice. Whether notice should be required for regular directors' meetings depends upon the size of the board, the directors' involvement in other corporate affairs, their proximity to the corporate offices, and their personal preferences. For example, formal notice is probably not required for a small group of directors who are also key employees of the corporation. However, notice may be necessary for a large board composed of advisory directors whose only corporate function is attendance at board meetings. Courtesy reminders should be given in any case. If formal notice is deemed desirable, the by-laws should specify the manner of giving notice and the period of time within which notice must be given.

> **EXAMPLE: Notice of a Directors' Regular Meeting**
> To: [*Name and address of director*]
> You are hereby notified that the regular quarterly meeting of the Board of Directors of Happiness, Inc. will be held at the principal office of said Company at 200 West 14th Avenue, Kearney, Nebraska, on the 1st day of August, 1992, at 2:00 o'clock A.M.
> [*Date*]
>
> _____, Secretary[31]

> **EXAMPLE: Notice of a Directors' Special Meeting**
> To: [*Name and address of director*]
> You are hereby notified that a special meeting of the Board of Directors of Happiness, Inc. has been called by the president of the Company, to be held at the principal office of the Company at 200 West 14th Avenue, Kearney, Nebraska, on Monday, the 9th day of September, 1992, at 10:00 o'clock A.M., to consider the question of selling the corporate stock of Trouble Corporation, and of authorizing the officers of this Company to make the transfer.
> [*Date*]
>
> _____, Secretary[32]

Unless the by-laws so require, the notice need not specify the purpose of the meeting. The Model Business Corporation Act requires two days' notice for special directors' meetings, but permits the articles or by-laws to specify a different notice period and to state whether the purpose of the meeting must be given in the notice.[33] It is common to provide a short period of notice for special meetings, since such meetings are usually called to consider urgent matters and a cumbersome notice procedure is likely detrimental to the best interests of the corporation.

The notice requirements are nullified somewhat by the statutory provisions that attendance at a meeting by a director constitutes waiver of notice, unless the director attends only for the purpose of objecting to the call of the meeting. In addition, most state statutes provide that whenever any notice is required to be given, a waiver of notice in writing signed by the person entitled to the notice, whether executed before or after the time stated therein, shall be equivalent to the giving of such notice. The Model Business Corporation Act contains this rule in Section 8.23.

> **EXAMPLE: Waiver of Notice**
> We, the undersigned, directors of Happiness, Inc., a Nebraska corporation, do hereby waive any and all notice required by the statutes of Nebraska, or by the Articles of Incorporation or By-laws of said Corporation, of a meeting to be held on the 10th day of August, 1992, at 4:00 o'clock P.M. for the purpose of authorizing the officers of said Corporation to execute a trust deed for the benefit of creditors.
> Dated August 10, 1992
>
> [*Signatures of all directors*][34]

Method of Voting. Voting by directors is usually conducted in an informal manner, but formal records should be kept, particularly on matters where there is disagreement among directors. There is no particular statutory regulation of director voting, but directors must vote in person and are not permitted to vote by proxy. The by-laws may prescribe any desirable voting procedure. It is good practice to specify a voting procedure for large boards. Directors express their vote by voice or written ballot on each resolution presented to the meeting, and the secretary of the meeting is responsible for recording the votes. If the vote is not unanimous on any particular issue, each director's position should be stated in the minutes of the meeting in case there may be a possibility of liability for the board's action.

SHAREHOLDER MEETINGS

Frequency

Shareholders' meetings are more strictly regulated by statute than are directors' meetings, to protect the shareholder voice in corporate matters. Moreover, shareholders have the responsibility of electing directors, and this is usually done on an annual basis. Consequently, the Model Business Corporation Act provides that an annual meeting of the shareholders *shall* be held at such time and place as may be fixed in the by-laws.[35] This statutory provision clearly indicates that a shareholder meeting must be held every year. Moreover, the act further provides that if the annual meeting is not held within six months after the end of the corporation's fiscal year or within fifteen months of the last annual meeting, any shareholder may apply to a court to summarily order a meeting to be held.

The various state statutes approach this issue differently. Nearly all states require annual meetings of shareholders, but failure to call such a meeting triggers various consequences. A few jurisdictions like the Model Business Corporation Act, allow shareholders to apply to a court to order the meeting.[36] Most states permit a certain number of the holders of the voting shares to call a meeting.[37] All states would agree that a failure to hold the shareholders' meeting does not invalidate the acts of the corporation, constitute grounds for dissolution, or otherwise impair the corporation's business operations.

In addition to the regular annual meeting, the Model Business Corporation Act states that special meetings of the shareholders may be called by the board of directors or the holders of not less than one-tenth of all the shares entitled to vote at the meeting. Further, the articles of incorporation or by-laws may authorize any other person to call a special shareholders' meeting.[38] The call is addressed to the secretary of the corporation, who is responsible for giving notice of the meeting.

> **EXAMPLE: Call of a Special Shareholders' Meeting**
> To Judi Wagner, Secretary:
>
> We, the undersigned, Stockholders of Happiness, Inc., owning the number of shares of stock set opposite our names, pursuant to provisions of the By-laws, do hereby call a special meeting of the Stockholders of said Company to be held at the corporate offices, on the 15th day of July, 1992, at 3:00 o'clock P.M. for the purpose of removing Charles Miser as a director and for the transaction of any or all business that may be brought before the meeting and we hereby authorize and direct that you notify the Stockholders of such meeting in accordance with the provisions of the By-laws.
>
> Dated_____, 19___.
>
> *Signature of Stockholders*   *Number of Shares*
>
> _____   _____
> _____   _____ [39]

State statutes specify different persons who are entitled to call a special meeting, and they particularly differ on the number of shareholders who must join in the call of their own special meeting. For example, the Ohio statute requires holders of 25% of the voting shares to join, and the articles of incorporation may require the concurrence of up to 50% of the voting shares to call a special meeting in that state.

Location

The by-laws may fix a particular place for the shareholders' meeting or they may authorize the board of directors to determine the meeting place from time to time. The latter authority facilitates a decision by the board of directors to hold the annual shareholders' meeting near the beaches of Florida if it is a winter meeting, or in the cool mountains of Colorful Colorado if it is scheduled in the summertime. State statutes usually provide that if the by-laws are silent on the matter, the meetings will be held at the principal office of the corporation.

Notice

Shareholders must receive notice of all meetings, and the statutory notice procedure may be burdensome, especially if the shareholder population is large. State statutes protect the shareholders by prescribing rules for determining the persons who are entitled to receive notice and setting the periods within which notice must be sent.

Persons Entitled to Receive Notice. To determine the shareholders entitled to receive notice of the meeting, the board of directors may set a date at which the corporation's stock transfer books will be closed. All persons listed in the stock record at that time are identified as *holders of record,* and those holders will be entitled to notice of the meeting. Instead of closing the stock transfer books, the board of directors may set a record date in advance of the meeting, and a list of shareholders entitled to receive notice will be prepared that day. Alternatively, the directors may simply direct that the notices will be mailed on a specified date, and all shareholders as of the close of business the day before that date will receive notice.[40] Since these determinative dates are all before the meeting, a person holding shares at the time the notice lists are prepared could sell those shares and no longer be a shareholder at the time of the annual meeting. Nevertheless, that person will receive the notice of the meeting and will be entitled to vote at the meeting. The voting determination procedure is founded on the proposition that the corporation must draw the line somewhere, and in the interests of orderly procedure the statute merely suggests a cutoff date.

The various state statutes have a few principal differences in determining the persons who are entitled to notice and to vote at the meeting. In some states, directors determine which shareholders are entitled to notice at a meeting by closing the stock transfer books before the meeting. In this procedure, the books must be closed during a period up to fifty days before a meeting, and the book may be closed for at least ten days immediately preceding the meeting. Thus, there is a period from ten to fifty days preceding the meeting within which the stock transfer books may be closed.

Instead of closing the stock transfer books, the by-laws or the board of directors may fix a *record date* for determination of the shareholders entitled to notice. Again, that date may not be more than a certain number of days before the date of the shareholders' meeting. Under the record date procedure, the transfer books are not closed, but an arbitrary date is fixed—say, thirty days before the scheduled meeting—and all persons who own shares as of that date will receive notice and be entitled to vote. Section 7.07 of the Model Business Corporation Act limits the period for setting the record date to seventy days before the meeting. In addition, Section 7.05 requires that notice of the meeting must be given no fewer then ten nor more than sixty days before the meeting date.

A final alternative is allowed: If the stock transfer books are not closed and no record date is set, then the day before the date that the notice is mailed to the shareholders will be considered to be the record date for determination of shareholders. Since the notice must be delivered no less than ten and no more than sixty days before the meeting,[41] roughly the same time periods apply to this alternative. Thus, the board of directors or by-laws may simply direct that notices will be sent on the thirtieth day preceding the meeting, and the thirty-first day before the meeting is then the record date. This last procedure is realistically feasible only if the notices are prepared and sent the same day.

The major variant in these provisions among the states is the period within which the books may be closed or the record date set. The Delaware statute allows the board of directors to fix a record date not more than sixty or less than ten days before the meeting and, like the Model Business Corporation Act, states that if no record date is fixed, the record date will be determined to be the close of business on the day preceding the day on which the notice is given. Most states have a minimum period of ten days. The longest maximum period for identifying holders of record is ninety days preceding the meeting in Maryland.

Advance Notice. Notice of the shareholder meeting must be written under most statutes, and should be written anyway. It must state the place, day, and hour of the meeting, and, for a special meeting, it usually must also indicate the purposes for which the meeting is called.[42] A few states require that notices for any meeting must state the purpose of the meeting.[43]

Notice for the meeting may be delivered to the shareholder either personally or by mail. If mailed, the notice is deemed to be delivered when deposited in the United States mail with postage prepaid and addressed to the shareholder at the shareholder's address as it appears on the stock transfer books of the corporation.

> **EXAMPLE: Notice of Annual Shareholders' Meeting**
> To the Stockholders of Happiness, Inc.:
>
> The Annual Meeting of the Stockholders of Happiness, Inc., will be held in the office of the Company, at 200 West 14th Avenue, Kearney, Nebraska, on Monday, September 9, 1992, at twelve o'clock noon, for the election of three directors and for the transaction of such other business as may properly come before the meeting.
>
> The stock transfer books of the Company will not be closed, but only stockholders of record at the close of business on August 20, 1992, will be entitled to vote.
>
> _____, Secretary[44]
>
> Dated_____, 19___.

> **EXAMPLE: Notice of Special Shareholders' Meeting**
> To the Stockholders of Happiness, Inc.
>
> Pursuant to vote of the Board of Directors a special meeting of the Stockholders of Happiness, Inc. is hereby called to be held on Wednesday, November 8, 1992, at 10 o'clock A.M., at the principal office of the Corporation, at 200 West 14th Avenue, Kearney, Nebraska, for the following purposes:
>
> 1. To consider and act upon the question of increasing the authorized capital stock of the Corporation and of amending the Certificate of Incorporation of the Corporation accordingly, as set forth in the following resolutions of the Board of Directors passed at a meeting of said Board held on the 3rd day of October, 1992, viz.:
>
> "Resolved, that it is advisable that the amount of the authorized capital stock of this Corporation be increased, by amendment of the Certificate of Incorporation, so as to authorize 100,000 additional shares of the common stock, of the par value of $1.00 each, and that for this purpose Article V of said Certificate of Incorporation should be amended by striking out the first two sentences thereof and substituting in lieu of said first two sentences the following, viz.: 'The total amount of the authorized capital stock of the Corporation is $500,000, divided into 500,000 shares, of the par value of $1.00 each. Of such authorized capital stock, 100,000 shares, amounting at par to $100,000, shall be preferred stock, and 400,000 shares, amounting at par to $400,000, shall be common stock.' Said Article V in all other respects to remain unchanged.
>
> "Further resolved, that a special meeting of the stockholders be called to be held at the principal and registered office of the Corporation, to wit, at the office of 200 West 14th Avenue, Kearney, Nebraska, on November 8. 1992, at 10 o'clock A.M. to take action on the foregoing resolution."
>
> 2. To transact any other business which may properly come before the meeting.
>
> The transfer books of the Corporation will be closed at the close of business on October 20, 1992, and reopened at 10 a.m., on November 8, 1992.
>
> By order of the Board of Directors.
>
> Dated_____, 19___.   _____, Secretary
>
> If you are unable to be present at the above meeting please sign and return the enclosed proxy.[45]

Under the Model Business Corporation Act, the notice must be given not less than ten nor more than sixty days before the meeting.[46] Although this time period is similar to the record date period used in many states, the rule is different from the one stated earlier for the determination of shareholders entitled to receive notice and to vote. The shareholders entitled to notice must first be determined, and then their notice must be properly delivered. Section 1.41 of the Model Business Corporation Act provides that written notice is effective when received by the shareholder, five days after its deposit in the mail (if mailed postpaid and correctly addressed), or upon the date shown on a written receipt (if sent by registered or certified mail, return receipt requested). Thus, for example, the board of directors is permitted to set a record date for determining shareholders entitled to receive notice anytime up to seventy days before the meeting, and it could legally establish the record date on the eleventh day before the meeting. However, if some notices were not received by the shareholders until the ninth day before the meeting, the delivery rule would be violated.

The time period within which the notice must be delivered varies by jurisdiction. The shortest statutory period for delivery of notice is five days' personal notice in Pennsylvania, and the earliest period prescribed is ninety days in Maryland. A few states say nothing about the time for notice, and Delaware allows the period to be changed in the by-laws.

Several jurisdictions have special notice rules if certain unusual matters are to be considered at the meeting. These statutes usually specify a longer minimum time within which the notice must be given, apparently so the shareholders will have a longer period of time to consider their vote. For example, many states still follow the original rules of the Model Business Corporation Act, which require a minimum of twenty days' notice when the shareholders' meeting is being called for the purpose of considering a plan of merger or consolidation or approval of the sale of assets not in the ordinary course of business.[47]

Having waded through the notice provisions and determined the precise procedure and timing of the notice, the giving of proper notice in practice can be a fulfilling event. But if you have become mired in these rules, the question may be asked, and not necessarily rhetorically, "What happens if we just ignore this requirement and hold the meeting anyway?"

Failure to give proper notice renders the meeting invalid and vulnerable to the challenge of any shareholder who did not receive proper notice. However, there are some saving provisions. Section 7.06 of the Model Business Corporation Act permits written waiver of notice by any shareholder entitled to receive such notice, and the waiver may be signed before or after the event. There is also a procedure for obtaining consent to action in writing, discussed in "Action without a Meeting" later in this chapter, which may be a solution to the inadequate notice problem for small corporations. As in the rule for directors' meetings,[48] a shareholder may attend a meeting for which no notice was given, and the attendance waives objection to the lack of notice unless the shareholder objects at the beginning of the meeting to the holding of the meeting without notice. If notice is given, but does not state the purposes of the meeting, a shareholder may also object to any consideration of a matter that was not mentioned in the notice.

> **EXAMPLE: Shareholders' Waiver of Notice**
> The undersigned, a shareholder of Happiness, Inc., hereby waives any and all notice required by the statutes of Nebraska, or the articles of incorporation or

bylaws of said corporation, for a meeting to be held on the 24th day of November, 1992 at 3:00 P.M. at the corporate offices for the purposes of increasing the authorized capital stock of the corporation and amending the certificate of incorporation of the corporation accordingly.

Dated November 24, 1992.

[Signature of the Shareholder]

Voting Lists

After the record date has been established, the corporation is required to prepare an alphabetical list of names of all of its shareholders who will be entitled to notice of the shareholders' meeting. This list is to be arranged by voting group, and must show the address of and number of shares held by each shareholder. The list is available for inspection by any shareholder, beginning two business days after notice of the meeting is given, and the list must be available at the corporation's principal office or another place identified in the notice. All shareholders are entitled to inspect the list during regular business hours. The purpose of the voting list is to permit shareholders to learn the identities of the other shareholders so they may discuss issues that are likely to arise at the meeting to see if all shareholders share the same concerns or are interested in voting their shares in a certain manner.

Proxies

Shareholders who are unable to be present at the shareholders' meeting may vote by proxy under most state laws. A proxy is a written authorization by a shareholder directing the proxy holder to vote the shareholder's shares on behalf of the shareholder. The proxy holder is bound to vote the shares in the manner directed by the shareholder in the proxy.

Proxies, like any other agreement, may contain any limiting or expanding provisions that the shareholder desires. The proxy form is usually furnished by the management and conforms to a standard form for general authorization to vote. The Model Business Corporation Act and other statutes regulating proxies require that they be written and signed by the shareholder. The act also permits the proxy to be signed by the shareholder's attorney-in-fact.[49]

A general proxy authorizes the proxy holder to vote on all matters properly presented to the shareholder meeting.

> **EXAMPLE: General Proxy for a Specified Meeting**
> I hereby constitute and appoint Ezra Brooks or Jack Daniels, or either one of them, and in place of either, in case of substitution, his substitute, attorneys and agent for me and in my name, place and stead, to vote as my proxy at the next Annual Meeting, and at any adjournment or adjournments thereof, of the Stockholders of Happiness, Inc., upon any question which may be brought before such meeting, including the election of directors, according to the number of votes I should be entitled to vote if then personally present, with full power to each of my said attorneys to appoint a substitute in his place.
> Dated_____, 19___.   _____[50]

The proxy may have a stated duration, in which case it is valid for the period of time stated. If no period is stated, it automatically expires after eleven months from the date of execution under the Model Business Corporation Act.

> **EXAMPLE: Continuing General Proxy**
>
> The undersigned hereby constitutes and appoints Jack Daniels, Bud Weiser, and John Walker, or any two of them acting jointly, as his, her, or their proxy to cast the votes of the undersigned at all general, special, and adjourned meetings of the Stockholders of Happiness, Inc. from time to time and from year to year, when the undersigned is not present at any such meeting and if present does not elect to vote in person. This proxy shall be effective for two years from the date hereof unless sooner revoked by written notice to the Secretary of the Corporation.
>
> Dated _____, 19___. _____ [51]

The statutory period of duration varies among the jurisdictions, but proxies are revocable at will, unless they are "coupled with an interest," such as when stock is pledged to a creditor to secure repayment of a loan, and a proxy to vote the shares is given to the creditor for the duration of the security interest. Section 7.22 of the Model Business Corporation Act recognizes that proxies may be made irrevocable in favor of a creditor (to whom the shares have been pledged), a person who has purchased the shares, an employee of the corporation who required the proxy as part of the employment contract, or a party to a voting agreement.

Proxies are most frequently used for large, publicly held corporations, where many shareholders will not be able to attend the meeting. The federal Securities Exchange Act of 1934 strictly regulates the solicitation of proxies for shareholders of a publicly held corporation.[52] A proxy in compliance with that act must satisfy special requirements as to wording and form.

> **EXAMPLE: Public Corporation Proxy**
>
> Happiness, Inc.
> Proxy Solicited by Management for Special Meeting
> of Stockholders, October 10, 1991
>
> P R O X Y
>
> The undersigned hereby appoints Jack Daniels, Bud Weiser and John Walker and each or any of them, attorneys, with powers the undersigned would possess if personally present, to vote all shares of Common Stock of the undersigned in Happiness, Inc. at the Special Meeting of its Stockholders to be held October 10, 1991 at 2:00 P.M., Central Daylight Saving Time, at Kearney, Nebraska, and at any adjournment thereof, upon the proposed amendment to the Certificate of Incorporation of the Company, which amendment is set forth in the Proxy Statement and has been declared advisable by the Board of Directors, and upon a split of each outstanding share of Common Stock of the par value of $5 into two shares of Common Stock of the par value of $5 each, and upon other matters properly coming before the meeting.
>
> The directors favor voting FOR the proposed amendment to the Certificate of Incorporation.
>
> *(Continued, and to be signed on the other side.)*
>
> *(Continued from the other side.)* Proxy No.
> The vote for the undersigned is to be cast (please indicate)
> FOR ☐   AGAINST ☐
>
> the proposed amendment to the Certificate of Incorporation and the split of each outstanding share of Common Stock of the par value of $5 into two shares of Common Stock of the par value of $5 each.
>
> UNLESS OTHERWISE DIRECTED THE VOTE OF THE UNDERSIGNED IS TO BE CAST "FOR" THE PROPOSED AMENDMENT TO THE CERTIFICATE OF INCORPORATION AND THE SPLIT OF EACH OUTSTANDING SHARE OF COMMON STOCK.
>
> Receipt of Notice of Special Meeting of Stockholders and the accompanying Proxy Statement is acknowledged.
>
> Date _____ 19___
>
> [Name and address of stockholder]
>
> _____
> _____
> _____
> Please sign above as name(s) appear(s) hereon.
>
> (When signing as attorney, executor, administrator, trustee, guardian, etc., give title as such. If joint account, each joint owner should sign.)[53]

Quorum

The Model Business Corporation Act states that the majority of shares entitled to vote (represented in person or by proxy) will constitute a quorum at a shareholder meeting unless otherwise provided in the articles of incorporation.[54] Most states have similar provisions, and permit the articles of incorporation to modify the quorum. Furthermore, in most states the quorum may not be reduced to less than one-third of the shareholders entitled to vote at the meeting, although Louisiana permits reduction to as low as one-quarter of the voting shares. The reduction in quorum requirements may be contained in the by-laws in some states.[55]

Voting of Shares

Unless the articles of incorporation provide otherwise, each outstanding share, regardless of class, is entitled to one vote. This is the provision in Section 7.21 of the Model Business Corporation Act, and most states take this approach to shareholder voting. A few jurisdictions extend voting to fractional shares, permitting a corresponding fractional vote on each matter submitted to the shareholders.[56]

Shareholder voting may be altered and concentrated through several devices. The articles of incorporation may provide that shares of different classes may have more or less than one vote per share—a principle called *weighted voting*.[57] To concentrate voting power, shareholders may predetermine how their shares will be voted by using a pooling agreement or voting trust.[58]

In most cases, the affirmative vote of the majority of shares present at the meeting and entitled to vote constitutes the act of shareholders. Again, this provision is subject to modification by the articles of incorporation or by-laws. Thus, if the corporation has 100,000 shares of voting stock outstanding, 50,001 shares constitute a quorum for a meeting, and shareholder action would be taken if 25,001 shares were voted in favor of the proposition. The articles of incorporation could provide that one-third of the shares entitled to vote would constitute a quorum, in which case 33,334 shares could hold a meeting and 16,668 shares could decide any issue. In both of these cases, the shares that carry the action are less than the majority of all shares entitled to vote. Conversely, if the articles of incorporation required that 80% of the voting shares must be represented to constitute a quorum, and 80% of the represented shares must vote affirmatively to carry an issue, an affirmative vote by a minimum of 64,000 shares is required to constitute shareholder action. Once a quorum is present, the rule is to apply the appropriate percentage to the shares represented.

The new Model Business Corporation Act and modern corporate statutes recognize that shareholders may be grouped together (other than simply divided among classes) into separate *voting groups,* which are entitled to vote and be counted together on certain specific corporate issues. For example, the articles of incorporation could designate Class A and Class B shareholders as a single voting group for purposes of approving a transaction involving a merger, but state that Class A, Class B, and Class C shareholders would be a single voting group to decide whether the corporation should dissolve. The voting group must be described in the articles of incorporation,[59] and, when designated, the quorum and voting requirements are then applied based upon each voting group. For example, if Class A and Class B shareholders are a voting group for purposes of approving a merger, the majority of those shareholders, counted together, would be required for a quorum, and a majority vote among the voting group of both Class A shareholders and Class B shareholders would be required to approve the action.[60]

A word of caution: A statute may require greater than a majority vote on certain matters. The necessary shareholder vote on individual issues is specified in the following section dealing with shareholder business.

The method of voting at a shareholder meeting is not generally prescribed by statute. Although any method is acceptable, including voice vote or written ballot, written ballot is the preferable procedure and a ballot may be required for the election of directors. Moreover, remember that shareholder action is taken by a specified percentage of shares represented at the meeting. A voice vote or show of hands indicates the shareholders' vote per *capita,* and if there is any disagreement a ballot will be necessary to determine the number of *shares* (not shareholders) voting in favor of the proposition. A ballot should specifically describe the matter being submitted to shareholder vote, and the secretary of the meeting is responsible for tallying the votes. Some states permit the appointment of impartial judges of election if requested by the shareholders or required in the by-laws.[61] These judges are responsible for determining whether the required shareholder vote has been received.

EXAMPLE: Ballot

For voting at a meeting of the Shareholders of Happiness, Inc., on November 24, 1992.

ISSUE NO._____

RESOLVED, [*here state resolution to be acted upon*]

Please record my vote:

_____ FOR

_____ AGAINST

_____ ABSTAIN

_____

Signature of Shareholder [optional]

_____

Number of Shares

SHAREHOLDER BUSINESS AND VOTE REQUIRED

Shareholders have an indirect voice in management, and, except in a close corporation, have very little direct control over the daily business affairs of the corporation. Their meetings, therefore, focus generally on receiving information about corporate business and taking action on matters that are within the ambit of shareholder control as specified in the statute, the articles of incorporation, and the by-laws.

The most important shareholder business is the election of directors. Through their right to elect directors, shareholders indirectly control the management policies and direction of their corporation. Moreover, shareholders are expected periodically to review management activities, and they may ratify and approve management acts at their annual shareholders' meeting. Most statutes also grant shareholders the right to vote directly on major decisions involving modifications in the structure of their corporation. These major fundamental changes usually significantly affect the ownership rights of the shareholder. It is also possible for the incorporators to grant greater control to the shareholders by special provisions in the articles of incorporation or by-laws. Shareholder involvement in each area of shareholder control depends on the particular structure of each corporation and the voting requirements imposed by the statute.

The agenda of a shareholder meeting, therefore, will vary considerably from corporation to corporation. Certain shareholder business, however, may be expected to be conducted in every case.

Special Matters over Which Shareholders Have Control

The articles of incorporation or by-laws may reserve to the shareholders certain items of business that would otherwise be determined by the directors. The reservation of control may be as extensive as allowing complete control over all management activities, as is permitted under the close corporation statutes enacted in Delaware and elsewhere,[62] or as limited as allowing the shareholders to amend and repeal by-laws. Depending upon the local statutory authority to place control with the shareholders, the articles of incorporation or by-laws may grant shareholders the right to select officers; fix compensation; determine the stated value of no par stock; adopt, amend, and repeal by-laws; and so forth. However, there are obvious practical limitations on shareholder control in these areas. If shareholders are cohesive and few, they may comfortably be vested with these responsibilities. On the other hand, the larger the group of shareholders, the more cumbersome it becomes to take action in these management areas.

The shareholders' vote necessary to carry action on matters reserved to their control is governed by statute and may be altered by the articles of incorporation or by-laws. The Model Business Corporation Act provides that shareholder action on a matter will be approved if the votes cast by the shareholders (or within a voting group, if one is designated) favoring the action exceed the votes cast opposing the action.[63] There is a subtle distinction here that is not found in most state statutes. Most states require that shareholder matters must be approved by a majority vote of the shareholders present constituting a quorum. For example, if 100 shares were entitled to vote on a matter, and 51 shares were represented at a meeting, a quorum would be present. Under most state statutes, 26 of those shares present must vote affirmatively to approve action by shareholders. Under the Model Business Corporation Act, fewer than a majority could approve the action if some shareholders abstained. Thus, if 20 shares voted in favor of the action, 19 shares voted against the action, and 12 shares abstained, the matter would be approved under the act, but would not be approved under most state statutes.

Election of Directors

The election of directors is usually an item of business at each annual shareholders' meeting, since the term of office for directors is generally until the next succeeding annual shareholders' meeting and until the successor directors have been elected and qualified.[64] Even if the board of directors is classified or staggered, a certain percentage of the board will be elected each year.

In previously discussing shareholder rights, it was noted that the shareholders may be able to cumulate their votes in the election of directors, depending upon the local statute and articles of incorporation. Some jurisdictions require the use of the cumulative voting procedure in the election of directors as a constitutional right of the shareholder. Others have statutes requiring cumulative voting unless the articles of incorporation specifically deny it. Delaware and other states deny cumulative voting under the corporation statute, but permit the articles of incorporation to grant it. The Model Business Corporation Act also takes this approach.[65]

Cumulative voting is a procedure for voting shares in the election of directors that is designed to secure representation of the minority shareholders on the board of directors. With straight voting, the holders of a majority of the stock should be able to elect the directors who will represent their interests, and if the interests of the majority are inconsistent with the interests of the minority, the minority group may suffer without representation on the board. With cumulative voting, each share carries as many votes as there are vacancies to be filled on the board of directors, and each shareholder is permitted to distribute the votes for all his or her shares among any candidates the shareholder desires to elect.

For example, suppose Bilko Building Company has three directors to be elected every year, and has 500 shares of stock outstanding, of which Anderson owns 300 shares, Bonner owns 100 shares, and Carlyle owns 100 shares. With straight voting, each person votes his or her shares for the candidates one at a time. Suppose three directors are to be elected at the meeting. If Anderson nominates Davis, Everett, and Ford as directors, and the minority shareholders nominate Girtler to represent their interests, the votes will probably be tallied as follows with straight voting.

Anderson's 300 shares	*Bonner's 100 shares*	*Carlyle's 100 shares*
X Davis	Davis	Davis
X Everett	X Everett	X Everett
X Ford	X Ford	X Ford
Girtler	X Girtler	X Girtler

The total votes for each candidate are as follows:

Davis	300
Everett	500
Ford	500
Girtler	200

Thus, Davis, Everett, and Ford are elected to fill the three director positions, and the minority shareholders have lost in their bid to elect Girtler.

Contrast the result of this election with a result using the cumulative voting procedure. Each shareholder is entitled to as many votes as shares owned, multiplied by the number of vacancies to be filled. Thus, Anderson has 900 votes (300 shares × 3 vacancies); Bonner has 300 votes (100 × 3); and Carlyle has 300 votes (100 × 3). Each shareholder may parcel his or her available votes in any manner, including applying all of them to one candidate. Therefore, if Bonner and Carlyle want to be certain to elect Girtler as their director, they may apply all of their votes for that purpose. Anderson cannot prevent Girtler's election no matter how Anderson votes. A cumulative voting ballot will look like this:

| Anderson's | | Bonner's | | Carlyle's | |
| 300 shares | | 100 shares | | 100 shares | |
(900 votes)		(300 votes)		(300 votes)	
300	Davis	0	Davis	0	Davis
300	Everett	0	Everett	0	Everett
300	Ford	0	Ford	0	Ford
0	Girtler	300	Girtler	300	Girtler

The total votes for the candidates are as follows:

Girtler	600
Davis	300
Everett	300
Ford	300

Thus, Girtler is elected, and a runoff election is necessary to determine the two remaining positions between Anderson's three nominees. Anderson could have applied 601 votes for one of the other candidates, thereby ensuring that one of those candidates would beat Girtler, but that would have left Anderson with only 299 shares for another candidate, and Girtler still would have been elected.

Notice that cumulative voting ensures minority representation on the board only if the minority shareholders are cohesive and determined in electing a representative. If Bonner and Carlyle could not have agreed on a suitable candidate to represent the minority, they may have lost the success of their combined vote.

Recall that the directors may be removed with or without cause by vote of the shareholders. If a director were elected to represent the minority interests under a cumulative voting procedure, the protection of cumulative voting could be nullified if the majority shareholders could remove the minority director after the election. Consequently, state statutes usually specify that if cumulative voting is in effect for the election of directors, no director may be removed unless the same cumulative voting procedure is used in the removal action. The director cannot be removed if the votes cast *against* the removal would be sufficient to elect the director if cumulatively voted at an election of the entire board of directors.[66] Thus, Bonner and Carlyle could vote cumulatively against Girtler's removal and prevent the removal the same way they elected Girtler.

Finally, recall that many states permit the board of directors to be classified or staggered, so that not all directors are elected each year.[67] When this classification procedure is combined with cumulative voting, it may neutralize the protective effect of cumulative voting. Suppose that in the previous example, the corporation's three directors are staggered over a three-year period. This means only one director is elected each year. Thus, cumulative voting, which authorizes the number of votes equal to the number of shares times the number of vacancies to be filled, gives Anderson 300 votes (300 shares × 1 vacancy); Bonner 100 votes (100 × 1); and Carlyle 100 votes (100 × 1). Anderson, therefore, can always defeat Bonner and Carlyle with 300 votes to their 200, just as with straight voting. For this reason, the Model Business Corporation Act permits staggering of the board only if the board consists of nine or more members.[68] That way, at least three directors will be elected each year, and the effect of cumulative voting is preserved.

The ballot for the election of directors should present all nominees, and, if cumulative voting is used, should explain how to use it.

EXAMPLE: Ballot for the Election of Directors Using Straight Voting

[STRAIGHT VOTING]

Annual Meeting of the Shareholders of Happiness, Inc. November 24, 1991.

The following persons have been nominated for the Board of Directors of Happiness, Inc. to serve until the next annual meeting of the Shareholders or until their successors have been elected and qualified.

<u>Slate of Directors</u>

[Nominee]
[Nominee]
[Nominee]
[Nominee]

Other nominations

_____

_____

[write in]

FOUR DIRECTORS ARE TO BE ELECTED. PLEASE CHECK ONLY FOUR SELECTIONS. IF MORE THAN FOUR SELECTIONS ARE MADE, THIS BALLOT WILL BE VOIDED [*or* ONLY THE FIRST FOUR SELECTIONS WILL BE COUNTED].

Please enter the number of shares you own: _____ Shares

<u>Voted for</u>	<u>Name of Nominee</u>
_____	[Nominee]
_____	[Nominee]
_____	[Nominee]
_____	[Nominee]
_____	_____ [write in]
_____	_____ [write in]

_____
Signature of Shareholder
[optional]

EXAMPLE: Ballot for the Election of Directors Using Cumulative Voting

[CUMULATIVE VOTING]

Annual meeting of the Shareholders of Happiness, Inc., November 24, 1991.

The following person have been nominated for the Board of Directors of Happiness, Inc., to serve until the next annual meeting of the Shareholders or until their successors have been elected.

Slate of Directors

[Nominee]
[Nominee]
[Nominee]
[Nominee]

Other nominations

_____

_____

[write in]

FOUR DIRECTORS ARE TO BE ELECTED. YOU ARE ENTITLED TO CUMULATE YOUR VOTES IN THIS ELECTION. PLEASE COMPUTE THE NUMBER OF VOTES TO WHICH YOU ARE ENTITLED AS FOLLOWS:

Number of shares owned _____ × 4 = _____
Number of Votes

You may cast these votes for any or all of the nominees, by writing the number of votes you wish to cast for each nominee next to the name of the nominee. THE TOTAL VOTES CAST MAY NOT EXCEED THE NUMBER OF VOTES COMPUTED ABOVE.

IF YOU CAST MORE VOTES THAN YOU ARE ALLOWED, OR IF THE NUMBER OF VOTES IS NOT ENTERED BELOW, THIS BALLOT WILL BE VOIDED.

Number of votes cast [write number]	Name of Nominee
_____	[Nominee]
_____	[Nominee]
_____	[Nominee]
_____	[Nominee]
_____	_____ [write in] _____

Total votes cast

_____

_____
Signature of Shareholder
[optional]

Approval of Extraordinary Matters

Certain structural changes of a corporation require the approval of the shareholders because the shareholders' ownership rights as investors may be materially affected by the action. These changes may involve major modifications to the organization or financial structure of the corporation, disposition of the corporation's assets, adjustments in the ownership characteristics of the shares, or termination of business.

The most frequent structural change in the corporation is the amendment of its articles of incorporation. The organization of the corporation is described in the articles of incorporation, and any amendment to those provisions modifies the structure and probably affects the ownership characteristics of the shareholders in some manner. An amendment as minor as changing the corporate name usually must be approved by the shareholders through the amendment procedure, although the actual effect on shareholder rights may be imperceptible. Other changes may have a more obvious effect on the character of the investment, such as amending the corporation's period of duration or diminishing the scope of the business it will conduct. Other typical changes directly concern the shares themselves. These include amendments to change the aggregate number of shares the corporation has authority to issue; to increase or decrease par value, or change par value shares into no par value shares and vice versa; to exchange, divide, reclassify, redesignate, or cancel shares; to create new classes, with special preferences; to modify preferences or change the authority of the board of directors to establish series of shares; and to limit, deny, or grant preemptive rights of shareholders.

Recognizing the cumbersome procedure required to approve amendments to the articles of incorporation, the new Model Business Corporation Act has begun a trend of permitting the board of directors to make certain changes without shareholder approval. The relaxed rules permit the board alone to extend the duration of the corporation, delete the names and addresses of directors and the registered agent, authorize a stock split by increasing the total number of shares, and make certain changes in the corporation's name.[69] In most states, however, any amendment to the articles of incorporation must be submitted to a vote of the shareholders.[70]

Merger and share exchange (also called consolidation) of the corporation and disposition of corporate assets other than in the ordinary course of business also require special shareholder approval. In a merger, one corporation joins another, the merging corporation ceases to exist, and the surviving corporation continues business with the assets, liabilities, and shareholders of both corporations. In a share exchange or consolidation, two corporations join to form a new corporation, and both of the original corporations may cease to exist. The ownership rights of the shareholders of the constituent corporations will be modified in these transactions. If their corporation is the survivor to the merger, it will probably issue new shares of stock to the shareholders of the merged corporation, and that may dilute their ownership interests. If their corporation has been merged into another corporation, the survivor corporation will probably exchange its shares for their shares in the old corporation. In a consolidation procedure, the new corporation resulting from the combination will issue new securities to shareholders of both old corporations. The shareholders should have some say in these matters. Similarly, if the directors of the corporation intend to sell or otherwise dispose of substantially all of the assets of the corporation, it may be necessary to consult the shareholders. This is not necessary when the corporation merely sells goods from inventory, such as when a department store sells television sets to its customers. However, when the sale of assets is outside the scope of the ordinary course of business, as when the department store sells its display counters, cash registers, and substantially all of its inventory in one transaction with another department store, the shareholders should be asked for their approval.

Finally, the shareholders' ownership rights will certainly be affected by a dissolution of their corporation. The directors are not vested with the authority to dissolve the corporation at will if shares have been issued; voluntary dissolution is regarded as a fundamental change requiring shareholder approval. Similarly, if the shareholders have approved dissolution of their corporation, the directors may not revoke the dissolution proceedings without affirmative shareholder approval of the revocation.

The specific procedures for the approval of these corporate structural modifications are discussed in a later chapter,[71] but the vote necessary for shareholder approval is discussed here. The Model Business Corporation Act originally provided that shareholder action on these matters would be carried by the affirmative vote of the holders of two-thirds of the shares entitled to vote on the issue. If a particular class was entitled to vote on the issue as a class,[72] the two-thirds affirmative vote of that class was also required. Many states still require this percentage of shareholder vote to approve structural modifications to the corporation. The Model Business Corporation Act, however, now merely requires a majority vote by the appropriate shares for approval, in order to comply with "contemporary practice in similar institutional matters." The act, like the other progressive jurisdictions that permit approval by the majority, allows the articles of incorporation to require a greater proportion of shareholder votes, if the extra shareholder protection is desired in these special areas. When a two-thirds vote is required for approval of the fundamental corporate changes, the minority shareholders holding more than one-third of the voting stock can successfully block such actions by the majority. Since the majority shareholders may be at odds with the minority, and there are cases where the majority stands to profit from such transactions, the extra protection for the minority shareholders may be important.

ACTION WITHOUT A MEETING

Notwithstanding the foregoing discussion intimating that shareholder and director meetings are necessary for effective corporate action, state law usually prescribes a written consent procedure for these intracorporate groups to take action without a formal meeting. The Model Business Corporation Act permits written consent by shareholders in Section 7.04 and by directors in Section 8.21. The act further provides that the articles of incorporation or by-laws can deny this procedure for directors, but it does not so condition action by shareholders. All states now have comparable provisions.

The statutory requirements for taking action without a meeting are that the proposed action would have been proper to submit to a regular meeting, and that consent in writing setting forth the proposed action must be obtained for all shareholders or all directors, as the case may be. The effect of the consent is unanimous approval of the particular action involved.

> **EXAMPLE: Unanimous Consent to Action of the Board of Directors**
> Pursuant to the provisions of the Nebraska Corporation Code, the following action is taken by the board of directors of Happiness, Inc., by unanimous written consent as if a meeting of the board of directors had been properly called pursuant to notice and all directors were present and voting in favor of such action.
>
>> RESOLVED, that the salary of the vice president be increased from the sum of $15,000.00 per year to the sum of $20,000.00 per year.
>
> IN WITNESS WHEREOF, we have executed this unanimous Consent of Action on the dates set forth after our respective names, effective November 10, 1991.

| _____ | _____ |
| [Director] | Date |

| _____ | _____ |
| [Director] | Date |

| _____ | _____ |
| [Director] | Date |

EXAMPLE: Unanimous Consent to Action of the Shareholders

Pursuant to the provisions of the Nebraska Corporation Code, the following action is taken by the shareholders of Happiness, Inc., by unanimous written consent, as if a meeting of the shareholders had been properly called pursuant to notice and all shareholders entitled to vote on the matters presented herein had been present and voting in favor of such action.

There are 100,000 shares entitled to vote on the matters presented herein, and the undersigned shareholders are the holders of record of all such shares on the date of this Unanimous Consent of the Shareholders.

> RESOLVED, that the action of the officers and directors of this corporation is making an investment in securities of Trouble, Inc., as set forth in the report which the corporation mailed to all stockholders of record on May 1, 1991, be and the same hereby is ratified.

IN WITNESS WHEREOF, the undersigned, constituting all of the shareholders of the corporation entitled to vote on the matters presented herein, have executed this unanimous Consent to Action of the Shareholders on the dates set forth after our respective names, effective November 10, 1991.

| _____ | _____ | _____ |
| [Shareholder] | [Number of shares] | [Date] |

| _____ | _____ | _____ |
| [Shareholder] | [Number of shares] | [Date] |

| _____ | _____ | _____ |
| [Shareholder] | [Number of shares] | [Date] |

| _____ | _____ | _____ |
| [Shareholder] | [Number of shares] | [Date] |

[etc.]

The only major variations among the statutes with consent to action provisions are whether the articles of incorporation or by-laws may deny this procedure for directors' meetings, and the percentage of shareholders required to file written consent in order to carry the shareholder action. Most states do not authorize a limitation on the directors' rights to file written consent and act without a meeting. The Model Business Corporation Act, Delaware, and New Jersey allow the certificate or articles of incorporation or by-laws to alter this provision.

Delaware allows for less-than-unanimous approval for shareholder consent. The statute provides that the holders of outstanding stock having at least the minimum number of votes that would be necessary to approve such action at a meeting may consent in writing and thereby bind the shareholders. The remaining shareholders are then entitled to notice of the action so taken.[73] Other states authorize the articles of incorporation to prescribe a less-than-unanimous number for shareholder written consent.[74] Otherwise, most states provide that all of the shareholders must file written consent to act without a meeting.

The use of shareholder consent without a meeting should be limited to small, close corporations. The requirements of unanimity and of obtaining the signatures of all shareholders make the procedure impracticable for large, publicly held corporations.

MINUTES

There is no mandatory procedure for conducting meetings of shareholders and directors. In many cases, these meetings are conducted in an informal manner, but they usually become more formal as the group becomes larger. The science of conducting a corporate meeting for a large intracorporate group has fortunately been reduced to writing in any easy-to-follow systematic procedure for corporate secretaries,[75] so formal meeting procedure escapes further elaboration here.

It is always necessary to follow the statutory requirements, such as notice, voting, and solicitation of proxies for every meeting. Consequently, the minutes of the meeting should always reflect that the statutory requirements have been observed. The minutes of the meeting constitute the permanent written record of the corporate history, and all matters considered at a meeting must be carefully recorded in order to trace the origin of all corporate actions.

The secretary of the corporation is usually given the privilege of keeping the minutes. The only guidelines for recording minutes are that the secretary must comply with instructions given by the board of directors and by the chairman of the meeting, and the secretary must compose the minutes in such a way that they constitute an accurate and complete transcription of the action taken by the intracorporate group at the particular meeting recorded. Otherwise, the secretary has broad discretion in the manner in which the minutes will be kept. Counsel may assist the secretary in establishing a corporate minute policy after formation of the corporation. As a general guide, all minutes should include at least the following:

1. Name of the corporation
2. Date
3. Place where the meeting is held
4. Special statutory, articles of incorporation, or by-law authority under which the meeting is called
5. Persons present, persons absent, or shares represented in person or by proxy
6. Statement that the meeting is held pursuant to a notice or waiver that is attached to the minutes
7. Nature of the meeting (regular or special)
8. Approval of minutes of previous meetings
9. Substance of the issues presented at the meeting, and description of how they were submitted and by whom
10. Decision and vote of the intracorporate group on each issue, in resolution form
11. Presentation of all reports, with copies attached if a report is written and a summary of the report if it is oral
12. Summary of the other business before the meeting[76]

If the meeting is a directors' meeting, the directors present and absent should be named. It is also important to report correctly the directors' vote on each resolution. If the vote is unanimous, that should be stated. If any director abstained or dissented, that director's name and vote should be stated, particularly if there is any possibility of the director's personal liability for action taken. For example, if the director were voting on the issuance of a dividend but funds were not legally available for payment of the dividend, the recording of a dissent may be necessary to relieve the director from liability for illegally declared dividends. If a director is "interested" in the particular action, as when the contract being considered by the board of directors is with another corporation in which the director is financially interested, it should be noted that the interested director did not vote or left the room during the discussion.[77]

The names of the shareholders present at a shareholder meeting and the number of shares they hold may be noted if the group is small. Otherwise, the number of shares represented in person and by proxy should be listed.

Informal activity that occurs during a meeting should not be described in unnecessary detail. It would not be appropriate, for example to list the persons who availed themselves of the corporate punch bowl at the meeting, or to record a discussion regarding a director's new house in the mountains. However, informal information about tentative corporate plans and current business conditions may be reported if it was discussed at the meeting. In this regard, if the chair obtains the informal consensus of the group on any particular matter, the minutes should express the affirmative reaction of those present.

NOTES

1. See Chapter 13.
2. See "Corporate Existence" in Chapter 6.
3. See M.B.C.A. § 2.05 (organizational meeting of incorporators or initial directors).
4. See "Formalities after Formation of a Corporation" in Chapter 6.
5. E.g., Pennsylvania, 15 Pa.Stat. § 210.
6. West's Modern Legal Forms §2852.
7. West's Modern Legal Forms § 2860.
8. West's Modern Legal Forms § 2861.
9. M.B.C.A. § 2.05.
10. West's Modern Legal Forms § 2886.
11. See "Certificates for Shares" in Chapter 7.
12. See "Ownership and Management of a Corporation" in Chapter 4 and "Preincorporation Share Subscriptions" in Chapter 6.
13. See "Preincorporation Share Subscriptions" in Chapter 6.
14. M.B.C.A. § 6.20.
15. West's Modern Legal Forms § 2896.
16. See "Approval of Action Taken at Previous Meetings" earlier in this section.
17. DeLano Service, Allegan, Mich. Form R-10.
18. West's Modern Legal Forms §§ 2892–93.
19. See "Selection and Registration of Corporate Name" in Chapter 6.
20. Int.Rev.Code of 1986, 26 U.S.C.A. § 1244(c)(3).
21. West's Modern Legal Forms § 2909.6.
22. See "Taxation of a Corporation" in Chapter 4.
23. Substantive elements of the Subchapter S election are discussed in "Taxation of a Corporation" in Chapter 4.
24. West's Modern Legal Forms § 2838.
25. See "By-laws" in Chapter 6.
26. M.B.C.A. § 8.20.

27. See the sample by-law provisions regulating directors' meetings in "By-laws" in Chapter 6 and Form 6Q in Appendix G.
28. See M.B.C.A. § 8.23.
29. See the by-law provisions in "By-laws" in Chapter 6 and Form 6Q in Appendix G, and the directors' resolution in "Directors' Regular and Special Meetings" earlier in this chapter.
30. West's Modern Legal Forms § 2855.
31. West's Modern Legal Forms § 2854.
32. West's Modern Legal Forms § 2857.
33. M.B.C.A. § 8.22.
34. West's Modern Legal Forms § 2858.
35. M.B.C.A. § 7.01.
36. E.g., Nebraska, Neb.Rev.Stat. § 21–2027 (application to a court after thirteen months without a meeting); Montana, Mont.Code Ann. § 35–1–501 (application to a court after eighteen months without a meeting).
37. The holders of one-tenth of the voting shares may call a special meeting if the annual meeting has not been held in Massachusetts, Mass.Gen.Laws Ann. ch. 156 § 30.
38. M.B.C.A. § 7.02.
39. West's Modern Legal Forms § 2831.
40. See M.B.C.A. §§ 7.05(d) and 7.07.
41. M.B.C.A. § 7.05.
42. M.B.C.A. § 7.05.
43. E.g., New Jersey, N.J.Stat.Ann. § 14A:5–4.
44. West's Modern Legal Forms § 2823.
45. West's Modern Legal Forms § 2825.
46. M.B.C.A. § 29.
47. For further elaboration on voting procedures for these transactions, see "Merger, Consolidation, and Exchange" and "Sale, Mortgage, or Other Disposition of Assets" in Chapter 13.
48. See "Directors' Regular and Special Meetings" earlier in this chapter.
49. M.B.C.A. § 7.22.
50. West's Modern Legal Forms § 2828.
51. West's Modern Legal Forms § 2828.1.
52. Securities Exchange Act of 1934, 15 U.S.C.A. § 78n, and the rules promulgated thereunder.
53. West's Modern Legal Forms § 2827.6. This proxy must be accompanied by a special notice and a proxy solicitation statement, prepared in accordance with the Securities Exchange Act of 1934. See West's Modern Legal Forms §§ 2827, 2827.1, and 2827.5.
54. M.B.C.A. § 7.25.
55. E.g., New York, McKinney Consol.Laws of N.Y.Bus.Corp.Law § 608.
56. M.B.C.A. § 6.04 (c).
57. Variations in voting rights between classes of shares are discussed in "Common Stock Rights" and "Preferred Stock Rights" in Chapter 7.
58. These shareholder agreements are most frequently found in close corporations. See "Concentration of Voting Power" in Chapter 11.
59. M.B.C.A. § 1.40(26).
60. M.B.C.A. §§ 7.25 and 7.26.
61. E.g., California, West's Ann.Calif.Corp.Code § 707; New York, McKinney Consol.Laws of N.Y.Bus.Corp.Law § 610.
62. See "Close Corporations" in Chapter 5.
63. M.B.C.A. § 7.25.
64. M.B.C.A. § 8.05.
65. M.B.C.A. § 7.28(b) and see "The Articles of Incorporation" in Chapter 6.
66. M.B.C.A. § 8.08.
67. See "Ownership and Management of a Corporation" in Chapter 4 and "The Articles of Incorporation" in Chapter 6.
68. M.B.C.A. § 8.06.
69. M.B.C.A. § 10.02.
70. Further elaboration on the procedure to amend the articles of incorporation is contained in "Amendment of the Articles of Incorporation" in Chapter 13.
71. See Chapter 13.
72. See "Preferred Stock Rights" in Chapter 7.

73. 8 Del.Code Ann. § 228.
74. E.g., New York, McKinney Consol.Laws of N.Y.Bus.Corp.Law § 615; Pennsylvania, 15 Pa.Stat. § 513.
75. B. M. Miller, 1 Manual and Guide for the Corporate Secretary, 3–35, 53–69, 107–137 (1969).
76. See the general forms for minutes of shareholder and director meetings, Forms 8A and 8B in Appendix G.
77. See M.B.C.A. § 8.31.

9 | CORPORATE DIVIDENDS AND OTHER DISTRIBUTIONS

TYPES OF CORPORATE DISTRIBUTIONS

One investment objective of share ownership is the receipt of profit distributions or dividends. The attractiveness of a stock investment is measured by this yield in addition to the projected value appreciation of the shares as the corporate business prospers. Shares are also entitled to receive a proportionate share of the assets of the corporation when the business is dissolved and liquidated. These distributions to shareholders are the subject matter of this chapter.

The revised Model Business Corporation Act has developed a series of financial provisions governing distributions from the corporation to its shareholders. Section 1.40 defines a *distribution* as a "direct or indirect transfer of money or other property (except its own shares) or the incurrence of an indebtedness by a corporation to or for the benefit of its shareholders in respect of any of its shares. A distribution may be in the form of a declaration or payment of a dividend; a purchase, redemption or other acquisition of shares; a distribution of indebtedness; or otherwise." Modern corporate practice is to refer to all of these payments to shareholders as distributions, regardless of whether they represent a distribution of corporate profits or a distribution of assets in liquidation. The term *dividends,* which represents the distribution of corporate profits to a corporation's shareholders, is being phased out of corporate parlance. However, this chapter will still use the term dividends to describe distributions of corporate profit to shareholders, and will reserve the term distributions to describe payments made to shareholders for other reasons.

The board of directors is vested with the authority and the discretion to declare dividends from time to time. Dividends may be paid in cash, property, or shares of the corporation, but payment is restricted to certain available funds in most states, or prohibited unless certain financial tests are met.[1] Generally, if the appropriate funds are available or if the financial condition of the corporation is satisfactory, the directors may distribute all sorts of desirable things to the shareholders.

Cash is always welcome, and the cash dividend is the most common corporate distribution. Cash dividends are declared by director resolution, which usually specifies a dollar amount per share and directs payment of the dividend to all shareholders entitled to receive it.

Property dividends are less common, but are equally available for use by the board of directors. If the corporation markets a desirable product, the product itself may be a dividend distribution. For example, R. J. Reynolds Tobacco Company once distributed a specially prepared package of its tobacco products to its shareholders as a dividend, and one famous corporate case involved a scramble to purchase shares of a distillery corporation that was reported to be preparing to issue a property dividend of its liquor products during World War II when liquor was scarce.[2] Property dividends occasionally include shares of stock of a subsidiary corporation owned by the parent corporation. There is no restriction on the type of property that may be distributed. If a corporation had a surplus of adding machine tape it could distribute that as a dividend, subject to the approval of the shareholder public relations department.

Dividends may also consist of more shares of the same corporation. Share dividends increase the number of shares owned by the receiving shareholder, but do not affect the shareholder's proportionate ownership interest. For example, the directors may declare a dividend of 1 share of common stock for every 100 shares outstanding. Each shareholder will receive 1 extra share of stock per 100 as a corporate distribution. Fractional shares[3] become relevant here. If Debbie Jaeger owns 125 shares and a one-for-one-hundred stock dividend is declared, she will be entitled to receive 1¼ shares in the dividend. The corporation may issue a stock certificate or scrip representing the fraction, it may pay the fair value of the quarter share in cash, or it may arrange for the sale of the fractional interest to another shareholder similarly situated.

Dividend distributions to shareholders do not necessarily come at regularly scheduled intervals. The board of directors may declare as many or as few dividends as it deems appropriate. It should be obvious, however, that directors who declare frequent dividends are usually popular with the shareholders. The practice of large corporations with established dividend policies is to declare a regular quarterly dividend on the corporate shares, as profits permit.

A dissolution distribution is usually a one-time distribution to shareholders when the corporate assets are liquidated and business is terminated. Partial liquidations are also possible, however, if the corporation ceases to operate one phase of its business and distributes assets from the discontinued operations to shareholders, continuing other active business operations thereafter.

The most important legal considerations regarding corporate distributions are the authority to declare or demand the distributions; the legally available funds out of which a distribution is paid; and the tax ramifications of distributions.

SOURCES OF FUNDS FOR DISTRIBUTION

All state statutes regulate the manner in which a corporation may distribute its assets to its shareholders, and each statute identifies particular accounts from which a distribution may be made. Common sources of dividend funds are earned surplus or retained earnings or profits. The Model Business Corporation Act was amended in 1979 to permit dividends from any source so long as the corporation remains solvent and its total assets remain greater than its total liabilities (plus any amounts payable as liquidation preferences).[4] Most state statutes use "unreserved and unrestricted earned surplus" as the main source for dividend distributions, and also allow dividends to be paid from other more specialized accounts. However, to understand the law of corporate distributions, the distinctions between sources of funds for distributions and the accounting principles used in creating these accounts should be explored. Consider the following accounts (which are defined this way in many state statutes):

1. *Net assets* means the amount by which the total assets of a corporation exceed the total debts of the corporation.

2. *Stated capital* means, at any particular time, the sum of (a) the par value of all shares of the corporation having a par value that have been issued; (b) the amount of the consideration received by the corporation for all shares of the corporation without par value that have been issued, except such part of the consideration therefor as may have been allocated to capital surplus in a manner permitted by law; and (c) such amounts not included in clauses a and b of this paragraph as have been transferred to stated capital of the corporation, whether upon the issue of shares as a share dividend or otherwise, minus all reductions from such sum as have been effected in a manner permitted by law.

3. *Surplus* means the excess of the net assets of a corporation over the corporation's stated capital.

4. *Earned surplus* means the portion of the surplus of a corporation equal to the balance of its net profits, income, gains, and losses from the date of incorporation, or from the latest date when a deficit was eliminated by an application of its capital surplus or stated capital or otherwise, after deducting subsequent distributions to shareholders and transfers to stated capital and capital surplus to the extent such distributions and transfers are made out of earned surplus. Earned surplus shall include also any portion of surplus allocated to earned surplus in mergers, consolidations, or acquisitions of all or substantially all of the outstanding shares or of the property and assets of another corporation, domestic or foreign.

5. *Capital surplus* means the entire surplus of a corporation other than its earned surplus.

Now review the following corporate balance sheet with these definitions in mind.

THE NOBLES COMPANY
BALANCE SHEET
December 31, 1990

ASSETS

Current Assets:

Cash	$ 5,000	
Marketable Securities		
Apex Telephone Company, at cost	8,000	
Accounts Receivable	2,000	
Inventory	5,000	
	$20,000	
Total Current Assets		$20,000
Property Plant and Equipment		58,000
Total Assets		$78,000

THE NOBLES COMPANY

BALANCE SHEET

December 31, 1990

LIABILITIES AND EQUITY

Current Liabilities:

Accounts Payable	$ 3,000		
Accrued Expenses Payable	3,000		
Total Current Liabilities		$ 6,000	
Bonds, First Mortgage 13½% Interest		20,000	
Total Liabilities			$26,000

Equity

Stated Capital

Common Shares, $1 par value; 50,000 authorized, 5,000 issued and outstanding	$ 5,000		
Preferred Shares, 5% cumulative, $100 par value; 100% of par liquidation preference; 10,000 authorized, 50 issued and outstanding	5,000		
Total Stated Capital		$10,000	
Capital Surplus		20,000	
Earned Surplus		22,000	
Total Equity			$52,000
Total Liabilities and Equity			$78,000

Following the statutory definitions, net assets is the amount by which the total assets, $78,000, exceed the total debts, $26,000. Thus, the net assets of the corporation in this case would be $52,000.

Stated capital in this example equals the par value of the 5,000 common shares plus the par value of the 50 preferred shares. The capital surplus results from the excess consideration for which the par value shares were sold. For example, the balance sheet shows capital surplus of $20,000, which could have resulted from selling the 5,000 common shares at $4 a share, allocating the $3 per share in excess of par to capital surplus, and selling the preferred shares at $200 per share, allocating the $100 per share excess to capital surplus.

Earned surplus represents accumulated corporate profits that have been earned during preceding accounting periods and retained in the corporation. The term surplus refers to the total amount of earned surplus and capital surplus. Thus, the total surplus of this corporation would be $42,000. The entire equity section of the balance sheet is also called *net worth*.

There is one other important definition for analyzing the legality of corporate distributions. A corporation is *insolvent* when it is unable to pay its debts as they become due in the usual course of business.[5]

The application of these terms may become clear as you consider the statutory provisions regulating corporate distributions.

CASH AND PROPERTY DIVIDENDS

As previously discussed, a dividend is a distribution of cash, other property, or shares to the stockholders of the corporation in the proportion of their share ownership. Recall that various classes of stock may be treated differently with respect to dividends. Dividend preferences are common in complex corporate financial structures, and preferences must always be observed. There is also a rule that dividends must be uniform within each class or series, meaning that each share of a given class or series will receive the same distribution as the other shares of that class or series. By way of illustration, consider the Nobles Company capital structure that was described previously with 5,000 shares of common stock and 50 shares of 5% cumulative preferred with $100.00 par value. Suppose the directors decided to issue a dividend and to distribute $2,000.00 in cash to the shareholders. The preferred shareholders are entitled to be paid their preferential dividends (5% of $100.00 per share), so they would receive $250.00 in dividends first. This leaves $1,750.00 for distribution to the common shareholders, who should receive $0.35 per share. Each shareholder of the particular class must be treated equally. The directors could not order a distribution of $0.50 per share to some common shareholders and $0.20 per share to others.

Shareholders' Rights to Dividends

The decision to distribute dividends is within the sole discretion of the board of directors, and no shareholder has a right to dividends until the board of directors declares it.[6] Cumulative preferred stock will accumulate dividends annually until they are finally paid, but even preferred shareholders have no right to dividends until they are declared by the board of directors. In the Nobles Company example, the 5% cumulative preferred stock will accumulate a dividend entitlement of five dollars per share per year, and if the board of directors ever declares a dividend, the arrearage must be paid before the common shareholders may receive dividends.

Once the board of directors has declared a dividend through an appropriate resolution, the shareholders have a right to the dividend and it becomes a debt from the corporation to the shareholders.

Section 6.40(f) of the Model Business Corporation Act makes this indebtedness to the shareholders equal to the corporation's indebtedness to other general, unsecured creditors, unless a shareholder has specifically agreed to subordinate the right to receive dividends to the claims of other creditors. The procedure for declaring a dividend is discussed after an exploration of the restrictions on sources of funds for dividends.

Restrictions on Payment of Dividends

Corporate statutes usually restrict the payment of dividends to funds contained in specified corporate accounts. There are also certain restrictions on payment even if funds appear to be available in the prescribed accounts. Section 6.40 of the Model Business Corporation Act prohibits the payment of dividends if the corporation is insolvent, or if the declaration or payment would be contrary to any restriction contained in the articles of incorporation.[7] If the organizers intend to restrict the directors' ability to declare and pay dividends, the law honors their restraints.

The act further provides that dividends may be declared only if the corporation's total assets exceed total liabilities and (unless provided otherwise in the articles of incorporation) the amounts payable to preferred shares having a preference to assets in liquidation. In the case of the Nobles Company, this excess is $47,000: total assets ($78,000) less total liabilities ($26,000) and amounts payable in liquidation to the preferred shares (100% of par, or $5,000). The asset and liabilities values are determined from the balance sheet or based on some other reasonable and fair valuation. Thus, if the Nobles Company's stock in Apex Telephone Company were valued in the market at $20,000, an additional $12,000 would be available for dividends.

In deciding whether the corporation would violate the rules restricting payment of dividends, the board of directors may rely upon the financial statements, fair market appraisals, or any other reasonable determination of value of the assets of the corporation. In measuring whether a dividend has the effect of causing insolvency or the reduction of net assets below the threshold amounts, the date the dividend is authorized is generally the date the determination is made. However, if the dividend is paid more than 120 days after the authorization of the dividend, the date of payment will be the relevant date for this determination.

Most states continue to permit dividends to be paid in cash or property only out of the unreserved and unrestricted earned surplus of the corporation, with a few exceptions, which are discussed in a moment. In those states, therefore, a corporation may pay dividends from available funds in its earned surplus account, and in the case of the hypothetical Nobles Company, $22,000 would be available for payment of dividends. However, there may be practical restrictions on the payment of such a dividend. A glance at the balance sheet should reveal that payment of a $22,000 dividend is unrealistic considering the relatively low cash position of the corporation and considering that the corporation's total liquid assets, including cash, securities, inventory, and accounts receivable, total only $20,000. The corporation would be unable to pay a full $22,000 dividend without liquidating part of its plant and equipment, even though the statutory funds are legally available for dividends up to $22,000. Thus, in every case, the maximum legal limits on dividends will be tempered by business advisability. The directors determine the latter within the bounds of the former.

Some states, including Delaware and Nevada, provide that in addition to the funds from earned surplus, dividends may be declared and paid out of the unreserved and unrestricted "net earnings for the current fiscal year and the next preceding fiscal year taken as a single period." This means that if the corporation has no historical earned surplus, but has earnings (profits) for the past two fiscal years, dividends may legally be paid from the profit funds, without regard to the balance in the earned surplus account.

In California, the availability of funds for dividends depends on a ratio of current assets to current liabilities, and management is allowed to *anticipate* receipts and expenses for the next year to make the computation.

Earned surplus generally represents the accumulated profits from corporate operations as determined by accepted accounting principles. Earned surplus or earnings may be restricted in several ways. Suppose a corporation has borrowed money from a bank or other financial institution, and the terms of the loan agreement require that earned surplus will be maintained at a minimum level of $10,000 for the duration of the loan. In accordance with the loan agreement, that amount of earned surplus should be restricted, and may not be used for the payment of dividends. A restriction would also be imposed when the corporation purchases its own shares from outside investors to hold as treasury shares. Most statutes require that the amount of earned surplus used to purchase treasury shares be restricted for as long as the shares remain treasury shares.[8] Many statutes ignore the distinction between ordinary surplus and reserved or restricted surplus, and permit dividends to be declared and paid notwithstanding such restrictions.

Sometimes dividends may be paid out of the depletion reserves of a corporation engaged in exploiting natural resources, such as minerals, oil and gas, and timber. The articles of incorporation also must expressly authorize such dividends.[9]

Cash and property dividend provisions vary extensively among the states. Most states couch their restrictions on legally available funds in terms of earned surplus or earnings during a prescribed period. Several other states add further restrictions to prohibit dividends from unrealized appreciation and depreciation.[10]

Procedure for Declaration, Payment, and Accounting

The board of directors has sole discretion to determine the amount to be paid as dividends by the corporation. Notice, however, that in the Nobles Company financial structure the directors must pay $5.00 per share for 50 shares of preferred stock as a cumulative dividend before any dividends may be paid to the common shares. If the directors declared a dividend of $3,000.00, they would first resolve to distribute $250.00 to the preferred shares, or $5.00 per share, and would then distribute the remaining $2,750.00 in a dividend of $0.55 per share for the common stock.

The decision to declare the dividend is made at a directors' meeting and is recorded as a resolution in the minutes.

> **EXAMPLE: Resolution to Declare a Cash Dividend**
> RESOLVED, that a dividend of $5.00 per share be declared and paid on the preferred stock and a dividend of $.55 per share be declared and paid on the common stock of this corporation out of the unreserved and unrestricted earned surplus to the holders of stock as shown by the records of the corporation on the 15th day of June, 1992, distributable on the 1st day of July, 1992, and that the treasurer is directed forthwith to mail checks for the same to the stockholders of record.[11]

An example of the resolution for a property dividend follows.

> **EXAMPLE: Resolution to Declare a Property Dividend**
> From the report furnished the meeting on the financial condition of the Company for the fiscal year ended December 31, 1991, and for each of the subsequent months, it appeared that the Company was in a position to declare and pay a dividend in property upon its outstanding shares of common stock.
>
> Thereupon, after discussion it was on motion duly made, seconded and unanimously adopted by the affirmative vote of the directors present:
>
> RESOLVED, that a dividend on the outstanding shares of common stock of this Corporation be and it hereby is declared and ordered to be paid in property of this Corporation, to-wit, shares of common stock of Apex Telephone Company owned by this Corporation at the rate of ten shares of common stock of said Apex Telephone Company for each share of common stock of this Corporation issued

> and outstanding. Said dividend to be payable on September 1, 1992 to the holders of record of said common stock of this Corporation at the close of business on August 10, 1992 from the net surplus of this Corporation as at the close of business on December 31, 1991, or from the net profits of this Corporation for its current fiscal year; and
>
> FURTHER RESOLVED, that the proper officers of the Corporation be and they hereby are authorized and directed in the name and on behalf of the Corporation to do or cause to be done all acts or things necessary or proper to carry out the foregoing resolution.[12]

Notice that the resolution sets a record date for a determination of stockholders who will be entitled to receive dividends. Nearly every state statute has certain rules to follow in fixing the record date, and in most states the rules are exactly the same as those regarding shareholder voting described earlier.[13] These rules permit the stock transfer books to be closed as early as fifty days before the dividend is paid. Alternatively, the directors may set a record date within the fifty-day period to determine which stockholders are entitled to receive dividends. If the books are not closed and if no date is set, the date for determining shareholders of record is the date that the board of directors adopted the resolution declaring the dividend. The Model Business Corporation Act gives the directors authority to fix a record date for determining shareholders entitled to a dividend, but if the directors fail to do so, the record date will be on the date the board of directors authorizes the distribution of the dividend.

When the dividend is paid in cash, the cash account will be reduced by $3,000, and the earned surplus account will be reduced by $3,000. This maintains the balance on the balance sheet. The dividend may also be paid in other property, such as the securities described in the foregoing property dividend example, which appear as current assets on the balance sheet. If the securities distributed were valued at $3,000, the earned surplus and the marketable securities accounts would be reduced by that amount. The value of the property distributed and charged to earned surplus is determined by the *book value,* which is the value shown on the balance sheet.

Tax Ramifications of Cash or Property Dividends

In the early discussion of the corporate form, it was observed that one disadvantage of corporate existence is the problem of double taxation. Dividends are at the heart of that problem. The corporation is taxed on its profits, and if the after-tax profits are distributed to shareholders as dividends, the dividends are income to the shareholders and are also taxed at the individual shareholder's rate. A corporation may avoid the problem of double taxation by paying salaries or consulting expenses to its shareholders wherever possible, since these items are deductible as expenses and the money thus expended is not taxed at the corporate level. Salaries are a viable alternative to dividends when the shareholders are employees of the corporation, as is frequently the case in small, close corporations. In large corporations, however, dividends are a necessary evil to provide the shareholders a return on their investment.

Cash dividends are declared on a shareholder's income tax return as income in the actual amount distributed. Property dividends are subject to a special rule. When property is distributed as a dividend, the shareholders must report as income the fair market value of the property received, even though the book value of the property may be less.[14] For example, if the distributed marketable securities of the Apex Telephone Company have a fair market value of $4,000, even though their book value is $3,000, the shareholder must report $4,000 as ordinary income.

Corporations that pay dividends aggregating more than $10 to any one person during the calendar year must file certain reports with the Internal Revenue Service, which uses those *informational reports* to determine whether the shareholders have reported the dividends on their individual income tax returns.

SHARE DIVIDENDS

A share dividend is a corporation's distribution of its own shares. The number of shares owned by the shareholders is increased, but the proportionate stock ownership of each shareholder does not change. A share dividend requires no modification in any of the characteristics of the shares, and it adds nothing to a shareholder's ownership interest; instead, it simply dilutes the shareholder's ownership interest by dividing the same investment into more shares.

Legal Restrictions

Most states permit share dividends from two sources: the corporation's treasury shares, if shares have been purchased and held in the treasury; and authorized-but-unissued shares. In either case, the earned surplus account must contain available funds, and it will be adjusted to reflect the dividend.

When authorized-but-unissued shares are used for share dividends, a transfer from surplus to stated capital occurs. The Model Business Corporation Act formerly required such a transfer, and many states still follow the rule.[15] If the shares have a par value, they must be issued at an amount equal to or greater than the par value. An amount of surplus equal to the aggregate par value of the dividend shares must then be transferred to stated capital at the time the dividend is paid. If the dividend shares have no par value, the shares are issued at a stated value fixed by a resolution of the board of directors, and stated capital receives an amount of surplus equal to the aggregate stated value. Further, the amount of surplus so transferred to stated capital must be disclosed to the shareholders when the dividend is paid.

To avoid dilution of one class in favor of another class, there is usually an additional restriction. No dividend payable in shares of any class may be paid to the holders of shares of any other class unless doing so is authorized by the articles of incorporation *or* by the affirmative vote or the written consent of the holders of at least a majority of the outstanding shares of the class in which the payment is to be made.

Using the Nobles Company as an example, note that the balance sheet reflects that 10,000 preferred shares with $100 par value are *authorized,* but only 50 of these shares are *issued and outstanding*. There are, therefore, 9,950 preferred shares authorized but unissued. The directors may consider issuing one share of preferred stock for each share of common stock as a share dividend, but they have two hurdles to jump: the authority to issue a share dividend to holders of one class in shares of another class, and the legally available funds for the dividend. If 5,000 shares of preferred were distributed to the common shareholders, the present holders of the 50 preferred shares would have their ownership interests severely diluted. Accordingly, either the articles of incorporation must authorize such a share dividend, or the preferred shareholders must approve the dividend. The second hurdle is insurmountable in this case, since each of the preferred shares has a par value of $100, and that amount must be transferred from surplus to stated capital for each distributed share. The surplus of the Nobles Company—the excess of net assets and stated capital—is only $42,000. To issue 5,000 shares of $100 par value stock, $50,000 in surplus must be transferred to stated capital. Consequently, this total share dividend could not be distributed; the greatest number of shares of preferred stocks that could be distributed is 4,200. Note that a share dividend of one class of shares to the holders of another class is rare. Usually a share dividend will be paid to holders of each class in shares of the same class.

If the corporation has no treasury shares, and if all of the authorized shares have been issued, the articles of incorporation must be amended to supply additional authorized shares before a share dividend may be declared.

Procedure for Declaration, Payment, and Accounting

The decision to declare a share dividend is made by the board of directors, which will adopt a resolution specifying the number of shares to be distributed, the proportion of distribution, record and payment dates for the persons to receive dividends, and authority for the transfer of surplus to stated capital.

> **EXAMPLE: Resolution to Declare a Stock Dividend**
> WHEREAS, there has been accumulated from undistributed profits of the company a surplus of $22,000.00, which in the opinion of the board of directors can be advantageously used for the benefit of stockholders.
>
> RESOLVED, that a stock dividend be and the same hereby is declared payable to stockholders of record as of the 10th day of July, 1992, one share of common stock of the par value of $1 per share to be distributed as such stock dividend to the holder of each outstanding share of common stock, and a like amount to the holder of each share of preferred stock of the par value of $100 each, said stock dividend to be extra and additional to any cash dividend now or hereinafter declared; and
>
> FURTHER RESOLVED, that $5,050.00 of said surplus be transferred to capital to accomplish said stock dividend, and 5,050 shares of common stock of the par value of $1 per share be issued and disbursed as hereinbefore provided.[16]

On the record date, the shareholders entitled to receive the shares are identified, and on the payment date, certificates are executed and distributed to those persons.

All accounting entries reflecting a stock dividend occur in the shareholders' equity section of the balance sheet, because the *payment* (the value of the shares) is transferred from the surplus accounts to the stated capital account. Stated capital receives the amount of the par value of the shares if the shares have a par value, or an amount determined by the board of directors for no par shares. For example, if the Nobles Company declared a 1-share-per-10 common stock dividend, 500 new shares of $1 par common stock would be issued as a dividend to the holders of the 5,000 outstanding shares. The stated capital would be increased by $500, the amount equal to the par value per share times the number of shares distributed as a dividend. The earned surplus account would be reduced by $500 since payment is theoretically made from there.

The New York Stock Exchange imposes a special accounting rule for stock dividends from companies listed on the exchange, and generally accepted accounting principles require the use of the rule for other corporations as well. Stated simply, the accounting for a stock dividend must recognize the fair market value of the shares being distributed. In the preceding Nobles Company distribution, suppose the 500 common shares, with $1 par value, had a fair market value of $10 per share. If the same shares were sold, $500 would be entered in stated capital and $4,500 would be transferred to capital surplus. When the shares are distributed as a stock dividend, the proper accounting entries would be $500 to stated capital, $4,500 to capital surplus, and $5,000 from earned surplus.

If you study these accounting entries, you may see why the issuance of a stock dividend adds nothing to the true economic interests of the shareholder. The shareholder's ownership interest in the corporation is represented by the shareholders' equity section of the balance sheet, including stated capital, capital surplus, and earned surplus. In issuing a stock dividend, the corporation is merely transferring funds within the shareholders' equity accounts, and is not distributing any assets of the corporation. The advantage of a stock dividend lies in the future; if the business continues to prosper, the value of each share of stock will increase. The eternal hope of shareholders is that all stock, including the shares distributed in a stock dividend, will appreciate in value, and the shareholders will realize huge capital gains when the stock is sold.

Tax Ramifications of Share Dividends

The tax ramifications of a stock dividend for shareholders is simple on its face, but complicated in its application. The dividend itself is a nontaxable transfer, since the shareholder receives no distribution of value from the stock dividend. Rather, the ownership interest is simply divided into more shares. Thus, no tax need be paid when a stock dividend is received. The tax problem comes later.

When the shares are sold, the shareholder must compute the *basis* for the shares—that is, their cost to the shareholder—in order to compute the capital gains. Stated very simply, if shares were purchased for $5.00 per share, and subsequently sold for $8.00 per share, the basis is the cost of the shares and the capital gain is $3.00 per share. Stock dividends complicate this computation, because they require an adjustment to the basis of the original shares. For example, suppose a shareholder purchased 100 shares of Nobles Company common stock at $5.00 per share, and subsequently received a one-for-ten stock dividend, resulting in a total of 110 shares for the original investment of $500.00. The shareholder's basis per share is now $4.545 per share, and that figure will be used to compute capital gains when the shares are sold. Further complications are apparent if the shareholder had purchased 10 shares in 1978 for $5.00 per share, 50 shares in 1979 for $6.00 per share, 25 shares in 1980 for $6.50 per share, and 15 shares in 1981 for $6.75 per share. When this shareholder later receives a 10-share stock dividend, all of these figures must be adjusted. A stock dividend may be most popular with the shareholder's accountant because of these confusing tax computations.

STOCK SPLITS

A stock split is very similar to a stock dividend inasmuch as it results in a greater division of the same ownership interest for each shareholder. However, a typical stock split usually involves some modification of the capital stock structure itself. If the corporation's shares have a par value, a split is normally accomplished by reducing the par value of the shares so that the aggregate stated capital of the corporation will be unaffected by the distribution. If the shares have no par value, the stock split effects a reduction of the stated value of each share.

The generally accepted distinction between stock splits and stock dividends stems from the mechanics of effecting the distribution. A stock *dividend* traditionally involves a transfer of surplus to stated capital within the shareholders' equity section of the balance sheet. By taking from surplus and adding to capital, one may consider the stock dividend to be a type of earnings distribution, although no value is actually distributed to the shareholders. A stock *split,* on the other hand, simply changes the total number of shares outstanding, and the stated capital remains the same. There are no shifting of funds and no distributions of earnings. This distinction between stock dividends and stock splits has very little practical effect, with the singular exception that in most states a true stock split will require an amendment to the articles of incorporation.

Like a share dividend, a stock split involves the issuance of a certain number of shares for each share currently held. Splits may be two-for-one, three-for-one, or even one-hundred-for-one. Under the new Model Business Corporation Act, there is no distinction in the corporate formalities required to issue a share dividend or to declare a stock split. In Section 6.23, the board of directors has the authority to issue a share dividend by simply declaring one. Under Section 10.02, the board of directors also has the authority to amend the articles of incorporation to change the total number of shares outstanding into a greater number of shares. There are two separate procedures for accomplishing a split. A modification of the par value of the shares is the common method. In a two-for-one split, the par value is halved, and twice as many shares are issued for the same amount of stated capital. In the case of the common shareholders of the Nobles Company, a two-for-one stock split will reduce the par value of the common shares to $0.50 per share, and result in a distribution of 5,000 additional shares for the 5,000 shares presently outstanding. There will then be 10,000 shares of common stock issued and outstanding represented by the same $5,000 in stated capital. The shareholders' equity section of the balance sheet will be changed only to indicate that there were 10,000 shares issued and outstanding, and that the par value is now $0.50 per share. An amendment to the articles of incorporation is necessary to reflect the new par value in the capital structure. The amendment may also require an increase in the authorized stock of the particular class. If the Nobles Company sought to issue an eleven-for-one stock split, the presently authorized shares would be insufficient for the distribution, since 55,000 shares would be needed. The extra shares may be authorized in the same amendment that changes par value.

Shares without par value may also be involved in a split, in which case an amendment to the articles may not be necessary since such shares remain no par value after the split. An amendment is required, however, if additional authorized shares are needed to accomplish the split. The initiative for the stock split begins with a resolution by the board of directors for an amendment to the articles of incorporation:

> **EXAMPLE:** **Resolution to Amend the Articles for a Stock Split**
> RESOLVED, that Article Fourth of the Articles of Incorporation be and the same is hereby amended as follows:
> "FOURTH: * * * one hundred thousand (100,000) shares shall be common stock with a par value of $.50 per share."

> At the time this amendment becomes effective, and without any further action on the part of the corporation or its stockholders, each share of common stock of a par value of $1.00 per share then issued and outstanding shall be changed and reclassified into two fully paid and nonassessable shares of common stock of a par value of $.50. The capital account of the corporation shall not be increased or decreased by such change and reclassification. To reflect the said change and reclassification, each certificate representing shares of common stock of a par value of $1.00 theretofore issued and outstanding shall be cancelled, and the holder of record of each such certificate shall be entitled to receive a new certificate representing two shares of common stock of a par value of $.50, so that upon this amendment becoming effective each holder of record of a certificate representing theretofore issued and outstanding common stock of the corporation will be entitled to certificates representing in the aggregate two shares of common stock of a par value of $.50 authorized by this amendment for each share of common stock of a par value of $1.00 per share of which he or she was the holder prior to the effectiveness of this amendment.[17]

In most states, this recommendation for an amendment to the articles of incorporation must be submitted to the shareholders for an appropriate vote. Section 10.02 of the new Model Business Corporation Act permits the board of directors to simply increase the total number of shares of a particular class without obtaining the approval of the shareholders.

The second method of declaring a stock split is the same procedure used to issue a share dividend. Instead of the par value of the shares by an amendment to the articles of incorporation, an amount may be transferred from surplus to stated capital, and the new shares may be issued for the increased stated capital. For example, the Nobles Company could accomplish a two-for-one split by transferring $5,000 from surplus to capital, thereby increasing stated capital to $10,000 and covering the issuance of 5,000 additional shares at the same par value. Although this is technically a distribution of earnings and is more appropriately described as a share dividend, it is generally referred to as a split because of the doubling of shares held by each shareholder. An amendment to the articles of incorporation may still be necessary if the remaining authorized but unissued shares are fewer than the additional shares required in the split.

In addition to the amendment procedure and transfer of surplus to capital methods of accomplishing stock splits, other rules may require capitalization of earnings in a stock distribution. The phrase "capitalization of earnings" refers to the second procedure of transferring surplus to stated capital. The rules of the New York Stock Exchange and the Securities Exchange Act of 1934 should be consulted for the circumstances requiring capitalization of earnings in a stock split.[18]

In all other respects, stock splits are treated the same as share dividends. Upon appropriate resolution of the board of directors, and amendment of the articles of incorporation, if necessary, new certificates are issued to shareholders reflecting the additional shares of the split. The tax ramifications for the shareholders are identical to the tax treatment of share dividends.

CORPORATION'S PURCHASE OF ITS OWN SHARES

The corporation may purchase its own shares from its shareholders if the board of directors authorizes the purchase and the applicable state statute so permits. The Model Business Corporation Act authorizes the repurchase of shares in Section

6.31, and Section 6.40 treats a repurchase as a distribution to shareholders, so that the same restrictions placed upon dividends also apply here. Most states regulate the repurchase of shares as dividends are regulated, so the funds used to purchase the shares are limited to unrestricted and unreserved earned surplus. Usually capital surplus may also be used if authorized by the articles of incorporation or by a majority vote of the shareholders.

The corporation's purchase of its own shares is a distribution to shareholders, since the corporation exchanges cash for shares. Because of the distribution characteristics, purchases of shares are regulated much the same way as other distributions. The law refuses permission to purchase shares if the corporation is insolvent or would be rendered insolvent by the purchase. However, there are some generally recognized exceptional cases when the corporation may reacquire its own shares without making a distribution subject to statutory regulation. These include the purchase of corporate shares to eliminate fractional shares,[19] to compromise or collect an indebtedness to the corporation, to pay dissenting shareholders entitled to payment under the law,[20] and to retire redeemable shares.[21] In all other cases, the corporate purchase of shares must be made from legally available funds, earned surplus or capital surplus in an appropriate case.

Consider the purchasing ability of the Nobles Company. Under the revised Model Business Corporation Act approach, the corporation may make a distribution only if it will be able to pay its debts as they come due and if total assets exceed (and after the distribution occurs will continue to exceed) total liabilities plus the amount payable to preferred shares as a liquidation preference. The balance sheet of the Nobles Company shows total assets of $78,000, total liabilities of $26,000, and a liquidation preference for preferred shares of $5,000. Thus, the corporation has a total of $47,000 in legal purchasing power, subject to its ability to pay debts as they come due. In states that use the earned surplus and capital surplus tests, the Nobles Company would have less purchasing power. The balance sheet shows unreserved and unrestricted earned surplus of $22,000, and that amount could be used by the board of directors to purchase shares. The balance sheet also shows $20,000 in capital surplus, which could be used if the articles of incorporation or the holders of the majority of voting shares authorized the action. However, the liquidity of the company may be a practical barrier to the purchase of shares. The corporation will be limited by the relatively low cash position shown on the balance sheet under both tests.

The shares purchased by the corporation may be returned to the status of authorized-and-unissued shares; cancelled; or, in most states, held by the corporation as treasury shares. Section 6.31 of the revised Model Business Corporation Act anticipates only that the shares would be returned to authorized-but-unissued status, or cancelled. If the shares are returned to authorized-but-unissued status, the amount paid for the shares is simply deducted from the asset side of the balance sheet, and the amount of the stated capital and capital surplus used to purchase the shares is deducted from the equity portion of the balance sheet.

When treasury shares are contemplated and permitted by statute, most states require that the surplus used to purchase the shares must be restricted in the amount required for the purchase, and the restriction must remain in effect as long as the shares are held as treasury shares. If the shares are subsequently sold or cancelled, the restriction may be removed. To illustrate, assume that the Nobles Company repurchased 1,000 shares of its common stock to hold as treasury shares at a price of $3.00 per share, using $3,000 of the earned surplus for the purchase.

The earned surplus account would reflect $19,000 in available earned surplus and $3,000 in restricted earned surplus, representing the 1,000 shares of common stock held in the treasury. Thereafter, the corporation may resell the treasury shares for any price (including a price below par value). When resold, the shares are no longer treasury shares and the restriction is lifted. If the corporation sells the shares for $2.50 per share, then only $2,500 will be added back to earned surplus and the loss of $500 will be permanently subtracted from that account. These transactions reflect that the corporation has suffered a loss by investing in its own shares.

Section 6.31 of the Model Business Corporation Act prescribes a streamlined procedure for cancelling the purchased shares. In most states, the board of directors adopts a resolution authorizing the cancellation of shares and a statement of cancellation is filed with the secretary of state. Under the new procedure, the board of directors (without shareholder approval) adopts articles of amendment that state the name of the corporation, the reduction in the number of authorized shares, and the total number of authorized shares after the reduction.[22] When the cancellation is completed, the stated capital account is reduced to reflect the cancellation and the earned surplus is adjusted to show that only the par value of the shares has been realized by the company. Thus, if the 1,000 shares reacquired by the Nobles Company for $3,000 were recorded as treasury shares first and later cancelled, the stated capital account would show 4,000 common shares issued and outstanding with $4,000 stated capital. The earned surplus account would be adjusted as follows:

After purchase, before cancellation:

Earned surplus		
Unrestricted		$19,000
Restricted		3,000
Total		$22,000

Cancellation:

Remove restriction—	
Add par value of cancelled shares	$ 1,000
Subtract purchase price of shares	(3,000)
Net reduction	$(2,000)

After cancellation:

Earned surplus	
Unrestricted	$20,000

You may have become uneasy about the corporation's purchase of its own shares, remembering that with dividend distributions, all shareholders of the same class must be treated equally. A relevant question at this point might be: Is the corporation required to purchase the entire class of stock if it intends to purchase any shares? The answer is no. The corporation may purchase all or any part of a particular class, and theoretically may select the shareholders from whom the purchase is made. However, there is a taint of unfairness if the selling shareholders happen to be the directors who authorized the purchase, and the plot thickens if the corporate business suddenly takes a turn for the worse right after the sale. There are laws that protect the other shareholders in such a case. Traditional common law principles of fraud apply here, and the shareholders are further protected through the fiduciary duties owed them by management. Finally, federal securities laws regulate insider trading by management, and those laws may also resolve the harm. Nevertheless, the corporate statutes do not require that all shareholders of a particular class be treated equally when the corporation purchases its own shares.

PARTIAL LIQUIDATIONS

A partial liquidation is a combination of a distribution of assets, usually cash, and the purchase of the corporation's own shares. In fact, any purchase of shares by a corporation is a partial liquidation. The concept of partial liquidation became popular when certain tax advantages were allowed for partial liquidations that qualified for special favorable tax treatment. The favorable tax consequences for partial liquidations have been eliminated in the federal tax law, but the term *partial liquidation* is still used whenever an identifiable segment of a business is distributed to the shareholders. This type of distribution could result from closing a particular division of a corporation and terminating the trade conducted by that division. After creditors are paid, the assets could be distributed as a partial liquidation to the shareholders. A partial liquidation may also result from a contraction of the corporation's business, such as the closing of certain selected manufacturing plants.

To illustrate a partial liquidation, the hypothetical Nobles Company could sell a portion of its plant and equipment, and liquidate the cash received in a distribution to the shareholders in exchange for stock. The transaction may occur as follows: The company sells $13,000 in plant equipment and continues its reduced business with the remaining plant and equipment available, and the net cash from the sale is distributed to the stockholders in exchange for a proportionate amount of stock. Since the $13,000 in plant and equipment equals approximately one-fourth of the net assets, the corporation may reacquire approximately one-quarter of the total outstanding stock in exchange for the distribution. The corporation has accomplished a purchase of stock by distributing cash assets received in a partial liquidation.

The procedure for a partial liquidation begins with a resolution of the board of directors.

> **EXAMPLE: Resolution to Partially Liquidate**
> Whereas, this Corporation presently is the owner of sundry producing and undeveloped oil and gas leases, drilling equipment, oil payments, and miscellaneous properties;
> Whereas, the Board of Directors deem it good business and advisable to make a partial liquidation of the Corporation and to pay out certain properties of the Corporation as a dividend in kind ratably to the stockholders of record on the 10th day of December, 1992; and
> Whereas, the payment of a partial liquidating dividend will not impair the capital stock of the Corporation.
> Now, therefore, be it resolved, that a partial liquidating dividend be declared and paid as of January 2, 1993, said dividend to be paid in properties in kind and consisting of the following described properties: [*Here describe.*]

Be it further resolved, that the Certificate of Incorporation of this Corporation be amended, reducing the capital stock of the Corporation from 5,000 shares of common stock of the par value of $1.00 per share to 3,750 shares of common stock of the par value of $1.00 per share, and from 50 shares of preferred stock of the par value of $100.00 per share to 37.5 shares of preferred stock of the par value of $100.00 per share; and that of the net book value of the assets paid out as a liquidating dividend, $1,250.00 of such amount be charged against the stated capital of the common shares and $1,250.00 of such amount be charged against the stated capital of the preferred shares, and the remainder be charged against the capital surplus account.[23]

DISSOLUTION AND LIQUIDATION

Distributions to shareholders are also involved in a complete dissolution of the corporation, since the shareholders are entitled to receive their proportionate ownership interests in the assets after corporate creditors have been paid. Shareholders of record are identified and notice is given to creditors permitting a reasonable period for filing claims.[24]

All shareholders participate ratably in the net assets of the corporation after payments to creditors, unless the articles of incorporation provide otherwise. The articles may authorize a capital stock structure with various classes or series of shares, one or more of which may be entitled to a preference to assets in liquidation. The preference will be honored before other classes of stock are entitled to their proportionate shares of assets.

Liquidation preferences are usually fixed as a percentage of par value or a specified dollar amount, and preferred shares, while entitled to the first priority to the assets, are limited to the liquidation amount specified. For example, observe that the preferred shares of the Nobles Company are entitled to a liquidation preference of 100% of par value per share. If dissolution occurred when the financial status of the corporation was as described earlier in the balance sheet, the net assets of the corporation would be $52,000.00 at dissolution. The preferred shares would be entitled to receive $5,000.00 of the assets (100% of $100.00 par value for 50 shares). The remaining $47,000.00 in assets would be distributed to the common shareholders, and the preferred shareholders would not share in this distribution. It is possible, however, to create participating preferred shares, so the preferred shareholders participate in the distribution of assets after receiving their preference. To illustrate, suppose that in addition to the 100% par value preference in liquidation, the articles of incorporation further provided that the preferrred shares would participate equally with the common shares in liquidation. The preferred shares would still receive the first $5,000.00, and the remaining $47,000.00 would be distributed equally among 5,050 shares (5,000 common and 50 preferred). Each share of each class would receive $9.31 in liquidation in the second distribution. Thus, the total liquidation distribution to the preferred shareholders would be $109.31 per share.

Classes of preferred stock that are entitled to cumulative *dividend* preferences may also have a preferred claim in liquidation to the extent of the dividend arrearages. This principle has undergone some tortured construction in litigation and is not firmly settled. However, the principle is simple and any interpretation problem could be avoided by careful drafting of the articles of incorporation. Again consider the example of the Nobles Company. Its preferred shares are entitled to a 5% cumulative dividend preference, meaning that dividends of $5 per share (5% of $100 par value) accumulate annually. When a dividend is finally declared, the total arrearage must be paid to the cumulative preferred shareholders before any other shareholders may receive dividends. Suppose the Nobles Company has not declared dividends for five years and is now being dissolved and liquidated. The dividends for the preferred shares have accumulated in the amount of $25 per share. The question is whether the preferred shareholders are entitled to receive their dividend arrearages as a preference in liquidation before other classes of stock are permitted to share the assets. The articles of incorporation could provide either way, but should be specific in any case. If it is intended that the preferred shares will be entitled to a liquidation preference for unpaid cumulative dividends, the articles should so specify, and should also define a dividend arrearage or accumulation as including unpaid amounts regardless of whether the corporation has ever declared a dividend or has had funds available for a declaration of a dividend. To negate the liquidation preference for unpaid cumulative dividends, the articles should specifically state that the right to unpaid accumulated dividends is lost if the corporation is dissolved and liquidated.

NOTES

1. See M.B.C.A. § 6.40.
2. Park & Tilford v. Schulte, 160 F.2d 984 (2d Cir. 1947).
3. See "Fractions of Shares or Scrip" in Chapter 7.
4. M.B.C.A. § 6.40.
5. See M.B.C.A. § 6.40(c).
6. M.B.C.A. § 6.40(a).
7. Dividend restrictions in the articles of incorporation were suggested as important considerations at the drafting stage. See "The Articles of Incorporation" in Chapter 6.
8. See "Corporation's Purchase of Its Own Shares" later in this chapter.
9. E.g., Nebraska, Neb.Rev.Stat. § 21-2043(2.)
10. E.g., California, West's Ann.Calif.Corp.Code § 500; and Idaho, Idaho Code Ann. § 30-1-45.
11. West's Modern Legal Forms § 2291 and 2292.
12. West's Modern Legal Forms § 2927.1.
13. See "Shareholder Meetings" in Chapter 8.
14. Internal Revenue Code of 1986, 26 U.S.C.A. § 301.
15. The 1979 revisions to the Model Business Corporation Act eliminated the concepts of treasury shares, stated capital, or surplus.
16. See also West's Modern Legal Forms § 2926 for a clause that authorizes the issuance of shares of one class to holders of shares of another class.
17. See West's Modern Legal Forms § 2835 for a form of resolution for a share split. The procedure to amend the articles of incorporation is detailed in "Amendment of the Articles of Incorporation" in Chapter 13.
18. See Rule 10(b)-12, Securities Exchange Act of 1934, 15 U.S.C.A. § 78(j.)
19. See "Fractions of Shares or Scrip" in Chapter 7.
20. See "Rights of Dissenting Shareholders" in Chapter 13.
21. See "Preferred Stock Rights" in Chapter 7.
22. A statement of cancellation of reacquired shares (as an amendment to the articles of incorporation) appears as Form 9A in Appendix G.
23. West's Modern Legal Forms § 2926.5.
24. The dissolution procedure in more fully discussed in "Voluntary Dissolution," "Involuntary Dissolution," and "Liquidation" in Chapter 13.

10 AGENTS, EMPLOYMENT, AND COMPENSATION

AGENCY

The operations of every business enterprise are conducted by agents and employees. Even in a sole proprietorship, the sole proprietor will hire other persons to perform certain duties, some as simple as cleaning up the premises and others as complex as managing the entire business. In a partnership, each partner is an agent for the partnership and for the other partners. And in a corporation, the firm can act only through agents. Although the corporation is a separate legal person, it can speak and hear only through its directors, officers, or shareholders. Therefore, the law of agency plays a role in each business enterprise.

The duties and responsibilities of each agent may be specifically described in an agreement between the agent and the enterprise. A brief discussion may help you understand some important principles of agency law and the context in which such agreements may be drafted.

Definition and Elements of Agency

An agency is a voluntary, consensual relationship between two persons. The relationship is created by law whenever one person, the principal, has a right to control the conduct of the agent, and the agent has the power to affect the legal relations of the principal. This relationship does not only occur in a business organization. Any time people ask other people to perform a task on their behalf, an agency relationship may be created. Your first experience with an agency relationship may have occurred when your mother asked you to go to the grocery store and buy a loaf of bread. In this context, your mother, as a principal, was authorizing you, as an agent, to perform a task for her, thereby giving you the authority to affect her legal relationship with the grocery store. In a business context, the legal relationship is more obvious. For example, the cashier at the counter in the local hardware store is an agent of the owner of the store, and has the authority to perform legal obligations (and incur legal liability) on behalf of the owner.

Agency relationships can arise in several other situations. Whenever a client asks an attorney to represent the client, the attorney is an agent for the client. The same is true with accountants and other consultants who perform services for individuals and businesses at their request.

It is not necessary that the agency relationship be formalized by a written document, although it frequently is. Agency authority can be granted informally, simply by asking someone to perform a task, or may be as formal as an extensive written agreement that details all duties and obligations of the principal and the agent. It is always advisable to use written documents to define and describe legal rights and obligations among the principal and the agent.

Types of Principals

The law of agency generally distinguishes three types of principals: disclosed, partially disclosed, and undisclosed. If an agent is conducting business for a principal, and the person with whom the agent is dealing knows the agent is acting for another and knows the person for whom the agent is acting, the principal is a disclosed principal. If a salesperson for IBM is selling hardware and software equipment to a purchaser, and the purchaser is aware that the salesperson is acting on behalf of IBM and that the equipment is manufactured and sold by IBM, IBM is a disclosed principal.

If an agent acts on behalf of a principal, but does not disclose the identity of the principal, the principal is partially disclosed. In this case, the person dealing with the agent knows that a principal exists, but does not know who the principal is. If Bill Schmidt wanted to purchase a new home in an exclusive subdivision, but was concerned about everyone in the community knowing that he could afford a home in this subdivision, Bill might authorize an agent to make inquiries of prospective sellers without disclosing Bill's identity. Those agents would approach sellers of property, explaining that they were acting for another, but saying that they wanted to keep the identity of their prospective purchaser anonymous until a particular property was selected and a purchase contract was negotiated. In these cases, the sellers of the property would realize that they were dealing with an agent, but would know that the agent was not personally interested in purchasing the property. Nevertheless, they would not be aware of the identity of Bill Schmidt until the agent had disclosed Bill's identity after a contract had been completed.

Whenever an agent is acting on behalf of another, but has not disclosed that fact or the identity of the person on whose behalf the agent is acting, the principal is undisclosed. If Bill Schmidt were worried that some prospective seller might learn his identity, he could authorize an agent to make inquiries concerning the purchase of property without disclosing that a principal was involved. In these cases, the agent would be giving prospective sellers an impression that the agent was personally interested in purchasing the property, and would negotiate a contract, according to Bill Schmidt's terms, without ever telling the seller that Bill was the actual purchaser. The sellers would thus be dealing with an undisclosed principal, since the only person they know is the agent.

Types of Agents

The law of agency generally distinguishes among several types of agents: general or special agents, servants or independent contractors, and subagents or subservants. A general agent is a person who is continuously employed to conduct a series of transactions. The cashier at the hardware store is employed on a daily basis to greet customers, record their purchases, and collect their money. This person has ongoing responsibilities for a series of transactions on behalf of the principal, and would be regarded as a general agent.

A special agent is a person who is employed to conduct a single transaction or a limited number of transactions. When Bill Schmidt authorizes an agent to negotiate and purchase a piece of property, the agent's task is limited to negotiating for a single transaction (to purchase the property for Bill). Similarly, if a principal asked an agent to negotiate the purchase of several pieces of property, the agent's duties would be limited to the transactions involving designated properties in which the principal is interested. These agents, with limited authority and specific transactional duties, are regarded as special agents.

A servant is an agent who agrees to devote time to the principal's business and affairs and whose physical conduct, during the performance of the employment, is subject to the control of the principal. Whether the principal has a right to control the activities of the agent is usually interpreted from various factors, including the type of business of the principal, the type of activities performed for the principal by the agent, and agreements between the principal and agent that describe the agent's authority. The cashier at the hardware store is probably a servant. This person follows directives given by the owner of the hardware store concerning the manner in which customers are to be greeted, prices are to be ascertained, and cash is to be collected and handled. Most activities of the cashier are subject to the control of the owner, and may frequently be changed or modified at the owner's whim and direction.

An independent contractor is a person who is conducting a transaction for the principal, but is not subject to the control of the principal. These persons are expected to exercise independent judgment, usually within their own professional guidelines and responsibilities, and, while they are acting on behalf of a principal, the principal does not have the right to tell them how to act or perform. The classic examples of independent contractors include attorneys, brokers, or consulting persons who have professional training and abilities to accomplish a transaction better than the principal can. For instance, a client will explain to an attorney many facts and issues relating to litigation, and the attorney is expected to exercise professional judgment and to conduct the litigation on behalf of the client to achieve the outcome the client desires. Independent contractor status usually arises with agents who have specialized training, but it is not necessary that an independent contractor have specialized or professional training to serve in that capacity. Whenever the relationship between a principal and an agent permits the agent to act individually according to the agent's own judgment, and particularly when an agent is hired for a specialized task that only the agent is capable of performing, an independent contractor status will arise.

Whenever one agent hires another to assist in the performance of duties for the principal, the second agent becomes a subagent. A subagent is created only if the first agent is authorized to hire the second. An agent may be authorized to hire other agents, based upon the scope of the work that the agent has been requested to perform. The authority may also come from a written agreement between the principal and the agent that grants authority to hire other persons to assist in the tasks the agent is expected to perform. For example, if the owner of a restaurant hired a manager to run the operations of the restaurant, the manager would have implied authority to hire a chef, dishwashers, waiters and waitresses, and other restaurant personnel. These persons would be subagents of the owner. If subagents are subject to the right of control by the principal, the subagents become subservants. Thus, if the owner of the restaurant can direct the activities of the chef who was hired by the manager, the chef becomes a subservant of the owner.

Duties and Obligations between the Principal and the Agent. The law of agency creates a fiduciary obligation between the principal and the agent. Consequently, the law implies certain duties that both parties must perform on behalf of the other, which may be amplified or supplemented by a written agreement.

Agents generally owe their principals the duties of obedience, care, and loyalty. An agent has a duty to obey a principal, and to perform all tasks the principal has directed, so long as those tasks are consistent with the engagement of the agent.

Each agent is expected to use reasonable care and diligence to accomplish the principal's objectives. This means an agent should use personal skill and knowledge and perform all tasks diligently while working for the principal. For example, an attorney would be required to know the law to be applied in the client's case, and an insurance agent would be expected not to permit a policy of insurance to expire or terminate without appropriate notice to the policy owner. Even if an agent is performing without compensation, the agent owes the principal the obligation to use due care and prudence in performing all duties. Consistent with the duty of care is an agent's duty to act in a manner that will not embarrass the principal or bring the principal into disrepute, and an agent always has a duty to provide full information concerning any matters the principal would want to know concerning the transaction undertaken by the agent.

The agent's duty of loyalty requires that the agent act solely for the interests of the principal while accomplishing the transactions for which the agent is employed. This duty requires the agent to account for any profits received by the agent on the principal's behalf, and to disclose fully any personal adverse or conflicting interests that would affect the agent's ability to act for the principal. Therefore, if an agent were engaged by a principal to find a particular parcel of property for the principal's business, and the agent also had an interest in acquiring a similar piece of property in the same area, the agent could not use negotiations for the principal to assist the agent in personal negotiations for the property, and the agent must disclose to the principal that the agent is also personally seeking a similar piece of property. An agent may not compete with the principal, and must disclose all confidential information received on the principal's behalf.

The principal also has obligations to the agent that are implied by law and that may be amplified or supplemented by an agreement. Generally, a principal is obligated to compensate an agent, according to the reasonable value of the agent's services, unless the agent has agreed to act without pay. The principal has a further obligation to provide the agent with the means to perform the agent's services, such as an office, samples of products the agent is expected to sell, transportation, or clerical assistance. The principal may also be obligated under an agreement with the agent to provide other benefits for the agent's service.

The principal has an additional obligation to indemnify the agent for any payments or liabilities incurred by the agent whenever the agent is performing a transaction on behalf of the principal. Since the agent is acting for the principal, any expenses or liabilities incurred belong to the principal, and the principal must pay them. Thus, if an agent incurs transportation costs or expenses entertaining the principal's customers, the principal must reimburse the agent under this duty.

The principal is also expected not to embarrass the agent or act in a manner that is harmful to the agent's reputation or self-esteem, and the principal must not interfere with the agent's performance by making the tasks more difficult or by sabotaging the agent's ability to perform the job. If the owner of the hardware store in the earlier example publicly berated the cashier in front of customers and other employees, or refused to provide the cashier with a workable cash register to record customer purchases, the owner would have violated these fiduciary duties to the cashier.

Agency Authority

Whenever a principal asks an agent to perform a task, the agent has authority to obligate the principal for legal rights and liabilities associated with that transaction. The law of agency has several distinctions concerning the types of authority the agent may enjoy and the rights and liabilities of the principal, the agent, and the other contracting parties whenever an agent negotiates a contract on the principal's behalf.

An agent is always authorized to do what the principal has told the agent to do. The agent may also reasonably infer authority to do acts required to perform the tasks assigned. General agents, who are engaged for a series of continuing transactions, may usually infer greater authority than a special agent, who is limited to the authority necessary to accomplish a single assigned transaction. The authority usually and reasonably needed to complete an assigned task is called *actual authority*. For example, if a truck company hires a truck driver to make interstate deliveries of goods, the truck driver has actual authority to operate the truck, and may reasonably infer authority to purchase gasoline and make repairs to the vehicle. However, the truck driver probably does not have actual authority to hire an assistant truck driver to help drive the truck, since that is not usually or reasonably inferred as being part of the truck driver's duties.

Even if the agent does not have actual authority, he or she may nevertheless obligate the principal in a transaction with a third party under the doctrine of *apparent authority*. Whenever conduct of the principal has caused a third party to believe that the agent has authority, the agent will have apparent authority to obligate the principal. This is true even when the agent knows there is no authority to obligate the principal. As long as the third party reasonably believes that the agent has authority, from appearances created by the principal, the principal will be obligated to the third party. For example, if the cashier at the hardware store has been told by the owner not to accept any returned merchandise, the cashier knows that there is no actual authority to accept returned merchandise from customers. Nevertheless, if the owner does not take steps to inform customers that the cashier does not have this authority, the customers may reasonably believe that the cashier could accept returned merchandise on behalf of the store. If a customer returns a defective lawn mower and the cashier refunds the purchase price, the owner of the store is obligated by that act. The appearances created by the owner are that the cashier has the authority to make those decisions, and the third person could reasonably believe that the cashier had that authority.

If an agent did not have either actual authority or apparent authority, the principal could nevertheless *ratify* a transaction the agent has negotiated. Through ratification, the principal will become obligated as if authority existed at the time the transaction was negotiated. Assume that an alert real estate broker knows Bill Schmidt is looking for a new home. Without contacting Bill, the broker negotiates with several sellers for homes in an area where Bill would like to live. The broker is acting without any authority from Bill in negotiating these contracts. However, once the broker receives terms from a seller and presents those terms to Bill for his consideration, Bill could ratify the contract negotiated by the broker, and agree to be obligated by that contract. Ratification requires that the principal have full knowledge of all material facts concerning the transaction, and the principal must indicate, through words or conduct, that he or she intends to be obligated in the transaction. In this case, even though the broker had no authority to negotiate on Bill's behalf, Bill's subsequent conduct in accepting the agreement would ratify the acts of the agent and obligate Bill to the contract.

Torts Committed by Agents

The creation of an agency is an extension of the personal life of the principal. Whenever an agent commits a tort or misdeed while performing duties for a principal, the law may require that the principal be liable for the injuries created through the agent's actions. This concept is called *vicarious liability*.

The first rule to learn is that the agent is always personally liable for any injury caused by the agent's acts. If a truck driver negligently causes an accident at a busy intersection, the truck driver will be personally liable, even though the truck driver was acting as an agent for the trucking company. Similarly, if the cashier at the hardware store steals a customer's credit card and uses it for personal purchases, the cashier is personally responsible for those actions, even though the cashier was acting as an agent of the hardware store.

In determining whether the principal will be liable for the acts of an agent, one must distinguish whether the agent is a servant or an independent contractor. Generally, the law requires that principals must be responsible for all acts of a servant, but injuries caused by independent contractors are not usually the responsibility of the principal.

Remember that a principal has the right to control the activities of a servant. Thus, if a servant negligently performs activities on behalf of the principal, the principal should have controlled the servant to be certain those activities did not cause harm. Consequently, if the truck driver injures a passenger in an automobile at an intersection, the owner of the trucking company will be liable if the owner had the right to control the truck driver's activities. The owner is responsible for giving the truck driver specific directions concerning driving in a busy intersection, and for hiring truck drivers who are capable of driving correctly and safely. However, the owner is not responsible for every act of a servant. The servant must be performing duties within the scope of employment for the owner to be held responsible.

The *scope of employment* is determined by the nature of the job the agent was engaged to perform, time and space limitations concerning the agent's whereabouts and activities, and whether the agent caused harm while performing duties that were intended to benefit the principal. For example, if the truck driver parked the truck overnight to rest in a motel, and then left the motel without paying the bill, it is questionable whether the motel owner could recover from the trucking company. The truck driver was hired to drive a truck, not to stay in a motel, and consequently, the motel transaction may not have been within the scope of the truck driver's employment. However, if the truck driver's duties required several days of driving to accomplish the delivery, staying in the motel *may* be part of the scope of employment. On the other hand, if the cashier at the hardware store negligently drove into the side of a vehicle while leaving the parking lot at work, the owner of the hardware store should not be liable, since the duties of the cashier have nothing to do with driving an automobile and driving a vehicle is not within the cashier's scope of employment.

Time and space limitations are imposed upon the agent's whereabouts and activities, to determine whether the agent was performing duties within the scope of employment. If the truck driver decided to deviate from an assigned route to visit an aunt in a nearby city, and while driving to the aunt's house caused an accident, the owner of the truck company should not be responsible because the truck driver was not on the assigned route at the time the accident occurred. This example raises an important distinction in the law of agency. The principal will be liable if the agent has merely "detoured" from the appointed tasks. As long as the agent is doing the assigned job, such as driving a truck, the owner may be liable wherever the agent may be driving, under the theory that the agent has merely detoured from the appointed route. On the other hand, if an agent "frolics," the principal will not be liable. An agent is frolicking when an agent's personal objectives become superior to the objectives of the principal. It could be argued that the truck driver's deviation from an assigned route to visit an aunt for personal purposes would make the trip a frolic, so that any accident that occurred under those circumstances would not result in liability of the principal. The most interesting cases usually involve an agent who stops to give aid and is negligent in parking or providing aid, when the agent had no authority or direction from the principal that stopping to give aid or assistance was part of the agent's assigned job.

Agents for a Business Enterprise

The foregoing rules can apply to any situation in which a person authorizes another to perform a task. In a business organization, those tasks usually relate to the operations of the business, such as performing the duties of a cashier or truck driver or acting as the attorney or accountant for the business.

Because of the significant obligations created under agency law, all business relationships that involve an agent should be reduced to writing and clearly defined so that the obligations and rights of the principal and the agent can be clearly understood and interpreted. Within a business organization, employees are agents and their duties and rights are generally based upon the principles of agency law discussed here. Most of these rules may be defined and supplemented by agreements, and both the employer and the employee generally desire a clear understanding concerning the nature of the employment, the duties to be performed, and the compensation and benefits to which the employee will be entitled. Several other issues may also be addressed in employment agreements to more clearly define the rights and responsibilities of the agent and the principal.

A corporation offers the most flexible employment and compensation possibilities of any form of business. Managerial talent may be widely distributed in the corporate structure, from directors and officers to other management executives and supervisory personnel, and the compensation schemes are equally varied, particularly because of the many tax advantages available through the corporate entity. This chapter is primarily devoted to employment arrangements with corporate employees, although much of what is said here also applies to employees of proprietorships and partnerships.

Most employees are hired on an informal basis, without any written contract, and they perform duties for a stated compensation, in salary or wages, until their employment is terminated. Certain personal motives may induce the employee's performance and provide compensatory incentives. The company may be a family business, and the employee, as a member of the family, may have a kindred incentive to do the job well. The employee also may be a shareholder, and therefore have a pecuniary interest in his or her own performance. If the employee's performance contributes to business successes, the employee's stock will become more valuable. These informal employee relationships do not require much planning or counsel, and, because of their simplicity, are appropriate arrangements for most proprietorships and many partnerships and corporations. However, they do not take advantage of the many special methods of preserving talent and compensation available through more elaborate employment agreements.

As the company structure becomes larger and more employees are needed, managerial talent becomes more important. Key employees become an integral part of the organization, and their compensation and incentives assume greater significance. The company must ensure that these people will remain employees in order to guarantee a smooth reliable business organization. Key employees are not necessarily executives. They include salespersons, research and development personnel, and any other employee with a special skill. The objectives of the company in retaining these people is selfish on two counts: first, without key employees the business may suffer mild to serious reverses until they are replaced; and second, if key employees decide to work for the corporation's competitors, the company not only loses valuable talent, but also risks the loss of important trade secrets and processes.

The employees also have some stake in their employment arrangements. Theirs is a question of job security, advancement, and compensation. These complementary objectives of a continuing employment relationship may be satisfied through many combinations of employee agreements, incentive compensation plans, and fringe benefits.

EMPLOYMENT AGREEMENTS

An employee's job security objectives may be assured by an employment contract by which the company promises to keep the employee employed for a period of time and the employee promises to perform the specified duties diligently for the specified period. It is generally recognized that employment contracts provide considerably greater protection for the employee than for the employer. In part, this attitude exists because courts generally refuse to force a person to perform against that person's will. Consequently, if the employee quits before the expiration of the employment term, the employer could not successfully petition a court to order the employee to continue working involuntarily. On the other hand, if the employer fires the employee before the expiration of the agreement the employee may recover the compensation he or she would have received had he or she been allowed to perform the agreement, unless the employer can prove good cause for termination. Nevertheless, an employer may gain some benefits from the employment contract insofar as the contract's terms prescribe incentive compensation to encourage the faithful continued performance of the employee. Further, the agreement may include noncompetition clauses that prohibit the employee's entry into a competing business upon termination, or it may reserve to the company any developments or ideas discovered by the employee during employment.

Like so many other areas of the law of business organizations, employment contracts must be tailored to the particular needs of the parties, and it would be unrealistic to attempt to cover every possibility. There are, however, certain general rules basic to each agreement. A typical employment agreement should contain clauses describing the employee's responsibilities and duties; provisions for compensation and reimbursement of expenses; a description of the duration of the agreement; provisions for termination of the agreement; and, in many cases, noncompetition clauses, death and disability clauses, and provisions for company rights to discovery and development during employment.

Employee Duties

The contractual language that details the duties and responsibilities of the employee always depends on the particular needs of the employer, the talent and position of the employee, and the exigencies of the business. The definition of duties is extremely important, considering the possibility of later disputes. Not only must the employee know what the employer expects, but the employer must have some definitive guidelines upon which to measure the employee's performance. If the employee is terminated involuntarily before the expiration of the term of the agreement, the employer must be prepared to show that the employee failed to perform the specified duties under the contract. If the duties described in the agreement are ambiguous or otherwise ill defined, this proof may be impossible.

The description of duties for top-level management positions necessarily must be broad. It would be very difficult to attempt to detail all the duties expected of a company executive since this person is hired to run the business. A general statement of management duties is unavoidable here.

> **EXAMPLE: Duties of a Manager**
> The Manager shall well and faithfully serve the Employer in such capacity as aforesaid, and shall at all times devote his whole time, attention, and energies to the management, superintendence, and improvement of said business to the utmost of his ability, and shall do and perform all such services, acts, and things connected therewith as the Employer shall from time to time direct and are of a kind properly belonging to the duties of a Manager.[1]

Other more specific provisions may be used for positions with definable boundaries. Consider the duties of a research chemist:

> **EXAMPLE: Duties and Inventions of a Research Chemist**
> The Corporation hereby employs the Employee as a research chemist. The Employee's duties shall include the application of her skill and knowledge as a chemist towards devising new pharmaceutical products and improving existing formulas, processes, and methods employed by the Corporation. All inventions, discoveries and improvements devised or discovered by the Employee while in the employ of the Corporation shall become and remain the sole and exclusive property of the Corporation, whether discovered during or after regular working hours.[2]

A manager of a merchandising outlet could have duties prescribed as follows:

> **EXAMPLE: Duties of a Merchandising Outlet Manager**
> The duties of the Manager shall be such as are assigned to him by the Company. Initially there shall be included among his duties and authority the selection of a stock of merchandise for this venture; schedule of purchases to be submitted and subject to advance approval by the Company and copies of proposed orders shall be submitted to the Company to be passed upon and approved. Selections for current replacements for stock and purchases for new season requirements shall likewise be made by the Manager subject to prior approval by and submission of orders to the Company, in the same manner as is above provided for the initial stock. The Manager shall also keep a perpetual inventory of merchandise on hand and take a monthly physical inventory. The Manager likewise shall have full authority to employ and discharge employees of the business, subject to approval of the Company. The Manager will refer all disputed claims, not allowed by him for adjustments or returns on complaints, to the Company. The duties and authority hereby conferred are subject to change at the pleasure of the Company.[3]

In preparing a description of duties, the employer (or, in some cases, the employee) should prepare a statement of job description, which includes all the specific items the employee is expected to do as part of employment. The initial job description prepared by the employer or the employee may then be modified to include other items related to the types of specific duties the employee expects to perform for the employer. The list of duties should begin with the most specific duties anticipated, and the duties should become more general as the list grows longer. It is important to attempt to identify all potential duties the employee is expected to perform, and to highlight technical duties that are unique to this particular employee. In addition, each description of duties must be tailored to the specific employee and to the position the employee will hold.

In representing the employer, it is advisable to include a phrase that permits additional duties to be assigned to the employee from time to time. For example, a duties clause may provide that the employee will perform certain duties and "all other matters connected therewith as the employer shall from time to time direct, and that are of a kind properly belonging to the duties of an employee of this type." Similarly, the duties clause may include a statement that says "the duties and authority hereby conferred are subject to change at the pleasure of the company." These catchall provisions are desirable from the employer's viewpoint in order to ensure that the talents of the employee may be directed to changing employment opportunities, and also to permit the employer to assign specific duties that may not have been contemplated at the time the agreement was negotiated, but which will better define a breach of the agreement should an employee fail to perform them.

Catchall provisions in a statement of duties work to the disadvantage of the employee, unless certain limits are placed upon them. On behalf of an employee, it would be important to provide that any additional duties assigned are to be "of a type that properly belongs to the duties of an employee in a particular position," or "reasonable duties." In this manner, the employee may avoid the assignment of duties that are not consistent with the overall employment or the assignment of inappropriate or distasteful duties to force the employee to breach the agreement.

The duties clause of the employment agreement may also serve to restrict authority and responsibility of the employee. Any limitations on the scope of the employee's authority should also be clearly defined. The agreement may reserve certain decisions or transactions to employees at a higher level for organizational purposes. The duties clause may also define territories, as in the case of sales personnel, or impose any other restrictions consistent with the employment relationship.

> **EXAMPLE: Limitations on Authority of District Manager**
> The District Manager shall possess no authority not herein expressly granted and is not authorized on behalf of the Companies to make, alter or discharge contracts or binders, except as may be directed in writing by the Companies, nor to waive forfeitures, grant permits, guarantee in dividends, if any, name extra rates, extend the time of payment of any premium, waive payment in cash, or to write receipts except for first premiums, or make any endorsements on the policies of the Companies, and shall receive no further remuneration for any service except as herein provided. It is expressly stipulated and agreed that the District Manager is not authorized to incur any indebtedness or liability in the name or in behalf of the Companies for any advertising, office rent, clerk hire, or any other purposes whatsoever or to receive any moneys due or to become due the Companies exclusive of the first premium, except as may be specifically directed by the Companies and the powers of the District Manager shall extend no farther than are herein expressly stated.

> **EXAMPLE: Restriction**
> The District Manager shall not make or permit to be made by any agent, any use of the radio or insert any advertisement respecting the Companies in any paper, or other matter, magazine, newspaper, periodical, or other publication or issue any circular or paper referring to the Companies without the written consent of the Companies.[4]

> **EXAMPLE: Reservation of Right to Reject Orders**
> No order shall be deemed binding upon the company until accepted by the company in its Illinois office in writing, and the company reserves the right to reject any order, or to cancel the same or any part thereof after acceptance, for credit or any other reason whatsoever deemed by the company to be sufficient.[5]

Compensation

The compensation clauses of an employment contract deserve special attention. In the first place, any ambiguity here is certain to become a matter of dispute since financial matters are of utmost concern to both parties to the agreement. Moreover, the compensation provisions of the contract offer the best opportunity for the employer to ensure continued faithful performance by the employee. Recall that courts are generally unwilling to force an employee to return to the job following a breach of an employment contract. Carefully planned incentive compensation provisions will motivate the employee to remain with the company. Finally, the compensation provisions may permit certain tax advantages for all parties, and these matters should be explored and explained to the client.

At this point the discussion is limited to basic compensation schemes applicable to all types of business organizations, and to current incentive provisions, which encourage immediate, rather than long-term performance. The exclusively corporate compensation schemes, such as stock options, and the long-term incentive provisions, such as deferred compensation and profit sharing, are discussed separately in later sections.

The most basic type of compensation for an employee is a salary arrangement, and contractual terms should specify at least the amount and frequency of payment.

> **EXAMPLE: Salary Compensation**
> In consideration of the service so to be performed the Employer agrees to pay to the Employee the sum of $25,000.00, payable in equal monthly installments for twelve consecutive months at the end of each month, until the termination of this agreement.[6]

A current incentive may supplement the salary agreement to encourage diligent performance by the employee.

> **EXAMPLE: Current Incentive Compensation**
> The Employer shall pay to the Manager a salary of Thirty thousand dollars per annum, payable by monthly installments of Two thousand five hundred dollars on the tenth day of each month and shall also pay to the manager a commission of two per cent per annum on the net profits of said business, such commission to be paid within ninety days after the year accounts have been certified by the accountants employed by the employer, whose certificate as to the amount of such net profits shall be conclusive.[7]

A percentage compensation agreement, a *commission,* is probably the best current incentive provision. The rate of compensation is based directly upon the employee's own performance, and the commission technique is used most effectively when applied to individual activities. However, this scheme may also be used to compensate management or supervisory employees whose performance depends in part on the efforts of others they control. For management employees, the percentage is frequently based upon profits produced under their direction. A definitional clause must define profits for application of the percentage. Moreover, since a determination of profits will not usually be made until the close of the business year, the employee will usually be permitted to withdraw specified sums in advance for current living expenses until the employee's percentage share has been determined. Examples of these provisions for executive compensation follow:

> **EXAMPLE: Executive Commission Compensation**
> The Company shall pay to the Manager as compensation for her services one-third of the net profits arising from the Chicago business.

> **EXAMPLE: Net Profits**
> In arriving at what shall be deemed the net profits arising from the Chicago business, the following items shall be paid out of the gross profits, viz.: The rents of the premises wherein the Chicago business shall be conducted and all repairs and alterations of the same, all taxes and payments for insurance, all salaries and wages of clerks and employees other than the Manager employed in or about the Chicago business, and all charges and expenses incurred in or about the same, all debts or other moneys which shall be payable on account of the Chicago business, the interest on the capital for the time being advanced by the Company, and all losses and damages incurred in or about the Chicago business.

> **EXAMPLE: Drawing Account**
> The Manager shall have the right to draw out for her own use the sum of $2,500.00 per month on account of her salary. The balance of her one-third share in the net profits shall not be withdrawn by her until after the annual general account hereinafter mentioned shall have been made and signed.[8]

Commission provisions for an individual employee's performance require a similar approach. However, instead of profit, the percentage is usually applied to sales obtained for the company by the employee, and that criterion creates another definitional problem. The sale of goods involves at least four transactional stages: the order is signed, the order is approved by the company, the goods are shipped, and the customer pays. One of these four stages, or some other reasonably ascertainable point, should be selected as the time the commission is earned. If any intermediate stage is selected, the company may further specify that the commission will be withdrawn or reduced if the customer fails to pay.

> **EXAMPLE: Compensation and Basis for Computing Commissions**
> In consideration of your services, we agree to pay you a commission of five percent on all sales during the term of your employment made to customers located in the territory covered by you. Such commissions shall be calculated on the net amount of sales, after deducting returns, allowances, freight charges, discounts, bad debts and similar items, and shall be deemed to be earned and payable only as and when orders have been shipped and actually paid for by customers. The prepayment of commissions shall not be deemed to be a waiver of the foregoing provisions, and in all cases in which commissions have been paid in advance of payment by the customer, or where returns or allowances are subsequently made, such appropriate adjustment as may be necessary shall thereafter be made.

> **EXAMPLE: Drawing Account and Traveling Expenses**
> You shall be entitled to receive and we agree to pay you a drawing account of $600 per week, which sum shall be applied against and deducted from commissions then or thereafter due you. You personally shall defray all traveling and other expenses incurred by you in connection with your employment.[9]

To be effective, current incentive programs should be directly related to the performance of the employee or of the persons under the employee's supervision. The employee has no control over unrelated performance and thus has no opportunity (or incentive) to improve it.

Current incentive programs pose special drafting problems to ensure absolute clarity. In the foregoing examples, the percentages, time for payment, formula for determining the amount to which the percentage is applied, and application of draws against earned compensation are all well defined. Each of these items must be unambiguous if the compensation provisions are to be effective. Some additional suggestions may be helpful:

1. A date or periodic date should be specified for the payment of incentive compensation. For example, if the incentive compensation is computed on an annual basis, it should be specified that payment will be made on a specific date of the following year, or within a certain number of days from the close of the business year. The exact date permits the employee to plan the receipt of income, and allows the employer to plan cash flow.

2. If accounting terms are used, such as *net profit* or *net sales,* they should be defined in the agreement. Specific expense items should be named if they are to be deducted from gross profit to reach net profit, or from gross sales to reach net sales. Moreover, the provisions should define profit as before or after income taxes are deducted, whichever represents the agreement of the parties.

3. The person or persons who determine the base amount against which the percentage is applied should be named. If the company has retained independent public accountants to audit its records, the accountants should be specified as the persons who will make these determinations, and it is common practice to specify that their determination is to be based upon "generally accepted accounting principles." However, keep in mind that generally accepted accounting principles are not well-defined rules, even for accountants. To avoid any disputes concerning computations in an employment agreement, it is preferable to provide that the amount will be determined "by the accountant then engaged by the company in the accountant's sole and exclusive judgment, which will be a conclusive determination for all purposes."

4. If the employee is permitted to draw against the incentive compensation, the agreement should cover the contingency that the draws may exceed the earned compensation. For example, suppose the manager is to receive one-third of the profits as determined at the end of the year, and the manager has drawn $30,000 during the year. If the profits total $99,000 when tallied, will the manager be required to repay the company $3,000, or will that amount accrue to be applied against the following year's profits, or will it be forgiven and deemed to be an expense of the company? The agreement should provide an answer.

5. If the incentive compensation is based upon periodic performance such as annual profits, the employee's commencement and termination during the period should be considered. A relatively small number of employees are hired on the first day of the business year. (A few more may quit on the last day, however, considering that the arduous task of taking inventory may be looming in the immediate future.) Nevertheless, some formula must be inserted for the employee who has not worked for the entire period upon which incentive compensation is based. A formula for this purpose may be drafted on any reasonable basis. For example, the employee's percentage may be applied to profit computed for the period of the year in which the employee actually worked. If the employee began working August 1, the actual profit would be computed from August 1 to December 31, and the percentage applied against that figure. Alternatively, the formula may specify a pro rata determination of profit for the entire year. Here, the entire year's profit would be reduced to five-twelfths, the fraction of the year from August 1 to December 31, and the percentages would be applied to that amount. Finally, a separate special formula for years of commencement and termination may be stated, such as one-sixth of the profit for these years, or no profit percentage if the employee works for less than half of any year, and so forth.

Closely related to the percentage compensation is a bonus plan based upon minimum performance of the employee, or the employee's division or department. The agreement may establish certain sums to be paid at a specified time following the close of the business year if the employee's individual performance or the employee's section of the organization produces results above a specified minimum. The bonus amounts may be periodically increased to reward continued performance. For example, the agreement with a manager of a retail store may provide that the manager shall receive a bonus of $1,000 the first year that net profits before taxes from the store exceed $10,000; $2,000 the second consecutive year that profits exceed that amount; and $3,000 the third and subsequent consecutive years that profits continue to exceed $10,000. The drafting considerations detailed earlier are equally applicable here. The agreement should define net profit or any other selected criterion, should specify the person who will determine the base figures, should provide for termination during the year, and should specify a date the bonus will be paid.

The bonus plan may be limited to an incentive for continuous employment, without considering the specific performance of the employee. For example, the agreement may discourage voluntary termination during the year.

> **EXAMPLE: Compensation and Bonus**
> The Employee shall receive a weekly salary of $1,000. In addition, the Corporation shall pay to the Employee at the end of each year of the term a year-end bonus of not less than $10,000 (less withholding taxes, social security and other required deductions); but no part of said bonus shall be payable if the Employee shall be in default under this agreement or shall not then be in the employ of the Corporation.[10]

The compensation section of the employment agreement is also an appropriate place to describe incidental financial benefits, such as reimbursement for expenses, vacation pay, and so forth.

> **EXAMPLE: Expense Reimbursement**
> Employer shall also pay to the Salesman his reasonable expenses of traveling, board and lodging, postage, and other expenses reasonably incurred by him as such Salesman in or about the business of the Employer.

> **EXAMPLE: Vacations**
> The Employee shall be entitled to vacations with pay in accordance with the established practices of the Corporation now or hereafter in effect for supervisory personnel.

The foregoing compensation plans are common to most employment agreements. Continued faithful performance of the employee may also be reasonably ensured by the use of several available special compensation techniques discussed in subsequent sections.

Term of the Agreement

The duration of the employment agreement should be specific and, as a general rule, should be reasonably short for the company's protection. If a continuing employment relationship is contemplated, it is far better to provide for options to renew the agreement than to leave the term indefinite.

The basic term of the agreement is always simple.

> **EXAMPLE: Duties and Term**
> The Employee agrees to give her undivided time and service in the employ of the Employer in such capacity as the Employer may direct, for the period of one year from and after the 1st day of December, 1993.[11]

Renewal provisions may be drafted one of three ways. First, the option to renew the agreement may be granted to the employer, with appropriate advance notice to the employee of the election to renew. Second, the option to renew may be vested with the employee, with appropriate advance notice to the employer of the election to renew. Third, the agreement may be automatically renewed for specified periods unless appropriate notice is given by either party to the other of the intention *not* to renew. The last provision is most common, and most adaptable to a continuing employment relationship.

> **EXAMPLE: Option to Renew**
> Employee grants Employer the option to renew this contract for a period of two years upon all the terms and conditions herein contained, except for the option to renew for a further period. This option may be exercised by Employer by giving Employee notice in writing at least thirty days prior to the expiration hereof; and such notice to Employee may be given by delivery to Employee personally or by mailing to Employee at the last known address.[12]

> **EXAMPLE: Initial Term and Automatic Renewal**
> The term of this employment shall commence February 1, 1991 and shall continue for a period of two years until January 31, 1993, and thereafter shall be deemed to be renewed automatically, upon the same terms and conditions, for successive periods of one year each, until either party, at least thirty days prior to the expiration of the original term or of any extended term, shall give written notice to the other of intention not to renew such employment.[13]

Provisions for notice should be tailored for specific circumstances. Written notice should always be required, and should be sent to a specified address of each party. For the employee, the address may be specified as "the last known address," or "the address on the records of the company." The time period for notice should be longer for a more specialized employee so that the employee may search for other employment if necessary, or so that the company may search for a replacement.

Termination of the Agreement

The employment agreement should be terminated or terminable upon the happening of certain contingent events. In many cases, salary continuation protection for an employee may be appropriate upon the happening of one of these events, and in cases where the event is also defined by an insurance policy, the employment agreement should use the definition from the insurance policy to be certain there is no conflict between the two definitions.

Cause for termination should be considered for the following contingent events:

1. If the employee is disabled for a period of time.
2. If the employee is bankrupt.
3. If the employee has been convicted of a crime.
4. If the employee is incarcerated.
5. If the employee is mentally disabled or otherwise unable to perform duties.
6. If the employee is suffering from alcoholism or drug-related disabilities.
7. If the employee breaches the agreement.
8. If the portion of the business in which the employee is employed is discontinued for any reason.
9. If the business is insolvent or bankrupt.
10. If a substantial portion of the business assets are destroyed.
11. If the business is sold, merged, consolidated, or dissolved for any reason.

12. If majority ownership of the business changes.
13. If any other matter arises that, considering the special duties of the employee, may constitute cause for termination under the agreement.

> **EXAMPLE: Termination of Manager with Cause**
> In the event of the illness of the Manager or other cause incapacitating him from attending to his duties as manager for six consecutive weeks, the Employer may terminate this agreement without notice upon payment to the Manager of five hundred dollars in addition to all arrears of salary and commission when ascertained up to the date of such termination. In the event of a breach of this agreement or of an act of bankruptcy on the part of the Manager, the Employer may terminate this agreement without notice or payment of salary or commission as hereinbefore provided.[14]

> **EXAMPLE: Termination with Cause**
> This agreement shall terminate in the event of the dissolution of the firm by death or otherwise, the appointment of a receiver or trustee in bankruptcy or the filing of a petition to reorganize under the Bankruptcy Act, or the destruction by fire of the firm's warehouse at South Bend, Indiana, notwithstanding the full term of one year may not, at the happening of any of said events, have fully expired.[15]

Finally, it is possible to agree to termination without cause with due notice.

> **EXAMPLE: Termination without Cause**
> The employment of the Editor may be terminated at any time (during the said period of two years) by either party giving to the other two calendar months' notice in writing of its or her intention to terminate the same, or by the Company upon its paying to the Editor a sum equal to two months' salary at the rate aforesaid in lieu of such notice.[16]

RESTRICTIVE AND PROPRIETARY COVENANTS

While the employer may be unsuccessful in persuading a court to order an employee to continue to work for the company against the employee's will, the employer may prevent the employee from exploiting the company by appropriating ideas that were developed during the employment for the employee's own benefit; leaving with trade secrets, specialized confidential knowledge, or customer lists; or working for competitors. Certain restrictive or proprietary covenants in the employment agreement may protect the employer from such abuse, and, if properly drafted, these covenants will receive court protection.

The covenants generally cover three areas of possible employee exploitation: (1) competing with the company after employment; (2) maintaining confidentiality of business secrets during and after employment; and (3) using developments, inventions, and ideas that the employee produced during the course of employment. Without an agreement on each of these points, under common law the employer risks the loss of significant market advantages through the acts of unfaithful employees.

No former employee would be prohibited from competing against a former employer without a specific agreement to that effect. The law has always favored fair and free competition, and there is nothing implicit in an employment relationship that requires the employee to withdraw from the marketplace after the employment is terminated. That is not to say, however, that the employee would be allowed to duplicate the former employer's secret practices and processes in future competition.

The law protects trade secrets, even without an agreement prohibiting their use, but the protection is somewhat elusive and unsatisfactory if left to common law resolution alone. First, it is difficult to determine which practices, procedures, and other matters are truly trade secrets entitled to protection. The employer will have the burden to prove that the company is the "owner" of the secret, meaning the secret was developed by or for the company, is not used by others, and is sufficiently unique so as to deserve proprietary protection. Further, the employer must show that the secret is known only to company employees in whom it must be confided for business purposes. Even if the matter is shown to be a trade secret, a court would have to be convinced that the employee's exploitation should be prohibited. The court would have to find that the employee's use or publication of the secret could cause irreparable harm to the employer. An agreement restricting the employee's use of trade secrets is essential for certainty of protection in this area.

The common law is also unpredictable on a question of the employer's rights in the employee's original ideas and developments discovered during the course of employment. Certainly, if the employee is hired to do research and create inventions, the employer has ownership rights in any productive research while the employee is on the job. But what happens if the employee dreams up an invention that is unrelated to the employer's research, or if the employee quits before research is productive, and subsequently produces an invention for the personal benefit of the employee? Specific provisions in the agreement may anticipate and resolve these problems.

EMPLOYER'S RIGHT TO EMPLOYEE WORK PRODUCT

The employer may have hired the employee for the express purpose of developing new products or business innovations. Certain specialized skills, such as research chemistry or engineering, are widely sought for this purpose and the employment relationship is directed to the production of inventions. The employee also may be hired to develop certain business practices and procedures that will increase efficiency and utilization of other employees' skills. These common cases should be distinguished by the test of a work product that can be legally protected. In the first case, an invention from the original thought of an engineer may be patentable and thereby have certain proprietary interests attached to it. In the second case, a particular procedural system devised by a time-and-motion expert may be unique, but will not be such an original creative product that a patent or copyright could be obtained. The employer's interest in each may be indistinguishable, however. The company obviously wants to retain proprietary rights in patentable inventions, and management may be equally concerned about reserving newly devised business procedures to themselves for the associated competitive advantages. The clauses suggested here will protect the company's rights to the patentable inventions, but they may not be adaptable to protection of other unpatentable work products. Rather, in the second case it would be more appropriate to describe the developed business procedure as a trade secret in the agreement and thereby ensure some confidentiality, or to prohibit the development of a similar system for a competitor through a noncompetitive covenant with the employee.

Work product clauses are most effective for inventions and other original creations that are capable of being patented or copyrighted. A work product clause should include at least the following general components:

1. A specific grant from the employee to the employer of the right to use such work product
2. A statement that the clause applies to any use to which the employer chooses to make of the work product
3. A statement that the clause applies to inventions, designs, procedures, and other matters in both their unperfected and improved states
4. A statement that the clause applies to inventions, designs, and other matters developed or obtained by the employee alone or severally or jointly with other persons
5. A statement that the clause applies to the entire period of the employment with the employer
6. A specific description of the employee's talents out of which inventions and designs are expected to be produced
7. A specific description of the type of inventions, designs, and other matters the employee is expected to develop
8. A general statement that other inventions, designs, and other matters that relate to the employee's product will be covered by the clause
9. A release by the employee of any legal or equitable right to the work product
10. A promise by the employee that all necessary documents for perfecting title will be executed and delivered to the employer on demand
11. A representation by the employee that such work product will not infringe upon any patents or other protected rights of others
12. Any special compensation arrangements that had been negotiated with the employee for subsequent use of the invention, design, or work product
13. Trade secret protection of the work product to protect against its publication before a patent, copyright, or other protected proprietary rights may be obtained
14. The relief or remedies to which the employer may be entitled for a breach of the clause, such as injunctions, liquidated damages, a constructive trust on all profits produced, and so forth

The scope of these provisions is usually determined by the nature of the employment. For example, if an employee is hired for the broad purpose of researching and developing improvements in elevators, a broad protective clause would be appropriate.

> **EXAMPLE: Grant of License**
> The Employee hereby grants to the Employer the exclusive license to manufacture, sell and deal in all inventions, designs, improvements and discoveries of the Employee, whether now perfected or whether invented, improved and discovered subsequent hereto, which pertain or relate to elevators and their appliances, or are capable of use in connection therewith.[17]

If the employment objective is more specific, such as the research and development of a valve and starter plug to improve elevator control, the clause may also be more specific.

> **EXAMPLE: Inventions Designated as the Property of the Employer**
> The Employee agrees that all inventions, improvements, ideas, and suggestions made by him and patents obtained by him severally or jointly with any other person or persons during the entire period of his employment, and any written renewal thereof made by him with the Employer, with relation to said valve and its appurtenances, including present starting plug, or method of elevator control, and all inventions of elevator valves, plugs, or methods of elevator control and valve appliances, and to machinery for manufacturing the same, are and shall be the sole property of the Employer, free from any legal or equitable title of the Employee, and that all necessary documents for perfecting such title shall be executed by the Employee and delivered to the Employer on demand.[18]

The specificity of the clause may be a matter for negotiation between the parties. The employee in the second example may have insisted upon the narrow description so that his or her subsequent development of an elevator door, for example, would not belong to the employer. However, the employee may be willing to consent to the broader provision for increased compensation. The employer's objective, of course, is to make the subject matter of the clause all-inclusive.

Work product protection clauses should always require the execution of any necessary documents for perfecting the employer's title to the inventions, as shown in the second example. This may obviate any need for an interpretation of the contract before the employer can market the invention, and the clause will place the employee in breach of the agreement if the employee fails to cooperate fully with the employer. It is also desirable to contract for trade secret protection of the invention to protect against the invention's publication before a patent may be obtained. A clause on these points follows.

> **EXAMPLE: Execution of Further Documents**
> I further agree, without charge to said company, but at its expense, to execute, acknowledge, and deliver all such further papers, including applications for patents, and to perform such other acts as I lawfully may, as may be necessary in the opinion of said company, to obtain or maintain patents for said inventions in any and all countries and to vest title thereto in said company, its successors and assigns; and I further agree that I will not divulge to others any information I may obtain during the course of my employment relating to the formulas, processes, methods, machines, manufacturers, compositions, or inventions of said company without first obtaining written permission from said company to do so.[19]

It may be appropriate (and necessary, if the employee skillfully negotiates the agreement) for the employer to compensate the employee based upon the profitable inventions the employee has created for the company. The percentage compensation scale would be tailored to the demands of the parties, and may look like this:

> **EXAMPLE: Compensation for Inventions**
> In order to recompense the above employee (hereinafter called the Employee) for meritorious inventions, the Corporation agrees on its part to examine the inventions disclosed to it by the Employee, and where said inventions, in the sole opinion of the Corporation, warrant such action, to cause United States patent applications to be filed through its attorneys covering the same, but without assuming any responsibility for the prosecution or defense of such patent

applications, and further agrees to give to the Employee in any cases where it decides to license said inventions, applications or patents to others, a percentage of any money royalties which it may receive from such licenses upon the following scale:

> Of the first $1,000.00 or part thereof collected in any one calendar year—40%
> Of the next $2,000.00 or part thereof collected in any one calendar year—30%
> Of the next $2,000.00 or part thereof collected in any one calendar year—20%
> Of the next $5,000.00 or part thereof collected in any one calendar year—15%
> Of all further sums collected in any one calendar year—10%

It is understood and agreed, however, that the question of when, how and to whom licenses shall be granted shall be in the sole discretion of the Corporation, and that in cases where the Corporation shall grant licenses involving, in addition to the Employee's inventions, the inventions of others, the Corporation shall have the sole right and authority to apportion the royalties received and the Employee shall receive the above percentage on the proportion awarded to his inventions.[20]

TRADE SECRET PROTECTION

Beginning with the truism that various companies have various secrets, some more important than others, trade secret protection must always be drafted to fit the particular exigencies of the company. A discount retail merchant may consider its supplier list to be a trade secret; a manufacturing company may consider the assembly process to be a trade secret; and a computer firm would treat its programs and techniques for interpretation as trade secrets. In each business, the "secret" is an integral part of the competitive advantage, and confidentiality is deemed to be crucial to continued success of the operation. One well-kept trade secret is the process and ingredients used to produce Coca-Cola. In part, this mystery is a result of using well-drafted employment agreements and never completely disclosing the secret process to anyone. (The Coca-Cola Company's Non-Disclosure Agreement appears as Form 10A in Appendix G.)

Several important rules should be followed in drafting trade secret clauses for employment contracts. First, the promise to keep the secrets should bind the employee during the employment *and* after termination of employment. Second, the clause should cover not only specific secrets that the employee uses in performing duties under the agreement, but also secrets the employee may have learned from alert observations or from other employees. Third, the agreement should broadly prohibit divulging any "trade secrets, procedures, processes, or knowledge of operations," and should also specifically itemize particular matters that are to be protected. Fourth, because of the difficulty of proving actual damages from the publication of a trade secret, an agreed damage clause, or *liquidated damages,* should be considered. A clause with all of these ingredients follows.

> **EXAMPLE: Trade Secrets**
> The Salesman further covenants not to communicate during the continuance of this agreement, or at any time subsequently, any trade secrets, processes, procedures or business operations, specifically including but not limited to information relating to the secrets of the traveling, advertising and canvassing departments, nor any knowledge or secrets which he then had or might from time to time acquire pertaining to other departments of the business of the Employer, to any person not a member of the Employer's firm, except as requested in writing by the Employer. In case of violation of this covenant, the Salesman agrees to pay the Employer or

its successors the sum of five thousand dollars as liquidated damages, but such payment is not to release the Salesman from the obligations undertaken, or from liability for further breach thereof.[21]

It would also be advisable to prohibit the employee's use of the secret as an individual, or the employee's direct or indirect benefit from the use of the secret, such as when a shareholder, partner, employee, consultant, creditor, or other participant in another business learns about or adopts the secret from the employee.

Customer lists commonly are protected by trade secret clauses, since courts are not likely to construe customer lists as a business secret under common law so as to shelter them without an agreement. However, in highly competitive businesses, the secrecy of customer lists is an important competitive advantage. A competitor who has obtained them will be spared considerable time and expenses in locating interested customers. Depending upon the nature of the business, customer list protection may not need to extend indefinitely after termination of employment. The list may change significantly within a year or two, and the contractual provision may be so limited.

> **EXAMPLE: Customer Lists**
>
> The Employee further agrees that during the period of one (1) year immediately after the termination of his employment with the Employer he will not, either directly or indirectly, make known or divulge the names or addresses of any of the customers or patrons of Employer at the time he entered the employ of Employer or with whom he became acquainted after entering the employ of Employer, to any person, firm or corporation, and that he will not, directly or indirectly, either for himself or for any other person, firm, company or corporation, call upon, solicit, divert, or take away, or attempt to solicit, divert or take away any of the customers, business or patrons of the Employer upon whom he called or whom he solicited or to whom he catered or with whom he became acquainted after his employment with the Employer.
>
> The Employee hereby consents and agrees that for any violation of any of the provisions of this agreement, a restraining order and/or an injunction may issue against him in addition to any other rights the Employer may have.
>
> In the event that the Employer is successful in any suit or proceeding brought or instituted by the Employer to enforce any of the provisions of the within agreement or on account of any damages sustained by the Employer by reason of the violation by the Employee of any of the terms and/or provisions of this Agreement to be performed by the Employee, the Employee agrees to pay to the Employer reasonable attorneys' fees to be fixed by the Court.[22]

COVENANTS NOT TO COMPETE

Unlike the foregoing restrictive provisions governing the employer's ownership rights to the employee's work product and the protection of trade secrets and other confidential information, a covenant not to compete does not endeavor to solidify the company's ownership rights. Rather, this covenant is designed to prevent the employee from using personal talents (which were probably developed or improved during the employment) against the former employer.

The negative objective causes some problems. Consider the plight of a research chemist who is an expert in industrial cleaning solutions. If he is a party to an employment contract that contains a clause forbidding future employment with any other industrial cleaner manufacturer, upon termination of his employment he will have lost his livelihood. His specialized technical knowledge significantly reduces his professional flexibility, and he must either breach the agreement or develop a new expertise. Of course, the company's objective is to prevent him from using his technical abilities to benefit a competitor, and the more specialized the skill, the more important it is for the company to discourage its marketability after termination. There is a bit of a tug of war here. If the restriction is too severe, a court simply won't enforce it. If it is too loose, the company can't enforce it.

Many courts are very reluctant to enforce noncompetition agreements for several reasons. First, a noncompetition agreement is a restraint of trade, which is normally illegal both in common law and under state and federal antitrust statutes. However, limited noncompetition covenants are sometimes lawful if they are ancillary to an otherwise legitimate agreement. Generally, a reasonable noncompetition agreement will be enforced if it is necessary for the protection of the employer, imposes no undue hardship on the employee, and does not injure the general public. Because courts are frequently reluctant to enforce noncompetition agreements, many states have adopted statutes that severely restrict the use of such covenants. In some, all restrictive competition covenants are void except when given in connection with the sale of a business or the dissolution of a partnership.[23] Other states permit such clauses in employment contracts, but limit the effectiveness to certain justifying characteristics, such as training or advertising expenses, a license to practice, executive or management personnel, or specific territory limitations.[24]

Almost uniformly, the enforceability of a covenant not to compete depends upon whether the covenant is "reasonable," which includes consideration of the following:

1. The legitimate needs of the employer for such protection
2. The interest of society in preventing monopolies or other excessive restrictions on competition
3. The burden placed upon the employee
4. Whether the employee has had frequent contacts with customers or clients of the employer
5. Whether the employer's business relied to a substantial degree on trade secrets to which the employee had access
6. Whether the employer provided training to the employee
7. Whether the employer's business is highly technical or complex
8. Whether the employer's business is highly competitive
9. Whether the employee, while employed, was a key employee, such as a manager or executive
10. Whether the employee provided unique services while employed by the employer
11. Whether the covenant exceeds boundaries of time, space, and type of activity that are reasonably required to give the employer the protection to which the employer is entitled
12. Whether there is a clear disparity of bargaining power between the employer and employee
13. Whether the employee understood the nature of the covenant at the time it was signed

Based upon these considerations drafting a noncompetition clause is a delicate operation.

One rule may be followed with impunity. A noncompetition clause may never prohibit the employee from engaging in competitive activity indefinitely. The protection of the clause must have a reasonable basis in fact, and no employer could convince a court that competitive activity by a certain employee will forever cause irreparable harm to the business. Consequently, the clause should be limited to a specified period during which the company will be justified in keeping the employee out of the market to preserve a competitive advantage.

From the employer's standpoint, the agreement should also provide that the employee is prohibited from competition upon termination "for any reason whatsoever." Certainly an employee who left to work for a competitor before the expiration of the agreement could not expect much sympathy from a court. However, an employee who was fired, and must now refrain from marketing personal talents, is in a different position. Without the language suggested above, a court may narrowly construe an employee's termination, and enforce the noncompetition clause only when termination results from the employee's initiative.

To enforce a noncompetitive agreement, the employer may have to show a court that the former employee's competitive activities are causing irreparable harm to the company. Doing so presents obvious difficulties in proof, which may be avoided by exacting a consent to injunctive relief against the employee should the employee violate the agreed provisions.

Finally, the competitive activities that are to be prohibited and the geographical limits of the prohibition should be specified with accuracy and clarity. If the provision is overly broad, it is less likely to be enforced in litigation involving its breach. Moreover, any ambiguity will always be resolved against the drafter, meaning the employer. For example, a provision that prohibits the employee from working in "the retail sales industry" is useless. A description of "retail sales of men's wear" is better but questionable. Equally unenforceable is a provision that prohibits the employee's competition in the "western part of the United States." The "South Dakota area" may be enforceable but requires a great deal of interpretation and would undoubtedly be limited to the boundaries of the state. The defined activities and geographical area should be consistent with the activities and market of the employer and should be specific. Consider the strengths and weaknesses of the following examples.

> **EXAMPLE: Agreement Not to Compete**
> I also agree that I will not work for any competitive company or for myself or sell directly or indirectly milk or milk products in the same territory covered by me either as route salesman or foreman of routes for a period of at least one year after severing relations with this Company.[25]

> **EXAMPLE: Covenant Not to Compete**
> It is further agreed by the Employee that the sale of the Employer's petroleum products in the trading area hereinbefore referred to is a valuable asset to the Employer and in order to promote the sales of petroleum products in said trading area the Employer will make expenditures through advertising and otherwise, and in consideration of the covenants and agreements herein contained the Employee agrees that in the event of the termination of this contract for any reason, with or without cause, that in such event, the Employee will not engage in the sale of

gasoline, fuel oils or petroleum products, directly or indirectly, either on her own account, or as an employee for any other person, firm or corporation, in the city of Chicago, Cook County, Illinois, for a period of five (5) years following the termination of this contract.[26]

EXAMPLE: Agreement and Covenant Not to Compete
The Employee further covenants and agrees that at no time during the term of this employment, or for two (2) years immediately following termination thereof (regardless of whether such termination is voluntary or involuntary) will he for himself or in behalf of any other person, partnership, corporation or company, engage in the pest control business or any business engaged in the eradication and control of rats, mice, roaches, bugs, vermin, termites, beetles and other insects within the territory known as cities of Spearfish, and Belle Fourche, South Dakota, and a radius of 25 miles of each of said cities, nor will he directly or indirectly for himself, or in behalf of or in conjunction with any other person, partnership, corporation or company, solicit or attempt to solicit the business or patronage of any person, corporation, company or partnership within the said territory for the purpose of selling a service for the eradication and control of rats, mice, roaches, bugs, vermin, termites, beetles and other insects, and such other incidental business and service now engaged in by the Company, nor will the Employee disclose to any person, whatsoever, any of the secrets, methods or systems used by the Company in and about its business.

The Employee hereby consents and agrees that for any violation of any of the provisions of this agreement, a restraining order and/or an injunction may issue against him in addition to any other rights the Employer may have.[27]

It is better practice to specifically define the boundaries in which competition is prohibited. For example, describing county lines or city limits is preferable to providing a point from which a radius will be computed. The larger the geographical area, the less likely it is that the covenant will be enforced. If the employer is engaged in the sale of goods within a particular city, it would be inadvisable to define noncompetition as including the entire state. This is true even if the employer plans to expand operations to the entire state, since a court will be more concerned with the actual needed protection at the time the covenant was signed than with speculating about expansion plans and potential competitive problems in the future.

The clause should provide that the employee understands the nature of the covenant, and consents to the covenant's prohibiting activities of the employee that may compete with the employer. Further, the covenant should specify that the employee understands that the clause is necessary for the employer's protection, and that the employee agrees that any violation of the clause will do irreparable harm to the employer.

The employee should be prohibited from directly or indirectly competing with the employer, either as an owner, manager, operator, or controlling person, or through being employed by, participating in, or being connected in any manner with the ownership, management, operations, or control of a competitor, including holding a position as a creditor. A classic avoidance technique for these covenants involves former employees who loan money to a new corporation that will compete with the former employer. In exchange for the loan, these "creditors" receive a convertible debenture that will be converted to common stock (and majority ownership of the corporation) the day after the former employee's covenant not to compete expires.

If the covenant will be regulated by a statute in the jurisdiction in which it is to be enforced, the specific statutory reason for the covenant (such as because the employee was trained by the employer, or because the employee is a member of the management or executive personnel) should be stated in the covenant.

The clause should contain *severability provisions,* which would allow for the removal of any objectionable portion of the clause, but not affect the enforcement of the remainder of the clause for the employer's protection.

Consideration should be given for penalties other than injunctive relief or damages, such as loss of accrued but unpaid commissions, loss of retirement or profit sharing incentives, and similar penalties that discourage but do not forbid one from entering into competition.

The fair objective of restrictive covenants in employment contracts is to protect the legitimate interests of the company, without unduly restricting the activities of the employee. Properly drafted restrictions will never exceed the limits of necessary company protection, and they will be firm and thorough on those points. They thereby will be afforded a better opportunity to do what they are supposed to do.

INCENTIVE COMPENSATION PLANS

Employee incentive is a key element to current performance and continued employment with the company. Individual incentive compensation terms for individual employment contracts were discussed previously.[28] It may be desirable, however, to use group incentive plans in lieu of or in addition to individual incentive provisions in each agreement. Of course, as the number of beneficiaries to an incentive compensation plan grows larger, the plan becomes less effective as a true incentive. For example, an individual salesperson can easily be motivated by a personal incentive based directly on individual sales, but personal motivation is more tenuous if the entire sales division, comprising many salespersons, is rewarded for the aggregate performance of all.

As with personal incentive plans, a cardinal rule for the effectiveness of a group incentive plan is that the compensation must be related directly to the performance of an ascertainable division of the company. In practice, these incentive plans are usually directed to key employees, since key employees motivate other employees to concentrate their efforts toward the employer's growth and profits, and further provide an incentive for other employees to remain with the company.

A group plan is properly administered under the direction of a committee, which, in the case of a corporation, may be composed of the directors but would not have to be. Persons who are entitled to compensation under the plan should not be members of the committee. The committee is usually vested with some discretion to determine the amount of the incentive awards and the recipients from among those eligible to participate in the plan.

The plan should begin with a statement of purpose, which usually indicates an intent to provide incentives to certain employees by enabling those employees to participate in the success of the company. The eligible participants in the plan must be clearly defined, as should the base accounts from which the amounts awarded under the plan will be determined. For example, if the participants under the plan are to receive a certain percentage of *profits,* that word must be defined, specifying whether taxes, allocations of overhead, contingent or unusual expenses, and so on are to be deducted. The formula for compensation under the plan may refer to multiple accounts, such as a percentage of the extent to which profits exceed capital, and all stated accounts should be clearly defined.

The membership of the committee is set forth in the plan, and the committee's duties and term of membership should be prescribed. If the committee is to have discretion in granting the incentive awards, a procedure for determination of the recipients, with specified guidelines for merit, may be provided. Alternatively, a formula could be drafted that would make the application of the awards a mechanical task for the committee, but the use of such a formula minimizes the flexibility of the plan by removing the committee's discretion from the incentive characteristics. True merit may be rewarded at the committee's discretion, but a formula may not account for that.

A method for determining the amount of the fund must be included in the plan. A percentage of the defined profits is the most simple method, and the complex formulas of other methods would defy the imagination. The fund is usually set aside in an Incentive Compensation Reserve account, awaiting the directions of the committee.

The payments under a corporate incentive plan may be made in cash or a stock equivalent, based upon the current market price of stock. If the stock is reported on a national exchange, a method is prescribed to compute market price, such as "the average daily opening price on the exchange during the calendar month preceding the month of award." The committee may decide whether the award is to be in cash or stock, and the committee should also have the authority to pay the award immediately or to defer payment in whole or in part. If deferral is permitted, separate accounts must be maintained for that purpose. The deferral of the award may provide certain tax benefits to the employees.[29]

Additional incentive thrust will result from imposing conditions upon payment of the compensation. For example, the terms of the plan may refuse payment to an eligible participant if that employee resigns during the year without the consent of the company. The plan may further deny deferred payments if a former employee is subsequently employed by a competitor of the company. It is also common to provide for forfeiture of any award if the employee is discharged for misconduct. The plan should specifically state that the employee has no claim or right to be granted an award under the plan, and the plan should not be construed as granting the participant a right to be retained in the employ of the company.

The company management should be granted authority to modify or suspend the plan at their discretion, but only prospectively. It should not be able to retroactively affect the rights of employees with respect to unpaid awards previously granted. Finally, a corporate incentive plan should be approved by the shareholders especially if it contemplates the issuance of stock as an incentive award.[30]

DEFERRED COMPENSATION

Key employees and executives may be plied with an incentive to remain with the company by a deferred compensation plan. These plans are designed to meet two important objectives in the employment relationship: (1) income for the employee is deferred until the employee retires or becomes incapacitated, providing necessary security and allowing receipt when the employee's income is taxed in a lower bracket; and (2) the employee is given an incentive to remain with the company to receive accumulated retirement benefits. The agreement for a deferred plan may be incorporated into an employee agreement or may be executed separately after a period of satisfactory employment.

The amounts of compensation to be deferred may be determined by a number of methods. A portion of base salary may be deferred, or a percentage of salary in addition to normal base salary may be used. Of course, the deferral provisions may also be tied to bonus or incentive plans, such as those described in the preceding section.

The deferred income is retained in a fund for the employee until payment at the prescribed time, usually following retirement or disability. Payment may be in a lump sum or in installments over a period of years.

> **EXAMPLE: Retirement Date**
> The Company agrees that Patricia Smith may retire from the active and daily service of the Company upon the first day of the month nearest her sixty-fifth birthday.

> **EXAMPLE: Retirement Compensation**
> The Company agrees that commencing with the date of such retirement it will pay to Patricia Smith the sum of $18,000.00 per annum payable in equal installments of $1,500.00 each, payable upon the first business day of each calendar month. The Company agrees that it will continue to make such payments to Patricia Smith during her lifetime, and with no liability to make payments to her legal representatives, for ten (10) years and until Patricia Smith shall have received one hundred twenty (120) monthly payments of $1,500.00 each; subject, however, to the conditions and limitations hereinafter set forth.[31]

The incentive to continue with the company results from the continual increase in the deferred fund and from the terms of the agreement, which typically conclude all rights and obligations under the agreement if the employee voluntarily terminates the employment relationship without the consent of the company.

> **EXAMPLE: Termination of Employment**
> If Patricia Smith shall voluntarily terminate her employment during her lifetime and prior to her said retirement, or if her employment shall be terminated for sufficient cause as determined by the Board of Directors of the Company, this Agreement shall automatically terminate and the Company shall have no further obligation hereunder.

These agreements also frequently prescribe a forfeiture of all benefits under the plan if the employee subsequently engages in competition with the company.

> **EXAMPLE: Covenant Not to Compete**
> Patricia Smith agrees that during such period of receipt of monthly payments from the Company she will not directly or indirectly enter into or in any manner take part in any business, profession or other endeavor either as an employee, agent, independent contractor, owner or otherwise in the City of Fort Lauderdale, Florida, which in the opinion of the directors of the Company shall be in competition with the business of the Company, which opinion of the directors shall be final and conclusive for the purposes hereof.

> **EXAMPLE: Forfeiture**
> Patricia Smith agrees that if she shall fail to observe any of the covenants hereof and shall continue to breach any covenant for a period of thirty (30) days after the Company shall have requested her to perform the same, or if she shall have entered any business described in the preceding paragraph and shall continue therein either directly or indirectly as aforesaid for a period of fifteen (15) days after the Company shall have notified her in writing at her home address that the directors of the Company have decided that such business is in competition with the Company; then, any of the provisions hereof to the contrary notwithstanding, Patricia Smith agrees that no further payments shall be due or payable by the Company hereunder either to Patricia Smith or to her spouse, and that the Company shall have no further liability hereunder.

In addition to their incentive character, the forfeiture clauses serve another useful purpose. The tax benefits from a deferred compensation plan may be generally stated to be that the company may deduct the payments to the deferred fund when paid, but the employee need not declare the payments as income until those payments are received. The latter rule is based upon the condition that the employee does not "constructively receive" the payments earlier—that is, the employee does not earn a vested right to the payments before they are paid. The conditions described earlier avoid the constructive receipt problem, since the employee's continuous performance and prohibition against competition are superimposed upon the employee's right to payment and prevent any vesting of the employee's interest until the conditions are satisfied.

The deferred compensation plan should divert the payment of the deferred income to the employee's heirs in the case of the employee's death.

> **EXAMPLE: Payments to Spouse if Employee Dies after Retirement**
> The Company agrees that if Patricia Smith shall so retire but shall die before receiving the said one hundred twenty (120) monthly payments, it will continue to make such monthly payments, to Fred Smith, her spouse, if he shall survive Patricia Smith, until the total payments made to Patricia Smith and her spouse shall equal $180,000.00; provided that if Fred Smith shall survive Patricia Smith but shall die before the said amount shall be paid by the Company, the Company shall have no liability to continue any payments hereunder beyond the first day of the month in which Fred Smith died.

> **EXAMPLE: Death of Spouse after Retirement**
> If Patricia Smith shall so retire and if her spouse shall not survive her, the Company shall not be required to continue any payments hereunder beyond the first day of the month in which Patricia Smith shall die.

> **EXAMPLE: Payments to Spouse if Employee Dies before Retirement**
> If Patricia Smith shall die before the aforesaid retirement date, and if her spouse shall survive her, the Company agrees to make the said monthly payments hereinbefore described to the said Fred Smith commencing with the first day of the month following the month in which Patricia Smith shall die and ending when one hundred twenty (120) monthly payments shall be made to the said Fred Smith or until and including the first day of the month in which he shall die, whichever event shall first occur.

> **EXAMPLE: Death of Employee before Retirement with No Spouse Surviving**
> If Patricia Smith shall die before the said retirement date and if Fred Smith shall not survive her, the Company shall not be required to make any payments hereunder.

PENSION AND PROFIT SHARING PLANS

Pension and profit sharing plans are deferred compensation plans, but they may produce additional tax benefits for the employer and the employee if they qualify under the Internal Revenue Code.[32] Both pension and profit sharing plans accumulate and defer income until some future date. The employer's objective is to induce the employee to remain with the company to receive accumulated retirement benefits. The profit sharing plan also adds a current performance incentive, since the amount contributed to the plan is based upon profits produced by the employee and the employee's co-workers.

Both profit sharing and pension plans are directed toward retirement or disability income and faithful performance. However, each reaches the objective by different means. The profit sharing plan is based upon profits, and the employer's contribution to the fund is couched in terms of a percentage of annual profit. From the employer's standpoint, a profit sharing plan is less onerous than a pension plan. It is subject to special tax rules, since the obligation to contribute depends upon the profitable operation of the business, and there is no fixed obligation to contribute annually. The contribution requirements reflect the economic cycles of the business, and as a result the plan is more flexible than a pension plan. The size of the fund will depend entirely upon the profits contributed throughout the duration of the plan. Allocation of the fund to individual employees is usually based upon employees' compensation during their periods of employment. These factors all result in a minimal burden for the employer and, if incentives are taken seriously, greater benefit to the employees. Young, aggressive employees who intend to remain with the company will particularly benefit. Their efforts in producing profit increase their compensation under the plan, and as they remain with the company, their share of the profits distributed to the fund will increase as their base compensation increases. Finally, it is possible to provide for periodic withdrawals from the profit sharing accounts in addition to distribution upon retirement, death, or disability.

Pension plans, on the other hand, are specifically directed toward retirement income, and the employer is usually obliged to contribute the necessary funds on an annual basis. Pension plans may be either defined benefit plans (where the exact benefits upon retirement are specified and contributions must be made to reach the specified benefits) or defined contribution plans (where a certain contribution is made by the employer each year and the benefits depend on the total funds available upon retirement). The benefits of the plan provide a specified income for the employee after retirement, and the employer contributions are fixed by an amount necessary to provide income for the specified period. The employer contributions are a fixed annual obligation and are not related to profits in any way. The contribution is, therefore, a charge on operations that must be considered in estimating costs and pricing. Moreover, the contribution is usually directly based upon the employee's length of service and age, since the contribution for an older employee must be higher to accumulate enough funds for that employee's specified retirement income under the plan. The allocation of funds among eligible employees under the plan will be in accordance with the prescribed pension, and young, aggressive employees are not particularly rewarded for their enthusiastic business achievements. However, the fixed obligation to contribute to the pension plan has some employee advantages that are not available with a profit sharing plan. The pension plan permits recognition of employment before the establishment of the plan, and accommodates immediate pensions for employees who have already reached retirement age when the plan is adopted.

The choice between a defined benefit or defined contribution pension plan or a profit sharing plan depends on many factors, the most important of which include the ability of the company to make the required contributions, the desired stimulation of incentive, and the characteristics of the employee group. For indecisive company managers, it may be suggested that a combination of both plans be used to benefit all employees.

Tax Ramifications

The tax treatment of profit sharing and pension plans is complicated, and should be thoroughly studied before recommending or drafting of a plan. Only a few of the most important provisions are generally covered here.

Tax-favored plans must be *qualified,* meaning they must satisfy the statutory requirements prescribed in the Internal Revenue Code.[33] A qualified plan results in tax benefits for both the employer and the employee. Subject to certain statutory limitations, the employer is permitted to deduct contributions to the plan in the year made, just as normal compensation would be deducted as an expense, even though the compensation is not actually paid to the employee during that year.[34] Therefore, the employer suffers no tax disadvantage by paying compensation to the plan, rather than paying directly to the employee. The funds paid into the plan may be accumulated and invested during the holding period, but the income earned on the investment is exempt from any tax.[35] The funds thereby increase much faster than if they were invested by the corporation without a qualified plan or by the individual employee. The employee-beneficiary of the plan is not taxed on any of the funds until those funds are distributed.[36] Thus, an executive who receives a substantial salary that elevates her tax bracket at the height of her earning power will not lose a proportionate amount of the compensation under the plan by having to pay tax on this deferred income in the years she is employed. Rather, she will pay tax on distributed amounts received in years of her retirement, when her other income is minimized and her tax bracket is much lower. Finally, the amounts contributed by the company and paid to heirs or beneficiaries upon the death of the employee can pass free of estate tax, since the employee may specify direct payment to named beneficiaries and the funds will not be included in the employee's estate.

The foregoing tax benefits increase the desirability of these plans as a part of the employee compensation scheme. Qualified plans permit the employer to minimize cost while maximizing employee compensation.

Qualification

The requirements of the Internal Revenue Code and the rulings thereunder are a maze of intricate rules with myriad exceptions, definitions, inclusions, and exclusions—all designed to describe the qualification procedure and standards of a profit sharing or pension plan. The purpose of the plan, amounts of benefits, participation, vesting of benefits, operation, contributions, and reporting must be structured in accordance with the statutory rules.

Few rules of life have changed as frequently as the rules regarding qualified profit sharing and pension plans. The Internal Revenue Code has been modified hundreds of times to attempt to balance the interests of the employer and the employee in providing tax-advantaged compensation plans that are fair, effective, and legitimate. Frequently, the rules will be modified on a prospective basis to encourage employment of certain classes of persons, such as persons over or under a certain age, persons with underemployed talents, persons involved in certain industries or professions, and so on. The rules that follow are general rules that may have changed or become subject to exceptions by the time you read them, but they generally illustrate the approach of the tax qualification procedures and the requirements necessary for qualified plans.

A qualified plan must be adopted for the purpose of offering the employees a share of the profits or income of the employer or for providing a fund that will be distributed to the employees or their beneficiaries after retirement. The plan must be established and maintained by the employer for the exclusive benefit of the employees. The funds cannot be diverted for any use other than the specified purposes.

The plan may not be qualified if it is intended to benefit only a few select employees. Section 401(a) of the Internal Revenue Code is extremely forceful in insisting that the qualified plan may not discriminate in favor of employees who are officers, shareholders, or highly compensated employees. Generally, the contributions to the plan should be allocated in proportion to and benefits awarded in relation to the total current compensation of the participants of the plan. It is possible to base contributions and benefits on less than all compensation of the employees so long as the plan remains nondiscriminatory.

Participation in the plan depends upon compliance with two general statutory tests: age and service requirements, and coverage requirements.

The material in this section describes these requirements, discusses how vesting affects the age and service requirements, outlines certain limitations on contributions to qualified plans, and explains the formalities associated with establishing a qualified plan.

Age and Service Requirements. Concerning the minimum age and service conditions, the qualified plan must permit participation for employees who have completed at least 1 year of service with the employer or who have reached age 21, whichever is later. One year of service means a 12-month period during which the employee works at least 1,000 hours. A part-time employee who works for more than a year but only logs 18 hours a week can be safely excluded under a qualified plan. But a full-time employee who works 40 hours a week and takes a 25-week vacation must be permitted to participate (unless, of course, the vacation turns out to be permanent and the vesting rules permit a forfeiture for the terminated employee). If the plan provides that employees who participate will be vested immediately with the benefits of the plan, an employer may provide for an eligibility waiting period (such as 2 years after employment begins). Older employees cannot be excluded from the plan simply because of age unless the plan is a defined (or target) benefit plan and an employee begins employment within 5 years of the normal retirement age specified in the plan. This last rule permits an employer to hire an employee who is near retirement without having to contribute large sums to the plan to provide the defined benefit amount when the employee does retire during the next 5 years.

Coverage Requirements. The rules for participation of certain classes of employees in a qualified plan are even more involved. Generally, a plan must pass one of four tests: a percentage test, a fair-cross-section test, a ratio test, or an average benefits test.

The *percentage test* requires that the plan cover either

1. 70% or more of all employees; or
2. 80% or more of all eligible employees, provided 70% or more of all employees are eligible.

The *fair-cross-section test* permits the plan to cover a classification of employees that is determined by the Internal Revenue Service not to be discriminatory in favor of officers, shareholders, or highly compensated employees. The test anticipates that the Internal Revenue Service will review the employees who are covered, make a determination that the plan is fair and not discriminatory, and approve the plan for qualification.

The *ratio test* compares highly compensated employees against non–highly compensated employees. The percentage of non–highly compensated employees covered must be at least 70% of the percentage of highly compensated employees covered by the plan.

The *average benefits test* combines the fair-cross-section test and the ratio test. The plan may benefit certain employees under a classification that the Internal Revenue Service has determined does not discriminate, and the average benefit percentage for non–highly compensated employees must be at least 70% of the average benefit for highly compensated employees.

A complex illustration may serve to explain these otherwise simple rules. Suppose a corporation has 80 regular employees who work full-time, and 5 part-time employees who work less than 1,000 hours in a 12-month period. The 80 regular employees may be classified as follows:

Age	*Served over 5 Years*	*Served 3–5 Years*	*Served 1–3 Years*	*Served Less Than 12 Months*
Over 60	7	2		
21–60	42	7	5	1
Under 21	3	4	2	7
	52	13	7	8

First, determine who will be potentially excludable under the age and service rules. The plan may exclude the 5 part-time employees because they work too few hours, and may exclude the 8 full-time employees who have served less than 12 months. The other 9 full-time employees who have not reached age 21 may be excluded. The plan could also exclude the 2 employees who are over 60 and who have served less than 5 years, but only if they began their employment when they were older than a specified age (say 60), *and* if the normal age of retirement is not more than 5 years older (say 65), *and* if the plan is a defined benefit plan where benefits are set in a certain amount after retirement and the employer would have to rapidly contribute great quantities of money for these employees in order to meet those benefits upon retirement.

As for coverage, the percentage test requires that a qualified plan must cover 70% of *all* employees or 80% or more of all *eligible* employees, provided 70% or more of all employees are eligible. In this case the plan must cover at least 56 employees (based upon 70% of all employees). It has already been determined that the plan excludes the 5 part-time employees, the 8 full-time employees who do not meet minimum service requirements, and the 9 full-time employees who are under age 21. This leaves 63 employees who meet the minimum age and service requirements (adequate to meet the 70% test). Under the second part of the percentage test, the plan could also be qualified if only 80% of all eligible employees are covered, as long as 70% of all employees are eligible. Thus, since 63 employees are eligible, as few as 51 (80% of those eligible) could be covered and the plan would still qualify for tax advantages.

If the plan provided that only employees who earned more than $30,000 per year would be included as participants, and if only 40 employees qualified under that test, the plan would not be qualified under the first part of the percentage test because of the participation formula rules. However, the plan might qualify under the fair-cross-section test if the Internal Revenue Service determines that even though only 40 employees are covered, the plan does not discriminate in favor of officers, shareholders, or highly compensated employees. This would require a determination that enough employees made substantially more than $30,000 per year that the threshold salary does not meet the "highly compensated" standard.

Suppose the corporation adopts a plan designed to cover only employees who work in a specified place, and only 20 employees meet that test. All is not lost even though the plan dismally fails the percentage test. The plan could still obtain special approval of the Internal Revenue Service if it is found not to be discriminatory in favor of officers, shareholders, or highly compensated employees. However, if the service learned that the "specified place" is corporate headquarters where management offices are located, the special classification would not likely succeed.

Try another example. Suppose the 80 regular employees are further classified as follows:

	Highly Compensated Employees	*Non–Highly Compensated Employees*
Eligible Employees	13	46
Noneligible Employees	4	17
Ratio of Eligible to Noneligible Employees	76%	73%

Using the ratio test, the plan would be qualified with the proportions of the employees specified in the table, since the non–highly compensated employees covered must be at least 70% of the highly compensated employees covered by the plan. Seventy-six percent of the highly compensated employees are eligible, and 73% of the non–highly compensated employees are eligible. This is a 96% ratio (70% to 73%).

The average benefits test compares the average benefits paid to non–highly compensated employees with the average benefits paid to highly compensated employees, based upon a classification approved by the Internal Revenue Service. Again in this case, the Internal Revenue Service reviews the average benefits paid to the respective groups and makes a determination whether the plan discriminates in favor of the highly compensated employees.

One final illustration to test your keen awareness of these rules. Could the corporation qualify a plan that covered only the 63 employees who work full-time, are over 21 years of age, and have worked at least 3 full years with the corporation? Yes. The plan meets the 70% test. Minimum age and service requirements are also met *if* the plan provides for immediate vesting.

Vesting. The qualified plan may meet one of two alternative vesting schedules under Section 411 of the Internal Revenue Code. Before these vesting schedules are reviewed, it should be noted that vesting is the employer's incentive hammer. So long as the benefits under the plan have not vested, the employer can reasonably expect that the employee will continue to work for the employer, hoping to enjoy vesting of the benefits one day. If the benefits have vested, the employee is absolutely entitled to them, and the incentive to remain with the company may be diminished. Consequently, most employers would prefer to defer vesting as long as possible. The vesting schedules state the *maximum* periods of time the plans may defer vesting and still be qualified.

The first alternative is called *five-year cliff vesting*. The plan may provide that no benefits will vest until five years of service have been completed, and then the benefits must be 100% vested and nonforfeitable. Under the second alternative, the plan may provide for three- to seven-year vesting. The employee may be required to complete at least three years before any benefits become vested. At the end of three years, 20% of the benefits vest, and each year 20% more of the benefits vest until the seventh year, when the benefits are 100% vested and nonforfeitable.

Limitations on Contributions. Section 415 of the Internal Revenue Code places certain limits on the benefits and contributions to qualified plans, which must be strictly observed. A defined benefit plan is generally limited to the lesser of $90,000 or 100% of the participant's average compensation for his or her highest three years. This $90,000 is adjusted for cost-of-living increases by the Treasury Department annually, and the limitation is also modified depending upon the age and years of service for each employee. The defined contribution plan is limited to the lesser of $30,000 or 25% of the participant's compensation for the annual contribution to the plan. This amount is also adjusted for cost-of-living increases, and employee contributions are taken into account in making the computation.

Formalities. The statutory formalities demand that the plan be permanent, in writing, and communicated to the employees. Its terms must contemplate a continuing program of contributions by the employer and distributions to the employees. While the plan may be terminated for business exigencies not within the employer's control, termination is always subject to careful scrutiny by the Internal Revenue Service to determine whether the plan was truly intended to be continuous at inception. Thus, there must be a valid business reason, unforeseeable when the plan was adopted, for the plan to be terminated. The written plan may be distributed to the employees, or, at least, a pamphlet describing its salient provisions should be available to the employees.

Finally, the operation of the plan is an important element to its qualification. The plan must be *funded*. The funding arrangements may be accomplished by a trust, requiring contributions from the employer to an institutional trustee, who will invest the funds and distribute them in accordance with the trust agreement. It is also possible to use the funds to purchase insurance contracts or other investment contracts for the benefit of the employee plan. In sum, there must be a formal contribution and investment arrangement, distinguishable from normal corporate activities by contractual provisions, preferably with an independent third party, to operate and administer the plan.[37]

INCENTIVE STOCK OPTIONS

Stock options that are offered as additional employee compensation may also perform an incentive function with tax advantages. However, rather than monetary remuneration, a stock option is designed to give the optionee-employee an ownership interest in the corporation-employer (the optionor).

A stock option is a written instrument in which a corporation offers the right to purchase stock in the corporation to an individual at a predetermined price at any time during a stated period. The individual is under no obligation to accept the offer to purchase. As you may expect, to benefit the recipient, the option offers the stock to the optionee at a price other than the market price. This feature has considerable incentive value, much as the carrot in front of the donkey does. The price is set at an amount higher than market price at first, encouraging the employee to produce profits so the market price will rise above the option price, and the employee will then have the option to purchase the stock at the discount option price. The incentive factor continues even after the employee exercises the option, since the value of the stock purchased should increase as the profits of the granting corporation increase.

An employee compensated by stock options should be motivated to work very hard on behalf of the corporation since the employee will eventually profit by holding the option until the market value of the stock exceeds the option price. By exercising the option, the employee makes a discount purchase of the stock and becomes a shareholder who has a pecuniary interest in the corporation's performance. Moreover, by using stock options, the corporation is compensating an employee without incurring any immediate expense, because the issuance of an option requires no direct payment to the employee. Of course, the ownership interest of existing shareholders is affected by stock options. The exercise of the option dilutes their proportionate ownership of the company. However, if the stock option motivates employees to continually strive for profits, the existing shareholders will also benefit from the resulting increase in stock values.

As a part of its compensation program, a corporation may adopt a stock option plan to benefit certain employees. Options granted under the plan give the recipients the right to purchase stock of the corporation at a specified price, the *option price,* for a specified period of time. The offer of stock to the employee may be accepted only during this period, and the act of acceptance is the exercise of the option. Upon payment of the option price to the corporation, the employee is entitled to receive certificates for the stock.

Tax Ramifications

Incentive stock options (ISOs) may receive special tax treatment under the Internal Revenue Code.[38] An incentive stock option is an option granted by a corporation to an individual based upon the individual's employment with the corporation.

When a corporation grants an incentive stock option to an employee, the employee does not realize any income at the time of the receipt of the option (even though the option may have value). If the corporation were to give the employee a cash payment equivalent to the value of the option, the payment would be treated as ordinary income and taxed immediately. Instead, with an incentive stock option plan, the employee will be taxed only when stock acquired through the exercise of the option is sold. This could be several years later, after the stock has substantially appreciated in value.

To obtain the benefits of an incentive stock option plan, the employee must not dispose of the stock for at least two years from the date the option was granted, and the employee must hold the stock for at least one year after purchasing it through the option. (These periods do not apply if the employee were to die.) The employee must also remain employed by the corporation from the time the option is granted until three months before the option's exercise. This is why these plans are regarded as *incentive* plans, since the employee must stay employed in order to realize the benefit of the stock option, the stock purchased, and the tax consequences.

When stock is purchased under an incentive stock option plan, the amount by which the fair market value of the stock at the time the option is exercised exceeds the option price is an item of *tax preference*. Tax preference income is subject to a surtax of an additional percentage. This additional tax does not usually constitute an onerous burden on most employees, since the tax preference surtax is charged only against employees who receive substantial benefits from the exercise of the option. To illustrate, consider Shelley Roberts, an employee of the Nobles Company, who has an option to buy 1,000 shares of corporate stock at $10 per share. When she exercises the option, the market price of the stock is $50 per share. In that year, she has tax preference income of $40,000, the difference between the market value and the option price. Further suppose that Shelley's tax preference income is taxed at 15%. The tax preference surtax is $6,000 in the year the option is exercised. If she holds the stock for more than three years, and sells it at $60 per share, her gain is $50,000, since she purchased the stock at $10 per share. The tax preference surtax does not diminish the desirability of the incentive stock option as a form of compensation. Shelley will have paid $6,000 in extra tax in the hypothetical transaction, but she has also profited $50,000. Who could complain about that?

Qualification

The Internal Revenue Code specifies several requirements for the qualification of tax-favored incentive stock option plans,[39] and, like qualified pension and profit sharing plans, the incentive stock option plan must strictly accord with the statutory rules. Generally, these requirements are concerned with the adoption and content of the option plan, the duration of the plan, the exercise of the option, the option price, and the employees covered by the plan.

An incentive stock option plan must state the number of shares that may be issued under the plan, and must describe the classes of employees who are eligible to receive options. The identification of shares to be issued under the plan should include the description of the shares from the articles of incorporation. The number may be specific, or a formula may be prescribed to establish the total number of shares that may be issued under the plan.

> **EXAMPLE: Shares Subject to the Plan**
> The Committee, from time to time, may provide for the option and sale in the aggregate of up to 100,000 shares of Common Stock of the Company, without par value. Shares shall be made available from authorized and unissued or reacquired Common Stock.[40]

For the tax benefits of the qualified stock option to be enjoyed, the option must be granted to a person employed at the time of the grant. Individuals who are employed by a parent or subsidiary corporation of the granting corporation would qualify, but a prospective employee would not. Moreover, the optionee must remain an employee at all times during the period from the date the option is granted to three months before the date the option is exercised. The continuous employment requirement does not apply to a deceased employee, but is strictly observed in all other cases. The plan may include this limitation in its provisions.

> **EXAMPLE: Rights in Event of Termination of Employment**
> In the event of termination of employment for any cause other than death, a participant's option shall expire within three months after his or her employment terminates. Nothing contained in the Plan shall confer upon any participant any right to be continued in the employ of the Company or any subsidiary of the Company or shall prevent the Company or any subsidiary from terminating the participant's employment at any time, with or without cause.

Of course, it is always possible to state in the plan that the stock options granted under the plan will expire immediately upon termination of employment. The Internal Revenue Code simply provides that the option may not extend beyond three months after termination to qualify for the advantageous tax treatment. The estate of a deceased employee is not so limited unless the option specifically so provides, and it may.

> **EXAMPLE: Rights in the Event of Death**
> In the event of the death of a participant while in the employ of the Company or a subsidiary, or within three months after termination of such employment, the option theretofore granted the participant shall be exercisable, in whole or in part, within the next three months succeeding the participant's death, if and to the extent the participant could have exercised it at the date of his or her death, by such person as shall have acquired the right to exercise such option by will or by the laws of descent and distribution.

The identification of employees covered by the plan may be satisfied by reasonably specific descriptions—for example, "supervisory employees," "all salaried employees," or "all employees of the corporation." The board of directors, or its delegates, usually has the power to determine the number of shares to be optioned to each employee within those described in the plan. Employees who own 10% or more of the voting stock of the corporation immediately before the option is granted are ineligible, unless the option price is at least 110% of the fair market value of the stock at the time the option is granted and the option terms require that the option must be exercised within a five-year period.

> **EXAMPLE: Participants**
> The Committee shall determine and designate from time to time those key employees (including employees who are also officers or directors) of the Company and its subsidiaries (as defined in section 425(f) of the Internal Revenue Code of 1986, as amended) to whom options are granted and who thereby become participants in the Plan. In selecting the individuals to whom options shall be granted, as well as in determining the number of shares subject to each option, the Committee shall weigh the positions and responsibilities of the individuals being considered, the nature of their services, their present and potential contributions

to the success of the Company, and such other factors as the Committee shall deem relevant to accomplish the purpose of the Plan. No option shall be granted to an employee who, immediately before such option is granted, owns stock possessing more than 10 percent of the total combined voting power or value of all classes of stock of the Company or its subsidiaries. Each grant of an option shall be evidenced by an option agreement which shall contain such terms and conditions as may be approved by the Committee and shall be signed by an officer of the Company and the employee.

An incentive stock option plan must be approved by the stockholders of the granting corporation within twelve months before or after the date the plan is adopted. A plan is usually adopted by an appropriate resolution of the board of directors.

EXAMPLE: Resolution to Adopt a Qualified Stock Option Plan
WHEREAS, it is the belief of the Board of Directors of this Corporation that its key employees would be interested in acquiring a part of the capital stock of this Corporation, and that ownership of stock of this Corporation by its key employees would be to the advantage of this Corporation, and

WHEREAS, by the recent increase in capital stock of this Corporation, there is available for further subscriptions a total of one hundred thousand (100,000) shares of the common stock, without par value, of this Corporation,

BE IT RESOLVED, That the Board of Directors do hereby adopt the Incentive Stock Option Plan, a copy of which is made a part of this resolution, subject to the approval of the common stockholders at their next regular meeting, and

RESOLVED FURTHER, That the Board of Directors of this Corporation do hereby recommend to the stockholders that they authorize the Board of Directors to set aside a total of ten thousand (10,000) shares of the common stock of this Corporation for sale to its key employees under said Incentive Stock Option Plan.[41]

The date of the resolution adopting the plan will be the date used to determine whether shareholder approval has been obtained within the statutory period. The required shareholder approval may come within twelve months before or after the adoption of the plan by the board of directors. Consequently, the shareholder action may be the impetus that causes the board to adopt a plan. As long as shareholder approval and board adoption occur within a twelve-month period, the plan may be qualified.

The federal tax law requires only that the plan be approved by the affirmative vote of the holders of the majority of the voting stock of the corporation. The vote is taken at a regular or special stockholders' meeting, and the normal shareholder voting provisions of the state corporate statute apply.[42] Further, there may be other requirements for shareholder action in the statute, articles of incorporation, or by-laws to obtain a waiver of any preemptive rights in the stock issued under the option. Shareholder approval of the plan must comply with those requirements.

An incentive stock option must be granted within ten years from the date on which the plan is adopted or the date on which the plan is approved by stockholders, whichever is earlier. Accordingly, the plan should contain an expiration date within the ten-year period. Of course, the expiration of the plan has no effect upon any options previously granted pursuant to the plan's terms.

EXAMPLE: Termination
The Plan shall terminate ten years after its effective date, or on such earlier date as the Board of Directors may determine.

The option may not be exercised after the expiration of ten years from the date it is granted. The plan should so state, and each option should recite a specified period for exercise within this limitation.

> **EXAMPLE: Option Period**
> The term of each option shall be such period as the Committee may determine, but not more than ten years from the date the option is granted.

Some quick mathematics should reveal that the period from first grant to last exercise under any qualified stock option plan may not exceed twenty years. If an option were granted just before the expiration of the ten-year period following adoption and shareholder approval of the plan, it would remain exercisable for ten additional years. Thus, the last option may be exercised almost twenty years after the plan takes effect.

The option price may not be less than the fair market value of the stock on the date the option is granted for the plan to qualify for special tax treatment. Thus, the employee can benefit only from the appreciation in the value of the stock following the grant of the option. This feature itself increases the incentive value of the option, since the employee's performance will be directed toward increasing the market value of the stock over the option price. The tax benefits of an incentive stock option will be lost if the option price is less than the market price when the option is granted.

The determination of the option price will generally be the responsibility of the board of directors or its appointed committee, and only a general statement regarding option price need be included in the option plan. It is absolutely necessary to specify that the option price will be not less than the market value of the stock on the date the option is granted. If the stock subject to the option has a par value, the option price must also be at least par value.

> **EXAMPLE: Option Price**
> Shares of Common Stock of the Company shall be offered from time to time at a price to be determined by the Stock Option Committee, which price shall be not less than the fair market value of the stock on the day the option is granted.
>
> Fair market value shall be the mean between the highest and lowest selling prices on the New York Stock Exchange on the valuation date. If there are no sales on such date, the value shall be determined by taking the mean between the highest and lowest sales upon the last preceding date on which such sales occurred. In no event shall the option price be less than the par value.

The remaining statutory requirements for qualification limit the employee-shareholder's ability to exercise other outstanding options, the ability to transfer the option to others, and the percentage ownership interest in the corporation and its affiliated corporations. The first rule is that an option may not be exercisable while there is outstanding an employee stock option previously granted to the same employee. This rule prevents the successive issuance of options at lower amounts when the market value of the company's stock is declining. The plan should recognize this limitation in its terms.

> **EXAMPLE: Prior Options**
> A subsequent option may not be exercised by a participant while that participant has outstanding any other prior stock options under this or prior stock option

plans which entitle him or her to purchase stock of the same class in the Company at a price higher than the option price of such subsequent option.

The Code also states that an incentive stock option may not be transferable by the employee—it may be exercised only by that employee. The singular exception to this rule is that transfers are permitted upon the death of the employee by the employee's will or by the laws of descent and distribution. The terms of the option should so state.

> **EXAMPLE: Nonassignability**
> Options are not transferable otherwise than by will or the laws of descent and distribution, and are exercisable during a participant's lifetime only by the participant.

Finally, the Internal Revenue Service frequently places various limitations on the amount of stock that may be subject to the option. Sometimes it states those limitations in terms of a *grant limitation,* so that an incentive stock option plan will not qualify if an employee is granted incentive stock options in excess of a certain amount (e.g., $100,000) in a calendar year. Sometimes those limitations are stated in terms of *exercise limitations,* so that an employee may not exercise incentive stock options in excess of a certain amount (e.g., $100,000) in any calendar year. Any limitations in the Internal Revenue Code must always be observed. When a limitation is changed, the prior limitation will usually apply for all options granted while the prior limitation was in effect, and the new limitations will apply only to options that are granted thereafter. Sometimes the machinations of the Internal Revenue Service can be a significant advantage to an employee. For example, an employee who is granted an option for $100,000 of stock in 1986 (when grant limitations applied) and was also granted an option for an additional $100,000 of stock in 1987 (when exercise limitations applied) may be able to purchase $200,000 of stock in 1987, since both the grant and exercise limitation rules for the applicable options are met.

Administration of the Plan

The terms of the plan will describe the persons who are to administer it. The board of directors could naturally serve in this capacity, but it may choose to delegate administration authority to a committee appointed by the board. The terms of the plan should also prescribe a procedure for the administrators' actions, and the authority granted or restricted in the administration of the plan.

> **EXAMPLE: Administration**
> The Plan shall be administered by a Stock Option Committee (herein called the Committee) consisting of three or more members of the Board of Directors of the Company who are not eligible to receive options under the Plan or who have waived their rights to receive options during such time as they are members of the Committee. The Committee shall be appointed annually by the Board of Directors, which may from time to time appoint additional members of the Committee or remove members and appoint new members in substitution for those previously appointed and fill vacancies however caused. A majority of the Committee shall constitute a quorum and the acts of a majority of the members present at any meeting at which a quorum is present, or acts approved in writing by all of the

members, shall be deemed the action of the Committee. Subject to the provisions of the Plan, the Committee is authorized to interpret it, to prescribe, amend and rescind rules and regulations relating to it, and to make all other determinations necessary or advisable for its administration. It is intended that all options granted under the Plan be "incentive stock options" under the Internal Revenue Code of 1986, as amended.

> **EXAMPLE: Allotment of Shares**
> The Committee shall determine the number of shares to be offered from time to time to each participant except that the maximum number of shares offered to any one participant upon the initial offering at the inception of the Plan shall not exceed 2,000 shares, and the maximum number of shares which any participant may purchase pursuant to the initial offering and all subsequent offerings under the Plan shall not exceed 5,000 shares. The Committee may also prescribe a minimum number of shares which may be purchased at any one time, and the time or times shares will be issued pursuant to the exercise of options. In any offering after the initial offering, the Committee may offer available shares to new participants or to then participants or to a greater or lesser number of participants, and may include previous participants in accordance with such determination as the Committee shall make from time to time.

The administrators should have authority to adjust the provisions of the option to account for subsequent capital adjustments in the corporation. For example, a stock split or stock dividend would accordingly reduce the market price, and may cause the option price to be unrealistic. An adjustment to the option will preserve its viability.

> **EXAMPLE: Adjustment upon Changes in Capitalization**
> In the event there is any change in the Common Stock of the Company by reason of stock dividends, stock split-ups, recapitalization, reorganizations, mergers, consolidations, combinations or exchanges of shares, or otherwise, the number of shares available for option and the shares subject to any option shall be appropriately adjusted by the Committee.

The plan should carefully limit the authority of the administration to modify its terms. If an amendment to the plan violates any of the statutory requirements for qualification, the qualified status of the plan and the options granted under it will be lost. Consequently, only technical amendments should be permitted, and the authority to amend should prohibit the types of changes that would result in a substantive modification affecting qualification.

> **EXAMPLE: Amendment**
> The Board of Directors may at any time suspend, rescind or terminate the Plan and may amend it from time to time in such respects as it may deem advisable, provided, however, that no such amendment shall, without further approval of the stockholders of the Company, except as provided herein, (a) increase the aggregate number of shares as to which options may be granted under the Plan either to all individuals or any one individual; (b) change the minimum option purchase price; (c) increase the maximum period during which options may be exercised; (d) extend the termination date of the plan; or (e) permit the granting of options to members of the Committee. No option may be granted during any suspension of the Plan or after the Plan has been rescinded or terminated and no amendment,

rescission, suspension or termination shall, without the participant's consent, alter or impair any of the rights or obligations under any option theretofore granted to that participant under the Plan.

In granting a stock option, the corporation is offering to issue securities that may have to be registered under federal and state securities laws. If the securities have been registered, the corporation should have no problem issuing the stock under the option. However, if the securities are not registered, it is quite important to obtain a representation from the employees that the stock is being purchased only for investment and not for distribution and resale to the general public. The sale of securities to key employees may be exempt from the registration requirements of the securities laws, but severe penalties are prescribed for sale of unregistered stock to the general public. This representation is designed to protect against these liabilities. The plan may contain a clause acknowledging the purpose of the purchase.

EXAMPLE: Purchase for Investment
All stock of the Company purchased pursuant to any option must be purchased for investment and not with the view to the distribution or resale thereof. Each option will be granted on the understanding that any shares purchased thereunder will be so purchased, and each employee to whom an option is granted shall be required to deliver to the Company a written representation and agreement to that effect.

Finally, the plan should recite the requirements of payment and other consideration to be given by the employee for the receipt and the exercise of the option. The plan may exact a promise from the employee that the employee will remain employed with the company for a period of time as a condition to the privilege of receiving the option.

EXAMPLE: Consideration for Option
Each participant shall, as consideration for the grant of the option, agree to remain in the continuous employ of the Company or one or more of its subsidiaries for at least two years from the date of the grant of such option.

EXAMPLE: Payment for Stock
Full payment for shares purchased shall be made at the time of exercising an option in whole or in part. No shares shall be issued until full payment therefor has been made and a participant shall have none of the rights of a stockholder until shares are issued to him or her.

INSURANCE PROGRAMS

Various programs of insurance coverage are available to a corporation for the benefit of its employees. Some of these programs have unique income tax advantages under the Internal Revenue Code, and all of them are intended to benefit the beneficiaries of an employee upon the employee's death with little or no cost to the employer.

Death benefit compensation programs are frequently used by corporations. Typically, the employer will promise to pay a portion of the employee's salary to the heirs for a period of time after death in consideration of the employee's continuous faithful performance. The amounts paid to the employee's heirs are tax free up to a certain amount[43] and the amounts paid are deductible to the corporation as business expenses. The corporation will normally apply for life insurance on the employee to cover this contingent liability, and will use the proceeds of the insurance to pay the agreed amounts to the heirs. For the employee, a death benefit agreement is like an insurance policy for the family, and the insurance is completely without cost to the employee.

Split-dollar insurance is another common plan used to benefit key personnel. The corporation and the employee join in the purchase of a life insurance policy on the life of the employee, and the employer-corporation pays a share of the premium, usually equal to the annual increase in the cash value of the policy. The employee pays the remaining premium. The corporation is named beneficiary to receive the amount of the premiums it has paid, and the employee will designate a beneficiary for the balance. When the employee dies, the corporation receives a return of all premiums paid, and the employee's beneficiary receives the remaining face value of the policy. The advantage to the employee is that the beneficiary will receive a considerable sum while the employee's share of the premiums has been minimal. The corporation will recover all it has paid, and will have no out-of-pocket costs to provide the insurance benefit.

EMPLOYEE EXPENSE REIMBURSEMENT PLANS

Many companies have instituted self-insured plans for employees as a method of supplementing group hospital insurance plans, major medical insurance, and other forms of reimbursement that may be provided to all employees. The variety of employee benefit plans is limited only by the imagination and generosity of the employer. Employers provide free transportation, buffet lunches, health and athletic club memberships, and a variety of other expense reimbursement provisions that encourage employees to remain loyal and dedicated to their work.

The Internal Revenue Code recognizes five statutory benefit plans that provide reimbursement of expenses to employees, and permits tax benefits for payments with respect to those plans provided the plans meet certain nondiscrimination requirements. The five statutory benefit plans that are subject to the nondiscrimination rules of Section 89 of the code are as follows:

1. Group term life insurance plans
2. Qualified group legal services plans
3. Educational assistance programs
4. Dependent care assistance programs
5. Accident or health plans (which involve reimbursement of medical expenses)

While the types of expenses reimbursed under these plans are different, the operations of the plans and the procedures for obtaining reimbursement are very similar. To illustrate how these plans are applied in a typical situation, this section concentrates on an accident and health plan for reimbursement of medical expenses.

Broad-based group medical insurance plans usually do not cover all expenses incurred by an employee. For example, certain amounts may not be reimbursed as a result of deductibles, coinsurance, and maximum benefit provisions. In addition, certain expenses such as private hospital room care, routine dental work, eyeglasses or contact lenses, and annual physical examinations are not covered under many group medical insurance plans covering employees generally. Employers may institute medical reimbursement plans under which all or some of these expenses are covered by the company.

Before 1978, the employer could choose, without adverse tax ramifications, the employee or group of employees who would participate in such a medical or dental expense reimbursement plan. The amounts reimbursed were not taxable to the employee but were deductible to the employer. If, on the other hand, an employee paid these expenses personally, the expenses would be tax deductible only to the extent that they exceeded a certain percentage of the employee's adjusted gross income (the amount currently allowed for a medical deduction on personal income tax returns). In the typical case, therefore, most or all of the expenses would not be tax deductible. These medical expense reimbursement plans were very popular in corporations before 1978 to provide a tax-free fringe benefit for special executives.

The Revenue Act of 1978 provided that all or a portion of the expenses reimbursed to an executive under a discriminatory, uninsured expense reimbursement plan will be taxed to the executive. The major concern is that such a plan is discriminatory in nature and not funded by insurance.

Between 1978 and 1986, the Internal Revenue Code was amended several times to apply separate nondiscrimination rules for all types of employee benefits. The Tax Reform Act of 1986 established a uniform, strict nondiscrimination rule for all fringe benefits and permitted the exclusion of such benefits from income only if the benefits are provided to a broad cross section of employees.

Comprehensive nondiscrimination rules are now applied to all statutory benefit plans. These rules are generally designed to avoid providing benefits to highly compensated employees to the exclusion of other employees. Benefits that do favor key or highly compensated employees must be included in the incomes of those employees. For a plan to provide tax-free benefits, it must meet several tests, including tests to determine whether eligibility for the plan is provided on a nondiscriminatory basis, whether the benefits received from the plan are provided on a nondiscriminatory basis, and whether the plan is valid.

Highly Compensated Employees

An employee is considered to be highly compensated in any year in which the employee

1. was a 5% owner of the employer;
2. earned more than $75,000 in annual compensation from the employer;
3. earned more than $50,000 in annual compensation from the employer and was a member of the top-paid group of the employer during the same year; or
4. was an officer of the company.

An officer is further defined as an individual who actually has the position of an officer and who received compensation more than 50% higher than the plan dollar limit in effect for that year. In a very large company, such as a multistate manufacturing company or a large national bank, hundreds of people could be officers and could meet that test. To avoid the problem that most of the employees are officers, the Internal Revenue Code limits the number of employees who are treated as officers to 50, regardless of the actual number who meet the test.

Consequently, if a corporation had 150 officers for purposes of the test, no more than 50 of them would be considered highly compensated employees for the discrimination rules. In a smaller company, where there are fewer than 50 officers, the rule is that no more than the greater of 3 employees or 10% of all employees are to be treated as officers. Thus, in a corporation with a president, vice-president, secretary and treasurer, and 25 other employees, only 3 persons would be considered officers for purposes of the nondiscrimination rule.

The dollar amounts of compensation increase annually according to cost of living increases established by the Treasury Department.

The top-paid group of employees includes active employees who are in the top 20% of all active employees based upon the compensation paid during the year. Certain employees may be excluded from this determination:

1. New employees who have not completed a certain period of service (e.g., 6 months or 1 year) or a shorter period as specified in the plan
2. Part-time employees who work less than 17½ hours per week or less than 6 months during a year (or such smaller periods as may be specified in the plan)
3. Employees who are part of a collective bargaining agreement with a union if there was good-faith bargaining by the union
4. Employees who are under age 21 (or an earlier age as specified in the plan)
5. Employees who are nonresident aliens and receive no earned income in the United States

For example, assume a corporation has 50 employees, 10 of whom are too new or too young to be included, are part-time, or are otherwise excludable. Of the 40 remaining employees, 10 earn more than $50,000, but on the basis of compensation paid, only 8 are in the top 20% of all active employees. Only 8 of those persons would then be included in the "highly compensated" definition.

Eligibility Test

The Internal Revenue Code provides a three-part eligibility test:

1. At least 50% of the employees eligible to participate in the plan must be non–highly compensated employees. This requirement will be met if the percentage of eligible highly compensated employees is not larger than the percentage of eligible non–highly compensated employees. For example, if a company has 20 employees, 15 of whom are highly compensated, the only way the company could satisfy this test is to make all employees eligible, so that the categories of highly compensated and non–highly compensated are the same—100%.
2. At least 90% of the non–highly compensated employees must be eligible for a benefit that is at least 50% as valuable as the benefit available to the highly compensated employees. For example, if the most valuable benefit under the plan for highly compensated employees is a payment of $2,500 per year toward medical expenses, at least 90% of the non–highly compensated employees must be able to have a benefit that is worth at least $1,250 during that calendar year.
3. The plan may not contain any eligibility provision that discriminates in favor of highly compensated employees. If a plan is designed to suit the highly individualized needs of one or more highly compensated employees, it may be discriminatory even if it applies to all employees. Thus, if the president of a company has a rare disease, and the company's plan agrees to pay 100% of all costs relating to that

particular disease, the plan would be discriminatory even if all employees were eligible to participate should they contract the disease.

Benefits Test

The plan will satisfy the benefits test if the average benefit received by non–highly compensated employees is at least 75% of the average employer benefit received by the highly compensated employees. For example, assume a company provides a medical benefit plan for all of its 500 employees, 75 of whom are highly compensated. The value of the benefits provided to the 425 non–highly compensated employees totals $255,000, or $600 per employee. The value of the benefits provided to the 75 highly compensated employees totals $56,250, or $750 per employee. The ratio between the $750 and the $600 determines whether discrimination occurs. Since this ratio is 80%, the plan meets the nondiscriminatory benefits requirements. If the benefits provided to the 75 highly compensated employees totalled $67,500, or $900 per employee, the plan would not qualify because it would miss the 75% test.

Alternative Test

For medical expense plans (accident and health) and group term life insurance plans, an alternative test is available. If these plans benefit at least 80% of the employer's non–highly compensated employees, the plan satisfies both the eligibility and benefits tests.

Drafting a Valid Plan

To avoid taxation of employer-provided benefits, the company must adopt a plan that meets at least five requirements:

1. The plan must be in writing
2. The plan must provide employees with reasonable notification of benefits available under the plan
3. The plan must be maintained for the exclusive benefit of employees, or spouses and dependents of employees where permissible
4. The employee's rights under the plan must be legally enforceable (which means that benefits under the plan may not be discretionary with the employer)
5. The employer must have intended to maintain the plan indefinitely when the plan was established

The following checklist should be followed for preparation of a plan.

1. An introduction to the plan should recite the plan's purpose, the plan's effective date, and the manner in which the plan will be administered.

> **EXAMPLE: Purpose, Effective Date, and Administration**
> MEDICAL AND DENTAL EXPENSE REIMBURSEMENT PLAN (the "Plan") has been established by Sickness And Health, Inc., a corporation (the "employer"), to provide for reimbursement of certain medical and dental expenses incurred by its eligible employees and their dependents.
> *Effective Date*
> The "effective date" of the Plan is July 1, 1992. The Plan year shall be the calendar year.

> *Administration of the Plan*
>
> The Plan will be administered by the employer. Any documents required to be filed with the employer will be given or filed properly if delivered or mailed by registered mail, postage prepaid, to the employer at 7561 South Cedar Street, Atlanta, Georgia.

2. The membership should be defined in accordance with the rules against discrimination.

> **EXAMPLE: Membership**
>
> Each employee of the employer will become a member in the Plan on the effective date, or on the first day of any calendar month during which the employee meets all of the following eligibility requirements, if such employee is not employed or does not meet such requirements, on the effective date:
>
> a) The employee is an employee who is customarily employed by the employer on a full time (customarily fifteen (15) hours or more per week) and permanent (customarily five (5) months or more per calendar year) basis;
> b) The employee has attained the age of twenty-one (21); and
> c) The employee has completed six (6) months of service with the employer. However, if the employer has not been in existence for such period upon meeting the other requirements hereof, then the employee shall qualify if such employee has been employed for the lesser period in which the employer has been in existence.

3. The plan benefits should be stated, with a maximum dollar limit.

> **EXAMPLE: Plan Benefits**
>
> Subject to the conditions and limitations of the Plan, each calendar year, beginning on the effective date, each member will be entitled to reimbursement from the employer of the medical care costs (as defined herein) incurred during that year with respect to that member's family unit (as defined herein) to the extent that such costs do not exceed an amount equal to the smallest of:
>
> a) The total medical care costs of the family unit paid during that calendar year; or
> b) $1,000.

4. A definition of medical care costs should be included.

> **EXAMPLE: Medical Care Costs**
>
> The term "medical care costs" as used in the Plan means amounts paid by a member (or any other individual included in that member's family unit) for:
>
> a) Diagnosis, cure, mitigation, treatment or prevention of disease, or for the purpose of affecting any structure or function of the body;
> b) Transportation primarily for and essential to medical care referred to in subparagraph (a) above;
> c) Insurance covering medical care referred to in subparagraphs (a) and (b) above; and
> d) Any other amounts paid which are included within the meaning of "medical care" as defined in Section 213 of the Internal Revenue Code of 1986, or any comparable provision of any future legislation that amends, supplements or supersedes that section.

5. The beneficiaries under the plan should be defined.

> **EXAMPLE: Family Unit**
> The term "family unit" as applied to any member means the member, the member's spouse and such other persons as are dependents within the meaning of Section 152 of the Internal Revenue Code of 1986, or any comparable provision of any future legislation that amends, supplements or supersedes that section.

6. The manner of making payments under the plan should be described.

> **EXAMPLE: Manner of Making Payments**
> By the end of each calendar year or within thirty (30) days thereafter, the employer shall reimburse each member for the portion of the member's family unit's medical care costs incurred during the year that is payable to that member, provided that by the end of that year or within thirty (30) days thereafter, the employer receives evidence acceptable to it that such medical care costs have been paid by the member or any other individual included in the member's family unit.

7. Provisions should be recited to avoid duplication of payments for the same expenses.

> **EXAMPLE: Nonduplication of Benefits**
> A member shall not be reimbursed for medical care costs under this Plan to the extent that such costs are paid to or for the benefit of the member, or to or for the benefit of any other individual included in the member's family unit, under the provisions of any public plan of health insurance or under the provisions of any other plan or insurance policy, the costs or premiums of which are directly or indirectly paid, in whole or part, by the employer.

8. If the employer is to pay all of the benefits under the plan, that should be stated.

> **EXAMPLE: Financing Plan Benefits**
> Subject to the provisions of [Amendment and Termination], the employer expects and intends to pay the entire cost of the benefits provided by this Plan. No member will be required or permitted to make contributions under the Plan.

9. Such items as the employer may require to document the charges should be described.

> **EXAMPLE: Information to Be Furnished by Members**
> Members must furnish to the employer such documents, evidence, data or information as the employer considers necessary or desirable for the purpose of administering the Plan or for the employer's protection. The benefits of the Plan for each member are on the condition that the member furnish full, true, and complete data, evidence or other information, and that the member will promptly sign any documents related to the Plan requested by the employer.

10. Any implication that the plan provides a continuing right of employment should be eliminated.

> **EXAMPLE: Employee Rights**
> The Plan does not constitute a contract of employment and participation in the Plan will not give any member the right to be retained in the employ of the employer, nor will participation in the Plan give any member any right or claim to any benefit under the Plan, unless such right or claim has specifically accrued under the terms of the Plan.

11. Someone (usually the employer) should be able to interpret the plan, with that person's decision being final.

> **EXAMPLE: Provision that Employer's Decision Is Final**
> Any interpretation of the Plan and any decision on any matter within the discretion of the employer made by the employer in good faith is binding on all persons. A misstatement or other mistake of fact shall be corrected when it becomes known, and the employer shall make such adjustments on account thereof as it considers equitable and practicable.

12. Provisions for terminated participating employees should be included.

> **EXAMPLE: Benefits of Terminated Participating Employees**
> If a member's employment by the employer is terminated by reason of the member's resignation or dismissal, then any amount payable to that member under the Plan immediately prior to the member's termination shall be paid to the member. If a member's participation in the Plan is terminated by reason of the member's death, then any amount that has become payable to the member under the Plan as of the date of his or her death shall, in the discretion of the employer, be paid to either the member's spouse or the member's estate.

13. Amendment and termination provisions should describe the manner in which an amendment occurs, the causes of termination, and provisions for notice of either.

> **EXAMPLE: Amendment and Termination**
> *General.* While the employer expects to continue the Plan, it must necessarily reserve and does reserve the right to amend the Plan from time to time or to terminate the Plan.
>
> *Amendment.* If the employer exercises its right to amend the Plan, any amount that has become payable under the Plan to any person prior to the date on which such amendment is adopted shall be paid by the employer in accordance with the terms of the Plan as in effect prior to that date.
>
> *Termination.* The Plan will terminate on the first to occur of the following:
>
> a) The date it is terminated by the employer;
> b) The date the employer is judicially declared bankrupt or insolvent; or
> c) The dissolution, merger, consolidation or reorganization of the employer, or the sale by the employer of all or substantially all of its assets, except that in any such event arrangements may be made whereby the Plan will be continued by any successor to the employer or by any purchaser of all or substantially all of the employer's assets, in which case the successor or purchaser will be substituted for the employer under the Plan.
>
> If the Plan is terminated in accordance with subparagraph (a) or (c) above, any amount that has become payable under the Plan to any person prior to the date of termination shall be paid by the employer in accordance with the terms of the Plan as in effect prior to its termination.
>
> *Notice of Amendment or Termination.* Members will be notified of an amendment or termination within a reasonable time.

NOTES

1. West's Modern Legal Forms § 8522.
2. West's Modern Legal Forms § 8573.
3. West's Modern Legal Forms § 8525.
4. West's Modern Legal Forms § 8524.
5. West's Modern Legal Forms § 8581.
6. West's Modern Legal Forms § 8526.
7. West's Modern Legal Forms § 8522.
8. West's Modern Legal Forms § 8523.
9. West's Modern Legal Forms § 8581.
10. West's Modern Legal Forms § 8573.
11. West's Modern Legal Forms § 8526.
12. West's Modern Legal Forms § 8537.
13. West's Modern Legal Forms § 8573.
14. West's Modern Legal Forms § 8522.
15. West's Modern Legal Forms § 8526.
16. West's Modern Legal Forms § 8527.
17. West's Modern Legal Forms § 8663.
18. West's Modern Legal Forms § 8664.
19. West's Modern Legal Forms § 8681.
20. West's Modern Legal Forms § 8682.
21. West's Modern Legal Forms § 8659.
22. West's Modern Legal Forms § 8658.
23. E.g., Cal.Bus. & Prof.Code §§ 16600–02; Mich.Comp.Laws Ann. §§ 445.761 and 445.766.
24. See Colo.Rev.Stat. § 8–2–113; Fla.Stat.Ann. § 542.12; and S.D. Compiled Laws Ann. § 53–9–8.
25. West's Modern Legal Forms § 8652.
26. West's Modern Legal Forms § 8656.
27. West's Modern Legal Forms §§ 8657 and 8658.
28. See "Employment Agreements" earlier in this chapter.
29. See "Deferred Compensation" later in this chapter.
30. A form for an incentive compensation plan appears in West's Modern Legal Forms § 3132.
31. All of the examples for this section are from West's Modern Legal Forms § 3149.
32. Int.Rev.Code of 1986, 26 U.S.C.A. § 401.
33. Ibid.
34. Int.Rev.Code of 1986, 26 U.S.C.A. § 404.
35. Int.Rev.Code of 1986, 26 U.S.C.A. §§ 401 and 501.
36. Int.Rev.Code of 1986, 26 U.S.C.A. § 402.
37. Forms for pension and profit sharing plans may be found in West's Modern Legal Forms §§ 6666–6687.15.
38. Int.Rev.Code of 1986, 26 U.S.C.A. § 422A.
39. Int.Rev.Code of 1986, 26 U.S.C.A. § 422A.
40. This clause and succeeding clauses in this section are taken from West's Modern Legal Forms § 3122, unless otherwise stated.
41. Prentice-Hall, Corporations, Forms ¶ 31,121.
42. The Model Business Corporation Act and most states require the affirmative vote of the holders of a majority of the voting stock to approve such action. See M.B.C.A. § 7.25 and "Shareholder Meetings—Voting of Shares" in Chapter 8.
43. Int.Rev.Code of 1986, 26 U.S.C.A. § 101(b).

11 AGREEMENTS REGARDING SHARE OWNERSHIP

PURPOSES AND LEGAL SUPPORT

In a previous discussion of special corporate forms, the close corporation was studied.[1] Ownership of the close corporation is usually held by a clique of shareholders, who may also be the acting management of the corporation. The control exercised by the shareholders is a significant characteristic of this special corporate form, and this exclusive control may be protected by various provisions and agreements that prevent the sale of stock to persons outside of the select shareholder group. Share transfer restrictions are designed to preserve present ownership interests, and these restrictions may be drafted as a limitation upon the capital stock structure in the articles of incorporation or may be the subject matter of a shareholder agreement to which all of the shareholders and the corporation are parties.

Restrictions on the transfer of shares are recognized as a viable and legal way to retain ownership control among a closed group of people, with one important limitation. Since corporate shares are personal property of the shareholder, and since the law will not enforce an agreement that completely nullifies property rights, an agreement restricting the transfer of shares may not completely and irrevocably prohibit the sale of the stock. An agreement may, however, impose all sorts of restrictions that discourage sale to outsiders, and it may require that the shares must first be offered to the corporation or the other shareholders before they may be sold elsewhere. Although the selling shareholder must be able to sell the stock in the end, the shareholder may be required to satisfy a maze of conditions before doing so.

There are also shareholder agreements designed to concentrate voting power, with a group of shareholders pooling their votes under a contract that prescribes in advance how their shares will be voted on certain matters. Whatever control can be wielded by the concerted action of the total shares represented by the agreement will be applied to a vote on the specified corporate issues. The typical issues covered by shareholder voting agreements include the election of directors, amendments to the articles of incorporation, mergers, consolidation, dissolution, and sales or other disposition of assets. Although these agreements are not unique to close corporations, they may be used in that setting to establish a predetermined voting position on such matters as salaries and dividends, especially where the shareholders are also employees of the corporation and are receiving salaries in lieu of dividends.

Shareholder voting agreements are commonly used to protect minority shareholders from abusive action by the majority shareholders. Recall that there are other provisions, statutory and by agreement, that protect the minority shareholders from the dangers of oppressive majority control. Cumulative voting is specifically designed to ensure minority shareholder representation on the board of directors (but an agreement among minority shareholders may still be necessary to effectively utilize cumulative voting).[2] The articles of incorporation may also require greater-than-majority voting requirements for shareholder action. For example, if the articles of incorporation exacted a 90% affirmative vote on all shareholder matters, an 11% minority shareholder could effectively veto any unwanted action. However, the majority shareholders may not appreciate this, and the incorporators must consider the potential dissatisfaction of majority shareholders when the articles are drafted. After all, the majority shareholders do invest the majority of capital. Some state statutes require a greater-than-majority vote for major changes in the corporate structure, such as amendments to the articles of incorporation, merger, and so forth,[3] and the minority shareholders receive some protection against modifications to their ownership interests in the corporation. Finally, judicial decisions support a cause of action by the minority shareholders against majority shareholders for oppression of the minority interest, but all would agree that it is far more desirable to avoid that oppression through concentrated voting power rather than by subsequent litigation.

The Model Business Corporation Act grants statutory approval of shareholder voting agreements. Section 7.31 states that such agreements shall be valid and specifically enforceable according to their terms. Common law has long recognized the ability of shareholders to predetermine their position by agreement on normal shareholder business, such as electing directors. A rule has developed, however, that frowns upon any shareholder agreement that impinges on the statutory rules or usurps the power of the board of directors. For example, shareholders cannot agree that a quorum for shareholder meetings shall be one-fourth of the total voting shares, since the minimum allowable by statute is one-third in most jurisdictions.[4] Similarly, a shareholder agreement that a particular person will be continuously maintained as an officer of the corporation may be ineffective because the authority to select officers belongs to the directors. Several states have adopted statutory rules that would permit the last agreement, but further add that the shareholders must bear full responsibility for managerial acts governed by their agreement.[5]

Leaving aside agreements that encroach upon director discretion or regulate other managerial acts, there is no question that shareholders may agree regarding the manner in which their shares will be voted on issues normally requiring shareholder action.

CONCENTRATION OF VOTING POWER

In addition to the statutory and chartered rules that protect the minority interest (cumulative voting and greater-than-majority voting requirements), shareholders may pool their votes in an agreement executed among themselves, and thereby concentrate their aggregate voting power on each shareholder issue. There are formal ways and informal ways to do this. The formal voting trust ensures a more reliable concentration of power, since it prevents the possibility of a divided position from a shareholder who subsequently decides to act independently. The informal voting or pooling agreement is much easier to operate and may exist for longer periods of time.

Voting Trust

The formal approach to the concentration of shareholder voting power is a device called the voting trust. Voting trusts are permitted under the Model Business Corporation Act and in most jurisdictions, and the statutory requirements must be strictly followed. The voting trust is a trust arrangement in every sense of the term. The shares represented by this agreement are placed in trust, out of the hands of the shareholders, and a designated voting trustee is directed to vote the shares represented by the trust in accordance with the terms of the agreement. The duration of a voting trust is limited to a period of 10 years under the Model Business Corporation Act.[6] A few states increase the term to 15 years,[7] and a couple permit a 21-year period.[8] Extensions for an additional period of 10 years are permitted in the Model Business Corporation Act and in several jurisdictions. The shareholders who are parties to a voting trust surrender their shares to the trust and the voting trustee becomes the record owner of those shares, thereby ensuring that the trustee is notified of every shareholder meeting and that the trustee will have the legal right to vote the shares at such meetings. The shareholder is issued a voting trust certificate rep_____ shares of stock he or she once held. Voting trust certificates may be _____ rtificates themselves, although the purchaser take_____ trust, which are stated on the certificate. The ce_____ he trustee and other important matters respecti_____

Under the Model Business Corporation Act, a voting trust becomes effective on the date that the first shares subject to the trust are registered in the trustee's name.[9] To meet the specific statutory requirements of most states and the act, the trust must be established as follows:

1. A written trust agreement must be prepared specifying the terms and conditions of the trust and conferring upon the trustee the right to vote the shares represented by the trust
2. The shares represented must be transferred to the trustee in return for voting trust certificates
3. The term of the agreement shall not be more than the statutory period
4. The trustee must keep a record of all beneficiaries (shareholders) with their names and addresses and the number of shares deposited with the trust
5. A counterpart of the trust agreement and the record of beneficiaries must be deposited with the corporation at its registered office

Several jurisdictions omit the requirement of the trustee's record of beneficiaries, but most of the other requirements are the same.

The voting trust agreement must strictly observe the statutory requirements, for a failure to do so may invalidate the trust. The agreement should specify its duration (within the statutory limit) and may provide for termination at any time by a prescribed vote of the beneficiaries. The designation of the trustees should state any qualifications the parties intend to impose, such as requiring the trustees to be shareholders or prohibiting any director of the corporation from acting as trustee. The description of authority should carefully detail the power of the trustees to vote the stock, naming specific issues if the trust is so limited, or granting total voting power of the stock to the trustees. The decisions of the trustees may be based upon the trustees' good judgment, or the agreement may require that the trustees obtain the consensus of a certain percentage of the beneficiaries before casting the trust vote. The trustees should also be excused from liability for their actions, except for gross negligence, and should be indemnified for expenses and liabilities incurred in the exercise of their trust power. The procedure for the transfer and issuance of voting trust certificates must also be detailed. Finally, ministerial duties of the trustees in receiving and paying dividends of the stock, filing documents with the corporation, and recording voting trust certificates may be specified.

A sample voting trust agreement with a voting trust certificate is Form 11A in Appendix G.

Stock Voting Agreement

Another agreement designed to concentrate shareholder voting power is a voting or pooling agreement, which may accomplish the same purpose as the voting trust, but usually is not subject to the same statutory regulation. Several shareholders join together and pool their respective voting interests, predetermining the manner in which the shares will be voted by the agreement.

Stock voting agreements may be quite informal and may vary depending upon the desires of the parties, since there is virtually no statutory regulation governing their formation and interpretation. Section 7.31 of the Model Business Corporation Act simply provides that "two or more shareholders may provide for the manner in which they will vote their shares by signing an agreement for that purpose." Voting agreements that are created under Section 7.31 are not subject to the rules concerning voting trusts in Section 7.30. In principle, then, a stock voting agreement could last indefinitely, as contrasted with the voting trust having a limited term. The voting agreement may also be a secret, if that is desirable, since no evidence of the agreement need be deposited with the corporation.

Stock voting agreements have traditionally suffered from one serious deficiency: their enforceability. Unlike voting trust agreements, stock voting agreements do not require shareholders to deposit their shares with anyone. The shareholders merely agree to vote the shares, which they still control, in the same manner as do the other parties to the agreement. Suppose Wagner, Naylor, and Shaklee enter into a stock pooling agreement that they will all vote the same way on shareholder matters, and the manner in which all votes will be cast will be determined by a majority vote among them. Suppose further that on a given issue Wagner and Naylor want the votes cast one way, but Shaklee dissents. If Shaklee refuses to abide by the decision, he may still cast the votes he controls any way he wants. The other parties may be able to sue him for breach of the pooling agreement, but the most important objective, the concentrated voting power, has been lost on that issue. This could not happen in a formal voting trust. In an effort to solve this problem, the new Model Business Corporation Act provides that a voting agreement will be specifically enforceable, meaning that a shareholder could be required by a court to cast his or her vote in conformity with the agreement. Very few states have adopted this provision.

Another problem unique to the voting agreement arises if one of the parties to the agreement decides to sell the stock. The concentrated voting power is lost if the purchaser is not obliged to abide by the agreement. A typical response to this problem is to impose a restriction on the transfer of stock held by the parties to the agreement requiring an offer to sell the stock to be directed to the other parties before the shares may be sold to a nonparty investor.

> **EXAMPLE: Restriction on Transfer of Stock**
> Neither party will sell any shares of stock in the corporation to any other person whomsoever, without first making a written offer to the other party hereto of all of the shares proposed to be sold, for the same price and upon the same terms and conditions as in such proposed sale, and allowing such other party a time of not less than 180 days from the date of such written offer within which to accept same.

The stock voting agreement requires joint action of the participants in exercising their voting rights. The joint action may be required on all matters submitted to the vote of the shareholders, or may be limited to certain issues where concentration of voting power is deemed to be important, such as amendments to the articles, election of directors, and so forth. An example of a joint action clause covering all shareholders' matters looks like this:

> **EXAMPLE: Joint Action**
> In exercising any voting rights to which either party may be entitled by virtue of ownership of stock held by them in the corporation each party will consult and confer with the other and the parties will act jointly in exercising such voting rights in accordance with such agreement as they may reach with respect to any matter calling for the exercise of such voting rights.[10]

The determination of how the votes will be cast is made by agreement of the participants, and, if there are more than two parties to the agreement, a formula should be prescribed for this determination. For example, the agreement could require the unanimous vote of the shareholders represented by the agreement, but this may be an impossible criterion to satisfy. A provision allowing the determination of position to be made by a majority of the shares represented by the agreement would be more practicable. If a deadlock is possible under the agreement, as it might be if only two shareholders were parties, a provision regarding arbitration is appropriate.

> **EXAMPLE: Arbitration**
> In the event the parties fail to agree with respect to any matter covered by the preceding paragraph the question in disagreement shall be submitted for arbitration to D. S. Charlton, of Montgomery, Alabama, as arbitrator and his decision thereon shall be binding upon the parties hereto. Such arbitration shall be exercised to the end of assuring good management for the corporation. The parties may at any time by written agreement designate any other individual to act as arbitrator in lieu of said D. S. Charlton.

Duration and termination provisions should be included, reflecting the desires of the parties as to such matters.

> **EXAMPLE: Duration**
> This agreement shall be in effect from the date hereof and shall continue in effect for a period of ten years unless sooner terminated by mutual agreement in writing by the parties hereto.[11]

Agreements to Secure Director Representation

Since corporate management is vested in the board of directors, and the board of directors is elected by the shareholders, the board is usually elected by the majority shareholders, particularly when cumulative voting is not in effect. Even if cumulative voting is used in the election of directors, the minority shareholders may have to unite to secure representation of the board.[12] Consequently, the minority shareholders frequently are not represented on the board of directors.

An assurance of minority representation on the board may be accomplished by agreement in two ways. With the first method, using the concentration of minority voting power, a shareholder voting agreement or voting trust may predetermine the manner in which the parties to the agreement will vote at the election of the directors. The terms of this agreement would provide that all parties to the agreement (or the trustee) would vote for a person who, according to a majority of the persons represented by the agreement (or other formula determination), would best represent the interests of the parties. With the second method, there would be an agreement among *all* shareholders that certain positions on the board of directors would be reserved to the nominee of the minority shareholders, and that all shareholders would vote to elect the minority nominee to the board at each election.

> **EXAMPLE: Agreement to Segregate the Board of Directors**
> That the number of the members of the Board of Directors of Trouble, Inc. be reduced from five, as it now is, to the number of four, that the number of members of said Board of Directors shall be maintained at four in number, of which at all times two thereof shall be such persons as shall be nominated or designated by the said parties of the first part and the other two thereof shall be such persons as shall be nominated or designated by the said party of the second part. And it is further mutually agreed between the parties that at all stockholders' meetings of the said Trouble, Inc. held for the purpose of election of directors or director (in case of vacancy of the Board of Directors), that all of the said shares of stock of parties of the first part and also of party of the second part and also any additional shares of stock of the Trouble, Inc. which may be subsequently acquired by the said parties or either of them, shall be voted in such manner and for such person or persons as will keep and maintain the Board of Directors four in number, of which two thereof shall be such persons as shall be nominated or designated by said parties of the first part and two thereof shall be such persons as shall be nominated or designated by the said party of the second part.[13]

Instead of the general description "minority nominee," it is possible to name a certain person in the shareholder agreement and agree that he or she will be continually elected as a director to represent the specialized shareholder interests. However, these agreements have been subjected to careful scrutiny by the courts, and have been declared invalid if they fail to leave room for the defeat of an incompetent director. On the other hand, a shareholder agreement will be enforceable if it states that a named director will be maintained in office as long as that person faithfully and conscientiously performs the duties of that office. Therefore, it is good practice to include a *savings clause* making the election of a particular director obligatory only if that person is competent to serve in that position.

SHARE TRANSFER RESTRICTIONS AND BUY-OUT AGREEMENTS

Shareholder agreements are frequently concerned with restrictions on the transfer of shares. These restrictions are not necessarily directed to the protection of special shareholder stock voting agreements. Usually the restrictions on transfer are intended to protect all shareholders who desire to avoid alienation or interference with corporate control. Minority shareholders could suffer greatly if majority shareholders were allowed to sell their shares and the associated control of the corporation to an outsider who is not sympathetic to the minority interest. Similarly, majority shareholders may suffer from the sale of even one share to a recalcitrant, argumentative shareholder, particularly in a close corporation where all of the shareholders must work closely to further the enterprise.

Restrictions on transfer of shares may be imposed in the articles of incorporation, the by-laws, or separate shareholder agreements. The corporation should also be a party to the restrictive agreement. The thrust of most restrictive agreements is to prohibit the transfer of shares to an outsider without first offering them for sale to the corporation or to the other shareholders.

Agreements affecting share ownership may also specify mandatory buy-out or sellout arrangements, directed to the corporation and the shareholders, but the objectives here are opposite from those of the share transfer restrictions. While share transfer restrictions are intended to discourage the transfer of shares, mandatory buy-out or sellout arrangements are designed to require the transfer of shares. The intracorporate groups may prefer to prohibit share ownership by a person who is not actively engaged in the business, and a mandatory sellout agreement may satisfy this objective. On the other hand, a shareholder may wish to ensure the existence of a market to sell his or her shares, and this can be accomplished through a mandatory buy-out agreement. In small, closely held corporations the shares may not be marketable, and without a mandatory buy-out agreement, a shareholder has no choice but to hold the shares indefinitely with no prospect of receiving a return of invested capital until the corporation is dissolved.

Restrictive Agreements

Section 6.27 of the Model Business Corporation Act provides statutory authority for an agreement among shareholders concerning restrictions on the transfer of shares of the corporation. The restrictions may be contained in the articles of incorporation, the by-laws, or a separate agreement. The share transfer restriction is authorized

1. to maintain the corporation's status when that status is dependent on the number or identity of the corporation's shareholders (such as when a corporation makes a Subchapter S election for tax purposes);

2. to preserve exemptions under federal or state laws (such as when a corporation offers shares privately to shareholders and does not register the shares with the Securities and Exchange Commission); and
3. to accomplish any other reasonable purpose.

The validity of a share transfer restriction will depend, in part, upon the nature and structure of the business conducted. The restriction must be adopted for a lawful purpose, and it may be necessary to show that there is a special need for a share transfer restriction in the particular type of business or in the particular relationship between shareholders. This should not be an onerous burden, but it should be considered when a share transfer restriction is adopted by the parties. There is ample reason to support the restriction in small, close corporations, but, in any case, the agreement should recite that its purpose is to further harmonious relations between the parties and to promote the best interests of the business.

The most effective way to ensure that no outsider will be admitted to a select shareholder group is to completely and forever prohibit the sale of the stock to any person at any time. This complete prohibition on transferability is certainly restrictive, but it is also unenforceable and against public policy. Agreements that indefinitely prohibit the exercise of personal rights are presumed to be unfair, and it is virtually impossible to muster any rational reason to support such a severe restriction.

The most common restriction used to control the transfer of shares grants the corporation or the other shareholders the first option to purchase shares before those shares may be sold to an outsider.

Events Triggering the Restriction. A stock transfer restriction is normally triggered when a selling shareholder has received a valid and sincere offer to purchase his or her shares. If the agreement does not provide for some method of determining whether an offer is valid and sincere, the shareholder may manipulate the agreement to force the corporation or the other shareholders either to buy the stock when the shareholder gives the appropriate notice, or to run the risk that the stock will be free from any transfer restriction if the corporation or the other shareholders fail to purchase the shares. Thus, some definition of a good-faith offer to purchase should be included in every restriction, and several possibilities exist for establishing the validity of a good-faith offer.

1. The agreement should provide that the offer to purchase the shares from an outside investor should be in writing.
2. The agreement may provide that the good-faith offer must be supported by an earnest-money deposit.
3. The agreement may provide that the good-faith offer must be supported by an escrow of the total purchase price, the terms of which would provide that in the event the corporation or the other shareholders fail to purchase their proportionate share of the selling shareholder's stock, the escrow proceeds would be distributed automatically to the selling shareholder and the stock would be deemed to have been purchased at that time.
4. The agreement may or may not provide for the disclosure of the identity of the good-faith purchaser, since the corporation or the other shareholders may be able to manipulate the agreement by ascertaining the identity of the good-faith purchaser and attempting to thwart the sale or sell other shares to this purchaser, thereby discouraging the purchase from the proposed selling shareholder.

> **EXAMPLE: Bona Fide Offer**
> Upon receipt of a bona fide offer to purchase the shares by a person not a shareholder of the corporation, a selling shareholder must follow the restrictions contained in this article prior to selling any shares of stock to the offeror. A bona fide offer shall require that the offeror place an amount equal to the purchase price of the stock in escrow, the terms of which shall require the release of said funds for the purchase of the stock if the corporation and other shareholders do not exercise their options hereunder, and contain an agreement from the offeror to be bound by the terms of these restrictions upon purchase of such shares.

Other events may also be the subject of a stock transfer restriction that prevents the free transferability of shares under certain conditions. For example, the death of a shareholder may require that the heirs or representatives of the deceased shareholder must offer the shares to the corporation or to the other shareholders. Similarly, retirement, disability, bankruptcy, or loss of a professional or occupational license necessary to the business of the corporation may trigger a stock transfer restriction. In these cases, however, it is more likely that the agreement would provide for a mandatory purchase or sale upon the happening of the event. These mandatory agreements are discussed in greater detail later in this section.

Option to Purchase. The usual option-to-purchase share transfer restriction requires that an offer to sell be directed first to the corporation, which has a right of refusal, and then to the other shareholders, who also have the right of refusal to purchase the shares. If both the corporation and the shareholders decline to purchase the shares, then the selling shareholder may sell to the outsider. Alternatively, the restriction may run only to the corporation, or may bypass the corporation and grant the option to purchase only to the other shareholders. When the other shareholders are granted the option to purchase, the shares will usually be offered to them in the same proportion as their present ownership interests in the corporation.

An example of a provision granting a right of refusal to the corporation and then to the remaining shareholders follows.

> **EXAMPLE: Option to Purchase Shares**
> Should any shareholder wish to dispose of his or her stock, it shall first be offered to the corporation at a price no greater than a bona fide offer by any third person, and in no event at a price greater than the par value and the proportionate share of any earned surplus, and said stock shall be available to the corporation for a period of thirty days. In the event that any of the said stock is not purchased by the corporation, it shall be offered to the remaining shareholders of the same class of stock in the same proportion as their respective stock interests in said class of stock, for a like price and for a similar period of time. In the event any of the remaining shareholders declines to purchase his or her proportionate share of said stock, that share shall be offered to the then remaining shareholders of the same class of stock for a like price and for a similar period of time. In the event that any of said stock is not purchased by the corporation or the shareholders, the remaining stock may then be sold by the shareholder at the price of the bona fide offer of the third person.

By way of illustration, suppose the Nobles Company has three shareholders: Dworet, who owns 100 shares; Rezabeck, who owns 200 shares; and Weiler, who owns 300 shares. If Dworet desires to sell her shares and receives a bona fide offer for the purchase, she must first offer to sell the shares to the corporation at the price determined by the formula, and the corporation shall have 30 days to reject or accept the offer. If the corporation rejects the offer, Dworet must then offer the shares to Rezabeck and Weiler, who own the same class of stock in a 2:3 ratio, since Rezabeck owns 200 shares and Weiler owns 300 shares. Rezabeck and Weiler may then purchase in that ratio, meaning that Rezabeck can purchase 40 shares and Weiler can purchase 60 shares. If Rezabeck declines to purchase the shares to which she is entitled, those shares must then be offered to Weiler, or vice versa, according to the sample provision. Only if the corporation and the other two shareholders decline to purchase the shares may Dworet sell the shares to the outsider.

Any variations in this scheme are permissible.

Considerations in Designating the Option to Purchase. There are a couple of practical observations to consider in drafting the restriction. The first offer to the corporation is desirable because a profitable corporation will probably have funds legally available to purchase the shares. Moreover, it is more convenient to make the offer to the corporation through a single notice than to notify all of the other shareholders. The remaining shareholders may also prefer that the purchase funds come from internal corporate operations rather than that they attempt to raise funds individually. However, there may be situations when the corporation is not permitted to buy its own shares because of statutory restrictions on the funds that must be used for that purpose. If funds are not legally available, the corporation must refuse the offer, and, to preserve the viability of the restriction, the offer should then run to the individual shareholders.

If the corporation is going to exercise an option to purchase or redeem its shares, it must do so in strict compliance with statutory restrictions on funds available for repurchase. Provided the corporation is solvent (and the purchase of shares will not render it insolvent), in many states the corporation may purchase its own shares only to the extent that it has unreserved and unrestricted surplus.[14] Under Section 6.40 of the Model Business Corporation Act, the corporation may acquire its own shares so long as the funds distributed for the purchase will not reduce the corporation's net assets below the aggregate amount payable to shareholders with liquidation rights upon involuntary liquidation and dissolution of the corporation.[15] The surplus requirements under the applicable statute have nothing to do with the availability of cash to effect a repurchase, except insofar as the corporation must be able to pay its debts and liabilities as they fall due after distributing a portion of its surplus. The corporation may have sufficient cash for the stock purchase, but insufficient surplus, or there may be enough surplus on the corporation's books, but no ready cash.

The corporation may use life insurance as a method of funding a buy-out agreement, especially when the event triggering the buy-out is death. Life insurance funding may also be used when the triggering event is retirement, disability, or termination of employment. These funding options are discussed in greater detail later.

The remaining shareholders may find raising funds to buy out a withdrawing shareholder a difficult task, particularly if they must come up with the cash immediately on a shareholder's death or some other triggering event. The problem may be alleviated if the agreement provides for installment payments.

The agreement should permit those who elect to purchase more than their pro rata shares to divide equitably among themselves any shares not taken on the first division. If some shares still remain, the agreement should provide whether the original number or only the untaken shares may be sold to an outsider. Another question is whether the selling shareholder may break his or her stock holdings into small blocks and offer them to several people, thus obtaining a higher price per share. If the parties wish to eliminate these possibilities, the agreement should specifically prohibit such actions.

All-or-Nothing Purchase. A choice must be made at the drafting stage between a restriction permitting a partial purchase of the offered stock or one requiring a purchase of all or nothing. Continuing with the example of the Nobles Company, presumably Dworet has received an offer from an outsider to buy her 100 shares at a price. The question now is whether the corporation or the other shareholders may purchase only a portion of her 100 shares in exercising the right of first refusal, or whether they must buy the entire block to exercise the option. Dworet is better protected if they must buy the entire block, since the outsider may not be interested in a purchase of only a portion of the 100 shares. However, the corporation and remaining shareholders have a greater guarantee against stock transfers if they are permitted to exercise their options in part, since they may then buy just enough of the stock to discourage the outsider, but they are not compelled to purchase all offered shares to prevent transfer. In the spirit of fairness, it is better practice to require the corporation to exercise its option in full or not at all. When the corporation refuses purchase, and the offer is made to remaining shareholders, the restriction should further specify a procedure to prevent portion purchases for the protection of the selling shareholder.

When more than one shareholder is entitled to an option to purchase, it is possible that some shareholders will exercise their options and others will not. In that case, a portion of the offered shares is available for sale to the outsider, but the outsider's interest in the purchase may dwindle after the number of shares has been reduced. To avoid this result, the restriction could provide that if all of the options are not exercised none of them may be, and this will preserve the block of stock intact. Alternatively, if the restrictions permit some shareholders to refuse the option without impairing the rights of the other shareholders to exercise their options, it should further specify that the shares that have been refused will be offered to the shareholders who intend to exercise their options. These last shareholders have evidenced an interest in purchasing their quota of the offered stock; perhaps they will also purchase the remaining shares. This second chance for internal sale, which also furthers the objectives of the remaining shareholders by granting another opportunity to avoid alienation of the shares, appears in the preceding example, "Option to Purchase Shares." Observe that if not all shares of the selling shareholder are purchased under the agreement, the amount paid by the corporation to the selling shareholder may be taxed as a dividend.[16]

In sum, the most fair and effective share transfer restriction will first grant the corporation the right to purchase all of the offered shares at a specified price. If the corporation refuses to buy all of the shares, then the other shareholders will have a right to purchase the offered shares according to their respective proportionate stock interests at a specified price. The restriction should then provide that if some shareholders do not exercise their options then none of them may, or that the remaining unpurchased shares must be offered to the shareholders who have exercised their options before they may be sold to an outsider.

Mandatory Buy-out or Sellout Provisions

The foregoing restrictions on transfer of shares are designed to avoid the alienation of shares and the potential loss of control of the corporation. Both goals are accomplished by granting the corporation or other shareholders the right of first refusal when shares are offered for sale. However, the shareholder may not be able to sell his or her shares to anybody (especially if the shareholder has invested in a small, closely held corporation), and then the shareholder deserves some protection. The shareholder agreement may *require* the corporation or the other shareholders to purchase the shares under certain circumstances. Conversely, the corporation may demand the right to purchase certain shares, such as when a shareholder-employee retires or quits. Thus, depending on the purpose to be served, mandatory buy or sell provisions may work both ways: the contract may require the corporation or other shareholders to purchase the shares, or it may require the shareholder to sell the shares.

Mandatory buy-out agreements reflect an *obligation* on the part of the corporation and other shareholders to purchase the selling shareholder's stock, as distinguished from an *option* on their part to buy under the share transfer restriction. These mandatory provisions are designed to guarantee a market for the stock, which may be needed particularly by a minority shareholder. The minority shareholder cannot sell if no willing purchasers are available, and the minority shareholder is powerless to force dissolution to recoup invested capital if the majority shareholders resist. The majority shareholders may also need the guarantee. Willing purchasers may be even harder to find for a larger block of stock, and while the majority shareholders could force dissolution, that may be an unwise business decision and may constitute oppression of the minority shareholders.

On the other hand, the mandatory buy-out agreement may also impose the *obligation* on the part of the shareholder or the shareholder's representatives upon the occurrence of a triggering event to sell the shares to the corporation or to the other shareholders. The corporation and the other shareholders may thereby protect against the ownership of shares by persons who are strangers to the enterprise, such as the heirs of a deceased shareholder, a trustee in bankruptcy, or the representatives of a disabled shareholder.

Events Commonly Triggering Buy-outs. A mandatory buy-out agreement is usually conditioned upon the death of a shareholder, the retirement of a shareholder at a certain age or after a specified length of service to the corporation, the disability of a shareholder, the bankruptcy of a shareholder, the loss of a shareholder's occupational license, or any attempt by a shareholder to force a dissolution of the corporation under statutory dissolution sections.[17]

The event triggering the buy-out should be clearly defined, and, in many cases where life insurance or other insurance is used to fund the buy-out agreement, the definition of the contingent event should contain the same terms as the definition of that event under the insurance policies that are expected to fund the purchase. For example, if the disability of a shareholder will trigger a buy-out, the agreement should define *disability* in the same method as the insurance policy defines the term, or the agreement should refer to the insurance policy definition. Further, after a specified period of time of continuous disability, again as defined in the insurance policy, a buy-out will occur with the proceeds of the insurance policy.

EXAMPLE: Purchase on Death
The Company will have the option, for a period commencing with the death of any shareholder and ending 60 days following the qualification of his or her executor or administrator, to purchase all of the shares owned by the decedent, at the price and terms provided in this agreement. The option shall be exercised by giving notice to the decedent's estate or other successor in interest in accordance with this agreement. If the option is not exercised within such 60-day period as to all shares owned by the decedent, the surviving shareholders shall have the option, for a period of 30 days commencing with the end of that 60-day period to purchase all of the shares owned by the decedent, at the price on the terms provided in this agreement. The option shall be exercised by giving notice, in accordance with this agreement, to the executor or administrator, stating the number of shares as to which it is exercised. If notice of exercise from the surviving shareholders specify in the aggregate more shares than are available for purchase by the shareholders, each shareholder shall have priority, up to the number of shares specified in his or her notice, to such proportion of those available shares as the number of Company shares he or she holds bears to the number of the Company shares held by all shareholders electing to purchase. The shares not purchased on such a priority basis shall be allocated in one or more successive allocations to those shareholders electing to purchase more than the number of shares to which they have a priority right, up to the number of shares specified in their respective notices, in the proportion that the number of shares held by each of them bears to the number of shares held by all of them. In the event this option is not exercised as to all of the shares owned by the decedent, his or her estate will hold those shares subject to the provisions of this agreement.

EXAMPLE: Purchase on Other Events
In the event any shareholder is adjudicated a bankrupt (voluntary or involuntary), or makes an assignment for the benefit of his or her creditors, or is physically or mentally incapacitated for more than three months, the event of incapacity as described in an insurance policy now owned by the corporation with the Equitable Life Insurance Corporation, Policy No. 40-82-123, the Company and the remaining shareholders shall have the option for a period of 90 days following notice of any such event to purchase all of the shares owned by the shareholder. Notice shall be given to the shareholder or his or her representative in accordance with this agreement. The option shall be exercisable first by the Company and thereafter by the remaining shareholders, and the price, terms of purchase, and methods of exercise of the option shall be the same as are provided in this agreement to apply in the event of death. In the event this option is not exercised as to all of the shares owned by the shareholder, he or she or his or her successor in interest will own the shares subject to the provisions of this agreement.

The compelling reasons for these types of agreements are easy to appreciate. The shares of a small corporation are not generally marketable and the beneficiaries or legatees of a deceased shareholder or the representatives of a disabled shareholder are not usually interested in holding shares in the business the shareholder enjoyed while the shareholder was productive in the business. Moreover, as an employee, the shareholder was probably receiving a salary instead of dividends, and dividends are rare in a small corporation anyway. Consequently, if the stock is not readily marketable, the salary is terminated, and since there are no dividends or other emoluments of share ownership, the beneficiaries or representatives of the shareholder will receive nothing from the share ownership, unless the corporation and the other shareholders are required to purchase the shares.

Mandatory sellout agreements are frequently adjunct to employment contracts, the terms of which contemplate issuance of shares as an incentive to performance. If the employee was misjudged and is subsequently terminated, the corporation has the right to buy back the shares. The agreement may also be separately executed to prevent continued stock ownership by any person for whatever reason. The shareholder is required to sell the shares to the corporation or to the other shareholders if they insist on the sale, with appropriate notice. The price is usually established in the agreement, as discussed in detail later, and provisions for surrender of shares should be included.

> **EXAMPLE: Common Stock of One Leaving Employ of Corporation May Be Purchased**
> In the event that any holder of the common stock of this corporation who may now or hereafter be an officer or employee of this corporation ceases, for any reason, to be such officer or employee, and provided further that the Board of Directors shall require it, by resolution passed at a special meeting called for that express purpose on not less than 2 days notice, the corporation or any officer or any common stockholder subscribing to this agreement shall have the option, within 30 days after such person shall cease to be an officer or employee, to purchase all of the common stock held by such person ceasing to be an officer or employee, at a price to be determined by the same method as hereinabove provided, and the tender of the amount of such purchase price shall operate to transfer and vest said shares of common stock in the corporation or officer or stockholder making such tender, and the common stockholder who has thus ceased to be an officer or employee shall, upon such payment or tender, transfer, assign and set over his or her common stock to the officer or common stockholder exercising such option.[18]

Considerations in Designating the Mandatory Purchase Requirement. The agreement should bind the corporation and the other shareholders to the purchase. However, the corporation's ability to purchase shares, even though required by the agreement, is limited by most state statutes, and the corporation may not have funds legally available for the purchase. In that event, the agreement should obligate the other shareholders to purchase their proportionate share of the stock, or to vote in favor of dissolution of the corporation. The latter provision would anticipate the possibility that the individual shareholders also cannot afford the purchase.

If the other shareholders are to buy the shares under the agreement, a procedure should be specified to proportion the shares they are permitted to purchase among them in the same ratio as their existing share ownership. (See the earlier example "Purchase on Death.")

Mechanics of the Agreement

Notice Procedure. The agreement should always establish a notice procedure to advise the corporation and the other shareholders of the intended sale (in the case of the stock transfer restriction) or to advise the persons holding the shares of a shareholder subject to a mandatory buy-out agreement that the option to purchase is being exercised. This notice procedure should further state a time period for a decision to purchase or refuse and for surrender of the shares.

> **EXAMPLE: Notice of Sale**
>
> The shareholder shall notify the directors of a desire to sell or transfer by notice in writing, which notice shall contain the price at which the shareholder is willing to sell. The directors shall within thirty days thereafter either accept or reject the offer by notice to the shareholder in writing. After the acceptance of the offer, the directors shall have thirty days within which to purchase the same at such valuation, but if at the expiration of thirty days, the corporation shall not have exercised the right to so purchase, the owner of the stock shall be at liberty to dispose of the same in any manner he or she may see fit.[19]

> **EXAMPLE: Notice to Purchase**
>
> The Company shall have the option, for a period commencing with the death of any shareholder and ending 30 days following the death of the shareholder, to purchase any part of the shares owned by the decedent, at the price and on the terms provided in this agreement. The option shall be exercised by giving notice of it to the decedent's estate or other successor in interest in writing. Such notice shall be deemed to have been duly given on the date of service if served personally on the party to whom notice is to be given, or within 72 hours after mailing if mailed to the party to whom notice is to be given by first class mail, registered or certified, postage prepaid and properly addressed to the party of his or her address set forth on the signature page of this agreement, or any other address that that party may designate by written notice to the other parties of this agreement.

Price Provisions. Any shareholder agreement involving the purchase and sale of stock must specify the price and payment terms applicable to the transaction. Restrictions on share transfer that require the offer of shares to the corporation and/or the remaining shareholders must establish a price for the offer. Similarly, mandatory buy-out or sellout agreements must specify the price to be paid.

Competing interests frequently arise in the negotiation of the price term. The shareholder would usually prefer to receive the highest price in cash as soon as possible, while the purchaser would usually prefer to pay the lowest price over the longest period of time. Many practical considerations also arise. For one thing, extended payment provisions always involve some risk for the selling shareholder, since the purchaser may become insolvent, may be unable to pay for another reason, or may simply refuse to pay. However, immediate payment in cash may be unrealistic depending upon the number of shares involved and the cash position of the purchaser.

The price provisions of the buy-out or restrictive agreement may accomplish several objectives. Depending upon the clients' desires, the following objective should be considered.

1. What price will estimate most accurately the value of the stock in case of a buy-out or sellout?
2. What price term will reflect most permanently the formula necessary to value the stock accurately?
3. What assets will be used to fund the stock purchase, and, if insurance proceeds are anticipated, will the price vary from the availability of the proceeds, and if so, in what manner?
4. Is there a desire to use the price provision as a further restriction upon the transfer of the shares?
5. Will the price provision be so unrealistic that the entire agreement will be unenforceable?

To be fair, the price provision of the stock purchase agreement should attempt to accurately reflect the true value of the stock at the time of purchase. Even if the parties intend to use the price provision as an additional restriction on the stock, so that no shareholder will be motivated to attempt to sell the stock because the price at which it must be sold under the stock transfer restriction would be prohibitive, it should be noted that courts are reluctant to enforce a stock transfer restriction that contains an unrealistically low price for the transfer of the stock. The effect of such price provisions are to prohibit the sale of the stock, since no shareholder would attempt to locate a buyer if it were necessary to sell the stock to other shareholders or to the corporation at an unrealistically low price.

There are several ways to prescribe the price and method of payment for stock purchase agreements. These terms are always subject to negotiation by the parties. Moreover, counsel who represents the corporation may not be able to represent ethically the interests of the individual shareholders who are intended to be parties to the agreement.

Firm Price. The agreement may establish a firm price to be paid for shares, such as fifty dollars a share, which will be applied to any purchase of stock for the duration of the agreement. This practice should be discouraged except for extremely short term agreements or at the early stages of the corporation (when the price is difficult to establish from other sources). It is probable that the stated price will become unrealistic one way or the other over an extended period of time.

> **EXAMPLE: Firm Price**
> The price at which the shares are to be offered to the corporation or to the remaining shareholders shall be $2.00 per share for the first year of this agreement.

Adjusted Stated Value. The agreement may provide for a stated value with a procedure for periodic adjustment. This method allows modifications in price to account for changed circumstances over an extended period of time. Usually a stated price will be coupled with a further agreement that the shareholders of the corporation will evaluate and reset the stated value on a periodic basis. Of course, as in any situation where people are negotiating for price, it is possible that the shareholders will not be able to agree on the adjustment. Therefore, the provision should include a certain formula to compute the adjustment to stated value in case the parties do not agree upon an adjustment to the price. For example, in the absence of shareholder agreement, the stated value may be increased or decreased by a percentage of the net income or loss, or a reevaluation of the assets. Alternatively, arbitration may be used to resolve issues that prevent an agreement on price of the shares.

> **EXAMPLE: Agreed Price with Arbitration**
> The purchase price to be paid for each of the shares subject to this agreement shall be equal to the agreed value of the Company divided by the total number of shares outstanding as of the date of the price to be determined. The initial agreed value of the Company is $185,000.00, and on January 20 of each year hereafter, the parties to this agreement shall review the Company's financial condition as of the end of the preceding fiscal year and shall determine by mutual agreement the Company's fair market value, which, if agreed upon, shall be the Company's value until a

different value is agreed on or otherwise established under the provisions of this agreement. If the parties are able to reach mutual agreement, they shall evidence it by placing their written and executed agreement in the minute book of the Company.

If no valuation has been agreed upon within two years before the date of the event requiring determination of value, the value of a selling shareholder's interest shall be agreed upon by the selling shareholder or that shareholder's successor in interest and the remaining shareholders. If they do not mutually agree on a value within 60 days after the date of the event requiring the determination, the value of the selling shareholder's interest shall be determined by arbitration as follows: The remaining shareholders and the selling shareholder or that shareholder's successor in interest shall each name an arbitrator. If the two arbitrators cannot agree on a value, they shall appoint a third, and the decision of the majority shall be binding on all parties. Arbitration shall be in accordance with the rules of the American Arbitration Association as such rules shall be in effect at the time of arbitration.

Earnings Multiple Formula. A preferred method of determining the price of the stock is to specify a formula that will account for the success of the business, the value of the assets, and the desirability of the stock if a market existed for its sale. A common formula for evaluation of stock is a *multiple of earnings* formula.

An earnings multiple formula establishes the price of corporate stock by multiplying the earnings of the corporation by a stated figure, which is set when the agreement is negotiated. The multiplier may fluctuate in the agreement, depending upon the number of years the shares have been held, or upon the number of shares held. For example, a multiplier of 3 times earnings may apply to blocks of 100 shares or less, held less than 2 years; a multiplier of 4 times earnings may apply for blocks of 100 to 200 shares held less than 2 years; and so forth. The definition of *earnings* deserves attention in the agreement, which should specify whether earnings refers to net earnings before or after tax, and whether the will be determined by an average of several years' earnings or a current income figure.

The earnings multiple formula probably has no relation to the actual market value of the stock, if one exists, or to the book value of the stock. It simply ensures that if the corporation has increased its earnings during the agreed period, the shareholder who desires to sell stock will realize some benefit from that increase. On the other hand, if earnings have decreased, the shareholder will have suffered by waiting to sell shares. In the event the corporation loses money and the earnings multiple produces a negative figure, the agreement may contain a *savings provision* that in no event will the stock be valued at any less than a stated amount. This ensures that the stock will always have some minimum value, and is obviously a desirable provision from the shareholder's standpoint.

The provisions that establish the earnings multiple formula should specify a person who will determine earnings conclusively from a specified source. The company's accountant, who has prepared the financial statements under generally accepted accounting principles, should perhaps be specified as the person who will determine and compute earnings as of the date of the buy-out agreement. Moreover, it may be necessary in small, closely held corporations, to specify certain adjustments to earnings that will more accurately reflect the true earnings of the corporation for the period averaged. In closely held corporations, it is common to pay shareholder-employees salaries that may be higher than those normally paid for similar employees. It is also common to provide for greater-than-normal lease payments for shareholder-owned equipment, and greater-than-normal interest payments for shareholder loans. These expense figures should be addressed and adjusted in the earnings formula computation, to reflect more accurately the true value of the stock based upon earnings.

The determination of an earnings multiple is frequently a negotiated matter, and ultimately depends upon a reasonable rate of return in the industry. Rates of return for certain industries are published from time to time by economic marketing sources and business brokers, and they may be used as a guide in determining the appropriate rate of return to set the multiple for earnings. The shareholders themselves are frequently capable of estimating a reasonable rate of return, which, if agreed to, may be used as the multiple in the earnings formula.

> **EXAMPLE: Capitalized Earnings Formula**
> The purchase price to be paid for each of the shares subject to this agreement shall be determined as follows:
>
> The net profits of the Company for each of the three complete fiscal years preceding the date of determination of price for purposes of this agreement shall be adjusted by deducting from the Company's profits state and federal income taxes, lease payments to shareholders, salary payments to shareholders, and interest payments on loans from shareholders. The net profit figures for the three years, thus adjusted, shall be added, and the total shall be divided by three. The average adjusted net profit figure so obtained shall be multiplied by 10, and the result shall be divided by the number of shares of the Company's capital stock then outstanding.

Book Value Formula. A book value formula may be a more accurate estimate of the actual value of the shares, depending upon the definition of book value and the nature of the business. Usually book value is determined by dividing the net assets (total assets less total liabilities) by the number of the outstanding shares of the corporation. This means that each shareholder is entitled to a proportionate share of the assets and the purchase price of the shares will be an amount equal to this proportionate interest. In this case, of course, the purchase price will increase as net assets increase, and vice versa. The accuracy of the formula is affected by the nature of the business. A highly profitable organization may operate with few assets, in which case the book value will be considerably lower than the fair market value of the shares. Conversely, it may be possible for a business with many assets to have high book value for shares that are virtually worthless.

The book value should be determined by a specified person, and the clause containing the book value formula should provide some guidance for the computation of book value. Again, if an independent accountant is used to prepare the corporate balance sheets in accordance with generally accepted accounting principles, that person may make the sole determination of the book value at a specified time. In addition, if certain assets are undervalued on the balance sheet, such as real estate that may have appreciated considerably from the time it was purchased, or if liabilities are overstated, such as contingent liabilities that are not likely to be realized by the corporation, the book value formula should direct the accountant to adjust those figures to reflect more accurately the true value or liability.

To minimize the cost of a determination of book value at any point in time, it is advisable to provide that book value will be determined as of the date of the last financial statement prepared before the occurrence of a contingent event. In this regard, the financial statements will be prepared on a regular basis and it is much less expensive for the corporation to be able to use a regular financial statement rather than attempting to prepare a new balance sheet only for the purpose of estimating the value of the stock for the contingent event that has triggered a buy-out. It may, of course, be provided that the values contained on the last financial statement should be adjusted, upward or downward, to reflect material changes in current operations.

Since book value includes all the assets of the corporation, care must be taken to be certain not to include the proceeds of insurance that may be payable to the corporation and that were intended to be used to purchase the shares under the shareholder agreement. For example, if the corporation is expecting to use proceeds of life insurance to fund a buy-out in case of a shareholder's death, the proceeds should be specifically excluded from a determination of book value, since the corporation will be entitled to them upon the death of the shareholder, and they will appropriately increase the corporation's net assets.

> **EXAMPLE: Book Value**
> The purchase price to be paid for the shares subject to this agreement shall be their book value determined as of the most recent financial statement prepared by the Company's accountants with additions or subtractions for current operations up to the end of the month preceding the month in which the event requiring determination of the purchase price occurs. Book value shall be determined from the books of the Company according to generally accepted principles of cash accounting applied in a consistent manner by the accountants of the Company who customarily prepare the Company's financial statements. The Company's book value shall be equal to its assets, excluding any proceeds of insurance policies, less its liabilities, and the amount thus determined shall be divided by all shares of the Company's capital stock then outstanding.

Combination of Formulas. Since earnings multiple and book value formulas rarely accurately reflect the true market value of the stock, it may be appropriate to combine these formulas together with others, to attempt to estimate accurately the true value of the stock at the time of the purchase.

> **EXAMPLE: Formula to Determine Value (Book Value with Earnings)**
> If any holder of any shares of the common stock of this Corporation desires to dispose of the same or any part thereof, that shareholder shall not transfer or otherwise dispose of the same to any person unless and until he or she has first complied with the provisions hereof and given the other common stockholders of the Corporation who are entitled to the benefits of this contract an opportunity to purchase the same, as herein provided. The common stockholder desiring to dispose of all or any of his or her stock shall give written notice of such desire to each of the officers of this Corporation within the State of Montana, stating the number of shares he or she desires to sell. Any officer or any other common stockholder of the Corporation entitled to the benefits of this contract may, within thirty days after the service of such notice upon the last officer to be served, elect to purchase any part or all of the common stock so offered, and, in the event of the exercise of such option, the common stockholder so giving such notice of a desire to sell shall forthwith sell, assign, transfer and set over said shares of common stock to the officer or common stockholder electing to purchase the same, and the officer or common stockholder to whom the shares are so transferred shall, at the same time, pay to the seller, as and for the purchase price thereof, the amount of the book value of said common stock as shown upon the last annual statement of the Corporation, and in addition thereto an amount equal to the stock's pro rata proportion of the net profits of the

business of the Corporation for such fractional part of the fiscal year as has elapsed since the date as of which the last annual statement was made, less any dividends declared during said fractional period.

For the purpose of determining said profits, the amount of the average annual net profits of the Corporation for the two fiscal years preceding the last annual statement shall be assumed to be the amount of the net profits which the Corporation shall earn during the current fiscal year, and the amount of the net profits of the Corporation for the fractional period of the year since the last annual statement shall be considered as that proportion of the average annual net profits of said two preceding years as the length of time which has lapsed since the last annual statement bears to the period of a full year. For the purposes of this contract, until the first annual statement of the Corporation is made, the book value shall be determined on the figures at which this Corporation has purchased the business and property of Everready Associates, a copartnership, and until this Corporation has completed two fiscal years which may be used as a basis for determining the average annual net profits, as aforesaid, the net earnings of the Corporation, for the purpose of this contract, shall be determined from the average net earnings during the preceding two fiscal years of the operation of said business either by this Corporation or by the copartnership from which its business was acquired, and, for that purpose, reference shall be had to the books of said copartnership for a sufficient period prior to the organization of this Corporation to produce a two year average. If it shall be necessary to use the net profits of the copartnership as a basis, proper adjustment and allowance shall be made for the fact that no salaries were paid by said copartnership, and that part of the capital of the Corporation is preferred stock. For the purposes of this contract, the annual statements of the Corporation shall be made up on the same plan and method as has heretofore been followed by said copartnership.[20]

Several other formulas may be used for determining the value of the shares, but they are mostly a product of the imagination of the drafter. Any formula that will establish a value for the shares and will serve the purposes of the agreement may be used. Note that the choice of the formula may significantly assist the effect of share transfer restrictions. If a share transfer restriction requires that all shares must be offered to the corporation at book value, and the book value considerably understates market price, the shareholder will be less likely to attempt to sell shares because the shareholder risks having to accept the book value price in any case. This provision does not run afoul of the rule that a complete restriction on sale is prohibited, since the shareholder does have the right to sell the stock. However, as a practical matter the shareholder is not likely to do so.

Matching a Bona Fide Offer. If a shareholder intends to sell stock and is subject to a share transfer restriction, the agreement may specify, in lieu of an agreed value, adjustable agreed value, or formula evaluation of price, that the corporation will be obliged to pay a price equal to that offered to the shareholder by the outsider investor. The selling shareholder benefits from this price determination since the shares will be purchased by the corporation at exactly the same price as would have been received from the outsider. A matching price provision should be used only in a case where the agreement also requires, as is usually the case, that the shareholder must have received a good-faith offer from an outsider and the offer is definite and provable to the corporation's satisfaction.

If one objective of the agreement is to discourage the transfer of shares to outsiders, the matching price provision is not the best alternative, because it ensures that the shareholder will receive the same consideration no matter who purchases the shares. Transfer is best discouraged by a clause giving the corporation or other shareholders the option to match the price, or to purchase at some other price, stated or determined by formula, *whichever is lower.*

> **EXAMPLE: Matching Offer**
> The price at which the shares are to be offered to the corporation or to the remaining shareholders shall be equal to the bona fide offer received from the offeror, or equal to book value as determined by the provisions of this agreement, whichever is lower.

Appraisal. An appraisal at the time of purchase may provide the most accurate but also the most expensive determination of value. The person who is to make the appraisal should be named in the agreement, or a procedure for naming appraisers should be described. For example, the agreement could name a mutually agreeable appraiser, or could provide for the selection of a panel of appraisers who will determine the value of the stock.

The clause providing for an appraiser should also specify the appraiser's qualifications, which should indicate some familiarity with the particular industry in which the corporation conducts its business. The clause should provide for the method of payment of the appraiser's expenses, and it is fair to provide that these expenses will be paid by the corporation (thereby absorbing the cost of the appraisal among all shareholders). In the last case, care should be taken to consider that when the corporation is paying the appraiser it may impair the appraiser's independence in determining the actual market value of the stock.

The method of appraisal should be specified, since business appraisers may use various methods to determine the value of the business. A liquidation value may be unrealistic, since it would include only the value of the assets less the payment of the liabilities, if the assets were immediately sold for a price. A preferable method would be an appraisal based upon *going-concern value,* which should include consideration of goodwill, business reputation, expected useful life of the assets, and liquidity of the company (its cash and current asset position projected over a period of time considering potential expenses and liabilities). Most business appraisers will apply a discount to the value of minority shares, since minority shareholders are rarely able to affect corporate policies. This potential discount for minority interests should be considered in the agreement, and if it is not desirable to discount shares simply because they represent a minority position, the discount should be excluded in the instructions to the appraiser.

> **EXAMPLE: Appraisal**
> The purchase price to be paid for each of the shares subject to this agreement shall be determined by appraisal. Within ten days after the occurrence of the event requiring the determination of the purchase price under this agreement, the Company shall cause Levine & Company, independent appraisers, to appraise the Company and determine its value. The appraisal fee shall be paid by the Company. In making the appraisal, the appraisers shall value real estate and improvements at fair market value; machinery and equipment shall be valued at replacement costs or fair market value, whichever is lower; finished inventory shall be valued at cost or market, whichever is lower; goods in process shall be valued at cost, using cost accounting procedures customarily employed by the Company in preparing financial statements; receivables shall be valued at their face amount, less an

allowance for uncollectable receivables that is reasonable in view of the past experience of the Company and the recent review of their collectability; all liabilities shall be deducted at their face value, and a reserve for contingent liabilities shall be established, if appropriate in the sole discretion of the appraiser. The value of other comparable companies, if known, shall also be considered. The value determined by appraisal shall be divided by the total number of shares of the Company's capital stock then outstanding. No discount shall be applied for the fact that the shares to be purchased under this agreement shall constitute less than 50% of the total shares then outstanding.

The appraisal provisions may be combined with other evaluation methods. The following clause uses a shareholder determination of stated value, but appraisal is used if the determination of the shareholders is not current.

> **EXAMPLE: Agreed Value or Appraisal to Determine Price**
> For the purposes of this agreement, each share of said stock shall be regarded as having a value of One hundred dollars ($100.00). The value of said stock as above determined may be changed from time to time by an endorsement over the signatures of the stockholders in the appendix to this agreement. A determination of value whether made in this clause or in the appendix shall remain vital and controlling for the period of one year from its effective date unless within such period it is superseded by a new determination. Should the death of a stockholder occur after one year from the effective date of the last determination of value, the value at the date of death shall be determined by three appraisers, one to be appointed by the surviving stockholder(s), one by the decedent's estate, and one by the two appraisers appointed as first provided. In their process of appraisement, the appraisers shall assume that the last valuation made by the stockholders, whether in this clause or in this appendix, was true and correct as of the date it was made, and with that assumption as a point of beginning, they shall proceed to redetermine such value with reference to the relevant facts and circumstances existing at the time of the decedent's death. Notwithstanding this provision for appraisement, the surviving stockholder(s) and the decedent's estate may elect to accept as controlling the last valuation made by the stockholders, even though such valuation was not made within the year preceding the date of the decedent's death.
> The value of the stock as above stated or as same may be determined from time to time hereafter is or shall be inclusive of any value referable to the good will of the corporation as a going concern.[21]

Arbitration. Rather than appraisal, the agreement may provide for an arbitration among independent arbitrators, who will conduct whatever investigation may be necessary to ascertain the value of the stock. This objective determination by independent third parties may be desirable, but probably is also expensive and will only serve to resolve a dispute rather than establish a true reflection of the value of the Company's stock.

> **EXAMPLE: Value Determined by Arbitration**
> The shareholder shall notify the corporation of the price at which he or she is willing to sell the stock, which notification shall contain the name of one arbitrator. The corporation shall, within thirty days thereafter, accept the offer, or by notice to the shareholder in writing, name a second arbitrator, and these two shall name a third. It shall then be the duty of the arbitrators to ascertain the value of the stock, and if any arbitrator shall neglect or refuse to appear at any meeting appointed by the arbitrators, a majority may act in the absence of such arbitrator.[22]

Terms of Payment. The agreement should specify the procedure and terms of payment when the transfer of shares is accomplished. As previously indicated, the purchasers may prefer to extend payment over a period of time, while the seller may prefer immediate cash. Full payment in cash rarely happens; the most common terms of payment provide for a cash down payment and installment payments for the balance, which may be represented by an interest-bearing promissory note. Installment payments may provide tax benefits to the seller, especially if a large block of valuable stock is the subject of the transfer and there are contingencies reflected that might change or eliminate the promised payments upon the occurrence of certain events. Whenever stock is sold, the seller is required to report any gain received in the year of the sale. A shareholder who sells a large block of stock at one time may incur considerable tax liability by receiving the payments in cash during the year of sale. However, if payments are to be made in installments, and future payments are contingent as to the amount (such as payments that vary depending on subsequent earnings or based upon asset levels of the corporation), the shareholder need report only the amount of the proportionate gain represented by the installments received during the year. This will spread the shareholder's profit on the shares being sold over the period of installments, which may be several years. The installment sale tax treatment now applies no matter how much of the purchase price is received during the year in which the sale is consummated and whether or not the payments extend over two or more installments.[23]

By agreeing to extend payments over a period of time, the selling shareholder risks the subsequent insolvency of the purchasers, or the purchasers' unwillingness to pay. This problem can be mitigated by providing the selling shareholder with some security to protect the payments. The security may be any property pledged as collateral to secure the note, but usually consists of the stock being sold. This means that the selling shareholder may repossess the stock upon default of the obligation. The agreement may specify this right of repossession or may establish an escrow arrangement by placing the shares being transferred in the hands of a third party pending payment of the full purchase price. Escrow terms require the return of the shares to the seller if the obligation is defaulted. If the obligation is paid in full, the shares will be delivered to the purchaser. A clause reciting the installment sale requirements and permitting a security interest in the stock follows.

> **EXAMPLE: Payment of Purchase Price**
> Not less than one-half the consideration required under the preceding clauses shall be paid in cash and, for the balance, a promissory note(s) of the kind hereinafter described may be given. On failure of the purchaser to settle in the manner required within the period of sixty (60) days from the election to purchase, the seller may rescind this agreement and re-establish the situation that would have existed had it never been made.
>
> A note given for part of the consideration shall provide for annual payments on the principal over a period not to exceed five (5) years from the date of the purchase, at the end of which time the unpaid portion of the principal shall be due and payable, and shall provide for interest at the rate of ten (10%) per centum per annum and for optional acceleration of maturity in event of a default in payment of principal or interest. The seller may require the purchaser to secure the payment of a note given for the purchase price by a pledge of all or a portion of the stock.[24]

Whether the selling shareholder will have the right to vote the shares that are security for the installment purchase is a subject of negotiation, but it is preferable to permit the selling shareholder to vote the shares unless some serious objection is raised to the contrary. It should also be recognized that the shares of the corporation, as security for the installment payment, may represent worthless collateral, since when the corporation ceases to pay on the installments, it is likely that the corporation's financial position will have deteriorated so much that the shares may be valueless. In representing a shareholder whose only security is the shares being sold, it is advisable to consider the following additional terms in the security agreement representing the shares.

1. Restrictions upon the payment of dividends, distributions in liquidation, or salaries during the time that the shares are held as security
2. The imposition of an asset-to-liability ratio during the period that the shares are security, so that the installment payments may be accelerated if the ratio is not maintained
3. Restrictions on the corporation's ability to borrow money, sell substantially all of its assets outside of the ordinary course of business, merge, consolidate, or dissolve during the period that the shares are subject to the restriction
4. Antidilution provisions that will adjust the shares held as security to reflect any stock splits, stock dividends, or other capital reorganization
5. Terms that facilitate the perfection of the security interest in the shares, such as a promise by the company to deliver necessary stock certificates or other documents that may be necessary to perfection of the security interest in the particular jurisdiction

> **EXAMPLE: Purchase with Security**
> The deferred portion of the purchase price for any shares purchased under this agreement shall be represented by a promissory note executed by all the purchasing shareholders providing for joint and several liability. Each maker agrees that he or she will pay his or her pro rata portion of each installment of principal and interest as it falls due. The note shall provide for payment of principal in 24 equal quarterly installments with interest on the unpaid balance at the rate of 18% per annum, with full privilege of prepayment of all or any part of the principal at any time without penalty or bonus. Any prepaid sums shall be applied against the installments thereafter falling due in inverse order of their maturity, or against all the remaining installments equally, at the option of the payers. The note shall provide that, in case of default, at the election of the holder the entire sum of principal and interest will immediately be due and payable, and that the makers shall pay reasonable attorneys' fees to the holder in the event that such suit is commenced because of default. The note shall be secured by a pledge of all the shares being purchased in the transaction to which the note relates, and of all other shares owned by the purchasing shareholders. The note shall further be secured by a deed of trust on the real property of the corporation, and a security interest in all personal property owned by the corporation. The pledge agreements and other agreements required to effect and execute such pledges shall contain such other terms and provisions as may be customary and reasonable. As long as no default occurs in payments on the note, the purchaser shall be entitled to vote the shares; however, dividends shall be paid to the holder of the note as a prepayment of principal. The purchaser shall expressly waive demand, notice of default, and notice of sale, and shall consent to public or private sale of the shares in the event of default, in whole or in lots at the option of the pledge holder, and the seller shall have the right to purchase at the sale.

It is preferable for the shareholder to obtain security other than the shares being transferred as collateral for installment payments under a share transfer agreement. The preceding example illustrates a security interest in personal property of the corporation and a mortgage on the corporation's real estate. If the corporation is not the purchaser, other personal or real property of the purchasing shareholders should be considered. Of course, the terms of the security must be negotiated, and the corporation's counsel should be sensitive particularly to the impairment on the corporation's borrowing power by the grant of a security to the shareholder whose shares are being purchased. Appropriate subordination provisions may be included in the security documents to permit the corporation to borrow for normal operating reasons.

Funding of the Agreement through Insurance. The corporation may use life insurance, disability insurance, or other insurance contracts as a method of funding a buy-out agreement. These funding techniques are especially effective if the event triggering the buy-out is death or disability. Other insurance contracts are also available for retirement or termination of employment.

A principal determination is whether all or some of the shareholders should or can be insured. A problem may arise when there are differences in ages, such as when one shareholder is over 65 and others are under 30, or when one or more of the shareholders is not insurable because of physical infirmities. When the corporation purchases the life insurance policies funding the buy-out agreement, the shareholders automatically bear the cost in proportion to their ownership interests in the corporation. If the majority shareholder is the oldest, that shareholder has a disadvantage. If all of the shareholders are roughly in the same age category for insurance purposes, the cost of insurance is spread more equitably. Advantages of corporation ownership of the policies include having fewer policies and more easily ensuring that the premiums are timely paid and that the policies remain in effect. The shareholders have statutory rights to access to the corporation's books and can verify the information given to them about the status of the policies.[25]

A buy-out agreement funded with life insurance usually causes the last survivor or survivors to come out ahead. The problem may be illustrated by the case of a corporation valued at $100,000.00 with four shareholders. The interest of each shareholder is worth $25,000.00, and the corporation purchases insurance policies for $25,000.00 on the life of each shareholder. The estate of the first shareholder to die receives $25,000.00, and each remaining shareholder then has a one-third interest, with a value of $33,333.33, in a corporation still worth $100,000.00. The last survivor gets the entire corporation. One way to avoid this problem is to increase the insurance on the survivors' lives, but this may be too expensive and does not entirely eliminate the windfall to the longer-surviving shareholders.

The corporation may not deduct life insurance premiums paid on policies on shareholders' lives if it is directly or indirectly a beneficiary under those policies.[26] This rule ordinarily prevents the corporation from deducting premiums for life insurance used to fund the corporation's purchase of its stock whether the corporation is the designated beneficiary or the indirect recipient of the proceeds through a trustee or a member of the decedent's family. If the shareholder is the beneficiary, some portion of the insurance proceeds may be included in the shareholder's gross estate for estate tax purposes.[27]

As alternative funding methods, the corporation may build up cash or liquid investments as a reserve with which to purchase the shareholder's interest. This creates an evaluation problem, especially when book value is considered the appropriate formula for determining the price of the purchased shares, in that the existence of the reserve enhances the value of the corporation and therefore may increase the amount to be paid at the buy-out. In addition, the corporation's inability to use the money in the reserve may handicap its day-to-day operations, and the fund may be reachable by its creditors. There is further risk that the accumulated earnings tax will be imposed on such a reserve under the Internal Revenue Code.[28]

Life insurance may also be used to fund a cross-purchase agreement of the shareholders, but the tax and nontax factors should be considered carefully. If the shareholders are employees, they may pay the premiums out of their corporate salaries, which are deductible by the corporation if the compensation is reasonable.[29] If the shareholders are using dividend income from the corporation to pay the premiums, the corporate deduction is not available. Direct payments of the insurance premiums by the corporation may be held to constitute dividends to a shareholder. To avoid estate tax problems, each shareholder should purchase insurance on the life of each other shareholder, but not on his or her own life.[30] A factor weighing against life insurance funding is the potential windfall for the surviving shareholders.

Especially when the cross-purchase agreement among shareholders is funded by life insurance, a trustee should be appointed to perform certain functions. Stock certificates may be deposited with the trustee and the trustee may receive payments and handle the paperwork attendant to such transfers. The trustee also may send notices and perform calculations as to the number of shares the offeree may purchase. The shareholders may prefer that a disinterested person perform these functions, and the agreement should provide the manner in which the trustee will be selected. The agreement should also provide the manner in which the cost for the trustee's services will be paid.

> **EXAMPLE: Cross-Purchase Insurance Agreement**
> In order to fund the payment of the purchase price for the shares to be purchased under this agreement on the death of any shareholder, each shareholder shall maintain in full force and effect a policy of life insurance on the life of each other shareholder in the face amount shown on Exhibit A to this agreement. Each such policy is listed and described in the Exhibit, and any additional policies hereafter acquired for the same purpose shall also be listed in the Exhibit. Each policy belongs solely to the shareholder who applied for it and, subject to the provisions of this agreement, the owner of each policy reserves all the powers and rights of ownership of it. Each such owner shall be named as the primary beneficiary of his or her respective policies, and shall pay all premiums on them as they become due. No shareholder shall exercise any of the powers of ownership of any of the policies by changing the named beneficiary, cancelling the policy, electing optional methods of payment, converting the policy, borrowing against it, or in any other way changing its nature, value, or the rights under the policy. Any dividends paid on any of the policies before maturity or the insured's death shall be paid to the policy owner and shall not be subject to this agreement. Receipts showing payment of premiums shall be delivered to the Secretary of the company no less than 20 days before each date upon which the respective premiums are due, and the receipts shall be held by the Secretary for inspection by all shareholders.

If one shareholder dies, that shareholder will have owned policies of insurance on the lives of fellow shareholders. Accordingly, it is desirable to provide for the disposition of any unneeded policies in the agreement.

> **EXAMPLE: Unneeded Insurance Policies**
> On the death of any shareholder, each of the surviving shareholders shall have the option for 90 days to purchase the policy of life insurance on the shareholder's life owned by the decedent. Each shareholder shall also have the right to purchase the policies on that shareholder's life within 90 days after the sale or transfer of all that shareholder's shares, or after termination of this agreement. This option shall be exercised by delivery of written notice of exercise to the decedent's personal representative or to the owner of the policy and paying the purchase price in cash. The purchase price shall be equal to the cash surrender value of the policy, reduced by any unpaid loans made against the policy. If the option is not exercised within that period, the policy owner may surrender the policy for its cash value or dispose of it in any other way he or she sees fit. The parties agree to execute such releases and assignments that may be necessary to effectuate the provisions of this paragraph.

Legend on Certificates. To ensure that shareholders will not violate the agreement and provide a purchase of the shares with stock certificates free from the transfer restrictions, it is necessary to place a conspicuous legend on each certificate for the shares, the terms of which should be specified by the agreement. Section 8–204 of the Uniform Commercial Code states that a purchaser of stock that is subject to a stock transfer restriction will purchase the shares free from the transfer restriction unless the certificate contains a conspicuous notation of the restriction or unless the purchaser has actual knowledge of the restriction. Section 6.27 of the Model Business Corporation Act also contains this rule.

The agreement should require that each shareholder shall surrender the certificate representing the shares to permit the inscription of an appropriate legend. The legend may provide the actual terms of the restriction, or simply say that the shares shall not be transferred, encumbered, or in any way alienated except under the terms of the agreement, referring to the agreement by date and indicating a place at which the agreement may be inspected.

> **EXAMPLE: Legend**
> Each share certificate, when issued, shall have a conspicuously endorsed legend on its face with the following words: "Sale, transfer, or hypothecation of the shares represented by this certificate is restricted by the provisions of a buy-out agreement among the shareholders and the Company dated November 28, 1992, a copy of which may be inspected at the principal office of the Company and all the provisions of which are incorporated by reference in this certificate." A copy of this agreement shall be delivered to the Secretary of the company, and shall be shown by the Secretary to any person making any inquiry about it.

Miscellaneous Provisions. Several additional considerations must be reviewed in preparing an agreement regarding share ownership. Since the transfer of shares under the agreement may have an effect on other corporate activities, and may be regulated with respect to securities law aspects by state and federal agencies, special issues concerning transfer of shares must be reviewed with the client and considered in drafting the agreement.

If the corporation has previously elected Subchapter S status for taxation, it may be desirable to continue the Subchapter S election even though shares are being transferred under a stock transfer agreement. Of course, each shareholder's consent is desirable to provide for taxation of the corporation under Subchapter S, and the agreement should provide that any transferee of the shares under the share transfer agreement will execute required documents and consent to the election.

> **EXAMPLE: Subchapter S Election**
> The Company and each of the shareholders agree to execute such documents and consents and to cause them to be delivered in a timely manner to the Internal Revenue Service in order to cause the Company to elect to be taxed as a small business corporation under section 1361 of the Internal Revenue Code of 1986. Each shareholder shall cause any transferee of any of his or her shares to file in a timely manner the required consent to the election. Notwithstanding any provision of this agreement to the contrary, no transfer of any of the Company's shares shall be made by any shareholder to any corporation, partnership, or trust, or to any other transferee, if the effect of the transfer would cause the election to be lost or revoked.

In the case of death or disability of a shareholder, the shareholder's spouse will have certain rights to assets of the shareholder. These assets would include the shares of stock owned by the shareholder. The agreement should contemplate the potential claims to be made by spouses and heirs of the shareholder, which may be inconsistent with the terms of the agreement. The shareholders should be required to take such steps that may be necessary to reconcile personal estate documents, such as wills and trusts, with the shareholder agreement.

> **EXAMPLE: Spouse's Consent**
> I acknowledge that I have read the foregoing agreement and that I know its contents. I am aware that by its provisions my spouse agrees to sell all of his or her shares to the Company, including my community interest in them, if any, on the occurrence of certain events. I hereby consent to the sale, approve of the provisions of the agreement, and agree that those shares and my interest in them are subject to the provisions of the agreement and that I will take no action at any time to hinder operation of the agreement on those shares or my interest in them.

> **EXAMPLE: Wills**
> Each shareholder agrees to include in his or her will a direction and authorization to his or her executor to comply with the provisions of this agreement and to sell his or her shares in accordance with this agreement; however, the failure of any shareholder to do so shall not affect the validity or enforceability of this agreement.

NOTES

1. See "Close Corporations" in Chapter 5.
2. See Sections "The Articles of Incorporation" in Chapter 6 and "Shareholder Business and Vote Required" in Chapter 8.
3. See Chapter 13.
4. See "Shareholder Meetings" in Chapter 8.
5. See M.S.C.C.S. § 20(c); Delaware's close corporation statute allows written shareholder agreements that interfere with the discretion of the directors, but the shareholders are responsible for acts controlled by the agreement. 8 Del.Code Ann. § 350.

6. M.B.C.A. § 7.30.
7. E.g., Minnesota, Minn.Stat.Ann. § 302A.453; Nevada, Nev.Rev.Stat. § 78.365.
8. New Jersey, N.J.Stat.Ann. § 14A:5–20; Maine, 13A Me.Rev.Stat.Ann. § 619.
9. M.B.C.A. § 7.30(b).
10. West's Modern Legal Forms § 3013.1.
11. West's Modern Legal Forms § 3013.
12. See the example described in "Shareholder Business and Vote Required" in Chapter 8.
13. West's Modern Legal Forms § 3013.5.
14. See "Corporation's Purchase of Its Own Shares" in Chapter 9.
15. See M.B.C.A. § 6.31.
16. Int.Rev.Code of 1986, 26 U.S.C.A. § 302.
17. See "Involuntary Dissolution" in Chapter 13.
18. West's Modern Legal Forms § 3013.
19. West's Modern Legal Forms § 2764.1.
20. West's Modern Legal Forms § 3013.
21. West's Modern Legal Forms § 3026.
22. West's Modern Legal Forms § 2764.1.
23. Int.Rev.Code of 1986, 26 U.S.C.A. § 453.
24. West's Modern Legal Forms § 3026.
25. M.B.C.A. § 16.02.
26. See Int.Rev.Code of 1986, 26 U.S.C.A. § 264(a).
27. See Int.Rev.Code of 1986, 26 U.S.C.A. § 2042.
28. See Int.Rev.Code of 1986, 26 U.S.C.A. § 531.
29. See Int.Rev.Code of 1986, 26 U.S.C.A. § 162(a)(1).
30. See Int.Rev.Code of 1986, 26 U.S.C.A. § 2042(2). Examples of agreements involving insurance-funded buy-out provisions may be found in West's Modern Legal Forms §§ 3027–3033.

12 CORPORATIONS IN FOREIGN JURISDICTIONS

SELECTION OF JURISDICTION

Early in the formation stages of a corporation, a particular jurisdiction will be selected as the situs of incorporation. The selection process was described in some detail in an earlier chapter,[1] and it was there recognized that a multistate business will have several jurisdictions to consider. A decision to form the multistate corporation in one particular state will usually be made after a comparison of the permissiveness and flexibility of the various statutes. The state of incorporation is the domestic state, and the corporation is a foreign corporation to every other state. The rule to be considered in this chapter is that a foreign corporation must *qualify* to do business in any state in which it intends to conduct business.

CONSTITUTIONAL BASIS FOR QUALIFICATION

A little history and legal theory of the corporate entity are important here. A corporation is a fictitious person created under the authority of a state statute, and, consequently, is a citizen of the state in which it has incorporated. Under the early common law, the corporation existed only in the state in which it incorporated, and it was not permitted to do business in any other jurisdiction. When corporate businesses began to outgrow the boundaries of their domestic states, a legal question arose as to whether a state could prevent a foreign corporation from doing business within its boundaries without incorporating therein. Alternatively, if incorporation could not be required, could a state place restrictions upon the foreign corporation's business and require the foreign corporation to satisfy certain conditions before it was entitled to do business in the foreign state?

The Constitution of the United States guarantees to all persons the ability to move freely among the states without restriction, and the question then became whether a corporation may be considered to be a "person" under these provisions of the Constitution. The Supreme Court eventually decided that a corporation, whether or not it is a person in the constitutional sense, could not be prevented from entering another state, but could be reasonably regulated by the foreign state, under the guise of the state's power to prescribe regulations to protect its own residents. If the regulations imposed were reasonable and designed to protect the local citizenry, the regulations were permitted.

If you keep this history in mind throughout this chapter, the current regulations on foreign corporations may be more easily understood. Most states require foreign corporations to disclose certain matters about their business structure by a public filing with a state official, so that the citizens of the state have access to necessary information about the organization with which they transact business. A separate area of regulation is concerned with litigation by and against the foreign corporation. These statutes are designed to subject the foreign organization to legal process within the state so that the citizens of a state may conveniently redress their complaints against the corporation. They further ensure compliance with qualification requirements before the corporation may use the state courts. In a constitutional sense, therefore, any state may impose regulations on foreign corporations, provided the regulations are reasonably directed to the state's responsibility and power to protect its own citizens.

AUTHORIZATION TO QUALIFY AS A FOREIGN CORPORATION

The authority to conduct business in a foreign state must come from within the corporation by official direction of the board of directors. Such management approval, which is usually accompanied by an enabling provision in the articles of incorporation, authorizes the corporation to submit to the necessary regulations in order to do business within a foreign jurisdiction.

The board of directors will usually adopt a resolution authorizing qualification at its organizational meeting if the plans for expansion are solidified at that time. The resolution states that the corporation may qualify to do business under the laws of other states, and that the officers of the corporation are empowered to execute any necessary documents and to pay all necessary taxes and fees in order to qualify the corporation as a foreign corporation.[2]

STATUTORY PROHIBITION FROM DOING BUSINESS WITHOUT QUALIFICATION

Every state has a statute pertaining to qualification of foreign corporations. Several states have adopted the Model Business Corporation Act approach, prohibiting any foreign corporation from transacting business within the boundaries of the state without qualifying and receiving a certificate of authority from the appropriate state official.[3] This is a strict provision. Nearly half of the states do not condition the right to transact business on the receipt of the certificate of authority, but they do specify a procedure for obtaining a certificate of authority, and further specify sanctions for failure to qualify.

It is not necessary that the foreign corporation be incorporated in a state whose laws are substantially similar to the laws of the state in which it seeks authority to do business. Indeed, many state statutes specifically prohibit denial of a certificate of authority simply because the laws of the state under which the foreign corporation is organized differ from the laws of the particular state in which it intends to qualify. Therefore, a corporation established under the permissive laws of Delaware, where the regulation of corporate management is very flexible, could not be denied admission to another state whose corporate statute restricts the activities of the intracorporate parties. However, the foreign corporation could be denied admission if it is organized for a purpose that is unlawful in the host state. For example, a Nevada corporation organized to conduct a gambling business may be denied admission to conduct gambling operations in a state where those activities are illegal. Otherwise, any corporation may qualify to do any business in any foreign jurisdiction.

TRANSACTING BUSINESS

The traditional statutory test for determining whether a corporation must qualify in a foreign jurisdiction is whether the corporation is "transacting business" within the foreign state. The transacting business test is not the most precise definition ever devised, and it has been responsible for considerable litigation. A sampling of the cases may illustrate the problem:

1. Would an Indiana corporation be doing business in Oklahoma by manufacturing equipment in Indiana, delivering it to Oklahoma, and installing it in Oklahoma?
2. Would a Delaware corporation be transacting business in New York by engaging an answering service and a soliciting salesman in New York?
3. Would an Arizona corporation be conducting business in Texas by sending salespeople and mechanics into Texas to solicit orders and to install and repair the machinery?
4. Would a Georgia corporation be doing business in Mississippi by hiring a local Mississippi mechanic to service an ice-cream dispenser for one year?

The answers from the cases considering these questions are as follows: (1) no, (2) yes, (3) no, (4) yes.

The judicial uncertainty surrounding this test is particularly unfortunate when the sanctions for failure to qualify are considered. A corporation may suffer severe penalties if it is found to have been conducting business without qualification. To obviate the problem, Section 15.01 of the Model Business Corporation Act enumerates certain activities that may be conducted by a foreign corporation without being considered to be transacting business. These activities are

(1) maintaining, defending, or settling any proceeding;
(2) holding meetings of the board of directors or shareholders or carrying on other activities concerning internal corporate affairs;
(3) maintaining bank accounts;
(4) maintaining offices or agencies for the transfer, exchange, and registration of the corporation's own securities or maintaining trustees or depositaries with respect to those securities;
(5) selling through independent contractors;
(6) soliciting or obtaining orders, whether by mail or through employees or agents or otherwise, if the orders require acceptance outside this state before they become contracts;
(7) creating or acquiring indebtedness, mortgages, and security interests in real or personal property;
(8) securing or collecting debts or enforcing mortgages and security interests in property securing the debts;
(9) owning, without more, real or personal property;

(10) conducting an isolated transaction that is completed within 30 days and that is not one in the course of repeated transactions of a like nature;
(11) transacting business in interstate commerce.

Only a few states detail such a comprehensive list, and many states have no list at all. Delaware provides a more specific list, which might be more helpful in solving the illustrative cases described earlier. The Delaware statute states that a foreign corporation shall not be required to qualify in the state under the following circumstances.

(1) If it is in the mail order or a similar business, merely receiving orders by mail or otherwise in pursuance of letters, circulars, catalogs, or other forms of advertising, or solicitation, accepting the orders outside this State, and filling them with goods shipped into this State;
(2) If it employs salesmen, either resident or traveling, to solicit orders in this State, either by display of samples or otherwise (whether or not maintaining sales offices in this State), all orders being subject to approval at the offices of the corporation without this State, and all goods applicable to the orders being shipped in pursuance thereof from without this State to the vendee or to the seller or his agent for delivery to the vendee, and if any samples kept within this State are for display or advertising purposes only, and no sales, repairs, or replacements are made from stock on hand in this State;
(3) If it sells, by contract consummated outside this State, and agrees, by the contract, to deliver into this State, machinery, plants or equipment, the construction, erection or installation of which within this State requires the supervision of technical engineers or skilled employees performing services not generally available, and as a part of the contract of sale agrees to furnish such services, and such services only, to the vendee at the time of construction, erection or installation;
(4) If its business operations within this State, although not falling within the terms of paragraphs (1), (2), and (3) of this subsection or any of them, are nevertheless wholly interstate in character;
(5) If it is an insurance company doing business in this State;
(6) If it creates, as borrower or lender, or acquires, evidences of debt, mortgages or liens on real or personal property;
(7) If it secures or collects debts or enforces any rights in property securing the same.[4]

Some statutory guidance may be available, therefore, on what does *not* constitute the transaction of business within the state. However, that is not to say that everything not enumerated in the statute *is* transacting business so as to require qualification. There is still room for judicial interpretation of the other corporate activities.

The safe approach should be obvious: If there is any question about the scope of the corporation's activities in a foreign jurisdiction, the corporation should apply for admission as a foreign corporation and obtain a certificate of authority. Failure to do so may subject the corporation to the statutory sanctions for failing to qualify. The safe approach is not always the most practical, however. Qualification does impose certain special burdens on the corporation, and corporate management may be unwilling to accept those burdens. Management should be fully advised on all ramifications of qualification, and the decision will be theirs, considering the costs, formalities, taxes, and fees on one hand, and the penalties for failure to qualify on the other.

SANCTIONS FOR NOT QUALIFYING

If a foreign corporation is transacting business within the state and has not received a certificate of authority from the host state, most state statutes impose certain interdictions and fines on the corporation or its management. Foreign corporations may be denied access to the local courts for any action, suit, or proceeding until a certificate of authority has been obtained. This sanction is found in the Model Business Corporation Act and in most jurisdictions. However, under the Model Business Corporation Act, the failure to qualify does not impair the validity of any contract or act of the corporation, and it does not prevent any corporation from *defending* any action in a court of the host state. Consequently, the practical drawback of failing to qualify under the Model Business Corporation Act is the inability of the corporation to maintain a suit in its own name. However, there are also pecuniary disadvantages. The failure to obtain a certificate renders the corporation liable to the state for all fees and taxes that would have been imposed had the corporation been qualified for the years during which it transacted business without a certificate of authority. In addition, the Model Business Corporation Act authorizes the imposition of any penalties normally levied for failure to pay the fees, and these fines also will be exacted from the foreign corporation. The attorney general is authorized to bring a suit to recover the amounts due under the statute.[5]

Although the prohibition from maintaining litigation and the collection of fees, taxes, and fines are severe sanctions, the Model Business Corporation Act is somewhat liberal by comparison with sanctions imposed in other states. Alabama provides that all acts of an unauthorized foreign corporation are void. Some state statutes say that any contract entered into by an unauthorized foreign corporation is not enforceable.[6] Certain jurisdictions impose fines, instead of the normal penalties for fees, and the amount of a fine may be as high as ten thousand dollars.[7] Fines may also be levied on corporate directors and officers. Other states authorize an action by the attorney general to enjoin the corporation from doing business.[8]

In the spirit of forgiveness, many states excuse the sanctions as soon as the corporation properly qualifies, although the relief may depend upon showing good cause for failure to qualify or obtaining court approval.

APPLICATION FOR CERTIFICATE OF AUTHORITY

All state statutes describe a procedure for the qualification of a foreign corporation. To acquire a certificate of authority in most states, the corporation must apply to the appropriate state official. The contents of the application vary among the jurisdictions, but there is a common purpose behind the qualification procedures. The applications reveal necessary information about the corporation's structure, its solvency, the location of its property, and its business potential. Foreign corporations are required to furnish essentially the same initial and periodic information as domestic corporations.

Section 15.02 of the Model Business Corporation Act includes the following items in an application for a certificate of authority.

1. The name of the foreign corporation
2. The state or country under the laws of which the corporation is incorporated
3. The date of incorporation and the period of duration
4. The street address of the corporation's principal office
5. The address of the corporation's registered office in the state, and the name of its registered agent at that office
6. The names and usual business addresses of the corporation's current directors and officers

In addition to the foregoing information, other state statutes expand the list of disclosable items to include the following:

1. A statement of the purpose or purposes the corporation proposes to pursue in the transaction of business in the host state
2. A statement of the aggregate number of shares the corporation has authority to issue, itemized by classes and series, if any, within a class
3. A statement of the aggregate number of issued shares itemized by classes and series, if any, within a class
4. An estimate, expressed in dollars, of the value of all property to be owned by the corporation for the following year, wherever located, and an estimate of the value of the property of the corporation to be located within the state during such year, and an estimate, expressed in dollars, of the gross amount of business that will be transacted by the corporation during such year, and an estimate of the gross amount thereof that will be transacted by the corporation at or from places of business in the state during such year
5. Such additional information as may be necessary or appropriate in order to enable the secretary of state to determine whether such corporation is entitled to a certificate of authority to transact business in the state and to determine and assess the fees and franchise taxes payable as prescribed in the applicable act.

A study of the requirements of the application for authority should suggest that those requirements are designed to facilitate the discovery and evaluation of corporate property within the state and to gauge the local productivity of the foreign corporation. This information is used to estimate the tax potential of the foreign corporation, and may also assist local citizens in their litigation against the corporation.

Each state statute should be consulted for local application requirements. In addition to supplying the typical information listed here, it may be necessary to file a list of other jurisdictions to which the corporation has been admitted.[9] Statements of good standing may be required from the corporation's home state,[10] and nearly half of the states require filing of the articles of incorporation duly authenticated by the domestic state officials. In Pennsylvania it is necessary, for tax purposes, to file a separate *registry statement* with the application.[11] Other unusual formalities include the following: the corporation may be required to state its assets and liabilities as of a recent date;[12] the corporation may have to stipulate an agent who is a local resident and a member of the local bar;[13] and statements regarding the amount of paid-in capital or paid-in surplus may be required.[14] Payment of fees and franchise taxes is almost always necessary, and some states require the filing of previous annual reports. To reiterate, as with other matters respecting corporate existence, it is necessary to carefully examine the statute of the state in which the corporation intends to do business, and to strictly comply with the statutory requirements.

The application for certificate of authority is prepared in duplicate or triplicate, as the statute requires, and executed by the president and secretary or one of their assistants. In many states, the application must be verified by one of the signatories.[15]

Most of the matters contained in the application for qualification are self-explanatory, but a couple of items deserve elaboration. The following material discusses requirements concerning the corporate name and the registered office and agent.

Corporate Name

The foreign corporation must comply with statutes regulating corporate names in the host state. The Model Business Corporation Act prescribes essentially the same name requirements for domestic and foreign corporations.[16] The name must contain the word *Corporation, Company, Incorporated,* or *Limited,* or an abbreviation of one of these words, and it may not contain any word or phrase that indicates or implies that the corporation is organized for any purpose other than the purposes enumerated in its articles of incorporation. Moreover, the name cannot be the same as, or deceptively similar to, the name of any domestic corporation existing under the laws of the state or of any foreign corporation already authorized to transact business in the state.

If the name under which the corporation is organized is not available in the host state, the corporation may use a fictitious name to transact business. Alternatively, a foreign corporation will be allowed to use the name of an existing corporation, already organized in the host state, if

1. the other corporation consents to the use of the name and agrees to change its name to a distinguishable name; or
2. the applicant has a court order establishing the applicant's right to use the name in the state.[17]

Suppose American Can Company is a New York corporation, and is seeking to qualify to do business in Tennessee, where there is an established domestic corporation by the same name. The name of the foreign corporation cannot be the same as that of a domestic corporation or a previously qualified foreign corporation. Therefore, the New York Corporation cannot be qualified in Tennessee under the circumstances. However, if the board of directors of the New York corporation adopts a *fictitious* name that is not deceptively similar to an existing name, then the corporation may be qualified under that fictitious name.

The foreign corporation seeking to qualify to do business will usually resist the fictitious name technique because the reputation of the corporate name, usually well established in other states, is lost by the adoption of an assumed name. One can only speculate at the business success of Xerox Corporation if it had been required to use the fictitious name of Copying Machines, Inc., in some of the foreign jurisdictions where it qualified to do business. However, many state officials have adopted informal tests for variations in fictitious names that will be acceptable. For example, if a domestic corporation had reserved the name Xerox Corp. and the real Xerox Corporation attempted to qualify to do business, many states would permit the fictitious name to be Xerox Corporation of Delaware, simply adding the name of the state of incorporation.

Corporations may also buy the right to use a particular name from its owner, and that is usually what must be done to obtain written consent for its use under the consent alternative. Law students who have studied this procedure have dreamed of making immediate and great fortunes by anticipating expansion of a large established corporation into their state, filing a reservation of the corporate name, and waiting to be approached for the consent.

The court order alternative is designed to give the corporation another choice if the price of the consent is excessive and a prior right to the name can be shown. For example, suppose Xerox Corporation had initially confined its business to the eastern states. Further suppose that an enterprising student of corporations, anticipating that Xerox would expand its business nationally, reserved the name Xerox Corporation in California, but did not actively conduct business under that name. Xerox probably could obtain a court order establishing its prior use of the name and eliminate the impediment of the name reservation in California.

The corporate name problem may be solved in advance with a little planning. Recall that all jurisdictions permit reservation of a corporate name and several permit registration of the name.[18] Registration is specifically designed for use by foreign corporations. An organized and existing corporation may file an application for registration of its corporate name with the secretary of state for a small fee. The name may be registered for calendar years, and the registration may be renewed. Corporate management, foreseeing corporate growth into foreign jurisdictions, would be well advised to pursue registration of the corporate name in states where registration is permitted.[19]

Registered Office and Agent

Each state requires that a qualified foreign corporation must maintain a registered office and appoint a registered agent to receive legal documents addressed to the corporation. The registered office may be, but need not be, the same as the corporation's place of business in the state; the registered agent may be either an individual resident in the state or a domestic corporation, or another foreign corporation authorized to transact business in the state. As is required of a domestic corporation, any changes in the office or agent of the foreign corporation must be filed in the office of the secretary of state.[20]

The purpose of the registered office and the agent is to facilitate the service of any process, notice, or demand required or permitted by law. A state may reasonably require a convenient way to notify a foreign corporation of any legal matters as a condition to its permission to do business in the state. For that reason, whenever a foreign corporation fails to appoint or maintain a registered agent in the state or whenever the registered agent cannot be found with due diligence, most statutes provide that the secretary of state will be deemed to be an agent of the corporation to receive legal documents. The secretary of state must send one copy of the document received by registered mail to the corporation at its principal office in the state of incorporation.[21] Section 15.10 of the Model Business Corporation Act has simplified this procedure. A foreign corporation that has failed to maintain a registered agent within the host state may be served by registered or certified mail directly addressed to the secretary of the foreign corporation at its principal office. This eliminates the burden placed upon the secretary of state to receive the document and to send it to the foreign corporation. Direct delivery is just as effective if the statute permits it. These provisions circumvent any potential escape from local complaints by failing to maintain a local agent and ensure the amenability of the foreign corporation to suit in local courts.

Several "registered agent" companies are available at the request of attorneys to act as registered agents for foreign corporations and to comply with the requirements of local laws on their behalf. They include the CT Corporation System; Prentice Hall, Inc.; and the United States Corporation Company.

CERTIFICATE OF AUTHORITY

Upon receipt of the application for a certificate of authority, the secretary of state or other appropriate official files the application and issues a certificate of authority. When the certificate is issued, the corporation is authorized to transact business in the state for the purposes set forth in its application as long as it remains in good standing.[22]

EFFECT OF QUALIFICATION

Once a foreign corporation has received authority to do business within the foreign state, it is entitled to enjoy the same rights and privileges as a domestic corporation organized for the same purposes. In addition, it is subject to the same duties, restrictions, penalties, and liabilities as a domestic corporation. In the host state, therefore, the foreign corporation will be treated like a native, receiving no better or worse treatment than the domestic corporations. The foreign corporation also remains subject to restrictions imposed by its home state, and it must observe those restrictions while operating in the host state.

Consider an Arkansas corporation that qualifies to do business in Pennsylvania. Suppose Arkansas law permits the corporation to be a general partner in another enterprise only if it is authorized to do so in the articles of incorporation or by vote of the shareholders. Pennsylvania law permits a corporation to be a general partner without any such authorization. If the articles of incorporation do not authorize the corporation's entry into a partnership, and the shareholders have not approved such a transaction, the Arkansas corporation could not become a general partner, even in Pennsylvania, where it would otherwise be treated like a domestic corporation. The restrictions placed upon the corporation in its home state are therefore superimposed upon its operations in the foreign state.

The reverse is not exactly the same. Consider a Nevada corporation that qualifies to do business in Pennsylvania. The Nevada corporation is authorized to conduct gambling activities in its home state, but Pennsylvania law would not permit gambling operations in Pennsylvania. The Nevada corporation must abide by the local laws, and it has no greater privileges in Pennsylvania than does a domestic Pennsylvania corporation. However, the internal affairs of the Nevada corporation will always be regulated by the law of Nevada. Thus, for example, if Pennsylvania law required a shareholder vote to change the name of the corporation, but Nevada law does not, the Nevada corporation will be entitled to change its name in Pennsylvania without a shareholder vote, since that matter would be an internal affair of the corporation.

In addition to the restrictions upon privileges and powers discussed here, a qualified foreign corporation also accepts other responsibilities within the host state. It agrees to certain requirements concerning service of process, taxes, and annual reports.

Service of Process

A foreign corporation authorized to transact business in a state is subjected to the jurisdiction of the courts of the host state. Consequently, service of documents relating to litigation upon the registered agent of the corporation is as effective as if the corporation were incorporated within the state and had been served at its principal office.

Taxes

By qualifying to do business within a state, a foreign corporation agrees to pay taxes to the host state. A state is permitted to tax a foreign corporation under the Constitution if the corporation has "substantial contacts" within the state. The law is now quite clear that by qualifying to do business within the state, the corporation creates those substantial contacts. The individual tax structures of the states are dissimilar, but several typical types of taxes are imposed upon foreign corporations.

Some states impose an initial franchise tax upon the filing of the application for a certificate of authority. This tax is generally based upon the aggregate amount of authorized capital stock of the corporation, similar to the measure for taxes imposed on a domestic corporation when its articles of incorporation are filed. A fee is also charged for filing the application of a foreign corporation.

Annual income taxes are also imposed upon foreign corporations. Generally, the tax formula used in any given state has been designed around the commercial character of the state and is intended to maximize tax revenues from foreign corporations. If the state is a recognized location for heavy industry, so that most foreign corporations have manufacturing or industrial plants there, the state will probably impose a tax on the value of the property of the foreign corporation located within the state. This tax formula maximizes revenue for states with an industrial character to their commerce. If the state is not heavily industrialized but has a high population, a tax may be imposed on the proportionate volume of business that the foreign corporation is transacting in the state. A tax on foreign corporations may also be computed by a formula based upon the total number of employees located within the state.

The tax provisions of each state play an important role in the selection of jurisdiction for a corporation anticipating a multistate business. At the formation stage, the choice between incorporating or qualifying to do business in a given jurisdiction will be influenced by that state's tax attitude. For example, if a corporation plans to locate a manufacturing plant in State X and intends to sell its products to customers primarily located in State Y, it would be a mistake to incorporate in State X, where the plant is located, if that state bases its foreign corporation tax on the volume of sales transacted within the state. The corporation should operate as a foreign corporation in State X, because that state's tax base depends upon volume of sales and this corporation will be making most of its sales out of state.

Annual Reports

Like domestic corporations, qualified foreign corporations must file annual reports with the state. The Model Business Corporation Act requires that the annual reports of domestic and foreign corporations contain the same information.[23] Most states require that the annual report contain certain standard information regarding the corporation, its registered offices and agents, its directors and officers, and the character of its business. The reported items typically used to levy taxes include the following:

1. A statement of the aggregate number of shares the corporation has authority to issue, itemized by classes and series, if any, within a class
2. A statement of the aggregate number of issued shares, itemized by classes and series
3. A statement, expressed in dollars, of the value of all the property of the corporation, wherever located, and the value of the property of the corporation located within the state, and the statement of the gross amount of business transacted by the corporation for the period of the report
4. Additional information as may be necessary or appropriate in order to enable the secretary of state to determine and assess the proper amount of franchise taxes payable by the corporation

The annual reports are intended to be used to assist the secretary of state in enforcing the corporation statute and ensuring compliance with its provisions, in fixing responsibility for any corporate transgressions on the named officers and directors, and in evaluating the appropriate tax to be assessed. Most states have the same reporting requirements for foreign and domestic corporations.

STRUCTURAL CHANGES OF A FOREIGN CORPORATION

Every state requires reporting of all corporate structural changes such as mergers, share exchanges, sale or exchange of assets, or amendments to the articles of incorporation for its domestic corporations. Similarly, qualified foreign corporations must follow certain procedures in the host state whenever a structural change occurs in the corporate organization.

Amendment to the Articles of Incorporation

Model Business Corporation Act Section 15.04 provides that a qualified foreign corporation must obtain an amended certificate of authority from the secretary of state of the host state if the corporation changes its name or the period of its duration. In addition, if the corporation changes the state or country in which it is incorporated, an amended certificate of authority must also be obtained.

In most states, any amendment to the articles of incorporation of the foreign corporation requires the filing of a statement with the secretary of state in the foreign jurisdiction. The time period for filing copies or statements of amendments differs among the states. Most states require that such an amendment be filed within 30 days, several states permit as long as 60 days,[24] and a few states have no time limit.[25] Again, careful study of the appropriate state law is important.

The filing procedure for amendments to the articles of incorporation of a foreign corporation is amplified if the amendment changes the corporate name or the period of duration. Merely filing copies of the amended articles of incorporation will not suffice to authorize the foreign corporation to use another name or to extend its longevity. The Model Business Corporation Act requires an amended certificate of authority to accomplish these changes.[26] A foreign corporation may change its corporate name or its duration by filing a new application for an amended certificate of authority. The form and contents of the application for an amended certificate and the procedure for issuance of the amended certificate are the same as those described for the original application for a certificate of authority.[27] Time limits on filing the application for the amended certificate are frequently imposed.[28]

There is an obvious problem if a foreign corporation changes its name by amending its articles of incorporation and the new name is not available in the host state. The drafters of the Model Business Corporation Act took a fairly firm stand on this issue. Under Section 15.06(e), if the new name is not available, the certificate of authority for the corporation will be suspended until the corporation again changes its name to one that is available. A few states soften the harshness of this rule by allowing an interim grace period of 180 days, during which the corporation may transact business under its old name, but by the end of the period the corporation must change its name to a name that is available under the laws of the state. If the corporation fails to change to an acceptable name but continues to transact business, its certificate of authority may be suspended.

Merger and Consolidation with the Foreign Corporation

A merger of a foreign corporation also requires certain additional filings in the host state when the foreign corporation is the surviving corporation after the merger. The legal consequences of a merger are considered in detail later,[29] but stated simply, a merger is a combination of two or more corporations into one corporate entity, whereby one of the corporate parties survives the transaction and the others cease to exist. In most state statutes, if the foreign corporation survives the merger, it must file a copy of the articles of merger with the secretary of state to make the merger effective.[30] It is not necessary for the surviving foreign corporation to procure an amended certificate of authority unless the corporation has changed its name under the merger or unless it has adopted a different period of duration than that authorized in its current certificate of authority. If either of those results are produced by the merger, the amendment procedure described earlier must be followed.

If a qualified foreign corporation merges with another foreign corporation that is not authorized to transact business within the host state, and the nonqualified corporation survives the merger, the surviving corporation must qualify in the foreign jurisdiction by filing an original application for a certificate of authority. The surviving corporation does not inherit the previously granted authority of the merged corporation through the merger.

If a foreign corporation merges with a domestic corporation, and the domestic corporation survives the merger, the articles of merger will be filed by the domestic corporation pursuant to the laws of the state.[31] However, if the foreign corporation survives the merger, certain other filings are required. The surviving foreign corporation may not be authorized to transact business within the state, and, if it intends to do so, it must file an original application for a certificate of authority. Even if it does not intend to do business within the state, the surviving foreign corporation is deemed, through the merger,

1. to appoint the secretary of state as its agent for service of process in a proceeding to enforce any obligation or the rights of dissenting shareholders of each domestic corporation that was a party to the merger or share exchange; and
2. to agree that it will promptly pay to the dissenting shareholders of each domestic corporation that was a party to the merger or share exchange the amount, if any, to which those shareholders are entitled under dissenting shareholders' rights.[32]

Many states require that the foreign corporation must file with the secretary of state a document that promises to perform these acts. However, if the surviving foreign corporation had been authorized to do business within the state, the terms of the corporation's authority theoretically include each of these items and no further filing should be required, and the Model Business Corporation Act now simply makes those consequences automatic.

Two or more corporations may also consolidate under most state statutes. Consolidation is a technique whereby the constituent corporations combine to form a single new corporation. If a qualified foreign corporation consolidates with another foreign corporation, whether qualified or unqualified, the new corporation must seek original authority to do business and does not inherit the qualified status enjoyed by any foreign corporation party to the consolidation.

Finally, a foreign corporation could enter into a share exchange with another corporation, either domestic or foreign. A share exchange is a transaction in which one corporation exchanges its shares for all or part of the shares of the other corporation. If the foreign corporation is the acquiring corporation in a share exchange, the procedure is exactly the same as if the foreign corporation were the surviving corporation in a merger.

WITHDRAWAL OF AUTHORITY

The management of a qualified foreign corporation may decide to discontinue business operations within the host state. However, this does not mean that they may simply pull up their tent and steal away. State regulation of foreign corporations is designed to require payment of fees and taxes and to ensure the availability of the foreign corporation for litigation commenced against it in the state. Consequently, the withdrawal of a foreign corporation is a formal procedure. The foreign corporation must file an application for withdrawal, which, under the Model Business Corporation Act, states that the corporation surrenders its authority to transact business in the state. It must further specifically revoke the authority of its registered agent to accept service of process and consent to service of process on the secretary of state for any proceeding based upon a cause of action arising during the time the corporation was operating within the state. The withdrawal application also includes a post office address to which the secretary of state may mail a copy of any process received for the corporation.[33] Many states also require other additional information that may be necessary to enable the secretary of state to assess any unpaid fees or franchise taxes.

State statutes governing withdrawal of foreign corporations are as varied as those pertaining to admission. Most statutes are directed toward full financial disclosure and amenability to service of process, and generally require that the foreign corporation tidy up its affairs before leaving the state. The statute may require proof that all corporate creditors within the state have been satisfied,[34] or a statement that the corporation no longer owns property within the state.[35] In all cases, taxes and fees must be paid as a condition to the approval of withdrawal.

Upon the filing of the application and the satisfaction of all statutory conditions, the appropriate state official will issue a certificate of withdrawal.[36]

REVOCATION OF CERTIFICATE OF AUTHORITY

A foreign corporation's authority to do business within a state may also cease by the revocation of authority by the host state. Generally, the certificate may be revoked whenever the foreign corporation has failed to comply with the law. For example, the corporation may have failed to file annual reports, or may have failed to pay fees, franchise taxes, or penalties. Other grounds for revocation include the corporation's failure to appoint and maintain a registered agent; failure to notify the state of a change in the agent or office; failure to file amendments to its articles of incorporation or articles of merger within the time prescribed; or misrepresentation in the material matter in any application, report, affidavit, or other document filed with the state. In addition to these grounds, some states add abusing or exceeding the corporation's authority; violating a state law; using an unauthorized name; or acting in a manner detrimental to the citizens of the state. The District of Columbia and Illinois have a revocation provision that looks like default: if the corporation does not conduct business or own tangible property within the state for a specified period, its certificate of authority may be revoked.

Most state statutes require notice to the corporation before the revocation of a certificate of authority. The Model Business Corporation Act directs the secretary of state to give the corporation 60 days' notice by mail addressed to the corporation's registered office in the state, and, if the corporation corrects the specified problem within the notice period, the certificate of authority may not be revoked. However, following the 60-day period if nothing is done, the secretary of state may issue a certificate of revocation.[37] The minimum notice period among the individual state statutes is 20 days,[38] and the maximum is 90 days.[39] Many states permit the remedy of the defect during the intermediate period.

A sample of a certificate of revocation appears as Form 12H in Appendix G. When the certificate is issued, the corporation's authority to transact business in the state ceases.

NOTES

1. "Selection of Jurisdiction" in Chapter 6.
2. See the sample resolution for organizational meetings of the board of directors in "Business Conducted at Organizational Meetings" in Chapter 8.
3. See M.B.C.A. § 15.01.
4. 8 Del.Code Ann. § 373(a).
5. M.B.C.A. § 15.02.
6. E.g., Georgia, Ga.Code Ann. § 14-2-331.
7. See the schedule of penalties for doing business without qualifying, 1 Prentice-Hall, Corporations ¶ 7103.

8. E.g., Delaware, 8 Del.Code Ann. § 384; and New York, McKinney Consol.Laws of N.Y.Bus.Corp.Law § 1303.
9. E.g., Illinois, Ill.Rev.Stat. c. 32 § 13.15; and Missouri, Vernon's Ann.Mo.Stat. § 351.580(1)(6).
10. E.g., Nebraska, Nev.Rev.Stat. § 21–20, 110.
11. 15 Pa.Stat. § 1004.
12. Oklahoma, 18 Okl.Stat.Ann. § 1130.
13. Virginia, Va.Code Ann. § 13.1–759.
14. E.g., Illinois, Ill.Rev.Stat. Ch. 32 § 13.15; and Wisconsin, Wis.Stat.Ann. § 180.813(I)(j) (paid-in capital); Missouri, Vernon's Ann.Mo.Stat. § 351.580(11) (paid-in surplus).
15. An example of an application for certificate of authority appears as Form 12A in Appendix G.
16. Compare M.B.C.A. §§ 4.01 and 15.06.
17. M.B.C.A. § 15.06.
18. See "Selection and Reservation of Corporate Name" in Chapter 6.
19. See M.B.C.A. § 4.03. Forms for registration and transfer of a corporate name appear as Forms 6I, 6J, 6K, and 6L in Appendix G.
20. See M.B.C.A. §§ 15.07 and 15.08. A statement for change of registered office or agent appears as Form 12B in Appendix G.
21. E.g., Georgia, Ga.Code Ann. § 14–2–319.
22. See M.B.C.A. § 15.05. An example of the certificate of authority is Form 12C in Appendix G.
23. M.B.C.A. § 16.22.
24. E.g., Arizona, Ariz.Rev.Stat. § 10–116(A); and Montana, Mont.Code Ann. § 35–1–1015.
25. E.g., Indiana, Burns' Ind.Ann.Stat. § 23–1–49–4.
26. M.B.C.A. § 15.04.
27. See "Application for Certificate of Authority" and "Certificate of Authority" earlier in this chapter, and M.B.C.A. § 15.04. Examples of an application for an amended certificate of authority are Forms 12D and 12E in Appendix G.
28. E.g., Missouri, 60 days, Vernon's Ann.Mo.Stat. § 351.600(1); and Georgia, 30 days, Ga.Code Ann. § 14–2–320.
29. See "Merger, Consolidation, and Exchange" in Chapter 13.
30. See M.B.C.A. §§ 11.05 and 11.07.
31. M.B.C.A. § 11.05.
32. M.B.C.A. § 11.07(b).
33. M.B.C.A. § 15.20.
34. E.g., Hawaii, Hawaii Rev.Stat. § 415–119.
35. E.g., Minnesota, Minn.Stat.Ann. § 303.16.
36. Examples of the application for withdrawal and the certificate of withdrawal are Forms 12F and 12G in Appendix G.
37. M.B.C.A. § 15.31.
38. E.g., Connecticut, Conn.Gen.Stat.Ann. § 33–409.
39. New Jersey, N.J.Stat.Ann. § 14A:13–10.

13 CHANGES IN CORPORATE STRUCTURE AND DISSOLUTION

Previous chapters considered corporate activities that occur in the ordinary course of business. It was noted earlier that the board of directors, and the officers to whom the directors delegate authority, are vested with continuing discretion in the management of business affairs, and that the shareholders exercise only indirect control over corporate operations through their election of the directors. However, this chapter is concerned with extraordinary corporate activity outside the scope of corporate business routine. Each extraordinary matter involves structural changes to the corporation, and, in most cases, affects the ownership rights of the shareholders. Consequently, a common characteristic in each transaction is the requirement for shareholder approval. Morever, the law governing extraordinary corporate activity grants special rights for shareholders in some cases, such as the right to have their shares appraised and purchased by the corporation if they disagree with the decision of management and their fellow shareholders. Special statutory procedures have been adopted by most states to regulate these structural changes, and this chapter is devoted to them.

AMENDMENT OF THE ARTICLES OF INCORPORATION

Any amendment of the articles of incorporation is a structural change of the corporation because the amendment changes the primary authorizing document for corporate existence. The corporation has the right to amend its articles of incorporation within the statutory guidelines established for the original articles of incorporation. Any provision may be inserted in an amendment if it would have been permitted in the original articles. The Model Business Corporation Act formerly detailed fifteen specific situations in which amendments to the articles of incorporation were required. In keeping with the modernization of corporate law, Section 10.01 of the new act simply states that "a corporation may amend its articles of incorporation at any time to add or change a provision that is required or permitted in the articles of incorporation or to delete a provision not required in the articles of incorporation."

Many states continue to follow the former Model Business Corporation Act provisions, and detail certain situations in which amendments will be required. Specifically, the corporation may change its name; its period of duration; its corporate purposes; its number of authorized shares and their par value; its par value shares to no par shares, and vice versa; and the designations, preferences, limitations, or other rights of its shares. The amendment may reclassify or cancel shares; create new classes of shares; divide classes of shares; authorize or revoke authorization of the board of directors to establish series shares; and cancel dividends accrued but not declared. The amendment may also limit, grant, or deny preemptive rights to shareholders.

The new Model Business Corporation Act's broad statutory power to amend is typical of most modern state statutes on the subject of amendments to the articles of incorporation. The power to amend on any issue that may be permitted in the original articles of incorporation may be safely inferred from the general statutory authority.

Procedure

Section 10.02 of the Model Business Corporation Act permits the corporation's board of directors to adopt certain amendments to the articles of incorporation without shareholder action, including amendments to accomplish the following:

1. Extend the duration of the corporation
2. Delete the names and addresses of the initial directors
3. Delete the name and address of the initial registered agent and registered office, if a statement of change is on file with the secretary of state
4. Change each issued and unissued authorized share of an outstanding class into a greater number of whole shares if the corporation has only shares of that class outstanding
5. Change the corporate name by substituting the word *corporation, incorporated, company,* or *limited,* or the abbreviation *Corp., Inc., Co.,* or *Ltd.,* or a similar word or abbreviation in the name, or by adding, deleting, or changing a geographical attribution for the name
6. Make any other changes permitted by the statute to be made without shareholder action (such as by cancelling shares reacquired by the corporation under Section 6.31 or by creating a series of shares under Section 6.02)

If the incorporators would prefer that the shareholders always be involved in approving amendments to the articles, the power of the board of directors to adopt these amendments without shareholder action may be denied expressly in the articles themselves.

In the usual amendment procedure, the board of directors adopts a resolution that sets forth the proposed amendment and directs that it be submitted to a vote at an annual or special meeting of the shareholders.[1]

> **EXAMPLE: Resolution to Change Corporate Name**
> RESOLVED, that Article I of the Articles of Incorporation of The Nobles Company be amended to read as follows:
> "The name of this corporation is The Nobility Company."
> FURTHER RESOLVED, that this amendment shall be submitted to the vote of the shareholders at a special meeting called for the purpose of considering the amendment.

Some states permit the shareholders to propose an amendment to the articles of incorporation.[2] The concerted action of a specified number of shareholders—for example, the holders of one-tenth of the outstanding voting stock of the corporation—is required, and those shareholders may petition the board of directors to propose the amendment or may request that the president of the company call a meeting of shareholders to consider the proposed amendment.

Written notice of the proposed amendment must be given within the statutory period to each shareholder of record entitled to vote upon the proposal.[3] A few states have added special notice requirements for certain amendments, such as those changing the number of authorized shares.[4] In many cases the proposal will be submitted to the shareholders at their annual meeting and the written proposal may be included in the notice of the annual meeting. If a special meeting is called, the notice must state the reason for the meeting—that is, to consider a proposed amendment to the articles of incorporation. In jurisdictions where the shareholders may unanimously consent in writing in lieu of a meeting, that procedure may be used to consider and approve the amendment.[5]

Adoption of the Amendment

The number of shareholder votes required to approve a proposed amendment to the articles of incorporation may be greater than the number required for routine shareholder matters. Moreover, if the amendment affects the rights of the shareholders of a certain class, those shareholders also must approve the amendment, even if they otherwise have no voting rights.

The Model Business Corporation Act formerly required the affirmative vote of the holders of two-thirds of the shares entitled to vote, but a recent amendment to the act reduced the vote to a majority. The reduced voting provision has been accepted in most of the jurisdictions that follow the act.

If a proposed amendment affects the rights of the holders of a certain class of shares, those shares are entitled to vote as a class on the amendment's adoption. An amendment is deemed to affect the rights of a particular class when it increases or decreases the aggregate number of authorized shares of the class, or modifies the number of shares held by shareholders of the class. Changing any of the designations, preferences, limitations, or rights of the shares of the class also qualifies for special approval. If the proposed amendment creates a new class having rights that are prior, superior, or substantially equal to the rights of the class, provides for an exchange of shares of another class into shares of the class, or divides the class into series, class voting applies. Finally, any amendment that limits or denies the preemptive rights of the shares of the class, or affects accrued but undeclared dividends of the class, must be approved by the class.[6] In most states, a change in the par value of the shares of the class will also require a class vote.

Some examples are appropriate. If the corporation has a class of common stock and a class of nonvoting 6% cumulative preferred stock with a par value of $100, the holders of the preferred shares would be entitled to vote on all amendments to accomplish the following:

1. Increase par value to $200 per share
2. Change dividends from cumulative to noncumulative, but only if dividends have accrued at the time the amendment is proposed
3. Add a new class of preferred stock with equal, prior, or superior liquidation preferences to the existing preferred class

4. Permit the directors to issue the remaining authorized shares of the preferred class in series
5. Add an additional one thousand authorized shares of the preferred class

Each of these amendments directly affects the preferred shareholders by diluting their ownership interest or altering their preferred status, and, in order to pass the amendment, the holders of a majority (or two-thirds, depending upon the jurisdiction) of the shares of the class must vote affirmatively. The class would not have a separate voice on other amendments, however. If the corporation changes its stated purposes, its number of directors, or its period of duration, the nonvoting class may not vote, even though these amendments may indirectly affect the value or quality of the shares.

Since shareholder approval is required for adoption of an amendment to the articles of incorporation, it would be difficult to amend the articles before any shares have been issued unless there were a separate procedure for that contingency. The Model Business Corporation Act has one in Section 10.05, and many states have comparable provisions. If shares have not been issued, an amendment to the articles of incorporation may be adopted by the resolution of the incorporators or the board of directors.

Articles of Amendment

The adopted amendment is set forth in the articles of amendment, which are filed with the appropriate state official. Additional fees and franchise taxes may be due under the state statute when the articles of amendment are filed.

In addition to the statement of the amendment, the Model Business Corporation Act requires that the articles of amendment contain information about the corporation, the number of shares entitled to vote on the amendment, the outcome of the vote, and other specified matters for special amendments.[7]

After examination of the articles of amendment to ensure conformity with the law, the state officer issues a certificate of amendment, and, under most state statutes, the amendment becomes effective upon the issuance of the certificate.[8] In a few states the amendment is effective upon filing,[9] and an even smaller number of states allow the amendment to be effective at a later date as specified in the amendment.[10]

Finally, the additional formalities for amendment of the articles of incorporation parallel the formalities for the articles of incorporation in each jurisdiction.[11] Thus, a jurisdiction that requires that the articles be filed with a county clerk in addition to the secretary of state will also require that the amendment to the articles be so filed. Similarly, if the state statute requires that the articles of incorporation must be published in a newspaper, the amendment to the articles must also be published.

Restated Articles of Incorporation

If the original articles of incorporation have been amended several times, it may be difficult to determine the current status of the articles by studying the files of the secretary of state. Consequently, most statutes permit a *restatement* or *composite* of the articles of incorporation whereby all past amendments are consolidated with the original articles of incorporation into a new document, which supersedes the original articles and the filed amendments. Under Section 10.07 of the Model Business Corporation Act, shareholder approval is not necessary to restate the articles of incorporation, since restatement is only a mechanical process of putting the corporation's file in order. Many states require shareholder approval, and, if a new amendment is to be added in connection with the restatement, shareholder approval would be required under the Model Business Corporation Act as well. The procedure for restatement is specified in the statute, and a restated certificate of incorporation is usually issued.[12]

MERGER, CONSOLIDATION, AND EXCHANGE

Merger and consolidation are statutory devices for the combination of two or more corporations into one corporate entity. The resulting corporation takes over the assets, liabilities, and businesses of the merging or consolidating corporations, and at least one of the corporations in the transaction will cease to exist. The corporate parties to a merger or consolidation are called *constituent* corporations, and that terminology will be used in the discussion of these transactions.

A merger is a device whereby one or more constituent corporations merge into and become a part of another constituent corporation. The corporations that merge into the other corporation cease to exist after the merger. The *surviving* corporation continues to exist after the merger, and takes over the assets and liabilities of the merging corporations. The survivor also takes over the stockholders, personnel, business contacts, and other normal business activities of the terminated corporations. To illustrate, suppose the ABC Corporation and the XYZ Corporation agree to merge, and their agreement provides that the XYZ Corporation will survive the merger. When the merger is accomplished, the ABC Corporation will no longer exist, and all of its assets, liabilities, and other business incidents will belong to XYZ Corporation, which maintains its original corporate structure throughout, unless the merger requires certain amendments to the structure.

A consolidation is different. In a consolidation transaction, one or more constituent corporations join together to form a new corporation, pooling their assets, liabilities, and business and transferring them to a new consolidated entity. The hypothetical ABC and XYZ Corporations could consolidate by forming the LMN Corporation, and transferring all of their respective business to this new corporation. In a consolidation, all constituent corporations cease to exist and the consolidation results in a fresh new corporate kid on the block.

The new Model Business Corporation Act has deleted all references to a consolidation. In modern corporate practice, consolidation transactions are obsolete since it is nearly always advantageous for one of the constituent corporations in the transaction to be the surviving corporation. If creation of a new entity is considered desirable, the new act provides that a new entity may be created for the merger and the disappearing constituent corporations are simply merged into it. Many state statutes still refer to a consolidation transaction, however, and provide a statutory procedure to accomplish it. Consequently, this text still refers to the consolidation as a separate transaction, although it will have limited usefulness in the future.

A more cautious combination than a merger or consolidation is an exchange. Neither corporation ceases to exist in an exchange, but some or all of the shares of one corporation will be exchanged for some or all of the shares of the other corporation. For example, the XYZ Corporation could exchange a certain number of its common shares for all of the preferred shares of ABC Corporation or all of the common shares of ABC Corporation, or it could complete some combination of those transactions. If XYZ Corporation exchanged shares of its common stock for *all* shares of ABC Corporation, common and preferred, the exchange would begin to look like a merger, and it may be necessary to follow merger rules.

Merger, consolidation, and exchange involve structural changes and affect share ownership in the constituent corporations. Consider the shareholders of the ABC Corporation in a merger with the XYZ Corporation. After the merger, their corporation will no longer exist, and they would rightfully expect to be consulted for their approval of the transaction. The shareholders of the expiring constituent corporation will usually receive a specified number of shares of the surviving corporation or cash in return for their original shares. The shareholders of the XYZ Corporation should also approve the transaction, because their share ownership will be diluted when shares are issued to all of the shareholders of the late ABC Corporation. Consolidation and exchange transactions involve the same equities, since shareholders of both constituent corporations will probably be receiving shares of the new consolidated corporation or in exchange for their original shares.

This section is devoted to the statutory procedures for effecting a merger, consolidation, and exchange. Before pressing on, permit a short digression in deference to the tax lawyer's approach to these problems. In tax parlance, the merger, consolidation, or exchange may be referred to as a *reorganization,* based upon definitions of the Internal Revenue Code.[13] The tax treatment of the transfers of assets depends upon the type of reorganization involved, and several different types of reorganizations are defined. The statutory merger or consolidation—that is, one accomplished under the state corporate statutes, as described in this section—is called an A Reorganization. Other important types of reorganization may involve the acquisition of one corporation by another or a combination of two corporations, but may fall short of the complete corporate law merger or consolidation. In a B Reorganization, one corporation swaps its voting shares for a controlling block (80% to 100%) of the shares of another corporation. This is an exchange transaction. Both corporations continue to exist, so full merger or consolidation is not accomplished. The acquired corporation becomes a subsidiary of the acquiring corporation, which maintains at least an 80% controlling interest in the subsidiary's stock. A C Reorganization involves an exchange of voting shares of the acquiring corporation for substantially all of the assets of the acquired corporation. Since both corporations continue to exist, this also is not a true merger or consolidation. Neither is it an exchange, because the stock was traded for assets, not for other stock. The tax statute identifies four other types of reorganizations—D, E, F, and G Reorganizations—which need not be described here, but detailed sources are available to help the inquisitive student learn the definitions and tax aspects of the reorganizations.[14]

With that cursory explanation of the tax terminology out of the way, now proceed with an analysis of the corporate practice requirements of a statutory merger or consolidation.

Procedure

The board of directors' resolution is the procedural starting point for a merger, consolidation, or exchange. The boards of directors of both corporations approve the transaction, stating the names of the constituent corporations; the terms of the proposed merger, consolidation, or exchange; and the manner and basis for converting the shares of the constituent corporations into shares of the exchanging corporation in an exchange, or shares or cash of the surviving corporation in a merger or the new corporation in a consolidation. The plan approved by resolution must also state changes to be made in the articles of incorporation of the surviving corporation for a merger, and the content of the articles of incorporation of the new corporation in a consolidation. The plan may further include any other terms necessary to accomplish the transaction.[15]

The resolution of the board of directors is the first statutory step toward approval of these transactions, and it is only the tip of the iceberg. Notice that the resolution must contain the terms and conditions of the proposed transaction. This unassuming requirement represents the culmination of several months (maybe years) of planning, drafting, and negotiation between the parties to establish those terms. Corporate management will have labored over a lengthy agreement containing terms of the structural changes that it believes will be acceptable to the shareholders and in the best business interests of all corporate parties. New corporate purposes must be drafted to account for the expanded business; the positions of the directors and officers of the constituent corporations must be placed or abandoned in the surviving or new corporation; the accounts of all corporate parties must be combined and reconciled; and by-laws must be harmonized. Certain restrictions regarding dividends, sales of stock, issuance of options, or other activities out of the ordinary course of business will usually be placed on the constituent corporations during the pendency of the transaction. During various stages of these negotiations, the corporate parties will frequently exchange *letters of intent,* which express in writing their respective understandings of the terms of the proposed agreement. Further negotiations are conducted based upon these stated positions, and eventually the negotiations will result in the final agreement, or in abandonment of the transaction if the negotiations reach an impasse. After acceptable terms are drafted,[16] a proposed closing date will be set, considering the other preparatory procedures that must be accomplished before closing. Rulings on the tax ramifications of the transaction are usually required, and the impact of the securities laws on the transfers of stock should be examined. Current accounting opinions should be scheduled and financial reports will be supplemented with current information. Documents must be reviewed by the attorneys, accountants, and other experts for all parties, and appropriate directors' and shareholders' meetings must be held in accordance with state law. That brings us back to the statutory requirements, which begin with the directors' resolution to approve the merger or consolidation plan.

The resolution should reflect that the plan of merger, consolidation, or exchange has been presented to the meeting of directors and approved by the directors, should authorize appropriate corporate officers to call a meeting of shareholders to consider the plan, and should further authorize the officers to file the necessary documents to accomplish the plan if the shareholders of the constituent corporations approve it.

> **EXAMPLE: Resolution to Approve Merger**
> RESOLVED, that the board of directors hereby recommends and approves the proposed Plan of Merger between this corporation and The Nobles Company, a Colorado corporation, substantially in the form presented to this meeting, and the

directors and officers of this corporation are hereby authorized to enter into said plan by executing the same, under the seal of this corporation, and

FURTHER RESOLVED, that said plan as entered into by the directors and officers of this corporation be submitted to the holders of the common stock of this corporation at a special meeting to be called for the purpose of considering and adopting said plan on August 15, 1991 at 2:00 P.M., at the offices of the corporation, and

FURTHER RESOLVED, that July 15, 1991, is hereby fixed as the record date for the determination of the holders of the common stock entitled to notice of and to vote at such special meeting, and

FURTHER RESOLVED, that in the event said plan shall be approved and adopted at the special meeting of the shareholders of this corporation in accordance with the statutory requirements of the State of Colorado, and shall also be approved and adopted by the shareholders of The Nobles Company in accordance with the statutory requirements of the State of Colorado, then the Secretary of this corporation is hereby authorized to certify upon said plan that it has been adopted, and the President and Secretary of this corporation are hereby authorized to execute articles of merger in the name and on behalf of this corporation and under its seal and to cause the same to be filed in the Office of the Secretary of State of the State of Colorado.

The Model Business Corporation Act requires shareholder approval by the shareholders of both corporations for any merger, consolidation, or exchange. Some states limit the approval of an exchange to only the shareholders of the corporation whose shares are being exchanged.

With respect to mergers, there are two important exceptions to the requirement or shareholder vote. The first exception is that under the new Model Business Corporation Act, a shareholder vote of the surviving corporation on a merger is not required if

1. the articles of incorporation of the surviving corporation will not change as a result of the merger;
2. each shareholder of the surviving corporation will have the same number of shares with the same rights after the merger;
3. the number of voting shares outstanding after the merger (plus the number issued as a result of the merger) will not exceed 20% of the total number of voting shares of the surviving corporation immediately before the merger; and
4. the number of participating shares outstanding immediately after the merger (plus the number of participating shares issued as a result of the merger) will not exceed 20% of the total number of participating shares outstanding immediately before the merger.[17]

This transaction is called a *small-impact merger;* the shareholders of the surviving corporation are not required to vote on the plan because it has such a small impact on their ownership rights. Following the merger, the shareholders of the surviving corporation will have essentially the same rights and shares, subject to a dissolution of up to 20%, but they are otherwise unaffected by the transaction.

The second exception is contained in Section 11.04 of the Model Business Corporation Act. If a parent corporation owns at least 90% of the outstanding shares of a subsidiary corporation, the parent may merge the subsidiary into itself without shareholder approval of either corporation. This is called a *short-form merger.* Since the parent corporation already owns at least 90% of the stock of the subsidiary, the two respective business organizations are practically merged anyway. In addition, a shareholder vote at the subsidiary corporation level would be useless, since the parent already owns 90% of the stock, and everyone knows how the parent corporation will vote.

Shareholder approval of a plan of merger, consolidation, or exchange is very similar to that required for amendment of the articles of incorporation and other structural changes. The plan may be considered at either a special or an annual meeting of shareholders. The Model Business Corporation Act requires notice to be given to every shareholder, whether or not entitled to vote, and the notice must always state that the plan of merger, consolidation, or exchange is to be considered at the meeting.[18] Most states require that notice be sent to every shareholder and that it contain a statement of the purpose of the meeting. Further, the notice may have to inform shareholders of their dissenting rights. The period of notice varies from 30 days[19] to 10 days.[20]

Because these transactions affect all corporate shares, many jurisdictions permit all shares to vote on the plan, whether or not they have the right to vote on other corporate matters. The Model Business Corporation Act originally demanded these expanded voting rights, but was later amended to include only regular voting shares on the theory that shareholders with nonvoting stock had waived the right to vote unless the shares of their particular class would be directly affected by the plan. Presently, Section 11.03 of the act requires the affirmative vote of the holders of the majority of voting stock and the affirmative vote of the holders of shares of each class entitled to vote, based upon the same tests for class voting as those applied to amendments to the articles of incorporation.[21] The majority vote concept is a relatively recent addition to the Model Business Corporation Act, and many states continue to require the affirmative vote of the holders of two-thirds of the voting shares.

Shareholders are almost uniformly granted the right to dissent to these transactions and to demand payment for their shares.[22]

Articles of Merger, Consolidation, or Exchange

Following the shareholder approval, articles of merger or articles of consolidation are prepared and filed with the appropriate state official. Many state statutes have no provision for separate articles and instead require that the plan of merger or consolidation, duly certified as having been approved, be filed. Publication may also be required, paralleling the formalities for the original articles of incorporation.[23]

Section 11.05 of the Model Business Corporation Act establishes the contents of the articles of merger or share exchange, including

1. the terms and conditions of the proposed transaction, which is usually contained in a plan that is attached to the articles and made a part thereof by reference;
2. if shareholder approval was not required, a statement to that effect;
3. if approval of the shareholders of one or more corporations party to the merger or share exchange was required,
   (a) the designation, number of outstanding shares, and number of votes entitled to be cast by each voting group entitled to vote separately on the plan as to each corporation, and
   (b) either the total number of votes cast for and against the plan by each voting group entitled to vote separately on the plan or the total number of undisputed

votes cast for the plan separately by each voting group and a statement that the number cast for the plan by each voting group was sufficient for approval by that voting group.

After the articles have been found to conform to law, and the necessary franchise taxes and fees have been paid, a certificate of merger, consolidation, or exchange is issued in most states. As with other matters involving a certificate from the secretary of state, these statutes make the transaction effective when the certificate is issued.[24] Nearly half of the jurisdictions date the effectiveness by the act of filing the required documents,[25] and many others, as well as the Model Business Corporation Act, also provide that the effectiveness of the transaction may be delayed until a date fixed in the plan.[26] The delayed effectiveness alternative is particularly desirable where filings are required in several states and simultaneous filing is impracticable. The effective date may be set at a specified time and all filings completed before that date.

Statutory Effect

When the merger or consolidation becomes effective, all constituent corporate parties to the plan become a single corporation (the designated survivor in a merger or the new corporation in a consolidation), and the other corporations cease to exist. The surviving or new corporation has all of the rights and privileges, is vested with all of the assets, and is responsible for all liabilities and obligations of the constituent corporations. The articles of incorporation of the surviving corporation are deemed amended to the extent provided in the merger plan, filed as a part of the articles of merger. Thus, if the plan requires modifications to the structure of the surviving corporation, there is no need to comply separately with the statutory procedure for amendments to the articles of incorporation.[27] In the case of consolidation, the articles of consolidation are deemed to be the articles of incorporation of the new consolidated corporation.

Hostile Takeovers

Not all business combination transactions are friendly. While many mergers, consolidations, and share exchanges result from negotiations among corporations that desire to combine their businesses, in some cases a corporation or individual will attempt to take over the operations of another corporation by using these statutory combinations against the will of the other corporation and its shareholders.

One corporation may perceive a profitable area for business expansion, but rather than develop its own operations for this purpose, it may attempt to take over another corporation that is already successfully engaged in that type of business. Another corporation's business may be deteriorating because management has lost interest or has been protecting its own expensive, personal objectives (such as high salaries or generous benefit plans). The performance of this corporation may be mediocre. Other companies or individuals may believe that if this corporation's management is replaced, the corporation would be substantially more profitable. These outsiders may see an opportunity to acquire control of the corporation, eliminate its existing management, and replace its management with more effective persons who will make the business profitable. In each of these situations, the prospect of a business combination becomes an adversary transaction. Existing management circles its wagons to protect its position and resist the potential takeover, while the acquiring parties aggressively attempt to secure control of the corporation to modify its business structure and objectives. The aggressors use statutory procedures to acquire the business operations for their own gain.

With public corporations, stock is readily available for purchase in the market. Consequently, a purchaser could buy enough shares of a publicly held corporation in the market to control the shareholder vote on a merger or similar transaction. Even in a closely held corporation, an outsider could acquire a substantial block of stock that would allow that outsider to control corporate activities. It is for this very reason that close corporations usually have shareholder agreements in place that prevent the sale of stock to outsiders without a first offering of the shares to other shareholders or to the company.

Not all acquisitions are for the altruistic business reason of improving the company. Many investors search for stock in companies that may be underpriced either because the market has responded negatively to publicity concerning the company or because the business of the company is in trouble and the market is reflecting uncertainty about the future of the company. These investors may purchase substantial blocks of stock to acquire control, and then use the stock as a basis upon which they will make a personal profit. An investor may sell control back to the company when the directors seek to protect their own positions without having to deal with new shareholders who may threaten their future. The term *greenmail* describes situations in which investors abuse their newly acquired control by selling it back to the corporation or to other interested shareholders at a premium.

Several corporate procedures and statutory rules have been developed to avoid abuses that are likely to occur in a hostile takeover.

Corporate Structure Defenses. When management of a corporation perceives that the corporation is vulnerable to a hostile takeover, certain structural changes can be made to the corporation to discourage the possibility of a takeover. Of course, the structure of the corporation can be changed only with the approval of the shareholders, but management frequently will convince the shareholders that the company's vulnerability could result in a substantial loss of the value of its shares if an outsider acquired control of the company through discount purchases of the company stock in a depressed market.

Usually, management will propose that the stock structure be altered to provide for special rights to existing stockholders in case of a potential takeover. These special rights are frequently called "poison pills" because the structure would permit existing stockholders to exercise them in the event of a takeover, which would cause the takeover to be ineffective. A new class of shares is created, and it has rights that are superior to those of all other shares in the corporation. The corporation declares a dividend, and distributes either the newly created shares or rights to purchase the newly created shares to its existing shareholders. These shares provide that in the event of a proposed merger, consolidation, or share exchange, the existing shareholders would have greater rights than any shareholder who purchased without having the newly created rights or shares. These plans come in various forms, but the general approach of each is to permit the existing shareholders to dilute an interest or acquire a substantially greater interest in the corporation as soon as a triggering event, such as a merger, consolidation, or share exchange, is proposed. Management of the corporation is given the right to redeem these special shares (and thereby neutralize the poison pill) in the event of a friendly takeover.

Management may be able to devise its own defense to a hostile takeover without involving its shareholders. All of the officers of a public company recently announced a "people pill" or "suicide pact" where these officers agreed that if *any* of them were demoted or fired after a change of control of their company, they would *all* resign. Any purchaser would have to choose between retaining all of the existing management without change or losing the entire executive staff at once.

Statutory Rules. Many states have adopted statutes designed to discourage hostile takeovers of their local corporations. These statutes recognize that a hostile takeover usually starts by a market acquisition of controlling shares. Once the *control shares* have been acquired by an investor, the investor can usually cause corporate action to be taken to merge, consolidate, or exchange shares with another company. Investors who purchase shares with this objective are called "sharks," and many of the statutory provisions and corporate structures that can be developed to prevent these takeovers are called "shark repellant." The effect of these statutory provisions will be to place any persons who acquire control shares at a disadvantage so long as they do not have the consensus of the other shareholders about their plans for the business.

One example of these new statutory provisions is the procedures for control share acquisitions found in several states, such as Florida and Indiana. Control shares are defined to mean the shares that would have voting power sufficient to entitle the owner to control the affairs of the corporation. They are usually described in terms of thresholds of percentage of voting power. For example, in Florida the restrictions on control shares are triggered whenever a shareholder acquires 20% of all voting power in a corporation. A second trigger occurs at the acquisition of 30%, and a third occurs when 50% of the voting power is acquired. In a publicly held corporation, only 20% of the entire voting power of the corporation could substantially control the outcome of a vote on a merger or consolidation, but certainly 50% will control the vote.

Whenever a person acquires sufficient control shares, the acquiring shareholder will not be entitled to vote the shares unless the other shareholders affirmatively decide to permit the shareholder to exercise voting power. Voting power is lost and must be affirmatively restored at each triggering event. In other words, the effect of the statute is to take away all votes of the shares acquired until the acquiring shareholder has been able to convince the other shareholders (and probably management) that his or her motives with respect to the control of that corporation are not adverse to the interests of the corporation and the other shareholders. The statute also allows the corporation's articles of incorporation or by-laws to provide that control shares acquired can be redeemed by the corporation at the fair value of the shares, permitting the corporation to buy out a hostile investor, rather than permitting the investor to vote the shares in a manner that will cause harm to other shareholders.

Another approach to statutory protection involves statutory rules relating to mergers, consolidations, and share exchanges with *affiliated corporations*. In a hostile takeover context, one corporation may acquire a substantial number of shares in another corporation. Once the corporation has acquired those shares, it may then elect to vote to merge or consolidate the acquired corporation into its own operations. Again, this could be against the business policies or best interests of the management and shareholders of the acquired corporation. Several state statutes provide that once one corporation acquires a certain percentage of the shares in another corporation, the corporations become affiliated. Then, to accomplish a business combination among the affiliated corporations, the shareholder vote is automatically increased from a majority to a two-thirds vote for that purpose. This gives the existing shareholders statutory protection that a potential shark will have to acquire a substantially larger number of shares to accomplish a business combination transaction if the other shareholders are not persuaded that the combination is in their best interests.

SALE, MORTGAGE, OR OTHER DISPOSITION OF ASSETS

If the corporation disposes of substantially all of its assets, a *corporate shell* results; while the basic corporate structure remains the same, the corporation becomes an organization without normal business assets. The sale, mortgage, lease, exchange, or other disposition of substantially all corporate assets is considered by most states to be a structural change in the corporation that requires shareholder approval.

This type of transaction may be part of a C Reorganization in tax language, where an acquiring corporation exchanges its voting stock for substantially all of the assets of the acquired corporation, or a D Reorganization, where substantially all of the assets are transferred to a corporation controlled by the transferring corporation or its shareholders.[28] These transactions are not statutory mergers or consolidations since all corporations survive the transaction. However, instead of owning business assets, the transferring corporation will own voting stock of the acquiring corporation. The management of the corporation could also sell the entire corporate business to a purchaser for cash, and subsequently dissolve the corporation, distributing the cash to its shareholders.

Statutes regulating these dispositions of assets are designed to secure shareholder approval if substantially all of the assets of the corporation are to be alienated from the business. To illustrate the equities of these statutes, suppose that the Nobles Company is engaged in the business of manufacturing and selling sporting goods. Its assets include all the machinery used for manufacture; the manufacturing plant; its inventory of skis, bicycles, and other sporting goods; accounts receivable; goodwill; and so forth. If substantially all of these assets are sold to another company for cash or stock, the Nobles Company shareholders will have an entirely different investment. Instead of owning an investment in a growing, successful sporting goods company, they may own a corporation holding cash, which will probably be distributed to them in exchange for their shares. Alternatively, their corporation may receive stock of the purchasing corporation, and while the business may be continued by the purchaser, it will operate under different management, which probably has different policies and interests. The character of the investment is thus changed. The law recognizes the fairness of consulting shareholders for their approval of such transactions.

The Model Business Corporation Act makes several distinctions regarding these transactions in Sections 12.01 and 12.02. First, the mortgage or pledge of corporate property never requires shareholder approval. Second, the sale, exchange, lease, or other disposition of substantially all of the property and assets in the regular course of business does not require shareholder approval. Third, no shareholder approval would be required for a corporation to transfer all of its assets to another corporation when the transferring corporation already owns all of the other corporation's shares (such as, where a parent corporation transfers all of its assets to a wholly owned subsidiary). Fourth, shareholder approval is required if substantially all of the corporate assets are sold, leased, exchanged, or disposed of in a transaction not within the ordinary course of business.

Most states permit the mortgage or pledge of corporate property without shareholder approval. In these transactions, the corporation continues to use the property, but has granted an interest in the property as collateral to secure a loan or other obligation. Business should continue as usual, and the property will be lost only if the corporation defaults on the obligation. The character of the shareholder's investment will not be affected if all goes as planned—that is, the corporate business will generate enough income to pay the obligation, the mortgage or pledge will be removed, and the corporate assets will remain intact. Consequently, there is no pressing need for shareholder protection here.

Several jurisdictions provide, as does the Model Business Corporation Act, that a sale or other disposition of substantially all of the corporate assets, if within the regular course of corporate business, may be accomplished by action of the board of directors without shareholder approval. The theory behind this rule is that if the transaction is within the ordinary course of corporate business, the board of directors is already authorized to proceed with it, and shareholder approval is never required for normal business transactions. On the other hand, other state statutes do not attempt to distinguish between transactions in or out of the ordinary course of business, perhaps because the distinction is difficult to apply. However, where the distinction exists, the normalcy of the transaction may be determined by the statement of purposes in the articles of incorporation. Suppose a corporation is organized for the purpose of purchasing and selling a single parcel of real estate, anticipating a profit from the sale. When the property is sold, the transaction is within the ordinary course of business, since that is exactly what the corporation was organized to do. Most cases are not that easy, however. If the articles of incorporation of the Nobles Company stated that one purpose of the corporation would be to "sell, lease, transfer, exchange, or otherwise deal in the assets of the corporation," the broad enabling authority may make a transfer of substantially all assets a normal corporate event, but that would certainly be subject to interpretation. From the standpoint of better corporate practice, any questionable transaction should be approved by the shareholders.

The transfer of all of the assets of a parent corporation to its subsidiary also should not involve shareholder approval. The shareholders own the shares of the parent, which already owns all of the shares of the subsidiary. When the parent's assets are distributed to the subsidiary, the same shareholders still own the assets, through their ownership of the parent.

Procedure

Once the sale or other disposition of assets is characterized as a structural change (as it is in every case where the transaction is not within the ordinary course of business), the procedure for approval of the transaction parallels the approval of a merger, consolidation, or share exchange. The board of directors adopts a resolution recommending the transaction and directing the submission of its terms to the shareholders for their approval.

> **EXAMPLE: Resolution for Sale of Assets Outside the Ordinary Course of Business**
>
> RESOLVED, that this Board do and hereby does declare that the consideration in the form of capital stock of The Nobles Company to be received in exchange for the hereinabove described properties and interests, is a full, fair and adequate consideration; that this Board do and hereby does ratify, confirm and approve all of the acts of its officers in making said agreement with The Nobles Company; and that this Board do and hereby does recommend to the stockholders of this Company that said agreement be approved by said stockholders; and
>
> FURTHER RESOLVED, that the question of approval of said agreement with The Nobles Company be submitted to the stockholders of this Company in a special meeting called for that purpose; and to that end it is
>
> FURTHER RESOLVED, that a special meeting of the stockholders of this Company be called to be held at the principal office of this Company in the City of Des Moines, State of Iowa, at 10:00 o'clock, a.m., on the 10th day of October, 1991; that the secretary of this Company be and he hereby is authorized and directed to give all the stockholders of this Company proper, timely and adequate notice of the time, place and purpose of said meeting; and that books for the transfer of stock will close at the conclusion of business on September 15, 1991, and will reopen on the day following the adjournment of said meeting.

The shareholders may consider the transaction at either an annual or special meeting.[29] Every shareholder, whether or not otherwise entitled to vote, must receive such notice. The period of notice is likely to be different in the several states, and some states require a statement of the shareholders' rights if they dissent to the transaction.[30] The Model Business Corporation Act requires an affirmative vote of the majority of the voting shares to approve the transaction, and authorizes class voting if the transaction affects the rights of the particular class. Many states continue to adhere to a two-thirds affirmative vote requirement, and some permit all outstanding shares to vote on the transaction.[31]

Bulk Transfer Requirements

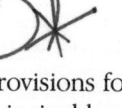

The Uniform Commercial Code contains provisions for the protection of business creditors whenever an enterprise whose principal business is to sell merchandise from stock (including one that manufactures what it sells) sells a major part of its assets out of the regular course of business. The Uniform Commercial Code (or portions of it) has been adopted in every state, so its provisions must be observed whenever a corporate *enterprise,* as defined, sells or otherwise transfers a major part of its assets outside the scope of ordinary business activities. The hypothetical Nobles Company, which is engaged in the manufacture and sale of sporting goods, is one such enterprise, and a transfer of its assets, including inventory, equipment, materials, and supplies, is subject to these requirements.

The bulk transfer requirements are concerned only with the creditors of the selling corporation who obviously have an interest in the assets of the business. If the business assets are sold in one transaction without the knowledge of those creditors, the creditors' chances of being paid may be significantly reduced.

To comply with the code, the seller must prepare an affidavit containing the names and business addresses of all creditors and the amounts owed to them as of the date of the transfer. The seller must also prepare a schedule identifying the property transferred. The list of creditors and the schedule identifying the property must be preserved by the purchaser for a period of six months following the transfer, and it must be available for inspection and copying by any business creditor.[32] In addition to the list and schedule, notice must be sent to every creditor of the business at least ten days before the buyer takes possession of the property or pays for it, whichever occurs first.[33] Only creditors who hold claims as of the date of the transfer should receive notice.

Failure to prepare and preserve the list and schedule or to give notice to creditors makes the transfer ineffective against the creditors of the business, meaning that the creditors may disregard the transfer and use the property to satisfy their claims. Of course, if the creditors are paid, they have no claim against the property. Moreover, the right to disregard the transfer does not last indefinitely. No creditor may reach the property more than 6 months after the transferee took possession of the goods, unless the transfer has been concealed, in which case the 6-month period runs from the date the transfer is discovered.[34]

RIGHTS OF DISSENTING SHAREHOLDERS

Under the Model Business Corporation Act and several statutes, nearly half of the outstanding shares may be voted *against* a merger, consolidation, share exchange, or sale of assets and the transaction will still be approved. The majority rule controls the holders of the dissenting shares, who must live with the decision of the majority, despite the effect the transaction may have on their shares. The statutory solution to this problem is to grant the dissenting shareholders the right to have their shares appraised and purchased, with limited exceptions, if they do not want to continue as investors in the corporation. In some states this is called the "shareholder's right of appraisal" or the "shareholder's right to demand payment of the value of the stock." Every state includes some rights of dissent and payment in its corporate statute.

Circumstances Giving Rise to Appraisal Rights

The Model Business Corporation Act grants the right to dissent in cases of mergers, share exchanges, and sales or exchange of substantially all assets outside the ordinary course of business. In addition, dissenters' rights will apply if the articles of incorporation are amended to materially affect the rights of a shareholder (such as by abolishing a preferential right, a preemptive right, a redemption right, or a voting right), and if the articles, by-laws, or resolutions of the board of directors so provide, they may apply to any transaction designated therein.[35]

The dissent and appraisal rights are limited by two important exceptions. They do not apply to shareholders of a surviving corporation whose votes were not necessary to approve the merger. This rule covers a merger of a subsidiary corporation into a parent corporation when the parent owned 90% or more of the stock of the subsidiary before the merger and a merger that will have a small impact upon the surviving corporation.[36] The Model Business Corporation Act formerly excluded holders of shares registered on a national securities exchange at the time the shareholders entitled to vote were identified, unless the articles of incorporation provided otherwise. Delaware and a few other states[37] have adopted such a rule, excepting holders of shares listed on a national exchange and holders of a class of shares that has 2,000 or more shareholders of record. The assumption that forms the basis for these rules is that the shares are readily salable if they are registered on a national securities exchange (or if 2,000 other shareholders exist), so the cumbersome appraisal procedure is not necessary to satisfy the dissenting shareholder. A shareholder should be able to sell shares at market if he or she decides to terminate an investment.

The Model Business Corporation Act includes another interesting provision allowing a shareholder to dissent as to less than all shares registered in the shareholder's name, in which case the dissenter's rights are to be determined as to the shares dissenting and the remaining shares are treated as if they belonged to different shareholders. On its face, the provision seems to be directed to an indecisive shareholder who is uncertain about the transaction and who will dissent as to some shares to recoup some of an investment, but will keep other shares in case the structural change turns out to be successful. Theoretically, this could happen, but the rule was designed to permit brokers, trustees, and agents holding shares for their clients to split the shares into approving and disapproving groups depending upon their clients' wishes.

Some states are more generous with dissenting shareholders' appraisal rights than is the Model Business Corporation Act. They extend the rights to certain other amendments to the articles of incorporation, such as changes in the corporate purposes, extension of corporate life, and changes in the capital stock structure.[38]

Procedure

Statutory provisions detailing the procedures for perfecting the shareholder's right to payment after dissent are quite complex. The first step is the notice of the shareholders meeting, which, when dissenters' rights apply, must state that shareholders may be entitled to assert dissenters' rights and must be accompanied by a copy of the statute that grants the rights.[39]

Then comes the dissent itself. The shareholder must file *written* notice of an intention to demand payment for shares before the vote is taken at the meeting of shareholders called to consider the transaction.[40] The objection must be made before the meeting in some states, and a few states require that the objection include a demand for appraisal and purchase of the shares.[41]

Of course, the shareholder must not vote in favor of the transaction at the meeting.[42]

Next assume the transaction is approved by the other shareholders and will eventually be consummated by the corporation. In most states, after approval, the shareholder has a certain period of time within which to demand payment of the fair value of the shares. This time period varies. The demand is addressed to the corporation in a sale of assets or a share exchange; to the surviving corporation in a merger; or to the new corporation in a consolidation. If the shareholder fails to object, to vote against the action, or to demand payment within the time provided, he or she loses the right to payment for shares, and is bound by the corporate action.

The revised Model Business Corporation Act now takes a little different approach. If the transaction is approved, the corporation must send notice of that fact to the shareholder who has demanded payment and voted properly (against or abstaining from the transaction), together with a form to use to demand payment and a copy of the statute, stating when the demand must be made and where the shares must be deposited. The time period in the notice cannot be less than 30 days or more than 60 days from the date the notice was delivered.[45] Failure to return the demand on time, with the shares, forfeits the shareholder's rights to dissent and sell shares to the corporation. If the shareholder demands payment and deposits the share certificates within the time period required by the notice, the shareholder will be entitled to continue to exercise shareholder rights until the rights are cancelled or modified by the taking of the proposed corporate action.[44]

The *fair value* of the shares is defined by the Model Business Corporation Act to be the value immediately before the effectuation of the corporate transaction, excluding appreciation or depreciation in anticipation of the transaction.[45] This test requires an evaluation of the impact of the publicity surrounding the transaction in the appraisal of the shares, and is extremely difficult to apply. For that reason, many states ignore appreciation or depreciation in value determination, or set the date for this appraisal at some other time farther removed from shareholder approval. The Model Business Corporation Act also recognizes that there are certain situations in which the exclusion of appreciation or depreciation would be inequitable. In those cases, the fair value is to be determined without considering appreciation or depreciation of the shares.

The corporation and the shareholder are encouraged to agree upon the value of the shares, but if fair value is disputed, the Model Business Corporation Act prescribes an elaborate procedure for resolving the issue. Once the corporation has delivered the dissenters' notice (no later than ten days after the corporate action was taken), the shareholders who wish to sell their shares must demand payment, certify their ownership of the shares, and deposit their certificates in accordance with the terms of the notice. The reason for the certification of ownership is to allow the corporation to determine whether a shareholder owned the shares before the public announcement of the proposed corporate action. If the shareholder purchased the shares after information concerning the proposed corporate action was available, the corporation may withhold payment for that shareholder's shares. This provision prevents shareholders from purchasing shares just before a corporation enters into a fundamental transaction so that they have an automatic market for the sale of their stock through dissenters' rights.[46]

Except for shares acquired after public information is available, the corporation must pay each dissenter the amount the corporation estimates to be a fair value of the shares, plus accrued interest. This payment must be accompanied by the corporation's recent financial statements, an estimate of the fair value from the corporation, an explanation of how the interest was calculated, and a statement of the dissenters' rights (usually including a copy of the statute itself).[47]

If a shareholder disagrees with the estimate of fair value the shareholder may file his or her own estimate with the corporation within 30 days. If the corporation cannot settle with the shareholder within 60 days after the shareholder's demand, the question of fair value will be referred to a court. The corporation must file the petition and, if it fails to do so, the corporation must pay the shareholder the price the shareholder demanded. If an action is filed with a court, all dissenters who dispute fair value are made parties to the action. The court may appoint appraisers to determine the fair value of the shares, and the court will enter a judgment for the value set by those appraisers.[48] The corporation is usually required to pay the expenses of the proceedings, but the court may assess the expenses against the dissenting shareholders if it finds that their rejection of the corporation's offered amount was arbitrary, vexatious, or not in good faith, and was without justification.[49]

Many states continue to base dissenters' rights on the old Model Business Corporation Act provisions, which also contained elaborate procedures for these disputes. To illustrate the differences between the old and new acts' sections, and to show dissenters' rights procedures as they exist in many states, the following table is offered.

Timetable #1 Days		Former Model Business Corporation Act	Revised Model Business Corporation Act
	−10	Date notice is sent to shareholders	Date corporation notifies shareholders of right to dissent
	−1	Date fair value determined	Date fair value determined
Date of meeting for shareholder approval	0	Latest date for written objection to action; shareholder must vote against action	Latest date for filing written objection; shareholder must not vote in favor of transaction
	10	Latest date for written demand for payment	If transaction is approved, date corporation sends notice to dissenters
	30	Latest date for submitting certificates representing shares to corporation for notation	Earliest date that corporation may require shareholder to demand payment and deposit certificates
	60		If transaction is not effected by now, date the corporation must return certificates
Date action is effected	0		Date corporation remits payment of fair value with information required by statute
	10	Latest date for corporation notice to shareholders with an offer at a specified price	
	30	Latest date for agreement	Latest date for dissenter's demand for dissenter's estimate of fair value
	60	Latest date for corporation to file petition on its own	
	90	Latest date for corporation to file petition on shareholder demand; date of payment if agreement reached on fair value	Latest date for corporation to settle with shareholder or file a petition with the court; failure to do one or the other requires payment to the dissenter at dissenter's price

Considering this complicated procedure, you may be able to understand why a corporate officer would equate the blessed glory of heaven with unanimous shareholder approval of the transaction. Further, in the spirit of this analogy, the dissenting shareholder, like a fallen angel, is banished from the corporate paradise, unless the shareholder repents. This remedy of the shareholder is said to be "exclusive," meaning that a demand for payment for shares is the only remedy a shareholder has if dissatisfied with the transaction. When the demand for payment is made, the shareholder loses the right to vote or to exercise any other rights as a shareholder. The shareholder is usually not entitled to withdraw the demand unless the corporation consents, and shareholder status is regained only upon withdrawal and consent, or if the corporation abandons the transaction, or if a court decides that the shareholder is not entitled to the right of payment for the shares.

VOLUNTARY DISSOLUTION

The dissolution of the corporation is a structural change that will affect the shareholders. Again, the shareholders must be consulted for their approval.

Procedure

The corporation may be dissolved at any time after it is formed by the appropriate concurrence of its aggregate membership. A decision to dissolve may be made immediately after formation, before the corporation commences business and before shares are issued. The incorporators (or the initial directors, if named in the articles of incorporation) constitute the total aggregate membership at this point, and an admission that the corporation was a bad idea is theirs to make. The Model Business Corporation Act procedure for dissolution before commencement of business and before the issuance of shares is very simple. The majority of the incorporators (or the initial directors) may execute and file articles of dissolution and a certificate of dissolution will be issued.[50]

A corporation that has commenced business and has issued shares may be dissolved through two typical procedures, which may originate with either the shareholders or the directors of the corporation. If the shareholders take the initiative, many states allow voluntary dissolution by the shareholders' unanimous written consent. All shareholders, whether or not they are otherwise entitled to vote, normally must join the consent, but a few states allow the holders of only the voting shares to make the decision.[51]

If the decision to dissolve eminates from the board of directors (as it must under the Model Business Corporation Act), or if unanimous shareholder consent to the dissolution is not feasible, the corporation may be dissolved by the usual procedure for corporate structural changes—that is, by the directors and the shareholders acting in their respective meetings. The board of directors adopts a resolution recommending that the corporation be dissolved and submits this resolution to the vote of the shareholders at either an annual or a special meeting.[52]

> **EXAMPLE: Resolution to Dissolve**
> The president made a statement as to the present plight of the Corporation, and after a confirmatory statement by the treasurer it was unanimously

RESOLVED, that the Board of Directors hereby recommend to the stockholders that in their interest this Corporation be dissolved and its affairs wound up; and

FURTHER RESOLVED, that a special meeting of the stockholders of the Corporation be held at the offices of the Corporation, on the 3rd day of December, 1991, at 3:00 o'clock p.m., to vote on the question as to whether this Corporation be dissolved, and that the secretary is hereby directed to give due notice of said meeting.[53]

The Model Business Corporation Act does not specify any unusual time period within which notice must be given, but the notice must state that the meeting will be for the purpose of considering the dissolution of the corporation.[54]

EXAMPLE: Notice of a Meeting for Dissolution

The stockholders of The Nobles Company are hereby notified that a special meeting of the stockholders of said Company will be held at the corporation's offices, 200 West 14th Avenue, Denver, Colorado, on the 3rd day of December, 1991, at 3:00 o'clock p.m., to vote on the question as to whether said Company should be dissolved.

Dated November 18, 1991.

_____, Secretary[55]

The shareholders must approve dissolution by a designated percentage of the vote. The Model Business Corporation Act originally required the affirmative vote of the holders of two-thirds of the outstanding shares entitled to vote on the issue, but the percentage was recently reduced to a majority of the voting shares. Class voting is also authorized under the act. Many states continue to adhere to the two-thirds vote requirement, and several jurisdictions allow every share to vote on the dissolution question, whether or not otherwise entitled to vote. The minutes of the shareholders' meeting would reflect the approval of the dissolution.

EXAMPLE: Resolution to Dissolve

WHEREAS, the Board of Directors believe this Corporation should be dissolved, and have called this special meeting of the stockholders to consider the matter; and

WHEREAS, after considering the statements of officers and a report of a committee of the stockholders, it appears to be for the best interests of the stockholders of this Corporation that its business should be terminated, the Corporation dissolved, and its assets distributed according to law:

NOW, THEREFORE, the holders of record of two-thirds of the outstanding shares of this Corporation entitled to vote therein concurring therein.

RESOLVED, that this Corporation hereby elects to dissolve, and that pursuant to the Colorado Corporation Law, the president and secretary, or other proper officers, are hereby authorized to execute and file the proper certificate of dissolution with the Secretary of State, that they duly publish the certificate of the Secretary of State of said filing, and that they and the other officers of this Corporation are hereby authorized and directed to take the steps prescribed by law to complete the dissolution and to wind up the affairs of this Corporation.[56]

A dissenting shareholder's appraisal remedy is rare in dissolution, and even if authorized, is usually limited to special circumstances surrounding the dissolution.

Statement of Intent to Dissolve

The dissolution procedure in most states has two sections designed to give advance public and private notice to outsiders that the corporation has initiated dissolution proceedings. These notices are intended to facilitate orderly liquidation of the corporation.

The statement of intent to dissolve, the first notice filed for dissolution of a going concern, is not required for dissolution by the incorporators since one prerequisite to that dissolution procedure is that the corporation has not yet commenced business, and thus protection of the public is not deemed to be necessary.

The statement of intent to dissolve must be executed and filed with the secretary of state if the dissolution has been approved by unanimous consent of the shareholders or by resolution of the board of directors with subsequent shareholder approval.[57] Many states require this first notice of the dissolution, although the statement may have to be published rather than filed.

Upon filing the statement, or beginning other specified statutory requirements for dissolution, the corporation must cease all normal business activity, and it may continue in business only for the purpose of winding up its affairs. The filing of the statement of intent does not terminate corporate existence. The corporate existence usually continues until a certificate of dissolution has been issued by the secretary of state or until a court has declared the corporation to be dissolved.

Notice to Creditors

After filing a statement of intent to dissolve, the corporation will proceed to collect its assets and to liquidate its business. As a part of the liquidation process, the corporation gives to each known creditor notice of its intent to dissolve. This is the private notice that complements the filed statement. Through these notices, everyone who cares about the corporation should have learned about the dissolution before it becomes effective. Some states require that the corporation advertise its intention to dissolve in a newspaper, rather than sending notices directly to creditors.

Articles of Dissolution

The new Model Business Corporation Act eliminates the prior filing of a statement of intent to dissolve and notice to creditors, and simply provides that after the dissolution is authorized, the corporation must deliver articles of dissolution to the secretary of state. In most states, these articles of dissolution will be filed only after payment of all corporate debts, liabilities, and obligations and after distribution of the remaining corporate property and assets to the shareholders. The articles of dissolution are executed and filed with the secretary of state with the same formality as are the original articles of incorporation. The articles of dissolution usually must state that the corporation has been liquidated. If the corporation had been a going concern, the articles of dissolution recite that all debts, obligations, and liabilities of the corporation have been paid and discharged or that adequate provisions have been made therefor, and that all the remaining property and assets of the corporation have been distributed among the shareholders in accordance with their respective rights and interests. If the voluntary dissolution occurred before the issuance of shares and commencement of business, the incorporators file articles of dissolution declaring those facts and confirming the return of amounts paid for subscriptions.

Upon the receipt and examination of the articles of dissolution, the secretary of state usually issues a certificate of dissolution, and at that point the existence of the corporation ceases. The new Model Business Corporation Act provides that the corporation is dissolved on the effective date stated in its articles of dissolution.[58]

A dissolved corporation continues its corporate existence, but may not carry on any business except to wind up its business affairs. Dissolution of the corporation does not affect title to the corporation's property, prevent transfer of the corporation's shares or securities, subject the corporation's directors and officers to personal liability, prevent commencement of a proceeding by or against the corporation in its name, or affect any proceedings that have been commenced by or against the corporation.[59] Section 14.06 of the Model Business Corporation Act requires that the dissolved corporation must notify any creditors or other claimants of the dissolution in writing after the dissolution has occurred. This notice will state a deadline, which cannot be fewer than 120 days from the date of the notice, by which claims will be considered. If a creditor does not make a claim within the stated time, the creditor may be barred from ever asserting the claim.[60] The dissolved corporation may also publish a notice of its dissolution for any persons who have claims that are not known to the corporation. This publication may state that any claim against the corporation will be barred after five years from the publication of the notice. Any timely filed claim may be enforced against the corporation (to the extent of its undistributed assets), or, if the assets have been distributed, against the shareholders who have received those assets on a pro rata basis.

Revocation of Voluntary Dissolution Proceedings

Just as the shareholders and the corporation approve voluntary dissolution, so may they revoke it. This indecision is expensive and time-consuming, but every statute gives the intracorporate parties the right to change their minds. The procedure for revocation usually duplicates the procedure for approval. If the shareholders consented to the dissolution (where permitted under local law), they may, by written consent any time before the issuance of a certificate of dissolution, revoke the dissolution proceedings by submitting a statement of revocation to the secretary of state. The revocation may also be accomplished by act of the corporation. The board of directors may submit to the vote of the shareholders a resolution revoking voluntary dissolution proceedings. Shareholder approval of revocation of voluntary dissolution requires the same vote (either majority or two-thirds) as that required for approval of dissolution.[61] When the statement of revocation is filed with the secretary of state, the corporation may again proceed to conduct business, as if nothing had ever happened. The revocation of voluntary dissolution proceedings must occur within 120 days of the effective date of dissolution under the Model Business Corporation Act, but most jurisdictions require the decision to be made before the articles of dissolution are filed.

INVOLUNTARY DISSOLUTION

By the State

A wayward corporation may be dragged, perhaps kicking and screaming, into dissolution by its creator, the state. The state is always entitled to enforce its laws, and if a corporation has failed to comply with the statutory requirements, the secretary of state or the attorney general may bring an action to force dissolution of the corporation. Typical corporate abuses that will justify involuntary dissolution include failing to file annual reports, failing to pay franchise taxes, procuring articles of incorporation through fraud, or abusing or exceeding authority granted by law.[62] Some jurisdictions add failure to appoint a registered agent or to notify regarding a change of the corporation's registered office within thirty days, insolvency, unfair competition or restraint of trade, persistent violations of state laws, or an existence that is detrimental to the public interest.

Most corporations will never run afoul of state law or commit other acts that support involuntary dissolution, but a few provisions in this area are to be approached with caution. Even otherwise conscientious corporate officers may delay annual reports, overlook payment of franchise taxes, or neglect to report changes of the registered office or registered agent. The procedures here should be explored, therefore, in an effort to save this creation, over which we have labored through nine chapters, from untimely demise for a mere oversight.

The Model Business Corporation Act provisions appear to take the fairest approach to these problems. Under Sections 14.20 and 14.21, the secretary of state sends notice of any alleged transgressions to the corporation at its registered office or, if it no longer maintains a registered office within the state, at its principal place of business. This notice may be sent if the corporation does not pay taxes, deliver its annual report, or maintain current information concerning its registered agent or registered office, or if the corporation's period of duration expires. Within sixty days after service of the notice, the corporation may satisfy the secretary of state that the matter has been resolved or that the grounds for the notice did not exist. If the corporation fails to respond to the notice, the secretary of state may administratively dissolve the corporation by issuing a certificate of dissolution. After the certificate of dissolution has been issued, the corporation may not carry on any business except to wind up and liquidate its affairs. At any time within two years after the effective date of an administrative dissolution, the corporation may apply to the secretary of state to be reinstated. Of course, a condition to reinstatement would be to resolve or eliminate any grounds that existed for dissolution at the time of the issuance of the certificate. If the secretary of state permits a reinstatement (or if a court orders reinstatement on appeal from the secretary of state's denial of an application for reinstatement), the reinstatement is retroactive and the corporation may resume its business as if the administrative dissolution had never occurred.[63]

Not all states are so forgiving. While many states require notice to the corporation, only about half of the jurisdictions allow the corporation to cure the defect after dissolution proceedings have actually been commenced.

By Shareholders

If corporate management refuses to consider dissolution and the unanimous consent of the shareholders cannot be obtained, voluntary dissolution is impossible, but an involuntary dissolution procedure may be invoked in special circumstances. This problem may arise in several situations. For example, under the Model Business Corporation Act, if the board of directors does not recommend a voluntary dissolution to the shareholders, the shareholders have no independent authority to dissolve the corporation alone. Even under jurisdictions that permit the shareholders to voluntarily dissolve their own corporation by unanimous consent, if the majority of the directors are also shareholders and oppose dissolution, no matter how many other shareholders favor dissolution, dissolution cannot be accomplished voluntarily. The approval of the directors-shareholders is necessary for unanimous shareholder consent and for a director resolution for dissolution. Dissolution by voluntary proceedings is also impossible if the directors or shareholders are deadlocked.

The statutory escape is the shareholders' application to a court for liquidation of the business and a decree of dissolution. Section 14.30 of the Model Business Corporation Act grants liquidation power to a court upon application of a shareholder who can establish an unbreakable director deadlock threatening irreparable injury to the corporation; oppressive, illegal, or fraudulent acts of those in control of the corporation; a shareholder deadlock in failing to elect new directors for a period of two years; or misapplication or waste of the corporate assets. These grounds are typical among corporate statutes granting the shareholder right to bring an action for involuntary liquidation and dissolution. Abandonment of the corporate business or persistent commission of ultra vires acts are also frequently specified grounds.

Some states have recently expanded the shareholders' authority to obtain a judicial decree of dissolution. In doing so, they recognize that majority shareholders or directors may take action against certain minority shareholders that may, at the least, put pressure on the minority shareholders to go along with the policies of the majority, and, at the worst, actually oppress the minority shareholders so that the corporation is not acting in their best interests. In these statutes, the shareholders may obtain a decree of dissolution by showing that the directors or those in control of the corporation are acting in a manner "unfairly prejudicial" to the shareholders in their capacity as shareholders, directors, or officers, or as employees of closely held corporations. These statutes also empower a court to order that the corporation buy out the complaining shareholder at a fair price, rather than dissolving the corporation.[64] The Model Business Corporation Act's Close Corporation Supplement provides for a similar remedy in Section 42, which would apply to closely held corporations.

If the shareholder proves the allegations in the action, the court proceeds to a judicially-supervised liquidation ending in a decree of dissolution.[65] However, if the problem is solved during the course of the liquidation proceedings, most state statutes require that the proceedings be discontinued, and all corporate property will be returned to the corporation.[66]

By a Creditor

Creditors may also force involuntary dissolution if the corporation is insolvent and the creditor's claim is undisputed. The Model Business Corporation Act deems claims that have been reduced to judgment and claims that have been admitted by the corporation in writing to be undisputed.[67] The creditor is in the frustrating position of owning an uncontested debt, which corporate management cannot pay because the corporation is insolvent. Moreover, management is resisting dissolution and liquidation whereby the creditor would receive some satisfaction from the assets. In such a case, the creditor may force judicial liquidation and involuntary dissolution.

LIQUIDATION

Closely associated with dissolution, whether voluntary or involuntary, is the process of collecting all corporate assets, completing or terminating unexecuted contracts, paying creditors and expenses, and distributing the remains to the owners. These activities are collectively referred to as liquidation. Under the Model Business Corporation Act, normal corporate business ceases when a decree of dissolution is entered by a court or when the secretary of state issues a certificate of dissolution.[68] The only corporate activities that may follow a dissolution are those necessary to wind up and liquidate the business and affairs of the corporation. Consequently, liquidation and winding-up precede final dissolution.

Nonjudicial Liquidation

When dissolution is voluntary and does not involve judicial proceedings, corporate management is responsible for winding up the corporate business and liquidating. In most states, this process is commenced after the statement of intent to dissolve is filed and must be completed before the articles of dissolution are filed, since the articles usually recite that all debts, obligations, and liabilities have been paid or provided for, and that the remaining assets have been distributed among the shareholders. There is no time limit on the liquidation process, but practical considerations encourage management to proceed as expeditiously as possible.

Nonjudicial liquidation may be conducted as informally as desired, as long as all creditors are paid and remaining assets are distributed. Special safeguards are inserted for creditors: The directors of the corporation may be personally liable if they distribute assets to the shareholders without providing for creditors,[69] and a forgotten creditor may enforce its claim against the corporation, directors, or shareholders for a period of time after dissolution.[70]

The new Model Business Corporation Act has expanded creditor protection in a dissolution of a corporation. Known creditors must receive notice of the dissolution instructing them about submitting claims within a period of time, no less than 120 days from the effective date of the notice. If a creditor does not deliver the claim, or if the claim is rejected and the creditor does not promptly commence a proceeding to enforce the claim, the claim will be barred.[71] For persons who may have a claim against the corporation but are not known at the time of dissolution, the dissolved corporation may publish notice of dissolution and request that persons with claims present them in accordance with the notice. Any person who does not respond to the published notice within five years after the publication date will not be entitled to assert a claim against the corporation.[72]

If the directors or officers become immersed in liquidation and discover dissatisfied shareholders, or hostile creditors, they may apply to have the liquidation supervised by a court.

Judicial Liquidation

Court-supervised liquidation is available to corporate management in voluntary dissolution proceedings and is also used when involuntary proceedings have been commenced by the state, the shareholders, or creditors of a corporation. The court may enjoin any person who threatens to interfere with orderly proceedings, and may appoint a receiver who will carry on the corporate business and preserve the corporation's assets during the proceedings. Creditors are usually required to file their claims under oath within a prescribed time, and a hearing will be held to finally determine the claims of all parties. A liquidating receiver is then appointed with authority to collect and sell the assets of the corporation, to apply the proceeds to the expenses of the liquidation and to creditors' claims, and then to distribute remaining funds to shareholders.[73]

Liquidation Distributions

In any liquidation of a corporation, judicially supervised or conducted by management, the corporate assets will be collected and may be sold, and the proceeds are used to pay first the expenses of liquidation and then the creditors of the corporation. Whatever remains belongs to the shareholders of the corporation. The remnants of the stockholders' corporation are distributed to them in accordance with their liquidation preferences.[74]

NOTES

1. M.B.C.A. § 10.03.
2. E.g., Pennsylvania, 15 Pa.Stat. § 1802.
3. See "Shareholder Meetings" in Chapter 8.
4. E.g., Colorado, Colo.Rev.Stat. § 7-2-107 (30 days' notice if the amendment increases the authorized number of shares).
5. See M.B.C.A. § 7.04 and "Action without a Meeting" in Chapter 8.
6. See M.B.C.A. § 10.04.
7. M.B.C.A. § 10.06. An example of articles of amendment appears as Form 13A in Appendix G.
8. E.g., New Mexico, N.M.Stat.Ann. § 53-13-5. An example of a certificate of amendment appears as Form 13B in Appendix G.
9. E.g., Nebraska, Neb.Rev.Stat. § 21-2062; and Pennsylvania, 15 Pa.Stat. § 809.
10. E.g., Florida, Fla.Stat.Ann. § 607.191(2) (not more than 90 days after filing); and N.J.Stat.Ann. § 14A:9-4(5) (not more than 30 days after filing).
11. See "Filing and Other Formalities" in Chapter 6.
12. Examples of restated articles and a restated certificate of incorporation are Forms 13C and 13D in Appendix G.
13. Int.Rev.Code of 1986, 25 U.S.C.A. § 368(a)(1).
14. See B. Bittker and J. Eustice, Federal Income Taxation of Corporations and Shareholders, Chapter 14 (1982); H. Henn and J. Alexander, Laws of Corporations § 351, 3d ed. (1983).
15. See M.B.C.A. §§ 11.01 and 11.02.
16. Sample agreements for statutory mergers and statutory consolidations may be found in West's Modern Legal Forms §§ 3044-3049.
17. M.B.C.A. § 11.03.
18. M.B.C.A. § 11.03.
19. E.g., Montana, Mont.Code.Ann. § 35-1-803.
20. E.g., Pennsylvania, 15 Pa.Stat. § 902.
21. See "Amendment of the Articles of Incorporation" earlier in this chapter.
22. See "Rights of Dissenting Shareholders" later in this chapter.
23. See "Filing and Other Formalities" in Chapter 6.
24. E.g., Alabama, Ala.Code Bus.Corp.Act § 87. Examples of articles of merger and articles of consolidation, and certificates of each, appear as Forms 13E to 13I in Appendix G.
25. E.g., California, West's Ann.Calif.Corp.Code § 1103; New York, McKinney Consol.Laws of N.Y.Bus.Corp.Law § 906; and Pennsylvania, 15 Pa.Stat. § 906.
26. M.B.C.A. § 11.05(G); e.g., Iowa, Iowa Code Ann. § 496A.73; and Michigan, Mich.Comp.Laws Ann. §§ 21.200(131) and 21.200(731) (no later than 90 days after filing).
27. M.B.C.A. § 11.06.
28. Int.Rev.Code of 1986, 26 U.S.C.A. § 368(1)(a).
29. M.B.C.A. § 79.
30. E.g., Georgia, Ga.Code Ann. § 14-2-231. See "Rights of Dissenting Shareholders" later in this chapter.
31. E.g., Connecticut, Conn.Gen.Stat.Ann. § 33-372; and North Carolina, N.C.Gen.Stat. § 55-112 (two-thirds of all outstanding shares necessary to approve the transaction).

32. Uniform Commercial Code (hereinafter cited as U.C.C.) § 6–104.
33. U.C.C. § 6–105. Examples of the affidavit and notice to creditors appears as Forms 13J and 13K in Appendix G.
34. U.C.C. § 6–111.
35. M.B.C.A. § 13.02. Dissenters' rights are not extended to mortgage, lease, or other disposition of substantially all of the corporate assets, unless so provided in the articles of incorporation or by-laws.
36. M.B.C.A. §§ 11.03, 11.04, and 13.02.
37. E.g., Florida, Fla.Stat.Ann. § 607.244.
38. E.g., Maryland, Md.Corps. & Assoc.Code Ann. § 3–202.
39. M.B.C.A. § 13.20.
40. M.B.C.A. § 13.21.
41. E.g., New Jersey, N.J.Stat.Ann. § 14A.11–2; and Texas, Vernon's Ann.Tex.Stat.Bus.Corp. Act art. 5.12.
42. M.B.C.A. § 13.21.
43. M.B.C.A. § 13.22.
44. M.B.C.A. § 13.23.
45. M.B.C.A. § 13.01(3).
46. M.B.C.A. § 13.27.
47. M.B.C.A. § 13.25.
48. M.B.C.A. § 13.20.
49. M.B.C.A. § 13.31.
50. M.B.C.A. § 14.01.
51. E.g., Delaware, 8 Del.Code Ann. § 275(c).
52. M.B.C.A. § 14.02.
53. West's Modern Legal Forms § 3082.
54. M.B.C.A. § 14.02.
55. West's Modern Legal Forms § 3083.
56. West's Modern Legal Forms § 3084.
57. Examples of statements of intent to dissolve are Forms 13L and 13M in Appendix G.
58. M.B.C.A. § 14.03.
59. M.B.C.A. § 14.05.
60. M.B.C.A. § 14.06.
61. M.B.C.A. § 14.04.
62. M.B.C.A. § 14.30.
63. M.B.C.A. §§ 14.22 and 14.23.
64. E.g., Minnesota, Minn.Stat.Ann. § 320A.751.
65. M.B.C.A. §§ 14.31–14.33.
66. See M.B.C.A. § 14.32.
67. M.B.C.A. § 14.30(3).
68. M.B.C.A. §§ 14.21 and 14.33.
69. M.B.C.A. § 8.33.
70. See, e.g., Nevada, Nev.Rev.Stat. § 78.585 (permitting creditor claims within 2 years after dissolution).
71. M.B.C.A. ;§ 14.06.
72. M.B.C.A. § 14.07.
73. M.B.C.A. § 14.32.
74. See "Dissolution and Liquidation" in Chapter 9.

APPENDIX A
UNIFORM PARTNERSHIP ACT

Part I Preliminary Provisions
Sec. 1 Name of Act.
Sec. 2 Definition of Terms.
Sec. 3 Interpretation of Knowledge and Notice.
Sec. 4 Rules of Construction.
Sec. 5 Rules for Cases Not Provided for in This Act.

Part II Nature of Partnership
Sec. 6 Partnership Defined.
Sec. 7 Rules for Determining the Existence of a Partnership.
Sec. 8 Partnership Property.

Part III Relations of Partners to Persons Dealing with the Partnership
Sec. 9 Partner Agent of Partnership as to Partnership Business.
Sec. 10 Conveyance of Real Property of the Partnership.
Sec. 11 Partnership Bound by Admission of Partner.
Sec. 12 Partnership Charged with Knowledge of or Notice to Partner.
Sec. 13 Partnership Bound by Partner's Wrongful Act.
Sec. 14 Partnership Bound by Partner's Breach of Trust.
Sec. 15 Nature of Partner's Liability.
Sec. 16 Partner by Estoppel.
Sec. 17 Liability of Incoming Partner.

Part IV Relations of Partners to One Another
Sec. 18 Rules Determining Rights and Duties of Partners.
Sec. 19 Partnership Books.
Sec. 20 Duty of Partners to Render Information.
Sec. 21 Partner Accountable as a Fiduciary.
Sec. 22 Rights to an Account.
Sec. 23 Continuation of Partnership Beyond Fixed Term.

Part V Property Rights of a Partner
Sec. 24 Extent of Property Rights of a Partner.
Sec. 25 Nature of a Partner's Right in Specific Partnership Property.
Sec. 26 Nature of Partner's Interest in the Partnership.
Sec. 27 Assignment of Partner's Interest.
Sec. 28 Partner's Interest Subject to Charging Order.

Part VI Dissolution and Winding Up
Sec. 29 Dissolution Defined.
Sec. 30 Partnership Not Terminated by Dissolution.
Sec. 31 Causes of Dissolution.
Sec. 32 Dissolution by Decree of Court.
Sec. 33 General Effect of Dissolution on Authority of Partner.
Sec. 34 Right of Partner to Contribution from Copartners after Dissolution.
Sec. 35 Power of Partner to Bind Partnership to Third Persons after Dissolution.
Sec. 36 Effect of Dissolution on Partner's Existing Liability.
Sec. 37 Right to Wind Up.
Sec. 38 Rights of Partners to Application of Partnership Property.
Sec. 39 Rights Where Partnership Is Dissolved for Fraud or Misrepresentation.

Sec. 40 Rules for Distribution.
Sec. 41 Liability of Persons Continuing the Business in Certain Cases.
Sec. 42 Rights of Retiring or Estate of Deceased Partner when the Business Is Continued.
Sec. 43 Accrual of Actions.

PART VII Miscellaneous Provisions
Sec. 44 When Act Takes Effect.
Sec. 45 Legislation Repealed.
(Adopted in 48 States, all except Georgia and Louisiana; the District of Columbia, the Virgin Islands, and Guam. The adoptions by Alabama and Nebraska do not follow the official text in every respect, but are substantially similar, with local variations.)

The Act consists of 7 Parts as follows:
I. Preliminary Provisions
II. Nature of Partnership
III. Relations of Partners to Persons Dealing with the Partnership
IV. Relations of Partners to One Another
V. Property Rights of a Partner
VI. Dissolution and Winding Up
VII. Miscellaneous Provisions
An Act to make uniform the Law of Partnerships
  Be it enacted, etc.:

PART I PRELIMINARY PROVISIONS
Sec. 1. Name of Act.
This act may be cited as Uniform Partnership Act.

Sec. 2. Definition of Terms.
In this act, "Court" includes every court and judge having jurisdiction in the case.
"Business" includes every trade, occupation, or profession.
"Person" includes individuals, partnerships, corporations, and other associations.
"Bankrupt" includes bankrupt under the Federal Bankruptcy Act or insolvent under any state insolvent act.
"Conveyance" includes every assignment, lease, mortgage, or encumbrance
"Real property" includes land and any interest or estate in land.

Sec. 3. Interpretation of Knowledge and Notice.
(1) A person has "knowledge" of a fact within the meaning of this act not only when he has actual knowledge thereof, but also when he has knowledge of such other facts as in the circumstances shows bad faith.
(2) A person has "notice" of a fact within the meaning of this act when the person who claims the benefit of the notice
  (a) States the fact to such person, or
  (b) Delivers through the mail, or by other means of communication, a written statement of the fact to such person or to a proper person at his place of business or residence.

Sec. 4. Rules of Construction.
(1) The rule that statutes in derogation of the common law are to be strictly construed shall have no application to this act.
(2) The law of estoppel shall apply under this act.
(3) The law of agency shall apply under this act.
(4) This act shall be so interpreted and construed as to effect its general purpose to make uniform the law of those states which enact it.
(5) This act shall not be construed so as to impair the obligations of any contract existing when the act goes into effect, nor to affect any action or proceedings begun or right accrued before this act takes effect.

Sec. 5. Rules for Cases Not Provided for in This Act.
In any case not provided for in this act the rules of law and equity, including the law merchant, shall govern.

PART II NATURE OF PARTNERSHIP
Sec. 6. Partnership Defined.
(1) A partnership is an association of two or more persons to carry on as co-owners a business for profit.
(2) But any association formed under any other statute of this state, or any statute adopted by authority, other than the authority of this state, is not a partnership under this act, unless such association would have been a partnership in this state prior to the adoption of this act; but this act shall apply to limited partnerships except in so far as the statutes relating to such partnerships are inconsistent herewith.

Sec. 7. Rules for Determining the Existence of a Partnership.
In determining whether a partnership exists, these rules shall apply:
(1) Except as provided by Section 16 persons who are not partners as to each other are not partners as to third persons.
(2) Joint tenancy, tenancy in common, tenancy by the entireties, joint property, common property, or part ownership does not of itself establish a partnership,

whether such co-owners do or do not share any profits made by the use of the property.

(3) The sharing of gross returns does not of itself establish a partnership, whether or not the persons sharing them have a joint or common right or interest in any property from which the returns are derived.

(4) The receipt by a person of a share of the profits of a business is prima facie evidence that he is a partner in the business, but no such inference shall be drawn if such profits were received in payment:

(a) As a debt by installments or otherwise,
(b) As wages of an employee or rent to a landlord,
(c) As an annuity to a widow or representative of a deceased partner,
(d) As interest on a loan, though the amount of payment vary with the profits of the business.
(e) As the consideration for the sale of a good-will of a business or other property by installments or otherwise.

Sec. 8. Partnership Property.
(1) All property originally brought into the partnership stock or subsequently acquired by purchase or otherwise, on account of the partnership, is partnership property.
(2) Unless the contrary intention appears, property acquired with partnership funds is partnership property.
(3) Any estate in real property may be acquired in the partnership name. Title so acquired can be conveyed only in the partnership name.
(4) A conveyance to a partnership in the partnership name, though without words of inheritance, passes the entire estate of the grantor unless a contrary intent appears.

PART III RELATIONS OF PARTNERS TO PERSONS DEALING WITH THE PARTNERSHIP

Sec. 9. Partner Agent of Partnership as to Partnership Business.
(1) Every partner is an agent of the partnership for the purpose of its business, and the act of every partner, including the execution in the partnership name of any instrument, for apparently carrying on in the usual way the business of the partnership of which he is a member binds the partnership, unless the partner so acting has in fact no authority to act for the partnership in the particular matter, and the person with whom he is dealing has knowledge of the fact that he has no such authority.
(2) An act of a partner which is not apparently for the carrying on of the business of the partnership in the usual way does not bind the partnership unless authorized by the other partners.
(3) Unless authorized by the other partners or unless they have abandoned the business, one or more but less than all the partners have no authority to:

(a) Assign the partnership property in trust for creditors or on the assignee's promise to pay the debts of the partnership,
(b) Dispose of the good-will of the business,
(c) Do any other act which would make it impossible to carry on the ordinary business of a partnership,
(d) Confess a judgment,
(e) Submit a partnership claim or liability to arbitration or reference.

(4) No act of a partner in contravention of a restriction on authority shall bind the partnership to persons having knowledge of the restriction.

Sec. 10. Conveyance of Real Property of the Partnership.
(1) Where title to real property is in the partnership name, any partner may convey title to such property by a conveyance executed in the partnership name; but the partnership may recover such property unless the partner's act binds the partnership under the provisions of paragraph (1) of section 9 or unless such property has been conveyed by the grantee or a person claiming through such grantee to a holder for value without knowledge that the partner, in making the conveyance, has exceeded his authority.
(2) Where title to real property is in the name of the partnership, a conveyance executed by a partner, in his own name, passes the equitable interest of the partnership, provided the act is one within the authority of the partner under the provisions of paragraph (1) of section 9.
(3) Where title to real property is in the name of one or more but not all the partners, and the record does not disclose the right of the partnership, the partners in whose name the title stands may convey title to such property, but the partnership may recover such property if the partners' act does not bind the partnership under the provisions of paragraph (1) of section 9, unless the purchaser or his assignee, is a holder for value, without knowledge.
(4) Where the title to real property is in the name of one or more or all the partners, or in a third person in trust for the partnership, a conveyance executed by a partner in the partnership name, or in his own name, passes the equitable interest of the partnership, provided the act is one within the authority of the partner under the provisions of paragraph (1) of section 9.

(5) Where the title to real property is in the names of all the partners a conveyance executed by all the partners passes all their rights in such property.

Sec. 11. Partnership Bound by Admission of Partner.
An admission or representation made by any partner concerning partnership affairs within the scope of his authority as conferred by this act is evidence against the partnership.

Sec. 12. Partnership Charged with Knowledge of or Notice to Partner.
Notice to any partner of any matter relating to partnership affairs, and the knowledge of the partner acting in the particular matter, acquired while a partner or then present to his mind, and the knowledge of any other partner who reasonably could and should have communicated it to the acting partner, operate as notice to or knowledge of the partnership, except in the case of a fraud on the partnership committed by or with the consent of that partner.

Sec. 13. Partnership Bound by Partner's Wrongful Act.
Where, by any wrongful act or omission of any partner acting in the ordinary course of the business of the partnership or with the authority of his copartners, loss or injury is caused to any person, not being a partner in the partnership, or any penalty is incurred, the partnership is liable therefor to the same extent as the partner so acting or omitting to act.

Sec. 14. Partnership Bound by Partner's Breach of Trust.
The partnership is bound to make good the loss:
(a) Where one partner acting within the scope of his apparent authority receives money or property of a third person and misapplies it; and
(b) Where the partnership in the course of its business receives money or property of a third person and the money or property so received is misapplied by any partner while it is in the custody of the partnership.

Sec. 15. Nature of Partner's Liability.
All partners are liable
(a) Jointly and severally for everything chargeable to the partnership under sections 13 and 14.
(b) Jointly for all other debts and obligations of the partnership; but any partner may enter into a separate obligation to perform a partnership contract.

Sec. 16. Partner by Estoppel.
(1) When a person, by words spoken or written or by conduct, represents himself, or consents to another representing him to any one, as a partner in an existing partnership or with one or more persons not actual partners, he is liable to any such person to whom such representation has been made, who has, on the faith of such representation, given credit to the actual or apparent partnership, and if he has made such representation or consented to its being made in a public manner he is liable to such person, whether the representation has or has not been made or communicated to such person so giving credit by or with the knowledge of the apparent partner making the representation or consenting to its being made.
 (a) When a partnership liability results, he is liable as though he were an actual member of the partnership.
 (b) When no partnership liability results, he is liable jointly with the other persons, if any, so consenting to the contract or representation as to incur liability, otherwise separately.
(2) When a person has been thus represented to be a partner in an existing partnership, or with one or more persons not actual partners, he is an agent of the persons consenting to such representation to bind them to the same extent and in the same manner as though he were a partner in fact, with respect to persons who rely upon the representation. Where all the members of the existing partnership consent to the representation, a partnership act or obligation results; but in all other cases it is the joint act or obligation of the person acting and the persons consenting to the representation.

Sec. 17. Liability of Incoming Partner.
A person admitted as a partner into an existing partnership is liable for all the obligations of the partnership arising before his admission as though he had been a partner when such obligations were incurred, except that this liability shall be satisfied only out of partnership property.

PART IV RELATIONS OF PARTNERS TO ONE ANOTHER
Sec. 18. Rules Determining Rights and Duties of Partners.
The rights and duties of the partners in relation to the partnership shall be determined, subject to any agreement between them, by the following rules:
(a) Each partner shall be repaid his contributions, whether by way of capital or advances to the partnership property and share equally in the profits and surplus remaining after all liabilities, including those to partners, are satisfied; and must contribute towards the losses, whether of capital or otherwise, sustained by the partnership according to his share in the profits.

(b) The partnership must indemnify every partner in respect of payments made and personal liabilities reasonably incurred by him in the ordinary and proper conduct of its business, or for the preservation of its business or property.

(c) A partner, who in aid of the partnership makes any payment or advance beyond the amount of capital which he agreed to contribute, shall be paid interest from the date of the payment or advance.

(d) A partner shall receive interest on the capital contributed by him only from the date when repayment should be made.

(e) All partners have equal rights in the management and conduct of the partnership business.

(f) No partner is entitled to remuneration for acting in the partnership business, except that a surviving partner is entitled to reasonable compensation for his services in winding up the partnership affairs.

(g) No person can become a member of a partnership without the consent of all the partners.

(h) Any difference arising as to ordinary matters connected with the partnership business may be decided by a majority of the partners; but no act in contraven tion of any agreement between the partners may be done rightfully without the consent of all the partners.

Sec. 19. Partnership Books.

The partnership books shall be kept, subject to any agreement between the partners, at the principal place of business of the partnership, and every partner shall at all times have access to and may inspect and copy any of them.

Sec. 20. Duty of Partners to Render Information.

Partners shall render on demand true and full information of all things affecting the partnership to any partner or the legal representative of any deceased partner or partner under legal disability.

Sec. 21. Partner Accountable as a Fiduciary.

(1) Every partner must account to the partnership for any benefit, and hold as trustee for it any profits derived by him without the consent of the other partners from any transaction connected with the formation, conduct, or liquidation of the partnership or from any use by him of its property.

(2) This section applies also to the representatives of a deceased partner engaged in the liquidation of the affairs of the partnership as the personal representatives of the last surviving partner.

Sec. 22. Right to an Account.

Any partner shall have the right to a formal account as to partnership affairs:

(a) If he is wrongfully excluded from the partnership business or possession of its property by his copartners,

(b) If the right exists under the terms of any agreement,

(c) As provided by section 21,

(d) Whenever other circumstances render it just and reasonable.

Sec. 23. Continuation of Partnership Beyond Fixed Term.

(1) When a partnership for a fixed term or particular undertaking is continued after the termination of such term or particular undertaking without any express agreement, the rights and duties of the partners remain the same as they were at such termination, so far as is consistent with a partnership at will.

(2) A continuation of the business by the partners or such of them as habitually acted therein during the term, without any settlement or liquidation of the partnership affairs, is prima facie evidence of a continuation of the partnership.

PART V PROPERTY RIGHTS OF A PARTNER

Sec. 24. Extent of Property Rights of a Partner.

The property rights of a partner are (1) his rights in specific partnership property, (2) his interest in the partnership, and (3) his right to participate in the management.

Sec. 25. Nature of a Partner's Right in Specific Partnership Property.

(1) A partner is co-owner with his partners of specific partnership property holding as a tenant in partnership.

(2) The incidents of this tenancy are such that:

(a) A partner, subject to the provisions of this act and to any agreement between the partners, has an equal right with his partners to posses specific partnership property for partnership purposes; but he has no right to possess such property for any other purpose without the consent of his partners.

(b) A partner's right in specific partnership property is not assignable except in connection with the assignment of rights of all the partners in the same property.

(c) A partner's right in specific partnership property is not subject to attachment or execution, except on a claim against the partnership. When partnership property is attached for a partnership debt the partners, or any of them, or the representatives of a deceased partner, cannot claim any right under the homestead or exemption laws.

(d) On the death of a partner his right in specific partnership property vests in the surviving partner or partners, except where the deceased was the last surviving partner, when his right in such property vests in his legal representative. Such surviving partner or partners, or the legal representative of the last surviving partner, has no right to possess the partnership property for any but a partnership purpose.

(e) A partner's right in specific partnership property is not subject to dower, curtesy, or allowances to widows, heirs, or next of kin.

Sec. 26. Nature of Partner's Interest in the Partnership.

A partner's interest in the partnership is his share of the profits and surplus, and the same is personal property.

Sec. 27. Assignment of Partner's Interest.

(1) A conveyance by a partner of his interest in the partnership does not of itself dissolve the partnership, nor, as against the other partners in the absence of agreement, entitle the assignee, during the continuance of the partnership to interfere in the management or administration of the partnership business or affairs, or to require any information or account of partnership transactions, or to inspect the partnership books; but it merely entitles the assignee to receive in accordance with his contract the profits to which the assigning partner would otherwise be entitled.

(2) In case of a dissolution of the partnership, the assignee is entitled to receive his assignor's interest and may require an account from the date only of the last account agreed to by all the partners.

Sec. 28. Partner's Interest Subject to Charging Order.

(1) On due application to a competent court by any judgment creditor of a partner, the court which entered the judgment, order, or decree, or any other court, may charge the interest of the debtor partner with payment of the unsatisfied amount of such judgment debt with interest thereon; and may then or later appoint a receiver of his share of the profits, and of any other money due or to fall due to him in respect of the partnership, and make all other orders, directions, accounts and inquiries which the debtor partner might have made, or which the circumstances of the case may require.

(2) The interest charged may be redeemed at any time before foreclosure, or in case of a sale being directed by the court may be purchased without thereby causing a dissolution:

(a) With separate property, by any one or more of the partners, or

(b) With partnership property, by any one or more of the partners with the consent of all the partners whose interests are not so charged or sold.

(3) Nothing in this act shall be held to deprive a partner of his right, if any, under the exemption laws, as regards his interest in the partnership.

PART VI DISSOLUTION AND WINDING UP

Sec. 29. Dissolution Defined.

The dissolution of a partnership is the change in the relation of the partners caused by any partner ceasing to be associated in the carrying on as distinguished from the winding up of the business.

Sec. 30. Partnership Not Terminated by Dissolution.

On dissolution the partnership is not terminated, but continues until the winding up of partnership affairs is completed.

Sec. 31. Causes of Dissolution.

Dissolution is caused:

(1) Without violation of the agreement between the partners,

(a) By the termination of the definite term or particular undertaking specified in the agreement,

(b) By the express will of any partner when no definite term or particular undertaking is specified,

(c) By the express will of all the partners who have not assigned their interests or suffered them to be charged for their separate debts, either before or after the termination of any specified term or particular undertaking.

(d) By the expulsion of any partner from the business bona fide in accordance with such a power conferred by the agreement between the partners;

(2) In contravention of the agreement between the partners, where the circumstances do not permit a dissolution under any other provision of this section, by the express will of any partner at any time;

(3) By any event which makes it unlawful for the business of the partnership to be carried on or for the members to carry it on in partnership;

(4) By the death of any partner;

(5) By the bankruptcy of any partner or the partnership;

(6) By decree of court under section 32.

Sec. 32. Dissolution by Decree of Court.

(1) On application by or for a partner the court shall decree a dissolution whenever:

(a) A partner has been declared a lunatic in any judicial proceeding or is shown to be of unsound mind,
(b) A partner becomes in any other way incapable of performing his part of the partnership contract,
(c) A partner has been guilty of such conduct as tends to affect prejudicially the carrying on of the business,
(d) A partner wilfully or persistently commits a breach of the partnership agreement, or otherwise so conducts himself in matters relating to the partnership business that it is not reasonably practicable to carry on the business in partnership with him,
(e) The business of the partnership can only be carried on at a loss,
(f) Other circumstances render a dissolution equitable.
(2) On the application of the purchaser of a partner's interest under section 27 or 28:
(a) After the termination of the specified term or particular undertaking,
(b) At any time if the partnership was a partnership at will when the interest was assigned or when the charging order was issued.

Sec. 33. General Effect of Dissolution on Authority of Partner.

Except so far as may be necessary to wind up partnership affairs or to complete transactions begun but not then finished, dissolution terminates all authority of any partner to act for the partnership,
(1) With respect to the partners,
(a) When the dissolution is not by the act, bankruptcy or death of a partner; or
(b) When the dissolution is by such act, bankruptcy or death of a partner, in cases where section 34 so requires.
(2) With respect to persons not partners, as declared in section 35.

Sec. 34. Right of Partner to Contribution from Copartners after Dissolution.

Where the dissolution is caused by the act, death or bankruptcy of a partner, each partner is liable to his copartners for his share of any liability created by any partner acting for the partnership as if the partnership had not been dissolved unless
(a) The dissolution being by act of any partner, the partner acting for the partnership had knowledge of the dissolution, or
(b) The dissolution being by the death or bankruptcy of a partner, the partner acting for the partnership had knowledge or notice of the death or bankruptcy.

Sec. 35. Power of Partner to Bind Partnership to Third Persons after Dissolution.

(1) After dissolution a partner can bind the partnership except as provided in Paragraph (3)
(a) By any act appropriate for winding up partnership affairs or completing transactions unfinished at dissolution;
(b) By any transaction which would bind the partnership if dissolution had not taken place, provided the other party to the transaction
(I) Had extended credit to the partnership prior to dissolution and had no knowledge or notice of the dissolution; or
(II) Though he had not so extended credit, had nevertheless known of the partnership prior to dissolution, and, having no knowledge or notice of dissolution, the fact of dissolution had not been advertised in a newspaper of general circulation in the place (or in each place if more than one) at which the partnership business was regularly carried on.
(2) The liability of a partner under paragraph (1b) shall be satisfied out of partnership assets alone when such partner had been prior to dissolution
(a) Unknown as a partner to the person with whom the contract is made; and
(b) So far unknown and inactive in partnership affairs that the business reputation of the partnership could not be said to have been in any degree due to his connection with it.
(3) The partnership is in no case bound by any act of a partner after dissolution
(a) Where the partnership is dissolved because it is unlawful to carry on the business, unless the act is appropriate for winding up partnership affairs; or
(b) Where the partner has become bankrupt; or
(c) Where the partner has no authority to wind up partnership affairs; except by a transaction with one who
(I) Had extended credit to the partnership prior to dissolution and had no knowledge or notice of his want of authority; or
(II) Had not extended credit to the partnership prior to dissolution, and, having no knowledge or notice of his want of authority, the fact of his want of authority has not been advertised in the manner provided for advertising the fact of dissolution in paragraph (1bII).
(4) Nothing in this section shall affect the liability under section 16 of any person who after dissolution represents himself or consents to another representing him as a partner in a partnership engaged in carrying on business.

Sec. 36. Effect of Dissolution on Partner's Existing Liability.

(1) The dissolution of the partnership does not of itself discharge the existing liability of any partner.

(2) A partner is discharged from any existing liability upon dissolution of the partnership by an agreement to that effect between himself, the partnership creditor and the person or partnership continuing the business; and such agreement may be inferred from the course of dealing between the creditor having knowledge of the dissolution and the person or partnership continuing the business.

(3) Where a person agrees to assume the existing obligations of a dissolved partnership, the partners whose obligations have been assumed shall be discharged from any liability to any creditor of the partnership who, knowing of the agreement, consents to a material alteration in the nature or time of payment of such obligations.

(4) The individual property of a deceased partner shall be liable for all obligations of the partnership incurred while he was a partner but subject to the prior payment of his separate debts.

Sec. 37. Right to Wind Up.

Unless otherwise agreed the partners who have not wrongfully dissolved the partnership or the legal representative of the last surviving partner, not bankrupt, has the right to wind up the partnership affairs; provided, however, that any partner, his legal representative or his assignee, upon cause shown, may obtain winding up by the court.

Sec. 38. Rights of Partners to Application of Partnership Property.

(1) When dissolution is caused in any way, except in contravention of the partnership agreement, each partner as against his co-partners and all persons claiming through them in respect of their interests in the partnership, unless otherwise agreed, may have the partnership property applied to discharge its liabilities, and the surplus applied to pay in cash the net amount owing to the respective partners. But if dissolution is caused by expulsion of a partner, bona fide under the partnership agreement and if the expelled partner is discharged from all partnership liabilities, either by payment or agreement under section 36(2), he shall receive in cash only the net amount due him from the partnership.

(2) When dissolution is caused in contravention of the partnership agreement the rights of the partners shall be as follows:

(a) Each partner who has not caused dissolution wrongfully shall have,

(I) All the rights specified in paragraph (1) of this section, and

(II) The right, as against each partner who has caused the dissolution wrongfully, to damages for breach of the agreement.

(b) The partners who have not caused the dissolution wrongfully, if they all desire to continue the business in the same name, either by themselves or jointly with others, may do so, during the agreed term for the partnership and for that purpose may possess the partnership property, provided they secure the payment by bond approved by the court, or pay to any partner who has caused the dissolution wrongfully, the value of his interest in the partnership at the dissolution, less any damages recoverable under clause (2aII) of the section, and in like manner indemnify him against all present or future partnership liabilities.

(c) A partner who has caused the dissolution wrongfully shall have:

(I) If the business is not continued under the provisions of paragraph (2b) all the rights of a partner under paragraph (1), subject to clause (2aII), of this section,

(II) If the business is continued under paragraph (2b) of this section the right as against his co-partners and all claiming through them in respect of their interests in the partnership, to have the value of his interest in the partnership, less any damages caused to his copartners by the dissolution, ascertained and paid to him in cash, or the payment secured by bond approved by the court, and to be released from all existing liabilities of the partnership; but in ascertaining the value of the partner's interest the value of the good-will of the business shall not be considered.

Sec. 39. Rights Where Partnership Is Dissolved for Fraud or Misrepresentation.

Where a partnership contract is rescinded on the ground of the fraud or misrepresentation of one of the parties thereto, the party entitled to rescind is, without prejudice to any other right, entitled,

(a) To a lien on, or right of retention of, the surplus of the partnership property after satisfying the partnership liabilities to third persons for any sum of money paid by him for the purchase of an interest in the partnership and for any capital or advances contributed by him; and

(b) To stand, after all liabilities to third persons have been satisfied, in the place of the creditors of the partnership for any payments made by him in respect of the partnership liabilities; and

(c) To be indemnified by the person guilty of the fraud or making the representation against all debts and liabilities of the partnership.

Sec. 40. Rules for Distribution.

In settling accounts between the partners after dissolution, the following rules shall be observed, subject to any agreement to the contrary:
(a) The assets of the partnership are:
   (I) The partnership property,
   (II) The contributions of the partners necessary for the payment of all the liabilities specified in clause (b) of this paragraph.
(b) The liabilities of the partnership shall rank in order of payment, as follows:
   (I) Those owing to creditors other than partners,
   (II) Those owning to partners other than for capital and profits,
   (III) Those owing to partners in respect of capital,
   (IV) Those owning to partners in respect of profits.
(c) The assets shall be applied in the order of their declaration in clause (a) of this paragraph to the satisfaction of the liabilities.
(d) The partners shall contribute, as provided by section 18(a) the amount necessary to satisfy the liabilities; but if any, but not all, of the partners are insolvent, or, not being subject to process, refuse to contribute, the other parties shall contribute their share of the liabilities, and, in the relative proportions in which they share the profits, the additional amount necessary to pay the liabilities.
(e) An assignee for the benefit of creditors or any person appointed by the court shall have the right to enforce the contributions specified in clause (d) of this paragraph.
(f) Any partner or his legal representative shall have the right to enforce the contributions specified in clause (d) of this paragraph, to the extent of the amount which he has paid in excess of his share of the liability.
(g) The individual property of a deceased partner shall be liable for the contributions specified in clause (d) of this paragraph.
(h) When partnership property and the individual properties of the partners are in possession of a court for distribution, partnership creditors shall have priority on partnership property and separate creditors on individual property, saving the rights of lien or secured creditors as heretofore.
(i) Where a partner has become bankrupt or his estate is insolvent the claims against his separate property shall rank in the following order:
   (I) Those owing to separate creditors,
   (II) Those owing to partnership creditors,
   (III) Those owing to partners by way of contribution.

Sec. 41. Liability of Persons Continuing the Business in Certain Cases.

(1) When any new partner is admitted into an existing partnership, or when any partner retires and assigns (or the representative of the deceased partner assigns) his rights in partnership property to two or more of the partners, or to one or more of the partners and one or more third persons, if the business is continued without liquidation of the partnership affairs, creditors of the first or dissolved partnership are also creditors of the partnership so continuing the business.
(2) When all but one partner retire and assign (or the representative of a deceased partner assigns) their rights in partnership property to the remaining partner, who continues the business without liquidation of partnership affairs, either alone or with others, creditors of the dissolved partnership are also creditors of the person or partnership so continuing the business.
(3) When any partner retires or dies and the business of the dissolved partnership is continued as set forth in paragraphs(1) and (2) of this section, with the consent of the retired partners or the representative of the deceased partner, but without any assignment of his right in partnership property, rights of creditors of the dissolved partnership and of the creditors of the person or partnership continuing the business shall be as if such assignment had been made.
(4) When all the partners or their representatives assign their rights in partnership property to one or more third persons who promise to pay the debts and who continue the business of the dissolved partnership, creditors of the dissolved partnership are also creditors of the person or partnership continuing the business.
(5) When any partner wrongfully causes a dissolution and the remaining partners continue the business under the provisions of section 38(2b), either alone or with others, and without liquidation of the partnership affairs, creditors of the dissolved partnership are also creditors of the person or partnership continuing the business.
(6) When a partner is expelled and the remaining partners continue the business either alone or with others, without liquidation of the partnership affairs, creditors of the dissolved partnership are also creditors of the person or partnership continuing the business.
(7) The liability of a third person becoming a partner in the partnership continuing the business, under this

section, to the creditors of the dissolved partnership shall be satisfied out of partnership property only.

(8) When the business of a partnership after dissolution is continued under any conditions set forth in this section the creditors of the dissolved partnership, as against the separate creditors of the retiring or deceased partner or the representative of the deceased partner, have a prior right to any claim of the retired partner or the representative of the deceased partner against the person or partnership continuing the business, on account of the retired or deceased partner's interest in the dissolved partnership or on account of any consideration promised for such interest or for his right in partnership property.

(9) Nothing in this section shall be held to modify any right of creditors to set aside any assignment on the ground of fraud.

(10) The use by the person or partnership continuing the business of the partnership name, or the name of a deceased partner as part thereof, shall not of itself make the individual property of the deceased partner liable for any debts contracted by such person or partnership.

Sec. 42. Rights of Retiring or Estate of Deceased Partner when the Business Is Continued.

When any partner retires or dies, and the business is continued under any of the conditions set forth in section 41 (1, 2, 3, 5, 6), or section 38(2b), without any settlement of accounts as between him or his estate and the person or partnership continuing the business, unless otherwise agreed, he or his legal representative as against such persons or partnership may have the value of his interest at the date of dissolution ascertained, and shall receive as an ordinary creditor an amount equal to the value of his interest in the dissolved partnership with interest, or, at his option or at the option of his legal representative, in lieu of interest, the profits attributable to the use of his right in the property of the dissolved partnership; provided that the creditors of the dissolved partnership as against the separate creditors, or the representative of the retired or deceased partner, shall have priority on any claim arising under this section, as provided by section 41(8) of this act.

Sec. 43. Accrual of Actions.

The right to an account of his interest shall accrue to any partner, or his legal representative, as against the winding up partners or the surviving partners or the person or partnership continuing the business, at the date of dissolution, in the absence of any agreement to the contrary.

PART VII MISCELLANEOUS PROVISIONS

Sec. 44. When Act Takes Effect.

This act shall take effect on the _____ day of _____ one thousand nine hundred and _____.

Sec. 45. Legislation Repealed.

All acts or parts of acts inconsistent with this act are hereby repealed.

APPENDIX B
UNIFORM LIMITED PARTNERSHIP ACT*

Sec. 1   Limited Partnership Defined.
Sec. 2   Formation
Sec. 3   Business Which May Be Carried On.
Sec. 4   Character of Limited Partner's Contribution.
Sec. 5   A Name Not to Contain Surname of Limited Partner, Exceptions.
Sec. 6. Liability for False Statements in Certificate.
Sec. 7   Limited Partner Not Liable to Creditors.
Sec. 8   Admission of Additional Limited Partners.
Sec. 9   Rights, Powers and Liabilities of a General Partner.
Sec. 10 Rights of a Limited Partner.
Sec. 11 Status of Person Erroneously Believing Himself a Limited Partner.
Sec. 12 One Person Both General and Limited Partner.
Sec. 13 Loans and Other Business Transactions with Limited Partner.
Sec. 14 Relation of Limited Partners Inter Se.
Sec. 15 Compensation of Limited Partner.
Sec. 16 Withdrawal or Reduction of Limited Partner's Contribution.
Sec. 17 Liability of Limited Partner to Partnership.
Sec. 18 Nature of Limited Partner's Interest in Partnership.
Sec. 19 Assignment of Limited Partner's Interest.
Sec. 20 Effect of Retirement, Death or Insanity of a General Partner.
Sec. 21 Death of Limited Partner.
Sec. 22 Rights of Creditors of Limited Partner.
Sec. 23 Distribution of Assets.
Sec. 24 When Certificate Shall Be Cancelled or Amended.
Sec. 25 Requirements for Amendment and for Cancellation of Certificate.
Sec. 26 Parties to Actions.
Sec. 27 Name of Act.
Sec. 28 Rules of Construction.
Sec. 29 Rules for Cases Not Provided for in This Act.
Sec. 30 Provisions for Existing Limited Partnerships.
Sec. 31 Act (Acts) Repealed.

(Adopted in 46 states, all except Connecticut, Minnesota, Wyoming and Louisiana; also in the District of Columbia, and the Virgin Islands.) An Act to Make Uniform the Law Relating to Limited Partnerships Be it enacted, etc., as follows:

Sec. 1. Limited Partnership Defined.
A limited partnership is a partnership formed by two or more persons under the provisions of Section 2, having as members one or more general partners and one or more limited partners. The limited partners as such shall not be bound by the obligations of the partnership.

Sec. 2. Formation.
(1) Two or more persons desiring to form a limited partnership shall
   (a) Sign and swear to a certificate, which shall state
      I. The name of the partnership,
      II. The character of the business,
      III. The location of the principal place of business,
      IV. The name and place of residence of each member; general and limited partners being respectively designated,

*The Uniform Limited Partnership Act was revised in 1976 and amended in 1985, but many states base their state statutes on the original version of the act. This is the original version; the revised act with amendments follows.

V. The term for which the partnership is to exist,

VI. The amount of cash and a description of and the agreed value of the other property contributed by each limited partner,

VII. The additional contributions, if any, agreed to be made by each limited partner and the times at which or events on the happening of which they shall be made,

VIII. The time, if agreed upon, when the contribution of each limited partner is to be returned,

IX. The share of the profits or the other compensation by way of income which each limited partner shall receive by reason of his contribution,

X. The right, if given, of a limited partner to substitute an assignee as contributor in his place, and the terms and conditions of the substitution,

XI. The right, if given, of the partners to admit additional limited partners,

XII. The right, if given, of one or more of the limited partners to priority over other limited partners, as to contributions or as to compensation by way of income, and the nature of such priority,

XIII. The right, if given, of the remaining general partner or partners to continue the business on the death, retirement or insanity of a general partner, and

XIV. The right, if given, of a limited partner to demand and receive property other than cash in return for his contribution.

(b) File for record the certificate in the office of (here designate the proper office).

(2) A limited partnership is formed if there has been substantial compliance in good faith with the requirements of paragraph (1).

Sec. 3. Business Which May Be Carried On.

A limited partnership may carry on any business which a partnership without limited partners may carry on, except (here designate the business to be prohibited).

Sec. 4. Character of Limited Partner's Contribution.

The contributions of a limited partner may be cash or other property, but not services.

Sec. 5. A Name Not to Contain Surname of Limited Partner, Exceptions.

(1) The surname of a limited partner shall not appear in the partnership name, unless

(a) It is also the surname of a general partner, or

(b) Prior to the time when the limited partner became such the business had been carried on under a name in which his surname appeared.

(2) A limited partner whose name appears in a partnership name contrary to the provisions of paragraph (1) is liable as a general partner to partnership creditors who extend credit to the partnership without actual knowledge that he is not a general partner.

Sec. 6. Liability for False Statements in Certificate.

If the certificate contains a false statement, one who suffers loss by reliance on such statement may hold liable any party to the certificate who knew the statement to be false

(a) At the time he signed the certificate, or

(b) Subsequently, but within a sufficient time before the statement was relied upon to enable him to cancel or amend the certificate, or to file a petition for its cancellation or amendment as provided in Section 25(3).

Sec. 7. Limited Partner Not Liable to Creditors.

A limited partner shall not become liable as a general partner unless, in addition to the exercise of his rights and powers as a limited partner, he takes part in the control of the business.

Sec. 8. Admission of Additional Limited Partners.

After the formation of a limited partnership, additional limited partners may be admitted upon filing an amendment to the original certificate in accordance with the requirements of Section 25.

Sec. 9. Rights, Powers and Liabilities of a General Partner.

(1) A general partner shall have all the rights and powers and be subject to all the restrictions and liabilities of a partner in a partnership without limited partners, except that without the written consent or ratification of the specific act by all the limited partners, a general partner or all of the general partners have no authority to

(a) Do any act in contravention of the certificate,

(b) Do any act which would make it impossible to carry on the ordinary business of the partnership,

(c) Confess a judgment against the partnership,

(d) Possess partnership property, or assign their rights in specific partnership property, for other than a partnership purpose,

(e) Admit a person as a general partner,

(f) Admit a person as a limited partner, unless the right so to do is given in the certificate,

(g) continue the business with partnership property on the death, retirement or insanity of a general partner, unless the right so to do is given in the certificate.

Sec. 10. Rights of a Limited Partner.
(1) A limited partner shall have the same rights as a general partner to
   (a) Have the partnership books kept at the principal place of business of the partnership, and at all times to inspect and copy any of them,
   (b) Have on demand true and full information of all things affecting the partnership, and a formal account of partnership affairs, whenever circumstances render it just and reasonable, and
   (c) Have dissolution and winding up by decree of court.
(2) A limited partner shall have the right to receive a share of the profits or other compensation by way of income, and to the return of his contribution as provided in Sections 15 and 16.

Sec. 11. Status of Person Erroneously Believing Himself a Limited Partner.
A person who has contributed to the capital of a business conducted by a person or partnership erroneously believing that he has become a limited partner in a limited partnership, is not, by reason of his exercise of the rights of a limited partner, a general partner with the person or in the partnership carrying on the business, or bound by the obligations of such person or partnership; provided that on ascertaining the mistake he promptly renounces his interest in the profits of the business, or other compensation by way of income.

Sec. 12. One Person Both General and Limited Partner.
(1) A person may be a general partner and a limited partner in the same partnership at the same time.
(2) A person who is a general, and also at the same time a limited partner, shall have all the rights and powers and be subject to all the restrictions of a general partner; except that, in respect to his contribution, he shall have the rights against the other members which he would have had if he were not also a general partner.

Sec. 13. Loans and Other Business Transactions with Limited Partner.
(1) A limited partner also may loan money to and transact other business with the partnership, and, unless he is also a general partner, receive on account of resulting claims against the partnership, with general creditors, a pro rata share of the assets. No limited partner shall in respect to any such claim
   (a) Receive or hold as collateral security any partnership property, or
   (b) Receive from a general partner or the partnership any payment, conveyance, or release from liability, if at the time the assets of the partnership are not sufficient to discharge partnership liabilities to persons not claiming as general or limited partners.
(2) The receiving of collateral security, or a payment, conveyance, or release in violation of the provisions of paragraph (1) is a fraud on the creditors of the partnership.

Sec. 14. Relation of Limited Partners Inter Se.
Where there are several limited partners the members may agree that one or more of the limited partners shall have a priority over other limited partners as to the return of their contributions, as to their compensation by way of income, or as to any other matter. If such an agreement is made it shall be stated in the certificate, and in the absence of such a statement all the limited partners shall stand upon equal footing.

Sec. 15. Compensation of Limited Partner.
A limited partner may receive from the partnership the share of the profits or the compensation by way of income stipulated for in the certificate; provided, that after such payment is made, whether from the property of the partnership or that of a general partner, the partnership assets are in excess of all liabilities of the partnership except liabilities to limited partners on account of their contributions and to general partners.

Sec. 16. Withdrawal or Reduction of Limited Partner's Contribution.
(1) A limited partner shall not receive from a general partner or out of partnership property any part of his contribution until
   (a) All liabilities of the partnership, except liabilities to general partners and to limited partners on account of their contributions, have been paid or there remains property of the partnership sufficient to pay them,
   (b) The consent of all members is had, unless the return of the contribution may be rightfully demanded under the provisions of paragraph (2), and
   (c) The certificate is cancelled or so amended as to set forth the withdrawal or reduction.
(2) Subject to the provisions of paragraph (1) a limited partner may rightfully demand the return of his contribution

(a) On the dissolution of a partnership, or
(b) When the date specified in the certificate for its return has arrived, or
(c) After he has given six months' notice in writing to all other members, if no time is specified in the certificate either for the return of the contribution or for the dissolution of the partnership.

(3) In the absence of any statement in the certificate to the contrary or the consent of all members, a limited partner, irrespective of the nature of his contribution, has only the right to demand and receive cash in return for his contribution.

(4) A limited partner may have the partnership dissolved and its affairs wound up when
(a) He rightfully but unsuccessfully demands the return of his contribution, or
(b) The other liabilities of the partnership have not been paid, or the partnership property is insufficient for their payment as required by paragraph (1a) and the limited partner would otherwise be entitled to the return of his contribution.

Sec. 17. Liability of Limited Partner to Partnership.

(1) A limited partner is liable to the partnership
(a) For the difference between his contribution as actually made and that stated in the certificate as having been made, and
(b) For any unpaid contribution which he agreed in the certificate to make in the future at the time and on the conditions stated in the certificate.

(2) A limited partner holds as trustee for the partnership
(a) Specific property stated in the certificate as contributed by him, but which was not contributed or which has been wrongfully returned, and
(b) Money or other property wrongfully paid or conveyed to him on account of his contribution.

(3) The liabilities of a limited partner as set forth in this section can be waived or compromised only by the consent of all members; but a waiver or compromise shall not affect the right of a creditor of a partnership, who extended credit or whose claim arose after the filing and before a cancellation or amendment of the certificate, to enforce such liabilities.

(4) When a contributor has rightfully received the return in whole or in part of the capital of his contribution, he is nevertheless liable to the partnership for any sum, not in excess of such return with interest, necessary to discharge its liabilities to all creditors who extended credit or whose claims arose before such return.

Sec. 18. Nature of Limited Partner's Interest in Partnership.

A limited partner's interest in the partnership is personal property.

Sec. 19. Assignment of Limited Partner's Interest.

(1) A limited partner's interest is assignable.

(2) A substituted limited partner is a person admitted to all the rights of a limited partner who has died or has assigned his interest in a partnership.

(3) An assignee, who does not become a substituted limited partner, has no right to require any information or account of the partnership transactions or to inspect the partnership books; he is only entitled to receive the share of the profits or other compensation by way of income, or the return of his contribution, to which his assignor would otherwise be entitled.

(4) An assignee shall have the right to become a substituted limited partner if all the members (except the assignor) consent thereto or if the assignor, being thereunto empowered by the certificate, gives the assignee that right.

(5) An assignee becomes a substituted limited partner when the certificate is appropriately amended in accordance with Section 25.

(6) The substituted limited partner has all the rights and powers, and is subject to all the restrictions and liabilities of his assignor, except those liabilities of which he was ignorant at the time he became a limited partner and which could not be ascertained from the certificate.

(7) The substitution of the assignee as a limited partner does not release the assignor from liability to the partnership under Sections 6 and 17.

Sec. 20. Effect of Retirement, Death or Insanity of a General Partner.

The retirement, death or insanity of a general partner dissolves the partnership, unless the business is continued by the remaining general partners
(a) Under a right so to do stated in the certificate, or
(b) With the consent of all members.

Sec. 21. Death of Limited Partner.

(1) On the death of a limited partner his executor or administrator shall have all the rights of a limited partner for the purpose of settling his estate, and such power as the deceased had to constitute his assignee a substituted limited partner.

(2) The estate of a deceased limited partner shall be liable for all his liabilities as a limited partner.

Sec. 22. Rights of Creditors of Limited Partner.

(1) On due application to a court of competent jurisdiction by any judgment creditor of a limited partner, the court may charge the interest of the indebted limited partner with payment of the unsatisfied amount of the judgment debt; and may appoint a receiver, and make all other orders, directions, and inquiries which the circumstances of the case may require.

In those states where a creditor on beginning an action can attach debts due the defendant before he has obtained a judgment against the defendant it is recommended that paragraph (1) of this section read as follows:

On due application to a court of competent jurisdiction by any creditor of a limited partner, the court may charge the interest of the indebted limited partner with payment of the unsatisfied amount of such claim; and may appoint a receiver, and make all other orders, directions, and inquires which the circumstances of the case may require.

(2) The interest may be redeemed with the separate property of any general partner, but may not be redeemed with partnership property.

(3) The remedies conferred by paragraph (1) shall not be deemed exclusive of others which may exist.

(4) Nothing in this act shall be held to deprive a limited partner of his statutory exemption.

Sec. 23. Distribution of Assets.

(1) In settling accounts after dissolution the liabilities of the partnership shall be entitled to payment in the following order:

(a) Those to creditors, in the order of priority as provided by law, except those to limited partners on account of their contributions, and to general partners,

(b) Those to limited partners in respect to their share of the profits and other compensation by way of income on their contributions,

(c) Those to limited partners in respect to the capital of their contributions,

(d) Those to general partners other than for capital and profits,

(e) Those to general partners in respect to profits,

(f) Those to general partners in respect to capital.

(2) Subject to any statement in the certificate or to subsequent agreement, limited partners share in the partnership assets in respect to their claims for capital, and in respect to their claims for profits or for compensation by way of income on their contributions respectively, in proportion to the respective amounts of such claims.

Sec. 24. When Certificate Shall Be Cancelled or Amended.

(1) The certificate shall be cancelled when the partnership is dissolved or all limited partners cease to be such.

(2) A certificate shall be amended when

(a) There is a change in the name of the partnership or in the amount or character of the contribution of any limited partner,

(b) A person is substituted as a limited partner,

(c) An additional limited partner is admitted,

(d) A person is admitted as a general partner,

(e) A general partner retires, dies or becomes insane, and the business is continued under section 20,

(f) There is a change in the character of the business of the partnership,

(g) There is a false or erroneous statement in the certificate,

(h) There is a change in the time as stated in the certificate for the dissolution of the partnership or for the return of a contribution,

(i) A time is fixed for the dissolution of the partnership, or the return of a contribution, no time having been specified in the certificate, or

(j) The members desire to make a change in any other statement in the certificate in order that it shall accurately represent the agreement between them.

Sec. 25. Requirements for Amendment and for Cancellation of Certificate.

(1) The writing to amend a certificate shall

(a) Conform to the requirements of Section 2(1a) as far as necessary to set forth clearly the change in the certificate which it is desired to make, and

(b) Be signed and sworn to by all members, and an amendment substituting a limited partner or adding a limited or general partner shall be signed also by the member to be substituted or added, and when a limited partner is to be substituted, the amendment shall also be signed by the assigning limited partner.

(2) The writing to cancel a certificate shall be signed by all members.

(3) A person desiring the cancellation or amendment of a certificate, if any person designated in paragraphs (1) and (2) as a person who must execute the writing refuses to do so, may petition the [here designate the proper court] to direct a cancellation or amendment thereof.

(4) If the court finds that the petitioner has a right to have the writing executed by a person who refuses to

do so, it shall order the [here designate the responsible official in the office designated in Section 2] in the office where the certificate is recorded to record the cancellation or amendment of the certificate; and where the certificate is to be amended, the court shall also cause to be filed for record in said office a certified copy of its decree setting forth the amendment.

(5) A certificate is amended or cancelled when there is filed for record in the office [here designate the office designated in Section 2] where the certificate is recorded

   (a) A writing in accordance with the provisions of paragraph (1), or (2) or

   (b) A certified copy of the order of court in accordance with the provisions of paragraph (4).

(6) After the certificate is duly amended in accordance with this section, the amended certificate shall thereafter be for all purposes the certificate provided for by this act.

Sec. 26. Parties to Actions.

A contributor, unless he is a general partner, is not a proper party to proceedings by or against a partnership, except where the object is to enforce a limited partner's right against or liability to the partnership.

Sec. 27. Name of Act.

This act may be cited as The Uniform Limited Partnership Act.

Sec. 28. Rules of Construction.

(1) The rule that statutes in derogation of the common law are to be strictly construed shall have no application to this act.

(2) This act shall be so interpreted and construed as to effect its general purpose to make uniform the law of those states which enact it.

(3) This act shall not be so construed as to impair the obligations of any contract existing when the act goes into effect, nor to affect any action on proceedings begun or right accrued before this act takes effect.

Sec. 29. Rules for Cases Not Provided for in This Act.

In any case not provided for in this act the rules of law and equity, including the law merchant, shall govern.

Sec. 30.[1] Provisions for Existing Limited Partnerships.

(1) A limited partnership formed under any statute of this state prior to the adoption of this act, may become a limited partnership under this act by complying with the provisions of Section 2; provided the certificate sets forth

   (a) The amount of the original contribution of each limited partner, and the time when the contribution was made, and

   (b) That the property of the partnership exceeds the amount sufficient to discharge its liabilities to persons not claiming as general or limited partners by an amount greater than the sum of the contributions of its limited partners.

(2) A limited partnership formed under any statute of this state prior to the adoption of this act, until or unless it becomes a limited partnership under this act, shall continue to be governed by the provisions of [here insert proper reference to the existing limited partnership act or acts], except that such partnership shall not be renewed unless so provided in the original agreement.

Sec. 31.[1] Act [Acts] Repealed.

Except as affecting existing limited partnerships to the extent set forth in Section 30, the act (acts) of [here designate the existing limited partnership act or acts] is (are) hereby repealed.

---

[1] Sections 30, 31, will be omitted in any state which has not previously had a limited partnership act.

APPENDIX C
REVISED UNIFORM LIMITED PARTNERSHIP ACT, 1976, WITH 1985 AMENDMENTS

ARTICLE 1 GENERAL PROVISIONS
Sec. 101 Definitions.
Sec. 102 Name.
Sec. 103 Reservation of Name.
Sec. 104 Specified Office and Agent.
Sec. 105 Records to Be Kept.
Sec. 106 Nature of Business.
Sec. 107 Business Transactions of Partner with Partnership.

ARTICLE 2 FORMATION: CERTIFICATE OF LIMITED PARTNERSHIP
Sec. 201 Certificate of Limited Partnership.
Sec. 202 Amendment to Certificate.
Sec. 203 Cancellation of Certificate.
Sec. 204 Execution of Certificates.
Sec. 205 Execution by Judicial Act.
Sec. 206 Filing in Office of Secretary of State.
Sec. 207 Liability for False Statement in Certificate.
Sec. 208 Scope of Notice.
Sec. 209 Delivery of Certificates to Limited Partners.

ARTICLE 3 LIMITED PARTNERS
Sec. 301 Admission of Additional Limited Partners.
Sec. 302 Voting.
Sec. 303 Liability to Third Parties.
Sec. 304 Person Erroneously Believing Himself [or Herself] Limited Partner.
Sec. 305 Information.

ARTICLE 4 GENERAL PARTNERS
Sec. 401 Admission of Additional General Partners.
Sec. 402 Events of Withdrawal.
Sec. 403 General Powers and Liabilities.
Sec. 404 Contributions by General Partner.
Sec. 405 Voting.

ARTICLE 5 FINANCE
Sec. 501 Form of Contribution.
Sec. 502 Liability for Contribution.
Sec. 503 Sharing of Profits and Losses.
Sec. 504 Sharing of Distributions.

ARTICLE 6 DISTRIBUTIONS AND WITHDRAWAL
Sec. 601 Interim Distributions.
Sec. 602 Withdrawal of General Partner.
Sec. 603 Withdrawal of Limited Partner.
Sec. 604 Distribution upon Withdrawal.
Sec. 605 Distribution in Kind.
Sec. 606 Right to Distribution.
Sec. 607 Limitations on Distribution.
Sec. 608 Liability upon Return of Contribution.

ARTICLE 7 ASSIGNMENT OF PARTNERSHIP INTERESTS
Sec. 701 Nature of Partnership Interest.
Sec. 702 Assignment of Partnership Interest.
Sec. 703 Rights of Creditor.
Sec. 704 Right of Assignee to Become Limited Partner.
Sec. 705 Power of Estate of Deceased or Incompetent Partner.

ARTICLE 8 DISSOLUTION
Sec. 801 Nonjudicial Dissolution.
Sec. 802 Judicial Dissolution.
Sec. 803 Winding Up.
Sec. 804 Distribution of Assets.

Article 9 FOREIGN LIMITED PARTNERSHIPS

Sec. 901 Law Governing.
Sec. 902 Registration.
Sec. 903 Issuance of Registration.
Sec. 904 Name.
Sec. 905 Changes and Amendments.
Sec. 906 Cancellation of Registration.
Sec. 907 Transaction of Business without Registration.
Sec. 908 Action by [Appropriate Official].

Article 10 DERIVATIVE ACTIONS

Sec. 1001 Right of Action.
Sec. 1002 Proper Plaintiff.
Sec. 1003 Pleading.
Sec. 1004 Expenses.

Article 11 MISCELLANEOUS

Sec. 1101 Construction and Application.
Sec. 1102 Short Title.
Sec. 1103 Severability.
Sec. 1104 Effective Date, Extended Effective Date, and Repeal.
Sec. 1105 Rules for Cases Not Provided for in This [Act].
Sec. 1106 Savings Clause.

ARTICLE 1 GENERAL PROVISIONS

§ 101. Definitions.

As used in this [Act], unless the context otherwise requires:

(1) "Certificate of limited partnership" means the certificate referred to in Section 201, and the certificate as amended or restated.

(2) "Contribution" means any cash, property, services rendered, or a promissory note or other binding obligation to contribute cash or property or to perform services, which a partner contributes to a limited partnership in his capacity as a partner.

(3) "Event of withdrawal of a general partner" means an event that causes a person to cease to be a general partner as provided in Section 402.

(4) "Foreign limited partnership" means a partnership formed under the laws of any state other than this State and having as partners one or more general partners and one or more limited partners.

(5) "General partner" means a person who has been admitted to a limited partnership as a general partner in accordance with the partnership agreement and named in the certificate of limited partnership as a general partner.

(6) "Limited partner" means a person who has been admitted to a limited partnership as a limited partner in accordance with the partnership agreement.

(7) "Limited partnership" and "domestic limited partnership" mean a partnership formed by two or more persons under the laws of this State and having one or more general partners and one or more limited partners.

(8) "Partner" means a limited or general partner.

(9) "Partnership agreement" means any valid agreement, written or oral, of the partners as to the affairs of a limited partnership and the conduct of its business.

(10) "*"Partnership interest" means a partner's share of the profits and losses of a limited partnership and the right to receive distributions of partnership assets.

(11) "Person" means a natural person, partnership, limited partnership (domestic or foreign), trust, estate, association, or corporation.

(12) "State" means a state, territory, or possession of the United States, the District of Columbia, or the Commonwealth of Puerto Rico.

§ 102. Name.

The name of each limited partnership as set forth in its certificate of limited partnership:

(1) shall contain without abbreviation the words "limited partnership";

(2) may not contain the name of a limited partner unless (i) it is also the name of a general partner or the corporate name of a corporate general partner, or (ii) the business of the limited partnership had been carried on under that name before the admission of that limited partner;

(3) may not be the same as, or deceptively similar to, the name of any corporation or limited partnership organized under the laws of this State or licensed or registered as a foreign corporation or limited partnership in this State; and

(4) may not contain the following words [here insert prohibited words].

§ 103. Reservation of Name.

(a) The exclusive right to the use of a name may be reserved by:

(1) any person intending to organize a limited partnership under this [Act] and to adopt that name;

(2) any domestic limited partnership or any foreign limited partnership registered in this State which, in either case, intends to adopt that name;

(3) any foreign limited partnership intending to register in this State and adopt that name; and

(4) any person intending to organize a foreign limited partnership and intending to have it register in this State and adopt that name.

(b) The reservation shall be made by filing with the Secretary of State an application, executed by the applicant, to reserve a specified name. If the Secretary of State finds that the name is available for use by a domestic or foreign limited partnership, he [or she] shall reserve the name for the exclusive use of the applicant for a period of 120 days. Once having so reserved a name, the same applicant may not again reserve the same name until more than 60 days after the expiration of the last 120-day period for which that applicant reserved that name. The right to the exclusive use of a reserved name may be transferred to any other person by filing in the office of the Secretary of State a notice of the transfer, executed by the applicant for whom the name was reserved and specifying the name and address of the transferee.

§ 104. Specified Office and Agent.

Each limited partnership shall continuously maintain in this State:

(1) an office, which may but need not be a place of its business in this State, at which shall be kept the records required by Section 105 to be maintained; and

(2) an agent for service of process on the limited partnership, which agent must be an individual resident of this State, a domestic corporation, or a foreign corporation authorized to do business in this State.

§ 105. Records to Be Kept.

(a) Each limited partnership shall keep at the office referred to in Section 104(1) the following:

(1) a current list of the full name and last known business address of each partner, separately identifying the general partners (in alphabetical order) and the limited partners (in alphabetical order);

(2) a copy of the certificate of limited partnership and all certificates of amendment thereto, together with executed copies of any powers of attorney pursuant to which any certificate has been executed;

(3) copies of the limited partnership's federal, state and local income tax returns and reports, if any, for the three most recent years;

(4) copies of any then effective written partnership agreements and of any financial statements of the limited partnership for the three most recent years; and

(5) unless contained in written partnership agreement, a writing setting out:

(i) the amount of cash and a description and statement of the agreed value of the other property or services contributed by each partner and which each partner has agreed to contribute;

(ii) the times at which or events on the happening of which any additional conrtibutionsagreed to be made by each partner are to be made;

(iii) any right of a partner to receive, or of a general partner to make, distributions to a partner which include a return of all or any part of the partner's contribution; and

(iv) any events upon the happening of which the limited partnership is to be dissolved and its affairs wound up.

(b) Records kept under this section are subject to inspection and copying at the reasonable request and at the expense, of any partner during ordinary business hours.

§ 106. Nature of Business.

A limited partnership may carry on any business that a partnership without limited partners may carry on except [here designate prohibited activities].

§ 107. Business Transactions of Partner with Partnership.

Except as provided in the partnership agreement, a partner may lend money to and transact other business with the limited partnership and, subject to other applicable law, has the same rights and obligations with respect thereto as a person who is not a partner.

ARTICLE 2 FORMATION; CERTIFICATE OF LIMITED PARTNERSHIP

§ 201. Certificate of Limited Partnership.

(a) In order to form a limited partnership, a certificate of limited partnership must be executed and filed in the office of the Secretary of State. The certificate shall set forth:

(1) the name of the limited partnership;

(2) the address of the office and the name and address of the agent for service of process required to be maintained by Section 104;

(3) the name and the business address of each general partner;

(4) the latest date upon which the limited partnership is to dissolve; and

(5) any other matters the general partners determine to include therein.

(b) A limited partnership is formed at the time of the filing of the certificate of limited partnership in the office of the Secretary of State or at any later time specified in the certificate of limited partnership if, in either case, there has been substantial compliance with the requirements of this section.

§ 202. Amendment to Certificate.

(a) A certificate of limited partnership is amended by filing a certificate of amendment thereto in the office of the Secretary of State. The certificate shall set forth:

(1) the name of the limited partnership;

(2) the date of filing the certificate; and

(3) the amendment to the certificate.

(b) Within 30 days after the happening of any of the following events, an amendment to a certificate of limited partnership reflecting the occurrence of the event or events shall be filed:

(1) the admission of a new general partner;

(2) the withdrawal of a general partner; or

(3) the continuation of the business under Section 801 after an event of withdrawal of a general partner.

(c) A general partner who becomes aware that any statement in a certificate of limited partnership was false when made or that any arrangements or other facts described have changed, making the certificate inaccurate in any respect, shall promptly amend the certificate.

(d) A certificate of limited partnership may be amended at any time for any other proper purpose the general partners determine.

(e) No person has any liability because an amendment to a certificate of limited partnership has not been filed to reflect the occurrence of any event referred to in subsection (b) of this section if the amendment is filed within the 30-day period specified in subsection (b).

(f) A restated certificate of limited partnership may be executed and filed in the same manner as a certificate of amendment.

§ 203. Cancellation of Certificate.

A certificate of limited partnership shall be cancelled upon the dissolution and the commencement of winding up of the partnership or at any other time there are no limited partners. A certificate of cancellation shall be filed in the office of the Secretary of State and set forth:

(1) the name of the limited partnership;

(2) the date of filing of its certificate of limited partnership;

(3) the reason for filing the certificate of cancellation;

(4) the effective date (which shall be a date certain) of cancellation if it is not to be effective upon the filing of the certificate; and

(5) any other information the general partners filing the certificate determine.

§ 204. Execution of Certificates.

(a) Each certificate required by this Article to be filed in the office of the Secretary of State shall be executed in the following manner:

(1) an original certificate of limited partnership must be signed by all general partners;

(2) a certificate of amendment must be signed by at least one general partner and by each other general partner designated in the certificate as a new general partner; and

(3) a certificate of cancellation must be signed by all general partners.

(b) Any person may sign a certificate by an attorney-in-fact, but a power of attorney to sign a certificate relating to the admission of a general partner must specifically describe the admission.

(c) The execution of a certificate by a general partner constitutes an affirmation under the penalties of perjury that the facts stated therein are true.

§ 205. Execution by Judicial Act.

If a person required by Section 204 to execute any certificate fails or refuses to do so, any other person who is adversely affected by the failure or refusal, may petition the [designate the appropriate court] to direct the execution of the certificate. If the court finds that it is proper for the certificate to be executed and that any person so designated has failed or refused to execute the certificate, it shall order the Secretary of State to record an appropriate certificate.

§ 206. Filing in Office of Secretary of State.

(a) Two signed copies of the certificate of limited partnership and of any certificates of amendment or cancellation (or of any judicial decree of amendment or cancellation) shall be delivered to the Secretary of State. A person who executes a certificate as an agent or fiduciary need not exhibit evidence of his [or her] authority as a prerequisite to filing. Unless the Secretary of State finds that any certificate does not conform to law, upon receipt of all filing fees required by law he [or she] shall:

(1) endorse on each duplicate original the word "Filed" and the day, month and year of the filing thereof;

(2) file one duplicate original in his [or her] office; and

(3) return the other duplicate original to the person who filed it or his [or her] representative.

(b) Upon the filing of a certificate of amendment (or judicial decree of amendment) in the office of the Secretary of State, the certificate of limited partnership shall be amended as set forth therein, and upon the effective date of a certificate of cancellation (or a judicial decree thereof), the certificate of limited partnership is cancelled.

§ 207. Liability for False Statement in Certificate.

If any certificate of limited partnership or certificate of amendment or cancellation contains a false statement, one who suffers loss by reliance on the statement may recover damages for the loss from:

(1) any person who executes the certificate, or causes another to execute it on his behalf, and knew, and any general partner who knew or should have known; the statement to be false at the time the certificate was executed; and

(2) any general partner who thereafter knows or should have known that any arrangement or other fact described in the certificate has changed, making the statement inaccurate in any respect within a sufficient time before the statement was relied upon reasonably to have enabled that general partner to cancel or amend the certificate, or to file a petition for its cancellation or amendment under Section 205.

§ 208. Scope of Notice.

The fact that a certificate of limited partnership is on file in the office of the Secretary of State is notice that the partnership is a limited partnership and the persons designated therein as general partners are general partners, but it is not notice of any other fact.

§ 209. Delivery of Certificates to Limited Partners.

Upon the return by the Secretary of State pursuant to Section 206 of a certificate marked "Filed", the general partners shall promptly deliver or mail a copy of the certificate of limited partnership and each certificate of amendment or cancellation to each limited partner unless the partnership agreement provides otherwise.

ARTICLE 3 LIMITED PARTNERS

§ 301. Admission of Additional Limited Partners.

(a) A person becomes a limited partner on the later of:
  (1) the date the original certificate of limited partnership is filed; or
  (2) the date stated in the records of the limited partnership as the date that person becomes a limited partner.

(b) After the filing of a limited partnership's original certificate of limited partnership, a person may be admitted as an additional limited partner:
  (1) in the case of a person acquiring a partnership interest directly from the limited partnership, upon compliance with the partnership agreement or, if the partnership agreement does not so provide, upon the written consent of all partners; and
  (2) in the case of an assignee of a partnership interest of a partner who has the power, as provided in Section 704, to grant the assignee the right to become a limited partner, upon the exercise of that power and compliance with any conditions limiting the grant or exercise of the power.

§ 302. Voting.

Subject to Section 303, the partnership agreement may grant to all or a specified group of the limited partners the right to vote (on a per capita or other basis) upon any matter.

§ 303. Liability to Third Parties.

(a) Except as provided in subsection (d), a limited partner is not liable for the obligations of a limited partnership unless he [or she] is also a general partner or, in addition to the exercise of his [or her] rights and powers as a limited partner, he [or she] participates in the control of the business. However, if the limited partner participates in the control of the business, he [or she] is liable only to persons who transact business with the limited partnership reasonably believing, based upon the limited partner's conduct, that the limited partner is a general partner.

(b) A limited partner does not participate in the control of the business within the meaning of subsection (a) solely by doing one or more of the following:
  (1) being a contractor for or an agent or employee of the limited partnership or of a general partner or being an officer, director, or shareholder of a general partner that is a corporation;
  (2) consulting with and advising a general partner with respect to the business of the limited partnership;
  (3) acting as surety for the limited partnership or guaranteeing or assuming one or more specific obligations of the limited partnership;
  (4) taking any action required or permitted by law to bring or pursue a derivative action in the right of the limited partnership;
  (5) requesting or attending a meeting of partners;
  (6) proposing, approving, or disapproving, by voting or otherwise, one or more of the following matters:
    (i) the dissolution and winding up of the limited partnership;
    (ii) the sale, exchange, lease, mortgage, pledge, or other transfer of all or substantially all of the assets of the limited partnership;
    (iii) the incurrence of indebtedness by the limited partnership other than in the ordinary course of its business;
    (iv) a change in the nature of the business;
    (v) the admission or removal of a general partner;
    (vi) the admission or removal of a limited partner;
    (vii) a transaction involving an actual or potential conflict of interest between a general partner and the limited partnership or the limited partners;

(viii) an amendment to the partnership agreement or certificate of limited partnership; or
(ix) matters related to the business of the limited partnership not otherwise enumerated in this subsection (b), which the partnership agreement states in writing may be subject to the approval or disapproval of limited partners;
(7) winding up the limited partnership pursuant to Section 803; or
(8) exercising any right or power permitted to limited partners under this [Act] and not specifically enumerated in this subsection (b).
(c) The enumeration in subsection (b) does not mean that the possession or exercise of any other powers by a limited partner constitutes participation by him [or her] in the business of the limited partnership.
(d) A limited partner who knowingly permits his [or her] name to be used in the name of the limited partnership, except under circumstances permitted by Section 102(2), is liable to creditors who extend credit to the limited partnership without actual knowledge that the limited partner is not a general partner.

§ 304. Person Erroneously Believing Himself [or Herself] Limited Partner.

(a) Except as provided in subsection (b), a person who makes a contribution to a business enterprise and erroneously but in good faith believes that he [or she] has become a limited partner in the enterprise is not a general partner in the enterprise and is not bound by its obligations by reason of making the contribution, receiving distributions from the enterprise, or exercising any rights of a limited partner, if, on ascertaining the mistake, he [or she]:
(1) causes an appropriate certificate of limited partnership or a certificate of amendment to be executed and filed; or
(2) withdraws from future equity participation in the enterprise by executing and filing in the office of the Secretary of State a certificate declaring withdrawal under this section.
(b) A person who makes a contribution of the kind described in subsection (a) is liable as a general partner to any third party who transacts business with the enterprise (i) before the person withdraws and an appropriate certificate is filed to show withdrawal, or (ii) before an appropriate certificate is filed to show that he [or she] is not a general partner, but in either case only if the third party actually believed in good faith that the person was a general partner at the time of the transaction.

§ 305. Information.

Each limited partner has the right to:
(1) inspect and copy any of the partnership records required to be maintained by Section 105; and
(2) obtain from the general partners from time to time upon reasonable demand (i) true and full information regarding the state of the business and financial condition of the limited partnership, (ii) promptly after becoming available, a copy of the limited partnership's federal, state and local income tax returns for each year, and (iii) other information regarding the affairs of the limited partnership as is just and reasonable.

ARTICLE 4 GENERAL PARTNERS

§ 401. Admission of Additional General Partners.

After the filing of a limited partnership's original certificate of limited partnership, additional general partners may be admitted as provided in writing in the partnership agreement or, if the partnership agreement does not provide in writing for the admission of additional general partners, with the written consent of all partners.

§ 402. Events of Withdrawal.

Except as approved by the specific written consent of all partners at the time, a person ceases to be a general partner of a limited partnership upon the happening of any of the following events:
(1) the general partner withdraws from the limited partnership as provided in Section 602;
(2) the general partner ceases to be a member of the limited partnership as provided in Section 702;
(3) the general partner is removed as a general partner in accordance with the partnership agreement;
(4) unless otherwise provided in writing in the partnership agreement, the general partner: (i) makes an assignment for the benefit of creditors; (ii) files a voluntary petition in bankruptcy; (iii) is adjudicated a bankrupt or insolvent; (iv) files a petition or answer seeking for himself [or herself] any reorganization, arrangement, composition, readjustment, liquidation, dissolution or similar relief under any statute, law, or regulation; (v) files an answer or other pleading admitting or failing to contest the material allegations of a petition filed against him [or her] in any proceeding of this nature; or (vi) seeks, consents to, or acquiesces in the appointment of a trustee, receiver, or liquidator of the general partner or of all or any substantial part of his [or her] properties;
(5) unless otherwise provided in writing in the partnership agreement, [120] days after the commencement of any proceeding against the general partner seeking reorganization, arrangement, composition, readjustment, liquidation, dissolution or similar relief under any statute, law, or regulation, the proceeding has not been dismissed, or if within [90] days after the appointment without his [or her] consent or acquiescence of a trustee, receiver, or liquidator of the

general partner or of all or any substantial part of his [or her] properties, the appointment is not vacated or stayed or within [90] days after the expiration of any such stay, the appointment is not vacated;

(6) in the case of a general partner who is a natural person,

    (i) his [or her] death; or

    (ii) the entry by a court of competent jurisdiction adjudicating him [or her] incompetent to manage his [or her] person or his [or her] estate;

(7) in the case of a general partner who is acting as a general partner by virtue of being a trustee of a trust, the termination of the trust (but not merely the substitution of a new trustee);

(8) in the case of a general partner that is a separate partnership, the dissolution and commencement of winding up of the separate partnership;

(9) in the case of a general partner that is a corporation, the filing of a certificate of dissolution, or its equivalent, for the corporation or the revocation of its charter; or

(10) in the case of an estate, the distribution by the fiduciary of the estate's entire interest in the partnership.

§ 403. General Powers and Liabilities.

(a) Except as provided in this [Act] or in the partnership agreement, a general partner of a limited partnership has the rights and powers and is subject to the restrictions of a partner in a partnership without limited partners.

(b) Except as provided in this [Act], a general partner of a limited partnership has the liabilities of a partner in a partnership without limited partners to persons other than the partnership and the other partners. Except as provided in this [Act] or in the partnership agreement, a general partner of a limited partnership has the liabilities of a partner in a partnership without limited partners to the partnership and to the other partners.

§ 404. Contributions by General Partner.

A general partner of a limited partnership may make contributions to the partnership and share in the profits and losses of, and in distributions from, the limited partnership as a general partner. A general partner also may make contributions to and share in profits, losses, and distributions as a limited partner. A person who is both a general partner and a limited partner has the rights and powers, and is subject to the restrictions and liabilities, of a general partner and, except as provided in the partnership agreement, also has the powers, and is subject to the restrictions, of a limited partner to the extent of his [or her] participation in the partnership as a limited partner.

§ 405. Voting.

The partnership agreement may grant to all or certain identified general partners the right to vote (on a per capita or any other basis), separately or with all or any class of the limited partners, on any matter.

ARTICLE 5 FINANCE

§ 501. Form of Contribution.

The contribution of a partner may be in cash, property, or services rendered, or a promissory note or other obligation to contribute cash or property or to perform services.

§ 502. Liability for Contribution.

(a) A promise by a limited partner to contribute to the limited partnership is not enforceable unless set out in a writing signed by the limited partner.

(b) Except as provided in the partnership agreement, a partner is obligated to the limited partnership to perform any enforceable promise to contribute cash or property or to perform services, even if he [or she] is unable to perform because of death, disability, or any other reason. If a partner does not make the required contribution of property or services, he [or she] is obligated at the option of the limited partnership to contribute cash equal to that portion of the value, as stated in the partnership records required to be kept pursuant to Section 105, of the stated contribution which has not been made.

(c) Unless otherwise provided in the partnership agreement, the obligation of a partner to make a contribution or return money or other property paid or distributed in violation of this [Act] may be compromised only by consent of all partners. Notwithstanding the compromise, a creditor of a limited partnership who extends credit or otherwise acts in reliance on that obligation after the partner signs a writing which reflects the obligation and before the amendment or cancellation thereof to reflect the compromise may enforce the original obligation.

§ 503. Sharing of Profits and Losses.

The profits and losses of a limited partnership shall be allocated among the partners, and among classes of partners, in the manner provided in writing in the partnership agreement. If the partnership agreement does not so provide in writing, profits and losses shall be allocated on the basis of the value, as stated in the partnership records required to be kept pursuant to Section 105, of the contributions made by each partner to the extent they have been received by the partnership and have not been returned.

§ 504. Sharing of Distributions.

Distributions of cash or other assets of a limited partnership shall be allocated among the partners and among classes of partners in the manner provided in writing in the partnership agreement. If the partnership agreement does not so provide in writing, distributions shall be made on the basis of the value, as stated in the partnership records required to be kept pursuant to Section 105, of the contributions made by each partner to the extent they have been received by the partnership and have not been returned.

ARTICLE 6 DISTRIBUTIONS AND WITHDRAWAL

§ 601. Interim Distributions.
Except as provided in this Article, a partner is entitled to receive distributions from a limited partnership before his [or her] withdrawal from the limited partnership and before the dissolution and winding up thereof.

To the extent and at the times or upon the happening of the events specified in the partnership agreement.

§ 602. Withdrawal of General Partner.
A general partner may withdraw from a limited partnership at any time by giving written notice to the other partners, but if the withdrawal violates the partnership agreement, the limited partnership may recover from the withdrawal general partner damages for breach of the partnership agreement and offset the damages against the amount otherwise distributable to him [or her].

§ 603. Withdrawal of Limited Partner.
A limited partner may withdraw from a limited partnership at the time or upon the happening of events specified in writing in the partnership agreement. If the agreement does not specify in writing the time or the events upon the happening of which a limited partner may withdraw or a definite time for the dissolution and winding up of the limited partnership, a limited partner may withdraw upon not less than six months' prior written notice to each general partner at his [or her] address on the books of the limited partnership at its office in this State.

§ 604. Distribution upon Withdrawal.
Except as provided in this Article, upon withdrawal any withdrawing partner is entitled to receive any distribution to which he [or she] is entitled under the partnership agreement and, if not otherwise provided in the agreement, he [or she] is entitled to receive, within a reasonable time after withdrawal, the fair value of his [or her] interest in the limited partnership as of the date of withdrawal based upon his [or her] right to share in distributions from the limited partnership.

§ 605. Distribution in Kind.
Except as provided in writing in the partnership agreement, a partner, regardless of the nature of his [or her] contribution, has no right to demand and receive any distribution from the limited partnership in any form other than cash. Except as provided in writing in the partnership agreement, a partner may not be compelled to accept a distribution of any asset in kind from a limited partnership to the extent that the percentage of the asset distributed to him [or her] exceeds a percentage of that asset which is equal to the percentage in which he [or she] shares in distributions from the limited partnership.

§ 606. Right to Distribution.
At the time a partner becomes entitled to receive a distribution, he [or she] has the status of, and is entitled to all remedies available to, a creditor of the limited partnership with respect to the distribution.

§ 607. Limitations on Distribution.
A partner may not receive a distribution from a limited partnership to the extent that, after giving effect to the distribution, all liabilities of the limited partnership, other than liabilities to partners on account of their partnership interest, exceed the fair value of the partnership assets.

§ 608. Liability upon Return of Contribution.
(a) If a partner has received the return of any part of his [or her] contribution without violation of the partnership agreement or this [Act], he [or she] is liable to the limited partnership for a period of one year thereafter for the amount of the returned contribution, but only to the extent necessary to discharge the limited partnership's liabilities to creditors who extended credit to the limited partnership during the period the contribution was held by the partnership.
(b) If a partner has received the return of any part of his [or her] contribution in violation of the partnership agreement or this [Act], he [or she] is liable to the limited partnership for a period of six years thereafter for the amount of the contribution wrongfully returned.
(c) A partner receives a return of his [or her] contribution to the extent that a distribution to him [or her] reduces his [or her] share of the fair value of the net assets of the limited partnership below the value, as set forth in the partnership records required to be kept pursuant to Section 105, of his [or her] contribution which has not been distributed to him [or her].

ARTICLE 7 ASSIGNMENT OF PARTNERSHIP INTERESTS

§ 701. Nature of Partnership Interest.
A partnership interest is personal property.

§ 702. Assignment of Partnership Interest.

Except as provided in the partnership agreement, a partnership interest is assignable in whole or in part. An assignment of a partnership interest does not dissolve a limited partnership or entitle the assignee to become or to exercise any rights of a partner. An assignment entitles the assignee to receive, to the extent assigned, only the distribution to which the assignor would be entitled. Except as provided in the partnership agreement, a partner ceases to be a partner upon assignment of all his [or her] partnership interest.

§ 703. Rights of Creditor.

On application to a court of competent jurisdiction by any judgment creditor of a partner, the court may charge the partnership interest of the partner with payment of the unsatisfied amount of the judgment with interest. To the extent so charged, the judgment creditor has only the rights of an assignee of the partnership interest. This [Act] does not deprive any partner of the benefit of any exemption laws applicable to his [or her] partnership interest.

§ 704. Right of Assignee to Become Limited Partner.

(a) An assignee of a partnership interest, including an assignee of a general partner, may become a limited partner if and to the extent that (i) the assignor gives the assignee that right in accordance with authority described in the partnership agreement, or (ii) all other partners consent.

(b) An assignee who has become a limited partner has, to the extent assigned, the rights and powers, and is subject to the restrictions and liabilities, of a limited partner under the partnership agreement and this [Act]. An assignee who becomes a limited partner also is liable for the obligations of his [or her] assignor to make and return contributions as provided in Articles 5 and 6. However, the assignee is not obligated for liabilities unknown to the assignee at the time he [or she] became a limited partner.

(c) If an assignee of a partnership interest becomes a limited partner, the assignor is not released from his [or her] liability to the limited partnership under Sections 207 and 502.

§ 705. Power of Estate of Deceased or Incompetent Partner.

If a partner who is an individual dies or a court of competent jurisdiction adjudges him [or her] to be incompetent to manage his [or her] person or his [or her] property, the partner's executor, administrator, guardian, conservator, or other legal representative may exercise all the partner's rights for the purpose of settling his [or her] estate or administering his [or her] property, including any power the partner had to give an assignee the right to become a limited partner. If a partner is a corporation, trust, or other entity and is dissolved or terminated, the powers of that partner may be exercised by its legal representative or successor.

ARTICLE 8 DISSOLUTION

§ 801. Nonjudicial Dissolution.

A limited partnership is dissolved and its affairs shall be wound up upon the happening of the first to occur of the following:

(1) at the time specified in the certificate of limited partnership;

(2) upon the happening of events specified in writing in the partnership agreement;

(3) written consent of all partners;

(4) an event of withdrawal of a general partner unless at the time there is at least one other general partner and the written provisions of the partnership agreement permit the business of the limited partnership to be carried on by the remaining general partner and that partner does so, but the limited partnership is not dissolved and is not required to be wound up by reason of any event of withdrawal, if within 90 days after the withdrawal, all partners agree in writing to continue the business of the limited partnership and to the appointment of one or more additional general partners if necessary or desired; or

(5) entry of a decree of judicial dissolution under Section 802.

§ 802. Judicial Dissolution.

On application by or for a partner the [designate the proper court] court may decree dissolution of a limited partnership whenever it is not reasonably practicable to carry on the business in conformity with the partnership agreement.

§ 803. Winding Up.

Except as provided in the partnership agreement, the general partners who have not wrongfully dissolved a limited partnership or, if none, the limited partners, may wind up the limited partnership's affairs; but the [designate the proper court] court may wind up the limited partnership's affairs upon application of any partner, his [or her] legal representative, or assignee.

§ 804. Distribution of Assets.

Upon the winding up of a limited partnership, the assets shall be distributed as follows:

(1) to creditors, including partners who are creditors, to the extent permitted by law, in satisfaction of liabilities of the limited partnership other than liabil-

ities for distributions to partners under Section 601 or 604;

(2) except as provided in the partnership agreement, to partners and former partners in satisfaction of liabilities for distributions under Section 601 or 604; and

(3) except as provided in the partnership agreement, to partners first for the return of their contributions and secondly respecting their partnership interests, in the proportions in which the partners share in distributions.

ARTICLE 9 FOREIGN LIMITED PARTNERSHIPS

§ 901. Law Governing.

Subject to the Constitution of this State, (i) the laws of the state under which a foreign limited partnership is organized govern its organization and internal affairs and the liability of its limited partners, and (ii) a foreign limited partnership may not be denied registration by reason of any difference between those laws and the laws of this State.

§ 902. Registration.

Before transacting business in this State, a foreign limited partnership shall register with the Secretary of State. In order to register, a foreign limited partnership shall submit to the Secretary of State, in duplicate, an application for registration as a foreign limited partnership, signed and sworn to by a general partner and setting forth:

(1) the name of the foreign limited partnership and, if different, the name under which it proposes to register and transact business in this State;

(2) the State and date of its formation;

(3) the name and address of any agent for service of process on the foreign limited partnership whom the foreign limited partnership elects to appoint; the agent must be an individual resident of this State, a domestic corporation, or a foreign corporation having a place of business in, and authorized to do business in, this State;

(4) a statement that the Secretary of State is appointed the agent of the foreign limited partnership for service of process if no agent has been appointed under paragraph (3) or, if appointed, the agent's authority has been revoked or if the agent cannot be found or served with the exercise of reasonable diligence;

(5) the address of the office required to be maintained in the state of its organization by the laws of that state or, if not so required, of the principal office of the foreign limited partnership;

(6) the name and business address of each general partner; and

(7) the address of the office at which is kept a list of the names and addresses of the limited partners and their capital contributions, together with an undertaking by the foreign limited partnership to keep those records until the foreign limited partnership;s registration in this State is cancelled or withdrawn.

§ 903. Issuance of Registration.

(a) If the Secretary of State finds that an application for registration conforms to law and all requisite fees have been paid, he [or she] shall:

(1) endorse on the application the word "Filed," and the month, day and year of the filing thereof;

(2) file in his [or her] office a duplicate original of the application; and

(3) issue a certificate of registration to transact business in this State.

(b) The certificate of registration, together with a duplicate original of the application, shall be returned to the person who filed the application or his [or her] representative.

§ 904. Name.

A foreign limited partnership may register with the Secretary of State under any name, whether or not it is the name under which it is registered in its state of organization, that includes without abbreviation the words "limited partnership" and that could be registered by a domestic limited partnership.

§ 905. Changes and Amendments.

If any statement in the application for registration of a foreign limited partnership was false when made or any arrangements or other facts described have changed, making the application inaccurate in any respect, the foreign limited partnership shall promptly file in the office of the Secretary of State a certificate, signed and sworn to by a general partner, correcting such statement.

§ 906. Cancellation of Registration.

A foreign limited partnership may cancel its registration by filing with the Secretary of State a certificate of cancellation signed and sworn to by a general partner. A cancellation does not terminate the authority of the Secretary of State to accept service of process on the foreign limited partnership with respect to [claims for relief] [causes of action] arising out of the transactions of business in this State.

§ 907. Transaction of Business without Registration.

(a) A foreign limited partnership transacting business in this State may not maintain any action, suit, or proceeding in any court of this State until it has registered in this State.

(b) The failure of a foreign limited partnership to register in this State does not impair the validity of any contract or act of the foreign limited partnership or prevent the foreign limited partnership from defending any action, suit, or proceeding in any court of this State.

(c) A limited partner of a foreign limited partnership is not liable as a general partner of the foreign limited partnership solely by reason of having transacted business in this State without registration.

(d) A foreign limited partnership, by transacting business in this State without registration, appoints the Secretary of State as its agent for service of process with respect to [claims for relief] [causes of action] arising out of the transaction of business in this State.

§ 908. Action by [Appropriate Official].
The [designate the appropriate official] may bring an action to restrain a foreign limited partnership from transacting business in this State in violation of this Article.

ARTICLE 10 DERIVATIVE ACTIONS
§ 1001. Right of Action.
A limited partner may bring an action in the right of a limited partnership to recover a judgment in its favor if general partners with authority to do so have refused to bring the action or if an effort to cause those general partners to bring the action is not likely to succeed.

§ 1002. Proper Plaintiff.
In a derivative action, the plaintiff must be a partner at the time of bringing the action and (i) must have been a partner at the time of the transaction of which he [or she] complains or (ii) his [or her] status as a partner must have had devolved upon him [or her] by operation of law or pursuant to the terms of the partnership agreement from a person who was a partner at the time of the transaction.

§ 1003. Pleading.
In a derivative action, the complaint shall set forth with particularity the effort of the plaintiff to secure initiation of the action by a general partner or the reasons for not making the effort.

§ 1004. Expenses.
If a derivative action is successful, in whole or in part, or if anything is received by the plaintiff as a result of a judgment, compromise or settlement of an action or claim, the court may award the plaintiff reasonable expenses, including reasonable attorney's fees, and shall direct him [or her] to remit to the limited partnership the remainder of those proceeds received by him [or her].

ARTICLE 11 MISCELLANEOUS
§ 1101. Construction and Application.
This [Act] shall be so applied and construed to effectuate its general purpose to make uniform the law with respect to the subject of this [Act] among states enacting it.

§ 1102. Short Title.
This [Act] may be cited as the Uniform Limited Partnership Act.

§ 1103 Severability.
If any provision of this [Act] or its application to any person or circumstance is held invalid, the invalidity does not affect other provisions or applications of the [Act] which can be given effect without the invalid provision or application, and to this end the provisions of this Act are severable.

§ 1104. Effective Date, Extended Effective Date, and Repeal.
Except as set forth below, the effective date of this [Act] is _____ and the following Acts [list existing limited partnership acts] are hereby repealed:

(1) The existing provisions for execution and filing of certificates of limited partnerships and amendments thereunder and cancellations thereof continue in effect until [specify time required to create central filing system], the extended effective date, and Sections 102, 103, 104, 105, 201, 202, 203, 204 and 206 are not effective until the extended effective date.

(2) Section 402, specifying the conditions under which a general partner ceases to be a member of a limited partnership, is not effective until the extended effective date, and the applicable provisions of existing law continue to govern until the extended effective date.

(3) Sections 501, 502 and 608 apply only to contributions and distributions made after the effective date of this [Act].

(4) Section 704 applies only to assignments made after the effective date of this [Act].

(5) Article 9, dealing with registration of foreign limited partnerships, is not effective until the extended effective date.

(6) Unless otherwise agreed by the partners, the applicable provisions of existing law governing allocation of profits and losses (rather than the provisions of Section 503), distributions to a withdrawing partner

(rather than the provisions of Section 604), and distribution of assets upon the winding up of a limited partnership (rather than the provisions of Section 804) govern limited partnerships formed before the effective date of this [Act].

§ 1105. Rules for Cases Not Provided for in This [Act].

In any case not provided for in this [Act] the provisions of the Uniform Partnership Act govern.

§ 1106. Savings Clause.

The repeal of any statutory provision by this Act does not impair, or otherwise affect, the organization or the continued existence of a limited partnership existing at the effective date of this Act, nor does the repeal of any existing statutory provision by this Act impair any contract or affect any right accrued before the effective date of this Act.

APPENDIX D

REVISED MODEL BUSINESS CORPORATION ACT

Chapter 1 General Provisions

Short Title and Reservation of Power
§ 1.01. Short Title
1.02. Reservation of Power to Amend or Repeal

Filing Documents
§ 1.20. Filing Requirements
1.21. Forms
1.22. Filing, Service, and Copying Fees
1.23. Effective Time and Date of Document
1.24. Correcting Filed Document
1.25. Filing Duty of Secretary of State
1.26. Appeal from Secretary of State's Refusal to File Document
1.27. Evidentiary Effect of Copy of Filed Document
1.28. Certificate of Existence
1.29. Penalty for Signing False Document

Secretary of State
§ 1.30. Powers

Definitions
§ 1.40. Act Definitions
1.41. Notice
1.42. Number of Shareholders

Chapter 2 Incorporation
§ 2.01. Incorporators
2.02. Articles of Incorporation
2.03. Incorporation
2.04. Liability for Preincorporation Transactions
2.05. Organization of Corporation
2.06. Bylaws
2.07. Emergency Bylaws

Chapter 3 Purposes and Powers
§ 3.01. Purposes
3.02. General Powers
3.03. Emergency Powers
3.04. Ultra Vires

Chapter 4 Name
§ 4.01. Corporate Name
4.02. Reserved Name
4.03. Registered Name

Chapter 5 Office and Agent
§ 5.01. Registered Office and Registered Agent
5.02. Change of Registered Office or Registered Agent
5.03. Resignation of Registered Agent
5.04. Service on Corporation

Chapter 6 Shares and Distributions

Shares
§ 6.01. Authorized Shares
6.02. Terms of Class or Series Determined by Board of Directors
6.03. Issued and Outstanding Shares
6.04. Fractional Shares

Issuance of Shares
§ 6.20. Subscription for Shares before Incorporation
6.21. Issuance of Shares
6.22. Liability of Shareholders
6.23. Share Dividends
6.24. Share Options
6.25. Form and Content of Certificates
6.26. Shares without Certificates
6.27. Restriction on Transfer of Shares and Other Securities
6.28. Expense of Issue

Subsequent Acquisition of Shares by Shareholders and Corporation
§ 6.30. Shareholders' Preemptive Rights
   6.31. Corporation's Acquisition of Its Own Shares

Distributions
§ 6.40. Distributions to Shareholders

Chapter 7 Shareholders

Meetings
§ 7.01. Annual Meeting
   7.02. Special Meeting
   7.03. Court-Ordered Meeting
   7.04. Action without Meeting
   7.05. Notice of Meeting
   7.06. Waiver of Notice
   7.07. Record Date

Voting
§ 7.20. Shareholders' List for Meeting
   7.21. Voting Entitlement of Shares
   7.22. Proxies
   7.23. Shares Held by Nominees
   7.24. Corporation's Acceptance of Votes
   7.25. Quorum and Voting Requirements for Voting Groups
   7.26. Action by Single and Multiple Voting Groups
   7.27. Greater Quorum or Voting Requirements
   7.28. Voting for Directors; Cumulative Voting

Voting Trusts and Agreements
§ 7.30. Voting Trusts
   7.31. Voting Agreements

Derivative Proceedings
§ 7.40. Procedure in Derivative Proceedings

Chapter 8 Directors and Officers

Board of Directors
§ 8.01. Requirement for and Duties of Board of Directors
   8.02. Qualifications of Directors
   8.03. Number and Election of Directors
   8.04. Election of Directors by Certain Classes of Shareholders
   8.05. Terms of Directors Generally
   8.06. Staggered Terms for Directors
   8.07. Resignation of Directors
   8.08. Removal of Directors by Shareholders
   8.09. Removal of Directors by Judicial Proceeding
   8.10. Vacancy on Board
   8.11. Compensation of Directors

Meetings and Action of the Board
§ 8.20. Meetings
   8.21. Action without Meeting
   8.22. Notice of Meeting
   8.23. Waiver of Notice
   8.24. Quorum and Voting
   8.25. Committees

Standards of Conduct
§ 8.30. General Standards for Directors
   8.31. Director Conflict of Interest
   8.32. Loans to Directors
   8.33. Liability for Unlawful Distributions

Officers
§ 8.40. Required Officers
   8.41. Duties of Officers
   8.42. Standards of Conduct for Officers
   8.43. Resignation and Removal of Officers
   8.44. Contract Rights of Officers

Indemnification
§ 8.50. Subchapter Definitions
   8.51. Authority to Indemnify
   8.52. Mandatory Indemnification
   8.53. Advance for Expenses
   8.54. Court-Ordered Indemnification
   8.55. Determination and Authorization of Indemnification
   8.56. Indemnification of Officers, Employees, and Agents
   8.57. Insurance
   8.58. Application of Subchapter

Chapter 9 [Reserved]

Chapter 10 Amendment of Articles of Incorporation and Bylaws

Amendment of Articles of Incorporation
§ 10.01. Authority to Amend
   10.02. Amendment by Board of Directors
   10.03. Amendment by Board of Directors and Shareholders

10.04. Voting on Amendments by Voting Groups
10.05. Amendment before Issuance of Shares
10.06. Articles of Amendment
10.07. Restated Articles of Incorporation
10.08. Amendment Pursuant to Reorganization
10.09. Effect of Amendment

Amendment of Bylaws

§ 10.20. Amendment by Board of Directors or Shareholders
10.21. Bylaw Increasing Quorum or Voting Requirement for Shareholders
10.22. Bylaw Increasing Quorum or Voting Requirement for Directors

CHAPTER 11 Merger and Share Exchange

§ 11.01. Merger
11.02. Share Exchange
11.03. Action on Plan
11.04. Merger of Subsidiary
11.05. Articles of Merger or Share Exchange
11.06. Effect of Merger or Share Exchange
11.07. Merger or Share Exchange with Foreign Corporation

CHAPTER 12 Sale of Assets

§ 12.01. Sale of Assets in Regular Course of Business and Mortgage of Assets
12.02. Sale of Assets Other than in Regular Course of Business

CHAPTER 13 Dissenters' Rights

Right to Dissent and Obtain Payment for Shares

§ 13.01. Definitions
13.02. Right to Dissent
13.03. Dissent by Nominees and Beneficial Owners

Procedure for Exercise of Dissenters' Rights

§ 13.20. Notice of Dissenters' Rights
13.21. Notice of Intent to Demand Payment
13.22. Dissenters' Notice
13.23. Duty to Demand Payment
13.24. Share Restrictions
13.25. Payment
13.26. Failure to Take Action
13.27. After-Acquired Shares
13.28. Procedure if Shareholder Dissatisfied with Payment or Offer

Judicial Appraisal of Shares

§ 13.30. Court Action
13.31. Court Costs and Counsel Fees

CHAPTER 14 Dissolution

Voluntary Dissolution

§ 14.01. Dissolution by Incorporators or Initial Directors
14.02. Dissolution by Board of Directors and Shareholders
14.03. Articles of Dissolution
14.04. Revocation of Dissolution
14.05. Effect of Dissolution
14.06. Known Claims against Dissolved Corporation
14.07. Unknown Claims against Dissolved Corporation

Administrative Dissolution

§ 14.20. Grounds for Administrative Dissolution
14.21. Procedure for and Effect of Administrative Dissolution
14.22. Reinstatement Following Administrative Dissolution
14.23. Appeal from Denial of Reinstatement

Judicial Dissolution

§ 14.30. Grounds for Judicial Dissolution
14.31. Procedure for Judicial Dissolution
14.32. Receivership or Custodianship
14.33. Decree of Dissolution

Miscellaneous

§ 14.40. Deposit with State Treasurer

CHAPTER 15 Foreign Corporations

Certificate of Authority

§ 15.01. Authority to Transact Business Required
15.02. Consequences of Transacting Business without Authority
15.03. Application for Certificate of Authority
15.04. Amended Certificate of Authority
15.05. Effect of Certificate of Authority
15.06. Corporate Name of Foreign Corporation
15.07. Registered Office and Registered Agent of Foreign Corporation

15.08. Change of Registered Office or Registered Agent of Foreign Corporation
15.09. Resignation of Registered Agent of Foreign Corporation
15.10. Service on Foreign Corporation

Withdrawal
§ 15.20. Withdrawal of Foreign Corporation

Revocation of Certificate of Authority
§ 15.30. Grounds for Revocation
15.31. Procedure for and Effect of Revocation
15.32. Appeal from Revocation

Chapter 16 Records and Reports

Records
§ 16.01. Corporate Records
16.02. Inspection of Records by Shareholders
16.03. Scope of Inspection Right
16.04. Court-Ordered Inspection

Reports
§ 16.20. Financial Statements for Shareholders
16.21. Other Reports to Shareholders
16.22. Annual Report for Secretary of State

Chapter 17 Transition Provisions
§ 17.01. Application to Existing Domestic Corporations
17.02. Application to Qualified Foreign Corporations
17.03. Saving Provisions
17.04. Severability
17.05. Repeal
17.06. Effective Date

CHAPTER 1 GENERAL PROVISIONS

Short Title and Reservation of Power
§ 1.01. Short Title
This Act shall be known and may be cited as the "[name of state] Business Corporation Act."

§ 1.02. Reservation of Power to Amend or Repeal
The [name of state legislature] has power to amend or repeal all or part of this Act at any time and all domestic and foreign corporations subject to this Act are governed by the amendment or repeal.

Filing Documents
§ 1.20. Filing Requirements
(a) A document must satisfy the requirements of this section, and of any other section that adds to or varies from these requirements, to be entitled to filing by the secretary of state.
(b) This Act must require or permit filing the document in the office of the secretary of state.
(c) The document must contain the information required by this Act. It may contain other information as well.
(d) The document must be typewritten or printed.
(e) The document must be in the English language. A corporate name need not be in English if written in English letters or Arabic or Roman numerals, and the certificate of existence required of foreign corporations need not be in English if accompanied by a reasonably authenticated English translation.
(f) The document must be executed:
   (1) by the chairman of the board of directors of a domestic or foreign corporation, by its president, or by another of its officers;
   (2) if directors have not been selected or the corporation has not been formed, by an incorporator; or
   (3) if the corporation is in the hands of a receiver, trustee, or other court-appointed fiduciary, by that fiduciary.
(g) The person executing the document shall sign it and state beneath or opposite his signature his name and the capacity in which he signs. The document may but need not contain: (1) the corporate seal, (2) an attestation by the secretary or an assistant secretary, (3) an acknowledgement, verification, or proof.
(h) If the secretary of state has prescribed a mandatory form for the document under section 1.21, the document must be in or on the prescribed form.
(i) The document must be delivered to the office of the secretary of state for filing and must be accompanied by one exact or conformed copy (except as provided in sections 5.03 and 15.09), the correct filing fee, and any franchise tax, license fee, or penalty required by this Act or other law.

§ 1.21. Forms
(a) The secretary of state may prescribe and furnish on request forms for: (1) an application for a certificate of existence, (2) a foreign corporation's application for a certificate of authority to transact business in this state, (3) a foreign corporation's application for a certificate of withdrawal, and (4) the annual report. If the secretary of state so requires, use of these forms is mandatory.

(b) The secretary of state may prescribe and furnish on request forms for other documents required or permitted to be filed by this Act but their use is not mandatory.

§ 1.22. Filing, Service, and Copying Fees

(a) The secretary of state shall collect the following fees when the documents described in this subsection are delivered to him for filing:

	Document	Fee
(1)	Articles of incorporation	$_____ .
(2)	Application for use of indistinguishable name	$_____ .
(3)	Application for reserved name	$_____ .
(4)	Notice of transfer of reserved name	$_____ .
(5)	Application for registered name	$_____ .
(6)	Application for renewal of registered name	$_____ .
(7)	Corporation's statement of change of registered agent or registered office or both	$_____ .
(8)	Agent's statement of change of registered office for each affected corporation not to exceed a total of	$_____ .
(9)	Agent's statement of resignation	No fee.
(10)	Amendment of articles of incorporation	$_____ .
(11)	Restatement of articles of incorporation with amendment of articles	$_____ .
(12)	Articles of merger or share exchange	$_____ .
(13)	Articles of dissolution	$_____ .
(14)	Articles of revocation of dissolution	$_____ .
(15)	Certificate of administrative dissolution	No fee.
(16)	Application for reinstatement following administrative dissolution	$_____ .
(17)	Certificate of reinstatement	No fee.
(18)	Certificate of judicial dissolution	No fee.
(19)	Application for certificate of authority	$_____ .
(20)	Application for amended certificate of authority	$_____ .
(21)	Application for certificate of withdrawal	$_____ .
(22)	Certificate of revocation of authority to transact business	No fee.
(23)	Annual report	$_____ .
(24)	Articles of correction	$_____ .
(25)	Application for certificate of existence or authorization	$_____ .
(26)	Any other document required or permitted to be filed by this Act	$_____ .

(b) The secretary of state shall collect a fee of $_____ each time process is served on him under this Act. The party to a proceeding causing service of process is entitled to recover this fee as costs if he prevails in the proceeding.

(c) The secretary of state shall collect the following fees for copying and certifying the copy of any filed document relating to a domestic or foreign corporation:

(1) $_____ a page for copying; and
(2) $_____ for the certificate.

§ 1.23. Effective Time and Date of Document

(a) Except as provided in subsection (b) and section 1.24(c), a document accepted for filing is effective:

(1) at the time of filing on the date it is filed, as evidenced by the secretary of state's date and time endorsement on the original document; or

(2) at the time specified in the document as its effective time on the date it is filed.

(b) A document may specify a delayed effective time and date, and if it does so the document becomes effective at the time and date specified. If a delayed effective date but no time is specified, the document is effective at the close of business on that date. A delayed effective date for a document may not be later than the 90th day after the date it is filed.

§ 1.24. Correcting Filed Document

(a) A domestic or foreign corporation may correct a document filed by the secretary of state if the document (1) contains an incorrect statement or (2) was defectively executed, attested, sealed, verified, or acknowledged.

(b) A document is corrected:

(1) by preparing articles of correction that (i) describe the document (including its filing date) or attach a copy of it to the articles, (ii) specify the incorrect statement and the reason it is incorrect or the manner in which the execution was defective, and (iii) correct the incorrect statement or defective execution; and

(2) by delivering the articles to the secretary of state for filing.

(c) Articles of correction are effective on the effective date of the document they correct except as to persons relying on the uncorrected document and adversely affected by the correction. As to those persons, articles of correction are effective when filed.

§ 1.25. Filing Duty of Secretary of State

(a) If a document delivered to the office of the secretary of state for filing satisfies the requirements of section 1.20, the secretary of state shall file it.

(b) The secretary of state files a document by stamping or otherwise endorsing "Filed," together with his name and official title and the date and time of receipt, on both the original and the document copy and on the receipt for the filing fee. After filing a document, except as provided in sections 5.03 and 15.10, the secretary of state shall deliver the document copy, with the filing fee receipt (or acknowledgement of receipt if no fee is required) attached, to the domestic or foreign corporation or its representative.

(c) If the secretary of state refuses to file a document, he shall return it to the domestic or foreign corporation or its representative within five days after the document was delivered, together with a brief, written explanation of the reason for his refusal.

(d) The secretary of state's duty to file documents under this section is ministerial. His filing or refusing to file a document does not:

(1) affect the validity or invalidity of the document in whole or part;

(2) relate to the correctness or incorrectness of information contained in the document;

(3) create a presumption that the document is valid or invalid or that information contained in the document is correct or incorrect.

§ 1.26. Appeal from Secretary of State's Refusal to File Document

(a) If the secretary of state refuses to file a document delivered to his office for filing, the domestic or foreign corporation may appeal the refusal within 30 days after the return of the document to the [name or describe] court [of the county where the corporation's principal office (or, if none in this state, its registered office) is or will be located] [of _____ county]. The appeal is commenced by petitioning the court to compel filing the document and by attaching to the petition the document and the secretary of state's explanation of his refusal to file.

(b) The court may summarily order the secretary of state to file the document or take other action the court considers appropriate.

(c) The court's final decision may be appealed as in other civil proceedings.

§ 1.27. Evidentiary Effect of Copy of Filed Document

A certificate attached to a copy of a document filed by the secretary of state, bearing his signature (which may be in facsimile) and the seal of this state, is conclusive evidence that the original document is on file with the secretary of state.

§ 1.28. Certificate of Existence

(a) Anyone may apply to the secretary of state to furnish a certificate of existence for a domestic corporation or a certificate of authorization for a foreign corporation.

(b) A certificate of existence or authorization sets forth:

(1) the domestic corporation's corporate name or the foreign corporation's corporate name used in this state;

(2) that (i) the domestic corporation is duly incorporated under the law of this state, the date of its incorporation, and the period of its duration if less than perpetual; or (ii) that the foreign corporation is authorized to transact business in this state;

(3) that all fees, taxes, and penalties owed to this state have been paid, if (i) payment is reflected in the records of the secretary of state and (ii) nonpayment affects the existence or authorization of the domestic or foreign corporation;

(4) that its most recent annual report required by section 16.22 has been delivered to the secretary of state;

(5) that articles of dissolution have not been filed; and

(6) other facts of record in the office of the secretary of state that may be requested by the applicant.

(c) Subject to any qualification stated in the certificate, a certificate of existence or authorization issued by the secretary of state may be relied upon as conclusive evidence that the domestic or foreign corporation is in existence or is authorized to transact business in this state.

§ 1.29. Penalty for Signing False Document

(a) A person commits an offense if he signs a document he knows is false in any material respect with intent that the document be delivered to the secretary of state for filing.

(b) An offense under this section is a [_____] misdemeanor [punishable by a fine of not to exceed $_____].

Secretary of State

§ 1.30. Powers

The secretary of state has the power reasonably necessary to perform the duties required of him by this Act.

Definitions
§ 1.40. Act Definitions
In this Act:

(1) "Articles of incorporation" include amended and restated articles of incorporation and articles of merger.

(2) "Authorized shares" means the shares of all classes a domestic or foreign corporation is authorized to issue.

(3) "Conspicuous" means so written that a reasonable person against whom the writing is to operate should have noticed it. For example, printing in italics or boldface or contrasting color, or typing in capitals or underlined, is conspicuous.

(4) "Corporation" or "domestic corporation" means a corporation for profit, which is not a foreign corporation, incorporated under or subject to the provisions of this Act.

(5) "Deliver" includes mail.

(6) "Distribution" means a direct or indirect transfer of money or other property (except its own shares) or incurrence of indebtedness by a corporation to or for the benefit of its shareholders in respect of any of its shares. A distribution may be in the form of a declaration or payment of a dividend; a purchase, redemption, or other acquisition of shares; a distribution of indebtedness; or otherwise.

(7) "Effective date of notice" is defined in section 1.41.

(8) "Employee" includes an officer but not a director. A director may accept duties that make him also an employee.

(9) "Entity" includes corporation and foreign corporation; not-for-profit corporation; profit and not-for-profit unincorporated association; business trust, estate, partnership, trust, and two or more persons having a joint or common economic interest; and state, United States, and foreign government.

(10) "Foreign corporation" means a corporation for profit incorporated under a law other than the law of this state.

(11) "Governmental subdivision" includes authority, county, district, and municipality.

(12) "Includes" denotes a partial definition.

(13) "Individual" includes the estate of an incompetent or deceased individual.

(14) "Means" denotes an exhaustive definition.

(15) "Notice" is defined in section 1.41.

(16) "Person" includes individual and entity.

(17) "Principal office" means the office (in or out of this state) so designated in the annual report where the principal executive offices of a domestic or foreign corporation are located.

(18) "Proceeding" includes civil suit and criminal, administrative, and investigatory action.

(19) "Record date" means the date established under chapter 6 or 7 on which a corporation determines the identity of its shareholders for purposes of this Act.

(20) "Secretary" means the corporate officer to whom the board of directors has delegated responsibility under section 8.40(c) for custody of the minutes of the meetings of the board of directors and of the shareholders and for authenticating records of the corporation.

(21) "Shares" means the units into which the proprietary interests in a corporation are divided.

(22) "Shareholder" means the person in whose name shares are registered in the records of a corporation or the beneficial owner of shares to the extent of the rights granted by a nominee certificate on file with a corporation.

(23) "State," when referring to a part of the United States, includes a state and commonwealth (and their agencies and governmental subdivisions) and a territory and insular possession (and their agencies and governmental subdivisions) of the United States.

(24) "Subscriber" means a person who subscribes for shares in a corporation, whether before or after incorporation.

(25) "United States" includes district, authority, bureau, commission, department, and any other agency of the United States.

(26) "Voting group" means all shares of one or more classes or series that under the articles of incorporation or this Act are entitled to vote and be counted together collectively on a matter at a meeting of shareholders. All shares entitled by the articles of incorporation or this Act to vote generally on the matter are for that purpose a single voting group.

§ 1.41. Notice

(a) Notice under this Act must be in writing unless oral notice is reasonable under the circumstances.

(b) Notice may be communicated in person; by telephone, telegraph, teletype, or other form of wire or wireless communication; or by mail or private carrier. If these forms of personal notice are impracticable, notice may be communicated by a newspaper of general circulation in the area where published; or by radio, television, or other form of public broadcast communication.

(c) Written notice by a domestic or foreign corporation to its shareholder, if in a comprehensible form, is effective when mailed, if mailed postpaid and correctly addressed to the shareholder's address shown in the corporation's current record of shareholders.

(d) Written notice to a domestic or foreign corporation (authorized to transact business in this state) may be addressed to its registered agent at its registered office or to the corporation or its secretary at its principal office shown in its most recent annual report or, in the case of a foreign corporation that has not yet delivered an annual report, in its application for a certificate of authority.

(e) Except as provided in subsection (c), written notice, if in a comprehensible form, is effective at the earliest of the following:
   (1) when received;
   (2) five days after its deposit in the United States Mail, as evidenced by the postmark, if mailed postpaid and correctly addressed;
   (3) on the date shown on the return receipt, if sent by registered or certified mail, return receipt requested, and the receipt is signed by or on behalf of the addressee.

(f) Oral notice is effective when communicated if communicated in a comprehensible manner.

(g) If this Act prescribes notice requirements for particular circumstances, those requirements govern. If articles of incorporation or bylaws prescribe notice requirements, not inconsistent with this section or other provisions of this Act, those requirements govern.

§ 1.42. Number of Shareholders

(a) For purposes of this Act, the following identified as a shareholder in a corporation's current record of shareholders constitutes one shareholder:
   (1) three or fewer coowners;
   (2) a corporation, partnership, trust, estate, or other entity;
   (3) the trustees, guardians, custodians, or other fiduciaries of a single trust, estate, or account.

(b) For purposes of this Act, shareholdings registered in substantially similar names constitute one shareholder if it is reasonable to believe that the names represent the same person.

CHAPTER 2 INCORPORATION

§ 2.01. Incorporators

One or more persons may act as the incorporator or incorporators of a corporation by delivering articles of incorporation to the secretary of state for filing.

§ 2.02. Articles of Incorporation

(a) The articles of incorporation must set forth:
   (1) a corporate name for the corporation that satisfies the requirements of section 4.01;
   (2) the number of shares the corporation is authorized to issue;
   (3) the street address of the corporation's initial registered office and the name of its initial registered agent at that office; and
   (4) the name and address of each incorporator.

(b) The articles of incorporation may set forth:
   (1) the names and addresses of the individuals who are to serve as the initial directors;
   (2) provisions not inconsistent with law regarding:
     (i) the purpose or purposes for which the corporation is organized;
     (ii) managing the business and regulating the affairs of the corporation;
     (iii) defining, limiting, and regulating the powers of the corporation, its board of directors, and shareholders;
     (iv) a par value for authorized shares or classes of shares;
     (v) the imposition of personal liability on shareholders for the debt of the corporation to a specified extent and upon specified conditions; and
   (3) any provision that under this Act is required or permitted to be set forth in the bylaws.

(c) The articles of incorporation need not set forth any of the corporate powers enumerated in this Act.

§ 2.03. Incorporation

(a) Unless a delayed effective date is specified, the corporate existence begins when the articles of incorporation are filed.

(b) The secretary of state's filing of the articles of incorporation is conclusive proof that the incorporators satisfied all conditions precedent to incorporation except in a proceeding by the state to cancel or revoke the incorporation or involuntarily dissolve the corporation.

§ 2.04. Liability for Preincorporation Transactions

All persons purporting to act as or on behalf of a corporation, knowing there was no incorporation under this Act, are jointly and severally liable for all liabilities created while so acting.

§ 2.05. Organization of Corporation

(a) After incorporation:
   (1) if initial directors are named in the articles of incorporation, the initial directors shall hold an organizational meeting, at the call of a majority of the directors, to complete the organization of the corporation by appointing officers, adopting bylaws, and carrying on any other business brought before the meeting;
   (2) if initial directors are not named in the articles, the incorporator or incorporators shall hold an organizational meeting at the call of a majority of the incorporators:
     (i) to elect directors and complete the organization of the corporation; or

(ii) to elect a board of directors who shall complete the organization of the corporation.
(b) Action required or permitted by this Act to be taken by incorporators at an organizational meeting may be taken without a meeting if the action taken is evidenced by one or more written consents describing the action taken and signed by each incorporator.
(c) An organizational meeting may be held in or out of this state.

§ 2.06. Bylaws
(a) The incorporators or board of directors of a corporation shall adopt initial bylaws for the corporation.
(b) The bylaws of a corporation may contain any provision for managing the business and regulating the affairs of the corporation that is not inconsistent with law or the articles of incorporation.

§ 2.07. Emergency Bylaws
(a) Unless the articles of incorporation provide otherwise, the board of directors of a corporation may adopt bylaws to be effective only in an emergency defined in subsection (d). The emergency bylaws, which are subject to amendment or repeal by the shareholders, may make all provisions necessary for managing the corporation during the emergency, including:
(1) procedures for calling a meeting of the board of directors;
(2) quorum requirements for the meeting; and
(3) designation of additional or substitute directors.
(b) All provisions of the regular bylaws consistent with the emergency bylaws remain effective during the emergency. The emergency bylaws are not effective after the emergency ends.
(c) Corporate action taken in good faith in accordance with the emergency bylaws:
(1) binds the corporation; and
(2) may not be used to impose liability on a corporate director, officer, employee, or agent.
(d) An emergency exists for purposes of this section if a quorum of the corporation's directors cannot readily be assembled because of some catastrophic event.

CHAPTER 3 PURPOSES AND POWERS
§ 3.01. Purposes
(a) Every corporation incorporated under this Act has the purpose of engaging in any lawful business unless a more limited purpose is set forth in the articles of incorporation.
(b) A corporation engaging in a business that is subject to regulation under another statute of this state may incorporate under this Act only if permitted by, and subject to all limitations of, the other statute.

§ 3.02. General Powers
Unless its articles of incorporation provide otherwise, every corporation has perpetual duration and succession in its corporate name and has the same powers as an individual to do all things necessary or convenient to carry out its business and affairs, including without limitation power:
(1) to sue and be sued, complain and defend in its corporate name;
(2) to have a corporate seal, which may be altered at will, and to use it, or a facsimile of it, by impressing or affixing it or in any other manner reproducing it;
(3) to make and amend bylaws, not inconsistent with its articles of incorporation or with the laws of this state, for managing the business and regulating the affairs of the corporation;
(4) to purchase, receive, lease, or otherwise acquire, and own, hold, improve, use, and otherwise deal with, real or personal property, or any legal or equitable interest in property, wherever located;
(5) to sell, convey, mortgage, pledge, lease, exchange, and otherwise dispose of all or any part of its property;
(6) to purchase, receive, subscribe for, or otherwise acquire; own, hold, vote, use, sell, mortgage, lend, pledge, or otherwise dispose of; and deal in and with shares or other interests in, or obligations of, any other entity;
(7) to make contracts and guarantees, incur liabilities, borrow money, issue its notes, bonds, and other obligations (which may be convertible into or include the option to purchase other securities of the corporation), and secure any of its obligations by mortgage or pledge of any of its property, franchises, or income;
(8) to lend money, invest and reinvest its funds, and receive and hold real and personal property as security for repayment;
(9) to be a promoter, partner, member, associate, or manager of any partnership, joint venture, trust, or other entity;
(10) to conduct its business, locate offices, and exercise the powers granted by this Act within or without this state;
(11) to elect directors and appoint officers, employees, and agents of the corporation, define their duties, fix their compensation, and lend them money and credit;
(12) to pay pensions and establish pension plans, pension trusts, profit sharing plans, share bonus plans, share option plans, and benefit or incentive plans for any or all of its current or former directors, officers, employees, and agents;
(13) to make donations for the public welfare or for charitable, scientific, or educational purposes;
(14) to transact any lawful business that will aid governmental policy;

(15) to make payments or donations, or do any other act, not inconsistent with law, that furthers the business and affairs of the corporation.

§ 3.03. Emergency Powers

(a) In anticipation of or during an emergency defined in subsection (d), the board of directors of a corporation may:

(1) modify lines of succession to accommodate the incapacity of any director, officer, employee, or agent; and

(2) relocate the principal office, designate alternative principal offices or regional offices, or authorize the officers to do so.

(b) During an emergency defined in subsection (d), unless emergency bylaws provide otherwise:

(1) notice of a meeting of the board of directors need be given only to those directors whom it is practicable to reach and may be given in any practicable manner, including by publication and radio; and

(2) one or more officers of the corporation present at a meeting of the board of directors may be deemed to be directors for the meeting, in order of rank and within the same rank in order of seniority, as necessary to achieve a quorum.

(c) Corporate action taken in good faith during an emergency under this section to further the ordinary business affairs of the corporation:

(1) binds the corporation; and

(2) may not be used to impose liability on a corporate director, officer, employee, or agent.

(d) An emergency exists for purposes of this section if a quorum of the corporation's directors cannot readily be assembled because of some catastrophic event.

§ 3.04. Ultra Vires

(a) Except as provided in subsection (b), the validity of corporate action may not be challenged on the ground that the corporation lacks or lacked power to act.

(b) A corporation's power to act may be challenged:

(1) in a proceeding by a shareholder against the corporation to enjoin the act;

(2) in a proceeding by the corporation, directly, derivatively, or through a receiver, trustee, or other legal representative, against an incumbent or former director, officer, employee, or agent of the corporation; or

(3) in a proceeding by the Attorney General under section 14.30.

(c) In a shareholder's proceeding under subsection (b)(1) to enjoin an unauthorized corporate act, the court may enjoin or set aside the act, if equitable and if all affected persons are parties to the proceeding, and may award damages for loss (other than anticipated profits) suffered by the corporation or another party because of enjoining the unauthorized act.

CHAPTER 4 NAME

§ 4.01. Corporate Name

(a) A corporate name:

(1) must contain the word "corporation," "incorporated," "company," or "limited," or the abbreviation "corp.," "inc.," "co.," or "ltd.," or words or abbreviations of like import in another language; and

(2) may not contain language stating or implying that the corporation is organized for a purpose other than that permitted by section 3.01 and its articles of incorporation.

(b) Except as authorized by subsections (c) and (d), a corporate name must be distinguishable upon the records of the secretary of state from:

(1) the corporate name of a corporation incorporated or authorized to transact business in this state;

(2) a corporate name reserved or registered under section 4.02 or 4.03;

(3) the fictitious name adopted by a foreign corporation authorized to transact business in this state because its real name is unavailable; and

(4) the corporate name of a not-for-profit corporation incorporated or authorized to transact business in this state.

(c) A corporation may apply to the secretary of state for authorization to use a name that is not distinguishable upon his records from one or more of the names described in subsection (b). The secretary of state shall authorize use of the name applied for if:

(1) the other corporation consents to the use in writing and submits an undertaking in form satisfactory to the secretary of state to change its name to a name that is distinguishable upon the records of the secretary of state from the name of the applying corporation; or

(2) the applicant delivers to the secretary of state a certified copy of the final judgment of a court of competent jurisdiction establishing the applicant's right to use the name applied for in this state.

(d) A corporation may use the name (including the fictitious name) of another domestic or foreign corporation that is used in this state if the other corporation is incorporated or authorized to transact business in this state and the proposed user corporation:

(1) has merged with the other corporation;

(2) has been formed by reorganization of the other corporation; or

(3) has acquired all or substantially all of the assets, including the corporate name, of the other corporation.

(e) This Act does not control the use of fictitious names.

§ 4.02. Reserved Name

(a) A person may reserve the exclusive use of a corporate name, including a fictitious name for a foreign corporation whose corporate name is not available, by delivering an application to the secretary of state for filing. The application must set forth the name and address of the applicant and the name proposed to be reserved. If the secretary of state finds that the corporate name applied for is available, he shall reserve the name for the applicant's exclusive use for a nonrenewable 120-day period.

(b) The owner of a reserved corporate name may transfer the reservation to another person by delivering to the secretary of state a signed notice of the transfer that states the name and address of the transferee.

§ 4.03. Registered Name

(a) A foreign corporation may register its corporate name, or its corporate name with any addition required by section 15.06, if the name is distinguishable upon the records of the secretary of state from the corporate names that are not available under section 4.01(b)(3).

(b) A foreign corporation registers its corporate name, or its corporate name with any addition required by section 15.06, by delivering to the secretary of state for filing an application:

(1) setting forth its corporate name, or its corporate name with any addition required by section 15.06, the state or country and date of its incorporation, and a brief description of the nature of the business in which it is engaged; and

(2) accompanied by a certificate of existence (or a document of similar import) from the state or country of incorporation.

(c) The name is registered for the applicant's exclusive use upon the effective date of the application.

(d) A foreign corporation whose registration is effective may renew it for successive years by delivering to the secretary of state for filing a renewal application, which complies with the requirements of subsection (b), between October 1 and December 31 of the preceding year. The renewal application when filed renews the registration for the following calendar year.

(e) A foreign corporation whose registration is effective may thereafter qualify as a foreign corporation under the registered name or consent in writing to the use of that name by a corporation thereafter incorporated under this Act or by another foreign corporation thereafter authorized to transact business in this state. The registration terminates when the domestic corporation is incorporated or the foreign corporation qualifies or consents to the qualification of another foreign corporation under the registered name.

CHAPTER 5 OFFICE AND AGENT

§ 5.01. Registered Office and Registered Agent

Each corporation must continuously maintain in this state:

(1) a registered office that may be the same as any of its places of business; and

(2) a registered agent, who may be:

(i) an individual who resides in this state and whose business office is identical with the registered office;

(ii) a domestic corporation or not-for-profit domestic corporation whose business office is identical with the registered office; or

(iii) a foreign corporation or not-for-profit foreign corporation authorized to transact business in this state whose business office is identical with the registered office.

§ 5.02. Change of Registered Office or Registered Agent

(a) A corporation may change its registered office or registered agent by delivering to the secretary of state for filing a statement of change that sets forth:

(1) the name of the corporation;

(2) the street address of its current registered office;

(3) if the current registered office is to be changed, the street address of the new registered office;

(4) the name of its current registered agent;

(5) if the current registered agent is to be changed, the name of the new registered agent and the new agent's written consent (either on the statement or attached to it) to the appointment; and

(6) that after the change or changes are made, the street addresses of its registered office and the business office of its registered agent will be identical.

(b) If a registered agent changes the street address of his business office, he may change the street address of the registered office of any corporation for which he is the registered agent by notifying the corporation in writing of the change and signing (either manually or in facsimile) and delivering to the secretary of state for filing a statement that complies with the requirements of subsection (a) and recites that the corporation has been notified of the change.

§ 5.03. Resignation of Registered Agent

(a) A registered agent may resign his agency appointment by signing and delivering to the secretary of state for filing the signed original and two exact or conformed copies of a statement of resignation. The statement may include a statement that the registered office is also discontinued.

(b) After filing the statement the secretary of state shall mail one copy to the registered office (if not discontinued) and the other copy to the corporation at its principal office.

(c) The agency appointment is terminated, and the registered office discontinued if so provided, on the 31st day after the date on which the statement was filed.

§ 5.04. Service on Corporation

(a) A corporation's registered agent is the corporation's agent for service of process, notice, or demand required or permitted by law to be served on the corporation.

(b) If a corporation has no registered agent, or the agent cannot with reasonable diligence be served, the corporation may be served by registered or certified mail, return receipt requested, addressed to the secretary of the corporation at its principal office. Service is perfected under this subsection at the earliest of:

(1) the date the corporation receives the mail;
(2) the date shown on the return receipt, if signed on behalf of the corporation; or
(3) five days after its deposit in the United States Mail, as evidenced by the postmark, if mailed postpaid and correctly addressed.

(c) This section does not prescribe the only means, or necessarily the required means, of serving a corporation.

CHAPTER 6 SHARES AND DISTRIBUTIONS

Shares

§ 6.01. Authorized Shares

(a) The articles of incorporation must prescribe the classes of shares and the number of shares of each class that the corporation is authorized to issue. If more than one class of shares is authorized, the articles of incorporation must prescribe a distinguishing designation for each class, and, prior to the issuance of shares of a class, the preferences, limitations, and relative rights of that class must be described in the articles of incorporation. All shares of a class must have preferences, limitations, and relative rights identical with those of other shares of the same class except to the extent otherwise permitted by section 6.02.

(b) The articles of incorporation must authorize (1) one or more classes of shares that together have unlimited voting rights, and (2) one or more classes of shares (which may be the same class or classes as those with voting rights) that together are entitled to receive the net assets of the corporation upon dissolution.

(c) The articles of incorporation may authorize one or more classes of shares that:

(1) have special, conditional, or limited voting rights, or no right to vote, except to the extent prohibited by this Act;
(2) are redeemable or convertible as specified in the articles of incorporation (i) at the option of the corporation, the shareholder, or another person or upon the occurrence of a designated event; (ii) for cash, indebtedness, securities, or other property; (iii) in a designated amount or in an amount determined in accordance with a designated formula or by reference to extrinsic data or events;
(3) entitle the holders to distributions calculated in any manner, including dividends that may be cumulative, noncumulative, or partially cumulative;
(4) have preference over any other class of shares with respect to distributions, including dividends and distributions upon the dissolution of the corporation.

(d) The description of the designations, preferences, limitations, and relative rights of share classes in subsection (c) is not exhaustive.

§ 6.02. Terms of Class or Series Determined by Board of Directors

(a) If the articles of incorporation so provide, the board of directors may determine, in whole or part, the preferences, limitations, and relative rights (within the limits set forth in section 6.01) of (1) any class of shares before the issuance of any shares of that class or (2) one or more series within a class before the issuance of any shares of that series.

(b) Each series of a class must be given a distinguishing designation.

(c) All shares of a series must have preferences, limitations, and relative rights identical with those of other shares of the same series and, except to the extent otherwise provided in the description of the series, with those of other series of the same class.

(d) Before issuing any shares of a class or series created under this section, the corporation must deliver to the secretary of state for filing articles of amendment, which are effective without shareholder action, that set forth:

(1) the name of the corporation;
(2) the text of the amendment determining the terms of the class or series of shares;
(3) the date it was adopted; and
(4) a statement that the amendment was duly adopted by the board of directors.

§ 6.03. Issued and Outstanding Shares

(a) A corporation may issue the number of shares of each class or series authorized by the articles of incorporation. Shares that are issued are outstanding shares until they are reacquired, redeemed, converted, or cancelled.

(b) The reacquisition, redemption, or conversion of outstanding shares is subject to the limitations of subsection (c) of this section and to section 6.40.

(c) At all times that shares of the corporation are outstanding, one or more shares that together have unlimited voting rights and one or more shares that together are entitled to receive the net assets of the corporation upon dissolution must be outstanding.

§ 6.04. Fractional Shares

(a) A corporation may:

(1) issue fractions of a share or pay in money the value of fractions of a share;

(2) arrange for disposition of fractional shares by the shareholders;

(3) issue scrip in registered or bearer form entitling the holder to receive a full share upon surrendering enough scrip to equal a full share.

(b) Each certificate representing scrip must be conspicuously labeled "scrip" and must contain the information required by section 6.25(b).

(c) The holder of a fractional share is entitled to exercise the rights of a shareholder, including the right to vote, to receive dividends, and to participate in the assets of the corporation upon liquidation. The holder of scrip is not entitled to any of these rights unless the scrip provides for them.

(d) The board of directors may authorize the issuance of scrip subject to any condition considered desirable, including:

(1) that the scrip will become void if not exchanged for full shares before a specified date; and

(2) that the shares for which the scrip is exchangeable may be sold and the proceeds paid to the scripholders.

Issuance of Shares

§ 6.20. Subscription for Shares before Incorporation

(a) A subscription for shares entered into before incorporation is irrevocable for six months unless the subscription agreement provides a longer or shorter period or all the subscribers agree to revocation.

(b) The board of directors may determine the payment terms of subscriptions for shares that were entered into before incorporation, unless the subscription agreement specifies them. A call for payment by the board of directors must be uniform so far as practicable as to all shares of the same class or series, unless the subscription agreement specifies otherwise.

(c) Shares issued pursuant to subscriptions entered into before incorporation are fully paid and nonassessable when the corporation receives the consideration specified in the subscription agreement.

(d) If a subscriber defaults in payment of money or property under a subscription agreement entered into before incorporation, the corporation may collect the amount owed as any other debt. Alternatively, unless the subscription agreement provides otherwise, the corporation may rescind the agreement and may sell the shares if the debt remains unpaid more than 20 days after the corporation sends written demand for payment to the subscriber.

(e) A subscription agreement entered into after incorporation is a contract between the subscriber and the corporation subject to section 6.21.

§ 6.21. Issuance of Shares

(a) The powers granted in this section to the board of directors may be reserved to the shareholders by the articles of incorporation.

(b) The board of directors may authorize shares to be issued for consideration consisting of any tangible or intangible property or benefit to the corporation, including cash, promissory notes, services performed, contracts for services to be performed, or other securities of the corporation.

(c) Before the corporation issues shares, the board of directors must determine that the consideration received or to be received for shares to be issued is adequate. That determination by the board of directors is conclusive insofar as the adequacy of consideration for the issuance of shares relates to whether the shares are validly issued, fully paid, and nonassessable.

(d) When the corporation receives the consideration for which the board of directors authorized the issuance of shares, the shares issued therefor are fully paid and nonassessable.

(e) The corporation may place in escrow shares issued for a contract for future services or benefits or a promissory note, or make other arrangements to restrict the transfer of the shares, and may credit distributions in respect of the shares against their purchase price, until the services are performed, the note is paid, or the benefits received. If the services are not performed, the note is not paid, or the benefits are not received, the shares escrowed or restricted and the distributions credited may be cancelled in whole or part.

§ 6.22. Liability of Shareholders

(a) A purchaser from a corporation of its own shares is not liable to the corporation or its creditors with respect to the shares except to pay the consideration for which the shares were authorized to be issued (section 6.21) or specified in the subscription agreement (section 6.20).

(b) Unless otherwise provided in the articles of incorporation, a shareholder of a corporation is not personally liable for the acts or debts of the corporation except that he may become personally liable by reason of his own acts or conduct.

§ 6.23. Share Dividends

(a) Unless the articles of incorporation provide otherwise, shares may be issued pro rata and without consideration to the corporation's shareholders or to the shareholders of one or more classes or series. An issuance of shares under this subsection is a share dividend.

(b) Shares of one class or series may not be issued as a share dividend in respect of shares of another class or series unless (1) the articles of incorporation so authorize, (2) a majority of the votes entitled to be cast by the class or series to be issued approve the issue, or (3) there are no outstanding shares of the class or series to be issued.

(c) If the board of directors does not fix the record date for determining shareholders entitled to a share dividend, it is the date the board of directors authorizes the share dividend.

§ 6.24. Share Options

A corporation may issue rights, options, or warrants for the purchase of shares of the corporation. The board of directors shall determine the terms upon which the rights, options, or warrants are issued, their form and content, and the consideration for which the shares are to be issued.

§ 6.25. Form and Content of Certificates

(a) Shares may but need not be represented by certificates. Unless this Act or another statute expressly provides otherwise, the rights and obligations of shareholders are identical whether or not their shares are represented by certificates.

(b) At a minimum each share certificate must state on its face:

(1) the name of the issuing corporation and that it is organized under the law of this state;

(2) the name of the person to whom issued; and

(3) the number and class of shares and the designation of the series, if any, the certificate represents.

(c) If the issuing corporation is authorized to issue different classes of shares or different series within a class, the designations, relative rights, preferences, and limitations applicable to each class and the variations in rights, preferences, and limitations determined for each series (and the authority of the board of directors to determine variations for future series) must be summarized on the front or back of each certificate. Alternatively, each certificate may state conspicuously on its front or back that the corporation will furnish the shareholder this information on request in writing and without charge.

(d) Each share certificate (1) must be signed (either manually or in facsimile) by two officers designated in the bylaws or by the board of directors and (2) may bear the corporate seal of its facsimile.

(e) If the person who signed (either manually or in facsimile) a share certificate no longer holds office when the certificate is issued, the certificate is nevertheless valid.

§ 6.26. Shares without Certificates

(a) Unless the articles of incorporation or bylaws provide otherwise, the board of directors of a corporation may authorize the issue of some or all of the shares of any or all of its classes or series without certificates. The authorization does not affect shares already represented by certificates until they are surrendered to the corporation.

(b) Within a reasonable time after the issue or transfer of shares without certificates, the corporation shall send the shareholder a written statement of the information required on certificates by section 6.25(b) and (c), and, if applicable, section 6.27.

§ 6.27. Restriction on Transfer of Shares and Other Securities

(a) The articles of incorporation, bylaws, an agreement among shareholders, or an agreement between shareholders and the corporation may impose restrictions on the transfer or registration of transfer of shares of the corporation. A restriction does not affect shares issued before the restriction was adopted unless the holders of the shares are parties to the restriction agreement or voted in favor of the restriction.

(b) A restriction on the transfer or registration of transfer of shares is valid and enforceable against the holder or a transferee of the holder if the restriction is authorized by this section and its existence is noted conspicuously on the front or back of the certificate or is contained in the information statement required by section 6.26(b). Unless so noted, a restriction is not enforceable against a person without knowledge of the restriction.

(c) A restriction on the transfer or registration of transfer of shares is authorized:

(1) to maintain the corporation's status when it is dependent on the number or identity of its shareholders;

(2) to preserve exemptions under federal or state securities law;
(3) for any other reasonable purpose.
(d) A restriction on the transfer or registration of transfer of shares may:
  (1) obligate the shareholder first to offer the corporation or other persons (separately, consecutively, or simultaneously) an opportunity to acquire the restricted shares;
  (2) obligate the corporation or other persons (separately, consecutively, or simultaneously) to acquire the restricted shares;
  (3) require the corporation, the holders of any class of its shares, or another person to approve the transfer of the restricted shares, if the requirement is not manifestly unreasonable;
  (4) prohibit the transfer of the restricted shares to designated persons or classes of persons, if the prohibition is not manifestly unreasonable.
(e) For purposes of this section, "shares" includes a security convertible into or carrying a right to subscribe for or acquire shares.

Subsequent Acquisition of Shares by Shareholders and Corporation
§ 6.28. Expense of Issue
A corporation may pay the expenses of selling or underwriting its shares, and of organizing or reorganizing the corporation, from the consideration received for shares.

§ 6.30. Shareholders' Preemptive Rights
(a) The shareholders of a corporation do not have a preemptive right to acquire the corporation's unissued shares except to the extent the articles of incorporation so provide.
(b) A statement included in the articles of incorporation that "the corporation elects to have preemptive rights" (or words of similar import) means that the following principles apply except to the extent the articles of incorporation expressly provide otherwise:
  (1) The shareholders of the corporation have a preemptive right, granted on uniform terms and conditions prescribed by the board of directors to provide a fair and reasonable opportunity to exercise the right, to acquire proportional amounts of the corporation's unissued shares upon the decision of the board of directors to issue them.
  (2) A shareholder may waive his preemptive right. A waiver evidenced by a writing is irrevocable even though it is not supported by consideration.
  (3) There is no preemptive right with respect to:
    (i) shares issued as compensation to directors, officers, agents, or employees of the corporation, its subsidiaries or affiliates;
    (ii) shares issued to satisfy conversion or option rights created to provide compensation to directors, officers, agents, or employees of the corporation, its subsidiaries or affiliates;
    (iii) shares authorized in articles of incorporation that are issued within six months from the effective date of incorporation;
    (iv) shares sold otherwise than for money.
  (4) Holders of shares of any class without general voting rights but with preferential rights to distributions or assets have no preemptive rights with respect to shares of any class.
  (5) Holders of shares of any class with general voting rights but without preferential rights to distributions or assets have no preemptive rights with respect to shares of any class with preferential rights to distributions or assets unless the shares with preferential rights are convertible into or carry a right to subscribe for or acquire shares without preferential rights.
  (6) Shares subject to preemptive rights that are not acquired by shareholders may be issued to any person for a period of one year after being offered to shareholders at a consideration set by the board of directors that is not lower than the consideration set for the exercise of preemptive rights. An offer at a lower consideration or after the expiration of one year is subject to the shareholders' preemptive rights.
(c) For purposes of this section, "shares" includes a security convertible into or carrying a right to subscribe for or acquire shares.

§ 6.31. Corporation's Acquisition of Its Own Shares
(a) A corporation may acquire its own shares and shares so acquired constitute authorized but unissued shares.
(b) If the articles of incorporation prohibit the reissue of acquired shares, the number of authorized shares is reduced by the number of shares acquired, effective upon amendment of the articles of incorporation.
(c) The board of directors may adopt articles of amendment under this section without shareholder action and deliver them to the secretary of state for filing. The articles must set forth:
  (1) the name of the corporation;
  (2) the reduction in the number of authorized shares, itemized by class and series; and
  (3) the total number of authorized shares, itemized by class and series, remaining after reduction of the shares.

Distributions

§ 6.40. Distributions to Shareholders

(a) A board of directors may authorize and the corporation may make distributions to its shareholders subject to restriction by the articles of incorporation and the limitation in subsection (c).

(b) If the board of directors does not fix the record date for determining shareholders entitled to a distribution (other than one involving a repurchase or reacquisition of shares), it is the date the board of directors authorizes the distribution.

(c) No distribution may be made if, after giving it effect:

> (1) the corporation would not be able to pay its debts as they become due in the usual course of business; or
>
> (2) the corporation's total assets would be less than the sum of its total liabilities plus (unless the articles of incorporation permit otherwise) the amount that would be needed, if the corporation were to be dissolved at the time of the distribution, to satisfy the preferential rights upon dissolution of shareholders whose preferential rights are superior to those receiving the distribution.

(d) The board of directors may base a determination that a distribution is not prohibited under subsection (c) either on financial statements prepared on the basis of accounting practices and principles that are reasonable in the circumstances or on a fair valuation or other method that is reasonable in the circumstances.

(e) The effect of a distribution under subsection (c) is measured:

> (1) in the case of distribution by purchase, redemption, or other acquisition of the corporation's shares, as of the earlier of (i) the date money or other property is transferred or debt incurred by the corporation or (ii) the date the shareholder ceases to be a shareholder with respect to the acquired shares;
>
> (2) in the case of any other distribution of indebtedness, as of the date the indebtedness is distributed;
>
> (3) in all other cases, as of (i) the date the distribution is authorized if the payment occurs within 120 days after the date of authorization or (ii) the date the payment is made if it occurs more than 120 days after the date of authorization.

(f) A corporation's indebtedness to a shareholder incurred by reason of a distribution made in accordance with this section is at parity with the corporation's indebtedness to its general, unsecured creditors except to the extent subordinated by agreement.

CHAPTER 7 SHAREHOLDERS

Meetings

§ 7.01. Annual Meeting

(a) A corporation shall hold a meeting of shareholders annually at a time stated in or fixed in accordance with the bylaws.

(b) Annual shareholders' meetings may be held in or out of this state at the place stated in or fixed in accordance with the bylaws. If no place is stated in or fixed in accordance with the bylaws, annual meetings shall be held at the corporation's principal office.

(c) The failure to hold an annual meeting at the time stated in or fixed in accordance with a corporation's bylaws does not affect the validity of any corporate action.

§ 7.02. Special Meeting

(a) A corporation shall hold a special meeting of shareholders:

> (1) on call of its board of directors or the person or persons authorized to do so by the articles of incorporation or bylaws; or
>
> (2) if the holders of at least 10 percent of all the votes entitled to be cast on any issue proposed to be considered at the proposed special meeting sign, date, and deliver to the corporation's secretary one or more written demands for the meeting describing the purpose or purposes for which it is to be held.

(b) If not otherwise fixed under section 7.03 or 7.07, the record date for determining shareholders entitled to demand a special meeting is the date the first shareholder signs the demand.

(c) Special shareholders' meetings may be held in or out of this state at the place stated in or fixed in accordance with the bylaws. If no place is stated or fixed in accordance with the bylaws, special meetings shall be held at the corporation's principal office.

(d) Only business within the purpose or purposes described in the meeting notice required by section 7.05(c) may be conducted at a special shareholders' meeting.

§ 7.03. Court-Ordered Meeting

(a) The [name or describe] court of the county where a corporation's principal office (or, if none in this state, its registered office) is located may summarily order a meeting to be held:

> (1) on application of any shareholder of the corporation entitled to participate in an annual meeting if an annual meeting was not held within the earlier of 6 months after the end of the corpora-

tion's fiscal year or 15 months after its last annual meeting; or

(2) on application of a shareholder who signed a demand for a special meeting valid under section 7.02, if:

(i) notice of the special meeting was not given within 30 days after the date the demand was delivered to the corporation's secretary; or

(ii) the special meeting was not held in accordance with the notice.

(b) The court may fix the time and place of the meeting, determine the shares entitled to participate in the meeting, specify a record date for determining shareholders entitled to notice of and to vote at the meeting, prescribe the form and content of the meeting notice, fix the quorum required for specific matters to be considered at the meeting (or direct that the votes represented at the meeting constitute a quorum for action on those matters), and enter other orders necessary to accomplish the purpose or purposes of the meeting.

§ 7.04. Action without Meeting

(a) Action required or permitted by this Act to be taken at a shareholders' meeting may be taken without a meeting if the action is taken by all the shareholders entitled to vote on the action. The action must be evidenced by one or more written consents describing the action taken, signed by all the shareholders entitled to vote on the action, and delivered to the corporation for inclusion in the minutes or filing with the corporate records.

(b) If not otherwise fixed under section 7.03 or 7.07, the record date for determining shareholders entitled to take action without a meeting is the date the first shareholder signs the consent under subsection (a).

(c) A consent signed under this section has the effect of a meeting vote and may be described as such in any document.

(d) If this Act requires that notice of proposed action be given to nonvoting shareholders and the action is to be taken by unanimous consent of the voting shareholders, the corporation must give its nonvoting shareholders written notice of the proposed action at least 10 days before the action is taken. The notice must contain or be accompanied by the same material that, under this Act, would have been required to be sent to nonvoting shareholders in a notice of meeting at which the proposed action would have been submitted to the shareholders for action.

§ 7.05. Notice of Meeting

(a) A corporation shall notify shareholders of the date, time, and place of each annual and special shareholders' meeting no fewer than 10 nor more than 60 days before the meeting date. Unless this Act or the articles of incorporation require otherwise, the corporation is required to give notice only to shareholders entitled to vote at the meeting.

(b) Unless this Act or the articles of incorporation require otherwise, notice of an annual meeting need not include a description of the purpose or purposes for which the meeting is called.

(c) Notice of a special meeting must include a description of the purpose or purposes for which the meeting is called.

(d) If not otherwise fixed under section 7.03 or 7.07, the record date for determining shareholders entitled to notice of and to vote at an annual or special shareholders' meeting is the close of business on the day before the first notice is delivered to shareholders.

(e) Unless the bylaws require otherwise, if an annual or special shareholders' meeting is adjourned to a different date, time, or place, notice need not be given of the new date, time, or place if the new date, time, or place is announced at the meeting before adjournment. If a new record date for the adjourned meeting is or must be fixed under section 7.07, however, notice of the adjourned meeting must be given under this section to persons who are shareholders as of the new record date.

§ 7.06. Waiver of Notice

(a) A shareholder may waive any notice required by this Act, the articles of incorporation, or bylaws before or after the date and time stated in the notice. The waiver must be in writing, be signed by the shareholder entitled to the notice, and be delivered to the corporation for inclusion in the minutes or filing with the corporate records.

(b) A shareholder's attendance at a meeting:

(1) waives objection to lack of notice or defective notice of the meeting, unless the shareholder at the beginning of the meeting objects to holding the meeting or transacting business at the meeting;

(2) waives objection to consideration of a particular matter at the meeting that is not within the purpose or purposes described in the meeting notice, unless the shareholder objects to considering the matter when it is presented.

§ 7.07. Record Date

(a) The bylaws may fix or provide the manner of fixing the record date for one or more voting groups in order to determine the shareholders entitled to notice of a shareholders' meeting, to demand a special meeting, to vote, or to take any other action. If the bylaws do not fix or provide for fixing a record date, the board of directors of the corporation may fix a future date as the record date.

(b) A record date fixed under this section may not be more than 70 days before the meeting or action requiring a determination of shareholders.

(c) A determination of shareholders entitled to notice of or to vote at a shareholders' meeting is effective for any adjournment of the meeting unless the board of directors fixes a new record date, which it must do if the meeting is adjourned to a date more than 120 days after the date fixed for the original meeting.

(d) If a court orders a meeting adjourned to a date more than 120 days after the date fixed for the original meeting, it may provide that the original record date continues in effect or it may fix a new record date.

Voting
§ 7.20. Shareholders' List for Meeting

(a) After fixing a record date for a meeting, a corporation shall prepare an alphabetical list of the names of all its shareholders who are entitled to notice of a shareholders' meeting. The list must be arranged by voting group (and within each voting group by class or series of shares) and show the address of and number of shares held by each shareholder.

(b) The shareholders' list must be available for inspection by any shareholder, beginning two business days after notice of the meeting is given for which the list was prepared and continuing through the meeting, at the corporation's principal office or at a place identified in the meeting notice in the city where the meeting will be held. A shareholder, his agent, or attorney is entitled on written demand to inspect and, subject to the requirements of section 16.02(c), to copy the list, during regular business hours and at his expense, during the period it is available for inspection.

(c) The corporation shall make the shareholders' list available at the meeting, and any shareholder, his agent, or attorney is entitled to inspect the list at any time during the meeting or any adjournment.

(d) If the corporation refuses to allow a shareholder, his agent, or attorney to inspect the shareholders' list before or at the meeting (or copy the list as permitted by subsection (b)), the [name or describe] court of the county where a corporation's principal office (or, if none in this state, its registered office) is located, on application of the shareholder, may summarily order the inspection or copying at the corporation's expense and may postpone the meeting for which the list was prepared until the inspection or copying is complete.

(e) Refusal or failure to prepare or make available the shareholders' list does not affect the validity of action taken at the meeting.

§ 7.21. Voting Entitlement of Shares

(a) Except as provided in subsections (b) and (c) or unless the articles of incorporation provide otherwise, each outstanding share, regardless of class, is entitled to one vote on each matter voted on at a shareholders' meeting. Only shares are entitled to vote.

(b) Absent special circumstances, the shares of a corporation are not entitled to vote if they are owned, directly or indirectly, by a second corporation, domestic or foreign, and the first corporation owns, directly or indirectly, a majority of the shares entitled to vote for directors of the second corporation.

(c) Subsection (b) does not limit the power of a corporation to vote any shares, including its own shares, held by it in a fiduciary capacity.

(d) Redeemable shares are not entitled to vote after notice of redemption is mailed to the holders and a sum sufficient to redeem the shares has been deposited with a bank, trust company, or other financial institution under an irrevocable obligation to pay the holders the redemption price on surrender of the shares.

§ 7.22. Proxies

(a) A shareholder may vote his shares in person or by proxy.

(b) A shareholder may appoint a proxy to vote or otherwise act for him by signing an appointment form, either personally or by his attorney-in-fact.

(c) An appointment of a proxy is effective when received by the secretary or other officer or agent authorized to tabulate votes. An appointment is valid for 11 months unless a longer period is expressly provided in the appointment form.

(d) An appointment of a proxy is revocable by the shareholder unless the appointment form conspicuously states that it is irrevocable and the appointment is coupled with an interest. Appointments coupled with an interest include the appointment of:

    (1) a pledge;

    (2) a person who purchased or agreed to purchase the shares;

    (3) a creditor of the corporation who extended it credit under terms requiring the appointment;

    (4) an employee of the corporation whose employment contract requires the appointment; or

    (5) a party to a voting agreement created under section 7.31.

(e) The death or incapacity of the shareholder appointing a proxy does not affect the right of the corporation to accept the proxy's authority unless notice of the death or incapacity is received by the secretary or other officer or agent authorized to tabulate votes before the proxy exercises his authority under the appointment.

(f) An appointment made irrevocable under subsection (d) is revoked when the interest with which it is coupled is extinguished.

(g) A transferee for value of shares subject to an irrevocable appointment may revoke the appointment if he did not know of its existence when he acquired the shares and the existence of the irrevocable appointment was not noted conspicuously on the certificate representing the shares or on the information statement for shares without certificates.

(h) Subject to section 7.24 and to any express limitation on the proxy's authority appearing on the face of the appointment form, a corporation is entitled to accept the proxy's vote or other action as that of the shareholder making the appointment.

§ 7.23. Shares Held by Nominees

(a) A corporation may establish a procedure by which the beneficial owner of shares that are registered in the name of a nominee is recognized by the corporation as the shareholder. The extent of this recognition may be determined in the procedure.

(b) The procedure may set forth:
   (1) the types of nominees to which it applies;
   (2) the rights or privileges that the corporation recognizes in a beneficial owner;
   (3) the manner in which the procedure is selected by the nominee;
   (4) the information that must be provided when the procedure is selected;
   (5) the period for which selection of the procedure is effective; and
   (6) other aspects of the rights and duties created.

§ 7.24. Corporation's Acceptance of Votes

(a) If the name signed on a vote, consent, waiver, or proxy appointment corresponds to the name of a shareholder, the corporation if acting in good faith is entitled to accept the vote, consent, waiver, or proxy appointment and give it effect as the act of the shareholder.

(b) If the name signed on a vote, consent, waiver, or proxy appointment does not correspond to the name of its shareholder, the corporation if acting in good faith is nevertheless entitled to accept the vote, consent, waiver, or proxy appointment and give it effect as the act of the shareholder if:
   (1) the shareholder is an entity and the name signed purports to be that of an officer or agent of the entity;
   (2) the name signed purports to be that of an administrator, executor, guardian, or conservator representing the shareholder and, if the corporation requests, evidence of fiduciary status acceptable to the corporation has been presented with respect to the vote, consent, waiver, or proxy appointment;
   (3) the name signed purports to be that of a receiver or trustee in bankruptcy of the shareholder and, if the corporation requests, evidence of this status acceptable to the corporation has been presented with respect to the vote, consent, waiver, or proxy appointment;
   (4) the name signed purports to be that of a pledgee, beneficial owner, or attorney-in-fact of the shareholder and, if the corporation requests, evidence acceptable to the corporation of the signatory's authority to sign for the shareholder has been presented with respect to the vote, consent, waiver, or proxy appointment;
   (5) two or more persons are the shareholder as cotenants or fiduciaries and the name signed purports to be the name of at least one of the coowners and the person signing appears to be acting on behalf of all the coowners.

(c) The corporation is entitled to reject a vote, consent, waiver, or proxy appointment if the secretary or other officer or agent authorized to tabulate votes, acting in good faith, has reasonable basis for doubt about the validity of the signature on it or about the signatory's authority to sign for the shareholder.

(d) The corporation and its officer or agent who accepts or rejects a vote, consent, waiver, or proxy appointment in good faith and in accordance with the standards of this section are not liable in damages to the shareholder for the consequences of the acceptance or rejection.

(e) Corporate action based on the acceptance or rejection of a vote, consent, waiver, or proxy appointment under this section is valid unless a court of competent jurisdiction determines otherwise.

§ 7.25. Quorum and Voting Requirements for Voting Groups

(a) Shares entitled to vote as a separate voting group may take action on a matter at a meeting only if a quorum of those shares exists with respect to that matter. Unless the articles of incorporation or this Act provide otherwise, a majority of the votes entitled to be cast on the matter by the voting group constitutes a quorum of that voting group for action on that matter.

(b) Once a share is represented for any purpose at a meeting, it is deemed present for quorum purposes for the remainder of the meeting and for any adjournment of that meeting unless a new record date is or must be set for that adjourned meeting.

(c) If a quorum exists, action on a matter (other than the election of directors) by a voting group is approved if the votes cast within the voting group favoring the action exceed the votes cast opposing the action, unless the articles of incorporation or this Act require a greater number of affirmative votes.

(d) An amendment of articles of incorporation adding, changing, or deleting a quorum or voting requirement for a voting group greater than specified in subsection (a) or (c) is governed by section 7.27.

(e) The election of directors is governed by section 7.28.

§ 7.26. Action by Single and Multiple Voting Groups

(a) If the articles of incorporation or this Act provide for voting by a single voting group on a matter, action on that matter is taken when voted upon by that voting group as provided in section 7.25.

(b) If the articles of incorporation or this Act provide for voting by two or more voting groups on a matter, action on that matter is taken only when voted upon by each of those voting groups counted separately as provided in section 7.25. Action may be taken by one voting group on a matter even though no action is taken by another voting group entitled to vote on the matter.

§ 7.27. Greater Quorum or Voting Requirements

(a) The articles of incorporation may provide for a greater quorum or voting requirement for shareholders (or voting groups of shareholders) than is provided for by this Act.

(b) An amendment to the articles of incorporation that adds, changes, or deletes a greater quorum or voting requirement must meet the same quorum requirement and be adopted by the same vote and voting groups required to take action under the quorum and voting requirements then in effect or proposed to be adopted, whichever is greater.

§ 7.28. Voting for Directors; Cumulative Voting

(a) Unless otherwise provided in the articles of incorporation, directors are elected by a plurality of the votes cast by the shares entitled to vote in the election at a meeting at which a quorum is present.

(b) Shareholders do not have a right to cumulate their votes for directors unless the articles of incorporation so provide.

(c) A statement included in the articles of incorporation that "[all] [a designated voting group of] shareholders are entitled to cumulate their votes for directors" (or words of similar import) means that the shareholders designated are entitled to multiply the number of votes they are entitled to cast by the number of directors for whom they are entitled to vote and cast the product for a single candidate or distribute the product among two or more candidates.

(d) Shares otherwise entitled to vote cumulatively may not be voted cumulatively at a particular meeting unless:

(1) the meeting notice or proxy statement accompanying the notice states conspicuously that cumulative voting is authorized; or

(2) a shareholder who has the right to cumulate his votes gives notice to the corporation not less than 48 hours before the time set for the meeting of his intent to cumulate his votes during the meeting, and if one shareholder gives this notice all other shareholders in the same voting group participating in the election are entitled to cumulate their votes without giving further notice.

Voting Trusts and Agreements
§ 7.30. Voting Trusts

(a) One or more shareholders may create a voting trust, conferring on a trustee the right to vote or otherwise act for them, by signing an agreement setting out the provisions of the trust (which may include anything consistent with its purpose) and transferring their shares to the trustee. When a voting trust agreement is signed, the trustee shall prepare a list of the names and addresses of all owners of beneficial interests in the trust, together with the number and class of shares each transferred to the trust, and deliver copies of the list and agreement to the corporation's principal office.

(b) A voting trust becomes effective on the date the first shares subject to the trust are registered in the trustee's name. A voting trust is valid for not more than 10 years after its effective date unless extended under subsection (c).

(c) All or some of the parties to a voting trust may extend it for additional terms of not more than 10 years each by signing an extension agreement and obtaining the voting trustee's written consent to the extension. An extension is valid for 10 years from the date the first shareholder signs the extension agreement. The voting trustee must deliver copies of the extension agreement and list of beneficial owners to the corporation's principal office. An extension agreement binds only those parties signing it.

§ 7.31. Voting Agreements

(a) Two or more shareholders may provide for the manner in which they will vote their shares by signing an agreement for that purpose. A voting agreement created under this section is not subject to the provisions of section 7.30.

(b) A voting agreement created under this section is specifically enforceable.

Derivative Proceedings
§ 7.40. Procedure in Derivative Proceedings

(a) A person may not commence a proceeding in the right of a domestic or foreign corporation unless he was a shareholder of the corporation when the transaction complained of occurred or unless he became a shareholder through transfer by operation of law from one who was a shareholder at that time.

(b) A complaint in a proceeding brought in the right of a corporation must be verified and allege with particularity the demand made, if any, to obtain action by the board of directors and either that the demand was refused or ignored or why he did not make the demand. Whether or not a demand for action was made, if the corporation commences an investigation of the changes made in the demand or complaint, the court may stay any proceeding until the investigation is completed.

(c) A proceeding commenced under this section may not be discontinued or settled without the court's approval. If the court determines that a proposed discontinuance or settlement will substantially affect the interest of the corporation's shareholders or a class of shareholders, the court shall direct that notice be given the shareholders affected.

(d) On termination of the proceeding the court may require the plaintiff to pay any defendant's reasonable expenses (including counsel fees) incurred in defending the proceeding if it finds that the proceeding was commenced without reasonable cause.

(e) For purposes of this section, "shareholder" includes a beneficial owner whose shares are held in a voting trust or held by a nominee on his behalf.

CHAPTER 8 DIRECTORS AND OFFICERS

Board of Directors
§ 8.01. Requirement for and Duties of Board of Directors

(a) Except as provided in subsection (c), each corporation must have a board of directors.

(b) All corporate powers shall be exercised by or under the authority of, and the business and affairs of the corporation managed under the direction of, its board of directors, subject to any limitation set forth in the articles of incorporation.

(c) A corporation having 50 or fewer shareholders may dispense with or limit the authority of a board of directors by describing in its articles of incorporation who will perform some or all of the duties of a board of directors.

§ 8.02. Qualifications of Directors

The articles of incorporation or bylaws may prescribe qualifications for directors. A director need not be a resident of this state or a shareholder of the corporation unless the articles of incorporation or bylaws so prescribe.

§ 8.03. Number and Election of Directors

(a) A board of directors must consist of one or more individuals, with the number specified in or fixed in accordance with the articles of incorporation or bylaws.

(b) If a board of directors has power to fix or change the number of directors, the board may increase or decrease by 30 percent or less the number of directors last approved by the shareholders, but only the shareholders may increase or decrease by more than 30 percent the number of directors last approved by the shareholders.

(c) The articles of incorporation or bylaws may establish a variable range for the size of the board of directors by fixing a minimum and maximum number of directors. If a variable range is established, the number of directors may be fixed or changed from time to time, within the minimum and maximum, by the shareholders or the board of directors. After shares are issued, only the shareholders may change the range for the size of the board or change from a fixed to a variable-range size board or vice versa.

(d) Directors are elected at the first annual shareholders' meeting and at each annual meeting thereafter unless their terms are staggered under section 8.06.

§ 8.04. Election of Directors by Certain Classes of Shareholders

If the articles of incorporation authorize dividing the shares into classes, the articles may also authorize the election of all or a specified number of directors by the holders of one or more authorized classes of shares. A class (or classes) of shares entitled to elect one or more directors is a separate voting group for purposes of the election of directors.

§ 8.05. Terms of Directors Generally

(a) The terms of the initial directors of a corporation expire at the first shareholders' meeting at which directors are elected.

(b) The terms of all other directors expire at the next annual shareholders' meeting following their election unless their terms are staggered under section 8.06.

(c) A decrease in the number of directors does not shorten an incumbent director's term.

(d) The term of a director elected to fill a vacancy expires at the next shareholders' meeting at which directors are elected.

(e) Despite the expiration of a director's term, he continues to serve until his successor is elected and qualifies or until there is a decrease in the number of directors.

§ 8.06. Staggered Terms for Directors

If there are nine or more directors, the articles of incorporation may provide for staggering their terms by dividing the total number of directors into two or three groups, with each group containing one half or one-third of the total, as near as may be. In that event, the terms of directors in the first group expire at the first annual shareholders' meeting after their election, the terms of the second group expire at the second annual shareholders' meeting after their election, and the terms of the third group, if any, expire at the third annual shareholders' meeting after their election. At each annual shareholders' meeting held thereafter, directors shall be chosen for a term of two years or three years, as the case may be, to succeed those whose terms expire.

§ 8.07. Resignation of Directors

(a) A director may resign at any time by delivering written notice to the board of directors, its chairman, or to the corporation.

(b) A resignation is effective when the notice is delivered unless the notice specifies a later effective date.

§ 8.08. Removal of Directors by Shareholders

(a) The shareholders may remove one or more directors with or without cause unless the articles of incorporation provide that directors may be removed only for cause.

(b) If a director is elected by a voting group of shareholders, only the shareholders of that voting group may participate in the vote to remove him.

(c) If cumulative voting is authorized, a director may not be removed if the number of votes sufficient to elect him under cumulative voting is voted against his removal. If cumulative voting is not authorized, a director may be removed only if the number of votes cast to remove him exceeds the number of votes cast not to remove him.

(d) A director may be removed by the shareholders only at a meeting called for the purpose of removing him and the meeting notice must state that the purpose, or one of the purposes, of the meeting is removal of the director.

§ 8.09. Removal of Directors by Judicial Proceeding

(a) The [name or describe] court of the county where a corporation's principal office (or, if none in this state, its registered office) is located may remove a director of the corporation from office in a proceeding commenced either by the corporation or by its shareholders holding at least 10 percent of the outstanding shares of any class if the court finds that (1) the director engaged in fraudulent or dishonest conduct, or gross abuse of authority or discretion, with respect to the corporation and (2) removal is in the best interest of the corporation.

(b) The court that removes a director may bar the director from reelection for a period prescribed by the court.

(c) If shareholders commence a proceeding under subsection (a), they shall make the corporation a party defendant.

§ 8.10. Vacancy on Board

(a) Unless the articles of incorporation provide otherwise, if a vacancy occurs on a board of directors, including a vacancy resulting from an increase in the number of directors:

    (1) the shareholders may fill the vacancy;

    (2) the board of directors may fill the vacancy; or

    (3) if the directors remaining in office constitute fewer than a quorum of the board, they may fill the vacancy by the affirmative vote of a majority of all the directors remaining in office.

(b) If the vacant office was held by a director elected by a voting group of shareholders, only the holders of shares of that voting group are entitled to vote to fill the vacancy if it is filled by the shareholders.

(c) A vacancy that will occur at a specific later date (by reason of a resignation effective at a later date under section 8.07(b) or otherwise) may be filled before the vacancy occurs but the new director may not take office until the vacancy occurs.

§ 8.11. Compensation of Directors

Unless the articles of incorporation or bylaws provide otherwise, the board of directors may fix the compensation of directors.

Meetings and Action of the Board
§ 8.20. Meetings

(a) The board of directors may hold regular or special meetings in or out of this state.

(b) Unless the articles of incorporation or bylaws provide otherwise, the board of directors may permit any or all directors to participate in a regular or special meeting by, or conduct the meeting through the use of, any means of communication by which all directors participating may simultaneously hear each other during the meeting. A director participating in a meeting by this means is deemed to be present in person at the meeting.

§ 8.21. Action without Meeting

(a) Unless the articles of incorporation or bylaws provide otherwise, action required or permitted by this Act to be taken at a board of directors' meeting may be taken without a meeting if the action is taken by all members of the board. The action must be evidenced by one or more written consents describing the action taken, signed by each director, and included in the minutes or filed with the corporate records reflecting the action taken.

(b) Action taken under this section is effective when the last director signs the consent, unless the consent specifies a different effective date.

(c) A consent signed under this section has the effect of a meeting vote and may be described as such in any document.

§ 8.22. Notice of Meeting

(a) Unless the articles of incorporation or bylaws provide otherwise, regular meetings of the board of directors may be held without notice of the date, time, place, or purpose of the meeting.

(b) Unless the articles of incorporation or bylaws provide for a longer or shorter period, special meetings of the board of directors must be preceded by at least two days notice of the date, time, and place of the meeting. The notice need not describe the purpose of the special meeting unless required by the articles of incorporation or bylaws.

§ 8.23. Waiver of Notice

(a) A director may waive any notice required by this Act, the articles of incorporation, or bylaws before or after the date and time stated in the notice. Except as provided by subsection (b), the waiver must be in writing, signed by the director entitled to the notice, and filed with the minutes or corporate records.

(b) A director's attendance at or participation in a meeting waives any required notice to him of the meeting unless the director at the beginning of the meeting (or promptly upon his arrival) objects to holding the meeting or transacting business at the meeting and does not thereafter vote for or assent to action taken at the meeting.

§ 8.24. Quorum and Voting

(a) Unless the articles of incorporation or bylaws require a greater number, a quorum of a board of directors consists of:

(1) a majority of the fixed number of directors if the corporation has a fixed board size; or

(2) a majority of the number of directors prescribed, or if no number is prescribed the number in office immediately before the meeting begins, if the corporation has a variable-range size board.

(b) The articles of incorporation or bylaws may authorize a quorum of a board of directors to consist of no fewer than one-third of the fixed or prescribed number of directors determined under subsection (a).

(c) If a quorum is present when a vote is taken, the affirmative vote of a majority of directors present is the act of the board of directors unless the articles of incorporation or bylaws require the vote of a greater number of directors.

(d) A director who is present at a meeting of the board of directors or a committee of the board of directors when corporate action is taken is deemed to have assented to the action taken unless: (1) he objects at the beginning of the meeting (or promptly upon his arrival) to holding it or transacting business at the meeting; (2) his dissent or abstention from the action taken is entered in the minutes of the meeting; or (3) he delivers written notice of his dissent or abstention to the presiding officer of the meeting before its adjournment or to the corporation immediately after adjournment of the meeting. The right of dissent or abstention is not available to a director who votes in favor of the action taken.

§ 8.25. Committees

(a) Unless the articles of incorporation or bylaws provide otherwise, a board of directors may create one or more committees and appoint members of the board of directors to serve on them. Each committee must have two or more members, who serve at the pleasure of the board of directors.

(b) The creation of a committee and appointment of members to it must be approved by the greater of (1) a majority of all the directors in office when the action is taken or (2) the number of directors required by the articles of incorporation or bylaws to take action under section 8.24.

(c) Sections 8.20 through 8.24, which govern meetings, action without meetings, notice and waiver of notice, and quorum and voting requirements of the board of directors, apply to committees and their members as well.

(d) To the extent specified by the board of directors or in the articles of incorporation or bylaws, each committee may exercise the authority of the board of directors under section 8.01.

(e) A committee may not, however:

(1) authorize distributions;

(2) approve or propose to shareholders action that this Act requires be approved by shareholders;
(3) fill vacancies on the board of directors or on any of its committees;
(4) amend articles of incorporation pursuant to section 10.02;
(5) adopt, amend, or repeal bylaws;
(6) approve a plan of merger not requiring shareholder approval;
(7) authorize or approve reacquisition of shares, except according to a formula or method prescribed by the board of directors; or
(8) authorize or approve the issuance or sale or contract for sale of shares, or determine the designation and relative rights, preferences, and limitations of a class or series of shares, except that the board of directors may authorize a committee (or a senior executive officer of the corporation) to do so within limits specifically prescribed by the board of directors.

(f) The creation of, delegation of authority to, or action by a committee does not alone constitute compliance by a director with the standards of conduct described in section 8.30.

Standards of Conduct
§ 8.30. General Standards for Directors
(a) A director shall discharge his duties as a director, including his duties as a member of a committee:
(1) in good faith;
(2) with the care an ordinary prudent person in a like position would exercise under similar circumstances; and
(3) in a manner he reasonably believes to be in the best interests of the corporation.

(b) In discharging his duties a director is entitled to rely on information, opinions, reports, or statements, including financial statements and other financial data, if prepared or presented by:
(1) one or more officers or employees of the corporation whom the director reasonably believes to be reliable and competent in the matters presented;
(2) legal counsel, public accountants, or other persons as to matters the director reasonably believes are within the person's professional or expert competence; or
(3) a committee of the board of directors of which he is not a member if the director reasonably believes the committee merits confidence.

(c) A director is not acting in good faith if he has knowledge concerning the matter in question that makes reliance otherwise permitted by subsection (b) unwarranted.

(d) A director is not liable for any action taken as a director, or any failure to take any action, if he performed the duties of his office in compliance with this section.

§ 8.31. Director Conflict of Interest
(a) A conflict of interest transaction is a transaction with the corporation in which a director of the corporation has a direct or indirect interest. A conflict of interest transaction is not voidable by the corporation solely because of the director's interest in the transaction if any one of the following is true:
(1) the material facts of the transaction and the director's interest were disclosed or known to the board of directors or a committee of the board of directors and the board of directors or committee authorized, approved, or ratified the transaction;
(2) the material facts of the transaction and the director's interest were disclosed or known to the shareholders entitled to vote and they authorized, approved, or ratified the transaction; or
(3) the transaction was fair to the corporation.

(b) For purposes of this section, a director of the corporation has an indirect interest in a transaction if (1) another entity in which he has a material financial interest or in which he is a general partner is a party to the transaction or (2) another entity of which he is a director, officer, or trustee is a party to the transaction and the transaction is or should be considered by the board of directors of the corporation.

(c) For purposes of subsection (a)(1), a conflict of interest transaction is authorized, approved, or ratified if it receives the affirmative vote of a majority of the directors on the board of directors (or on the committee) who have no direct or indirect interest in the transaction, but a transaction may not be authorized, approved, or ratified under this section by a single director. If a majority of the directors who have no direct or indirect interest in the transaction voted to authorize, approve, or ratify the transaction, a quorum is present for the purpose of taking action under this section. The presence of, or a vote cast by, a director with a direct or indirect interest in the transaction does not affect the validity of any action taken under subsection (a)(1) if the transaction is otherwise authorized, approved, or ratified as provided in that subsection.

(d) For purposes of subsection (a)(2), a conflict of interest transaction is authorized, approved, or ratified if it receives the vote of a majority of the shares entitled to be counted under this subsection. Shares owned by or voted under the control of a director who has a direct or indirect interest in the transaction, and shares owned by or voted under the control of an entity described in subsection (b)(1), may not be counted in a vote of shareholders to determine whether to authorize, approve, or ratify a conflict of interest transaction under subsection (a)(2). The vote of those shares, however, is counted in determining whether the transaction is approved under other sections of this Act. A majority of the shares, whether or not present, that are entitled to be counted in a vote on the transaction under this subsection constitutes a quorum for the purpose of taking action under this section.

§ 8.32. Loans to Directors

(a) Except as provided by subsection (c), a corporation may not lend money to or guarantee the obligation of a director of the corporation unless:

(1) the particular loan or guarantee is approved by a majority of the votes represented by the outstanding voting shares of all classes, voting as a single voting group, except the votes of shares owned by or voted under the control of the benefited director; or

(2) the corporation's board of directors determines that the loan or guarantee benefits the corporation and either approves the specific loan or guarantee or a general plan authorizing loans and guarantees.

(b) The fact that a loan or guarantee is made in violation of this section does not affect the borrower's liability on the loan.

(c) This section does not apply to loans and guarantees authorized by statute regulating any special class of corporations.

§ 8.33. Liability for Unlawful Distributions

(a) Unless he complies with the applicable standards of conduct described in section 8.30, a director who votes for or assents to a distribution made in violation of this Act or the articles of incorporation is personally liable to the corporation for the amount of the distribution that exceeds what could have been distributed without violating this Act or the articles of incorporation.

(b) A director held liable for an unlawful distribution under subsection (a) is entitled to contribution:

(1) from every other director who voted for or assented to the distribution without complying with the applicable standards of conduct described in section 8.30; and

(2) from each shareholder for the amount the shareholder accepted knowing the distribution was made in violation of this Act or the articles of incorporation.

Officers

§ 8.40. Required Officers

(a) A corporation has the officers described in its bylaws or appointed by the board of directors in accordance with the bylaws.

(b) A duly appointed officer may appoint one or more officers or assistant officers if authorized by the bylaws or the board of directors.

(c) The bylaws or the board of directors shall delegate to one of the officers responsibility for preparing minutes of the directors' and shareholders' meetings and for authenticating records of the corporation.

(d) The same individual may simultaneously hold more than one office in a corporation.

§ 8.41. Duties of Officers

Each officer has the authority and shall perform the duties set forth in the bylaws or, to the extent consistent with the bylaws, the duties prescribed by the board of directors or by direction of an officer authorized by the board of directors to prescribe the duties of other officers.

§ 8.42. Standards of Conduct for Officers

(a) An officer with discretionary authority shall discharge his duties under that authority:

(1) in good faith;

(2) with the care an ordinarily prudent person in a like position would exercise under similar circumstances; and

(3) in a manner he reasonably believes to be in the best interests of the corporation.

(b) In discharging his duties an officer is entitled to rely on information, opinions, reports, or statements, including financial statements and other financial data, if prepared or presented by:

(1) one or more officers or employees of the corporation whom the officer reasonably believes to be reliable and competent in the matters presented; or

(2) legal counsel, public accountants, or other persons as to matters the officer reasonably believes are within the person's professional or expert competence.

(c) An officer is not acting in good faith if he has knowledge concerning the matter in question that makes reliance otherwise permitted by subsection (b) unwarranted.

(d) An officer is not liable for any action taken as an officer, or any failure to take any action, if he performed the duties of his office in compliance with this section.

§ 8.43. Resignation and Removal of Officers

(a) An officer may resign at any time by delivering notice to the corporation. A resignation is effective when the notice is delivered unless the notice specifies a later effective date. If a resignation is made effective at a later date and the corporation accepts the future effective date, its board of directors may fill the pending vacancy before the effective date if the board of directors provides that the successor does not take office until the effective date.

(b) A board of directors may remove any officer at any time with or without cause.

§ 8.44. Contract Rights of Officers

(a) The appointment of an officer does not itself create contract rights.

(b) An officer's removal does not affect the officer's contract rights, if any, with the corporation. An officer's resignation does not affect the corporation's contract rights, if any, with the officer.

Indemnification

§ 8.50. Subchapter Definitions

In this subchapter:

(1) "Corporation" includes any domestic or foreign predecessor entity of a corporation in a merger or other transaction in which the predecessor's existence ceased upon consummation of the transaction.

(2) "Director" means an individual who is or was a director of a corporation or an individual who, while a director of a corporation, is or was serving at the corporation's request as a director, officer, partner, trustee, employee, or agent of another foreign or domestic corporation, partnership, joint venture, trust, employee benefit plan, or other enterprise. A director is considered to be serving an employee benefit plan at the corporation's request if his duties to the corporation also impose duties on, or otherwise involve services by, him to the plan or to participants in or beneficiaries of the plan. "Director" includes, unless the context requires otherwise, the estate or personal representative of a director.

(3) "Expenses" include counsel fees.

(4) "Liability" means the obligation to pay a judgment, settlement, penalty, fine (including an excise tax assessed with respect to an employee benefit plan), or reasonable expenses incurred with respect to a proceeding.

(5) "Official capacity" means: (i) when used with respect to a director, the office of director in a corporation; and (ii) when used with respect to an individual other than a director, as contemplated in section 8.56, the office in a corporation held by the officer or the employment or agency relationship undertaken by the employee or agent on behalf of the corporation. "Official capacity" does not include service for any other foreign or domestic corporation or any partnership, joint venture, trust, employee benefit plan, or other enterprise.

(6) "Party" includes an individual who was, is, or is threatened to be made a named defendant or respondent in a proceeding.

(7) "Proceeding" means any threatened, pending, or completed action, suit, or proceeding, whether civil, criminal, administrative, or investigative and whether formal or informal.

§ 8.51. Authority to Indemnify

(a) Except as provided in subsection (d), a corporation may indemnify an individual made a party to a proceeding because he is or was a director against liability incurred in the proceeding if:

(1) he conducted himself in good faith; and
(2) he reasonably believed:
 (i) in the case of conduct in his official capacity with the corporation, that his conduct was in its best interests; and
 (ii) in all other cases, that his conduct was at least not opposed to its best interests; and
(3) in the case of any criminal proceeding, he had no reasonable cause to believe his conduct was unlawful.

(b) A director's conduct with respect to an employee benefit plan for a purpose he reasonably believed to be in the interests of the participants in and beneficiaries of the plan is conduct that satisfies the requirement of subsection (a)(2)(ii).

(c) The termination of a proceeding by judgment, order, settlement, conviction, or upon a plea of nolo contendere or its equivalent is not, of itself, determinative that the director did not meet the standard of conduct described in this section.

(d) A corporation may not indemnify a director under this section:

(1) in connection with a proceeding by or in the right of the corporation in which the director was adjudged liable to the corporation; or
(2) in connection with any other proceeding charging improper personal benefit to him, whether or not involving action in his official capacity, in which he was adjudged liable on the basis that personal benefit was improperly received by him.

(e) Indemnification permitted under this section in connection with a proceeding by or in the right of the corporation is limited to reasonable expenses incurred in connection with the proceeding.

§ 8.52. Mandatory Indemnification

Unless limited by its articles of incorporation, a corporation shall indemnify a director who was wholly successful, on the merits or otherwise, in the defense of any proceeding to which he was a party because he is or was a director of the corporation against reasonable expenses incurred by him in connection with the proceeding.

§ 8.53. Advance for Expenses

(a) A corporation may pay for or reimburse the reasonable expenses incurred by a director who is a party to a proceeding in advance of final disposition of the proceeding if:

(1) the director furnishes the corporation a written affirmation of his good faith belief that he has met the standard of conduct described in section 8.51;
(2) the director furnishes the corporation a written undertaking, executed personally or on his behalf, to repay the advance if it is ultimately determined that he did not meet the standard of conduct; and
(3) a determination is made that the facts then known to those making the determination would not preclude indemnification under this subchapter.

(b) The undertaking required by subsection (a)(2) must be an unlimited general obligation of the director but need not be secured and may be accepted without reference to financial ability to make repayment.

(c) Determinations and authorizations of payments under this section shall be made in the manner specified in section 8.55.

§ 8.54. Court-Ordered Indemnification

Unless a corporation's articles of incorporation provide otherwise, a director of the corporation who is a party to a proceeding may apply for indemnification to the court conducting the proceeding or to another court of competent jurisdiction. On receipt of an application, the court after giving any notice the court considers necessary may order indemnification if it determines:

(1) the director is entitled to mandatory indemnification under section 8.52, in which case the court shall also order the corporation to pay the director's reasonable expenses incurred to obtain court-ordered indemnification; or
(2) the director is fairly and reasonably entitled to indemnification in view of all the relevant circumstances, whether or not he met the standard of conduct set forth in section 8.51 or was adjudged liable as described in section 8.51(d), but if he was adjudged so liable his indemnification is limited to reasonable expenses incurred.

§ 8.55 Determination and Authorization of Indemnification

(a) A corporation may not indemnify a director under section 8.51 unless authorized in the specific case after a determination has been made that indemnification of the director is permissible in the circumstances because he has met the standard of conduct set forth in section 8.51.

(b) The determination shall be made:

(1) by the board of directors by majority vote of a quorum consisting of directors not at the time parties to the proceeding;
(2) if a quorum cannot be obtained under subdivision (1), by majority vote of a committee duly designated by the board of directors (in which designation directors who are parties may participate), consisting solely of two or more directors not at the time parties to the proceeding;
(3) by special legal counsel:
  (i) selected by the board of directors or its committee in the manner prescribed in subdivision (1) or (2); or
  (ii) if a quorum of the board of directors cannot be obtained under subdivision (1) and a committee cannot be designated under subdivision (2), selected by majority vote of the full board of directors (in which selection directors who are parties may participate); or
(4) by the shareholders, but shares owned by or voted under the control of directors who are at the time parties to the proceeding may not be voted on the determination.

(c) Authorization of indemnification and evaluation as to reasonableness of expenses shall be made in the same manner as the determination that indemnification is permissible, except that if the determination is made by special legal counsel, authorization of indemnification and evaluation as to reasonableness of expenses shall be made by those entitled under subsection (b)(3) to select counsel.

§ 8.56. Indemnification of Officers, Employees, and Agents

Unless a corporation's articles of incorporation provide otherwise:

(1) an officer of the corporation who is not a director is entitled to mandatory indemnification under section 8.52, and is entitled to apply for court-ordered indemnification under section 8.54, in each case to the same extent as a director;
(2) the corporation may indemnify and advance expenses under this subchapter to an officer, employee, or agent of the corporation who is not a director to the same extent as to a director; and

(3) a corporation may also indemnify and advance expenses to an officer, employee, or agent who is not a director to the extent, consistent with public policy, that may be provided by its articles of incorporation, bylaws, general or special action of its board of directors, or contract.

§ 8.57. Insurance

A corporation may purchase and maintain insurance on behalf of an individual who is or was a director, officer, employee, or agent of the corporation, or who, while a director, officer, employee, or agent of the corporation, is or was serving at the request of the corporation as a director, officer, partner, trustee, employee, or agent of another foreign or domestic corporation, partnership, joint venture, trust, employee benefit plan, or other enterprise, against liability asserted against or incurred by him in that capacity or arising from his status as a director, officer, employee, or agent, whether or not the corporation would have power to indemnify him against the same liability under section 8.51 or 8.52.

§ 8.58. Application of Subchapter

(a) A provision treating a corporation's indemnification of or advance for expenses to directors that is contained in its articles of incorporation, bylaws, a resolution of its shareholders or board of directors, or in a contract or otherwise, is valid only if and to the extent the provision is consistent with this subchapter. If articles of incorporation limit indemnification or advance for expenses, indemnification and advance for expenses are valid only to the extent consistent with the articles.

(b) This subchapter does not limit a corporation's power to pay or reimburse expenses incurred by a director in connection with his appearance as a witness in a proceeding at a time when he has not been made a named defendant or respondent to the proceeding.

CHAPTER 9 [RESERVED]

CHAPTER 10 AMENDMENT OF ARTICLES OF INCORPORATION AND BYLAWS

Amendment of Articles of Incorporation
§ 10.01. Authority to Amend

(a) A corporation may amend its articles of incorporation at any time to add or change a provision that is required or permitted in the articles of incorporation or to delete a provision not required in the articles of incorporation. Whether a provision is required or permitted in the articles of incorporation is determined as of the effective date of the amendment.

(b) A shareholder of the corporation does not have a vested property right resulting from any provision in the articles of incorporation, including provisions relating to management, control, capital structure, dividend entitlement, or purpose or duration of the corporation.

§ 10.02. Amendment by Board of Directors

Unless the articles of incorporation provide otherwise, a corporation's board of directors may adopt one or more amendments to the corporation's articles of incorporation without shareholder action:

(1) to extend the duration of the corporation if it was incorporated at a time when limited duration was required by law;

(2) to delete the names and addresses of the initial directors;

(3) to delete the name and address of the initial registered agent or registered office, if a statement of change is on file with the secretary of state;

(4) to change each issued and unissued authorized share of an outstanding class into a greater number of whole shares if the corporation has only shares of that class outstanding;

(5) to change the corporate name by substituting the word "corporation," "incorporated," "company," "limited," or the abbreviation "corp.," "inc.," "co.," or "ltd.," for a similar word or abbreviation in the name, or by adding, deleting, or changing a geographical attribution for the name; or

(6) to make any other change expressly permitted by this Act to be made without shareholder action.

§ 10.03. Amendment by Board of Directors and Shareholders

(a) A corporation's board of directors may propose one or more amendments to the articles of incorporation for submission to the shareholders.

(b) For the amendment to be adopted:

(1) the board of directors must recommend the amendment to the shareholders unless the board of directors determines that because of conflict of interest or other special circumstances it should make no recommendation and communicate the basis for its determination to the shareholders with the amendment; and

(2) the shareholders entitled to vote on the amendment must approve the amendment as provided in subsection (e).

(c) The board of directors may condition its submission of the proposed amendment on any basis.

(d) The corporation shall notify each shareholder, whether or not entitled to vote, of the proposed shareholders' meeting in accordance with section

7.05. The notice of meeting must also state that the purpose, or one of the purposes, of the meeting is to consider the proposed amendment and contain or be accompanied by a copy or summary of the amendment.

(e) Unless this Act, the articles of incorporation, or the board of directors (acting pursuant to subsection (c)) require a greater vote or a vote by voting groups, the amendment to be adopted must be approved by:

(1) a majority of the votes entitled to be cast on the amendment by any voting group with respect to which the amendment would create dissenters' rights; and

(2) the votes required by sections 7.25 and 7.26 by every other voting group entitled to vote on the amendment.

§ 10.04. Voting on Amendments by Voting Groups

(a) The holders of the outstanding shares of a class are entitled to vote as a separate voting group (if shareholder voting is otherwise required by this Act) on a proposed amendment if the amendment would:

(1) increase or decrease the aggregate number of authorized shares of the class;

(2) effect an exchange or reclassification of all or part of the shares of the class into shares of another class;

(3) effect an exchange or reclassification, or create the right of exchange, of all or part of the shares of another class into shares of the class;

(4) change the designation, rights, preferences, or limitations of all or part of the shares of the class;

(5) change the shares of all or part of the class into a different number of shares of the same class;

(6) create a new class of shares having rights or preferences with respect to distributions or to dissolution that are prior, superior, or substantially equal to the shares of the class;

(7) increase the rights, preferences, or number of authorized shares of any class that, after giving effect to the amendment, having rights or preferences with respect to distributions or to dissolution that are prior, superior, or substantially equal to the shares of the class;

(8) limit or deny an existing preemptive right of all or part of the shares of the class; or

(9) cancel or otherwise affect rights to distributions or dividends that have accumulated but not yet been declared on all or part of the shares of the class.

(b) If a proposed amendment would affect a series of a class of shares in one or more of the ways described in subsection (a), the shares of that series are entitled to vote as a separate voting group on the proposed amendment.

(c) If a proposed amendment that entitles two or more series of shares to vote as separate voting groups under this section would affect those two or more series in the same or a substantially similar way, the shares of all the series so affected must vote together as a single voting group on the proposed amendment.

(d) A class or series of shares is entitled to the voting rights granted by this section although the articles of incorporation provide that the shares are nonvoting shares.

§ 10.05. Amendment before Issuance of Shares

If a corporation has not yet issued shares, its incorporators or board of directors may adopt one or more amendments to the corporation's articles of incorporation.

§ 10.06. Articles of Amendment

A corporation amending its articles of incorporation shall deliver to the secretary of state for filing articles of amendment setting forth:

(1) the name of the corporation;

(2) the text of each amendment adopted;

(3) if an amendment provides for an exchange, reclassification, or cancellation of issued shares, provisions for implementing the amendment if not contained in the amendment itself;

(4) the date of each amendment's adoption;

(5) if an amendment was adopted by the incorporators or board of directors without shareholder action, a statement to that effect and that shareholder action was not required;

(6) if an amendment was approved by the shareholders:

(i) the designation, number of outstanding shares, number of votes entitled to be cast by each voting group entitled to vote separately on the amendment, and number of votes of each voting group indisputably represented at the meeting;

(ii) either the total number of votes cast for and against the amendment by each voting group entitled to vote separately on the amendment or the total number of undisputed votes cast for the amendment by each voting group and a statement that the number cast for the amendment by each voting group was sufficient for approval by that voting group.

§ 10.07. Restated Articles of Incorporation

(a) A corporation's board of directors may restate its articles of incorporation at any time with or without shareholder action.

(b) The restatement may include one or more amendments to the articles. If the restatement includes an amendment requiring shareholder approval, it must be adopted as provided in section 10.03.

(c) If the board of directors submits a restatement for shareholder action, the corporation shall notify each shareholder, whether or not entitled to vote, of the proposed shareholders' meeting in accordance with section 7.05. The notice must also state that the purpose, or one of the purposes, of the meeting is to consider the proposed restatement and contain or be accompanied by a copy of the restatement that identifies any amendment or other change it would make in the articles.

(d) A corporation restating its articles of incorporation shall deliver to the secretary of state for filing articles of restatement setting forth the name of the corporation and the text of the restated articles of incorporation together with a certificate setting forth:

(1) whether the restatement contains an amendment to the articles requiring shareholder approval and, if it does not, that the board of directors adopted the restatement; or

(2) if the restatement contains an amendment to the articles requiring shareholder approval, the information required by section 10.06.

(e) Duly adopted restated articles of incorporation supersede the original articles of incorporation and all amendments to them.

(f) The secretary of state may certify restated articles of incorporation, as the articles of incorporation currently in effect, without including the certificate information required by subsection (d).

§ 10.08. Amendment Pursuant to Reorganization

(a) A corporation's articles of incorporation may be amended without action by the board of directors or shareholders to carry out a plan of reorganization ordered or decreed by a court of competent jurisdiction under federal statute if the articles of incorporation after amendment contain only provisions required or permitted by section 2.02.

(b) The individual or individuals designated by the court shall deliver to the secretary of state for filing articles of amendment setting forth:

(1) the name of the corporation;

(2) the text of each amendment approved by the court;

(3) the date of the court's order or decree approving the articles of amendment;

(4) the title of the reorganization proceeding in which the order or decree was entered; and

(5) a statement that the court has jurisdiction of the proceeding under federal statute.

(c) Shareholders of a corporation undergoing reorganization do not have dissenters' rights except as and to the extent provided in the reorganization plan.

(d) This section does not apply after entry of a final decree in the reorganization proceeding even though the court retains jurisdiction of the proceeding for limited purposes unrelated to consummation of the reorganization plan.

§ 10.09. Effect of Amendment

An amendment to articles of incorporation does not affect a cause of action existing against or in favor of the corporation, a proceeding to which the corporation is a party, or the existing rights of persons other than shareholders of the corporation. An amendment changing a corporation's name does not abate a proceeding brought by or against the corporation in its former name.

Amendment of Bylaws

§ 10.20. Amendment by Board of Directors or Shareholders

(a) A corporation's board of directors may amend or repeal the corporation's bylaws unless:

(1) the articles of incorporation or this Act reserve this power exclusively to the shareholders in whole or part; or

(2) the shareholders in amending or repealing a particular bylaw provide expressly that the board of directors may not amend or repeal that bylaw.

(b) A corporation's shareholders may amend or repeal the corporation's bylaws even though the bylaws may also be amended or repealed by its board of directors.

§ 10.21. Bylaw Increasing Quorum or Voting Requirement for Shareholders

(a) If authorized by the articles of incorporation, the shareholders may adopt or amend a bylaw that fixes a greater quorum or voting requirement for shareholders (or voting groups of shareholders) than is required by this Act. The adoption or amendment of a bylaw that adds, changes, or deletes a greater quorum or voting requirement for shareholders must meet the same quorum requirement and be adopted by the same vote and voting groups required to take action under the quorum and voting requirement then in effect or proposed to be adopted, whichever is greater.

(b) A bylaw that fixes a greater quorum or voting requirement for shareholders under subsection (a) may not be adopted, amended, or repealed by the board of directors.

§ 10.22. Bylaw Increasing Quorum or Voting Requirement for Directors

(a) A bylaw that fixes a greater quorum or voting requirement for the board of directors may be amended or repealed:

(1) if originally adopted by the shareholders, only by the shareholders;

(2) if originally adopted by the board of directors, either by the shareholders or by the board of directors.

(b) A bylaw adopted or amended by the shareholders that fixes a greater quorum or voting requirement for the board of directors may provide that it may be amended or repealed only by a specified vote of either the shareholders or the board of directors.

(c) Action by the board of directors under subsection (a)(2) to adopt or amend a bylaw that changes the quorum or voting requirement for the board of directors must meet the same quorum requirement and be adopted by the same vote required to take action under the quorum and voting requirement then in effect or proposed to be adopted, whichever is greater.

CHAPTER 11 MERGER AND SHARE EXCHANGE

§ 11.01. Merger

(a) One or more corporations may merge into another corporation if the board of directors of each corporation adopts and its shareholders (if required by section 11.03) approve a plan of merger.

(b) The plan of merger must set forth:

(1) the name of each corporation planning to merge and the name of the surviving corporation into which each other corporation plans to merge;

(2) the terms and conditions of the merger; and

(3) the manner and basis of converting the shares of each corporation into shares, obligations, or other securities of the surviving or any other corporation or into cash or other property in whole or part.

(c) The plan of merger may set forth:

(1) amendments to the articles of incorporation of the surviving corporation; and

(2) other provisions relating to the merger.

§ 11.02. Share Exchange

(a) A corporation may acquire all of the outstanding shares of one or more classes or series of another corporation if the board of directors of each corporation adopts and its shareholders (if required by section 11.03) approve the exchange.

(b) The plan of exchange must set forth:

(1) the name of the corporation whose shares will be acquired and the name of the acquiring corporation;

(2) the terms and conditions of the exchange;

(3) the manner and basis of exchanging the shares to be acquired for shares, obligations, or other securities of the acquiring or any other corporation or for cash or other property in whole or part.

(c) The plan of exchange may set forth other provisions relating to the exchange.

(d) This section does not limit the power of a corporation to acquire all or part of the shares of one or more classes or series of another corporation through a voluntary exchange or otherwise.

§ 11.03. Action on Plan

(a) After adopting a plan of merger or share exchange, the board of directors of each corporation party to the merger, and the board of directors of the corporation whose shares will be acquired in the share exchange, shall submit the plan of merger (except as provided in subsection (g)) or share exchange for approval by its shareholders.

(b) For a plan of merger or share exchange to be approved:

(1) the board of directors must recommend the plan of merger or share exchange to the shareholders, unless the board of directors determines that because of conflict of interest or other special circumstances it should make no recommendation and communicates the basis for its determination to the shareholders with the plan; and

(2) the shareholders entitled to vote must approve the plan.

(c) The board of directors may condition its submission of the proposed merger or share exchange on any basis.

(d) The corporation shall notify each shareholder, whether or not entitled to vote, of the proposed shareholders' meeting in accordance with section 7.05. The notice must also state that the purpose, or one of the purposes, of the meeting is to consider the plan of merger or share exchange and contain or be accompanied by a copy or summary of the plan.

(e) Unless this Act, the articles of incorporation, or the board of directors (acting pursuant to subsection (c)) require a greater vote or a vote by voting groups, the plan of merger or share exchange to be authorized must be approved by each voting group entitled to vote separately on the plan by a majority of all the votes entitled to be cast on the plan by that voting group.

(f) Separate voting by voting groups is required:

(1) on a plan of merger if the plan contains a provision that, if contained in a proposed amendment to articles of incorporation, would require action by one or more separate voting groups on the proposed amendment under section 10.04;

(2) on a plan of share exchange by each class or series of shares included in the exchange, with each class or series constituting a separate voting group.

(g) Action by the shareholders of the surviving corporation on a plan of merger is not required if:

(1) the articles of incorporation of the surviving corporation will not differ (except for amendments enumerated in section 10.02) from its articles before the merger;

(2) each shareholder of the surviving corporation whose shares were outstanding immediately before the effective date of the merger will hold the same number of shares, with identical designations, preferences, limitations, and relative rights, immediately after;

(3) the number of voting shares outstanding immediately after the merger, plus the number of voting shares issuable as a result of the merger (either by the conversion of securities issued pursuant to the merger or the exercise of rights and warrants issued pursuant to the merger), will not exceed by more than 20 percent the total number of voting shares of the surviving corporation outstanding immediately before the merger; and

(4) the number of participating shares outstanding immediately after the merger, plus the number of participating shares issuable as a result of the merger (either by the conversion of securities issued pursuant to the merger or the exercise of rights and warrants issued pursuant to the merger), will not exceed by more than 20 percent the total number of participating shares outstanding immediately before the merger.

(h) As used in subsection (g):

(1) "Participating shares" means shares that entitle their holders to participate without limitation in distributions.

(2) "Voting shares" means shares that entitle their holders to vote unconditionally in elections of directors.

(i) After a merger or share exchange is authorized, and at any time before articles of merger or share exchange are filed, the planned merger or share exchange may be abandoned (subject to any contractual rights), without further shareholder action, in accordance with the procedure set forth in the plan of merger or share exchange or, if none is set forth, in the manner determined by the board of directors.

§ 11.04. Merger of Subsidiary

(a) A parent corporation owning at least 90 percent of the outstanding shares of each class of a subsidiary corporation may merge the subsidiary into itself without approval of the shareholders of the parent or subsidiary.

(b) The board of directors of the parent shall adopt a plan of merger that sets forth:

(1) the names of the parent and subsidiary; and

(2) the manner and basis of converting the shares of the subsidiary into shares, obligations, or other securities of the parent or any other corporation or into cash or other property in whole or part.

(c) The parent shall mail a copy or summary of the plan of merger to each shareholder of the subsidiary who does not waive the mailing requirement in writing.

(d) The parent may not deliver articles of merger to the secretary of state for filing until at least 30 days after the date it mailed a copy of the plan of merger to each shareholder of the subsidiary who did not waive the mailing requirement.

(e) Articles of merger under this section may not contain amendments to the articles of incorporation of the parent corporation (except for amendments enumerated in section 10.02).

§ 11.05. Articles of Merger or Share Exchange

(a) After a plan of merger or share exchange is approved by the shareholders, or adopted by the board of directors if shareholder approval is not required, the surviving or acquiring corporation shall deliver to the secretary of state for filing articles of merger or share exchange setting forth:

(1) the plan of merger or share exchange;

(2) if shareholder approval was not required, a statement to that effect;

(3) if approval of the shareholders of one or more corporations party to the merger or share exchange was required:

(i) the designation, number of outstanding shares, and number of votes entitled to be cast by each voting group entitled to vote separately on the plan as to each corporation; and

(ii) either the total number of votes cast for and against the plan by each voting group entitled to vote separately on the plan or the total number of undisputed votes cast for the plan separately by each voting group and a statement that the number cast for the plan by each voting group was sufficient for approval by that voting group.

(b) A merger or share exchange takes effect upon the effective date of the articles of merger or share exchange.

§ 11.06. Effect of Merger or Share Exchange

(a) When a merger takes effect:

(1) every other corporation party to the merger merges into the surviving corporation and the

separate existence of every corporation except the surviving corporation ceases;

(2) the title to all real estate and other property owned by each corporation party to the merger is vested in the surviving corporation without reversion or impairment;

(3) the surviving corporation has all liabilities of each corporation party to the merger;

(4) a proceeding pending against any corporation party to the merger may be continued as if the merger did not occur or the surviving corporation may be substituted in the proceeding for the corporation whose existence ceased;

(5) the articles of incorporation of the surviving corporation are amended to the extent provided in the plan of merger; and

(6) the shares of each corporation party to the merger that are to be converted into shares, obligations, or other securities of the surviving or any other corporation or into cash or other property are converted, and the former holders of the shares are entitled only to the rights provided in the articles of merger or to their rights under chapter 13.

(b) When a share exchange takes effect, the shares of each acquired corporation are exchanged as provided in the plan, and the former holders of the shares are entitled only to the exchange rights provided in the articles of share exchange or to their rights under chapter 13.

§ 11.07. Merger or Share Exchange with Foreign Corporation

(a) One or more foreign corporations may merge or enter into a share exchange with one or more domestic corporations if:

(1) in a merger, the merger is permitted by the law of the state or country under whose law each foreign corporation is incorporated and each foreign corporation complies with that law in effecting the merger;

(2) in a share exchange, the corporation whose shares will be acquired is a domestic corporation, whether or not a share exchange is permitted by the law of the state or country under whose law the acquiring corporation is incorporated;

(3) the foreign corporation complies with section 11.05 if it is the surviving corporation of the merger or acquiring corporation of the share exchange; and

(4) each domestic corporation complies with the applicable provisions of sections 11.01 through 11.04 and, if it is the surviving corporation of the merger or acquiring corporation of the share exchange, with section 11.05.

(b) Upon the merger or share exchange taking effect, the surviving foreign corporation of a merger and the acquiring foreign corporation of a share exchange is deemed:

(1) to appoint the secretary of state as its agent for service of process in a proceeding to enforce any obligation or the rights of dissenting shareholders of each domestic corporation party to the merger or share exchange; and

(2) to agree that it will promptly pay to the dissenting shareholders of each domestic corporation party to the merger or share exchange the amount, if any, to which they are entitled under chapter 13.

(c) This section does not limit the power of a foreign corporation to acquire all or part of the shares of one or more classes or series of a domestic corporation through a voluntary exchange or otherwise.

CHAPTER 12 SALE OF ASSETS

§ 12.01. Sale of Assets in Regular Course of Business and Mortgage of Assets

(a) A corporation may, on the terms and conditions and for the consideration determined by the board of directors:

(1) sell, lease, exchange, or otherwise dispose of all, or substantially all, of its property in the usual and regular course of business;

(2) mortgage, pledge, dedicate to the repayment of indebtedness (whether with or without recourse), or otherwise encumber any or all of its property whether or not in the usual and regular course of business; or

(3) transfer any or all of its property to a corporation all the shares of which are owned by the corporation.

(b) Unless the articles of incorporation require it, approval by the shareholders of a transaction described in subsection (a) is not required.

§ 12.02. Sale of Assets Other than in Regular Course of Business

(a) A corporation may sell, lease, exchange, or otherwise dispose of all, or substantially all, of its property (with or without the good will), otherwise than in the usual and regular course of business, on the terms and conditions and for the consideration determined by the corporation's board of directors, if the board of directors proposes and its shareholders approve the proposed transaction.

(b) For a transaction to be authorized:

(1) the board of directors must recommend the proposed transaction to the shareholders unless the board of directors determines that because of conflict of interest or other special circumstances it should make no recommendation and commu-

nicates the basis for its determination to the shareholders with the submission of the proposed transaction; and

(2) the shareholders entitled to vote must approve the transaction.

(c) The board of directors may condition its submission of the proposed transaction on any basis.

(d) The corporation shall notify each shareholder, whether or not entitled to vote, of the proposed shareholders' meeting in accordance with section 7.05. The notice must also state that the purpose, or one of the purposes, of the meeting is to consider the sale, lease, exchange, or other disposition of all, or substantially all, the property of the corporation and contain or be accompanied by a description of the transaction.

(e) Unless the articles of incorporation or the board of directors (acting pursuant to subsection (c)) require a greater vote or a vote by voting groups, the transaction to be authorized must be approved by a majority of all the votes entitled to be cast on the transaction.

(f) After a sale, lease, exchange, or other disposition of property is authorized, the transaction may be abandoned (subject to any contractual rights) without further shareholder action.

(g) A transaction that constitutes a distribution is governed by section 6.40 and not by this section.

CHAPTER 13 DISSENTERS' RIGHTS

Right to Dissent and Obtain Payment for Shares

§ 13.01. Definitions

In this chapter:

(1) "Corporation" means the issuer of the shares held by a dissenter before the corporate action, or the surviving or acquiring corporation by merger or share exchange of that issuer.

(2) "Dissenter" means a shareholder who is entitled to dissent from corporate action under section 13.02 and who exercises that right when and in the manner required by sections 13.20 through 13.28.

(3) "Fair value," with respect to a dissenter's shares, means the value of the shares immediately before the effectuation of the corporate action to which the dissenter objects, excluding any appreciation or depreciation in anticipation of the corporate action unless exclusion would be inequitable.

(4) "Interest" means interest from the effective date of the corporate action until the date of payment, at the average rate currently paid by the corporation on its principal bank loans or, if none, at a rate that is fair and equitable under all the circumstances.

(5) "Record shareholder" means the person in whose name shares are registered in the records of a corporation or the beneficial owner of shares to the extent of the rights granted by a nominee certificate on file with a corporation.

(6) "Beneficial shareholder" means the person who is a beneficial owner of shares held by a nominee as the record shareholder.

(7) "Shareholder" means the record shareholder or the beneficial shareholder.

§ 13.02. Right to Dissent

(a) A shareholder is entitled to dissent from, and obtain payment of the fair value of his shares in the event of, any of the following corporate actions:

(1) consummation of a plan of merger to which the corporation is a party (i) if shareholder approval is required for the merger by section 11.03 or the articles of incorporation and the shareholder is entitled to vote on the merger or (ii) if the corporation is a subsidiary that is merged with its parent under section 11.04;

(2) consummation of a plan of share exchange to which the corporation is a party as the corporation whose shares will be acquired, if the shareholder is entitled to vote on the plan;

(3) consummation of a sale or exchange of all, or substantially all, of the property of the corporation other than in the usual and regular course of business, if the shareholder is entitled to vote on the sale or exchange, including a sale in dissolution, but not including a sale pursuant to court order or a sale for cash pursuant to a plan by which all or substantially all of the net proceeds of the sale will be distributed to the shareholders within one year after the date of sale;

(4) an amendment of the articles of incorporation that materially and adversely affects rights in respect of a dissenter's shares because it:

(i) alters or abolishes a preferential right of the shares;

(ii) creates, alters, or abolishes a right in respect of redemption, including a provision respecting a sinking fund for the redemption or repurchase, of the shares;

(iii) alters or abolishes a redemptive right of the holder of the shares to acquire shares or other securities;

(iv) excludes or limits the right of the shares to vote on any matter, or to cumulate votes, other than a limitation by dilution through issuance of shares or other securities with similar voting rights; or

(v) reduces the number of shares owned by the shareholder to a fraction of a share if the fractional share so created is to be acquired for cash under section 6.04; or

(5) any corporate action taken pursuant to a shareholder vote to the extent the articles of incorporation, bylaws, or a resolution of the board of directors provides that voting or nonvoting shareholders are entitled to dissent and obtain payment for their shares.

(b) A shareholder entitled to dissent and obtain payment for his shares under this chapter may not challenge the corporate action creating his entitlement unless the action is unlawful or fraudulent with respect to the shareholder or the corporation.

§ 13.03. Dissent by Nominees and Beneficial Owners

(a) A record shareholder may assert dissenters' rights as to fewer than all the shares registered in his name only if he dissents with respect to all shares beneficially owned by any one person and notifies the corporation in writing of the name and address of each person on whose behalf he asserts dissenters' rights. The rights of a partial dissenter under this subsection are determined as if the shares as to which he dissents and his other shares are registered in the names of different shareholders.

(b) A beneficial shareholder may assert dissenters' rights as to shares held on his behalf only if:

(1) he submits to the corporation the record shareholder's written consent to the dissent not later than the time the beneficial shareholder asserts dissenters' rights; and

(2) he does so with respect to all shares of which he is the beneficial shareholder or over which he has power to direct the vote.

Procedure for Exercise of Dissenters' Rights

§ 13.20. Notice of Dissenters' Rights

(a) If proposed corporate action creating dissenters' rights under section 13.02 is submitted to a vote at a shareholders' meeting, the meeting notice must state that shareholders are or may be entitled to assert dissenters' rights under this chapter and be accompanied by a copy of this chapter.

(b) If corporate action creating dissenters' rights under section 13.02 is taken without a vote of shareholders, the corporation shall notify in writing all shareholders entitled to assert dissenters' rights that the action was taken and send them the dissenters' notice described in section 13.22.

§ 13.21. Notice of Intent to Demand Payment

(a) If proposed corporate action creating dissenters' rights under section 13.02 is submitted to a vote at a shareholders' meeting, a shareholder who wishes to assert dissenters' rights (1) must deliver to the corporation before the vote is taken written notice of his intent to demand payment for his shares if the proposed action is effectuated and (2) must not vote his shares in favor of the proposed action.

(b) A shareholder who does not satisfy the requirements of subsection (a) is not entitled to payment for his shares under this chapter.

§ 13.22. Dissenters' Notice

(a) If proposed corporate action creating dissenters' rights under section 13.02 is authorized at a shareholders' meeting, the corporation shall deliver a written dissenters' notice to all shareholders who satisfied the requirements of section 13.21.

(b) The dissenters' notice must be sent no later than 10 days after the corporate action was taken, and must:

(a) state where the payment demand must be sent and where and when certificates for certificated shares must be deposited;

(2) inform holders of uncertificated shares to what extent transfer of the shares will be restricted after the payment demand is received;

(3) supply a form for demanding payment that includes the date of the first announcement to news media or to shareholders of the terms of the proposed corporate action and requires that the person asserting dissenters' rights certify whether or not he acquired beneficial ownership of the shares before that date;

(4) set a date by which the corporation must receive the payment demand, which date may not be fewer than 30 nor more than 60 days after the date the subsection (a) notice is delivered; and

(5) be accompanied by a copy of this chapter.

§ 13.23. Duty to Demand Payment

(a) A shareholder sent a dissenters' notice described in section 13.22 must demand payment, certify whether he acquired beneficial ownership of the shares before the date required to be set forth in the dissenters' notice pursuant to section 13.22(b)(3), and deposit his certificates in accordance with the terms of the notice.

(b) The shareholder who demands payment and deposits his share certificates under section (a) retains all other rights of a shareholder until these rights are cancelled or modified by the taking of the proposed corporate action.

(c) A shareholder who does not demand payment or deposit his share certificates where required, each by the date set in the dissenters' notice, is not entitled to payment for his shares under this chapter.

§ 13.24. Share Restrictions

(a) The corporation may restrict the transfer of uncertificated shares from the date the demand for their payment is received until the proposed corporate action is taken or the restrictions released under section 13.26.

(b) The person for whom dissenters' rights are asserted as to uncertificated shares retains all other rights of a shareholder until these rights are cancelled or modified by the taking of the proposed corporate action.

§ 13.25. Payment

(a) Except as provided in section 13.27, as soon as the proposed corporate action is taken, or upon receipt of a payment demand, the corporation shall pay each dissenter who complied with section 13.23 the amount the corporation estimates to be the fair value of his shares, plus accrued interest.

(b) The payment must be accompanied by:
   (1) the corporation's balance sheet as of the end of a fiscal year ending not more than 16 months before the date of payment, an income statement for that year, a statement of changes in shareholders' equity for that year, and the latest available interim financial statements, if any;
   (2) a statement of the corporation's estimate of the fair value of the shares;
   (3) an explanation of how the interest was calculated;
   (4) a statement of the dissenter's right to demand payment under section 13.28; and
   (5) a copy of this chapter.

§ 13.26. Failure to Take Action

(a) If the corporation does not take the proposed action within 60 days after the date set for demanding payment and depositing share certificates, the corporation shall return the deposited certificates and release the transfer restrictions imposed on uncertificated shares.

(b) If after returning deposited certificates and releasing transfer restrictions, the corporation takes the proposed action, it must send a new dissenters' notice under section 13.22 and repeat the payment demand procedure.

§ 13.27. After-Acquired Shares

(a) A corporation may elect to withhold payment required by section 13.25 from a dissenter unless he was the beneficial owner of the shares before the date set forth in the dissenters' notice as the date of the first announcement to news media or to shareholders of the terms of the proposed corporate action.

(b) To the extent the corporation elects to withhold payment under subsection (a), after taking the proposed corporate action, it shall estimate the fair value of the shares, plus accrued interest, and shall pay this amount to each dissenter who agrees to accept it in full satisfaction of his demand. The corporation shall send with its offer a statement of its estimate of the fair value of the shares, an explanation of how the interest was calculated, and a statement of the dissenter's right to demand payment under section 13.28.

§ 13.28. Procedure if Shareholder Dissatisfied with Payment or Offer

(a) A dissenter may notify the corporation in writing of his own estimate of the fair value of his shares and amount of interest due, and demand payment of his estimate (less any payment under section 13.25), or reject the corporation's offer under section 13.27 and demand payment of the fair value of his shares and interest due, if:
   (1) the dissenter believes that the amount paid under section 13.25 or offered under section 13.27 is less than the fair value of his shares or that the interest due is incorrectly calculated;
   (2) the corporation fails to make payment under section 13.25 within 60 days after the date set for demanding payment; or
   (3) the corporation, having failed to take the proposed action, does not return the deposited certificates or release the transfer restrictions imposed on uncertificated shares within 60 days after the date set for demanding payment.

(b) A dissenter waives his right to demand payment under this section unless he notifies the corporation of his demand in writing under subsection (a) within 30 days after the corporation made or offered payment for his shares.

Judicial Appraisal of Shares

§ 13.30. Court Action

(a) If a demand for payment under section 13.28 remains unsettled, the corporation shall commence a proceeding within 60 days after receiving the payment demand and petition the court to determine the fair value of the shares and accrued interest. If the corporation does not commence the proceeding within the 60-day period, it shall pay each dissenter whose demand remains unsettled the amount demanded.

(b) The corporation shall commence the proceeding in the [name or describe] court of the county where a corporation's principal office (or, if none in this state, its registered office) is located. If the corporation is a foreign corporation without a registered office in this state, it shall commence the proceeding in the county in this state where the registered office of the domestic corporation merged with or whose shares were acquired by the foreign corporation was located.

(c) The corporation shall make all dissenters (whether or not residents of this state) whose demands remain unsettled parties to the proceeding as in an action against their shares and all parties must be served with a copy of the petition. Nonresidents may be served by registered or certified mail or by publication as provided by law.

(d) The jurisdiction of the court in which the proceeding is commenced under subsection (b) is plenary and exclusive. The court may appoint one or more persons as appraisers to receive evidence and recommend decision on the question of fair value. The appraisers have the powers described in the order appointing them, or in any amendment to it. The dissenters are entitled to the same discovery rights as parties in other civil proceedings.

(e) Each dissenter made a party to the proceeding is entitled to judgment (1) for the amount, if any, by which the court finds the fair value of his shares, plus interest, exceeds the amount paid by the corporation or (2) for the fair value, plus accrued interest, of his after-acquired shares for which the corporation elected to withhold payment under section 13.27.

§ 13.31. Court Costs and Counsel Fees

(a) The court in an appraisal proceeding commenced under section 13.30 shall determine all costs of the proceeding, including the reasonable compensation and expenses of appraisers appointed by the court. The court shall assess the costs against the corporation, except that the court may assess costs against all or some of the dissenters, in amounts the court finds equitable, to the extent the court finds the dissenters acted arbitrarily, vexatiously, or not in good faith in demanding payment under section 13.28.

(b) The court may also assess the fees and expenses of counsel and experts for the respective parties, in amounts the court finds equitable:

(1) against the corporation and in favor of any or all dissenters if the court finds the corporation did not substantially comply with the requirements of sections 13.20 through 13.28; or

(2) against either the corporation or a dissenter, in favor of any other party, if the court finds that the party against whom the fees and expenses are assessed acted arbitrarily, vexatiously, or not in good faith with respect to the rights provided by this chapter.

(c) If the court finds that the services of counsel for any dissenter were of substantial benefit to other dissenters similarly situated, and that the fees for those services should not be assessed against the corporation, the court may award to these counsel reasonable fees to be paid out of the amounts awarded the dissenters who were benefited.

CHAPTER 14 DISSOLUTION

Voluntary Dissolution

§ 14.01. Dissolution by Incorporators or Initial Directors

A majority of the incorporators or initial directors of a corporation that has not issued shares or has not commenced business may dissolve the corporation by delivering to the secretary of state for filing articles of dissolution that set forth:

(1) the name of the corporation;

(2) the date of its incorporation;

(3) either (i) that none of the corporation's shares has been issued or (ii) that the corporation has not commenced business;

(4) that no debt of the corporation remains unpaid;

(5) that the net assets of the corporation remaining after winding up have been distributed to the shareholders, if shares were issued; and

(6) that a majority of the incorporators or initial directors authorized the dissolution.

§ 14.02. Dissolution by Board of Directors and Shareholders

(a) A corporation's board of directors may propose dissolution for submission to the shareholders.

(b) For a proposal to dissolve to be adopted:

(1) the board of directors must recommend dissolution to the shareholders unless the board of directors determines that because of conflict of interest or other special circumstances it should make no recommendation and communicates the basis for its determination to the shareholders; and

(2) the shareholders entitled to vote must approve the proposal to dissolve as provided in subsection (e).

(c) The board of directors may condition its submission of the proposal for dissolution on any basis.

(d) The corporation shall notify each shareholder, whether or not entitled to vote, of the proposed shareholders' meeting in accordance with section 7.05. The notice must also state that the purpose, or one of the purposes, of the meeting is to consider dissolving the corporation.

(e) Unless the articles of incorporation or the board of directors (acting pursuant to subsection (c)) require a greater vote or a vote by voting groups, the proposal to dissolve to be adopted must be approved by a majority of all the votes entitled to be cast on that proposal.

§ 14.03. Articles of Dissolution

(a) At any time after dissolution is authorized, the corporation may dissolve by delivering to the secretary of state for filing articles of dissolution setting forth:

(1) the name of the corporation;
(2) the date dissolution was authorized;
(3) if dissolution was approved by the shareholders:
 (i) the number of votes entitled to be cast on the proposal to dissolve; and
 (ii) either the total number of votes cast for and against dissolution or the total number of undisputed votes cast for dissolution and a statement that the number cast for dissolution was sufficient for approval.
(4) If voting by voting groups was required, the information required by subparagraph (3) must be separately provided for each voting group entitled to vote separately on the plan to dissolve.
(b) A corporation is dissolved upon the effective date of its articles of dissolution.

§ 14.04. Revocation of Dissolution

(a) A corporation may revoke its dissolution within 120 days of its effective date.
(b) Revocation of dissolution must be authorized in the same manner as the dissolution was authorized unless that authorization permitted revocation by action of the board of directors alone, in which event the board of directors may revoke the dissolution without shareholder action.
(c) After the revocation of dissolution is authorized, the corporation may revoke the dissolution by delivering to the secretary of state for filing articles of revocation of dissolution, together with a copy of its articles of dissolution, that set forth:
(1) the name of the corporation;
(2) the effective date of the dissolution that was revoked;
(3) the date that the revocation of dissolution was authorized;
(4) if the corporation's board of directors (or incorporators) revoked the dissolution, a statement to that effect;
(5) if the corporation's board of directors revoked a dissolution authorized by the shareholders, a statement that revocation was permitted by action by the board of directors alone pursuant to that authorization; and
(6) if shareholder action was required to revoke the dissolution, the information required by section 14.03(a)(3) or (4).
(d) Revocation of dissolution is effective upon the effective date of the articles of revocation of dissolution.
(e) When the revocation of dissolution is effective, it relates back to and takes effect as of the effective date of the dissolution and the corporation resumes carrying on its business as if dissolution had never occurred.

§ 14.05. Effect of Dissolution

(a) A dissolved corporation continues its corporate existence but may not carry on any business except that appropriate to wind up and liquidate its business and affairs, including:
(1) collecting its assets;
(2) disposing of its properties that will not be distributed in kind to its shareholders;
(3) discharging or making provision for discharging its liabilities;
(4) distributing its remaining property among its shareholders according to their interests; and
(5) doing every other act necessary to wind up and liquidate its business and affairs.
(b) Dissolution of a corporation does not:
(1) transfer title to the corporation's property;
(2) prevent transfer of its shares or securities, although the authorization to dissolve may provide for closing the corporation's share transfer records;
(3) subject its directors or officers to standards of conduct different from those prescribed in chapter 8;
(4) change quorum or voting requirements for its board of directors or shareholders; change provisions for selection, resignation, or removal of its directors or officers or both; or change provisions for amending its bylaws;
(5) prevent commencement of a proceeding by or against the corporation in its corporate name;
(6) abate or suspend a proceeding pending by or against the corporation on the effective date of dissolution; or
(7) terminate the authority of the registered agent of the corporation.

§ 14.06. Known Claims Against Dissolved Corporation

(a) A dissolved corporation may dispose of the known claims against it by following the procedure described in this section.
(b) The dissolved corporation shall notify its known claimants in writing of the dissolution at any time after its effective date. The written notice must:
(1) describe information that must be included in a claim;
(2) provide a mailing address where a claim may be sent;
(3) state the deadline, which may not be fewer than 120 days from the effective date of the written notice, by which the dissolved corporation must receive the claim; and

(4) state that the claim will be barred if not received by the deadline.

(c) A claim against the dissolved corporation is barred:

(1) if a claimant who was given written notice under subsection (b) does not deliver the claim to the dissolved corporation by the deadline;

(2) if a claimant whose claim was rejected by the dissolved corporation does not commence a proceeding to enforce the claim within 90 days from the effective date of the rejection notice.

(d) For purposes of this section, "claim" does not include a contingent liability or a claim based on an event occurring after the effective date of dissolution.

§ 14.07. Unknown Claims against Dissolved Corporation

(a) A dissolved corporation may also publish notice of its dissolution and request that persons with claims against the corporation present them in accordance with the notice.

(b) The notice must:

(1) be published one time in a newspaper of general circulation in the county where the dissolved corporation's principal office (or, if none in this state, its registered office) is or was last located;

(2) describe the information that must be included in a claim and provide a mailing address where the claim may be sent; and

(3) state that a claim against the corporation will be barred unless a proceeding to enforce the claim is commenced within five years after the publication of the notice.

(c) If the dissolved corporation publishes a newspaper notice in accordance with subsection (b), the claim of each of the following claimants is barred unless the claimant commences a proceeding to enforce the claim against the dissolved corporation within five years after the publication date of the newspaper notice:

(1) a claimant who did not receive written notice under section 14.06;

(2) a claimant whose claim was timely sent to the dissolved corporation but not acted on;

(3) a claimant whose claim is contingent or based on an event occurring after the effective date of dissolution.

(d) A claim may be enforced under this section:

(1) against the dissolved corporation, to the extent of its undistributed assets; or

(2) if the assets have been distributed in liquidation, against a shareholder of the dissolved corporation to the extent of his pro rata share of the claim or the corporate assets distributed to him in liquidation, whichever is less, but a shareholder's total liability for all claims under this section may not exceed the total amount of assets distributed to him.

Administrative Dissolution
§ 14.20. Grounds for Administrative Dissolution

The secretary of state may commence a proceeding under section 14.21 to administratively dissolve a corporation if:

(1) the corporation does not pay within 60 days after they are due any franchise taxes or penalties imposed by this Act or other law;

(2) the corporation does not deliver its annual report to the secretary of state within 60 days after it is due;

(3) the corporation is without a registered agent or registered office in this state for 60 days or more;

(4) the corporation does not notify the secretary of state within 60 days that its registered agent or registered office has been changed, that its registered agent has resigned, or that its registered office has been discontinued; or

(5) the corporation's period of duration stated in its articles of incorporation expires.

§ 14.21. Procedure for and Effect of Administrative Dissolution

(a) If the secretary of state determines that one or more grounds exist under section 14.20 for dissolving a corporation, he shall serve the corporation with written notice of his determination under section 5.04.

(b) If the corporation does not correct each ground for dissolution or demonstrate to the reasonable satisfaction of the secretary of state that each ground determined by the secretary of state does not exist within 60 days after service of the notice is perfected under section 5.04, the secretary of state shall administratively dissolve the corporation by signing a certificate of dissolution that recites the ground or grounds for dissolution and its effective date. The secretary of state shall file the original of the certificate and serve a copy on the corporation under section 5.04.

(c) A corporation administratively dissolved continues its corporate existence but may not carry on business except that necessary to wind up and liquidate its business and affairs under section 14.05 and notify claimants under sections 14.06 and 14.07.

(d) The administrative dissolution of a corporation does not terminate the authority of its registered agent.

§ 14.22. Reinstatement Following Administrative Dissolution

(a) A corporation administratively dissolved under section 14.21 may apply to the secretary of state for reinstatement within two years after the effective date of dissolution. The application must:
  (1) recite the name of the corporation and the effective date of its administrative dissolution;
  (2) state that the ground or grounds for dissolution either did not exist or have been eliminated;
  (3) state that the corporation's name satisfies the requirements of section 4.01; and
  (4) contain a certificate from the [taxing authority] reciting that all taxes owed by the corporation have been paid.

(b) If the secretary of state determines that the application contains the information required by subsection (a) and that the information is correct, he shall cancel the certificate of dissolution and prepare a certificate of reinstatement that recites his determination and the effective date of reinstatement, file the original of the certificate, and serve a copy on the corporation under section 5.04.

(c) When the reinstatement is effective, it relates back to and takes effect as of the effective date of the administrative dissolution and the corporation resumes carrying on its business as if the administrative dissolution had never occurred.

§ 14.23. Appeal from Denial of Reinstatement

(a) If the secretary of state denies a corporation's application for reinstatement following administrative dissolution, he shall serve the corporation under section 5.04 with a written notice that explains the reason or reasons for denial.

(b) The corporation may appeal the denial of reinstatement to the [name or describe] court within 30 days after service of the notice of denial is perfected. The corporation appeals by petitioning the court to set aside the dissolution and attaching to the petition copies of the secretary of state's certificate of dissolution, the corporation's application for reinstatement, and the secretary of state's notice of denial.

(c) The court may summarily order the secretary of state to reinstate the dissolved corporation or may take other action the court considers appropriate.

(d) The court's final decision may be appealed as in other civil proceedings.

Judicial Dissolution

§ 14.30. Grounds for Judicial Dissolution

The [name or describe court or courts] may dissolve a corporation:

(1) in a proceeding by the attorney general if it is established that:
  (i) the corporation obtained its articles of incorporation through fraud; or
  (ii) the corporation has continued to exceed or abuse the authority conferred upon it by law;

(2) in a proceeding by a shareholder if it is established that:
  (i) the directors are deadlocked in the management of the corporate affairs, the shareholders are unable to break the deadlock, and irreparable injury to the corporation is threatened or being suffered, or the business and affairs of the corporation can no longer be conducted to the advantage of the shareholders generally, because of the deadlock;
  (ii) the directors or those in control of the corporation have acted, are acting, or will act in a manner that is illegal, oppressive, or fraudulent;
  (iii) the shareholders are deadlocked in voting power and have failed, for a period that includes at least two consecutive annual meeting dates, to elect successors to directors whose terms have expired; or
  (iv) the corporate assets are being misapplied or wasted;

(3) in a proceeding by a creditor if it is established that:
  (i) the creditor's claim has been reduced to judgment, the execution on the judgment returned unsatisfied, and the corporation is insolvent; or
  (ii) the corporation has admitted in writing that the creditor's claim is due and owing and the corporation is insolvent; or

(4) in a proceeding by the corporation to have its voluntary dissolution continued under court supervision.

§ 14.31. Procedure for Judical Dissolution

(a) Venue for a proceeding by the attorney general to dissolve a corporation lies in [name the county or counties]. Venue for a proceeding brought by any other party named in section 14.30 lies in the county where a corporation's principal office (or, if none in this state, its registered office) is or was last located.

(b) It is not necessary to make shareholders parties to a proceeding to dissolve a corporation unless relief is sought against them individually.

(c) A court in a proceeding brought to dissolve a corporation may issue injunctions, appoint a receiver or custodian pendente lite with all powers and duties the court directs, take other action required to preserve the corporate assets wherever located, and carry on the business of the corporation until a full hearing can be held.

§ 14.32. Receivership or Custodianship
(a) A court in a judicial proceeding brought to dissolve a corporation may appoint one or more receivers to wind up and liquidate, or one or more custodians to manage, the business and affairs of the corporation. The court shall hold a hearing, after notifying all parties to the proceeding and any interested persons designated by the court, before appointing a receiver or custodian. The court appointing a receiver or custodian has exclusive jurisdiction over the corporation and all of its property wherever located.
(b) The court may appoint an individual or a domestic or foreign corporation (authorized to transact business in this state) as a receiver or custodian. The court may require the receiver or custodian to post bond, with or without sureties, in an amount the court directs.
(c) The court shall describe the powers and duties of the receiver or custodian in its appointing order, which may be amended from time to time. Among other powers:
(1) the receiver (i) may dispose of all or any part of the assets of the corporation wherever located, at a public or private sale, if authorized by the court; and (ii) may sue and defend in his own name as receiver of the corporation in all courts of this state;
(2) the custodian may exercise all of the powers of the corporation, through or in place of its board of directors or officers, to the extent necessary to manage the affairs of the corporation in the best interests of its shareholders and creditors.
(d) The court during a receivership may redesignate the receiver a custodian, and during a custodianship may redesignate the custodian a receiver, if doing so is in the best interests of the corporation, its shareholders, and creditors.
(e) The court from time to time during the receivership or custodianship may order compensation paid and expense disbursements or reimbursements made to the receiver or custodian and his counsel from the assets of the corporation or proceeds from the sale of the assets.

§ 14.33. Decree of Dissolution
(a) If after a hearing the court determines that one or more grounds for judicial dissolution described in section 14.30 exist, it may enter a decree dissolving the corporation and specifying the effective date of the dissolution, and the clerk of the court shall deliver a certified copy of the decree to the secretary of state, who shall file it.
(b) After entering the decree of dissolution, the court shall direct the winding up and liquidation of the corporation's business and affairs in accordance with section 14.05 and the notification of claimants in accordance with sections 14.06 and 14.07.

Miscellaneous
§ 14.40. Deposit with State Treasurer
Assets of a dissolved corporation that should be transferred to a creditor, claimant, or shareholder of the corporation who cannot be found or who is not competent to receive them shall be reduced to cash and deposited with the state treasurer or other appropriate state official for safekeeping. When the creditor, claimant, or shareholder furnishes satisfactory proof of entitlement to the amount deposited, the state treasurer or other appropriate state official shall pay him or his representative that amount.

CHAPTER 15 FOREIGN CORPORATIONS

Certificate of Authority
§ 15.01. Authority to Transact Business Required
(a) A foreign corporation may not transact business in this state until it obtains a certificate of authority from the secretary of state.
(b) The following activities, among others, do not constitute transacting business within the meaning of subsection (a):
(1) maintaining, defending, or settling any proceeding;
(2) holding meetings of the board of directors or shareholders or carrying on other activities concerning internal corporate affairs;
(3) maintaining bank accounts;
(4) maintaining offices or agencies for the transfer, exchange, and registration of the corporation's own securities or maintaining trustees or depositaries with respect to those securities;
(5) selling through independent contractors;
(6) soliciting or obtaining orders, whether by mail or through employees or agents or otherwise, if the orders require acceptance outside this state before they become contracts;
(7) creating or acquiring indebtedness, mortgages, and security interests in real or personal property;
(8) securing or collecting debts or enforcing mortgages and security interests in property securing the debts;

(9) owning, without more, real or personal property;
(10) conducting an isolated transaction that is completed within 30 days and that is not one in the course of repeated transactions of a like nature;
(11) transacting business in interstate commerce.
(c) The list of activities in subsection (b) is not exhaustive.

§ 15.02. Consequences of Transacting Business without Authority

(a) A foreign corporation transacting business in this state without a certificate of authority may not maintain a proceeding in any court in this state until it obtains a certificate of authority.
(b) The successor to a foreign corporation that transacted business in this state without a certificate of authority and the assignee of a cause of action arising out of that business may not maintain a proceeding based on that cause of action in any court in this state until the foreign corporation or its successor obtains a certificate of authority.
(c) A court may stay a proceeding commenced by a foreign corporation, its successor, or assignee until it determines whether the foreign corporation or its successor requires a certificate of authority. If it so determines, the court may further stay the proceeding until the foreign corporation or its successor obtains the certificate.
(d) A foreign corporation is liable for a civil penalty of $_____ for each day, but not to exceed a total of $_____ for each year, it transacts business in this state without a certificate of authority. The attorney general may collect all penalties due under this subsection.
(e) Notwithstanding subsections (a) and (b), the failure of a foreign corporation to obtain a certificate of authority does not impair the validity of its corporate acts or prevent it from defending any proceeding in this state.

§ 15.03. Application for Certificate of Authority

(a) A foreign corporation may apply for a certificate of authority to transact business in this state by delivering an application to the secretary of state for filing. The application must set forth:
(1) the name of the foreign corporation or, if its name is unavailable for use in this state, a corporate name that satisfies the requirements of section 15.06;
(2) the name of the state or country under whose law it is incorporated;
(3) its date of incorporation and period of duration;
(4) the street address of its principal office;
(5) the address of its registered office in this state and the name of its registered agent at that office; and
(6) the names and usual business addresses of its current directors and officers.
(b) The foreign corporation shall deliver with the completed application a certificate of existence (or a document of similar import) duly authenticated by the secretary of state or other official having custody of corporate records in the state or country under whose law it is incorporated.

§ 15.04. Amended Certificate of Authority

(a) A foreign corporation authorized to transact business in this state must obtain an amended certificate of authority from the secretary of state if it changes:
(1) its corporate name;
(2) the period of its duration; or
(3) the state or country of its incorporation.
(b) The requirements of section 15.03 for obtaining an original certificate of authority apply to obtaining an amended certificate under this section.

§ 15.05. Effect of Certificate of Authority

(a) A certificate of authority authorizes the foreign corporation to which it is issued to transact business in this state subject, however, to the right of the state to revoke the certificate as provided in this Act.
(b) A foreign corporation with a valid certificate of authority has the same but no greater rights and has the same but no greater privileges as, and except as otherwise provided by this Act is subject to the same duties, restrictions, penalties, and liabilities now or later imposed on, a domestic corporation of like character.
(c) This Act does not authorize this state to regulate the organization or internal affairs of a foreign corporation authorized to transact business in this state.

§ 15.06. Corporate Name of Foreign Corporation

(a) If the corporate name of a foreign corporation does not satisfy the requirements of section 4.01, the foreign corporation to obtain or maintain a certificate of authority to transact business in this state:
(1) may add the word "corporation," "incorporated," "company," or "limited," or the abbreviation "corp.," "inc.," "co.," or "ltd.," to its corporate name for use in this state; or
(2) may use a fictitious name to transact business in this state if its real name is unavailable and it

delivers to the secretary of state for filing a copy of the resolution of its board of directors, certified by its secretary, adopting the fictitious name.

(b) Except as authorized by subsections (c) and (d), the corporate name (including a fictitious name) of a foreign corporation must be distinguishable upon the records of the secretary of state from:

(1) the corporate name of a corporation incorporated or authorized to transact business in this state;

(2) a corporate name reserved or registered under section 4.02 or 4.03;

(3) the fictitious name of another foreign corporation authorized to transact business in this state; and

(4) the corporate name of a not-for-profit corporation incorporated or authorized to transact business in this state.

(c) A foreign corporation may apply to the secretary of state for authorization to use in this state the name of another corporation (incorporated or authorized to transact business in this state) that is not distinguishable upon his records from the name applied for. The secretary of state shall authorize use of the name applied for if:

(1) the other corporation consents to the use in writing and submits an undertaking in form satisfactory to the secretary of state to change its name to a name that is distinguishable upon the records of the secretary of state from the name of the applying corporation; or

(2) the applicant delivers to the secretary of state a certified copy of a final judgment of a court of competent jurisdiction establishing the applicant's right to use the name applied for in this state.

(d) A foreign corporation may use in this state the name (including the fictitious name) of another domestic or foreign corporation that is used in this state if the other corporation is incorporated or authorized to transact business in this state and the foreign corporation:

(1) has merged with the other corporation;

(2) has been formed by reorganization of the other corporation; or

(3) has acquired all or substantially all of the assets, including the corporate name, of the other corporation.

(e) If a foreign corporation authorized to transact business in this state changes its corporate name to one that does not satisfy the requirements of section 4.01, it may not transact business in this state under the changed name until it adopts a name satisfying the requirements of section 4.01 and obtains an amended certificate of authority under section 15.04.

§ 15.07. Registered Office and Registered Agent of Foreign Corporation

Each foreign corporation authorized to transact business in this state must continuously maintain in this state:

(1) a registered office that may be the same as any of its places of business; and

(2) a registered agent, who may be:

(i) an individual who resides in this state and whose business office is identical with the registered office;

(ii) a domestic corporation or not-for-profit domestic corporation whose business office is identical with the registered office; or

(iii) a foreign corporation or foreign not-for-profit corporation authorized to transact business in this state whose business office is identical with the registered office.

§ 15.08. Change of Registered Office or Registered Agent of Foreign Corporation

(a) A foreign corporation authorized to transact business in this state may change its registered office or registered agent by delivering to the secretary of state for filing a statement of change that sets forth:

(1) its name;

(2) the street address of its current registered office;

(3) if the current registered office is to be changed, the street address of its new registered office;

(4) the name of its current registered agent;

(5) if the current registered agent is to be changed, the name of its new registered agent and the new agent's written consent (either on the statement or attached to it) to the appointment; and

(6) that after the change or changes are made, the street addresses of its registered office and the business office of its registered agent will be identical.

(b) If a registered agent changes the street address of his business office, he may change the street address of the registered office of any foreign corporation for which he is the registered agent by notifying the corporation in writing of the change and signing (either manually or in facsimile) and delivering to the secretary of state for filing a statement of change that complies with the requirements of subsection (a) and recites that the corporation has been notified of the change.

§ 15.09. Resignation of Registered Agent of Foreign Corporation

(a) The registered agent of a foreign corporation may resign his agency appointment by signing and delivering to the secretary of state for filing the original and two exact or conformed copies of a statement of resignation. The statement of resignation may include a statement that the registered office is also discontinued.

(b) After filing the statement, the secretary of state shall attach the filing receipt to one copy and mail the copy and receipt to the registered office if not discontinued. The secretary of state shall mail the other copy to the foreign corporation at its principal office address shown in its most recent annual report.

(c) The agency appointment is terminated, and the registered office discontinued if so provided, on the 31st day after the date on which the statement was filed.

§ 15.10. Service on Foreign Corporation

(a) The registered agent of a foreign corporation authorized to transact business in this state is the corporation's agent for service of process, notice, or demand required or permitted by law to be served on the foreign corporation.

(b) A foreign corporation may be served by registered or certified mail, return receipt requested, addressed to the secretary of the foreign corporation at its principal office shown in its application for a certificate of authority or in its most recent annual report if the foreign corporation:

(1) has no registered agent or its registered agent cannot with reasonable diligence be served;

(2) has withdrawn from transacting business in this state under section 15.20; or

(3) has had its certificate of authority revoked under section 15.31.

(c) Service is perfected under subsection (b) at the earliest of:

(1) the date the foreign corporation receives the mail;

(2) the date shown on the return receipt, if signed on behalf of the foreign corporation; or

(3) five days after its deposit in the United States Mail, as evidenced by the postmark, if mailed postpaid and correctly addressed.

(d) This section does not prescribe the only means, or necessarily the required means, of serving a foreign corporation.

Withdrawal

§ 15.20. Withdrawal of Foreign Corporation

(a) A foreign corporation authorized to transact business in this state may not withdraw from this state until it obtains a certificate of withdrawal from the secretary of state.

(b) A foreign corporation authorized to transact business in this state may apply for a certificate of withdrawal by delivering an application to the secretary of state for filing. The application must set forth:

(1) the name of the foreign corporation and the name of the state or country under whose law it is incorporated;

(2) that it is not transacting business in this state and that it surrenders its authority to transact business in this state;

(3) that it revokes the authority of its registered agent to accept service on its behalf and appoints the secretary of state as its agent for service of process in any proceeding based on a cause of action arising during the time it was authorized to transact business in this state;

(4) a mailing address to which the secretary of state may mail a copy of any process served on him under subdivision (3); and

(5) a commitment to notify the secretary of state in the future of any change in its mailing address.

(c) After the withdrawal of the corporation is effective, service of process on the secretary of state under this section is service on the foreign corporation. Upon receipt of process, the secretary of state shall mail a copy of the process to the foreign corporation at the mailing address set forth under subsection (b).

Revocation of Certificate of Authority

§ 15.30. Grounds for Revocation

The secretary of state may commence a proceeding under section 15.31 to revoke the certificate of authority of a foreign corporation authorized to transact business in this state if:

(1) the foreign corporation does not deliver its annual report to the secretary of state within 60 days after it is due;

(2) the foreign corporation does not pay within 60 days after they are due any franchise taxes or penalties imposed by this Act or other law;

(3) the foreign corporation is without a registered agent or registered office in this state for 60 days or more;

(4) the foreign corporation does not inform the secretary of state under section 15.08 or 15.09 that its registered agent or registered office has changed, that its registered agent has resigned, or that its registered office has been discontinued within 60 days of the change, resignation, or discontinuance;

(5) an incorporator, director, officer, or agent of the foreign corporation signed a document he knew was false in any material respect with intent that the document be delivered to the secretary of state for filing;

(6) the secretary of state receives a duly authenticated certificate from the secretary of state or other official having custody of corporate records in the state or

country under whose law the foreign corporation is incorporated stating that it has been dissolved or disappeared as the result of a merger.

§ 15.31. Procedure for and Effect of Revocation

(a) If the secretary of state determines that one or more grounds exist under section 15.30 for revocation of a certificate of authority, he shall serve the foreign corporation with written notice of his determination under section 15.10.

(b) If the foreign corporation does not correct each ground for revocation or demonstrate to the reasonable satisfaction of the secretary of state that each ground determined by the secretary of state does not exist within 60 days after service of the notice is perfected under section 15.10, the secretary of state may revoke the foreign corporation's certificate of authority by signing a certificate of revocation that recites the ground or grounds for revocation and its effective date. The secretary of state shall file the original of the certificate and serve a copy on the foreign corporation under section 15.10.

(c) The authority of a foreign corporation to transact business in this state ceases on the date shown on the certificate revoking its certificate of authority.

(d) The secretary of state's revocation of a foreign corporation's certificate of authority appoints the secretary of state the foreign corporation's agent for service of process in any proceeding based on a cause of action which arose during the time the foreign corporation was authorized to transact business in this state. Service of process on the secretary of state under this subsection is service on the foreign corporation. Upon receipt of process, the secretary of state shall mail a copy of the process to the secretary of the foreign corporation at its principal office shown on its most recent annual report or in any subsequent communication received from the corporation stating the current mailing address of its principal office or, if none are on file, in its application for a certificate of authority.

(e) Revocation of a foreign corporation's certificate of authority does not terminate the authority of the registered agent of the corporation.

§ 15.32. Appeal from Revocation

(a) A foreign corporation may appeal the secretary of state's revocation of its certificate of authority to the [name or describe] court within 30 days after service of the certificate of revocation is perfected under section 15.10. The foreign corporation appeals by petitioning the court to set aside the revocation and attaching to the petition copies of its certificate of authority and the secretary of state's certificate of revocation.

(b) The court may summarily order the secretary of state to reinstate the certificate of authority or may take any other action the court considers appropriate.

(c) The court's final decision may be appealed as in other civil proceedings.

CHAPTER 16 RECORDS AND REPORTS

Records

§ 16.01. Corporate Records

(a) A corporation shall keep as permanent records minutes of all meetings of its shareholders and board of directors, a record of all actions taken by the shareholders or board of directors without a meeting, and a record of all actions taken by a committee of the board of directors in place of the board of directors on behalf of the corporation.

(b) A corporation shall maintain appropriate accounting records.

(c) A corporation or its agent shall maintain a record of its shareholders, in a form that permits preparation of a list of the names and addresses of all shareholders, in alphabetical order by class of shares showing the number and class of shares held by each.

(d) A corporation shall maintain its records in written form or in another form capable of conversion into written form within a reasonable time.

(e) A corporation shall keep a copy of the following records at its principal office:

(1) its articles or restated articles of incorporation and all amendments to them currently in effect;

(2) its bylaws or restated bylaws and all amendments to them currently in effect;

(3) resolutions adopted by its board of directors creating one or more classes or series of shares, and fixing their relative rights, preferences, and limitations, if shares issued pursuant to those resolutions are outstanding;

(4) the minutes of all shareholders' meetings, and records of all action taken by shareholders without a meeting, for the past three years;

(5) all written communications to shareholders generally within the past three years, including the financial statements furnished for the past three years under section 16.20;

(6) a list of the names and business addresses of its current directors and officers; and

(7) its most recent annual report delivered to the secretary of state under section 16.22.

§ 16.02. Inspection of Records by Shareholders

(a) A shareholder of a corporation is entitled to inspect and copy, during regular business hours at the corporation's principal office, any of the records of the corporation described in section 16.01(e) if he gives the corporation written notice of his demand at least five business days before the date on which he wishes to inspect and copy.

(b) A shareholder of a corporation is entitled to inspect and copy, during regular business hours at a reasonable location specified by the corporation, any of the following records of the corporation if the shareholder meets the requirements of subsection (c) and gives the corporation written notice of his demand at least five business days before the date on which he wishes to inspect and copy:

(1) excerpts from minutes of any meeting of the board of directors, records of any action of a committee of the board of directors while acting in place of the board of directors on behalf of the corporation, minutes of any meeting of the shareholders, and records of action taken by the shareholders or board of directors without a meeting, to the extent not subject to inspection under section 16.02(a);

(2) accounting records of the corporation; and

(3) the record of shareholders.

(c) A shareholder may inspect and copy the records described in subsection (b) only if:

(1) his demand is made in good faith and for a proper purpose;

(2) he describes with reasonable particularity his purpose and the records he desires to inspect; and

(3) the records are directly connected with his purpose.

(d) The right of inspection granted by this section may not be abolished or limited by a corporation's articles of incorporation or bylaws.

(e) This section does not affect:

(1) the right of a shareholder to inspect records under section 7.20 or, if the shareholder is in litigation with the corporation, to the same extent as any other litigant;

(2) the power of a court, independently of this Act, to compel the production of corporate records for examination.

§ 16.03. Scope of Inspection Right

(a) A shareholder's agent or attorney has the same inspection and copying rights as the shareholder he represents.

(b) The right to copy records under section 16.02 includes, if reasonable, the right to receive copies made by photographic, xerographic, or other means.

(c) The corporation may impose a reasonable charge, covering the costs of labor and material, for copies of any documents provided to the shareholder. The charge may not exceed the estimated cost of production or reproduction of the records.

(d) The corporation may comply with a shareholder's demand to inspect the record of shareholders under section 16.02(b)(3) by providing him with a list of its shareholders that was compiled no earlier than the date of the shareholder's demand.

§ 16.04. Court-Ordered Inspection

(a) If a corporation does not allow a shareholder who complies with section 16.02(a) to inspect and copy any records required by that subsection to be available for inspection, the [name or describe court] of the county where the corporation's principal office (or, if none in this state, its registered office) is located may summarily order inspection and copying of the records demanded at the corporation's expense upon application of the shareholder.

(b) If a corporation does not within a reasonable time allow a shareholder to inspect and copy any other record, the shareholder who complies with section 16.02(b) and (c) may apply to the [name or describe court] in the county where the corporation's principal office (or, if none in this state, its registered office) is located for an order to permit inspection and copying of the records demanded. The court shall dispose of an application under this subsection on an expedited basis.

(c) If the court orders inspection and copying of the records demanded, it shall also order the corporation to pay the shareholder's costs (including reasonable counsel fees) incurred to obtain the order unless the corporation proves that it refused inspection in good faith because it had a reasonable basis for doubt about the right of the shareholder to inspect the records demanded.

(d) If the court orders inspection and copying of the records demanded, it may impose reasonable restrictions on the use or distribution of the records by the demanding shareholder.

Reports

§ 16.20. Financial Statements for Shareholders

(a) A corporation shall furnish its shareholders annual financial statements, which may be consolidated or combined statements of the corporation and one or more of its subsidiaries, as appropriate, that include a balance sheet as of the end of the fiscal year, an income statement for that year, and a statement of changes in shareholders' equity for the year unless that information appears elsewhere in the financial statements. If financial statements are prepared for the corporation on the basis of generally accepted accounting principles, the annual financial statements must also be prepared on that basis.

(b) If the annual financial statements are reported upon by a public accountant, his report must accompany them. If not, the statements must be accompanied by a statement of the president or the person responsible for the corporation's accounting records:

(1) stating his reasonable belief whether the statements were prepared on the basis of generally accepted accounting principles and, if not, describing the basis of preparation; and

(2) describing any respects in which the statements were not prepared on a basis of accounting consistent with the statements prepared for the preceding year.

(c) A corporation shall mail the annual financial statements to each shareholder within 120 days after the close of each fiscal year. Thereafter, on written request from a shareholder who was not mailed the statements, the corporation shall mail him the latest financial statements.

§ 16.21. Other Reports to Shareholders

(a) If a corporation indemnifies or advances expenses to a director under section 8.51, 8.52, 8.53, or 8.54 in connection with a proceeding by or in the right of the corporation, the corporation shall report the indemnification or advance in writing to the shareholders with or before the notice of the next shareholders' meeting.

(b) If a corporation issues or authorizes the issuance of shares for promissory notes or for promises to render services in the future, the corporation shall report in writing to the shareholders the number of shares authorized or issued, and the consideration received by the corporation, with or before the notice of the next shareholders' meeting.

§ 16.22. Annual Report for Secretary of State

(a) Each domestic corporation, and each foreign corporation authorized to transact business in this state, shall deliver to the secretary of state for filing an annual report that sets forth:

(1) the name of the corporation and the state or country under whose law it is incorporated;

(2) the address of its registered office and the name of its registered agent at that office in this state;

(3) the address of its principal office;

(4) the names and business addresses of its directors and principal officers;

(5) a brief description of the nature of its business;

(6) the total number of authorized shares, itemized by class and series, if any, within each class; and

(7) the total number of issued and outstanding shares, itemized by class and series, if any, within each class.

(b) Information in the annual report must be current as of the date the annual report is executed on behalf of the corporation.

(c) The first annual report must be delivered to the secretary of state between January 1 and April 1 of the year following the calendar year in which a domestic corporation was incorporated or a foreign corporation was authorized to transact business. Subsequent annual reports must be delivered to the secretary of state between January 1 and April 1 of the following calendar years.

(d) If an annual report does not contain the information required by this section, the secretary of state shall promptly notify the reporting domestic or foreign corporation in writing and return the report to it for correction. If the report is corrected to contain the information required by this section and delivered to the secretary of state within 30 days after the effective date of notice, it is deemed to be timely filed.

CHAPTER 17 TRANSITION PROVISIONS

§ 17.01. Application to Existing Domestic Corporations

This Act applies to all domestic corporations in existence on its effective date that were incorporated under any general statute of this state providing for incorporation of corporations for profit if power to amend or repeal the statute under which the corporation was incorporated was reserved.

§ 17.02. Application to Qualified Foreign Corporations

A foreign corporation authorized to transact business in this state on the effective date of this Act is subject to this Act but is not required to obtain a new certificate of authority to transact business under this Act.

§ 17.03. Saving Provisions

(a) Except as provided in subsection (b), the repeal of a statute by this Act does not affect:

(1) the operation of the statute or any action taken under it before its repeal;

(2) any ratification, right, remedy, privilege, obligation, or liability acquired, accrued, or incurred under the statute before its repeal;

(3) any violation of the statute, or any penalty, forfeiture, or punishment incurred because of the violation, before its repeal;

(4) any proceeding, reorganization, or dissolution commenced under the statute before its repeal, and the proceeding, reorganization, or dissolution may be completed in accordance with the statute as if it had not been repealed.

(b) If a penalty or punishment imposed for violation of a statute repealed by this Act is reduced by this Act, the penalty or punishment if not already imposed shall be imposed in accordance with this Act.

§ 17.04. Severability
If any provision of this Act or its application to any person or circumstance is held invalid by a court of competent jurisdiction, the invalidity does not affect other provisions or applications of the Act that can be given effect without the invalid provision or application, and to this end the provisions of the Act are severable.

§ 17.05. Repeal
The following laws and parts of laws are repealed: [to be inserted].

§ 17.06. Effective Date
This Act takes effect _____.

APPENDIX E
MODEL STATUTORY CLOSE CORPORATION SUPPLEMENT

Creation
§ 1. Short Title
2. Application of [Model] Business Corporation Act and [Model] Professional Corporation Supplement
3. Definition and Election of Statutory Close Corporation Status

Shares
§ 10. Notice of Statutory Close Corporation Status on Issued Shares
11. Share Transfer Prohibition
12. Share Transfer after First Refusal by Corporation
13. Attempted Share Transfer in Breach of Prohibition
14. Compulsory Purchase of Shares after Death of Shareholder
15. Exercise of Compulsory Purchase Right
16. Court Action to Compel Purchase
17. Court Costs and Other Expenses

Governance
§ 20. Shareholder Agreements
21. Elimination of Board of Directors
22. Bylaws
23. Annual Meeting
24. Execution of Documents in More than One Capacity
25. Limited Liability

Reorganization and Termination
§ 30. Merger, Share Exchange, and Sale of Assets
31. Termination of Statutory Close Corporation Status
32. Effect of Termination of Statutory Close Corporation Status
33. Shareholder Option to Dissolve Corporation

Judicial Supervision
§ 40. Court Action to Protect Shareholders
41. Ordinary Relief
42. Extraordinary Relief: Share Purchase
43. Extraordinary Relief: Dissolution

Transition Provisions
§ 50. Application to Existing Corporations
51. Reservation of Power to Amend or Repeal
52. Saving Provisions
53. Severability
54. Repeal
55. Effective Date

Creation

§ 1. Short Title

This Supplement shall be known and may be cited as the "[name of state] Statutory Close Corporation Supplement."

§ 2. Application of [Model] Business Corporation Act and [Model] Professional Corporation Supplement

(a) The [Model] Business Corporation Act applies to statutory close corporations to the extent not inconsistent with the provisions of this Supplement.

(b) This Supplement applies to a professional corporation organized under the [Model] Professional Corporation Supplement whose articles of incorporation contain the statement required by section 3(a), except insofar as the [Model] Professional Corporation Supplement contains inconsistent provisions.

(c) This Supplement does not repeal or modify any statute or rule of law that is or would apply to a corporation that is organized under the [Model] Business Corporation Act or the [Model] Professional Corporation Supplement and that does not elect to become a statutory close corporation under section 3.

§ 3. Definition and Election of Statutory Close Corporation Status

(a) A statutory close corporation is a corporation whose articles of incorporation contain a statement that the corporation is a statutory close corporation.

(b) A corporation having 50 or fewer shareholders may become a statutory close corporation by amending its articles of incorporation to include the statement required by subsection (a). The amendment must be approved by the holders of at least two-thirds of the votes of each class or series of shares of the corporation, voting as separate voting groups, whether or not otherwise entitled to vote on amendments. If the amendment is adopted, a shareholder who voted against the amendment is entitled to assert dissenters' rights under [MBCA ch. 13].

Shares
§ 10. Notice of Statutory Close Corporation Status on Issued Shares

(a) The following statement must appear conspicuously on each share certificate issued by a statutory close corporation:

> The rights of shareholders in a statutory close corporation may differ materially from the rights of shareholders in other corporations. Copies of the articles of incorporation and bylaws, shareholders' agreements, and other documents, any of which may restrict transfers and affect voting and other rights, may be obtained by a shareholder on written request to the corporation.

(b) Within a reasonable time after the issuance or transfer of uncertificated shares, the corporation shall send to the shareholders a written notice containing the information required by subsection (a).

(c) The notice required by this section satisfies all requirements of this Act and of [MBCA § 6.27] that notice of share transfer restrictions be given.

(d) A person claiming an interest in shares of a statutory close corporation which has complied with the notice requirement of this section is bound by the documents referred to in the notice. A person claiming an interest in shares of a statutory close corporation which has not complied with the notice requirement of this section is bound by any documents of which he, or a person through whom he claims, has knowledge or notice.

(e) A corporation shall provide to any shareholder upon his written request and without charge copies of provisions that restrict transfer or affect voting or other rights of shareholders appearing in articles of incorporation, bylaws, or shareholders' or voting trust agreements filed with the corporation.

§ 11. Share Transfer Prohibition

(a) An interest in shares of a statutory close corporation may not be voluntarily or involuntarily transferred, by operation of law or otherwise, except to the extent permitted by the articles of incorporation or under section 12.

(b) Except to the extent the articles of incorporation provide otherwise, this section does not apply to a transfer:

(1) to the corporation or to any other holder of the same class or series of shares;

(2) to members of the shareholder's immediate family (or to a trust, all of whose beneficiaries are members of the shareholder's immediate family), which immediate family consists of his spouse, parents, lineal descendants (including adopted children and stepchildren) and the spouse of any lineal descendant, and brothers and sisters;

(3) that has been approved in writing by all of the holders of the corporation's shares having general voting rights;

(4) to an executor or administrator upon the death of a shareholder or to a trustee or receiver as the result of a bankruptcy, insolvency, dissolution, or similar proceeding brought by or against a shareholder;

(5) by merger or share exchange [under MBCA ch. 11] or an exchange of existing shares for other shares of a different class or series in the corporation;

(6) by a pledge as collateral for a loan that does not grant the pledgee any voting rights possessed by the pledgor;

(7) made after termination of the corporation's status as a statutory close corporation.

§ 12. Share Transfer after First Refusal by Corporation

(a) A person desiring to transfer shares of a statutory close corporation subject to the transfer prohibition of section 11 must first offer them to the corporation by obtaining an offer to purchase the shares for cash from a third person who is eligible to purchase the shares under subsection (b). The offer by the third person must be in writing and state the offeror's name and address, the number and class (or series) of shares offered, the offering price per share, and the other terms of the offer.

(b) A third person is eligible to purchase the shares if:
(1) he is eligible to become a qualified shareholder under any federal or state tax statute the corporation has adopted and he agrees in writing not to terminate his qualification without the approval of the remaining shareholders; and
(2) his purchase of the shares will not impose a personal holding company tax or similar federal or state penalty tax on the corporation.
(c) The person desiring to transfer shares shall deliver the offer to the corporation, and by doing so offers to sell the shares to the corporation on the terms of the offer. Within 20 days after the corporation receives the offer, the corporation shall call a special shareholders' meeting, to be held not more than 40 days after the call, to decide whether the corporation should purchase all (but not less than all) of the offered shares. The offer must be approved by the affirmative vote of the holders of a majority of votes entitled to be cast at the meeting, excluding votes in respect of the shares covered by the offer.
(d) The corporation must deliver to the offering shareholder written notice of acceptance within 75 days after receiving the offer or the offer is rejected. If the corporation makes a counteroffer, the shareholder must deliver to the corporation written notice of acceptance within 15 days after receiving the counteroffer or the counteroffer is rejected. If the corporation accepts the original offer or the shareholder accepts the corporation's counteroffer, the shareholder shall deliver to the corporation duly endorsed certificates for the shares, or instruct the corporation in writing to transfer the shares if uncertificated, within 20 days after the effective date of the notice of acceptance. The corporation may specifically enforce the shareholder's delivery or instruction obligation under this subsection.
(e) A corporation accepting an offer to purchase shares under this section may allocate some or all of the shares to one or more of its shareholders or to other persons if all the shareholders voting in favor of the purchase approve the allocation. If the corporation has more than one class (or series) of shares, however, the remaining holders of the class (or series) of shares being purchased are entitled to a first option to purchase the shares not purchased by the corporation in proportion to their shareholdings or in some other proportion agreed to by all the shareholders participating in the purchase.
(f) If an offer to purchase shares under this section is rejected, the offering shareholder, for a period of 120 days after the corporation received his offer, is entitled to transfer to the third person offeror all (but not less than all) of the offered shares in accordance with the terms of his offer to the corporation.

§ 13. Attempted Share Transfer in Breach of Prohibition

(a) An attempt to transfer shares in a statutory close corporation in violation of a prohibition against transfer binding on the transferee is ineffective.
(b) An attempt to transfer shares in a statutory close corporation in violation of a prohibition against transfer that is not binding on the transferee, either because the notice required by section 10 was not given or because the prohibition is held unenforceable by a court, gives the corporation an option to purchase the shares from the transferee for the same price and on the same terms that he purchased them. To exercise its option, the corporation must give the transferee written notice within 30 days after they are presented for registration in the transferee's name. The corporation may specifically enforce the transferee's sale obligation upon exercise of its purchase option.

§ 14. Compulsory Purchase of Shares after Death of Shareholder

(a) This section, and sections 15 through 17, apply to a statutory close corporation only if so provided in its articles of incorporation. If these sections apply, the executor or administrator of the estate of a deceased shareholder may require the corporation to purchase or cause to be purchased all (but not less than all) of the decedent's shares or to be dissolved.
(b) The provisions of sections 15 through 17 may be modified only if the modification is set forth or referred to in the articles of incorporation.
(c) An amendment to the articles of incorporation to provide for application of sections 15 through 17, or to modify or delete the provisions of these sections, must be approved by the holders of at least two-thirds of the votes of each class or series of shares of the statutory close corporation, voting as separate voting groups, whether or not otherwise entitled to vote on amendments. If the corporation has no shareholders when the amendment is proposed, it must be approved by at least two-thirds of the subscribers for shares, if any, or, if none, by all of the incorporators.
(d) A shareholder who votes against an amendment to modify or delete the provisions of sections 15 through 17 is entitled to dissenters' rights under [MBCA chapter 13] if the amendment upon adoption terminates or substantially alters his existing rights under these sections to have his shares purchased.
(e) A shareholder may waive his and his estate's rights under sections 15 through 17 by a signed writing.
(f) Sections 15 through 17 do not prohibit any other agreement providing for the purchase of shares upon a shareholder's death, nor do they prevent a shareholder from enforcing any remedy he has independently of these sections.

§ 15. Exercise of Compulsory Purchase Right

(a) A person entitled and desiring to exercise the compulsory purchase right described in section 14 must deliver a written notice to the corporation, within 120 days after the death of the shareholder, describing the number and class or series of shares beneficially owned by the decedent and requesting that the corporation offer to purchase the shares.

(b) Within 20 days after the effective date of the notice, the corporation shall call a special shareholders' meeting, to be held not more than 40 days after the call, to decide whether the corporation should offer to purchase the shares. A purchase offer must be approved by the affirmative vote of the holders of a majority of votes entitled to be cast at the meeting, excluding votes in respect of the shares covered by the notice.

(c) The corporation must deliver a purchase offer to the person requesting it within 75 days after the effective date of the request notice. A purchase offer must be accompanied by the corporation's balance sheet as of the end of a fiscal year ending not more than 16 months before the effective date of the request notice, an income statement for that year, a statement of changes in shareholders' equity for that year, and the latest available interim financial statements, if any. The person must accept the purchase offer in writing within 15 days after receiving it or the offer is rejected.

(d) A corporation agreeing to purchase shares under this section may allocate some or all of the shares to one or more of its shareholders or to other persons if all the shareholders voting in favor of the purchase offer approve the allocation. If the corporation has more than one class or series of shares, however, the remaining holders of the class or series of shares being purchased are entitled to a first option to purchase the shares not purchased by the corporation in proportion to their shareholdings or in some other proportion agreed to by all the shareholders participating in the purchase.

(e) If price and other terms of a compulsory purchase of shares are fixed or are to be determined by the articles of incorporation, bylaws, or a written agreement, the price and terms so fixed or determined govern the compulsory purchase unless the purchaser defaults, in which event the buyer is entitled to commence a proceeding for dissolution under section 16.

§ 16. Court Action to Compel Purchase

(a) If an offer to purchase shares made under section 15 is rejected, or if no offer is made, the person exercising the compulsory purchase right may commence a proceeding against the corporation to compel the purchase in the [name or describe] court of the county where the corporation's principal office (or, if none in this state, its registered office) is located. The corporation at its expense shall notify in writing all of its shareholders, and any other person the court directs, of the commencement of the proceeding. The jurisdiction of the court in which the proceeding is commenced under this subsection is plenary and exclusive.

(b) The court shall determine the fair value of the shares subject to compulsory purchase in accordance with the standards set forth in section 42 together with terms for the purchase. Upon making these determinations the court shall order the corporation to purchase or cause the purchase of the shares or empower the person exercising the compulsory purchase right to have the corporation dissolved.

(c) After the purchase order is entered, the corporation may petition the court to modify the terms of purchase and the court may do so if it finds that changes in the financial or legal ability of the corporation or other purchaser to complete the purchase justify a modification.

(d) If the corporation or other purchaser does not make a payment required by the court's order within 30 days of its due date, the seller may petition the court to dissolve the corporation and, absent a showing of good cause for not making the payment, the court shall do so.

(e) A person making a payment to prevent or cure a default by the corporation or other purchaser is entitled to recover the payment from the defaulter.

§ 17. Court Costs and Other Expenses

(a) The court in a proceeding commenced under section 16 shall determine the total costs of the proceeding, including the reasonable compensation and expenses of appraisers appointed by the court and of counsel and experts employed by the parties. Except as provided in subsection (b), the court shall assess these costs equally against the corporation and the party exercising the compulsory purchase right.

(b) The court may assess all or a portion of the total costs of the proceeding:

(1) against the person exercising the compulsory purchase right if the court finds that the fair value of the shares does not substantially exceed the corporation's last purchase offer made before commencement of the proceeding and that the person's failure to accept the offer was arbitrary, vexatious, or otherwise not in good faith; or

(2) against the corporation if the court finds that the fair value of the shares substantially exceeds

the corporation's last sale offer made before commencement of the proceeding and that the offer was arbitrary, vexatious, or otherwise not made in good faith.

Governance
§ 20. Shareholder Agreements
(a) All the shareholders of a statutory close corporation may agree in writing to regulate the exercise of the corporate powers and the management of the business and affairs of the corporation or the relationship among the shareholders of the corporation.

(b) An agreement authorized by this section is effective although:
- (1) it eliminates a board of directors;
- (2) it restricts the discretion or powers of the board or authorizes director proxies or weighted voting rights;
- (3) its effect is to treat the corporation as a partnership; or
- (4) it creates a relationship among the shareholders or between the shareholders and the corporation that would otherwise be appropriate only among partners.

(c) If the corporation has a board of directors, an agreement authorized by this section restricting the discretion or powers of the board relieves directors of liability imposed by law, and imposes that liability on each person in whom the board's discretion or power is vested, to the extent that the discretion or powers of the board of directors are governed by the agreement.

(d) A provision eliminating a board of directors is an agreement authorized by this section is not effective unless the articles of incorporation contain a statement to that effect as required by section 21.

(e) A provision entitling one or more shareholders to dissolve the corporation under section 33 is effective only if a statement of this right is contained in the articles of incorporation.

(f) To amend an agreement authorized by this section, all the shareholders must approve the amendment in writing unless the agreement provides otherwise.

(g) Subscribers for shares may act as shareholders with respect to an agreement authorized by this section if shares are not issued when the agreement was made.

(h) This section does not prohibit any other agreement between or among shareholders in a statutory close corporation.

§ 21. Elimination of Board of Directors
(a) A statutory close corporation may operate without a board of directors if its articles of incorporation contain a statement to that effect.

(b) An amendment to articles of incorporation eliminating a board of directors must be approved by all the shareholders of the corporation, whether or not otherwise entitled to vote on amendments, or if no shares have been issued, by all the subscribers for shares, if any, or if none, by all the incorporators.

(c) While a corporation is operating without a board of directors as authorized by subsection (a):
- (1) all corporate powers shall be exercised by or under the authority of, and the business and affairs of the corporation managed under the direction of, the shareholders;
- (2) unless the articles of incorporation provide otherwise, (i) action requiring director approval or both director and shareholder approval is authorized if approved by the shareholders and (ii) action requiring a majority or greater percentage vote of the board of directors is authorized if approved by the majority or greater percentage of the votes of shareholders entitled to vote on the action;
- (3) a shareholder is not liable for his act or omission, although a director would be, unless the shareholder was entitled to vote on the action;
- (4) a requirement by a state or the United States that a document delivered for filing contain a statement that specified action has been taken by the board of directors is satisfied by a statement that the corporation is a statutory close corporation without a board of directors and that the action was approved by the shareholders;
- (5) the shareholders by resolution may appoint one or more shareholders to sign documents as "designated directors."

(d) An amendment to articles of incorporation deleting the statement eliminating a board of directors must be approved by the holders of at least two-thirds of the votes of each class or series of shares of the corporation, voting as separate voting groups, whether or not otherwise entitled to vote on amendments. The amendment must also specify the number, names, and addresses of the corporation's directors or describe who will perform the duties of a board under [MBCA § 8.01].

§ 22. Bylaws
(a) A statutory close corporation need not adopt bylaws if provisions required by law to be contained in bylaws are contained in either the articles of incorporation or a shareholder agreement authorized by section 20.

(b) If a corporation does not have bylaws when its statutory close corporation status terminates under section 31, the corporation shall immediately adopt bylaws under [MBCA § 2.06].

§ 23. Annual Meeting

(a) The annual meeting date for a statutory close corporation is the first business day after May 31st unless its articles of incorporation, bylaws, or a shareholder agreement authorized by section 20 fixes a different date.

(b) A statutory close corporation need not hold an annual meeting unless one or more shareholders deliver written notice to the corporation requesting a meeting at least 30 days before the meeting date determined under subsection (a).

§ 24. Execution of Documents in More than One Capacity

Notwithstanding any law to the contrary, an individual who holds more than one office in a statutory close corporation may execute, acknowledge, or verify in more than one capacity any document required to be executed, acknowledged, or verified by the holders of two or more offices.

§ 25. Limited Liability

The failure of a statutory close corporation to observe the usual corporate formalities or requirements relating to the exercise of its corporate powers or management of its business and affairs is not a ground for imposing personal liability on the shareholders for liabilities of the corporation.

Reorganization and Termination

§ 30. Merger, Share Exchange, and Sale of Assets

(a) A plan of merger or share exchange:

(1) that if effected would terminate statutory close corporation status must be approved by the holders of at least two-thirds of the votes of each class or series of shares of the statutory close corporation, voting as separate voting groups, whether or not the holders are otherwise entitled to vote on the plan;

(2) that if effected would create the surviving corporation as a statutory close corporation must be approved by the holders of at least two-thirds of the votes of each class or series of shares of the surviving corporation, voting as separate voting groups, whether or not the holders are otherwise entitled to vote on the plan.

(b) A sale, lease, exchange, or other disposition of all or substantially all of the property (with or without the good will) of a statutory close corporation, if not made in the usual and regular course of business, must be approved by the holders of at least two-thirds of the votes of each class or series of shares of the corporation, voting as separate voting groups, whether or not the holders are otherwise entitled to vote on the transaction.

§ 31. Termination of Statutory Close Corporation Status

(a) A statutory close corporation may terminate its statutory close corporation status by amending its articles of incorporation to delete the statement that it is a statutory close corporation. If the statutory close corporation has elected to operate without a board of directors under section 21, the amendment must either comply with [MBCA § 8.01] or delete the statement dispensing with the board of directors from its articles of incorporation.

(b) An amendment terminating statutory close corporation status must be approved by the holders of at least two-thirds of the votes of each class or series of shares of the corporation, voting as separate voting groups, whether or not the holders are otherwise entitled to vote on amendments.

(c) If an amendment to terminate statutory close corporation status is adopted, each shareholder who voted against the amendment is entitled to assert dissenters' rights under [MBCA ch. 13].

§ 32. Effect of Termination of Statutory Close Corporation Status

(a) A corporation that terminates its status as a statutory close corporation is thereafter subject to all provisions of the [Model] Business Corporation Act or, if incorporated under the [Model] Professional Corporation Supplement, to all provisions of that Supplement.

(b) Termination of statutory close corporation status does not affect any right of a shareholder or of the corporation under an agreement or the articles of incorporation unless this Act, the [Model] Business Corporation Act, or another law of this state invalidates the right.

§ 33. Shareholder Option to Dissolve Corporation

(a) The articles of incorporation of a statutory close corporation may authorize one or more shareholders, or the holders of a specified number or percentage of shares of any class or series, to dissolve the corporation at will or upon the occurrence of a specified event or contingency. The shareholder or shareholders exercising this authority must give written notice of the intent to dissolve to all the other shareholders. Thirty-one days after the effective date of the notice, the corporation shall begin to wind up and liquidate its business and affairs and file articles of dissolution under [MBCA sections 14.03 through 14.07].

(b) Unless the articles of incorporation provide otherwise, an amendment to the articles of incorporation to add, change, or delete the authority to dissolve described in subsection (a) must be approved by the holders of all the outstanding shares, whether or not otherwise entitled to vote on amendments, or if no shares have been issued, by all the subscribers for shares, if any, or if none, by all the incorporators.

Judicial Supervision
§ 40. Court Action to Protect Shareholders
(a) Subject to satisfying the conditions of subsections (c) and (d), a shareholder of a statutory close corporation may petition the [name or describe] court for any of the relief described in section 41, 42, or 43 if:
 (1) the directors or those in control of the corporation have acted, or are acting, or will act in a manner that is illegal, oppressive, fraudulent, or unfairly prejudicial to the petitioner, whether in his capacity as shareholder, director, or officer, of the corporation;
 (2) the directors or those in control of the corporation are deadlocked in the management of the corporation's affairs, the shareholders are unable to break the deadlock, and the corporation is suffering or will suffer irreparable injury or the business and affairs of the corporation can no longer be conducted to the advantage of the shareholders generally because of the deadlock; or
 (3) there exists one or more grounds for judicial dissolution of the corporation under [MBCA § 14.30].
(b) A shareholder must commence a proceeding under subsection (a) in the [name or describe] court of the county where the corporation's principal office (or, if none in this state, its registered office) is located. The jurisdiction of the court in which the proceeding is commenced is plenary and exclusive.
(c) If a shareholder has agreed in writing to pursue a nonjudicial remedy to resolve disputed matters, he may not commence a proceeding under this section with respect to the matters until he has exhausted the nonjudicial remedy.
(d) If a shareholder has dissenters' rights under this Act or [MBCA ch. 13] with respect to proposed corporate action, he must commence a proceeding under this section before he is required to give notice of his intent to demand payment under [MBCA § 13.21] or to demand payment under [MBCA § 13.23] or the proceeding is barred.
(e) Except as provided in subsections (c) and (d), a shareholder's right to commence a proceeding under this section and the remedies available under sections 41 through 43 are in addition to any other right or remedy he may have.

§ 41. Ordinary Relief
(a) If the court finds that one or more of the grounds for relief described in section 40(a) exist, it may order one or more of the following types of relief:
 (1) the performance, prohibition, alteration, or setting aside of any action of the corporation or of its shareholders, directors, or officers of or any other party to the proceeding;
 (2) the cancellation or alteration of any provision in the corporation's articles of incorporation or bylaws;
 (3) the removal from office of any director or officer;
 (4) the appointment of any individual as a director or officer;
 (5) an accounting with respect to any matter in dispute;
 (6) the appointment of a custodian to manage the business and affairs of the corporation;
 (7) the appointment of a provisional director (who has all the rights, powers, and duties of a duly elected director) to serve for the term and under the conditions prescribed by the court;
 (8) the payment of dividends;
 (9) the award of damages to any aggrieved party.
(b) If the court finds that a party to the proceeding acted arbitrarily, vexatiously, or otherwise not in good faith, it may award one or more other parties their reasonable expenses, including counsel fees and the expenses of appraisers or other experts, incurred in the proceeding.

§ 42. Extraordinary Relief: Share Purchase
(a) If the court finds that the ordinary relief described in section 41(a) is or would be inadequate or inappropriate, it may order the corporation dissolved under section 43 unless the corporation or one or more of its shareholders purchases all the shares of the shareholder for their fair value and on terms determined under subsection (b).
(b) If the court orders a share purchase, it shall:
 (1) determine the fair value of the shares, considering among other relevant evidence the going concern value of the corporation, any agreement among some or all of the shareholders fixing the price or specifying a formula for determining share value for any purpose, the recommendations of appraisers (if any) appointed by the court, and any legal constraints on the corporation's ability to purchase the shares;

(2) specify the terms of the purchase, including if appropriate terms for installment payments, subordination of the purchase obligation to the rights of the corporation's other creditors, security for a deferred purchase price, and a covenant not to compete or other restriction on the seller;

(3) require the seller to deliver all his shares to the purchaser upon receipt of the purchase price or the first installment of the purchase price;

(4) provide that after the seller delivers his shares he has no further claim against the corporation, its directors, officers, or shareholders, other than a claim to any unpaid balance of the purchase price and a claim under any agreement with the corporation or the remaining shareholders that is not terminated by the court; and

(5) provide that if the purchase is not completed in accordance with the specified terms, the corporation is to be dissolved under section 43.

(c) After the purchase order is entered, any party may petition the court to modify the terms of the purchase and the court may do so if it finds that changes in the financial or legal ability of the corporation or other purchaser to complete the purchase justify a modification.

(d) If the corporation is dissolved because the share purchase was not completed in accordance with the court's order, the selling shareholder has the same rights and priorities in the corporation's assets as if the sale had not been ordered.

§ 43. Extraordinary Relief: Dissolution

(a) The court may dissolve the corporation if it finds:
(1) there are one or more grounds for judicial dissolution under [MBCA § 14.30]; or
(2) all other relief ordered by the court under section 41 or 42 has failed to resolve the matters in dispute.

(b) In determining whether to dissolve the corporation, the court shall consider among other relevant evidence the financial condition of the corporation but may not refuse to dissolve solely because the corporation has accumulated earnings or current operating profits.

Transition Provisions

§ 50. Application to Existing Corporations

(a) This Supplement applies to all corporations electing statutory close corporation status under section 3 after its effective date.

(b) [If Sec. 54 repeals an integrated close corporation statute enacted before this Supplement, this and additional subsections should provide a cutoff date by which corporations qualified under the repealed statute must elect whether to be covered by this Supplement, the procedure for making the election, and the effect of the election on existing agreements among shareholders. Cf. MBCA ch. 17 and Model Professional Corporation Supplement sec. 70.]

§ 51. Reservation of Power to Amend or Repeal

The [name of state legislature] has power to amend or repeal all or part of this Supplement at any time and all corporations subject to this Supplement are governed by the amendment or repeal.

§ 52. Saving Provisions

(a) The repeal of a statute by this Supplement does not affect:
(1) the operation of the statute or any action taken under it before its repeal;
(2) any ratification, right, remedy, privilege, obligation, or liability acquired, accrued, or incurred under the statute before its repeal;
(3) any violation of the statute, or any penalty, forfeiture, or punishment incurred because of the violation, before its repeal;
(4) any proceeding, reorganization, or dissolution commenced under the statute before its repeal, and the proceeding, reorganization, or dissolution may be completed in accordance with the statute as if it had not been repealed.

§ 53. Severability

If any provision of this Supplement or its application to any person or circumstance is held invalid by a court of competent jurisdiction, the invalidity does not affect other provisions or applications of the Supplement that can be given effect without the invalid provision or application, and to this end the provisions of the Supplement are severable.

§ 54. Repeal

The following laws and parts of laws are repealed: _____.

§ 55. Effective Date

This Supplement takes effect _____.

APPENDIX F
MODEL PROFESSIONAL CORPORATION SUPPLEMENT (1984)

General Provisions
- § 1. Short Title
- 2. Application of [Model] Business Corporation Act
- 3. Supplement Definitions

Creation
- § 10. Election of Professional Corporation Status
- 11. Purposes
- 12. General Powers
- 13. Rendering Professional Services
- 14. Prohibited Activities
- 15. Corporate Name

Shares
- § 20. Issuance of Shares
- 21. Notice of Professional Corporation Status on Shares
- 22. Share Transfer Restriction
- 23. Compulsory Acquisition of Shares after Death or Disqualification of Shareholder
- 24. Acquisition Procedure
- 25. Court Action to Appraise Shares
- 26. Court Costs and Fees of Experts
- 27. Cancellation of Disqualified Shares

Governance
- § 30. Directors and Officers
- 31. Voting of Shares
- 32. Confidential Relationship
- 33. Privileged Communications
- 34. Responsibility for Professional Services

Reorganization and Termination
- § 40. Merger
- 41. Termination of Professional [Activities]
- 42. Judicial Dissolution

Foreign Professional Corporations
- § 50. Authority to Transact Business
- 51. Application for Certificate of Authority
- 52. Revocation of Certificate of Authority

Miscellaneous Regulatory Provisions
- § 60. Articles of Incorporation for Licensing Authority
- 61. Annual Qualification Statement for Licensing Authority
- 62. Annual Report for Secretary of State
- 63. Rulemaking by Licensing Authority
- 64. Licensing Authority's Regulatory Jurisdiction
- 65. Penalty for Signing False Document

Transition Provisions
- § 70. Application to Existing Corporations
- 71. Reservation of Power to Amend or Repeal
- 72. Saving Provisions
- 73. Severability
- 74. Repeal
- 75. Effective Date

General Provisions

§ 1. Short Title

This Act shall be known and may be cited as the "[name of state] Professional Corporation Supplement."

§ 2. Application of [Model] Business Corporation Act

The [Model] Business Corporation Act applies to professional corporations, both domestic and foreign, to the extent not inconsistent with the provisions of this Supplement.

§ 3. Supplement Definitions
In this supplement:

(1) "Disqualified person" means an individual or entity that for any reason is or becomes ineligible under this Supplement to be issued shares by a professional corporation.

(2) "Domestic professional corporation" means a professional corporation.

(3) "Foreign professional corporation" means a corporation or association for profit incorporated for the purpose of rendering professional services under a law other than the law of this state.

(4) "Law" includes rules promulgated in accordance with section 63.

(5) "Licensing authority" means the officer, board, agency, court, or other authority in this state empowered to license or otherwise authorize the rendition of a professional service.

(6) "Professional corporation" means a corporation for profit, other than a foreign professional corporation, subject to the provisions of this Supplement.

(7) "Professional service" means a service that may be lawfully rendered only by a person licensed or otherwise authorized by a licensing authority in this state to render the service and that may not be lawfully rendered by a corporation under the [Model] Business Corporation Act.

(8) "Qualified person" means an individual, general partnership, or professional corporation that is eligible under this Supplement to be issued shares by a professional corporation. [*Reviser's note:* the phrase "or professional corporation" should be deleted if Alternative 2 or 3 of section 34(c) or (c) and (d) is chosen.]

Creation

§ 10. Election of Professional Corporation Status

(a) One or more persons may incorporate a professional corporation by delivering to the secretary of state for filing articles of incorporation that state (1) it is a professional corporation and (2) its purpose is to render the specified professional services.

(b) A corporation incorporated under a general law of this state that is not repealed by this Supplement may elect professional corporation status by amending its articles of incorporation to comply with subsection (a) and section 15.

§ 11. Purposes

(a) Except to the extent authorized by subsection (b), a corporation may elect professional corporation status under section 10 solely for the purpose of rendering professional services (including services ancillary to them) and solely within a single profession.

(b) A corporation may elect professional corporation status under section 10 for the purpose of rendering professional services within two or more professions, and for the purpose of engaging in any lawful business authorized by [MBCA § 3.01], to the extent the combination of professional purposes or of professional and business purposes is authorized by the licensing law of this state applicable to each profession in the combination.

§ 12. General Powers

(a) Except as provided in subsection (b), a professional corporation has the powers enumerated in [MBCA § 3.02].

(b) A professional corporation may be a promoter, general partner, member, associate, or manager of a partnership, joint venture, trust, or other entity only if the entity is engaged solely in rendering professional services or in carrying on business authorized by the professional corporation's articles of incorporation.

§ 13. Rendering Professional Services

(a) A domestic or foreign corporation may render professional services in this state only through individuals licensed or otherwise authorized in this state to render the services.

(b) Subsection (a) does not:

(1) require an individual employed by a professional corporation to be licensed to perform services for the corporation if a license is not otherwise required;

(2) prohibit a licensed individual from rendering professional services in his individual capacity although he is a shareholder, director, officer, employee, or agent of a domestic or foreign professional corporation;

(3) prohibit an individual licensed in another state from rendering professional services for a domestic or foreign professional corporation in this state if not prohibited by the licensing authority.

§ 14. Prohibited Activities

(a) A professional corporation may not render any professional service or engage in any business other than the professional service and business authorized by its articles of incorporation.

(b) Subsection (a) does not prohibit a professional corporation from investing its funds in real estate, mortgages, securities, or any other type of investment.

§ 15. Corporate Name

(a) The name of a domestic professional corporation and of a foreign professional corporation authorized to transact business in this state, in addition to satisfying the requirements of [MBCA §§ 4.01 and 15.06]:

(1) must contain the words "professional corporation," "professional association," or "service cor-

poration" or the abbreviation "P.C.," "P.A.," or "S.C.";

(2) may not contain language stating or implying that it is incorporated for a purpose other than that authorized by section 11 and its articles of incorporation; and

(3) must conform with any rule promulgated by the licensing authority having jurisdiction over a professional service described in the corporation's articles of incorporation.

(b) [MBCA §§ 4.01 and 15.06] do not prevent the use of a name otherwise prohibited by those sections if it is the personal name of a shareholder or former shareholder of the domestic or foreign professional corporation or the name of an individual who was associated with a predecessor of the corporation.

Shares

§ 20. Issuance of Shares

(a) A professional corporation may issue shares, fractional shares, and rights or options to purchase shares only to:

(1) individuals who are authorized by law in this or another state to render a professional service described in the corporation's articles of incorporation;

(2) general partnerships in which all the partners are qualified persons with respect to the professional corporation and in which at least one partner is authorized by law in this state to render a professional service described in the corporation's articles of incorporation;

(3) professional corporations, domestic or foreign, authorized by law in this state to render a professional service described in the corporation's articles of incorporation. [*Reviser's note:* Subsection (3) should be deleted if Alternative 2 or 3 of section 34(c) or (c) and (d) is chosen.]

(b) If a licensing authority with jurisdiction over a profession considers it necessary to prevent violation of the ethical standards of the profession, the authority may by rule restrict or condition, or revoke in part, the authority of professional corporations subject to its jurisdiction to issue shares. A rule promulgated under this section does not, of itself, make a shareholder of a professional corporation at the time the rule becomes effective a disqualified person.

(c) Shares issued in violation of this section or a rule promulgated under this section are void.

§ 21. Notice of Professional Corporation Status on Shares

(a) The following statement must appear conspicuously on each share certificate issued by a professional corporation:

The transfer of shares of a professional corporation is restricted by the [Model Professional Corporation Supplement] and is subject to further restriction imposed from time to time by the licensing authority. Shares of a professional corporation are also subject to a statutory compulsory repurchase obligation.

(b) Within a reasonable time after the issuance or transfer of uncertificated shares of a professional corporation, the corporation shall send the shareholders a written notice containing the statement required by subsection (a).

§ 22. Share Transfer Restriction

(a) A shareholder of a professional corporation may transfer or pledge shares, fractional shares, and rights or options to purchase shares of the corporation only to individuals, general partnerships, and professional corporations qualified under section 20 to be issued shares. [*Reviser's note:* The phrase "and professional corporations" should be deleted if Alternative 2 or 3 of section 34(c) or (c) and (d) is chosen.]

(b) A transfer of shares made in violation of subsection (a), except one made by operation of law or court judgment, is void.

§ 23. Compulsory Acquisition of Shares after Death or Disqualification of Shareholder

(a) A professional corporation must acquire (or cause to be acquired by a qualified person) the shares of its shareholder, at a price the corporation believes represents their fair value as of the date of death, disqualification, or transfer, if:

(1) the shareholder dies;

(2) the shareholder becomes a disqualified person, except as provided in subsection (c); or

(3) the shares are transferred by operation of law or court judgment to a disqualified person, except as provided in subsection (c).

(b) If a price for the shares is fixed in accordance with the articles of incorporation or bylaws or by private agreement, that price controls. If the price is not so fixed, the corporation shall acquire the shares in accordance with section 24. If the disqualified person rejects the corporation's purchase offer, either the person or the corporation may commence a proceeding under section 25 to determine the fair value of the shares.

(c) This section does not require the acquisition of shares in the event of disqualification if the disqualification lasts no more than five months from the date the disqualification or transfer occurs.

(d) This section, and section 24, do not prevent or relieve a professional corporation from paying pension benefits or other deferred compensation for services rendered to a former shareholder if otherwise permitted by law.

(e) A provision for the acquisition of shares contained in a professional corporation's articles of incorporation or bylaws, or in a private agreement, is specifically enforceable.

§ 24. Acquisition Procedure

(a) If shares must be acquired under section 23, the professional corporation shall deliver a written notice to the executor or administrator of the estate of its deceased shareholder, or to the disqualified person or transferee, offering to purchase the shares at a price the corporation believes represents their fair value as of the date of death, disqualification, or transfer. The offer notice must be accompanied by the corporation's balance sheet for a fiscal year ending not more than 16 months before the effective date of the offer notice, an income statement for that year, a statement of changes in shareholders' equity for that year, and the latest available interim financial statements, if any.

(b) The disqualified person has 30 days from the effective date of the notice to accept the corporation's offer or demand that the corporation commence a proceeding under section 25 to determine the fair value of his shares. If he accepts the offer, the corporation shall make payment for the shares within 60 days from the effective date of the offer notice (unless a later date is agreed on) upon the disqualified person's surrender of his shares to the corporation.

(c) After the corporation makes payment for the shares, the disqualified person has no further interest in them.

§ 25. Court Action to Appraise Shares

(a) If the disqualified shareholder does not accept the professional corporation's offer under section 24(b) within the 30 day period, the shareholder during the following 30 day period may deliver a written notice to the corporation demanding that it commence a proceeding to determine the fair value of the shares. The corporation may commence a proceeding at any time during the 60 days following the effective date of its offer notice. If it does not do so, the shareholder may commence a proceeding against the corporation to determine the fair value of his shares.

(b) The corporation or disqualified shareholder shall commence the proceeding in the [name or describe] court of the county where the corporation's principal office (or, if none in this state, its registered office) is located. The corporation shall make the disqualified shareholder a party to the proceeding as in an action against his shares. The jurisdiction of the court in which the proceeding is commenced is plenary and exclusive.

(c) The court may appoint one or more persons as appraisers to receive evidence and recommend decision on the question of fair value. The appraisers have the power described in the order appointing them, or in any amendment to it.

(d) The disqualified shareholder is entitled to judgment for the fair value of his shares determined by the court as of the date of death, disqualification, or transfer together with interest from that date at a rate found by the court to be fair and equitable.

(e) The court may order the judgment paid in installments determined by the court.

§ 26. Court Costs and Fees of Experts

(a) The court in an appraisal proceeding commenced under section 25 shall determine all costs of the proceeding, including the reasonable compensation and expenses of appraisers appointed by the court, and shall assess the costs against the professional corporation. But the court may assess costs against the disqualified shareholder, in an amount the court finds equitable, if the court finds the shareholder acted arbitrarily, vexatiously, or not in good faith in refusing to accept the corporation's offer.

(b) The court may also assess the fees and expenses of counsel and experts for the disqualified shareholder against the corporation and in favor of the shareholder if the court finds that the fair value of his shares substantially exceeded the amount offered by the corporation or that the corporation did not make an offer.

§ 27. Cancellation of Disqualified Shares

If the shares of a disqualified person are not acquired under section 24 or 25 within 10 months after the death of the shareholder or within 5 months after the disqualification or transfer, the professional corporation shall immediately cancel the shares on its books and the disqualified person has no further interest as a shareholder in the corporation other than his right to payment of the fair value of the shares under section 24 or 25.

Governance

§ 30. Directors and Officers

Not less than one-half of the directors of a professional corporation, and all of its officers except the secretary and treasurer (if any), must be qualified persons with respect to the corporation.

§ 31. Voting of Shares

(a) Only a qualified person may be appointed a proxy to vote shares of a professional corporation.

(b) A voting trust with respect to shares of a professional corporation is not valid [unless all of its trustees and beneficiaries are qualified persons. But if a beneficiary who is a qualified person dies or becomes disqualified, a voting trust valid under this subsection continues to be valid for 10 months after the date of death or for 5 months after the disqualification occurred.] [*Reviser's note:* The bracketed text should be deleted if Alternative 2 or 3 of section 34(c) or (c) and (d) is chosen.]

§ 32. Confidential Relationship
(a) The relationship between an individual rendering professional services as an employee of a domestic or foreign professional corporation and his client or patient is the same as if the individual were rendering the services as a sole practitioner.
(b) The relationship between a domestic or foreign professional corporation and the client or patient for whom its employee is rendering professional services is the same as that between the client or patient and the employee.

§ 33. Privileged Communications
A privilege applicable to communications between an individual rendering professional services and the person receiving the services recognized under the statute or common law of this state is not affected by this Supplement. The privilege applies to a domestic or foreign professional corporation and to its employees in all situations in which it applies to communications between an individual rendering professional services on behalf of the corporation and the person receiving the services.

§ 34. Responsibility for Professional Services
(a) Each individual who renders professional services as an employee of a domestic or foreign professional corporation is liable for a negligent or wrongful act or omission in which he personally participates to the same extent as if he rendered the services as a sole practitioner. An employee of a domestic or foreign professional corporation is not liable, however, for the conduct of other employees of the corporation unless he is at fault in appointing, supervising, or cooperating with them.
(b) A domestic or foreign professional corporation whose employees perform professional services within the scope of their employment or of their apparent authority to act for the corporation is liable to the same extent as its employees.

Alternative 1
(c) Except as otherwise provided by statute, the personal liability of a shareholder of a domestic or foreign professional corporation is no greater in any respect than the liability of a shareholder of a corporation incorporated under the [Model] Business Corporation Act.

Alternative 2
(c) Except as otherwise provided by statute, if a domestic or foreign professional corporation is liable under subsection (b), every shareholder of the corporation is liable to the same extent as if he were a partner in a partnership and the services creating liability were rendered on behalf of the partnership.

Alternative 3
(c) If a domestic or foreign professional corporation is liable under subsection (b), every shareholder of the corporation is liable to the same extent as if he were a partner in a partnership and the services creating liability were rendered on behalf of the partnership:
   (1) except as otherwise provided by statute; or
   (2) unless the corporation has provided security for professional responsibility under subsection (d) and the liability is satisfied to the extent provided by the security.
(d) A domestic or foreign professional corporation may provide security for professional responsibility by obtaining insurance or a surety bond. The licensing authority with jurisdiction over a profession may determine by rule the amount, coverage, and form of insurance or bond required based on the number of shareholders, type of practice, and other variables considered appropriate by the authority for the profession. If a licensing authority has not determined the amount of security required for the profession, the amount is the product of $_____$ multiplied by the number of shareholders of the corporation rendering services in that profession.

Reorganization and Termination
§ 40. Merger
(a) If all the shareholders of the disappearing and surviving corporations are qualified to be shareholders of the surviving corporation, a professional corporation may merge with another domestic or foreign professional corporation or with a domestic or foreign business corporation.
(b) If the surviving corporation is to render professional services in this state, it must comply with this Supplement.

§ 41. Termination of Professional Activities
If a professional corporation ceases to render professional services, it must amend its articles of incorporation to delete references to rendering professional

services and to conform its corporate name to the requirements of [MBCA § 4.01]. After the amendment becomes effective the corporation may continue in existence as a business corporation under the [MBCA] and it is no longer subject to this Supplement.

§ 42. Judicial Dissolution

The attorney general may commence a proceeding under [MBCA §§ 14.30–14.33] to dissolve a professional corporation if:

(1) the secretary of state or a licensing authority with jurisdiction over a professional service described in the corporation's articles of incorporation serves written notice on the corporation under [MBCA § 5.04] that it has violated or is violating a provision of this Supplement;

(2) the corporation does not correct each alleged violation, or demonstrate to the reasonable satisfaction of the secretary of state or licensing authority that it did not occur, within 60 days after service of the notice is perfected under [MBCA § 5.04]; and

(3) the secretary of state or licensing authority certifies to the attorney general a description of the violation, that it notified the corporation of the violation, and that the corporation did not correct it, or demonstrate that it did not occur, within 60 days after perfection of service of the notice.

Foreign Professional Corporations

§ 50. Authority to Transact Business

(a) Except as provided in subsection (c), a foreign professional corporation may not transact business in this state until it obtains a certificate of authority from the secretary of state.

(b) A foreign professional corporation may not obtain a certificate of authority unless:

(1) its corporate name satisfies the requirements of section 15;

(2) it is incorporated for one or more of the purposes described in section 11; and

(3) all of its shareholders, not less than one-half of its directors, and all of its officers other than its secretary and treasurer (if any) are licensed in one or more states to render a professional service described in its articles of incorporation.

(c) A foreign professional corporation is not required to obtain a certificate of authority to transact business in this state unless it maintains or intends to maintain an office in this state for conduct of business or professional practice.

§ 51. Application for Certificate of Authority

The application of a foreign professional corporation for a certificate of authority to render professional services in this state must contain the information called for by [MBCA § 15.03] and in addition include a statement that all of its shareholders, not less than one-half of its directors, and all of its officers other than its secretary and treasurer (if any), are licensed in one or more states to render a professional service described in its articles of incorporation.

§ 52. Revocation of Certificate of Authority

The secretary of state may administratively revoke under [MBCA §§ 15.30–15.32] the certificate of authority of a foreign professional corporation authorized to transact business in this state if a licensing authority with jurisdiction over a professional service described in the corporation's articles of incorporation certifies to the secretary of state that the corporation has violated or is violating a provision of this Supplement and describes the violation in the certificate.

Miscellaneous Regulatory Provisions

§ 60. Articles of Incorporation for Licensing Authority

A domestic or foreign professional corporation authorized to transact business in this state may not render professional services in this state until it delivers a certified copy of its articles of incorporation for filing to each licensing authority with jurisdiction over a professional service described in the articles.

§ 61. Annual Qualification Statement for Licensing Authority

(a) Each domestic professional corporation, and each foreign professional corporation authorized to transact business in this state, shall deliver for filing to each licensing authority having jurisdiction over a professional service described in the corporation's articles of incorporation an annual statement of qualification setting forth:

(1) the names and usual business addresses of its directors and officers; and

(2) information required by rule promulgated by the licensing authority to determine compliance with this Supplement and other rules promulgated under it.

(b) The first qualification statement must be delivered to the licensing authority between January 1 and April 1 of the year following the calendar year in which a domestic corporation became a professional corporation or a foreign professional corporation was authorized to transact business in this state. Subsequent qualification statements must be delivered to the licensing authority between January 1 and April 1 of the following calendar years.

(c) The licensing authority shall collect a fee of $_____ when a qualification statement is delivered to it for filing.

§ 62. Annual Report for Secretary of State

The annual report required by [MBCA § 16.22] for each domestic professional corporation, and for each foreign professional corporation authorized to transact business in this state, must include a statement that all of its shareholders, not less than one-half of its directors, and all of its officers other than its secretary and treasurer (if any), are qualified persons with respect to the corporation.

§ 63. Rulemaking by Licensing Authority

Each licensing authority is empowered to promulgate rules expressly authorized by this Supplement if the rules are consistent with the public interest or required by the public health or welfare or by generally recognized standards of professional conduct.

§ 64. Licensing Authority's Regulatory Jurisdiction

This Supplement does not restrict the jurisdiction of a licensing authority over individuals rendering a professional service within the jurisdiction of the licensing authority, nor does it affect the interpretation or application of any law pertaining to standards of professional conduct.

§ 65. Penalty for Signing False Document

(a) A person commits an offense if he signs a document he knows is false in any material respect with intent that the document be delivered to the licensing authority for filing.
(b) An offense under this section is a [___] misdemeanor [punishable by a fine of not to exceed $_____].
(c) The offense created by this section is in addition to any other offense created by law for the same conduct.

Transition Provisions

§ 70. Application to Existing Corporations

(a) This Supplement applies to every corporation incorporated under a general law of this state that is repealed by this Supplement. If an existing corporation to which this Supplement applies must amend its articles of incorporation to comply with this Supplement, it shall do so within 90 days after the effective date of this Supplement.
(b) This Supplement does not apply to a corporation now existing or later incorporated under a law of this state that is not repealed by this Supplement unless the corporation elects professional corporation status under section 10.
(c) This Supplement does not affect an existing or future right or privilege to render professional services through the use of any other form of business entity.

§ 71. Reservation of Power to Amend or Repeal

The [name of state legislature] has power to amend or repeal all or part of this Supplement at any time and all domestic and foreign professional corporations subject to this Supplement are governed by the amendment or repeal.

§ 72. Saving Provisions

(a) Except as provided in subsection (b), the repeal of a statute by this Supplement does not affect:
 (1) the operation of the statute or any action taken under it before its repeal;
 (2) any ratification, right, remedy, privilege, obligation, or liability acquired, accrued, or incurred under the statute before its repeal;
 (3) any violation of the statute, or any penalty, forfeiture, or punishment incurred because of the violation, before its repeal;
 (4) any proceeding, reorganization, or dissolution commenced under the statute before its repeal, and the proceeding, reorganization, or dissolution may be completed in accordance with the statute as if it had not been repealed.
(b) If a penalty or punishment imposed for violation of a statute repealed by this Supplement is reduced by this Supplement, the penalty or punishment if not already imposed shall be imposed in accordance with this Supplement.

§ 73. Severability

If any provision of this Supplement or its application to any person or circumstance is held invalid by a court of competent jurisdiction, the invalidity does not affect other provisions or applications of the Supplement that can be given effect without the invalid provision or application, and to this end the provisions of the Supplement are severable.

§ 74. Repeal

The following laws and parts of laws are repealed: _____.

§ 75. Effective Date

This Supplement takes effect _____.

APPENDIX G
FORMS

FORM 1A
TRADE NAME AFFIDAVIT
(COLORADO)

Recorded at................o'clock...........M., ...

Reception No................................. ....Recorder.

STATE OF COLORADO, } ss.
............County of..................

....of the

..................County of..................., in the State of Colorado, ...

....being first duly sworn, upon oath deposes and says that..

....

is the name under which a business or trade is being carried on at..........................

in the..................County of..................., and State of Colorado.

That the full Christian and surname and address of all the persons who are represented by the said name of..is as follows, to wit:

....

....

....

....

....

That the affiant................the person..........carrying on said business or trade under the name or style aforesaid.

....

Subscribed and sworn to before me, this............day of..................................., 19......

My commission expires.., 19......

Witness my hand and official seal.

....
Notary Public.

NOTE—All co-partnerships and every person doing business otherwise than in his own full name should make this affidavit, which must be filed in the county in which the firm carries on its trade or business, and must be refiled whenever there is any change in the membership of the firm; and no suit can be prosecuted by such firm for the collection of any debts until such affidavit is filed.

No. 298. TRADE NAME AFFIDAVIT. Bradford Publishing Co., 1824-46 Stout Street, Denver, Colorado—2-73

No..

TRADE NAME AFFIDAVIT
OF

....

....

....

....

Trading or doing business under the name of

....

....

at ....

....................County of.....................................
State of Colorado.

STATE OF COLORADO } ss.
....................County of.....................

Office of County Clerk and Recorder

I hereby certify that the within instrument was filed for record in my office at........o'clock........M., ..., 19........, and was duly recorded in book............, page............

....
Recorder.

By ....
Deputy.

Fees, $..

BRADFORD PUBLISHING CO., DENVER

FORM 1B

FICTITIOUS NAME STATEMENT
(CALIFORNIA)

Original Copy for Filing with County Clerk of _____ County

FICTITIOUS BUSINESS NAME STATEMENT

The following person (persons) is (are) doing business as:

(*) _____
(FICTITIOUS BUSINESS NAME)

at (**) _____
_____

(***) 1. _____ 2. _____
        (FULL NAME - TYPE/PRINT)   (FULL NAME - TYPE/PRINT)

        _____   _____
        (ADDRESS)   (ADDRESS)

        _____   _____
        (CITY)   (CITY)

     3. _____ 4. _____
        (FULL NAME - TYPE/PRINT)   (FULL NAME - TYPE/PRINT)

        _____   _____
        (ADDRESS)   (ADDRESS)

        _____   _____
        (CITY)   (CITY)

(****) This business is conducted by _____
(i) "an individual," (ii) "a general partnership," (iii) "a limited partnership," (iv) "an unincorporated association other than a partnership," (v) "a corporation," (vi) "a business trust."

Signed _____

Signature Must Also Be Typed or Printed _____

This statement was filed with the County Clerk of _____ County on _____
                                                                              (Date)

Attorney or Bank or Agent

Name _____   FILE NO. _____

Address _____

City _____

Telephone _____

Statutory Filing Fee — $10.00
(Includes one Certification—See Page 3)

Statement Expires 5 years from Dec. 31 of year
in which filed and must be Renewed then with a
new Statement

- -

for FREE FORMS—

PHONE (213) 625-2141

CALIFORNIA
NEWSPAPER SERVICE BUREAU, Inc.
ESTABLISHED 1934
210 South Spring Street
Los Angeles, Calif. 90012

**Affiliated with The Los Angeles Daily Journal
and the Sacramento Daily Recorder**

THE BELOW INSTRUCTIONS ARE NOT TO BE PUBLISHED (Sec. 17924 B&P)

INSTRUCTIONS FOR COMPLETION OF STATEMENT
Section 17913 Business & Professions Code

(*) **The Fictitious Name under which business is being conducted.**

(**) If the registrant has a place of business in this State, insert the street address of his principal place of business in this State. If the registrant has no place of business in this State, insert the street address of his principal place of business outside this State.

(***) If the registrant is an individual, insert his full name and residence address. If the registrant is a partnership or other association of persons, insert the full name and residence address of *each general* partner. If the registrant is a business trust, insert the full name and residence address of each trustee. If the registrant is a corporation, insert the name of the corporation as set forth in its articles of incorporation and the State of incorporation. (Attach additional sheet if necessary.)

(****) Insert whichever of the following best describes the nature of the business: "an individual", "a general partnership", "a limited partnership", "an unincorporated association other than a partnership", "a corporation", or a "business trust."

A FICTITIOUS BUSINESS NAME STATEMENT EXPIRES AT THE END OF FIVE YEARS FROM DECEMBER, 31 OF THE YEAR IN WHICH IT WAS FILED. Except as provided in Section 17923, B&P Code, it expires *40 days after any change in the facts set forth in the statement;* except that a change in the residence address of an individual, general partner, or trustee does not cause the statement to expire.

The statement expires upon the filing of a statement of abandonment.

NOTICE TO REGISTRANT · Section 17924 Business & Professions Code

(1) Your fictitious business name statement must be published in a newspaper once a week for four successive weeks and an affidavit of publication filed with the county clerk within 30 days after publication has been accomplished. The statement should be published in a newspaper of general circulation in the county where the principal place of business is located. The statement should be published in such county in a newspaper that circulates in the area where the business is to be conducted (Sec. 17917 B&P Code)

(2) Any person who executes, files, or publishes any fictitious business name statement, knowing that such statement is false, in whole or in part, is guilty of a misdemeanor and upon conviction thereof shall be fined not to exceed five hundred dollars ($500) (Sec. 17930 B&P Code).

THE LAW...

(1) Where the asterisk (*) appears in the form, insert the fictitious business name.

(2) Where the two asterisks (**) appear in the form: If the registrant has a place of business in this state, insert the street address of his principal place of business in this state. If the registrant has no place of business in this state, insert the street address of his principal place of business outside this state.

(3) Where the three asterisks (***) appear in the form: If the registrant is an individual, insert his full name and residence address. If the registrant is a partnership or other association of persons, insert the full name and residence address of each general partner. If the registrant is a business trust, insert the full name and residence address of each trustee. If the registrant is a corporation, insert the name of the corporation as set out in its articles of incorporation and the state of incorporation.

(4) Where the four asterisks (****) appear in the form, insert whichever of the following best describes the nature of the business: (i) "an individual," (ii) "a general partnership," (iii) "a limited partnership," (iv) "an unincorporated association other than a partnership," (v) "a corporation," (vi) "a business trust."

17914. If the registrant is an individual, the statement shall be signed by the individual; if a partnership or other association of persons, by a general partner; if a business trust, by a trustee; if a corporation, by an officer.

17915. The fictitious business name statement shall be filed with the clerk of the county in which the registrant has his principal place of business in this state or, if he has no place of business in this state, with the Clerk of Sacramento County.

17916. Presentation for filing of a fictitious business name statement and one copy, tender of the filing fee, and acceptance of the statement by the county clerk constitute filing under this chapter. The county clerk shall note on the copy the file number and the date of filing the original and shall certify and deliver or send the copy to the registrant.

For Laws on Publication See Reverse Side of Attached Duplicate (Pink) Copy of This Form.

FORMS   467

FORM 1C

PUBLICATION OF FICTITIOUS NAME
(CALIFORNIA)

Duplicate Copy for Publication in the _____

FICTITIOUS BUSINESS NAME STATEMENT
The following person (persons) is (are) doing business as:

(*) _____
(FICTITIOUS BUSINESS NAME)

at (**) _____

_____

(***) 1 _____ 2. _____
(FULL NAME - TYPE/PRINT)   (FULL NAME - TYPE/PRINT)

_____   _____
(ADDRESS)   (ADDRESS)

_____   _____
(CITY)   (CITY)

3 _____   4 _____
(FULL NAME - TYPE/PRINT)   (FULL NAME - TYPE/PRINT)

_____   _____
(ADDRESS)   (ADDRESS)

_____   _____
(CITY)   (CITY)

(****) This business is conducted by _____
(i) "an individual," (ii) "a general partnership," (iii) "a limited partnership," (iv) "an unincorporated association other than a partnership," (v) "a corporation," (vi) "a business trust."

Signed _____
Signature Must Also Be Typed or Printed _____

This statement was filed with the County Clerk of _____ County on _____
                                                                        (Date)

Attorney or Bank or Agent   FILE NO. _____

Name _____

Address _____

City _____

Telephone _____

PUBLISH ALL ITEMS IN DOUBLE BRACKETS ABOVE

See Reverse of This Form for Publication Instructions and Law.

- -

for FREE FORMS—
PHONE (213) 625-2141

CALIFORNIA
NEWSPAPER SERVICE BUREAU, Inc.
ESTABLISHED 1934
210 South Spring Street
Los Angeles, Calif. 90012
Affiliated with The Los Angeles Daily Journal
and the Sacramento Daily Recorder

THE BELOW INSTRUCTIONS ARE NOT TO BE PUBLISHED (Sec. 17924 B&P)

INSTRUCTIONS FOR COMPLETION OF STATEMENT
Section 17913 Business & Professions Code

(*) The Fictitious Name under which business is being conducted.

(**) If the registrant has a place of business in this State, insert the street address of his principal place of business in this State. If the registrant has no place of business in this State, insert the street address of his principal place of business outside this State.

(***) If the registrant is an individual, insert his full name and residence address. If the registrant is a partnership or other association of persons, insert the full name and residence address of *each general* partner. If the registrant is a business trust, insert the full name and residence address of each trustee. If the registrant is a corporation, insert the name of the corporation as set forth in its articles of incorporation and the State of incorporation. (Attach additional sheet if necessary.)

(****) Insert whichever of the following best describes the nature of the business: "an individual", "a general partnership", "a limited partnership", "an unincorporated association other than a partnership", "a corporation", or a "business trust."

A FICTITIOUS BUSINESS NAME STATEMENT EXPIRES AT THE END OF FIVE YEARS FROM DECEMBER 31 OF THE YEAR IN WHICH IT WAS FILED. Except as provided in Section 17923, B&P Code, it expires *40 days after any change in the facts set forth in the statement;* except that a change in the residence address of an individual, general partner, or trustee does not cause the statement to expire.

The statement expires upon the filing of a statement of abandonment.

NOTICE TO REGISTRANT - Section 17924 Business & Professions Code

(1) Your fictitious business name statement must be published in a newspaper once a week for four successive weeks and an affidavit of publication filed with the county clerk within 30 days after publication has been accomplished. The statement should be published in a newspaper of general circulation in the county where the principal place of business is located. The statement should be published in such county in a newspaper that circulates in the area where the business is to be conducted (Sec. 17917 B&P Code)

(2) Any person who executes, files, or publishes any fictitious business name statement, knowing that such statement is false, in whole or in part, is guilty of a misdemeanor and upon conviction thereof shall be fined not to exceed five hundred dollars ($500) (Sec. 17930 B&P Code).

THE LAW...

17915. The fictitious business name statement shall be filed with the clerk of the county in which the registrant has his principal place of business in this state or, if he has no place of business in this state, with the Clerk of Sacramento County.

17916. Presentation for filing of a fictitious business name statement and one copy, tender of the filing fee, and acceptance of the statement by the county clerk constitute filing under this chapter. The county clerk shall note on the copy the file number and the date of filing the original and shall certify and deliver or send the copy to the registrant.

17917. (a) Within 30 days after a fictitious business name statement has been filed pursuant to this chapter, the registrant shall cause a statement in the form prescribed by subdivision (a) of Section 17913 to be published pursuant to Government Code Section 6064 in a newspaper of general circulation in the county in which the principal place of business of the registrant is located or, if there is no such newspaper in that county, then in a newspaper of general circulation in an adjoining county. If the registrant does not have a place of business in this state, the notice shall be published in a newspaper of general circulation in Sacramento County.

(b) Subject to the requirements of subdivision (a), the newspaper selected for the publication of the statement should be one that circulates in the area where the business is to be conducted.

(c) Where a new statement is required because the prior statement has expired under subdivision (a) of Section 17920, the new statement need not be published unless there has been a change in the information required in the expired statement.

(d) An affidavit showing the publication of the statement shall be filed with the county clerk within 30 days after the completion of the publication.

FORM 1D
BUSINESS CERTIFICATE
(NEW YORK)

201 — Certificate of Conducting Business under an Assumed Name For Individual   b   JULIUS BLUMBERG, INC., LAW BLANK PUBLISHERS 80 EXCHANGE PLACE AT BROADWAY, NEW YORK

Business Certificate

I HEREBY CERTIFY that I am conducting or transacting business under the name or designation of

at

City or Town of   County of   State of New York.

My full name is*
and I reside at

I FURTHER CERTIFY that I am the successor in interest to

the person or persons heretofore using such name or names to carry on or conduct or transact business.

IN WITNESS WHEREOF, I have this   day of   19   , made and signed this certificate.

....

* Print or type name.
* If under 21 years of age, state "I am .... years of age".

STATE OF NEW YORK
COUNTY OF   } ss.:

On this   day of   19   , before me personally appeared

to me known and known to me to be the individual described in and who executed the foregoing certificate, and he thereupon duly acknowledged to me that he executed the same.

FORM 1E

ABANDONMENT OF FICTITIOUS NAME
(CALIFORNIA)

CERTIFICATE OF DISCONTINUANCE OF USE AND/OR ABANDONMENT OF FICTITIOUS NAME

THE UNDERSIGNED _____ hereby certify that, effective _____
                (Do) (Does)   (Date)

_____ ceased to do business under the fictitious firm name of _____
(They) (He) (She)

_____
(Exact Name of Business Only)

at _____ California,
   (Number)   (Street)   (City)

which business was formerly composed of the following person__, whose name__ in full and place__ of residence

_____ as follows, to-wit:
(Is) (Are)

_____

_____

_____

_____

_____

    Certificate for transaction of business under the above fictitious name, and affidavit of publication thereof, are on file in the office of the County Clerk of.................................County, under the provisions of Section 2466 of the Civil Code.

    WITNESS _____ hand__ this _____ day of _____, 19____.
              (Our) (My)

                                                    Signatures: _____

_____, Atty(s).

County Clerk's File No. _____

For publication in the proper newspaper and for filing of the affidavit of publication with the appropriate County Clerk please mail two copies of this notice to

THE LOS ANGELES DAILY JOURNAL
ESTABLISHED 1888
220 W. FIRST STREET, LOS ANGELES, CALIF. 90012
TELEPHONE: MAdison 5-2141

LOS ANGELES NEWSPAPER SERVICE BUREAU, INC.
STATEWIDE LEGAL ADVERTISING CLEARING HOUSE SINCE 1934
224 W. FIRST ST., LOS ANGELES, CALIF. 90012
TELEPHONE: MAdison 5-2541

5M—8/67—A-73-74

FORM 2A

ASSIGNMENT OF PARTNER'S INTEREST IN FIRM

Know All Men by These Presents, that for and in consideration of the sum of One Dollar ($1) and other good and valuable considerations to me in hand paid, receipt of which is hereby acknowledged, I, _____, of _____, do hereby assign to _____, of _____, all of my right, title and interest in and to a certain agreement of partnership bearing date the _____ day of _____, 19__, made and entered into by and between _____, _____, and myself; and I do hereby authorize and direct _____ to account to and with _____ for all profits, issues and income arising under the partnership agreement in the same manner and with the same force and effect as if such accounting were had and made with me personally.

In Witness Whereof, I have hereunto set my hand and seal this _____ day of _____, 19__.

_____ [*Seal*] [1]

1. West's Modern Legal Forms § 6411. Other examples of an assignment of a partner's interest in the firm, and a form for consent of the other partners to an assignment appear in West's Modern Legal Forms §§ 6412–6415.

FORM 2B

PERSONAL NOTICE OF DISSOLUTION OF PARTNERSHIP

To: _____   Date: _____

Please be advised that the partnership between A.B., C.D. and E.F. was dissolved on the _____ day of _____, 19__, and that E.F. is no longer a member of the firm. Your account, in the amount of $_____, according to our books, will be settled with A.B. and C.D. who will continue the business under the firm name of B & D.

[*Signatures of the partners*]

FORM 2C

NOTICE OF DISSOLUTION OF PARTNERSHIP BY PUBLICATION

Notice is hereby given that the partnership between A.B., C.D. and E.F. was dissolved on the _____ day of _____, 19__, so far as relates to E.F. All debts due to the partnership, and those due by them, will be settled with and by the remaining partners who will continue the business under the firm name of B. & D.

[*Date*] [*Signatures of the partners*] [2]

2. West's Modern Legal Forms § 6446.

FORM 2D

PRELIMINARY NOTICE OF EXPULSION TO PARTNER

To [*Name and address of partner*]

We hereby give you notice that we propose to exercise the power given to us by paragraph _____ of the agreement of partnership, dated the _____ day of _____, 19__, under which we are now carrying on business in partnership with you, of terminating the partnership so far as you are concerned on the ground that you have acted in a manner inconsistent with the good faith observable between partners [*or* that you have been guilty of conduct such as would be a ground for an application to the court for a dissolution of the partnership].

In order to afford you an opportunity of explaining and, if possible, satisfying us that no good cause of complaint exists, we hereby invite you to attend a meeting of the partners, to be held at _____, on _____ next, at _____ o'clock.

If you are unable to attend such meeting, we must ask you to arrange for another meeting with us, to be held at an early date and in any case within [*one week*] from the date of this notice.

Dated _____, 19__. [*Signatures of partners*] [3]

3. West's Modern Legal Forms § 6439.

FORM 2E

NOTICE OF EXPULSION TO PARTNER

To [*Name and address of partner*]

Referring to our notice to you, dated the _____ day of _____, 19__, and to the meeting of the partners held pursuant to such notice on the _____ day of _____, 19__, [*or* and in view of the fact that you neither attended the meeting to which we invited you in such notice nor have taken any other steps to meet us or explain matters], we regret to inform you that we are unable to accept as satisfactory the explanations offered by you at such meeting after hearing from us exactly what was our cause of complaint against you, and accordingly, we hereby give you notice that in exercise of the power for this purpose given to us by paragraph _____ of the agreement of partnership, dated the _____ day of _____, 19__, under which we have heretofore carried on business in partnership with you, we hereby terminate the partnership so far as you are concerned as of the date of this notice on the ground generally that [*repeat the ground as stated in the preliminary notice and add*] and more particularly on the ground that [*state shortly the facts relied on as constituting the general ground previously stated*].

Dated _____, 19__.   [*Signatures of partners*] [4]

4. West's Modern Legal Forms §.6440.

FORM 2F

COMPLEX PARTNERSHIP AGREEMENT

ARTICLE I. GENERAL PROVISIONS

A. Recitals.
B. Parties.
C. Purpose.
D. Firm Name.
E. Term.
F. Location of Principal Place of Business.

ARTICLE II. CAPITAL

A. Original Capital Contributed by Partners.
B. Annual Additional Contributions to Capital.
C. Reserve for Capital Expenditures; Other Reserves.
D. Annual Reimbursements on Contributions to Capital.

ARTICLE III. PROFITS AND LOSSES OF THE FIRM; PARTICIPATION OF PARTNERS THEREIN; DRAWINGS; BONUSES

A. Units of Participation in Profits and Losses by the Respective Partners.
B. Drawing Accounts of the Respective Partners and the Extent to Which Any are Guaranteed.
C. Reserve for Bonuses and Payments Therefrom.

ARTICLE IV. MEETINGS AND VOTING OF PARTNERS

A. Meetings of Partners; Voting at Such Meetings.
B. Percentage of Votes Required for Certain Partnership Meetings; Requirement of Recommendation of the Management Committee in Advance of Certain Partnership Decisions.

ARTICLE V. CHANGES AS TO PARTNERS

A. No Classes of Partners.
B. Addition of Partners.
C. Death or Permanent Disability of a Partner.
　1. Death.
　2. Permanent Disability.
D. Permanent Withdrawal of a Partner.
　1. Notice of Withdrawal and Effective Date of Withdrawal.
　2. Possible Termination of the Firm Superseding Withdrawal Notice.
　3. Partition with and Payments to the Withdrawing Partner.
E. Retirement of Partners; Gradual Steps toward Retirement; Retirement Plans for Partners.
　1. Retired Partners; Plans for their Compensation.
　2. When a Partner Retires.
　3. Gradual Steps toward Retirement.
F. Expulsion of a Partner.
　1. Expulsion for Cause.
　2. Effects of Expulsion for Cause.
　3. Expulsion without Determining Any Cause Therefor.
　4. Effects of Expulsion without Determining Any Cause Therefor.
G. Temporary Incapacity; Leave of Absence; Temporary Withdrawal; Vacations.
　1. Temporary Incapacity or Illness.
　2. Leave of Absence.
　3. Temporary Withdrawal.
　4. Vacations.

ARTICLE VI. DUTIES OF PARTNERS

A. Devotion to Duty.
B. Charging for Services.

ARTICLE VII. MANAGEMENT

A. Authority and Membership of the Management Committee.
B. Functioning of the Management Committee and Its Subcommittees.
C. Membership in Subcommittees of the Management Committee.

ARTICLE VIII. INSURANCE; INVESTMENTS

A. Life Insurance.
B. Other Insurance.
C. Investments.

ARTICLE IX. PROPERTIES AND RECORDS

A. Firm Properties.
B. Accounting Records.

ARTICLE X. TERMINATION AND LIQUIDATION OF FIRM

A. Termination of the Firm by Voluntary Vote or Otherwise.
B. Pending Employments on Termination.
C. Liquidation of Assets.
D. Prior Opportunity of Partners to Bid for Purchase of Assets Being Liquidated.
E. Distribution of Proceeds from Liquidation.

ARTICLE XI. LEGAL EFFECT OF PROVISIONS; ARBITRATION

A. Governing Law.
B. Persons Bound.
C. Rights of Partners Not Assignable; Not to be Pledged.
D. Finality of Decisions within the Firm; Effect of Divergent or Adverse Interest Personally of Any Partner.
E. Arbitration.
F. Severability.

ARTICLE XII. AMENDMENTS

ARTICLES OF PARTNERSHIP FOR THE FIRM OF A, B & C

ARTICLE I. GENERAL PROVISIONS

Section A. Recitals. 1. The undersigned parties hereby agree this _____ day of _____, 19__, to organize a partnership under the firm name of A, B & C.

2. The effective date of this Agreement is the _____ day of _____, 19__.

Section B. Parties. A, B, C; D, E and F constitute the original partners of the firm.

Section C. Purpose. The purpose of this partnership is to engage in [*here set out nature of the business*], and any other business related thereto.

Section D. Firm Name. The name of the partnership "A, B & C" shall continue until changed in accordance with the provisions of this Agreement.

Section E. Term. The partnership shall continue from the effective date of this Agreement until dissolved in accordance with the terms hereof.

Section F. Location of Principal Place of Business. The principal place of business of the partnership shall be at _____, or at such other place or places as the partners shall hereafter determine.

ARTICLE II. CAPITAL

Section A. Original Capital Contributed by Partners. The original capital contributions of the respective partners hereunder are shown on Exhibit A attached hereto. It reflects cash contributed and property, the title of which is transferred to the firm at the current agreed market value of each item. The firm agrees to repay to each partner, at the time and as hereinafter provided, the aggregate amount he has thus contributed as original capital plus interest thereon at the rate of _____ per cent per annum on all unpaid balances.

Section B. Annual Additional Contributions to Capital. Five per cent of the net income of the firm for each fiscal year shall be withheld from distribution and credited, as additional contributions to capital, to partners, in the amount that each would have received had that sum been distributed. Interest shall be paid by the firm on all unreimbursed balances of all these additional contributions to capital at the rate of _____ per cent per annum until fully repaid.

Section C. Reserve for Capital Expenditures; Other Reserves.
1. Out of the sums contributed as additional contributions to capital for each fiscal year, there shall be set aside as of the beginning of the new fiscal year that amount, in addition to any unexpended balance in that reserve fund left over from the last year, estimated to be needed for capital expenditures of the firm during the new fiscal year. As such expenditures are incurred during that year they shall be paid for out of that reserve fund.

2. Out of the remainder of the sums contributed as additional contributions to capital for each fiscal year, there shall be set aside that amount for any other reserve fund, or to add to any existing reserve fund, estimated to be needed to meet any other anticipated obligations or commitments of the firm. As such expenditures are incurred they may be paid out of the appropriate reserve fund.

Section D. Annual Reimbursements on Contributions to Capital.
1. At the end of each fiscal year there shall be charged to firm expense for that year the amount of depreciation accrued for the year,

which the firm for federal income tax purposes is entitled to deduct from firm income, and the amount of interest accrued for the year on the unreimbursed balances of contributions to capital.

2. At the end of each fiscal year, (i) the amount of such interest shall be paid to the partners entitled thereto; and (ii) cash sums aggregating the amount of such depreciation shall be paid ratably in reimbursement of contributions to capital.

3. Any amounts remaining out of the annual contributions to capital provided for in Section B of this Article, after the deduction of the reserves as provided in Section C of this Article, shall be paid to partners to reimburse them for their contributions to capital. Such reimbursements shall be made for the oldest contributions first, all repayments for contributions as of the same time being made ratably as to them.

ARTICLE III. PROFITS AND LOSSES OF THE FIRM; PARTICIPATION OF PARTNERS THEREIN; DRAWINGS; BONUSES

Section A. Units of Participation in Profits and Losses Held by the Respective Partners. Except as otherwise expressly provided in this Article, participation of partners in net profits and losses shall be on the basis of the units of participation held by each partner, which shall be as follows:

- A: 30 units
- B: 20 units
- C: 20 units
- D: 12 units
- E: 8 units
- F: 5 units

Upon termination of all interest in the partnership as to any partner, his units of participation and all rights thereunder shall expire. No amendment of this Agreement shall be required therefor. Otherwise no change in the aggregate number of units held by partners or in the number held by any partner shall be effected except by an appropriate amendment of this Agreement.

Section B. Drawing Accounts and the Extent to Which Any are Guaranteed. 1. The firm shall carry on its books a drawing account for each partner. As of the end of each calendar month he shall be paid the sum indicated below, which shall thereupon be charged to his drawing account.

- A: $2,400.00 per month
- B: 1,600.00 per month
- C: 1,600.00 per month
- D: 1,000.00 per month
- E: 800.00 per month
- F: 800.00 per month

2. As of close of each fiscal year there shall be credited to the drawing account of each partner his share of the net profits computed as provided in this Article III, less the amount of his annual contribution to capital of the firm; any reimbursements to him of contributions shall be so credited and all other debits and credits between the partner and the firm to date shall be included in the calculation. Any excess of credits over debits shall thereupon be paid to the partner.

3. If at the end of the fiscal year, after crediting to the drawing accounts of partners E and F the participation of each such partner in the net profits, there remains a deficit in his drawing account, he shall not be required to pay the amount of that deficit to the firm, but as an expense of the firm (to be shared ratably by the remaining partners who do not have the benefit of this guaranty) his account shall be credited in the amount of such deficit. Thus E and F each is guaranteed that he shall receive as a minimum his drawing account for each month of the year. Moreover, if the net profits of the year aggregate as much as the total of the drawing accounts of all partners plus any amounts credited in balancing the drawing accounts of E and F, all of the other partners shall retain the amounts of their respective drawing accounts. But, if the net profits aggregate less than the total paid in the drawing accounts plus the said amounts credited to the accounts of E and F, then A, B, C and D shall share ratably all such deficits for the year in the proportion of their respective drawing accounts, except however that D shall not be required to pay back to the firm any more than the amount that he has received in excess of the stated amounts of the drawing accounts of E and F.

4. If at the end of the fiscal year there are net profits for distribution over and above the aggregate of all the stipulated monthly drawings and payments made as the agreed annual additional contributions to capital, then the portion of such net profits not transferred to the reserve for bonuses, as provided for in the next section hereof, shall be applied first to payments to those partners who have received in their monthly drawings less than their ratable share of net profits; and thereafter the balance of net profits shall be distributed ratably to all partners in proportion to their respective units of participation.

Section C. Reserve for Bonuses and Payments Therefrom. The net profits of the firm remaining for each fiscal year after paying (or setting aside funds for paying) all expenses of the year and after paying fully the stipulated monthly drawings and making the annual agreed additional contributions to capital, shall be distributed as follows: seventy five per cent of such remaining net profits shall be distributed as heretofore provided (Sections A and B of this Article) and the remaining twenty five per cent shall be placed in a "bonus reserve". The management committee shall as promptly as convenient recommend to all partners the uses to which this fund of twenty five per cent shall be placed, and thereupon at a meeting of the firm it shall be determined to whom and in what amounts such reserved funds shall be paid. It is anticipated that normally, unless some anticipated need for the reserve fund seems to require other use of such funds in the new fiscal year immediately ahead, said reserve fund will be used for extra distributions to partners as achievement bonuses.

ARTICLE IV. MEETINGS AND VOTING OF PARTNERS

Section A. Meetings of Partners; Voting at Such Meetings. 1. A meeting of partners shall be held at any time on call of the management committee or at any time after written notice at least 10 days in advance jointly signed by any three partners, specifying the hour and purposes of the meeting. The call by the management committee may be written or oral and need not be made any period of time in advance of the meeting, nor need it specify the purposes of the meeting; except, however, that in those instances where written notice for at least a specified period of time is required by any provision of these Articles, every call or notice of such meeting shall comply with such requirement.

2. At each meeting of partners every partner shall have one vote for each unit of participation held by him, as specified in Section A of Article III of this document; a quorum for any issue at any meeting shall exist if partners holding a majority of such units are present in person or voting by proxy or written instruction. Any partner may vote on any matter (subject to provisions of paragraph 3, this Section) if not present, by general or specific proxy to a partner present or by specific instructions in writing.

3. A partner shall not vote, however, and the number of outstanding units shall be deemed to be reduced by the number he holds (for the purposes of determining on any such issue whether quorum exists or whether the requisite percentage of outstanding units have been voted in the affirmative), when he is the partner affected by any of the following issues:

(a) If the partner has given a notice of withdrawal from the firm and the partnership meeting is voting on a proposal to terminate the firm and liquidate its affairs (see Article V, Section D) the person whose notice of withdrawal is pending shall not vote and the percentage of votes for termination and liquidation shall be determined as though that partner's units of participation did not exist.

(b) If the issue before the partnership is whether a partner (i) is under permanent disability, or (ii) should be expelled from the firm, whether for cause or without determining that a cause exists or (iii) should be permitted to retire or to attain retirement by gradual steps, or (iv) should be granted a temporary withdrawal from the firm (see Article V, Sections C, E, F and G), then as to each such issue the partner involved shall not vote and the percentage of votes shall be determined as though his units of participation did not exist.

4. Excepting only as provided in paragraph 3 of this Section A of Article IV or in Section D of Article XI of this Agreement, no partner shall be disqualified from voting on any issue, notwithstanding any interest he may have therein which differs from the interest of the firm or the other partners.

Section B. Percentage of Votes Required for Certain Partnership Decisions; Requirement of Recommendation of the Management Committee in Advance of Certain Partnership Decisions.

1. As provided by Article V of this Agreement, it may be determined by partnership vote that one presently a partner (i) is under permanent disability, (ii) should be expelled from the firm, (iii) should be permitted to retire or to attain retirement by gradual steps, or (iv) should be granted temporary withdrawal from the firm; or that one not a partner presently be added as a partner (see Article V, Sections B, C, E, F and G). As to each such issue (subject in each instance to the provisions of paragraph 3 of Section A of this Article), it is required that for so determining that issue in the affirmative, affirmative votes shall be cast by partners holding at least two-thirds of the outstanding units of participation that can be voted on that issue. An affirmative recommendation of the management committee in advance is required for a vote of the partners on the addition of a new partner (see Article V, Section B) or for a vote on payments out of the bonus reserve (see Article III, Section C).

2. As provided by Article X of this Agreement, decision may be made that the firm be terminated and its affairs liquidated at any meeting held for the specific purpose of determining whether this shall be done, on the written call of the management committee or of any three partners stating the purpose of the meeting and giving at least three days' notice. For determining this issue in the affirmative (subject to the provisions of paragraph 3(a) of Section A of this Article) votes in the affirmative of partners holding at least two-thirds of the outstanding units of participation that can be voted on that issue, shall be required.

3. As provided in Article XII of this Agreement, these Articles of Partnership may be amended upon affirmative votes of partners holding at least two-thirds of the outstanding units of participation that can be voted on that issue, provided that the proposed amendment and the recommendation of the management committee with reference thereto are attached to the written notice of the meeting at which the proposed amendment is to be considered.

4. A majority of the votes cast, a quorum being present, may determine any other issue at a partnership meeting, provided no such determination shall be contrary to a provision of law or of this Agreement.

ARTICLE V. CHANGES AS TO PARTNERS

Section A. No Classes of Partners. Though their contractual rights differ, as provided in this instrument, all partners are of the same class and have identical and equal rights except as herein otherwise provided.

Section B. Addition of Partners. The management committee may from time to time propose that additional partners be invited to join the partnership, and may propose the units of participation and the drawing accounts for each, together with the proposed amendment to the Articles of Partnership, specifically providing for any drawing account, guaranties and other provisions. In each such instance:

1. There shall be given to each partner a notice of at least ten days of a meeting for all partners at which each partner shall be entitled to discuss the proposal fully; each partner shall be entitled to a postponement of that meeting up to a date not less than thirty days after the giving of the ten-day notice.

2. At that meeting the partners may by their affirmative votes (as provided in paragraph 1 of Section B of Article IV) determine that the invitation shall be extended as proposed by the management committee or with such revisions as are determined upon.

3. If the invitation is accepted, the new partner and prior partners holding at least two-thirds of the participating units entitled to vote at the meeting referred to in paragraphs 1 and 2 of this Section B, shall join in executing an amendment to these Articles of Partnership providing for the change in the partnership thus effected.

Section C. Death or Permanent Disability of a Partner.

1. *Death.* The death of a partner shall terminate all his interest in the partnership, its property and assets. The continuing firm shall pay in cash to his estate (or to his nominee or nominees in accordance with the provisions of any separate agreement entered into between him and the management committee acting for the firm) the following amounts to be paid in installments at the times indicated:

(a) On or before thirty days after the date of his death, the net amount of his capital in the firm as of the date of death plus interest on his capital to that date.

(b) Within ninety days from the date of death, an amount computed as follows:

(i) Start with his pro rata share of seventy five percent of the net profits (after reducing said profits by interest on the capital accounts of all partners to date of death) of the firm for that portion of its then current year ending with the date of death;

(ii) Add thereto any part of the remaining twenty five percent of the firm's net profits which the management committee in its discretion determines to be his fair share of such net profits as a bonus payment to him, based on the same considerations for that part of the year as are provided for any full year in Section C of Article III hereof;

(iii) Deduct from the total arrived at in (ii) above, all distributions the deceased partner had received from the firm on account of net earnings during the year; and

(iv) Adjust the remaining balance by debiting and crediting all sums owing to the firm by him or by the firm to him immediately prior to his death. If the result is a minus balance, it shall be deducted from the aggregate amount payable in monthly installments as provided in subparagraph (c) of Section C, paragraph 1.

(c) In a series of forty-two consecutive monthly installments, beginning on or before one hundred twenty days after the date of his death, a further amount which (except as otherwise herein provided) shall be the average of the sums paid to him as a partner of the firm during each of the last three complete fiscal years of the firm during which he was a partner.

(i) The computation of the sums so paid to him each year shall include all distributions to him out of net income of the firm, but without any deductions for contributions to its capital or any additions for reimbursements therefor or interest on unreimbursed contributions. If he became a retired partner or temporarily withdrawn partner, the years of retirement or of temporary withdrawal are not to be included in the computation. If he had not been a member of the firm for as long as three complete fiscal years, then there shall be paid the average of sums paid to him for two such years, and if not a member for as long as two such years, then the sums so paid to him for one year. If he had not been a member one full year, no sums shall be paid under this subparagraph (c).

(ii) The first six installments of the amount thus to be paid by the continuing firm shall each be as much as decedent's current agreed monthly drawing at the time of his death and may, at the option of the firm, be as much more as the firm shall elect. The remainder of the sum payable by the continuing firm, if any (after the payment of the first six installments) shall be paid in thirty-six monthly installments, approximately equal, beginning three hundred days after death, with interest added to each of these installments at the rate of five percent per annum from date of death until paid.

2. *Permanent Disability.* (a) The determination that a partner is permanently disabled shall terminate all his interests in the partnership and his units of participation as a partner. That determination shall be made only upon the affirmative vote by partners holding at least two-thirds of all units of participation, not including the partner whose disability is in issue or the units held by him, all in accordance with the provisions of Article IV of this agreement.

(b) As of the time of the determination of permanent disability of a partner, he shall no longer be a partner and shall no longer have any duties to perform with respect to any professional employment of the firm, nor shall he be privileged to perform any services in any such matter. His units of participation shall expire as of that time, and hence no votes at any partnership meeting may thereafter be cast by him, and he shall not be entitled to any share of profits or losses thereafter. Except for sums to be paid to him by the continuing firm as provided for in subparagraph (c) of this paragraph 2, he shall not be entitled to any payments from the firm and shall have no rights or interests in any of its properties or assets from the time of such determination. However, the partners in their discretion may vote to bestow upon him some purely honorary title such as "Partner Emeritus," without compensation.

(c) The amounts payable by the continuing firm to or for the account of a partner determined to be permanently disabled shall be computed in the same way and paid in the same manner as if he had died on the date of the determination of his permanent disability. His death before all such payments have been made shall not interrupt the continued payments by the continuing firm; but no further sums shall be owing by the firm because of his death.

Section D. Permanent Withdrawal of a Partner.

1. *Notice of Withdrawal and Effective Date of Withdrawal.* Any partner may voluntarily withdraw from the partnership at any time on notice of thirty days to the other partners. As of the expiration of the thirty day period, or sooner if mutually agreed upon, the withdrawal shall be effective.

2. *Possible Termination of the Firm Superseding Withdrawal Notice.* At any time during the pendency of a withdrawal notice and before the effective date of withdrawal, a termination of the firm may be voted in accordance with the provisions of Article X of this Agreement. If this is done, the dissolution proceedings, the liquidation of assets, and the distribution of proceeds shall ensue, and the notice of withdrawal shall be of no effect.

3. *Partition with and Payments to the Withdrawing Partner.* The withdrawing partner's right, title, and interest in the firm shall

be extinguished in consideration of the partition with and the payments to him by the continuing firm on the following bases:

(a) On the effective date of withdrawal he shall be paid the amount of his net capital in the firm plus interest thereon to that date. This payment shall be in cash unless the firm at its option elects to set aside for him and deliver to him in kind his pro rata share of all its capital assets. In the event the firm sets aside property for him it shall have a discretion as to what items to set aside, all items being valued for the purposes of partition, either by agreement between the firm and the withdrawing partner or by an independent appraisal, at current market prices.

(b) Within ninety days after the effective date of withdrawal an amount in cash shall be paid computed as follows:

(i) Start with his pro rata share of seventy-five per cent of the net profits (after reducing said profits by interest on the capital accounts of all partners to the effective date of withdrawal) of the firm for that portion of its then current year ending on the effective date of withdrawal;

(ii) Add thereto any part of the twenty-five per cent of the firm's net profits for said portion of its then current year, which the management committee fairly determines to be his fair share of such net profits as a bonus payment to him based on the same considerations for that portion of the year that are provided in Section C of Article III for any full year, and bearing in mind that the same part of twenty-five per cent of the profits from receipts of the portion of the current year, will be applied to future receipts from fees charged for services rendered before the withdrawal, pursuant to the provisions of subparagraph (c) (ii) of this paragraph 3;

(iii) Deduct from the total arrived at in (ii) above all distributions the withdrawing partner had received from the firm on account of net earnings during the year;

(iv) Adjust the balance thus arrived at by debiting the discounted value at that time of his ratable share of payments yet to accrue against the firm on account of the prior death or permanent disability of a partner; and

(v) Adjust the balance thus arrived at by debiting and crediting all sums owing to the firm by him or by the firm to him immediately prior to the effective date of withdrawal.

If the foregoing computations result in a minus balance it shall be debited against each quarterly payment later accruing to him under the provisions of subparagraphs (c) and (d); and if the debt is not thus discharged, it shall be owing by the withdrawing partner to the continuing firm.

(c) In quarter-annual installments following the withdrawal, a share of the fees collected by the firm during each quarter thereafter for services rendered by the firm prior to the effective date of withdrawal shall be paid, the amount of these quarter-annual payments to be computed as follows:

(i) Start with his pro rata share of seventy-five per cent of the gross amount of such fees collected during such quarter (after reducing same by the amount if any which the management committee of the continuing firm fairly determines to represent the share of all fees earned during that quarter by the firm which were prepaid by the client prior to the effective date of withdrawal);

(ii) Add thereto an amount which is that percentage of the figure computed under (i) immediately above, which the amount computed under (b) (ii) of this paragraph 3 bears to the figure computed under paragraph (b) (i) of this paragraph 3; and

(iii) The total amount thus arrived at shall be paid to the withdrawing partner with an accounting to him at that time of how the amount is arrived at, provided he then makes a like accounting and payment if any is due by him to the firm, in accordance with the provisions of subparagraph (d) immediately following.

(d) Subject to the right of each client to direct that any or all of his pending matters in which the firm is employed on the effective date of withdrawal shall be handled for him by the continuing firm rather than the withdrawing partner, the withdrawing partner, at his option, as to each of the current employments of the firm pending on that date for which he was the responsible partner in charge, shall then be entitled (provided he then pays the firm for all its expenditures on behalf of the client in connection with such matter for which the client then is or would later be indebted to the firm) to assume all further responsibilities to the client for that matter and to take with him all files and documents pertaining wholly to that employment. Thereafter, the withdrawing partner shall bill the client for and be entitled to collect for disbursements theretofore made and services theretofore rendered in connection with that matter as well as for subsequent services and disbursements. The withdrawing partner shall account to the continuing firm with respect to his gross collections of fees for services rendered on each such matter by the firm prior to the effective date of withdrawal, and shall pay the firm in cash, in quarter-annual installments from such collections, amounts calculated on the same basis, or as nearly as possible on the same basis, as the firm shall be accounting to the withdrawing partner and paying him in accordance with the provisions of sub-paragraph (c) immediately above.

Agreement as to Tax Effects

In view of the differences in tax results dependent upon distinctions which may not be readily apparent to lawyers outside the tax field, it is quite important that contracts with reference to the liquidation or sale of the interest of a withdrawing or disabled partner, and especially of a deceased partner, should clearly express the intention of the parties as to the tax effects anticipated by the parties to flow from their agreement. Naturally, they should be careful to see that the agreement does what they think it does. As an addition to the agreement, therefore, we suggest a paragraph pertinent to all provisions of Sections C and D of Article V:

It is contemplated by the parties to this Agreement that any payments hereunder for the interest in the firm of a withdrawing or permanently disabled or deceased partner are, to the extent that they represent payment for partnership properties, capital payments falling under Section 736(b) of the Internal Revenue Code. All other payments for the interests of such persons, including so-called "interest" payments on capital invested, are intended by the partners as payments of partnership income under Section 736(a) of the Internal Revenue Code. Each partner covenants for himself and his heirs and assigns that he will make no claims or representations with reference to the income tax nature of any such amounts that are inconsistent with the intent expressed in this subparagraph.

Section E. Retirement of Partners; Gradual Steps toward Retirement; Retirement Plans for Partners.

1. *Retired Partners; Plans for Their Compensation.* (a) A retired partner shall receive no current compensation from the firm in payment for current services, either by way of participation in distribution of net profits of the firm or agreed monthly drawings. He may receive bonuses or specifically agreed fees or shares of fees. He shall be offered, at the expense of the firm, so long as he is able and wishes to use same for at least twenty percent of the business time of each year, an office in the offices of the firm and a secretary to give him such secretarial assistance as he may require; in consideration of which he shall, whenever convenient to him, advise with and serve as consultant to any of the partners or associates of the firm. His name shall be carried on firm letterheads, in legal directories and otherwise not as an active partner of the firm but under the heading, "Of Counsel."

(b) The management committee in its discretion is authorized to pay during any year, to each retired partner as a "retirement bonus", up to twenty-five percent of his average annual income for the last three full years during which he was an active partner of the firm.

2. *When a Partner Retires.* Any partner may retire at any time upon approval by the partners, in accordance with provisions of

Article IV of this Agreement, of his request to retire. Any partner who has attained the age of seventy-five shall retire if and when requested to do so by partners holding at least two-thirds of the units or participation entitled to vote.

3. *Gradual Steps toward Retirement.* If the request of a partner that he be permitted to enter upon and carry out a plan for gradual retirement is approved by vote of the partners in accordance with the provisions of Article IV of this Agreement, a program of gradual steps toward his retirement shall be entered into and consummated, as agreed between him and the firm. Such a plan may be required of any partner at any time after he attains the age of seventy. The adoption of such a plan as to any partner will involve a program over a period of the following ten years (provided his interest in the firm is not meanwhile terminated by death, total disability, withdrawal, or expulsion; and provided said interest is not modified by an agreement between him and the firm approved by vote of the partners). During that ten-year period his duties shall be gradually reduced and hence, his units of participation and thus his share of net profits or losses, and his voting rights shall be reduced from what they are at the start of the period by eight per cent at the end of each of the first nine fiscal years, of the period, and his remaining interest in the firm shall be terminated by effecting his retirement at the end of the tenth year.

Section F. Expulsion of a Partner.

1. *Expulsion for Cause.* A partner shall be expelled for cause when it has been determined by vote of partners in accordance with the provisions of Article IV of this Agreement, that any of the following reasons for his expulsion exist:

(a) Disbarment, suspension or other major disciplinary action of any duly constituted authority.

(b) Professional misconduct or violation of the canons of professional ethics, if such misconduct continues after its desistance has been requested by the management committee.

(c) Action that injures the professional standing of the firm, if such action continues after its desistance is requested by the management committee.

(d) Insolvency or bankruptcy or assignment of assets for the benefit of creditors.

(e) Breach of any provision of the Articles of Partnership of the firm, which all other partners expressly agree is a major provision, if, after the breach has been specified as a prospective ground for expulsion by written notice given by the management committee, the same breach continues or occurs again.

(f) Any other reason which the other partners unanimously agree warrants expulsion.

2. *Effects of Expulsion for Cause.* Upon a determination that a partner be expelled for cause he shall thereby be so expelled and shall have no right or interest thereafter in the firm or any of its assets, clientele, files or records, or affairs. He shall have thereafter no further duties to the firm or any of its clients and shall be privileged to serve none of them thereafter. He shall immediately remove himself and his personal effects from the firm offices. Upon any such expulsion, the expelled partner shall be obligated not to accept employments for services from any who have been clients of the firm during the last five years preceding the determination of expulsion, the obligation not to accept such employments being a continuing one for a term of the next ensuing five years. From the time of the expulsion, the expelled partner shall have no participation whatever in the income or losses of the firm or any distribution or drawings from the net income. Realizing that the existence of any such cause for expulsion may bring disgrace on the firm and damage the firm in amounts and ways that cannot be calculated or become liquidated in amount, each partner agrees that the firm shall succeed to all of the rights of the expelled partner as hereinabove set forth and shall retain all sums unpaid by it to the expelled partner, whether accrued or not at that time; further, that the receipt and retention by the firm of all such rights and sums shall satisfy and discharge the damages of the firm, being retained as and thereby determined to be liquidated damages; no other indebtedness of the expelled partner to the firm being discharged.

3. *Expulsion without Determining Any Cause Therefor.* A partner shall be expelled immediately when, on recommendation of the management committee, it is determined by a vote of the partners as provided in Article IV that he shall be expelled without determination of any cause therefor. This method of expulsion may be employed notwithstanding the fact that grounds may exist for expulsion for cause.

4. *Effects of Expulsion without Determining Any Cause Therefor.* Upon such expulsion without determining a cause therefor, the partner so expelled shall have no right or interest thereafter in the firm or any of its assets, clientele, files or records, or affairs. He shall have thereafter no further duties to the firm or any of its clients and shall be privileged to serve none of them thereafter. He shall immediately remove himself and his personal effects from the firm offices. Except as otherwise provided in this paragraph, a partner so expelled shall be entitled to the same rights, the same payments by, and be subject to the same duties to the continuing firm as if he were then voluntarily withdrawing from the firm.

Section G. Temporary Incapacity; Leave of Absence; Temporary Withdrawal; Vacations.

1. *Temporary Incapacity or Illness.* In the event of any interruption of the performance of any partner's services to the firm or to

its clients on account of any temporary incapacity or illness, or any other reason not voluntary with him, the management committee may, in its complete discretion, make any arrangements it deems fair to the partner and to the firm, as to the period of his absence and his compensation during that period.

2. *Leave of Absence.* In the event any partner desires an interruption of the performance of his services to the firm or its clients, for any reason voluntary with him, his request shall be submitted to and may be approved by the management committee which, if the interruption shall not be for more than one year, may in its complete discretion make any arrangements it deems fair to the partner and to the firm, as to the period of his absence and his compensation during that period.

3. *Temporary Withdrawal.* If any partner desires an interruption of his services to the firm and its clients for a period longer than the management committee can, or feels that it should, approve under either of the last two paragraphs of this instrument, he may apply to the firm for a temporary withdrawal. The firm, by vote of the partners in accordance with provisions of Article IV of this document, shall determine whether the request shall be granted and if so, on what terms and conditions. During the period of any temporary withdrawal, there shall be a suspension and not a termination of the units of participation of the partner involved. Such a temporary withdrawal unless extended under the same procedure by which it was originally granted shall be for a specific time, at the expiration of which the temporarily withdrawing partner shall resume his services.

4. *Vacations.* All decisions of the firm with reference to vacations of partners in excess of _____ weeks a year for each partner are to be wholly within the discretion of the management committee.

ARTICLE VI. DUTIES OF PARTNERS

Section A. Devotion to Duty. Each partner shall devote his best efforts to serving professionally the firm and its clients. Subject to any exceptions provided in rules of the firm adopted in accordance with the provisions of Article VII, Section A of this Agreement, or any other exceptions consented to by the management committee, each partner shall devote substantially all his normal business time to such services.

Section B. Charging for Services. 1. Each partner shall charge reasonably for all services rendered by him, following generally the policies of the firm as to fees charged. However, each partner may serve without charge any member of his own family, and with the consent of the management committee any partner may serve without charge, or at less than regular charge, any civic, educational, religious, or charitable organization or project.

2. Each partner will follow rules and policies of the firm adopted in accordance with the provisions of Section A of Article VII of this Agreement relating to consideration by the firm, rather than one partner only, of fees on substantial services rendered by the firm.

3. No salaries, commissions, fees or gratuities of any substantial significance shall be accepted, directly or indirectly, by any partner personally from any client or prospective client of the firm, unless with the express consent in advance of the management committee, and the fair value of any such item received with such consent, though retained by the partner, shall be treated for accounting purposes as compensation to the firm and shall be charged against such partner as an advance on the next maturing installment or installments of his drawing account. The management committee may agree, however, to any exception to any provision of this paragraph.

ARTICLE VII. MANAGEMENT

Section A. Authority and Membership of the Management Committee. 1. Subject to the express terms of this Agreement, which as to certain specific matters provides that decisions of the firm shall be determined by the vote of the partners holding required units of participation, the complete and sole management of the firm is hereby vested in the management committee.

2. Any part or parts of the power, right, and authority vested in the management committee may, at any time and from time to time, be delegated by it to a subcommittee of one or more chosen by it. Such authority may be delegated with power in the subcommittee only to recommend to the management committee what action should be taken, or with power to act; in the latter event, action of the subcommittee shall be the action of the management committee. Any delegation may be terminated by the management committee at any time.

3. It may from time to time cause a set of the rules and policies of the firm to be distributed in an office manual to all partners, associated attorneys and employees of the firm.

4. The management committee shall consist of three partners. No one of them shall be retired (though he may be participating in gradual steps toward retirement) or the subject of pending action for expulsion. Partners subject to any of the stated disabilities shall be disqualified from election to or from acting on the management committee. Upon any such event that disqualifies from continued service a member of the committee, he shall automatically cease to be a member of the committee and shall not serve thereafter unless and until (when qualified) re-elected to fill a vacancy on the committee. There shall be an alternate member elected by the partners, and if there is a

vacancy on the committee because of death, resignation, or disqualification, the alternate shall become a member of the committee. In the event of any temporary absence of a member, the alternate may serve as a member of the committee during the period of the absence. As soon as convenient the partners shall meet and choose a successor to fill any vacancy (other than a vacancy resulting from a temporary absence of one of the four elected). In the event of any vacancy not yet filled by vote of the partners, the management committee may on its own account call on any qualified partner of its choice to serve temporarily with the committee. The tenure of one so chosen shall expire when the partners elect a successor.

5. The management committee, from the effective date of this instrument, shall consist of A, C, and E. The named alternate shall be B. Each of the four shall serve respectively until his tenure is terminated by death, resignation, disqualification, or a determination by vote of the partners that his term shall expire.

6. The tenure of every member of the committee and every alternate member shall be subject to termination without cause, by requisite vote of the partners in accordance with the provisions of Article IV of this document.

Section B. Functioning of the Management Committee and Its Subcommittees. 1. Members of the management committee shall make every reasonable effort to keep each other and the alternate advised of all pending problems, prospective decisions, and actions taken. Action of the committee shall be by majority vote. It shall not be necessary that any notice be given of the time or place of decision or of the matter to be decided. Any decision of the committee may be reversed prospectively by any subsequent action of the committee.

2. Though the committee has no obligation so to do, it may refer any matter on which all members of the committee are not in agreement to a meeting of the partners for decision.

Section C. Membership in Subcommittees of the Management Committee. The management committee shall decide what subcommittees there shall be from time to time, how many members (one or more) there shall be of each subcommittee, who the members shall be, and what the subcommittee's functions and authority shall be. The management committee may at any time modify or revise prospectively any authorized decision of any subcommittee. Any partner or any full time employee may be a member of any subcommittee.

ARTICLE VIII. INSURANCE; INVESTMENTS

Section A. Life Insurance. The management committee in its discretion shall determine from time to time what life insurance, if any, shall be carried on the lives of partners for benefit of the firm.

Section B. Other Insurance. The management committee in its discretion shall determine from time to time what other insurance, if any, the firm shall carry.

Section C. Investments. The management committee in its discretion shall determine from time to time what investments, if any, the firm shall make and all matters with reference to the proceeds of such investments, and with reference to reinvestments or changes in investment policies.

ARTICLE IX. PROPERTIES AND RECORDS

The management committee in its discretion shall make all decisions of the firm from time to time on the following subjects:

Section A. Firm Properties. [Some firms in their Articles limit the authority of the management committee or its equivalent with respect to properties. Examples:

(i) Require that the purchase of all properties, except supplies, be approved by partnership vote; or

(ii) Require such a vote for purchase of properties costing more than a specific amount; or

(iii) Require such a vote for purchase of an office site or office building; or any property not deemed necessary to the practice of law; or

(iv) Limit the amount to be spent in a year, without a partnership vote for replacements, repairs or upkeep.]

Section B. Accounting Records. [Many firms have express provisions in their partnership agreements covering one or more of the following points on this subject.

(i) Specifically requiring that the books of account be kept on a cash basis;

(ii) Specifically defining the fiscal year of the firm;

(iii) Specifically defining what financial statements shall be prepared with copies given to each partner;

(iv) Specifically requiring that partnership income tax returns be prepared and filed regularly and a copy of the same given to each partner a specific period, say at least one week, before each return is filed, and a specific period, say at least two weeks, before his personal return is due;

(v) Specifically requiring that all accounting records of the firm shall be open to inspection by each partner at any time during business hours;

(vi) Specifically requiring that the financial records of the firm shall be retained for an agreed period and shall be available for inspection or copying by anyone who was a partner at the time that such records were prepared, including one who at the time of the inspection is a former partner.]

ARTICLE X. TERMINATION AND LIQUIDATION OF FIRM

Section A. Termination of the Firm by Voluntary Vote or Otherwise. The partnership may be terminated at any time by affirmative vote of the partners at a partnership meeting, in accordance with the provisions of Article IV of this Agreement.

Section B. Pending Employments on Termination. In the event of termination of the partnership, no further services shall be rendered in the partnership name and no further business transacted for the partnership except action necessary for the winding up of its affairs, the distribution or liquidation of its assets, and the distribution of the proceeds of the liquidation. Maintenance of offices to effectuate or facilitate the winding up of the partnership affairs shall not be construed to involve a continuation of the partnership. In advance of the effective date of the termination of the partnership the management committee shall assign every uncompleted service to one or another of the partners on such terms as shall be agreeable to the clients involved and the partners to whom such matters are assigned; and the rendition of services from the effective date of the termination shall henceforth be by such individuals and other law firms, if any, in which they may respectively become partners.

Section C. Liquidation of Assets. The members of the management committee (but not including alternate members) on the effective date of the termination of the partnership, shall be the agents of the terminated partnership in liquidation, and of the individual partners, for winding up all its affairs and all business transactions of the partnership, other than the performance of incomplete professional services referred to in Section B above. Said members of the management committee shall continue to serve (unless death, incapacity, or resignation shall intervene) until the completion of the winding up and liquidation. The committee shall act by majority vote or votes. In the event of any temporary or permanent vacancy in the committee, the remaining members shall choose a third member of the committee. Members of the management committee shall not be paid for their services after the termination of the partnership in the winding up or liquidation operations. They may, out of the assets and proceeds of the assets on hand, employ such assistants as they determine appropriate, and the committee may so employ and pay any one of its members to take any such actions and render any such services in the winding up and liquidation.

Section D. Prior Opportunity of Partners to Bid for Purchase of Assets Being Liquidated. The partners holding units of participation immediately prior to the termination of the partnership may, in the discretion of the management committee, be given first opportunity over any other prospective bidder for the purchase of any of the assets, all such partners being given an equal opportunity, so that they respectively as individuals or jointly or in groups, may bid; and if the best bid by any of them, in the opinion of the management committee, is at least ninety-five per cent of the highest and best bid otherwise received, then such best bid by any partner or partners may be accepted.

Section E. Distribution of Proceeds from Liquidation. The business affairs of the partnership, in the event of the termination of the partnership, shall be wound up and liquidated as promptly as business circumstances and orderly business practices will permit. After payment of expenses incurred, the net assets and the proceeds of the liquidation shall be applied in the following order:

1. To the payment of the debts and liabilities of the partnership owing to the creditors other than partners, and the expenses of liquidation.

2. To the payment of the debts and liabilities owing to the partners other than for (i) capital, (ii) profits and (iii) any unmatured installments yet to be paid on account of the death, permanent disability, retirement (or death following retirement) or withdrawal of a partner. It is agreed that all sums to become due on installments referred to in (iii) shall be assumed ratably by each partner at the date of termination and that each shall thereafter pay his ratable share of each such installment as it becomes due.

3. To the repayment to each of the partners of his capital contributions to the firm.

4. To the payment to partners (computed on the basis of their respective units of participation at the date of termination of the firm) of all the remaining net of assets and proceeds, if any, first in whatever amounts are necessary to complete a ratable distribution for the current year, to each partner to the full extent of distributions previously received by each other partner; and second, to ratable distributions to all partners.

5. If the assets and proceeds of the liquidation are insufficient to pay all of the items referred to in paragraphs 1 and 2, but not including (i), (ii) and (iii) referred to in paragraph 2, then the management committee shall make an assessment against the partners to cover net losses of the firm and such assessments shall be paid and applied to the satisfaction of the items covered by paragraphs 1 and 2.

ARTICLE XI. LEGAL EFFECT OF PROVISIONS; ARBITRATION

Section A. Governing Law. All provisions of this Agreement shall be construed, shall be given effect and shall be enforced according to the laws of the State of _____.

Section B. Persons Bound. Each of the partners executes this Agreement with the understanding and agreement that each has hereby bound and obligated himself, his estate, and any and all claiming by, through, or under him.

Section C. Rights of Partners Not Assignable; Not to be Pledged. No partner and no one acting by authority of or for a partner may pledge, hypothecate, or in any manner transfer his interest in the partnership, or his interest in any of its assets, receivables, records, documents, files, or clientele, all such rights and interests of each partner being personal to him and non-transferable and non-assignable (except that other partners of the firm may succeed to such rights or some of them in accordance with the terms of this Agreement).

Section D. Finality of Decisions within the Firm; Effect of Personal Diverse or Adverse Interest of Any Partner. Every final decision of the firm on any matter affecting any party hereto or anyone claiming by, through or under any party, by vote of the partners or by decision of the management committee, when in accordance with the terms and provisions of this Agreement, shall be binding and conclusive. Except where it is expressly provided in this Agreement that one shall not be permitted to vote as to any such decision, there shall be no disqualification of anyone from voting who shall be entitled to vote according to the terms and provisions of this Agreement, notwithstanding any adverse or divergent interest that he may personally have in the decision; and the decision shall, nevertheless, be binding and final notwithstanding any such adverse or divergent interest held by anyone so voting. It is understood that individual partners and that members of the management committee will doubtless have divergent and may have adverse, or arguably adverse, personal interests from one another on some matters that are to be determined according to the provisions of this Agreement and have diverse or adverse interests personally from those of some party affected by the decision; all this is agreed to and waived as a disqualification. Nonetheless, anyone entitled to such a vote on any such matter may recuse himself from voting and thereupon the decision shall be made on the computation of votes to the same effect as if the one so recusing himself had as to that matter, no right to vote; and if the vote is by the partners, as if he held no units of participation. Each party having any vote on any such matters shall recuse himself on any vote if requested so to do by joint action of partners holding a majority of the units of participation then outstanding.

Section E. Arbitration. Any controversy or claim arising out of or relating to any provision of this Agreement or the breach thereof, shall be settled by arbitration in accordance with the rules then in effect of the American Arbitration Association, to the extent consistent with the laws of the State of _____. It is agreed that any party to any award rendered in any such arbitration proceedings may seek a judgment upon the award and that judgment may be entered thereon by any court having jurisdiction.

Section F. Severability. It is agreed that the invalidity or unenforceability of any Article, Section, paragraph or provision of this Agreement shall not affect the validity or enforceability of any one or more of the other Articles, Sections, paragraphs or provisions; and that the parties hereto will execute any further instruments or perform any acts which are or may be necessary to effectuate all and each of the terms and provisions of this agreement.

ARTICLE XII. AMENDMENTS

An amendment hereto may alter, revise, delete or add to any provision or provisions of this agreement. No amendment to this instrument shall be adopted or become effective unless and until it (i) has been voted in accordance with the provisions of paragraph 3 of **Section B of Article IV of this Agreement;** and (ii) has been executed and attached to this Agreement as a part of same.

In Witness Whereof, the parties have signed this Agreement.

[*Signatures*] [5]

---

5. West's Modern Legal Forms § 6257. This agreement was prepared by Paul Carrington and William A. Sutherland for the American Bar Association Standing Committee on Economics of Law Practice. The original draft printed in the ABA Economics of Law Practice Series Pamphlet Number 6, November 1961, contained the helpful comments of the authors, omitted here to save space. The authors emphasized the need to tailor each partnership agreement to the clients, and cautioned their readers to consider the various provisions of this agreement as merely suggestions for comparison and study.

FORM 3A

ASSIGNMENT OF A LIMITED PARTNER'S INTEREST

For value received, I, the undersigned, of _____, hereby assign to _____, of _____, the whole of my interest in the limited partnership of _____, conducting business under a partnership agreement dated _____, 19__. Effective upon the signing of this instrument the assignee shall be entitled to receive the share of the profits or other compensation by way of income to which I would otherwise be entitled, and to the return of my contribution to the capital of the partnership. In the event that all the other members of the partnership consent thereto, the assignee shall be entitled to all the rights which I, as a limited partner, had in the partnership.

Dated _____, 19__. [*Signature*]

[*Acknowledgment*] [6]

6. West's Modern Legal Forms § 6456.

FORM 3B

CONSENT TO SUBSTITUTION OF A LIMITED PARTNER

We, the undersigned, being all the members of the limited partnership of _____, except _____, who by an instrument dated _____, 19__, and duly acknowledged by her, has assigned her entire interest as a limited partner in this partnership to _____, of _____, do hereby consent that _____ be substituted as a limited partner in the place of _____, and entitled to all the rights which _____ had as a limited partner in this partnership pursuant to the terms of the partnership agreement dated _____, 19__.

Dated _____, 19__. [*Signatures*] [7]

7. West's Modern Legal Forms § 6457.

FORM 3C

LIMITED PARTNERSHIP AGREEMENT

Agreement of Limited Partnership made this _____ day of _____, 19__, between _____ and _____, both of _____ (herein referred to as general partners), and _____ of _____, and _____ of _____ (herein referred to as limited partners).

1. **Formation.** The parties hereby form a limited partnership pursuant to sections _____ of the [Revised Statutes] of the State of _____, known as the Uniform Limited Partnership Act.

2. **Certificate.** The parties shall forthwith sign and swear to a certificate prepared in accordance with the provisions of the Uniform Limited Partnership Act cited above, and cause the same to be filed for record in the office of [*here designate the proper office*].

3. **Name.** The name of the partnership is _____.

4. **Business.** The purpose of the partnership shall be to engage in the business of _____, and in any other business necessary and related to it.

5. **Place of Business.** The principal place of business of the partnership shall be at _____, but additional places of business may be established as the general partners shall determine.

6. **Term.** The partnership shall commence on _____, 19__, and shall continue until terminated as herein provided.

7. **Capital.** The initial capital of the partnership shall be $_____. Each of the partners shall contribute in cash or in property the amount set opposite his name.

General Partners	Cash Contributions	Agreed Value of Property Contributions
_____	$_____	$_____
_____	_____	_____
Limited Partners		
_____	_____	_____
_____	_____	_____

The property contributed is described in a separate instrument attached hereto as Exhibit A.

8. **Additional Contributions to Capital.** The general partners shall make, and the limited partners shall each have the option of making, additional contributions to the capital of the partnership in such amount as the general partners deem necessary to carry on the business of the partnership.

9. **Withdrawal of Capital.** Neither a general nor a limited partner may withdraw all or any part of his capital contribution without the consent of all the general partners, provided that each limited partner may rightfully demand the return of all or part of his contribution after he has given six months' notice in writing to all the other partners. Upon any withdrawal by a limited partner the certificate of limited partnership shall be amended to reflect this change in his capital contribution.

10. **Profits and Losses.** The net profits of the partnership during each fiscal year shall be credited, and the net losses incurred by the partnership during any fiscal year shall be debited, as of the close thereof, to the capital accounts of the partners in the proportions set opposite their respective names.

General Partners	Percentage
_____	_____%
_____	_____%
Limited Partners	
_____	_____%
_____	_____%

Notwithstanding anything to the contrary herein contained, no limited partner shall be liable for any of the debts of the partnership or any of its losses in excess of his capital contributions to the partnership.

11. **Capital Accounts.** An individual capital account shall be maintained for each partner, to which shall be credited his contributions to capital and to which shall be debited his withdrawals from capital and his share of partnership losses.

12. **Salaries.** Each of the general partners shall receive such reasonable salaries as may from time to time be agreed upon by the general partners. These salaries shall be treated as an expense of the partnership in determining the net profit or loss in any fiscal year.

13. **Drawing Accounts.** An individual drawing account may be maintained for each partner in an amount fixed by the general part-

ners, but such drawing accounts shall be in the proportion to which the partners are entitled to share in the profits of the partnership.

14. **Management.** The general partners shall have equal rights in the management of the partnership business.

15. **Devotion to Business.** Each general partner shall devote all his normal business time and best efforts to the conduct of the business of the partnership.

16. **Limitations on General Partners' Powers.** No general partner shall, without the written consent or ratification of the specific act by all the other partners:

(a) Assign, transfer, or pledge any of the claims of or debts due to the partnership except upon payment in full, or arbitrate or consent to the arbitration of any disputes or controversies of the partnership;

(b) Make, execute, or deliver any assignment for the benefit of creditors, or sign any bond, confession of judgment, security agreement, deed, guarantee, indemnity bond, surety bond, or contract to sell or contract of sale of all or substantially all profit of the partnership;

(c) Lease or mortgage any part of partnership real estate or any interest therein, or enter into any contract for any such purpose;

(d) Pledge or hypothecate or in any manner transfer his interest in the partnership, except to the parties of this agreement;

(e) Become a surety, guarantor or accommodation party to any obligation except for partnership business;

(f) Do any act prohibited by law to be done by a single partner.

17. **Books of Account.** The partnership shall maintain adequate accounting records. All books, records and accounts of the partnership shall be kept at its principal place of business and shall be open at all times to inspection by all the partners.

18. **Accounting Basis.** The books of account shall be kept on a cash [*or* an accrual] basis.

19. **Fiscal Year.** The fiscal year of the partnership shall be the calendar year. The net profit or net loss of the partnership shall be determined in accordance with generally accepted accounting principles as soon as practicable after the close of each fiscal year.

20. **Annual Audit.** The books of account shall be audited as of the close of each fiscal year by a certified public accountant chosen by all the partners.

21. **Banking.** All the funds of the partnership shall be deposited in its name in such checking account or accounts as shall be designated

by the general partners. Checks shall be drawn on such accounts for partnership purposes only and shall be signed by any of the general partners.

22. **Assignment by Limited Partner.** Each limited partner may assign his interest in the partnership, and the assignee shall have the right to become a substituted limited partner and entitled to all the rights of the assignor if all the partners (except the assignor) consent thereto. Otherwise the assignee is only entitled to receive the share of the profits to which his assignor would be entitled.

23. **Retirement of a General Partner.** A general partner may retire from the partnership at the end of any fiscal year by giving at least 90 days' notice in writing to all the other partners.

24. **Effect of Retirement, Death or Insanity of a General Partner.** The retirement, death or insanity of a general partner dissolves the partnership, unless the business is continued by the remaining partners as herein provided.

25. **Distribution of Assets on Dissolution.** Upon dissolution of the partnership by mutual agreement or for any other reason its liabilities to creditors shall be paid in the order of priority provided by law, and the remaining assets, or the proceeds of their sale, shall be distributed in the following order:

(a) To the limited partners in proportion to their share of the profits;

(b) To the limited partners in proportion to their capital contributions;

(c) To the general partners other than for capital and profits;

(d) To the general partners in proportion to their share of the profits;

(e) To the general partners in proportion to their capital contributions.

26. **Election of Remaining Partners to Continue Business.** In the event of the retirement, death or insanity of a general partner, the remaining partners shall have the right to continue the business of the partnership under its present name either by themselves or in conjunction with any other person or persons they may select, but they shall pay to the retiring partner, or to the legal representatives of the deceased or insane partner, as the case may be, the value of his interest in the partnership, as provided in paragraph 28.

27. **Notice of Election to Continue Business.** If the remaining partners elect to continue the business of the partnership they shall

serve notice in writing of such election upon the retiring partner within two months after receipt of his notice of intention to retire, or upon the legal representatives of the deceased or insane partner within three months after the death of the decedent or the adjudication of insanity, as the case may be. If at the time of such election no legal representative has been appointed notice shall be sent to the last known address of the decedent or insane partner.

28. **Valuation of Partner's Interest.** The value of the interest of a retiring, deceased or insane partner shall be the sum of (a) his capital account, (b) his drawing account, and (c) his proportionate share of accrued net profits. If a net loss has been incurred to the date of dissolution, his share of such net loss shall be deducted. The assets of the partnership shall be valued at book value and no value shall be attributed to good will.

29. **Payment of Purchase Price.** The value of the partner's interest as determined in the above paragraph shall be paid without interest to the retiring partner, or to the legal representatives of the deceased or insane partner, as the case may be, in _____ monthly installments, commencing on the first day of the second month after the effective date of the purchase.

30. **Death of a Limited Partner.** In the event of the death of a limited partner, his personal representative during the period of administration of his estate shall succeed to his rights hereunder as a limited partner, and this interest as a limited partner may be assigned to any member of the family of the limited partner in distribution of his estate, or to any person in pursuance of a bequest in his last will and testament, and such member of the family [or person, if made by will] to whom such assignment or bequest is made, shall thereupon succeed to his interest as a limited partner and have all the rights of a substituted limited partner.

In Witness Whereof, the parties have signed and sealed this agreement.

[*Signatures and seals*] [8]

8. West's Modern Legal Forms § 6452.

FORM 3D

LIMITED PARTNERSHIP CERTIFICATE

We, the undersigned, for the purpose of forming a limited partnership pursuant to the Uniform Limited Partnership Act as set forth in Sections _____ of the _____ Code, hereby certify:

1. **Name.** The name of the partnership is _____.

2. **Character of Business.** The character of the business to be carried on is to engage in the business of _____.

3. **Place of Business.** The location of the principal place of business of the partnership is _____.

4. **General Partners.** The name and place of residence of each general partner are:

_____   _____

_____   _____

Limited Partners. The name and place of residence of each limited partner are:

_____   _____

_____   _____

5. **Term.** The term for which the partnership is to exist is indefinite [*or* from _____, 19__, to the close of business on _____, 19__, and thereafter from year to year].

6. **Initial Contribution of Each Limited Partner.** The amount of cash and a description of and the agreed value of the other property contributed by each limited partner are:

Name	Cash	Description of Other Property	Agreed Value of Other Property
_____	_____	_____	_____
_____	_____	_____	_____

7. **Additional Contributions of Each Limited Partner.** Each limited partner may (but shall not be obliged to) make such additional contributions to the capital of the partnership as may from time to time be agreed upon by the general partners.

8. **Return of Contribution to Each Limited Partner.** The contribution of each limited partner is to be returned to him as may from time to time be agreed upon by the general partners.

9. **Profit Shares of Each Limited Partner.** The share of the profits or other compensation by way of income which each limited partner shall receive by reason of his contribution is:

_____   _____%

_____   _____%

10. **Assignment of Limited Partner's Interest.** Each limited partner is given the right to substitute an assignee as contributor in his place, provided that the assignment is approved by all the general partners.

11. **Admission of Additional Limited Partners.** The general partners are given the right to admit additional limited partners, provided that the admissions are approved by all the general partners, but in no event other than upon a cash contribution to the partnership and upon the same terms as herein expressed.

12. **Death, Retirement or Insanity of General Partner.** In the event of the death, retirement or insanity of a general partner, the remaining general partners shall have the right to continue the business of the partnership under the same name by themselves or in conjunction with any other person or persons they may select.

13. **Right of Limited Partner to Receive Property Other Than Cash.** Each limited partner is given the right to demand and receive property other than cash in return for his contribution, and the value of such property shall be that shown on the books of the partnership.

Signed the _____ day of _____, 19___.

[*Signatures of general and limited partners*]

Subscribed and sworn to before me this _____ day of _____, 19___.

_____ [9]
Notary Public

---

[9]. West's Modern Legal Forms § 6455.

FORM 3E

LIMITED PARTNERSHIP CERTIFICATE

(REVISED UNIFORM LIMITED
PARTNERSHIP ACT)

We, the undersigned, for the purpose of forming a limited partnership pursuant to the Revised Uniform Limited Partnership Act as set forth in Sections _____ of the _____ Code, hereby certify:

1. **Name.** The name of the partnership is _____.

2. **Character of Business.** The character of the business to be carried on is to engage in the business of _____.

3. **Address and Agent.** The address of the office of the partnership is _____, and the agent for service of process upon the partnership is _____.

4. **Members.** The name and the business address of each member of the partnership are as follows:

Name	Business Address	Type of Member
_____	_____	[General]
_____	_____	[Limited]
_____	_____	[Limited]

5. **Initial Contribution of Each Partner.** The amount of cash and a description and statement of the agreed value of other property or services contributed by each partner are as follows:

Name	Cash	Description of Property or Services	Agreed Value of Property or Services
_____	_____	_____	_____
_____	_____	_____	_____

6. **Additional Contributions.** The times or events which will require additional contributions to be made by each partner are as follows: _____

7. **Assignment of a Limited Partner's Interest.** Each limited partner is given the right to substitute an assignee as contributor in his or her place, provided that the assignment is approved by the general partners.

8. **Termination of Membership.** With sixty (60) days written notice to the general partners, any member of the partnership may terminate his or her membership in the partnership and receive a full distribution of his or her partnership interest in cash, provided, however, that no such distribution shall be made unless the assets of the partnership exceed the liabilities of the partnership on a ratio of at least 2:1.

9. **Distributions.** The partners may receive from the partnership from time to time such property of the partnership, including cash, as may be agreed upon by the general partners.

10. **Return of a Capital Contribution.** The general partners may, from time to time, as they agree distribute to the other partners such portions of the capital contributions of the other partners as the general partners may deem appropriate.

11. **Dissolution.** The partnership shall be dissolved and its affairs wound up upon the happening of any of the following:

    a. Unanimous agreement by all members.

    b. Death, insanity, disability or retirement of a general partner without a successor general partner having been elected within 90 days.

    c. Sale or disposition of substantially all of the partnership property.

    d. Any event which, in the opinion of the general partners, prevents the partnership from carrying on its ordinary business.

12. **Continuation of Business.** Notwithstanding any event of dissolution, the remaining members of the partnership may continue the business of the partnership without liquidation of the partnership by electing a successor or replacement general partner within 90 days from the event which causes the dissolution.

13. **Other Matters.** _____

_____

_____

Dated this _____ day of _____, 19___.

[Signatures of general and limited partners]

Subscribed and sworn to before me this ___ day of _____, 19 ___.

_____

Notary Public

FORM 3F

AMENDMENT OF LIMITED PARTNERSHIP CERTIFICATE

We, the undersigned, for the purpose of amending the certificate of limited partnership of _____, filed in the office of _____ on _____, 19__, hereby certify:

Whereas, the limited partner, _____, has assigned the whole of her interest in the limited partnership of _____ to _____, and _____ has been substituted as a limited partner in such partnership,

Paragraph 4 of the certificate of limited partnership is amended to read as follows:

"4. **General Partners.** The name and place of residence of each general partner are:

_____   _____

_____   _____

"**Limited Partners.** The name and place of residence of each limited partner are:

_____   _____

_____   _____ "

Signed the _____ day of _____, 19__.

[*Signatures of general and limited partners including the substituted limited partner and the assigning limited partner*]

Subscribed and sworn to before me this _____ day of _____, 19__.

_____ [10]
Notary Public

---

10. West's Modern Legal Forms § 6458.

FORM 3G

STATEMENT OF CANCELLATION

    Notice is hereby given that the limited partnership heretofore existing between _____, _____ and _____, under the firm name of _____, and doing the business of _____
_____
is hereby dissolved by mutual consent.

    Dated this _____ day of _____, 19___, at _____, _____.

_____	_____
_____	_____
_____	_____
_____	_____
(General Partners)	(Limited Partners)

FORM 4A

SHAREHOLDER'S STATEMENT OF CONSENT AS TO TAXABLE STATUS UNDER SUBCHAPTER S

    _____, the undersigned, as a stockholder of _____ CORPORATION, hereby consents and agrees to the Corporation's election under Section 1372(a) to be treated as a "Small Business Corporation" for income tax purposes. It has been explained to me that the taxable income of the Corporation, to the extent that it exceeds dividends distributed in money out of earnings and profits of the taxable year, will be taxed directly to shareholders (rather than to the Corporation) to the extent that it would have constituted a dividend if it had been distributed on the last day of the Corporation's taxable year.

                                                _____
                                                        Shareholder

FORM 4B

Form 2553
(Rev. February 1986)
Department of the Treasury
Internal Revenue Service

Election by a Small Business Corporation
(Under section 1362 of the Internal Revenue Code)
▶ For Paperwork Reduction Act Notice, see page 1 of instructions.
▶ See separate instructions.

OMB No. 1545-0146
Expires 1-31-89

Note: *This election, to be treated as an "S corporation," can be approved only if all the tests in Instruction B are met.*

Part I Election Information

Name of corporation (see instructions)	Employer identification number (see instructions)	Principal business activity and principal product or service (see instructions)
Number and street		Election is to be effective for tax year beginning (month, day, year)
City or town, state and ZIP code		Number of shares issued and outstanding (see instructions)

Is the corporation the outgrowth or continuation of any form of predecessor? . . . . ☐ Yes ☐ No   Date and place of incorporation
If "Yes," state name of predecessor, type of organization, and period of its existence ▶ ....

A If this election takes effect for the first tax year the corporation exists, enter the earliest of the following: (1) date the corporation first had shareholders, (2) date the corporation first had assets, or (3) date the corporation began doing business. ▶

B Selected tax year: Annual return will be filed for tax year ending (month and day) ▶ ....
See instructions before entering your tax year. If the tax year ends any date other than December 31, you must complete Part II or Part IV on back. You may want to complete Part III to make a back-up request.

C Name of each shareholder, person having a community property interest in the corporation's stock, and each tenant in common, joint tenant, and tenant by the entirety. (A husband and wife (and their estates) are counted as one shareholder in determining the number of shareholders without regard to the manner in which the stock is owned.)	D Shareholders' Consent Statement. We, the undersigned shareholders, consent to the corporation's election to be treated as an "S corporation" under section 1362(a). (Shareholders sign and date below.)*	E Stock owned		F Social security number (employer identification number for estates or trust)	G Tax year ends (month and day)
		Number of shares	Dates acquired		

*For this election to be valid, the consent of each shareholder, person having a community property interest in the corporation's stock, and each tenant in common, joint tenant, and tenant by the entirety must either appear above or be attached to this form. (See instructions for Column D, if continuation sheet or a separate consent statement is needed.)

Under penalties of perjury, I declare that I have examined this election, including accompanying schedules, and statements, and to the best of my knowledge and belief, it is true, correct, and complete.

Signature and
Title of Officer ▶   Date ▶

See Parts II, III, and IV on back.   Form **2553** (Rev. 2-86)

Form 2553 (Rev. 2-86) Page 2

Part II Selection of Tax Year Under Revenue Procedure 83-25

H Check the applicable box below to indicate whether the corporation is:
☐ Adopting the tax year entered in item B, Part I.
☐ Retaining the tax year entered in item B, Part I.
☐ Changing to the tax year entered in item B, Part I.

I Check the applicable box below to indicate the representation statement the corporation is making as required under section 7.01 (item 4) of Revenue Procedure 83-25, 1983-1 C.B. 689.

☐ Under penalties of perjury, I represent that shareholders holding more than half of the shares of the stock (as of the first day of the tax year to which the request relates) of the corporation have the same tax year or are concurrently changing to the tax year that the corporation adopts, retains, or changes to per item B, Part I.

☐ Under penalties of perjury, I represent that shareholders holding more than half of the shares of the stock (as of the first day of the tax year to which the request relates) of the corporation have a tax year or are concurrently changing to a tax year that, although different from the tax year the corporation is adopting, retaining, or changing to per item B, Part I, results in a deferment of income to each of these shareholders of three months or less.

☐ Under penalties of perjury, I represent that the corporation is adopting, retaining, or changing to a tax year that coincides with its natural business year as verified by its satisfaction of the requirements of section 4.042(a), (b), (c), and (d) of Revenue Procedure 83-25.

J Check here ☐ if the tax year entered in item B, Part I, is requested under the provisions of section 8 of Revenue Procedure 83-25. Attach to Form 2553 a statement and other necessary information pursuant to the ruling request requirements of Revenue Procedure 85-1. The statement must include the business purpose for the desired tax year. See instructions.

Part III Back-Up Request by Certain Corporations Initially Selecting a Fiscal Year (See Instructions.)

Check here ☐ if the corporation agrees to adopt or to change to a tax year ending December 31 if necessary for IRS to accept this election for S corporation status (temporary regulations section 18.1378-1(b)(2)(ii)(A)). This back-up request does not apply if the fiscal tax year request is approved by IRS or if the election to be an S corporation is not accepted.

Part IV Request by Corporation for Tax Year Determination by IRS (See Instructions.)

Check here ☐ if the corporation requests the IRS to determine the permitted tax year for the corporation based on information submitted in Part I (and attached schedules). This request is made under provisions of temporary regulations section 18.1378-1(d).

★ U.S.G.P.O.: 1986-491-473/20122

FORM 4C

RESOLUTION AUTHORIZING ISSUANCE OF SECTION 1244 STOCK

Whereas, the Corporation is authorized to offer and issue 500 shares of common stock, no par value, none of which has yet been issued, and the directors desire to hereafter issue 100 shares of said common stock for $20,000;

Whereas, A_____ B_____ and C_____ D_____ have expressed the wish that each be permitted to subscribe for 50 shares of said common stock at a price of $200 a share; and

Whereas, the Corporation is a domestic corporation meeting the definition of a "small business corporation" contained in section 1244 (c) (2) of the Internal Revenue Code of 1954;

Upon motion duly made, seconded, and unanimously carried, it was

Resolved, that the Corporation hereby adopts a plan, effective this date, to offer 50 shares of common stock, no par value, each to A_____ B_____ and C_____ D_____ in consideration of $10,000 to be paid by each only in money and property acceptable to the Corporation (other than stock or securities), provided, however, the said A_____ B_____ and C_____ D_____ shall within two weeks after the date of adoption of this plan notify the Corporation in writing of the acceptance of this offer, and during the said two week period the Corporation shall offer and issue only such common stock. The maximum amount to be received by the Corporation in consideration of the stock to be issued pursuant to this plan shall be $20,000. It is the intention of the officers and directors of the Corporation to comply in every respect with section 1244 of the Internal Revenue Code of 1954 pertaining to "Losses on Small Business Stock", and any questions concerning the interpretation or operation of this plan shall be resolved in such manner as will qualify the plan under said law. The officers of the Corporation are hereby authorized, empowered and directed to do and perform any and all acts and deeds necessary to carry out the plan.[11]

---

11. West's Modern Legal Forms § 2909.-5.

FORM 4D

PLAN FOR ISSUANCE OF SECTION 1244 STOCK

1. The corporation shall offer and issue under this Plan, a maximum of _____ shares of its common stock at a maximum price of _____ ($_____) per share.

2. This offer shall terminate, unless sooner terminated by: ___

   (a) Complete issuance of all shares offered hereunder, or

   (b) Appropriate action terminating the same by the Board

of Directors and the Stockholders, or

   (c) By the adoption of a new Plan by the Stockholders for the issuance of additional stock under Section 1244, Internal Revenue Code.

3. No increase in the basis of outstanding stock shall result from a contribution to capital hereunder.

4. No stock offered hereunder shall be issued on the exercise of a stock right, stock warrant, or stock option, unless such right, warrant, or option is applicable solely to unissued stock offered under the Plan and is exercised during the period of the Plan.

5. Stock subscribed for prior to the adoption of the Plan, including stock subscribed for prior to the date the corporation comes into existence, may be issued hereunder, provided however, that the said stock is not in fact issued prior to the adoption of such Plan.

6. No stock shall be issued hereunder for a payment which, along or together with prior payments, exceeds the maximum amount that may be received under the Plan.

7. Any offering or portion of an offer outstanding which is unissued at the time of the adoption of this Plan is herewith withdrawn. Stock rights, stock warrants, stock options or securities convertible into stock, which are outstanding at the time this Plan is adopted, are likewise herewith withdrawn.

8. Stock issued hereunder shall be in exchange for money or other property except for stock or securities. Stock issued hereunder shall not be in return for services rendered or to be rendered to, or for the benefit of, the corporation. Stock may be issued hereunder however, in consideration for cancellation of indebtedness of the corporation unless such indebtedness is evidenced by a security, or arises out of the performance of personal services.

9. Any matters pertaining to this issue not covered under the provisions of this Plan shall be resolved in favor of the applicable

law and regulations in order to qualify such issue under Section 1244 of the Internal Revenue Code. If any shares issued hereunder are finally determined not to be so qualified, such shares, and only such shares shall be deemed not to be in this Plan, and such other shares issued hereunder shall not be affected thereby.

10. The sum of the aggregate amount offered hereunder plus the equity capital of the corporation amounts to $_____.

11. The date of adoption of this Plan is _____, 19___.[12]

[12]. See West's Modern Legal Forms 2909.6.

FORM 5A

CONTRACT BETWEEN STOCKHOLDERS ORGANIZING A CLOSE CORPORATION

Agreement, made this _____ day of _____, 19___, between A_____ B_____ of _____, and C_____ D_____ of _____ (hereinafter referred to as the "Shareholders").

Whereas, the Shareholders have caused _____ Corporation to be organized as a corporation under the laws of the State of _____, and have agreed that it shall be financed and its business conducted subject to the provisions of this agreement.

Now, therefore, in consideration of the mutual covenants herein contained, it is agreed:

1. **Subscription to Stock.** The Shareholders each subscribe for and agree to purchase _____ shares each of the capital stock of the Corporation at $_____ per share. These shares shall be issued and paid for within _____ days after the organization of the Corporation.

2. **Loan to Corporation.** The Shareholders each agree to loan to the Corporation the sum of $_____, to be used for the purposes of the business of the Corporation, such loan to be repaid at the convenience of the Corporation, with interest thereon at _____ per cent per annum.

3. **Employment.** The Corporation shall employ A_____ B_____ and C_____ D_____ each at a salary of $_____ per week. A_____

B____ and C____ D____ each agree to accept such employment, to devote their full time and best efforts to the business of the Corporation, and not to engage in any other competing business, directly or indirectly. Such salary shall be subject to increase or decrease and the term of employment of A____ B____ and C____ D____ may be terminated only by vote of the Board of Directors of the Corporation in accordance with the provisions contained in the Certificate of Incorporation.

4. **First Option on Termination of Employment.** In the event that either A____ B____ or C____ D____ shall at any time, for any reason whatsoever, leave the employ of the Corporation or cease to be actively engaged in the business of the Corporation, all of the shares owned by such Shareholder shall be offered for sale to the other Shareholder, who is hereby given an option for a period of _____ days from the date on which such employment or activity shall terminate, to purchase all of such shares at a price equal to the book value thereof. Book value of shares shall be computed from the books of the Corporation maintained by its regular accountant in accordance with generally accepted principles of accounting. The option hereby given shall relate to all of such shares of the offeror, and the offeree shall not have the right to purchase only part thereof. If the aforesaid offer is accepted, notwithstanding any of the foregoing provisions of this paragraph, the offeror shall receive from the offeree not less than the value of his investment in the Corporation plus the amount of any unpaid loan theretofore made by the offeror to the Corporation, with appropriate interest thereon to the date of purchase. Payments to be made under this paragraph shall be made as follows: _____ upon the acceptance of the offer; _____ _____ months thereafter; and the final _____ _____ months thereafter. Title to the shares shall pass to the offeree only upon the completion of all payments. After the payment of the first installment, the offeror shall hold such shares only as security for payment of the remaining installments, and the offeree shall have the sole right to vote the shares and to collect all dividends and other distributions thereon. Upon payment of the last installment, the shares shall be transferred of record to the offeree.

5. **Restriction on Transfer of Stock.** Each of the Shareholders expressly agrees not to transfer, sell, assign, pledge or otherwise in any manner dispose of or encumber any of his shares unless and until he shall have offered to sell all of his shares to the other Shareholder at a price to be computed and to be paid as specified in paragraph 4 above. Such offer shall be made in writing and shall continue for _____ days from the date thereof.

6. **Legend on Stock Certificates.** All stock certificates issued by the Corporation shall have marked on the face thereof "Subject to

provisions of Stockholders Agreement dated _____, 19__ restricting transfer." No dividend shall be paid on any shares transferred, pledged, assigned or encumbered in breach of this agreement.

7. **Death and Disability.** Upon the death of any Shareholder who is also an employee, his salary shall be paid to his widow or next of kin for _____ weeks following such death. If any Shareholder shall become physically incapacitated and unable to attend to his duties as an employee of the Corporation, he shall continue to receive his full salary (less the sum required to employ a substitute in his place) for a period of _____ months after the commencement of such incapacity. In the event of the death, or incapacity of any shareholder-employee for more than _____ months, the other Shareholder shall have the option, for _____ days after such death or expiration of said _____ month period, to purchase his shares at the price and on the terms provided for in paragraph 4 hereof. The life of the other Shareholder shall be insured for the benefit of the other Shareholder for $_____, or for such other amount as the Shareholders may jointly agree upon. If the proceeds of such insurance payable to any Shareholder are equal to at least _____ per cent of the purchase price of the stock of the deceased Shareholder as computed in accordance with the provisions of paragraph 4, such Shareholder agrees that he will exercise his option to purchase all of the shares from the estate of the deceased Shareholder as herein provided. Upon the receipt of any such proceeds, any then remaining unpaid installments of such purchase price shall be prepaid by the purchaser, to at least the extent of such proceeds.

8. **Election of Directors.** Each Shareholder agrees, so long as he shall remain a Shareholder, to vote his shares for the election of the following four persons as Directors of the Corporation:

A____ B____ (or such other person as is designated by A____ B____)

C____ D____ (or such other person as is designated by C____ D____)

and generally to so vote at directors' and stockholders' meetings of the Corporation as to carry out and make effective all the terms and provisions of this agreement.

9. **Appointment of Officers.** So long as they are faithful, efficient and competent in the performance of their duties, the following persons shall be supported by the Shareholders for election to offices of the Corporation:

President and Treasurer	A____ B____
Vice President and Secretary	C____ D____

10. **Arbitration.** All disputes, differences and controversies arising under and in connection with this agreement shall be settled and finally determined by arbitration in the City of _____ according to the rules of the American Arbitration Association now in force or hereafter adopted.

11. **Duration.** This agreement shall continue in force during the entire period of the life of the Corporation.

12. **Successors.** This agreement and all provisions hereof shall enure to the benefit of and shall be binding upon the heirs, executors, legal representatives, next of kin, transferees and assigns of the parties hereto.

13. **Severability.** If for any reason any provision hereof shall be inoperative, the validity and effect of all other provisions shall not be affected thereby.

14. **Modifications.** No modification or waiver of any provision of this agreement shall be valid unless in writing signed by all of the parties.

In witness whereof, the parties have signed this agreement on the day and year first above written.

_____
_____

Confirmed and Agreed to:
_____ Corporation

_____
President

Attest:

_____ [13]
Secretary

13. West's Modern Legal Forms § 2432.-15.

FORM 5B

ARTICLES OF INCORPORATION OF A MEDICAL CORPORATION

ARTICLES OF INCORPORATION
OF

_____

We, the undersigned, hereby associate ourselves together for the purpose of becoming a professional corporation for profit under the provisions of _____, Statutes, as amended by "The Professional Service Corporation Act" of the State of _____, and pursuant to the following Articles of Incorporation:

ARTICLE I. NAME

The name of this corporation shall be _____.

ARTICLE II. PURPOSE

The general nature of the business to be transacted by the corporation shall be and is to engage in every aspect of the general practice of medicine. The professional services involved in the corporation's practice of medicine may be rendered only through its officers, agent and employees who are duly authorized and licensed to practice medicine in the State of _____.

This corporation shall not engage in any business other than the practice of medicine. However, this corporation may invest its funds in real estate, mortgages, stocks, bonds, and other types of investments, and may own real and personal property necessary for the rendering of the professional services authorized hereby.

ARTICLE III. CAPITAL STOCK

The maximum number of shares of stock that the corporation is authorized to have outstanding at any time shall be _____ shares of the par value of one dollar ($1.00) per share, all of which shall be common stock of the same class. All stock issued shall be fully paid and non-assessable. The stockholders shall have no pre-emptive rights with respect to the stock of the corporation, and the corporation may issue and sell its common stock from time to time without offering such shares to the stockholders then holding shares of common stock. Shares of the corporation's stock and certificates therefore shall be issued only to doctors authorized and licensed to practice medicine in the State of _____.

ARTICLE IV. INITIAL CAPITAL

The amount of capital with which this corporation will begin business shall be and is the sum of _____ dollars.

ARTICLE V. DURATION

The corporation shall have perpetual existence.

ARTICLE VI. PRINCIPAL OFFICE

The principal office of this corporation shall be located in the City of _____, County of _____, State of _____, and the post office address of said principal office of the corporation shall be _____.

ARTICLE VII. NUMBER OF DIRECTORS

The number of directors of this corporation shall be not less than three (3) nor more than five (5).

ARTICLE VIII. INITIAL BOARD OF DIRECTORS

The names and post office addresses of the members of the first Board of Directors, who, subject to the provisions of the Bylaws and these Articles of Incorporation, shall hold office for the first year of the corporation's existence or until their successors are elected and have qualified, are as follows:

Names	**Addresses**
_____	_____
_____	_____
_____	_____
_____	_____

ARTICLE IX. SUBSCRIBERS

The name and post office address of each subscriber of these Articles of Incorporation are as follows:

Names	**Addresses**
_____	_____
_____	_____
_____	_____
_____	_____

The subscribers certify that the proceeds of the stock subscribed for will not be less than the amount of capital with which the corporation will begin business, as set forth in Article IV hereinabove.

ARTICLE X. STOCKHOLDERS

The stock of this corporation may be issued, owned and registered only in the name or names of an individual or individuals who are duly authorized and licensed to practice medicine in the State of _____ and who are employees, officers or agents of this corporation. In the event that a stockholder;

(a) becomes disqualified to practice medicine in this State, or

(b) is elected to a public office or accepts employment, that pursuant to law, places restrictions or limitations upon his continued rendering of professional services as a medical doctor, or

(c) ceases to be an employee, officer or agent of the corporation, or

(d) sells, transfers, hypothecates or pledges, or attempts to sell, transfer, hypothecate or pledge any shares of stock in this corporation to any person ineligible by law or by virtue of these Articles to be a shareholder in this corporation, or if such sale, transfer, hypothecation or pledge or attempt to sell, transfer, hypothecate or pledge is made in a manner prohibited by law, or in a manner inconsistent with the provisions of these Articles, or the Bylaws of this corporation, or

(e) suffers an execution to be levied upon his stock, or such stock is subjected to judicial sale or other process, the effect of which is to vest any legal or equitable interest in such stock in some person other than the stockholder,

then the stock of such stockholder shall immediately stand forfeited and such stock shall be immediately cancelled by this corporation and the stockholder or other person in possession of such stock shall be entitled only to receive payment for the value of such stock, which said value shall be the book value thereof as of the last day of the month preceding the month in which any of the events above enumerated occurs. The stockholder whose stock so becomes forfeit and is cancelled by the corporation, shall forthwith cease to be an employee, officer, director or agent of the corporation and except to receive payment for his stock in accordance with the foregoing and payment of any other sums then lawfully due and owing to said stockholder by the corporation, such stockholder shall then and thereafter have no further financial interest of any kind in this corporation.

ARTICLE XI. DEATH OF STOCKHOLDER

Upon the death of a stockholder, his stock shall be subject to purchase by the corporation or by the other stockholders at such price and upon such terms and conditions and in such manner as may be provided for in the Bylaws of this corporation, in a manner consistent with law and these Articles.

ARTICLE XII. SALE OF STOCK

No stockholder of this corporation may sell or transfer any of such stockholder's shares of stock in this corporation except to another individual who is then duly authorized and licensed to practice medicine in the State of _____ and then only after the proposed sale or transfer shall have been first approved, at a stockholders' meeting specially called for such purpose, by such proportion, not less than a majority, of the outstanding stock excluding the shares of stock proposed to be sold or transferred, as may be provided from time to time in the Bylaws. In such stockholders' meeting, the shares of stock proposed to be sold or transferred may not be voted or counted for any purpose.

The corporation's shareholders are specifically authorized from time to time to adopt Bylaws not inconsistent herewith restraining the alienation of shares of stock of this corporation and providing for the purchase or redemption by the corporation of its shares of stock.

ARTICLE XIII. REGULATION OF BUSINESS

In furtherance of and not in limitation of the powers conferred by statute, the following specific provisions are made for the regulation of the business and the conduct of the affairs of the corporation:

1. **Management.** Subject to such restrictions, if any, as are herein expressed and such further restrictions, if any, as may be set forth in the Bylaws, the Board of Directors shall have the general management and control of the business and may exercise all of the powers of the corporation except such as may be by statute, or by the articles of incorporation or amendment thereto, or by the Bylaws as constituted from time to time, expressly conferred upon or reserved to the stockholders.

2. **Officers.** The corporation shall have such officers as may from time to time be provided in the Bylaws and such officers shall be designated in such manner and shall hold their offices for such terms and shall have such powers and duties as may be prescribed by the Bylaws or as may be determined from time to time by the Board of Directors subject to the Bylaws.

3. **Contracts.** No contract or other transaction between the corporation and any other firm, association or corporation shall be affected or invalidated by the fact that any one or more of the directors of the corporation is or are interested in or is a member, director or officer or are members, directors or officers of such firm or corporation and any director or directors individually or jointly

may be a party or parties to or may be interested in any contract or transaction of the corporation or in which the corporation is interested; and no contract, act or transaction of the corporation with any person, firm, association or corporation shall be affected or invalidated by the fact that any director or directors of the corporation is a party or are parties to or interested in such contract, act or transaction or in any way connected with such person, firm, association or corporation, and each and every person who may become a director of the corporation is hereby relieved from any liability that might otherwise exist from contracting with the corporation for the benefit of himself or any firm, association or corporation in which he may in any way be interested.

ARTICLE XIV. AMENDMENTS

This corporation reserves the right to amend, alter, change, or repeal any provision contained herein in the manner now or hereafter prescribed by law, and all rights conferred on stockholders herein are granted subject to this reservation.

In Witness Whereof, each subscriber has signed these Articles of Incorporation.

[*Acknowledgment*] [14]

14. West's Modern Legal Forms § 3158.-7.

FORM 5C

APPLICATION FOR REGISTRATION OF PROFESSIONAL CORPORATION (CALIFORNIA)

File No. _____
(To be filled in by Board)
Fee: $100.00

APPLICATION

for issuance of

CERTIFICATE OF REGISTRATION AS A MEDICAL CORPORATION

(Section 2501 of the Business and Professions Code)

1. _____
   (Name of Applicant)

   a professional corporation, hereby requests issuance to it of a Certificate of Registration as a medical corporation.

2. Applicant will do business as (fictitious name) _____

   (See Section 2393 of the Business and Professions Code and Section 13409 of the Corporations Code)

3. The corporation number assigned to the applicant by the California Secretary of State is _____.

4. Date of incorporation _____.

5. A. The address of applicant's principal office is:
   _____

   B. The address of all other offices of applicant are:
   _____
   _____
   _____

   C. Applicant's telephone number is: _____
                                       (Area Code)   (Number)

6. The directors of the applicant are:

NAME	ADDRESS	PROFESSIONAL LICENSE NUMBER

(File supplemental sheet if more space required)

7. The officers of the applicant are:

    (If any officers are not licensed persons, so indicate. See Section 13403 of the Corporations Code.)

NAME	ADDRESS	PROFESSIONAL LICENSE NUMBER
President	_____	_____
Vice-President	_____	_____
Secretary	_____	_____
Treasurer	_____	_____
Asst. Secretary	_____	_____

    (Need not be a licensed person. See Section 2501 of the Business and Professions Code.)

Asst. Treasurer _____

    (Need not be a licensed person. See Section 2501 of the Business and Professions Code.)

8. The shareholders of the applicant are:

NAME	ADDRESS	PROFESSIONAL LICENSE NUMBER
(1)	_____	_____
(2)	_____	_____
(3)	_____	_____
(4)	_____	_____
(5)	_____	_____

    (File supplemental sheet if more space required)

9. The employees of the applicant rendering professional services are:

NAME	ADDRESS	PROFESSIONAL LICENSE NUMBER
(1)	_____	_____
(2)	_____	_____
(3)	_____	_____
(4)	_____	_____
(5)	_____	_____

    (File supplemental sheet if more space required)

10. The bylaws of the applicant adopted on _____ comply with Medical Corporation Rule 1378.6 in that:

    (a) Ownership of shares of the applicant may be owned only by a medical corporation, or by a licensed physician and surgeon or podiatrist, as the case may be.

(b) The income of the applicant attributable to medical services rendered while a shareholder is a disqualified person shall not in any manner accrue to the benefit of such shareholder or his shares.

(c) The share certificates of the applicant contain a legend setting forth the restrictions of sections (a) and (b) above, and, where applicable, the restrictions of section (d) below.

and, where applicable:

(d) Where there are two or more shareholders in the corporation and one of the shareholders:

(1) Dies;

(2) Ceases to be an eligible shareholder; or

(3) Becomes a disqualified person as defined in Section 13401(d) of the Corporations Code, for a period exceeding ninety (90) days,

his shares shall be sold and transferred to the corporation, its shareholders, or other eligible persons, on such terms as are agreed upon. Such sale or transfer shall be not later than six (6) months after any such death and not later than ninety (90) days after the date he ceases to be an eligible shareholder, or ninety (90) days after the date he becomes a disqualified person. The requirements of subsections (a) and (b) of this section shall be set forth in the medical corporation's articles of incorporation or bylaws, except that the terms of the sale or transfer provided for in said subsection (b) need not be set forth in said articles or bylaws if they are set forth in a written agreement.

(e) The applicant and its shareholders may, but need not, agree that shares sold to it by a person who becomes a disqualified person may be resold to such person if and when he again becomes an eligible shareholder.

11. Security for claims against applicant.
(Check one)

☐ Applicant is insured as provided in Section 1378.5(a) of the Medical Corporation Rules as evidenced by the Cerificate of insurance attached as Exhibit C.

☐ Applicant is not insured.

(NOTE: Under Section 1378.5(b) of the Medical Corporation Rules all shareholders of the corporation shall be jointly and severally liable for all claims established against the corporation by its patients arising out of the rendering of, or failure to render, medical services up to the minimum amounts specified for insurance under subsection (a) hereof except during periods of time when the corporation shall provide and maintain insurance for claims against it by its patients arising out of the rendering of, or failure to render medical services.)

12. Applicant is an existing corporation and its organization, bylaws, articles of incorporation and general plan of operation are such that its affairs will be conducted in compliance with the Medical Practice Act, the Professional Corporations Act, and other applicable provisions of the Corporations Code, the Medical Corporation Rules of the Board of Medical Examiners and such other law, rules and regulations as may be applicable.

13. Enclosed herewith are the following exhibits:

   A. Articles of Incorporation, certified by the Secretary of State. (Section 2501 of the Business and Professions Code.)

   B. Bylaws certified by the Secretary of the applicant corporation. (Section 2501 of the Business and Professions Code.)

   C. Certificate of insurance.
      (Must be filed if applicant is insured. Section 1378.5(a) Medical Corporation Rules.)

   D. Notice of Liability of Shareholders (Section 1378.5(b) Medical Corporation Rules.)

   Executed this _____ day of _____, 19__.

                                   _____
                                   [Name of Corporation]

                             By   _____
                                   [Type name]

                                   _____
                                   [Title of person executing]

                                   _____
                                   [Signature]

DECLARATION

I am an officer of _____, and as such make this declara-
                    (Name of Applicant)

tion for and on behalf of said corporation. I have read the foregoing application and all attachments thereto and know the contents thereof, and the same are true of my own knowledge. I declare, under penalty of perjury, that the foregoing is true and correct.

Executed at _____, California, this _____ day of _____, 19__.

_____
(Signature)

_____[15]
(Title)

[15]. West's Modern Legal Forms § 3158.-4.

FORM 6A

PRE-INCORPORATION AGENDA AND INFORMATION SHEET

These forms are intended for use at an initial client interview as information gathering forms, and as external checklists to assist the attorney in following up with the client, the accountant, the insurance agent and others so that all aspects of the incorporation are accomplished in a timely fashion and without duplication of effort.

These forms should be filled out during the client interview and reviewed with the legal assistant when the assignment is made. A copy is to be mailed to the client, the accountant and insurance agent when acknowledging the engagement.

The Agenda should be kept in the file and reviewed periodically during the incorporation process; follow-up letters may be generated by these reviews.

PRE-INCORPORATION AGENDA
FOR
_____

Item	Responsibility	To Be Completed	Date Completed
1. Reserve Corporate Name			
2. Draft and File Articles of Incorporation			
3. Prepare Initial Organizational Consent or Minutes			
4. Prepare Bylaws			
5. Additional Organization Documents:			
a) Employment Agreements			
b) Service Agreements			
c) Medical and Dental Expense Reimbursement Plan			
d) Shareholders Agreement			
e) Share Certificates			
f) Transfer Documents			
g) Bank Resolution			
h) Subchapter S Election			
6. Order Corporate Kit			
7. Send Explanatory Transmittal Letter			
8. Other:			

Client: _____
File No.: _____

PRE-INCORPORATION
INFORMATION SHEET

1. Date Information Supplied: _____
   Parties Present: _____
      Lawyer: _____
      Client: _____
   Other Parties: _____
2. State of Incorporation: _____
3. Proposed Date of Incorporation: _____
4. Name of Corporation: _____
   Alternative Name: _____ / _____
   Trade Name: _____
5. Name Reserved? YES (__) NO (__) SHOULD BE (__)
6. Will be Incorporating a Going Business? _____
   If so, describe generally: _____

   Any Patents, Copyrights or Trademarks to be Registered or Transferred: _____
7. Principal Purpose of Corporation: _____

   (State broadly, but with sufficient specificity to meet statutory requirements.)
8. Principal Place of Business: _____
   ☐ Own   ☐ Lease
   Other places of significant business activity or presence:
   Address   **Description**   **Own/Lease**

9. Qualification in other states required. YES (__) NO (__)
   If so, what states: _____

10. Registered Agent and Office in State: _____

    Registered Agent and Office in states in which qualified:
    _____

    (Do not commit lawyer to be registered agent.)

11. Common Stock (if preferred, explain details):

Class	Number of Shares	Par Value	Issue Price
_____	_____	_____	_____
_____	_____	_____	_____

Explain details: _____

Will there be a formal stock subscription agreement: _____

If no par value, amount of consideration to be allocated to capital surplus: _____

Note: If stock is no par value, stated capital of the company will be equal to actual consideration paid for issued stock except that part of consideration that directors may allocate to capital surplus.

12. Anticipated Shareholders:

Name and Phone	Address	Zip Code
(1) _____	_____	_____
(2) _____	_____	_____
(3) _____	_____	_____
(4) _____	_____	_____

13. Section 1244 Plan: _____
    Date of Commencement of Offer: _____

Note: Section 1244 stock permits deduction of capital losses, if any, upon sale of such stock as ordinary losses against ordinary income of Section 1244 stock owner. See Section 1244 of the Internal Revenue Code for details.

14. Share Ownership and Consideration (corresponding to above stockholders):

Number of Shares	Consideration	Date to be Paid
(1) _____	_____	_____
(2) _____	_____	_____
(3) _____	_____	_____
(4) _____	_____	_____

15. Initial Indebtedness: Secured $_____ Unsecured $_____

Note: (1) If capital structure of the company will involve debt, advised debt equity ratio should not be in excess of 3/1 and recommend 2/1 if workable for participants. Point out that any debt must specifically be treated as debt by the company, or the IRS is likely to characterize any such debt securities as stock.

Note: (2) If prospective contributor to corporate capital will take back note to secure corporate debt, make sure note will qualify as a "long-term security" under § 351 of the Internal Revenue Code. Otherwise, transfer of property to company may constitute a taxable event (i. e., a "sale") which will cause realization of probable capital gain to taxpayer-transferror.

16. Incorporators:

Name	Address (If not shown above.)	Zip Code
_____	_____	_____
_____	_____	_____
_____	_____	_____
_____	_____	_____

17. Directors:

Name and Phone	Address (If not shown above.)	Zip Code
_____	_____	_____
_____	_____	_____
_____	_____	_____

18. Officers:

Name	Office	Address
_____	President	_____
_____	Treasurer	_____
_____	Secretary	_____
_____		

19. Preemptive Rights. YES (____) NO (____) Restrictions_____

Note: See explanatory material in Corporate Law Notebook or in B. M. Miller, *Manual and Guide for the Corporate Secretary* 815-844 (1969), for background prior to client conference.

20. Cumulative Voting. YES (____) NO (____)

Note: See explanatory material in Corporate Law Notebook or in B. M. Miller, *supra* at 89-94, for background prior to client conference.

21. Date and Time of Annual Meeting: _____
_____
(e. g.: "____ days following close of fiscal year" or "held each year prior to the ____ day of _____.")
For provision in Bylaws: "In the event the Board of Directors fails to so fix the date and time of such meeting, it shall be held on the ____ in _____ at ____ a. m. (e. g., on the first Tuesday in March at 10:00 a. m.)

22. Bank: _____
    Signatories: _____
    Limitations: _____
       Should we obtain banking resolutions: YES (____) NO (____)

23. Commencement of Employment, if any: _____

Note: If business is already in progress, obtain Employer Identification Number: _____

24. Date of First Meeting of Board of Directors: _____

25. Stock Transfer Restrictions? YES (____) NO (____) Special provisions: _____
_____

Insurance Funded: YES (____) NO (____)
Insurance Company or Agent _____
26. Ownership of Real Property (list states and counties): _____
_____

Ownership of Personal Property: _____
_____

27. Custody of Corporate Minute Book, Stock Book, and Seal:
Client (____) Us (____)
Other Custodian: _____
28. Supplemental Checklist
    ☐ COMPARE FEATURES OF CORPORATION LAWS OF FOLLOWING STATES: _____
    ☐ COMPARE ORGANIZATION FEES AND TAXES
    ☐ CHECK COSTS OF QUALIFICATION IN FOREIGN STATES
    ☐ CHECK ANNUAL FEES AND TAXES
    ☐ CHECK STATE TAX SAVINGS WHICH MAY BE EFFECTED BY SCHEDULING INCORPORATION (AND ANY QUALIFICATIONS) BEFORE OR AFTER CERTAIN DATES
29. Miscellaneous Advice to Include in Cover Letter to Client:
    (a) Securities Laws Considerations (*i.e.*, investment letter): ____
    _____

    (b) Retail Sales Tax, Use Tax, and Store Licenses: _____
    _____

    (c) State License to do Business Compliance: _____
    _____

    (d) Qualification in Other States: _____
    _____

    (e) State Workmen's Compensation Insurance Compliance: ____
    _____

    (f) State Unemployment Insurance Compliance: _____
    _____

    (g) Obtain Federal Employer Identification Number: _____
    _____

    (h) Employer's Tax Guide re Withholding Requirements (Federal and State): _____
    _____

(i) State Consumer Credit Compliance (Notification): _____

(j) Local Retail Sales Tax License: _____

(k) Local Use Tax License: _____

(l) Local Occupational Privilege Tax Compliance: _____

(m) "Tax Information on Subchapter S Corporations" (IRS Publication 589): _____

(n) "Corporations and the Federal Income Tax" (IRS Publication 542): _____

(o) Other Matters: _____

NOTES AND COMMENTS

Attorney handling
Incorporation

FORM 6B

AGREEMENT BETWEEN PROMOTERS

Agreement, made this _____ day of _____, 19__, between A____ B____ of _____, C____ D____ of _____, and E____ F____ of _____.

Whereas, the parties desire to form a corporation upon the terms and conditions set forth in this agreement.

Now, therefore, it is agreed:

1. **Formation of the Corporation.** The parties shall as soon as possible form a corporation under the laws of the State of _____.

2. **Certificate of Incorporation.** The certificate of incorporation shall provide substantially as follows:

(a) The name of the corporation shall be _____, or if this name is not available such other name as the parties shall select.

(b) The principal office or place of business of the corporation shall be located at _____. The name and address of its resident agent shall be _____.

(c) The purpose of the corporation shall be the manufacture and wholesale distribution of textile fabrics. The corporation shall have such powers as may be appropriate in connection with such a business.

(d) The names and places of residence of each of the incorporators are:

_____   _____
_____   _____
_____

(e) The corporation shall have perpetual existence.

(f) The minimum amount of capital with which the corporation shall commence business is $1,000.

(g) The total number of shares of stock shall be 1,000, divided into two classes as follows:

Common Stock, $10 par value	5000 shares
Preferred Stock, $100 par value	500 shares

(h) The designations, the powers, preferences and rights, and the qualifications, limitations or restrictions of such stock are: [*Here describe*].

3. **Subscriptions of Parties.** The parties subscribe for shares of stock of the proposed corporation, as follows:

(a) Within one week after the certificate of incorporation has been filed and recorded the corporation shall issue to A____ B____

_____ shares of common stock of the corporation, $10 par value, in consideration of the simultaneous execution and delivery to the corporation of a deed transferring marketable title to the following described real property, free and clear of liens: [*Here describe*].

(b) Within one week after the certificate of incorporation has been filed and recorded the corporation shall issue to C_____ D_____ _____ shares of common stock of the corporation, $10 par value, in consideration of the simultaneous execution of an agreement assigning to the corporation the inventions of C_____ D_____ relating to _____ as set forth in applications filed in the United States Patent Office and identified as follows: [*Here describe*].

(c) Within one week after the certificate of incorporation has been filed and recorded the corporation shall issue to E_____ F_____ _____ shares of preferred stock of the corporation, $100 par value, in consideration of the simultaneous payment by E_____ F_____ to the corporation of the sum of $_____ in cash.

4. **Agreement to Purchase Additional Stock.** E_____ F_____ agrees to purchase additional preferred stock not to exceed $_____ in par value if during the first two years of the operation of the corporation its net profits do not equal at least $_____.

5. **Stock to Promoter for Services.** The corporation shall issue to _____ of _____, _____ shares of common stock of the corporation, par value $_____, in consideration for his services in organizing the corporation.

6. **First Directors of Corporation.** The directors of the corporation for the first year shall be _____, _____ and _____.

7. **Employment Contracts.** The corporation shall employ A_____ B_____ as president and general manager and C_____ D_____ as secretary-treasurer, each for a term of 5 years, at a salary of $_____ per year for A_____ B_____ and $_____ per year for C_____ D_____. Their employment shall not be terminated without cause and their salary shall not be increased or decreased without unanimous approval of all directors. Written employment contracts shall be entered into with A_____ B_____ and C_____ D_____ wherein they agree to devote their time and best efforts exclusively to the business and interests of the corporation.

8. **Restrictions on Transfer of Stock.** Each of the parties agrees not to transfer, sell, assign, pledge or otherwise dispose of his shares of stock of the corporation without first obtaining the written consent of the other parties to the sale or other disposition, or without first offering to sell the shares to the corporation at a value to be determined by a board of 3 appraisers one of whom shall be appointed by each of the parties, A_____ B_____, C_____ D_____ and E_____ F_____.

The offer shall be in writing and shall remain open for 30 days. If the corporation fails to accept the offer within that period, a second offer also in writing shall then be made to sell the shares on similar terms to the other parties to this agreement pro-rata. If the offer be not accepted by either the corporation or the other parties the shares shall thereafter be freely transferable.

9. **Designation of Incorporators.** The parties appoint and designate _____ and _____ to act as the incorporators of the corporation and to take whatever steps are necessary to organize the corporation in accordance with the applicable laws of the State of _____. The authority which is hereby granted shall extend to the preparation, execution, and filing of such documents and other papers as are necessary in the incorporation process to carry out the terms and conditions of this agreement.

10. **Organization Expenses.** Each of the parties shall advance to _____ his pro-rata share of the funds which shall be necessary to pay the expenses and costs of incorporation. As soon as practicable after it commences business the corporation shall reimburse each of the parties for such advances.

11. **Arbitration.** All disputes, differences and controversies arising under or in connection with this agreement shall be settled and finally determined by arbitration in the City of _____ according to the Rules of the American Arbitration Association now in force or hereafter adopted.

12. **Non-Assignability of Agreement.** This agreement shall not be assignable by either party without the written consent of the other parties.

13. **Persons Bound.** The terms and conditions of this agreement shall be binding upon the parties and their respective legal representatives, successors and assigns. However, if one of the parties dies prior to the time the corporation comes into existence, this agreement shall automatically terminate.

Executed in triplicate on the date first above written.

_____
_____
_____[17]

17. West's Modern Legal Forms § 2432.-10.

FORM 6C

CERTIFICATE OF PAID-IN CAPITAL
(NEW JERSEY)

Form C-109—10-31-61 5 M

Filing $5.00
Recording $2.00
Total $7.00

Certificate of Payment of Capital Stock

of the .... Company.

    The location of the principal office in this State is at No. .... Street, in the .... of .... County of ....

    The name of the agent therein and in charge thereof, upon whom process against this corporation may be served, is ....

    In accordance with the provisions of Section 14:8-16 of the Revised Statutes, we ....

.... President,

and .... Secretary of the

.... Company,

a corporation of the State of New Jersey, do hereby certify that ....

.... dollars, being the ....

....

....

of capital stock of said company, as authorized by its Certificate of Incorporation filed in the Department of State on the .... day of ....

A. D. 19...., has been fully paid in: ....

dollars thereof by the purchase of property and ....

dollars thereof in cash. The capital stock of said company previously paid and reported is

$ .... of Common Stock and .... of Preferred Stock.

    WITNESS our hands the .... day of ....

A. D. 19....

.... *President.*

.... *Secretary.*

STATE OF .... } ss.
COUNTY OF ....

...., President,

and .... Secretary of the

.... Company.

Being severally duly sworn, on their respective oaths depose and say that the foregoing certificate by them signed is true.

    Subscribed and sworn to before me,

this ....

.... *President.*

day of .... A. D. 19....

.... *Secretary.*

Certificate of Payment

of

Capital Stock

of the

....

....

....

.... Company.

Filed ...., 19....

....
Secretary of State.

FORM 6D

CHECKLIST FOR SELECTION OF JURISDICTION

(1) Are there express provisions for preincorporation share subscriptions?

(2) May a corporation be formed for perpetual or limited duration?

(3) How restrictive are the provisions concerning corporate names?

(4) Are there express provisions permitting use of a similar corporate name with the consent of the existing corporation? In the case of affiliated corporations? Otherwise?

(5) Is reservation of a corporate name possible? By express statutory provisions? By administrative courtesy?

(6) For what period may a corporate name be reserved?

(7) What renewals of reservation of corporate name are possible?

(8) Is a single incorporator permissible?

(9) Are there any requirements that the incorporator or incorporators subscribe for shares? What are the qualifications required of an incorporator or incorporators with respect to: Residence? Citizenship? Age? Otherwise?

(10) May a corporation serve as an incorporator?

(11) Are there express provisions for informal action by the incorporator(s)?

(12) For what purposes may a corporation be incorporated?

(13) Are broad purposes permissible?

(14) Must specified purposes be set forth in the articles of incorporation?

(15) Are there any constitutional or statutory restrictions on corporate ownership of real property? Agricultural land? Personal property? Shares in other corporations? Are there any constitutional or statutory debt limitations?

(16) Are there express provisions on the ultra vires doctrine?

(17) How broad are the statutory general corporate powers? Do they include power to make charitable contributions irrespective of corporate benefit? To carry out retirement, incentive and benefit plans for directors, officers, and employees? To be a partner? To adopt emergency bylaws? Must the statutory general corporate powers be set forth in the articles of incorporation?

(18) What are the fees for filing or recording the articles of incorporation?

(19) What are the organization taxes? Other initial taxes?

(20) Do such taxes discriminate against shares without par value?

(21) Are filings subject to close administrative scrutiny and conservatism, with resulting delays?

(22) Is there a state stamp tax on the issuance of securities?

(23) Are "blue sky" law requirements burdensome?

(24) What, if any, is the minimum authorized or paid-in capital requirement? Must evidence of compliance be filed? Who are liable, and to what extent, for noncompliance?

(25) What qualitative and quantitative consideration requirements apply to par value shares? To shares without par value? With respect to the valuation of property or services, does the "true value" or "good faith" rule apply? Do preincorporation services satisfy such consideration requirements?

(26) To what extent may a portion of the consideration received for shares be allocated to capital surplus? Within what period after the issuance of the shares may this be done?

(27) May partly-paid shares be issued? May certificates for partly-paid shares be issued?

(28) Are there express provisions for fractions of shares? Scrip?

(29) What provisions may be made with respect to: Dividend preferences? Liquidation preferences?

(30) When two or more classes of shares are authorized, must the provisions concerning them be stated or summarized on the share certificates?

(31) Are express provisions made for issuing preferred or other "special" classes of shares in series? What are the limitations on permissible variations between series of the same class?

(32) To what extent may preferred shares be made redeemable? To what extent may common shares be made redeemable?

(33) To what extent may shares be made convertible?

(34) What are the record date provisions? Are bearer shares permissible? What rights attach to them?

(35) What are the express statutory provisions for, and judicial and administrative attitudes toward, close corporations?

(36) To what extent may voting rights of shareholders be denied or limited? Absolutely? Contingently? May shares carry multiple votes? Fractional votes?

(37) What are the minimum quorum requirements for shareholder action?

(38) Are there express provisions permitting greater-than-normal requirements for: Shareholder quorum? Shareholder vote?

(39) Are there express provisions for holding shareholder meetings outside the state? On dates to be set by board of directors? What are the notice requirements?

(40) Are there express provisions for informal action by shareholders? Unanimously? By required percentages?

(41) Is cumulative voting permissive or mandatory?

(42) What are the provisions for shareholder class voting for directors?

(43) Are there express provisions for shareholder voting agreements?

(44) Are there express provisions permitting shareholder control of directors?

(45) Are there express provisions for irrevocable proxies?

(46) Are there express provisions for voting trusts, permitting closed voting trusts and renewals?

(47) Are there express provisions for purchase and redemption by the corporation of its own shares, including use of stated capital if the purchase is made for specified purposes?

(48) Are there provisions concerning the validity and enforceability of agreements by the corporation to purchase its own shares?

(49) Is insolvency, in either the equity or the bankruptcy sense, a limitation on the redemption or purchase by the corporation of its own shares?

(50) Are there express provisions for rights and options to purchase shares, including the issuance of shares, and the share certificates therefor, even partly-paid, to directors, officers and employees? What are the judicial attitudes with respect thereto?

(51) Is shareholder approval required for the issuance of share options, either generally or to directors, officers and employees?

(52) Do preemptive rights exist or not exist absent provision in the articles of incorporation? Are they adequately defined? May they be denied, limited, amplified, or altered in the articles of incorporation?

(58) What is the minimum number of authorized directors?

(59) What are the qualifications required of directors with respect to: Residence? Citizenship? Shareholding? Age? Otherwise?

(60) May the board of directors be classified? Staggered?

(61) What are the minimum quorum requirements for board of directors action?

(62) Are there express provisions permitting greater-than-normal requirements for: Board of directors quorum? Board of directors vote?

(63) Are there express provisions for holding board of directors meetings outside the state?

(64) Are there express provisions for informal action by the board of directors? By means of conference telephone or some comparable communication technique:

(65) What are the provisions for removal of directors? For cause? Without cause?

(66) Are there express provisions for filling vacancies on the board of directors? By shareholder action? By board of directors action?

(67) Are there provisions for increasing the size of the board of directors? By shareholder action? By board of directors action?

(68) Are there provisions for filling newly-created directorships? By shareholder action? By board of directors action?

(69) Are there express provisions for executive committees of the board of directors? Other committees of the board of directors? Informal action by committees? What powers may be exercised by committees? What is the minimum number of committee members?

(70) Are there express interested directors/officers provisions?

(71) What corporate officers are required?

(72) May the same person hold more than one office?

(73) What are the required qualifications of the various officers with respect to: Residence? Citizenship? Shareholding? Being a director? Age? Otherwise?

(74) Are there provisions for the election of officers by shareholders? For the removal of officers by shareholders?

(75) To what standards are directors and officers held accountable? Standard of care? Fiduciary standards? Statutory duties? What are the possible liabilities of directors? Officers?

(76) To what extent may directors immunize themselves from liability by filing their written dissents? By reliance on records?

(77) What are the express provisions for deadlock, arbitration, and dissolution, and the judicial attitudes concerning the same?

(78) Are cash and property dividends payable out of surplus? Capital surplus? Earned surplus? Net profits?

(79) Is insolvency, in either the equity or the bankruptcy sense, a limitation on cash or property dividends?

(80) Are unrealized appreciation and depreciation recognized in computing surplus? Capital surplus? Earned surplus?

(81) Are there express "wasting assets" corporation dividend provisions?

(82) Are there express provisions for share dividends? Share splits? Other share distributions?

(83) To what extent do statutory requirements of notice or disclosure to shareholders apply in the event of: Cash or property dividends or other distributions from sources other than earned surplus? Share distributions? Reduction of stated capital by cancellation of reacquired shares? Reduction of stated capital made by board of directors? Elimination of deficit in earned surplus account by application of capital surplus ("quasi-reorganization")? Conversion of shares? Who are liable for noncompliance? Corporation? Directors or officers for subjecting corporation to liability?

(84) What are the provisions for shareholder class voting for extraordinary corporate matters? May filings effecting exordinary corporate matters have delayed effective dates?

(85) What shareholder approval is required for a sale, lease, exchange, or other disposition of corporate assets?

(86) What shareholder approval is required for a corporate mortgage or pledge?

(87) What shareholder approval is required for a corporate guaranty?

(88) Do the statutory provisions provide for expeditious amendment of the articles of incorporation? Including elimination of preemptive rights? Elimination of cumulative voting? Elimination of cumulative preferred dividend arrearages? Making nonredeemable shares redeemable? Are there provisions for "restated" articles of incorporation?

(89) What are the statutory provisions permitting merger or consolidation?

(90) Are there provisions for short-merger of a subsidiary into a parent corporation? Of a parent into a subsidiary corporation?

(91) What are the statutory provisions concerning nonjudicial dissolution?

(92) What are the statutory provisions concerning judicial dissolution?

(93) How extensive are the appraisal remedies afforded dissenting shareholders? To what extent are appraisal remedies exclusive?

(94) What are the express provisions relating to shareholder derivative actions?

(95) Are there express provisions for derivative actions by a director? By an officer? By a creditor? By others?

(96) Is there statutory differentiation between shareholder derivative actions and other actions brought by shareholders?

(97) What are the provisions for indemnification for litigation expenses of directors? Of officers? Of other corporate personnel? Are there provisions for insurance?

(98) Are the statutory indemnification provisions exclusive or not with respect to directors? Officers? Other corporate personnel?

(99) What books and records must be kept within the state?

(100) What are the requirements with respect to annual and other reports?

(101) What are the annual franchise tax rates?

(102) What are the state share transfer tax rates?

(103) Are nonresident security holders subject to local taxes? Personal property taxes? Inheritance taxes?

(104) Are there express provisions to accommodate small business investment companies?

(105) Are there express provisions to accommodate open-end investment companies ("mutual funds")?

(106) To what extent are foreign corporations doing business in the state subject to the corporate statute's regulatory provisions? Local "blue sky" laws? Local fees and taxes?

(107) To what extent has the corporate statute been construed by the courts? Are judicial and administrative attitudes sympathetic?

(108) Does the state have a statute or regulations similar to Subchapter S?[18]

---

18. Reprinted with permission from H. Henn, Handbook of the Law of Corporations and Other Business Enterprises 134–138 (2d ed. 1970), Copyright © 1970 by West Publishing Company.

FORM 6E

APPLICATION OF RESERVATION OF CORPORATE NAME
(NEW JERSEY)

Form C-120
Rev. 7-1-71

APPLICATION FOR RESERVATION OF CORPORATE NAME

UNDER SECTION 14A:2-3, CORPORATIONS,

GENERAL, OF THE NEW JERSEY STATUTES

(For Use by Domestic or Foreign Corporations)

To: The Secretary of State
    State of New Jersey

Pursuant to the provisions of Section 14A:2-3, Corporations, General, of the New Jersey Statutes, the undersigned applicant hereby applies for the reservation of a corporate name in New Jersey for a period of one hundred twenty (120) days, and for that purpose submits the following application:

1. The corporate name to be reserved is _____
_____ .

2. The name and address* of the applicant is _____
_____ .
(*Include zip code)

Dated: The _____ day of _____ , 19_____ .

_____
(Applicant)

_____
(Print or Type Name and Title)

FOR USE BY DOMESTIC OR FOREIGN CORPORATIONS

PLEASE READ CAREFULLY

BEFORE COMPLETING THIS FORM

14A:2-3. Reserved Name.

(1) The exclusive right to the use of a corporate name may be reserved upon compliance with the provisions of this section.

(2) The reservation shall be made by filing in the office of the Secretary of State an application to reserve a specified corporate name, executed by or on behalf of the applicant and setting forth the name and address of the applicant. If the Secretary of State finds that the name complies with the provisions of Section 14A:2-2, he shall reserve it for the exclusive use of the applicant for a period of 120 days from the date of filing of the application and shall issue a certificate of reservation.

(3) The right to the exclusive use of a specified corporate name so reserved may be transferred by filing in the office of the Secretary of State a notice of such transfer, executed by or on behalf of the applicant for whom the name was reserved, and specifying the name and address of the transferee.

Fees for filing in Office of the Secretary of State, State House, Trenton, N.J., 08625.

Filing Fee $20.00

NOTE: 1. All checks drawn on Out-of-State Banks must be certified.
        2. No recording fees will be assessed.

FORM 6F
CERTIFICATE OF RESERVATION OF CORPORATE NAME
(SOUTH DAKOTA)

State of South Dakota
Office of The Secretary of State

Certificate of Reservation of Corporate Name

I, LORNA B. HERSETH, Secretary of State of the State of South Dakota, hereby certify that the corporate name of .... has been reserved in this office for the exclusive use of ....
....
for a period of one hundred twenty days after the date hereof, which period shall not be extended, pursuant to the provisions of the South Dakota corporation acts.

IN TESTIMONY WHEREOF, I have hereunto set my hand and affixed the Great Seal of the State of South Dakota, at Pierre, the Capital, this .... day of .... A.D. 19......

....
Secretary of State
....
Assistant

APPENDIX G

FORM 6G
NOTICE OF TRANSFER OF RESERVED NAME
(NEW JERSEY)

Form C-121
Rev. 7-1-71

NOTICE OF TRANSFER OF RESERVED CORPORATE NAME

(FOR USE BY DOMESTIC OR FOREIGN CORPORATIONS)

To: The Secretary of State

State of New Jersey

Pursuant to the provisions of Section 14A:2-3(3), Corporations, General, of the New Jersey Statutes, the undersigned hereby transfers to

_____
(Name of transferee)

_____
(Address of transferee, including zip code)

all rights in the following reserved corporate name:

_____

The period of reservation will expire on _____.
(Date)

Dated at _____ this ____ day of _____, 19___.

_____
(Transferor)

_____
(Print or Type Name and Title)

FOR USE BY DOMESTIC OR FOREIGN CORPORATIONS

PLEASE READ CAREFULLY

BEFORE COMPLETING THIS FORM

14A:2-3. Reserved Name.

(1) The exclusive right to the use of a corporate name may be reserved upon compliance with the provisions of this section.

(2) The reservation shall be made by filing in the office of the Secretary of State an application to reserve a specified corporate name, executed by or on behalf of the applicant and setting forth the name and address of the applicant. If the Secretary of State finds that the name complies with the provisions of section 14A:2-2, he shall reserve it for the exclusive use of the applicant for a period of 120 days from the date of filing of the application and shall issue a certificate of reservation.

(3) The right to the exclusive use of a specified corporate name so reserved may be transferred by filing in the office of the Secretary of State a notice of such transfer, executed by or on behalf of the applicant for whom the name was reserved, and specifying the name and address of the transferee.

Fees for filing in Office of the Secretary of State, State House, Trenton, N.J. 08625.

Filing Fee $10.00

NOTE: 1. No recording fee will be assessed.
2. All checks drawn on Out-of-State Banks must be certified.

FORM 6H

CERTIFICATE OF TRANSFER OF RESERVED CORPORATE NAME
(MODEL ACT)

STATE OF _____
OFFICE OF THE SECRETARY OF STATE

**CERTIFICATE OF
TRANSFER OF RESERVED CORPORATE NAME
OF**

_____

The undersigned, as Secretary of State of the State of _____ _____, hereby certifies that the corporate name of _____ _____, which was reserved in this office on _____, 19___, for a period of one hundred twenty days thereafter, has been transferred to _____ _____, whose address is _____, pursuant to the provisions of Section 9 of the _____ Business Corporation Act.

Dated _____, 19___.

_____
Secretary of State

FORM 6I

APPLICATION FOR REGISTRATION OF CORPORATE NAME
(OREGON)

Application for Registration of Corporate Name

of

_____

To the Corporation Commissioner
of the State of Oregon:

Pursuant to the provisions of ORS 57.055 of the Oregon Business Corporation Act, the undersigned corporation hereby applies for the registration of its corporate name to and including December 31, 19____, and submits the following statement:

FIRST: The name of the corporation is _____

_____

SECOND: It is incorporated under the laws of _____

THIRD: The date of its incorporation is _____

FOURTH: It is carrying on or doing business, **but does not intend to and will not transact business of an intrastate character within the State of Oregon.**

FIFTH: The business in which it is engaged is _____

_____

_____

SIXTH: This Application is accompanied by (a) a certificate setting forth that the corporation is in good standing under the laws of _____, wherein it is incorporated, executed by the official having custody of the records pertaining to corporations in that _____; and (b) a registration fee of $_____ as required by ORS 57.055.

I, the undersigned officer, declare under penalties of perjury that I have examined the foregoing and to the best of my knowledge and belief, it is true, correct and complete.

_____

By _____

Dated _____, 19____.   Its _____

This application should be accompanied by a fee of $1.00 for each month, or fraction thereof, between date of filing and the following December 31, and forwarded to: Corporation Commissioner, Salem, Oregon 97310.

FORM 6J
CERTIFICATE OF REGISTRATION OF CORPORATE NAME
(SOUTH DAKOTA)

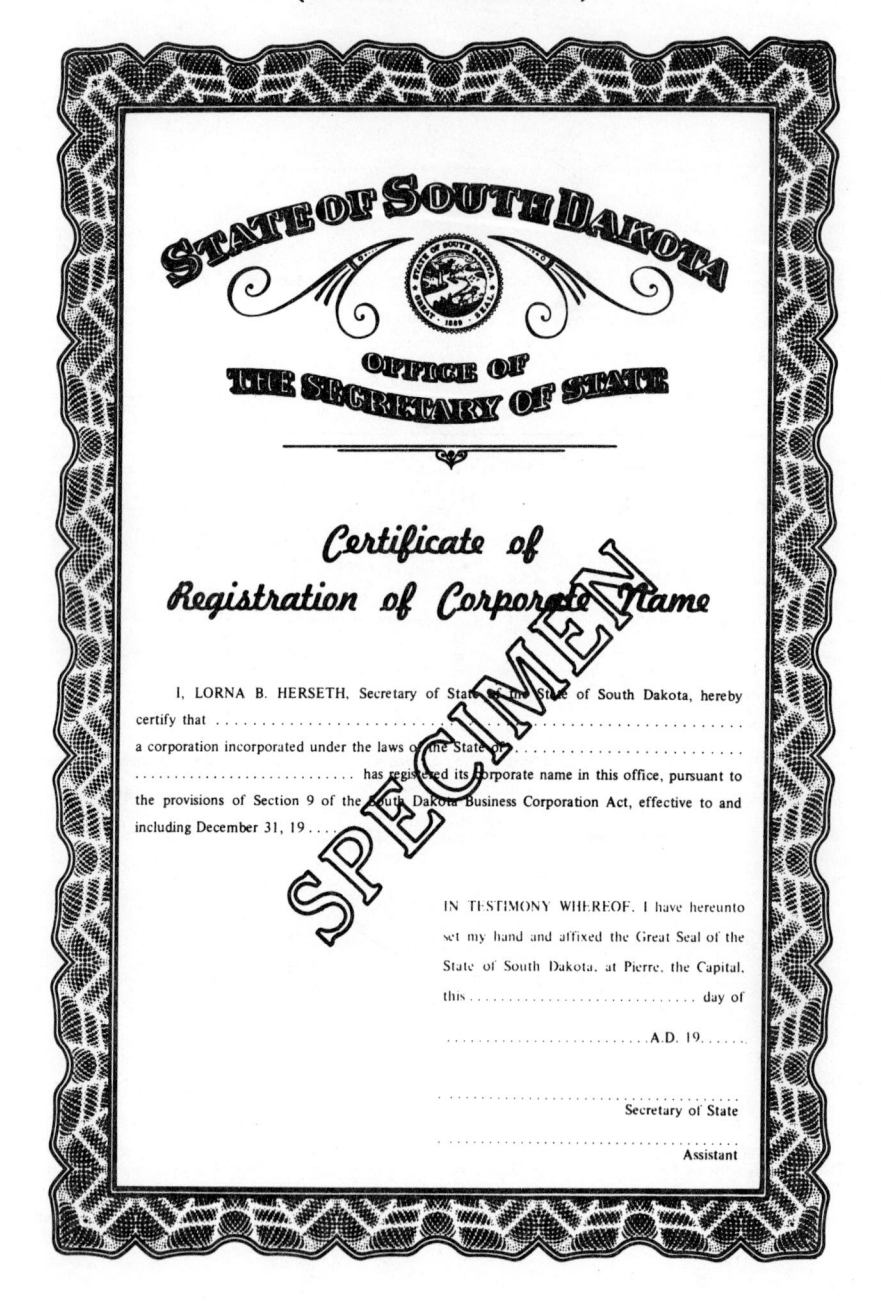

STATE OF SOUTH DAKOTA
OFFICE OF THE SECRETARY OF STATE

Certificate of Registration of Corporate Name

I, LORNA B. HERSETH, Secretary of State of the State of South Dakota, hereby certify that .... a corporation incorporated under the laws of the State of .... has registered its corporate name in this office, pursuant to the provisions of Section 9 of the South Dakota Business Corporation Act, effective to and including December 31, 19.....

IN TESTIMONY WHEREOF, I have hereunto set my hand and affixed the Great Seal of the State of South Dakota, at Pierre, the Capital, this .... day of .... A.D. 19......

....
Secretary of State
....
Assistant

FORM 6K

APPLICATION FOR RENEWAL OF REGISTERED NAME
(OREGON)

**Application for
Renewal of Registration of Corporate Name**

OF

_____

To the Corporation Commissioner
of the State of Oregon:

Pursuant to the provisions of ORS 57.060 of the Oregon Business Corporation Act, the undersigned corporation hereby applies for a renewal of the registration of its corporate name to and including December 31, 19____, and submits the following statements:

FIRST: The name of the corporation is _____

_____

SECOND: It is incorporated under the laws of _____

THIRD: The date of its incorporation is _____

FOURTH: It is carrying on or doing business, <u>but does not intend to and will not transact business of an intrastate character within the State of Oregon.</u>

FIFTH: The business in which it is engaged is _____

_____

_____

_____

SIXTH: This Application is accompanied by (a) a certificate setting forth that the corporation is in good standing under the law of _____, wherein it is incorporated, executed by the official having custody of the records pertaining to corporations in that jurisdiction; and (b) a registration fee of $10 as required by said ORS 57.060.

Dated _____, 19____.

_____

By _____

Its _____

FORM 6L
CERTIFICATE OF RENEWAL OF REGISTERED NAME
(SOUTH DAKOTA)

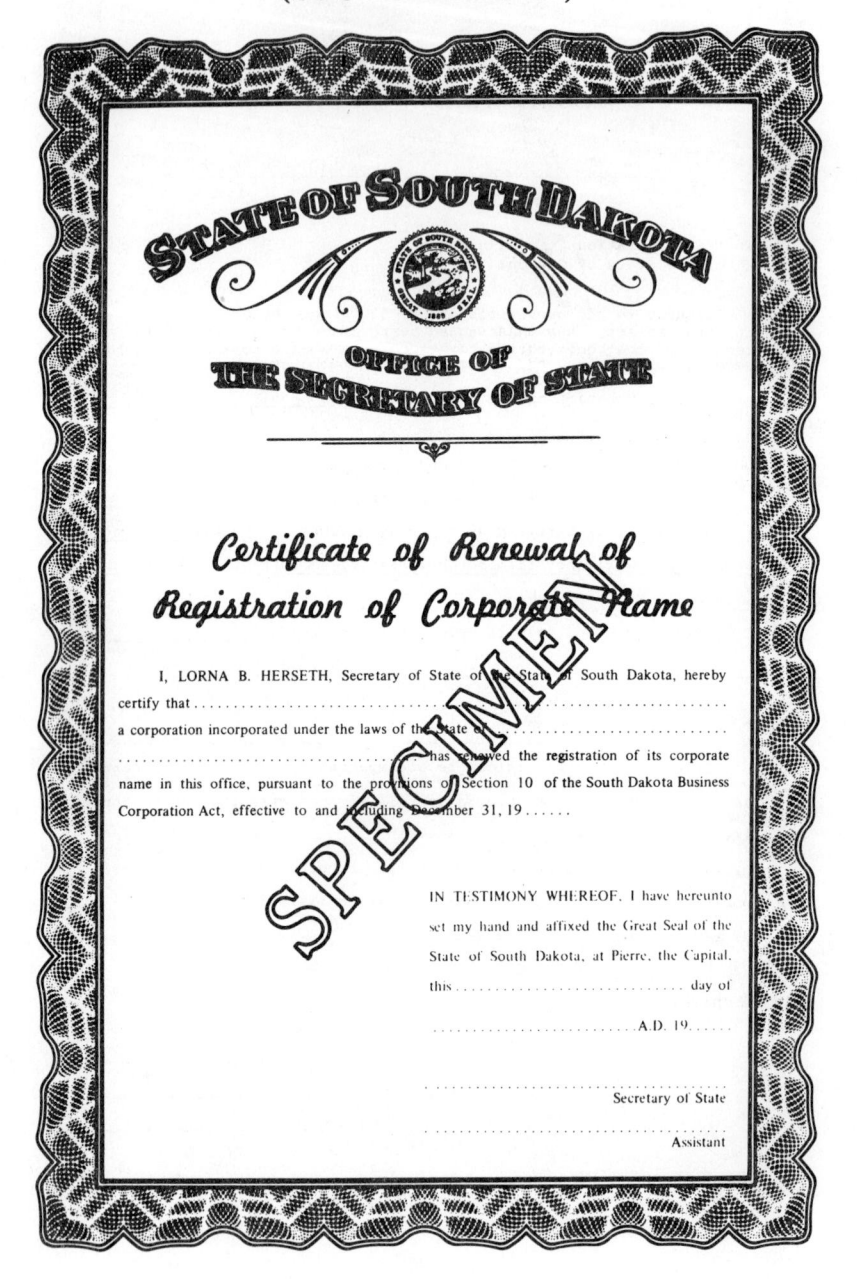

STATE OF SOUTH DAKOTA
OFFICE OF THE SECRETARY OF STATE

Certificate of Renewal of Registration of Corporate Name

I, LORNA B. HERSETH, Secretary of State of the State of South Dakota, hereby certify that .... a corporation incorporated under the laws of the State of .... has renewed the registration of its corporate name in this office, pursuant to the provisions of Section 10 of the South Dakota Business Corporation Act, effective to and including December 31, 19......

IN TESTIMONY WHEREOF, I have hereunto set my hand and affixed the Great Seal of the State of South Dakota, at Pierre, the Capital, this .... day of .... A.D. 19......

....
Secretary of State

....
Assistant

FORM 6M

STATEMENT OF ASSUMED NAME BY CORPORATION

SS: AN-TN-1
(Rev. 7/75)

STATE OF COLORADO)
) SS   CERTIFICATE OF
COUNTY OF   )   ASSUMED OR TRADE NAME

...., a Colorado corporation, being desirous of transacting a portion of its business under an assumed or trade name as permitted by 7-71-101, Colorado Revised Statutes 1973, hereby certifies:

1. The corporate name and location of the principal office of said corporation is:

2. The name, other than its own corporate name, under which such business is carried on is:*

3. A brief description of the kind of business transacted and to be transacted under such assumed or trade name is:

IN WITNESS WHEREOF, The undersigned President and Secretary of said corporation, have this day executed this Certificate ...., 19..........

....
By..
                                        President

Attest:

....
            Secretary

Subscribed and sworn to before me this..............day of.., 19.......... .
My commission expires.. .

....
                Notary Public

*Any assumed name so used by any such corporation shall contain one of the words "corporation" "incorporated," "limited," or one of the abbreviations "Corp.", "Inc." or "Ltd."

SUBMIT THE ORIGINAL TYPED FORM ONLY.
Filing fee $10.00

FORM 6N

CHECKLIST FOR ARTICLES OF INCORPORATION

1. Corporate name
   (a) Clear intended name with Secretary of State of state of incorporation
   (b) Clear intended name with Secretary of State of other states where corporation intends to transact business
   (c) Desirability of trade-mark search of intended name
   (d) Desirability of filing name as a trade name
2. Location of principal office
   (a) County
   (b) City
   (c) Street and number
3. Resident agent
   (a) Name of individual or corporation
   (b) Address (including street and number)
4. Purposes
   (a) Nature of business in general
   (b) Scope of activities in detail
5. Powers
   (a) Is it desired to set out the statutory powers?
   (b) Are there to be any limitations of the customary powers, such as the right to deal in real and personal property, to borrow money, to deal in securities, etc.?
6. Capital stock
   (a) Total number of shares of all classes
   (b) Number of shares of each class having a par value
   Common
   Preferred
   Other
   (c) Par value of each class
   Common
   Preferred
   Other
   (d) Number of shares without par value
   Common
   Preferred
   Other
   (e) Price at which par value stock is to be sold
   Common
   Preferred
   Other

    (f) Price at which no par value stock is to be sold
        Common
        Preferred
        Other
    (g) Are incorporators planning to exchange property for stock; if so, description and agreed value of property
    (h) How is the price at which subsequently issued stock shall be sold to be determined?

7. Characteristics of preferred stock
    (a) Dividends
        Source
        Rate
        Dates of payment
        Cumulative or noncumulative
    (b) Redemption
        Price
        Notice
        Manner
    (c) Priority of shares in event of dissolution
    (d) Conversion rights of preferred stock
    (e) Sinking fund for redemption or retirement

8. Minimum amount of capital with which corporation will commence business

9. Incorporators
    (a) Names and addresses of each of the incorporators (dummies or principals)

10. Period of duration
    (a) Is corporation to have perpetual existence?
    (b) If for a fixed term, commencing _____; ceasing _____

11. Liability of stockholders
    (a) Is private property of stockholders to be subject to payment of corporate debts?

12. Is the certificate to include the provision for compromises and arrangements between the corporation and its creditors?

13. Is the preemptive right of stockholders to be denied?

14. Are there special situations, such as a sale of assets, which should require the approval of more than a majority of the outstanding stock?

15. Voting rights
    (a) Any limitations on the right of each stockholder to one vote for each share of stock
    (b) Is the preferred stock to have full, limited, or no voting power?

16. Is the transfer of stock to be restricted?

17. Is there to be a provision for a stock option plan?
18. Are the directors to have the power to amend bylaws?
19. Are the directors to have the power to set apart reserves?
20. Is the requirement that directors be elected by ballot to be eliminated? [19]

19. West's Modern Legal Forms § 2491.1.

FORM 60

DELAWARE ARTICLES OF INCORPORATION

CERTIFICATE OF INCORPORATION
OF
FINE FABRICS CORPORATION

1. **Name.** The name of the Corporation is Fine Fabrics Corporation.

2. **Registered Office and Registered Agent.** The address of the Corporation's registered office in Delaware is 100 _____ Street in the City of Wilmington and County of New Castle, and the name of its registered agent at such address is _____ Trust Company.

3. **Purposes.** The purpose of the Corporation is to engage in any lawful act or activity for which corporations may be now or hereafter organized under the General Corporation Law of Delaware.

4. **Capital Stock** [*providing for one class of par value stock*]. The Corporation is authorized to issue only one class of stock. The total number of such shares is ten thousand and the par value of each of such shares is ten dollars.

[**Alternate**] 4. **Capital Stock** [*providing for two classes of stock, one voting and one non-voting*]. The total number of shares of all classes of stock which the Corporation shall have authority to issue is ten thousand, all of which are to be without par value. Five thousand of such shares shall be Class A voting shares and five thousand of such shares shall be Class B non-voting shares. The Class A shares and the Class B shares shall have identical rights except that the Class B shares shall not entitle the holder thereof to vote on any matter unless specifically required by law.

[**Alternate**] 4. **Capital Stock** [*providing for two classes of stock, preferred and common*]. The total number of shares of all classes of capital stock which the Corporation shall have authority to issue is twenty-six million shares, of which one million shares shall be shares of Preferred Stock without par value (hereinafter called

"Preferred Stock"), and twenty-five million shares shall be shares of Common Stock of the par value of $5 per share (hereinafter called "Common Stock").

Any amendment to the Certificate of Incorporation which shall increase or decrease the authorized capital stock of the Corporation may be adopted by the affirmative vote of the holders of a majority of the outstanding shares of stock of the Corporation entitled to vote.

The designations and the powers, preferences and rights, and the qualifications, limitations or restrictions thereof, of the Preferred Stock shall be as follows:

(1) The Board of Directors is expressly authorized at any time, and from time to time, to provide for the issuance of shares of Preferred Stock in one or more series, with such voting powers, full or limited but not to exceed one vote per share, or without voting powers and with such designations, preferences and relative, participating, optional or other special rights, and qualifications, limitations or restrictions thereof, as shall be expressed in the resolution or resolutions providing for the issue thereof adopted by the Board of Directors and as are not expressed in this Certificate of Incorporation or any amendment thereto, in-including (but without limiting the generality of the foregoing) the following:

(a) the designation of such series;

(b) The dividend rate of such series, the conditions and dates upon which such dividends shall be payable, the preference or relation which such dividends shall bear to the dividends payable on any other class or classes or on any other series of any class or classes of capital stock of the Corporation, and whether such dividends shall be cumulative or non-cumulative;

(c) whether the shares of such series shall be subject to redemption by the Corporation, and, if made subject to such redemption, the times, prices and other terms and conditions of such redemption;

(d) the terms and amount of any sinking fund provided for the purchase or redemption of the shares of such series;

(e) whether the shares of such series shall be convertible into or exchangeable for shares of any other class or classes or of any other series of any class or classes of capital stock of the Corporation, and, if provision be made for conversion or exchange, the times, prices, rates, adjustments, and other terms and conditions of such conversion or exchange;

(f) the extent, if any, to which the holders of the shares of such series shall be entitled to vote as a class or otherwise with respect to the election of directors or otherwise; provided, however, that in no event shall any holder of any series of Preferred Stock be entitled to more than one vote for each share of such Preferred Stock held by him;

(g) the restrictions and conditions, if any, upon the issue or reissue of any additional Preferred Stock ranking on a parity with or prior to such shares as to dividends or upon dissolution;

(h) the rights of the holders of the shares of such series upon the dissolution of, or upon the distribution of assets of, the Corporation, which rights may be different in the case of a voluntary dissolution than in the case of an involuntary dissolution.

(2) Except as otherwise required by law and except for such voting powers with respect to the election of directors or other matters as may be stated in the resolutions of the Board of Directors creating any series of Preferred Stock, the holders of any such series shall have no voting power whatsoever.

5. **Incorporators.** The names and mailing addresses of the incorporators are:

Name	Mailing Address
_____	_____
_____	_____

[Optional] 6. **Initial Directors** [*if the powers of the incorporator or incorporators are to terminate upon the filing of the certificate of incorporation*]. The names and mailing addresses of the persons who are to serve as directors until the first annual meeting of stockholders or until their successors are elected and qualify are:

Name	Mailing Address
_____	_____
_____	_____

[Optional] 7. **Regulatory Provisions.** The following additional provisions are inserted for the management of the business and for the conduct of the affairs of the Corporation, and creating, defining, limiting, and regulating the powers of the Corporation, the directors, and the stockholders, or any class of stockholders:

(a) *Power of Directors to Amend Bylaws*. The Board of Directors is authorized and empowered from time to time in its discretion to make, alter or repeal the bylaws of the Corporation, except as such power may be limited by any one or more bylaws of the Corporation adopted by the stockholders.

(b) *Books.* The books of the Corporation (subject to the provisions of the laws of the State of Delaware) may be kept outside of the State of Delaware at such places as from time to time may be designated by the Board of Directors.

(c) *Cumulative Voting.* At all elections of directors of the Corporation, each stockholder shall be entitled to as many votes as shall equal the number of votes which he would be entitled to cast for the election of directors with respect to his shares of stock multiplied by the number of directors to be elected, and that he may cast all of such votes for a single director or may distribute them among the number to be voted for, or for any two or more of them as he may see fit.

(d) *Consent of Stockholders in Lieu of Meeting.* Whenever the vote of stockholders at a meeting thereof is required or permitted to be taken for or in connection with any corporate action by any provision of the General Corporation Law of the State of Delaware the meeting and vote of stockholders may be dispensed with if such action is taken with the written consent of the holders of not less than a majority of all the stock entitled to be voted upon such action if a meeting were held; provided that in no case shall the written consent be by the holders of stock having less than the minimum percentage of the vote required by statute for such action, and provided that prompt notice is given to all stockholders of the taking of corporate action without a meeting and by less than unanimous written consent.

(e) *Elections of Directors.* Elections of directors need not be by written ballot.

(f) *Removal of Directors.* The stockholders may at any time, at a meeting expressly called for that purpose, remove any or all of the directors, with or without cause, by a vote of the holders of a majority of the shares then entitled to vote at an election of directors. No director may be removed when the votes cast against his removal would be sufficient to elect him if voted cumulatively at an election at which the same total number of votes were cast and the entire board were then being elected. [When by the provisions of the certificate of incorporation the holders of the shares of any class or series, voting as a class, are entitled to elect one or more directors, any director so elected may be removed only by the applicable vote of the holders of the shares of that class or series, voting as a class.]

[Optional] 8. **Creditor Arrangements.** Whenever a compromise or arrangement is proposed between this corporation and its creditors or any class of them and/or between this corporation and its stockholders or any class of them, any court of equitable jurisdiction within the State of Delaware may, on the application in a summary way of this corporation or of any creditor or stockholder thereof or on the application of any receiver or receivers appointed for this corporation under the provisions of section 291 of Title 8 of the Delaware Code or on the application of trustees in dissolution or of any receiver or receivers appointed for this corporation under the provisions of section 279 of Title 8 of the Delaware Code order a meeting of the creditors or class of creditors, and/or of the stockholders or class of stockholders of this corporation, as the case may be, to be summoned in such manner as the said court directs. If a majority in number representing three-fourths in value of the creditors or class of creditors, and/or of the stockholders or class of stockholders of this corporation, as the case may be, agree to any compromise or arrangement and to any reorganization of this corporation as consequence of such compromise or arrangement, the said compromise or arrangement and the said reorganization shall, if sanctioned by the court to which the said application has been made, be binding on all the creditors or class of creditors, and/or on all the stockholders or class of stockholders, of this corporation, as the case may be, and also on this corporation.

[Optional] 9. **Preemptive Rights.** The holders from time to time of the shares of the Corporation shall have the preemptive right to purchase, at such respective equitable prices, terms, and conditions as shall be fixed by the Board of Directors, such of the shares of the Corporation as may be issued, from time to time, over and above the issue of the first 5,000 shares of the Corporation which have never previously been sold. Such preemptive right shall apply to all shares issued after such first 5,000 shares, whether such additional shares constitute a part of the shares presently or subsequently authorized or constitute shares held in the treasury of the Corporation, and shall be exercised in the respective ratio which the number of shares held by each stockholder at the time of such issue bears to the total number of shares outstanding in the names of all stockholders at such time.

[Optional] 10. **Greater Voting Requirements.** The affirmative vote of a majority of the directors shall be necessary for the transaction of any business at any meeting of directors, except in the case of a proposal to borrow money on the Corporation's credit, in which case the favorable vote of all of the directors shall be necessary.

[Optional] 11. **Duration.** The duration of the Corporation's existence shall extend for the period beginning on the date the certificate of incorporation of the Corporation is filed with the Secretary of State of Delaware, and ending December 31, 1977.

[Optional] 12. **Personal Liability.** The stockholders shall be liable for the debts of the Corporation in the proportion that their stock bears to the total outstanding stock of the Corporation.

13. **Amendment.** The Corporation reserves the right to amend, alter, change or repeal any provision contained in the Certificate of Incorporation, in the manner now or hereafter prescribed by statute, and all rights conferred upon stockholders herein are granted subject to this reservation.

We, the undersigned, being all of the incorporators above named, for the purpose of forming a corporation pursuant to the General Corporation Law of Delaware, sign and acknowledge this certificate of incorporation this 1st day of September, 1968.

_____

_____

Acknowledgment

State of _____ } ss.
County of _____

On this 1st day of September, 1968, before me personally came _____, one of the persons who signed the foregoing certificate of incorporation, known to me personally to be such, and acknowledged that the said certificate is his act and deed and that the facts stated therein are true.

_____ [20]

Notary Public

[Seal]

20. West's Modern Legal Forms § 2509.1.

FORM 6P

ARTICLES OF INCORPORATION
(NORTH DAKOTA)

CORPORATION FOR PROFIT
SUBMIT DUPLICATE ORIGINALS

ARTICLES OF INCORPORATION
OF

_____

We, the undersigned natural persons of the age of twenty-one years or more, acting as incorporators of a corporation under the North Dakota Business Corporation Act, adopt the following Articles of Incorporation for such corporation:

Article 1. The name of said corporation shall be: _____
(Shall contain the word "corporation", "company", "incorporated",
or "limited", or shall contain an abbreviation of one such words)

Article 2. The period of its duration is: _____
("Perpetual unless limited")

Article 3. The purposes for which the corporation is organized are:

Article 4. The aggregate number of shares which the corporation shall have authority to issue is: _____
(If shares consist of one class only, insert statement of par value of shares, or that all are without par value. If shares are divided into classes, insert number of shares of each class)

Total authorized capitalization is: _____

Article 5. The corporation will not commence business until at least one thousand dollars has been received by it as consideration for the issuance of shares.

Article 6. Provisions limiting or denying to shareholders the preemptive right to acquire additional or treasury shares of the corporation are: _____
(If preemptive rights are not to be limited or desired, insert the word "none")

Article 7. Provisions for the regulation of the internal affairs of the corporation are: _____
(If no provisions for the regulation of the internal affairs of the corporation are set forth, insert the word "none")

Article 8. The address of the initial registered office of the corporation is: _____
(Street Address and City)

and the name of its initial registered agent at such address is: _____

Article 9. The number of directors constituting the initial board of directors of the corporation is _____
(State definite number—not less than 3 nor more than 15)

and the names and addresses of the persons who are to serve as directors until the first annual meeting of shareholders or until their successors are elected and shall qualify are:

Name	Street Address	City	State

Article 10. The name and address of each incorporator is:
(Not less than three)

Name	Street Address	City	State
_____	_____	____	____
_____	_____	____	____
_____	_____	____	____
_____	_____	____	____
_____	_____	____	____

We, the above named incorporators, being first duly sworn, say that we each have read the foregoing Articles of Incorporation and know the contents thereof, and verily believe the statements made therein to be true.

_____   _____
_____   _____
_____   _____
_____   _____

Dated _____ 19____.

Subscribed and sworn to before me this _____ day of _____ 19____.

NOTARIAL SEAL

_____
Notary Public

State of _____

My Commission Expires _____ 19____.

Certificate No. _____

Filing Date _____ 19____.

_____
(Secretary of State)

_____
(By Deputy)

Fees:
$25,000 capitalization or less $25.00
$25,000 to $50,000 capitalization — an additional 50.00
For each $10,000 or fraction thereof over
 $50,000 capitalization 5.00
Filing fee in addition to above fees 16.00

TOTAL FEES: $ _____

"Buy North Dakota Products"

State of North Dakota

Certificate No. ....

CERTIFICATE OF INCORPORATION
OF

....

   The undersigned, as Secretary of State of the State of North Dakota, hereby certifies that duplicate originals of Articles of Incorporation for the incorporation of ....

....

duly signed and verified pursuant to the provisions of the North Dakota .... Corporation Act, have been received in this office and are found to conform to law.

   ACCORDINGLY the undersigned, as such Secretary of State, and by virtue of the authority vested in him by law, hereby issues this Certificate of Incorporation to

....

and attaches hereto a duplicate original of the Articles of Incorporation.

In Testimony Whereof, I have hereunto set my hand and affixed the Great Seal of the State at the Capitol in the City of Bismarck, this .... day of .... A. D., 19......

....
Secretary of State.

By ....
Deputy.

"Buy North Dakota Products"

FORM 6Q
DELAWARE BY-LAWS

BYLAWS
OF
FINE FABRICS CORPORATION

A Delaware Corporation

ARTICLE I

Offices

The principal office of the Corporation shall be in Wilmington, Delaware. The Corporation may have offices at such other places within or without the State of Delaware as the Board of Directors may from time to time establish.

ARTICLE II

Meetings of Stockholders

Section 1. *Annual Meetings.* The annual meeting of the stockholders for the election of directors and for the transaction of such other business as properly may come before such meeting shall be held at two o'clock in the afternoon on the second Wednesday of March in each year, if not a legal holiday, or, if a legal holiday, then on the next succeeding day not a legal holiday.

Section 2. *Special Meetings.* A special meeting of the stockholders may be called at any time by the President or the Board of Directors, and shall be called by the President upon the written request of stockholders of record holding in the aggregate one-fifth or more of the outstanding shares of stock of the Corporation entitled to vote, such written request to state the purpose or purposes of the meeting and to be delivered to the President.

Section 3. *Place of Meetings.* All meetings of the stockholders shall be held at the office of the Corporation in Lincoln, Nebraska, or at such other place, within or without the State of Delaware, as shall be determined from time to time by the Board of Directors of the stockholders of the Corporation.

Section 4. *Change in Time or Place of Meetings.* The time and place specified in this Article II for the meetings of stockholders for the election of directors shall not be changed within sixty days next before the day on which such election is to be held. A notice of any such change shall be given to each stockholder at least twenty days before the election is held, in person or by letter mailed to his last known post office address.

Section 5. *Notice of Meetings.* Except as otherwise required by statute, written or printed notice of each meeting of the stockholders, whether annual or special, stating the place, day and hour thereof and the purposes for which the meeting is called, shall be given by or under the direction of the Secretary at least ten but not more than fifty days before the date fixed for such meeting, to each stockholder entitled to vote at such meeting, of record at the close of business on the day fixed by the Board of Directors as a record date for the determination of the stockholders entitled to vote at such meetings, or if no such date has been fixed, of record at the close of business on the day next preceding the day on which notice is given, by leaving such notice with him or at his residence or usual place of business or by mailing it, postage prepaid and addressed to him at his post office address as it appears on the books of the Corporation. A waiver of such notice in writing, signed by the person or persons entitled to said notice, whether before or after the time stated therein, shall be deemed equivalent to such notice. Except as otherwise required by statute, notice of any adjourned meeting of the stockholders shall not be required.

Section 6. *Quorum.* Except as otherwise required by statute, the presence at any meeting, in person or by proxy, of the holders of record of a majority of the shares then issued and outstanding and entitled to vote shall be necessary and sufficient to constitute a quorum for the transaction of business. In the absence of a quorum, a majority in interest of the stockholders entitled to vote, present in person or by proxy, or, if no stockholder entitled to vote is present in person or by proxy, any officer entitled to preside or act as secretary of such meeting, may adjourn the meeting from time to time for a period not exceeding twenty days in any one case. At any such adjourned meeting at which a quorum may be present, any business may be transacted which might have been transacted at the meeting as originally called.

Section 7. *List of Stockholders Entitled to Vote.* The officer who has charge of the stock ledger of the Corporation shall prepare and make, at least ten days before every election of directors, a complete list of the stockholders entitled to vote at said election, arranged in alphabetical order, and showing the address of each stockholder and the number of shares registered in the name of each stockholder. Such list shall be open to the examination of any stockholder during ordinary business hours, for a period of at least ten days prior to the election, either at a place within the city, town or village where the election is to be held and which place shall be specified in the notice of the meeting, or, if not so specified, at the place where said meeting is to be held, and the list shall be produced and kept at the time and place of election during the whole time thereof, and subject to the inspection of any stockholder who may be present.

Section 8. *Voting.* Except as otherwise provided by statute or by the Certificate of Incorporation, and subject to the provisions of Section 4 of Article VIII of these Bylaws, each stockholder shall at every meeting of the stockholders be entitled to one vote in person or by proxy for each share of the capital stock having voting power held by such stockholder, but no proxy shall be voted on after three years from its date, unless the proxy provides for a longer period.

At all meetings of the stockholders, except as otherwise required by statute, by the Certificate of Incorporation, or by these Bylaws, all matters shall be decided by the vote of a majority in interest of the stockholders entitled to vote present in person or by proxy.

Persons holding stock in a fiduciary capacity shall be entitled to vote the shares so held, and persons whose stock is pledged shall be entitled to vote, unless in the transfer by the pledgor on the books of the Corporation he shall have expressly empowered the pledgee to vote thereon, in which case only the pledgee or his proxy may represent said stock and vote thereon.

Shares of the capital stock of the Corporation belonging to the Corporation shall not be voted upon directly or indirectly.

Section 9. *Consent of Stockholders in Lieu of Meeting.* Whenever the vote of stockholders at a meeting thereof is required or permitted to be taken in connection with any corporate action, by any provisions of the statutes or of the Certificate of Incorporation, the meeting and vote of stockholders may be dispensed with, if all the stockholders who would have been entitled to vote upon the action if such meeting were held, shall consent in writing to such corporate action being taken.

ARTICLE III

Board of Directors

Section 1. *General Powers.* The business of the Corporation shall be managed by the Board of Directors, except as otherwise provided by statute or by the Certificate of Incorporation.

Section 2. *Number and Qualifications.* The Board of Directors shall consist of five members. Except as provided in the Certificate of Incorporation this number can be changed only by the vote or written consent of the holders of 90 per cent of the stock of the Corporation outstanding and entitled to vote. This number cannot be changed by amendment of the Bylaws of the Corporation. No director need be a stockholder.

[Alternative Clause: Indefinite Number of Directors]

Section 2. *Number and Qualifications.* The number of directors shall be not less than three nor more than fifteen, except that in case all the shares of the Corporation are owned beneficially and of record by either one or two stockholders, the number of directors may be less than three but not less than the number of stockholders. Within the limits specified, the number of directors for each corporate year shall be fixed by vote at the meeting at which they are elected. No director need be a stockholder.

Section 3. *Election and Term of Office.* The directors shall be elected annually by the stockholders, and shall hold office until their successors are respectively elected and qualified.

At all elections for directors each stockholder shall be entitled to as many votes as shall equal the number of his shares of stock multiplied by the number of directors to be elected, and he may cast all of such votes for a single director, or may distribute them among the number to be voted for, or any two or more of them, as he may see fit.

Elections of directors need not be by ballot.

Section 4. *Compensation.* The members of the Board of Directors shall be paid a fee of $_____ for attendance at all annual, regular, special and adjourned meetings of the Board. No such fee shall be paid any director if absent. Any director of the Corporation may also serve the Corporation in any other capacity, and receive compensation therefor in any form. Members of special or standing committees may be allowed like compensation for attending committee meetings.

Section 5. *Removals and Resignations.* The stockholders may, at any meeting called for the purpose, by vote of two-thirds of the capital stock issued and outstanding, remove any director from office, with or without cause; provided, however, that no director shall be removed in case the votes of a sufficient number of shares are cast against his removal, which if cumulatively voted at an election of directors would be sufficient to elect him.

The stockholders may, at any meeting, by vote of a majority of such stock represented at such meeting, accept the resignation of any director.

Section 6. *Vacancies.* Any vacancy occurring in the office of director may be filled by a majority of the directors then in office, though less than a quorum, and the directors so chosen shall hold office until the next annual election and until their successors are duly elected and qualified, unless sooner displaced.

When one or more directors resign from the Board, effective at a future date, a majority of the directors then in office, including those who have so resigned, shall have power to fill such vacancy or vacancies, the vote thereon to take effect when such resignation or resignations shall become effective, and each director so chosen shall hold office as herein provided in the filling of other vacancies.

ARTICLE IV

Meetings of Board of Directors

Section 1. *Regular Meetings.* A regular meeting of the Board of Directors may be held without call or formal notice immediately after and at the same place as the annual meeting of the stockholders or any special meeting of the stockholders at which a Board of Directors is elected. Other regular meetings of the Board of Directors may be held without call or formal notice at such places within or without the State of Delaware and at such times as the Board may by vote from time to time determine.

Section 2. *Special Meetings.* Special meetings of the Board of Directors may be held at any place either within or without the State of Delaware at any time when called by the President, Treasurer, Secretary or two or more directors. Notice of the time and place thereof shall be given to each director at least three days before the meeting if by mail or at least twenty-four hours if in person or by telephone or telegraph. A waiver of such notice in writing, signed by the person or persons entitled to said notice, either before or after the time stated therein, shall be deemed equivalent to such notice. Notice of any adjourned meeting of the Board of Directors need not be given.

Section 3. *Quorum.* The presence, at any meeting, of one-third of the total number of directors, but in no case less than two directors, shall be necessary and sufficient to constitute a quorum for the transaction of business except that when a Board of one director is authorized, then one director shall constitute a quorum. Except as otherwise required by statute or by the Certificate of Incorporation, the act of a majority of the directors present at a meeting at which a quorum is present shall be the act of the Board of Directors. In the absence of a quorum, a majority of the directors present at the time and place of any meeting may adjourn such meeting from time to time until a quorum be present.

Section 4. *Consent of Directors in Lieu of Meeting.* Unless otherwise restricted by the Certificate of Incorporation, any action required or permitted to be taken at any meeting of the Board of Directors or any committee thereof may be taken without a meeting, if prior to such action a written consent thereto is signed by all members of the Board or committee, and such written consent is filed with the minutes of proceedings of the Board or committee.

ARTICLE V

Committees of Board of Directors

The Board of Directors may, by resolution passed by a majority of the whole Board, designate one or more committees, each committee to consist of two or more of the directors of the Corporation, which, to the extent provided in the resolution, shall have and may exercise the powers of the Board of Directors in the management of the business and affairs of the Corporation, and may authorize the seal of the Corporation to be affixed to all papers which may require it. Such committee or committees shall have such name or names as may be determined from time to time by resolution adopted by the Board of Directors.

The committees of the Board of Directors shall keep regular minutes of their proceedings and report the same to the Board of Directors when required.

ARTICLE VI

Officers

Section 1. *Number.* The corporation shall have a President, one or more Vice Presidents, a Secretary and a Treasurer, and such other officers, agents and factors as may be deemed necessary. One person may hold any two offices except the offices of President and Vice President and the offices of President and Secretary.

Section 2. *Election, Term of Office and Qualifications.* The officers specifically designated in Section 1 of this Article VI shall be chosen annually by the Board of Directors and shall hold office until their successors are chosen and qualified. No officer need be a director.

Section 3. *Subordinate Officers.* The Board of Directors from time to time may appoint other officers and agents, including one or more Assistant Secretaries and one or more Assistant Treasurers, each of whom shall hold office for such period, have such authority and perform such duties as are provided in these Bylaws or as the Board of Directors from time to time may determine. The Board of Directors may delegate to any officer the power to appoint any such subordinate officers, agents and factors and to prescribe their respective authorities and duties.

Section 4. *Removals and Resignations.* The Board of Directors may at any meeting called for the purpose, by vote of a majority of their entire number, remove from office any officer or agent of the Corporation, or any member of any committee appointed by the Board of Directors.

The Board of Directors may at any meeting, by vote of a majority of the directors present at such meeting, accept the resignation of any officer of the Corporation.

Section 5. *Vacancies.* Any vacancy occurring in the office of President, Vice President, Secretary, Treasurer or any other office by death, resignation, removal, or otherwise shall be filled for the unexpired portion of the term in the manner prescribed by these Bylaws for the regular election or appointment to such office.

Section 6. *The President.* The President shall be the chief executive officer of the Corporation and, subject to the direction and under the supervision of the Board of Directors, shall have general charge of the business, affairs and property of the Corporation, and control over its officers, agents and employees. The President shall preside at all meetings of the stockholders and of the Board of Directors at which he is present. The President shall do and perform such other duties and may exercise such other powers as from time to time may be assigned to him by these Bylaws or by the Board of Directors.

Section 7. *The Vice President.* At the request of the President or in the event of his absence or disability, the Vice President, or in case there shall be more than one Vice President, the Vice President designated by the President, or in the absence of such designation, the Vice President designated by the Board of Directors, shall perform all the duties of the President, and when so acting, shall have all the powers of, and be subject to all the restrictions upon, the President. Any Vice President shall perform such other duties and may exercise such other powers as from time to time may be assigned to him by these Bylaws or by the Board of Directors or the President.

Section 8. *The Secretary.* The Secretary shall

(a) record all the proceedings of the meetings of the Corporation and directors in a book to be kept for that purpose;

(b) have charge of the stock ledger (which may, however, be kept by any transfer agent or agents of the Corporation under the direction of the Secretary), an original or duplicate of which shall be kept at the principal office or place of business of the Corporation in the State of _____;

(c) prepare and make, at least ten days before every election of directors, a complete list of the stockholders entitled to vote at said election, arranged in alphabetical order;

(d) see that all notices are duly given in accordance with the provisions of these Bylaws or as required by statute;

(e) be custodian of the records of the Corporation and the Board of Directors, and of the seal of the Corporation, and see that the seal is affixed to all stock certificates prior to their issuance and to all documents the execution of which on behalf of the Corporation under its seal shall have been duly authorized;

(f) see that all books, reports, statements, certificates and the other documents and records required by law to be kept or filed are properly kept or filed; and

(g) in general, perform all duties and have all powers incident to the office of Secretary and perform such other duties and have such other powers as from time to time may be assigned to him by these Bylaws or by the Board of Directors or the President.

Section 9. *The Treasurer.* The Treasurer shall

(a) have supervision over the funds, securities, receipts, and disbursements of the Corporation;

(b) cause all moneys and other valuable effects of the Corporation to be deposited in its name and to its credit, in such depositaries as shall be selected by the Board of Directors or pursuant to authority conferred by the Board of Directors;

(c) cause the funds of the Corporation to be disbursed by checks or drafts upon the authorized depositaries of the Corporation, when such disbursements shall have been duly authorized;

(d) cause to be taken and preserved proper vouchers for all moneys disbursed;

(e) cause to be kept at the principal office of the Corporation correct books of account of all its business and transactions;

(f) render to the President or the Board of Directors, whenever requested, an account of the financial condition of the Corporation and of his transactions as Treasurer;

(g) be empowered to require from the officers or agents of the Corporation reports or statements giving such information as he may desire with respect to any and all financial transactions of the Corporation; and

(h) in general, perform all duties and have all powers incident to the office of Treasurer and perform such other duties and have such other powers as from time to time may be assigned to him by these Bylaws or by the Board of Directors or the President.

Section 10. *Assistant Secretaries and Assistant Treasurers.* The Assistant Secretaries and Assistant Treasurers shall have such duties as from time to time may be assigned to them by the Board of Directors or the President.

Section 11. *Salaries.* The salaries of the officers of the Corporation shall be fixed from time to time by the Board of Directors, except that the Board of Directors may delegate to any person the power to fix the salaries or other compensation of any officers or agents appointed in accordance with the provisions of Section 3 of this Article VI. No officer shall be prevented from receiving such salary by reason of the fact that he is also a director of the Corporation.

Section 12. *Surety Bond.* The Board of Directors may secure the fidelity of any or all of the officers of the Corporation by bond or otherwise.

ARTICLE VII

Execution of Instruments

Section 1. *Execution of Instruments Generally.* All documents, instruments or writings of any nature shall be signed, executed, verified, acknowledged and delivered by such officer or officers or such agent or agents of the Corporation and in such manner as the Board of Directors from time to time may determine.

Section 2. *Checks, Drafts, Etc.* All notes, drafts, acceptances, checks, endorsements, and all evidence of indebtedness of the Corporation whatsoever, shall be signed by such officer or officers or such agent or agents of the Corporation and in such manner as the Board of Directors from time to time may determine. Endorsements for deposit to the credit of the Corporation in any of its duly authorized depositaries shall be made in such manner as the Board of Directors from time to time may determine.

Section 3. *Proxies.* Proxies to vote with respect to shares of stock of other corporations owned by or standing in the name of the Corporation may be executed and delivered from time to time on behalf of the Corporation by the President or a Vice President and the Secretary or an Assistant Secretary of the Corporation or by any other person or persons duly authorized by the Board of Directors.

ARTICLE VIII

Capital Stock

Section 1. *Certificates of Stock.* Every holder of stock in the Corporation shall be entitled to have a certificate, signed in the name of the Corporation by the Chairman or Vice Chairman of the Board of Directors, the President or a Vice President and by the Treasurer or an Assistant Treasurer, or the Secretary or an Assistant Secretary of the Corporation, certifying the number of shares owned by him in the Corporation; provided, however, that where such certificate is signed by a transfer agent or an assistant transfer agent or by a transfer clerk acting on behalf of the Corporation and a registrar, the signature of any such Chairman or Vice Chairman of the Board of Directors, President, Vice President, Treasurer, Assistant Treasurer, Secretary or Assistant Secretary may be facsimile. In case any officer or officers who shall have signed, or whose facsimile signature or signatures shall have been used on, any such certificate or certificates shall cease to be such officer or officers of the Corporation, whether because of death, resignation or otherwise, before such certificate or certificates shall have been delivered by the Corporation, such certificate or certificates may nevertheless be adopted by the Corporation and be issued and delivered as though the person or persons who signed such certificate or certificates, or whose facsimile signature or signatures shall have been used thereon, had not ceased to be such officer or officers of the Corporation, and any such delivery shall be regarded as an adoption by the Corporation of such certificate or certificates.

Certificates of stock shall be in such form as shall, in conformity to law, be prescribed from time to time by the Board of Directors.

Section 2. *Transfer of Stock.* Shares of stock of the Corporation shall only be transferred on the books of the Corporation by the holder of record thereof or by his attorney duly authorized in writing, upon surrender to the Corporation of the certificates for such shares endorsed by the appropriate person or persons, with such evidence of the authenticity of such endorsement, transfer, authorization and other matters as the Corporation may reasonably require, and accompanied by all necessary stock transfer tax stamps. In that event it shall be the duty of the Corporation to issue a new certificate to the person entitled thereto, cancel the old certificate, and record the transaction on its books.

Section 3. *Rights of Corporation with Respect to Registered Owners.* Prior to the surrender to the Corporation of the certificates for shares of stock with a request to record the transfer of such shares, the Corporation may treat the registered owner as the person entitled to receive dividends, to vote, to receive notifications, and otherwise to exercise all the rights and powers of an owner.

Section 4. *Closing Stock Transfer Book.* The Board of Directors may close the Stock Transfer Book of the Corporation for a period not exceeding fifty days preceding the date of any meeting of stockholders or the date for payment of any dividend or the date for the allotment of rights or the date when any change or conversion or exchange of capital stock shall go into effect or for a period of not exceeding fifty days in connection with obtaining the consent of stockholders for any purpose. However, in lieu of closing the Stock Transfer Book, the Board of Directors may fix in advance a date, not exceeding fifty days preceding the date of any meeting of stockholders, or the date for the payment of any dividend, or the date for the allotment of rights, or the date when any change or conversion or exchange of capital stock shall go into effect, or a date in connection with obtaining such consent, as a record date for the determination of the stockholders entitled to notice of, and to vote at, any such meeting and any adjournment thereof, or entitled to receive payment of any such dividend, or to any such allotment of rights, or to exercise the rights in respect of any such change, conversion or exchange of capital stock, or to give such consent, and in such case such stockholders, and only such stockholders as shall be stockholders of record on the date so fixed shall be entitled to such notice of, and to vote at, such meeting and any adjournment thereof, or to receive payment of such dividend, or to receive such allotment of rights, or to exercise such rights, or to give such consent, as the case may be, notwithstanding any transfer of any stock on the books of the Corporation after any such record date fixed as aforesaid.

Section 5. *Lost, Destroyed and Stolen Certificates.* Where the owner of a certificate for shares claims that such certificate has been lost, destroyed or wrongfully taken, the Corporation shall issue a new certificate in place of the original certificate if the owner (a) so requests before the Corporation has notice that the shares have been acquired by a bona fide purchaser; (b) files with the Corporation a sufficient indemnity bond; and (c) satisfies such other reasonable requirements, including evidence of such loss, destruction, or wrongful taking, as may be imposed by the Corporation.

ARTICLE IX

Dividends

Section 1. *Sources of Dividends.* The directors of the Corporation, subject to any restrictions contained in the statutes and Certificate of Incorporation, may declare and pay dividends upon the shares of the capital stock of the Corporation either (a) out of its net assets in excess of its capital, or (b) in case there shall be no such excess, out of its net profits for the fiscal year then current or the current and preceding fiscal year.

Section 2. *Reserves.* Before the payment of any dividend, the directors of the Corporation may set apart out of any of the funds of the Corporation available for dividends a reserve or reserves for any proper purpose, and the directors may abolish any such reserve in the manner in which it was created.

Section 3. *Reliance on Corporate Records.* A director shall be fully protected in relying in good faith upon the books of account of the Corporation or statements prepared by any of its officials as to the value and amount of the assets, liabilities and net profits of the Corporation, or any other facts pertinent to the existence and amount of surplus or other funds from which dividends might properly be declared and paid.

Section 4. *Manner of Payment.* Dividends may be paid in cash, in property, or in shares of the capital stock of the Corporation at par.

ARTICLE X

Seal

The corporate seal, subject to alteration by the Board of Directors, shall be in the form of a circle and shall bear the name of the Corporation and the year of its incorporation and shall indicate its formation under the laws of the State of Delaware. Such seal may be used by causing it or a facsimile thereof to be impressed or affixed or reproduced or otherwise.

ARTICLE XI

Fiscal Year

Except as from time to time otherwise provided by the Board of Directors, the fiscal year of the Corporation shall be the calendar year.

ARTICLE XII

Amendments

Section 1. *By the Stockholders.* Except as otherwise provided in the Certificate of Incorporation or in these Bylaws, these Bylaws may be amended or repealed, or new Bylaws may be made and adopted, by a majority vote of all the stock of the Corporation issued and outstanding and entitled to vote at any annual or special meeting of the stockholders, provided that notice of intention to amend shall have been contained in the notice of meeting.

Section 2. *By the Directors.* Except as otherwise provided in the Certificate of Incorporation or in these Bylaws, these Bylaws, including amendments adopted by the stockholders, may be amended or repealed by a majority vote of the whole Board of Directors at any regular or special meeting of the Board, provided that the stockholders may from time to time specify particular provisions of the Bylaws which shall not be amended by the Board of Directors.[21]

21. West's Modern Legal Forms § 2793.

FORM 7A
BOND AND SHARE CERTIFICATES

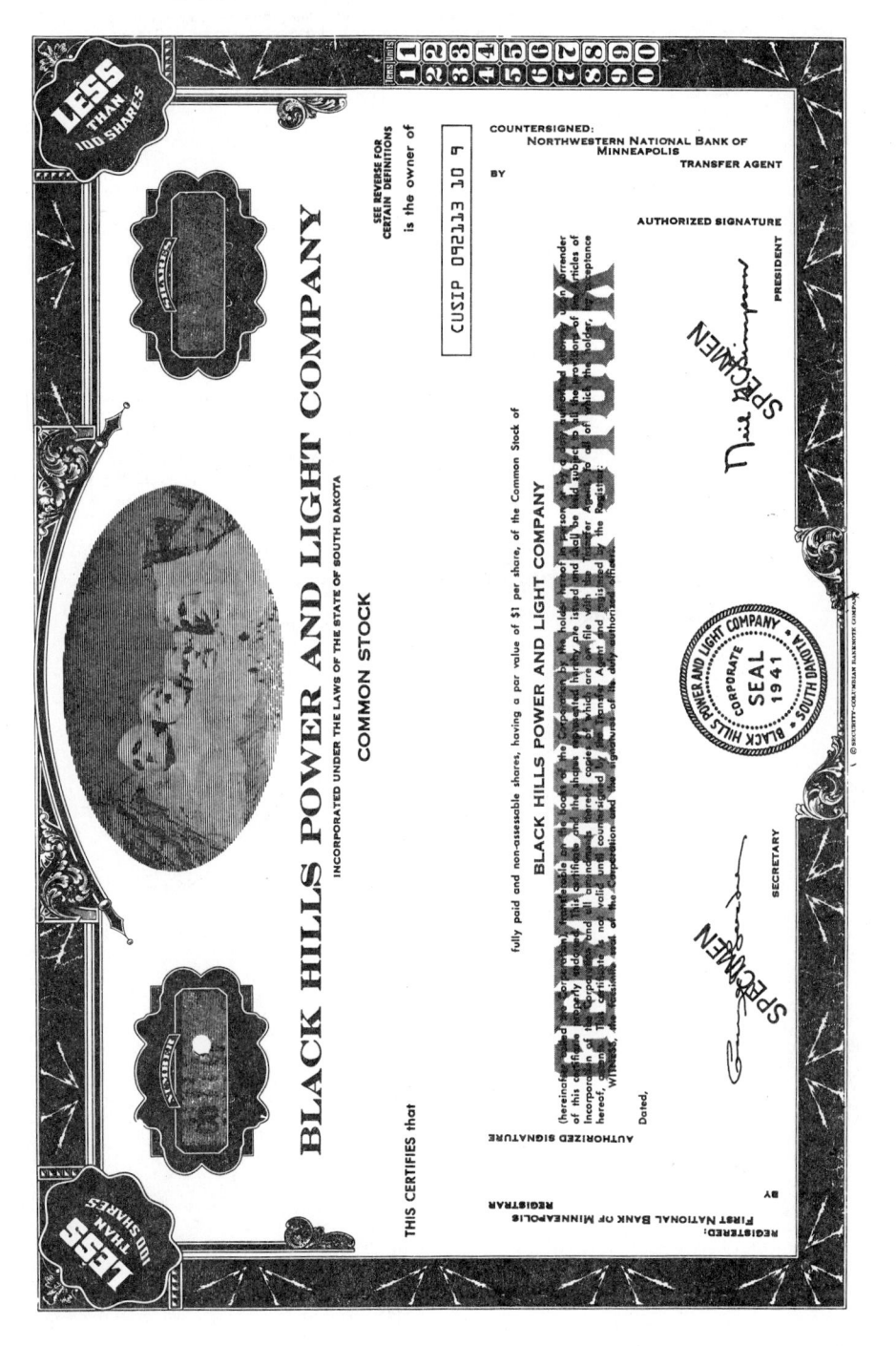

BLACK HILLS POWER AND LIGHT COMPANY

Notice: The Corporation will furnish to any shareholder upon request and without charge, a full statement of the designations, preferences, limitations, and relative rights of the shares of each class of stock authorized to be issued, and a like full statement relative to any preferred or special class of stock in series which the Corporation is or may be authorized to issue, or has issued, as to the variations in the relative rights and preferences between the shares of each such series so far as the same have been fixed and determined and the authority of the Board of Directors to fix and determine the relative rights and preferences of subsequent series.

The following abbreviations, when used in the inscription on the face of this certificate, shall be construed as though they were written out in full according to applicable laws or regulations:

TEN COM — as tenants in common
TEN ENT — as tenants by the entirety
JT TEN — as joint tenants with right of survivorship and not as tenants in common

UNIF GIFT MIN ACT — _____ Custodian _____
         (Cust)   (Minor)
    under Uniform Gifts to Minors
    Act _____
      (State)

Additional abbreviations may also be used though not in the above list.

For Value Received, _____ *hereby sell, assign and transfer unto*

PLEASE INSERT SOCIAL SECURITY OR OTHER IDENTIFYING NUMBER OF ASSIGNEE

_____
(PLEASE PRINT OR TYPEWRITE NAME AND ADDRESS OF ASSIGNEE)

_____

_____ *Shares of the Stock represented by the within certificate, and do hereby irrevocably constitute and appoint*

_____ *attorney, to transfer the same on the books of the within-named Corporation, with full power of substitution in the premises.*

Dated _____

Notice: The signature to this assignment must correspond with the name as written upon the face of the certificate in every particular, without alteration or enlargement or any change whatever.

SIGNATURE GUARANTEED BY:

_____

THIS SPACE MUST NOT BE COVERED IN ANY WAY

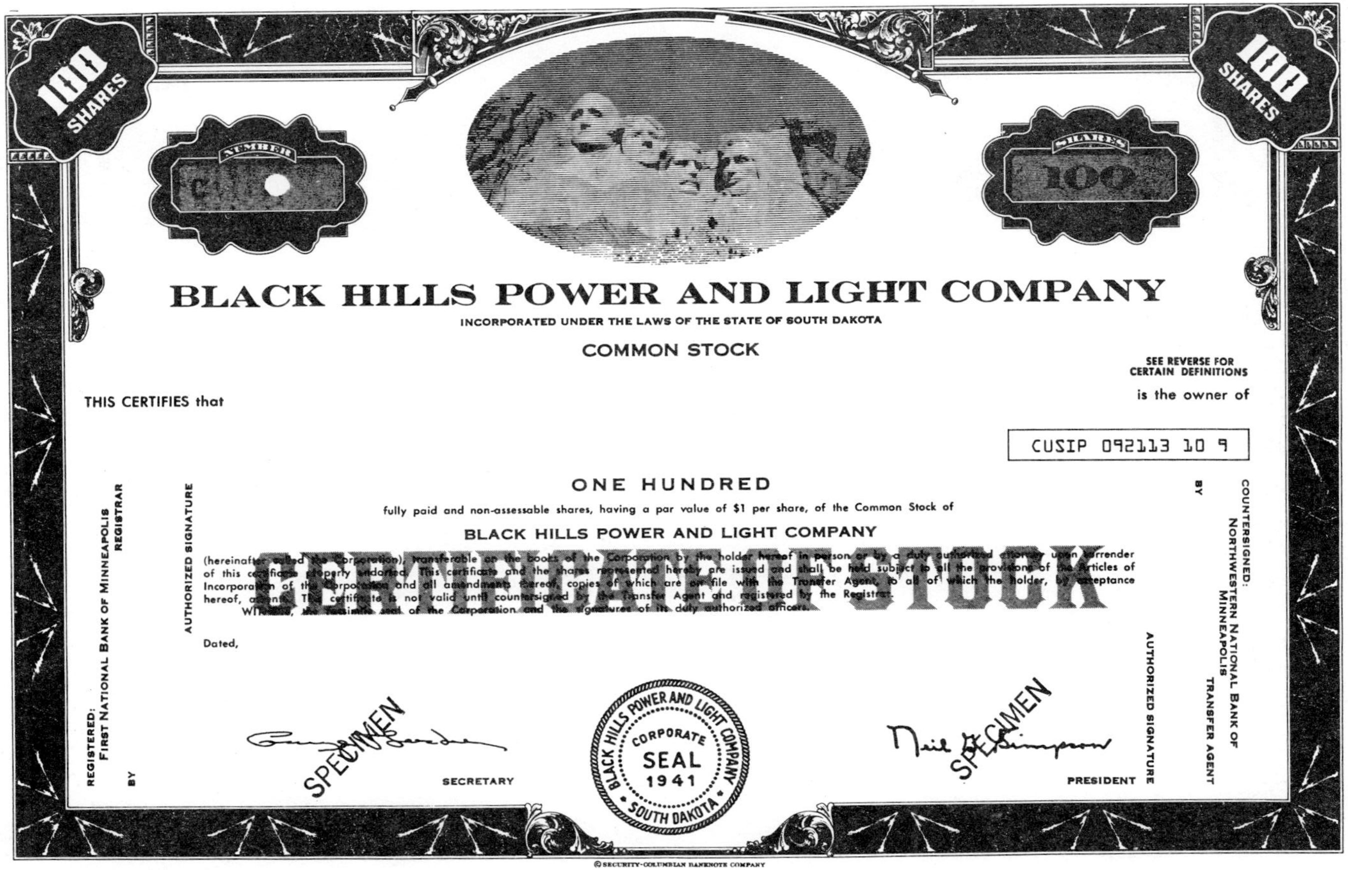

FORMS 581

100 SHARES

BLACK HILLS POWER AND LIGHT COMPANY
INCORPORATED UNDER THE LAWS OF THE STATE OF SOUTH DAKOTA

COMMON STOCK

SEE REVERSE FOR CERTAIN DEFINITIONS

CUSIP 092113 10 9

COUNTERSIGNED:
NORTHWESTERN NATIONAL BANK OF MINNEAPOLIS
TRANSFER AGENT

BY

AUTHORIZED SIGNATURE

THIS CERTIFIES that

is the owner of

ONE HUNDRED

fully paid and non-assessable shares, having a par value of $1 per share, of the Common Stock of

BLACK HILLS POWER AND LIGHT COMPANY

(hereinafter called the Corporation) transferable on the books of the Corporation by the holder hereof in person or by duly authorized attorney upon surrender of this certificate properly endorsed. This certificate and the shares represented hereby are issued and shall be held subject to all of the provisions of the Articles of Incorporation of the Corporation and all amendments thereto, copies of which are on file with the Transfer Agent, to all of which the holder, by acceptance hereof, consents. This certificate is not valid until countersigned and registered by the Transfer Agent and Registrar.

Dated,

SPECIMEN
SECRETARY

SPECIMEN
PRESIDENT

BLACK HILLS POWER AND LIGHT COMPANY
CORPORATE SEAL
1941
SOUTH DAKOTA

REGISTERED:
FIRST NATIONAL BANK OF MINNEAPOLIS
REGISTRAR

BY

AUTHORIZED SIGNATURE

BLACK HILLS POWER AND LIGHT COMPANY

Notice: The Corporation will furnish to any shareholder upon request and without charge, a full statement of the designations, preferences, limitations, and relative rights of the shares of each class of stock authorized to be issued, and a like full statement relative to any preferred or special class of stock in series which the Corporation is or may be authorized to issue, or has issued, as to the variations in the relative rights and preferences between the shares of each such series so far as the same have been fixed and determined and the authority of the Board of Directors to fix and determine the relative rights and preferences of subsequent series.

The following abbreviations, when used in the inscription on the face of this certificate, shall be construed as though they were written out in full according to applicable laws or regulations:

TEN COM — as tenants in common	UNIF GIFT MIN ACT — _____ Custodian _____
TEN ENT — as tenants by the entirety	(Cust) (Minor)
JT TEN — as joint tenants with right of survivorship and not as tenants in common	under Uniform Gifts to Minors Act _____ (State)

Additional abbreviations may also be used though not in the above list.

For Value Received, _____ hereby sell, assign and transfer unto

PLEASE INSERT SOCIAL SECURITY OR OTHER IDENTIFYING NUMBER OF ASSIGNEE

_____
(PLEASE PRINT OR TYPEWRITE NAME AND ADDRESS OF ASSIGNEE)

_____ Shares of the Stock represented by the within certificate, and do hereby irrevocably constitute and appoint

_____ attorney, to transfer the same on the books of the within-named Corporation, with full power of substitution in the premises.

Dated _____

Notice: The signature to this assignment must correspond with the name as written upon the face of the certificate in every particular, without alteration or enlargement or any change whatever.

SIGNATURE GUARANTEED BY:

THIS SPACE MUST NOT BE COVERED IN ANY WAY

FORMS 583

The Company will furnish to any shareholder, upon request to its principal office or to any of its transfer offices and without charge, a full statement of the designation, relative rights, preferences and limitations of its common and preferred shares, and of each series of its preferred shares so far as the same have been fixed and the authority of the board of directors to designate and fix the relative rights, preferences and limitations of other series of its preferred shares. **As specified in such statement, the affirmative vote or consent of two-thirds of the holders of preferred shares or a series of preferred shares is required in order to take certain actions affecting preferred shares.**

For Value received, _____ hereby sell, assign and transfer _____ Shares represented by the within Certificate unto

PLEASE PRINT OR TYPE TAXPAYER-IDENTIFYING NUMBER AND NAME AND ADDRESS OF ASSIGNEE	FOR AT&T USE ONLY:
	RIN:
SHARES	CTF. NOTE: / YR. H ☐
	CLASS ACCT: / E ☐

PLEASE PRINT OR TYPE TAXPAYER-IDENTIFYING NUMBER AND NAME AND ADDRESS OF ASSIGNEE	
	RIN:
SHARES	CTF. NOTE: / YR. H ☐
	CLASS ACCT: / E ☐

PLEASE PRINT OR TYPE TAXPAYER-IDENTIFYING NUMBER AND NAME AND ADDRESS OF ASSIGNEE	
	RIN:
SHARES	CTF. NOTE: / YR. H ☐
	CLASS ACCT: / E ☐

and do hereby irrevocably constitute and appoint _____ Attorney to transfer the said shares on the records of the within named Company with full power of substitution in the premises.

Dated, _____

The following abbreviations shall be construed as though the words set forth below opposite each abbreviation were written out in full where such abbreviation appears:

TEN COM — as tenants in common
TEN ENT — as tenants by the entireties
JT TEN — as joint tenants with right of survivor-ship and not as tenants in common

(Name) CUST (Name) UNIF - (Name) under the GIFT MIN ACT (State) (State) Uniform Gifts to Minors Act / (Name) as Custodian for (Name) under the (State) Uniform Gifts to Minors Act

Additional abbreviations may also be used though not in the above list.

IMPORTANT { BEFORE SIGNING, READ AND COMPLY CAREFULLY WITH REQUIREMENTS PRINTED BELOW.

THE SIGNATURE(S) TO THIS ASSIGNMENT MUST CORRESPOND WITH THE NAME(S) AS WRITTEN UPON THE FACE OF THE CERTIFICATE IN EVERY PARTICULAR WITHOUT ALTERATION OR ENLARGEMENT OR ANY CHANGE WHATEVER. THE SIGNATURE(S) SHOULD BE GUARANTEED BY A COMMERCIAL BANK OR TRUST COMPANY, OR BY A NEW YORK, BOSTON, MIDWEST, PBW OR PACIFIC STOCK EXCHANGE MEMBER FIRM, WHOSE SIGNATURE IS KNOWN TO THE TRANSFER OFFICE.

FORMS 585

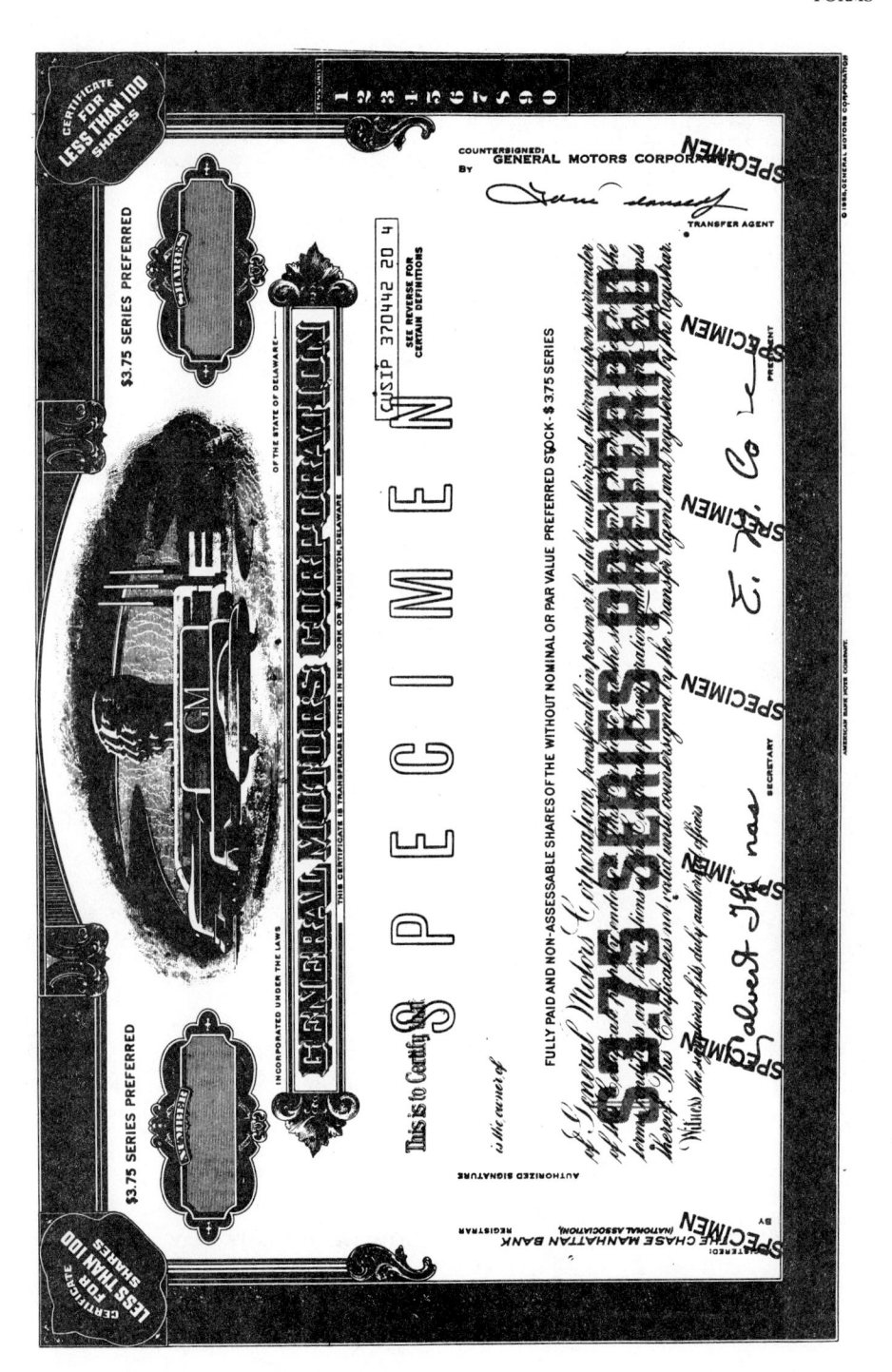

GENERAL MOTORS CORPORATION

The following abbreviations, when used in the inscription on the face of this certificate, shall be construed as though they were written out in full according to applicable laws or regulations:

TEN COM	— as tenants in common	UNIF GIFT MIN ACT —	
TEN ENT	— as tenants by the entireties	_____ Custodian _____	
JT TEN	— as joint tenants with right of survivorship and not as tenants in common	(Cust) (Minor) under Uniform Gifts to Minors Act_____ (State)	

Additional abbreviations may also be used though not in the above list.

THE CORPORATION WILL FURNISH WITHOUT CHARGE TO EACH STOCKHOLDER WHO SO REQUESTS A STATEMENT OF THE RIGHTS, PRIVILEGES, RESTRICTIONS, VOTING POWERS, LIMITATIONS AND QUALIFICATIONS OF THE SEVERAL CLASSES OF STOCK OF THE CORPORATION. REQUESTS MAY BE DIRECTED TO THE TRANSFER AGENT, GENERAL MOTORS CORPORATION, 767 FIFTH AVENUE, NEW YORK, NEW YORK 10022.

FOR VALUE RECEIVED, THE UNDERSIGNED HEREBY SELLS, ASSIGNS AND TRANSFERS THE SHARES OF THE CAPITAL STOCK REPRESENTED BY THE WITHIN CERTIFICATE AS FOLLOWS:

PLEASE INSERT SOCIAL SECURITY OR OTHER IDENTIFYING NUMBER OF ASSIGNEE

_____UNTO_____
SHARES   FULL NAME AND ADDRESS (INCLUDING ZIP CODE) OF ASSIGNEE SHOULD BE TYPEWRITTEN OR PRINTED LEGIBLY

AND HEREBY IRREVOCABLY CONSTITUTES AND APPOINTS
_____ATTORNEY
TO TRANSFER THE SAID STOCK ON THE BOOKS OF THE WITHIN-NAMED CORPORATION WITH FULL POWER OF SUBSTITUTION IN THE PREMISES.

DATED_____

SIGN HERE_____
SIGNATURE MUST CORRESPOND WITH NAME ON FACE OF CERTIFICATE

SIGNATURE GUARANTEED

NOTICE: THE SIGNATURE TO THIS ASSIGNMENT MUST CORRESPOND WITH THE NAME AS WRITTEN UPON THE FACE OF THE CERTIFICATE IN EVERY PARTICULAR WITHOUT ENLARGEMENT OR ANY CHANGE WHATEVER.

THIS SPACE MUST NOT BE COVERED IN ANY WAY

AMERICAN TELEPHONE AND TELEGRAPH COMPANY

THIRTY YEAR 8¾% DEBENTURE, DUE MAY 15, 2000

8¾%
DUE MAY 15, 2000

SPECIMEN

Number

SEE REVERSE FOR ABBREVIATIONS

THIS CERTIFICATE IS TRANSFERABLE AT THE OFFICE OF THE COMPANY IN NEW YORK CITY

CUSIP 030177 AX 7

American Telephone and Telegraph Company, a New York corporation (herein referred to as the "Company") for value received, hereby promises to pay to

A registered assigns, at the office or agency of the Company in the Borough of Manhattan, The City of New York, State of New York, the principal sum of

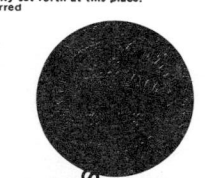

on May 15, 2000, in such coin or currency of the United States of America at the time of payment shall be legal tender for the payment of public and private debts, and to pay interest, semi-annually on May 15 and November 15, on said principal sum at the rate per annum specified in the title of this Debenture, at said office or agency, from the fifteenth day of May or November, as the case may be, to which interest on Debentures has been paid preceding the date hereof, unless the date hereof is May 15 or a November 15 to which interest has been paid, in which case from the date hereof, or unless the date hereof is prior to the first payment of interest, in which case from May 18, 1970) until payment of said principal sum has been made or duly provided for. Notwithstanding the foregoing, unless this Debenture shall be authenticated at a time when there is an existing default in the payment of interest on the Debentures, if the date hereof is after April 15 and before the next following May 15 or is after October 15 and before the next following November 15, this Debenture shall bear interest from such May 15 or November 15, provided, however, that if the Company shall default in the payment of interest due on such May 15 or November 15, then this Debenture shall bear interest from the next preceding November 15 or May 15, as the case may be. The interest so payable on any May 15 or November 15 will, subject to certain exceptions provided in the Indenture referred to on the reverse hereof, be paid to the person in whose name this Debenture shall be registered at the close of business on the April 15 or the October 15 prior to such November 15, whether or not such April 15 or October 15 shall be a business day.

Reference is hereby made to the further provisions of this Debenture set forth on the reverse hereof, and such further provisions shall for all purposes have the same effect as though fully set forth at this place.

This Debenture shall not be valid or become obligatory for any purpose until the certificate of authentication hereon shall have been executed by the Trustee under the Indenture referred to on the reverse hereof.

In Witness Whereof, American Telephone and Telegraph Company has caused this Debenture to be signed by its Chairman of the Board by its President and by its Treasurer, each by a facsimile of his signature, and has caused a facsimile of its corporate seal to be affixed hereunto or imprinted hereon.

DATED

American Telephone and Telegraph Company

By
Treasurer   Chairman of the Board

TRUSTEE'S CERTIFICATE OF AUTHENTICATION
This is one of the Debentures described in the within-mentioned Indenture.

Chemical Bank, As Trustee

By
Authorized Officer

AMERICAN TELEPHONE AND TELEGRAPH COMPANY

This Debenture is one of a duly authorized issue of Debentures of the Company, designated as set forth on the face hereof (herein referred to as the "Debentures"), limited to the aggregate principal amount of $1,569,327,000, all issued or to be issued under and pursuant to an Indenture dated May 18, 1970 (herein referred to as the "Indenture"), duly executed and delivered by the Company to Chemical Bank, Trustee (herein referred to as the "Trustee"), which Indenture and all Indentures supplemental thereto are hereby incorporated by reference in and made a part of this instrument and are hereby referred to for a description of the rights, limitation of rights, obligations, duties and immunities thereunder of the Trustee, the Company and the holders (the words "holders" or "holder" meaning the registered holders or registered holder) of the Debentures.

In case an Event of Default, as defined in the Indenture, shall have occurred and be continuing, the principal hereof may be declared, and upon such declaration shall become, due and payable, in the manner, with the effect and subject to the conditions provided in the Indenture.

The Indenture contains provisions permitting the Company and the Trustee, with the consent of the holders of not less than 66-2/3% in aggregate principal amount of the Debentures at the time outstanding, evidenced as in the Indenture provided, to execute supplemental Indentures adding any provisions to or changing in any manner or eliminating any of the provisions of the Indenture or of any supplemental indenture or modifying in any manner the rights of the holders of the Debentures; provided, however, that no such supplemental indenture shall (i) extend the fixed maturity of any Debentures, or reduce the principal amount thereof, or reduce the rate or extend the time of payment of interest thereon, or reduce any premium payable upon the redemption thereof, without the consent of the holder of each Debenture so affected, or (ii) reduce the aforesaid percentage of Debentures, the consent of the holders of which is required for any such supplemental indenture, without the consent of the holders of all Debentures then outstanding. It is also provided in the Indenture that, under certain circumstances, the holders of a majority in aggregate principal amount of the Debentures at the time outstanding may on behalf of the holders of all of the Debentures waive any past default under the Indenture and its consequences, except a default in the payment of the principal of (or premium, if any) or interest on any of the Debentures. Any such consent or waiver by the holder of this Debenture (unless revoked as provided in the Indenture) shall be conclusive and binding upon such holder and upon all future holders and owners of this Debenture and of any Debenture issued in exchange or substitution therefor, irrespective of whether or not any notation of such consent or waiver is made upon this Debenture or such other Debenture.

No reference herein to the Indenture and no provision of this Debenture or of the Indenture shall alter or impair the obligation of the Company, which is absolute and unconditional, to pay the principal of (and premium, if any) and interest on this Debenture at the place, at the respective times, at the rate and in the coin or currency herein prescribed.

The Debentures are issuable as registered Debentures without coupons in denominations of $100 and any multiple of $100. At the office or agency of the Company referred to on the face hereof and in the manner and subject to the limitations provided in the Indenture, Debentures may be exchanged without a service charge for a like aggregate principal amount of Debentures of other authorized denominations.

The Debentures may be redeemed, at the option of the Company, as a whole or from time to time in part (selected by lot or otherwise in such manner as the Trustee may deem appropriate and fair), on or after May 15, 1975 and prior to maturity, upon the notice referred to below, at the following redemption prices (expressed in percentages of the principal amount): during the 12 months' periods ending May 14:

1976......	107.00%	1983......	104.55%	1990......	102.10%
1977......	106.65	1984......	104.20	1991......	101.75
1978......	106.30	1985......	103.85	1992......	101.40
1979......	105.95	1986......	103.50	1993......	101.05
1980......	105.60	1987......	103.15	1994......	100.70
1981......	105.25	1988......	102.80	1995......	100.35
1982......	104.90	1989......	102.45		

and thereafter, 100%, together in each case with accrued interest to the date fixed for redemption. As provided in the Indenture, notice of redemption to the holders of Debentures to be redeemed as a whole or in part shall be given by mailing a notice of such redemption not less than thirty nor more than ninety days prior to the date fixed for redemption to their last addresses as they shall appear upon the register kept for that purpose.

Upon due presentment for registration of transfer of this Debenture at the above-mentioned office or agency of the Company, a new Debenture or Debentures, of authorized denominations, for a like aggregate principal amount, will be issued to the transferee as provided in the Indenture. No service charge shall be made for any such transfer, but the Company may require payment of a sum sufficient to cover any tax or other governmental charge that may be imposed in relation thereto.

The Company, the Trustee, any paying agent and any Debenture registrar may deem and treat the holder hereof as the absolute owner hereof (whether or not this Debenture shall be overdue and notwithstanding any notation of ownership or other writing hereon) for the purpose of receiving payment of or on account of the principal hereof (and premium, if any) and, subject to the provisions on the face hereof, interest hereon, and for all other purposes, and neither the Company nor the Trustee nor any paying agent nor any Debenture registrar shall be affected by any notice to the contrary.

No recourse shall be had for the payment of the principal of (or premium, if any) or the interest on this Debenture, or for any claim based hereon, or otherwise in respect hereof, or based on or in respect of the Indenture or any indenture supplemental thereto, against any incorporator, shareholder, officer or director, as such, past, present or future, of the Company or of any successor corporation, either directly or through the Company or any successor corporation, whether by virtue of any constitution, statute or rule of law or by the enforcement of any assessment or penalty or otherwise, all such liability being, by the acceptance hereof and as part of the consideration for the issue hereof, expressly waived and released.

The following abbreviations shall be construed as though the words set forth below opposite each abbreviation were written out in full where such abbreviation appears:

TEN COM — as tenants in common
TEN ENT — as tenants by the entireties
JT TEN — as joint tenants with right of survivorship and not as tenants in common

(Name) CUST (Name) UNIF GIFT MIN ACT (State) — (Name) as Custodian for (Name) under the (State) Uniform Gifts to Minors Act

Additional abbreviations may also be used though not in the above list.

FOR VALUE RECEIVED, the undersigned sells, assigns and transfers unto

PLEASE PRINT OR TYPE TAXPAYER-IDENTIFYING NUMBER | NAME AND ADDRESS INCLUDING ZIP CODE OF ASSIGNEE

RESERVED FOR A.T.&T. CO. USE

RIN

TRANS CODE	DEB NOTE	TOWN CODE	CLASS NON-DOM.
61			
NA 1			
CC 2			4

the within Debenture of AMERICAN TELEPHONE AND TELEGRAPH COMPANY and hereby irrevocably constitutes and appoints

_____ Attorney

to transfer said Debenture on the books of said Company with full power of substitution in the premises.

Dated _____

THE SIGNATURE(S) TO THIS ASSIGNMENT MUST CORRESPOND WITH THE NAME(S) AS WRITTEN UPON THE FACE OF THE DEBENTURE IN EVERY PARTICULAR WITHOUT ALTERATION OR ENLARGEMENT OR ANY CHANGE WHATEVER. THE SIGNATURE(S) SHOULD BE GUARANTEED BY A COMMERCIAL BANK OR TRUST COMPANY, OR BY A NEW YORK, BOSTON, MIDWEST, PHILADELPHIA-BALTIMORE-WASHINGTON OR PACIFIC COAST STOCK EXCHANGE MEMBER OR FIRM WHOSE SIGNATURE IS KNOWN TO THE TRANSFER OFFICE.

GENERAL MOTORS CORPORATION

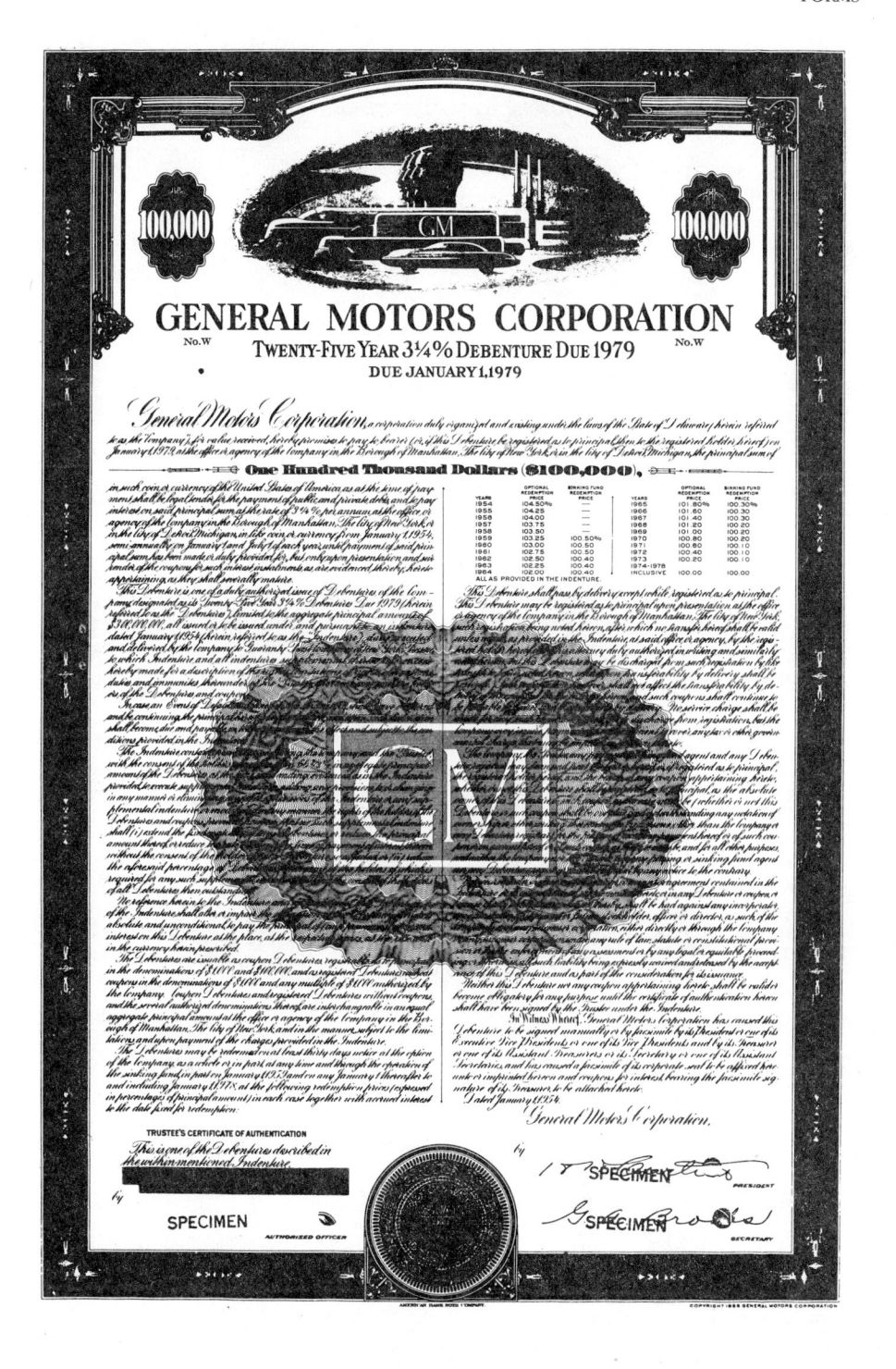

TWENTY-FIVE YEAR 3¼% DEBENTURE DUE 1979
DUE JANUARY 1, 1979

No. W   No. W

100,000   **100,000**

General Motors Corporation, a corporation duly organized and existing under the laws of the State of Delaware (herein referred to as the "Company"), for value received, hereby promises to pay to bearer (or, if this Debenture be registered, to the registered holder hereof) on January 1, 1979 at the office or agency of the Company in the Borough of Manhattan, The City of New York, or in the City of Detroit, Michigan, as like coin or currency, from January 1, 1954, the principal sum of

One Hundred Thousand Dollars ($100,000),

YEARS	OPTIONAL REDEMPTION PRICE	SINKING FUND REDEMPTION PRICE	YEARS	OPTIONAL REDEMPTION PRICE	SINKING FUND REDEMPTION PRICE
1954	104.50%	—	1965	101.80%	100.30%
1955	104.25	—	1966	101.60	100.30
1956	104.00	—	1967	101.40	100.30
1957	103.75	—	1968	101.20	100.20
1958	103.50	—	1969	101.00	100.20
1959	103.25	100.50%	1970	100.80	100.20
1960	103.00	100.50	1971	100.60	100.10
1961	102.75	100.50	1972	100.40	100.10
1962	102.50	100.40	1973	100.20	100.10
1963	102.25	100.40	1974–1978		
1964	102.00	100.40	INCLUSIVE	100.00	100.00

ALL AS PROVIDED IN THE INDENTURE.

Dated January 1, 1954.

General Motors Corporation.

by   SPECIMEN   PRESIDENT

SPECIMEN   SECRETARY

TRUSTEE'S CERTIFICATE OF AUTHENTICATION

This is one of the Debentures described in the within-mentioned Indenture.

by   SPECIMEN   AUTHORIZED OFFICER

APPENDIX G

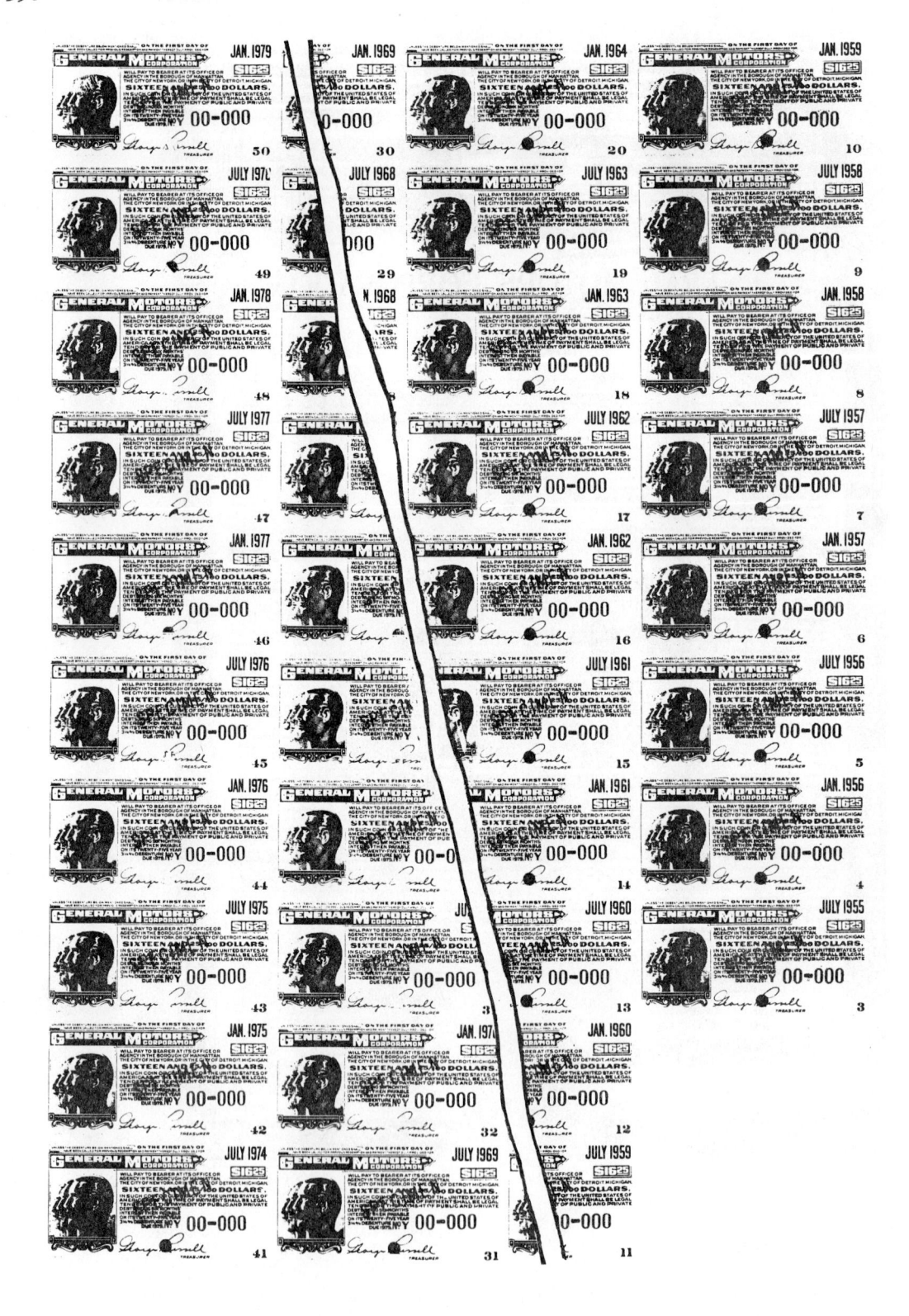

FORMS 591

GENERAL MOTORS CORPORATION

NO. W

$1,000,000

TWENTY-FIVE YEAR 3½% GOLD DEBENTURE DUE 1979

DUE JANUARY 1, 1979

INTEREST PAYABLE JANUARY 1 AND JULY 1

PRINCIPAL AND INTEREST PAYABLE IN THE BOROUGH OF MANHATTAN, THE CITY OF NEW YORK, OR IN THE CITY OF DETROIT, MICHIGAN.

UNITED STATES INTERNAL REVENUE STAMPS REQUIRED BY LAW HAVE BEEN AFFIXED TO THE WITHIN-MENTIONED DEBENTURE AND DULY CANCELLED.

NOTICE: NO WRITING BELOW EXCEPT BY DEBENTURE REGISTRAR.

DATE OF REGISTRATION AS TO PRINCIPAL	NAME OF REGISTERED OWNER	SIGNATURE OF REGISTRAR

592 APPENDIX G

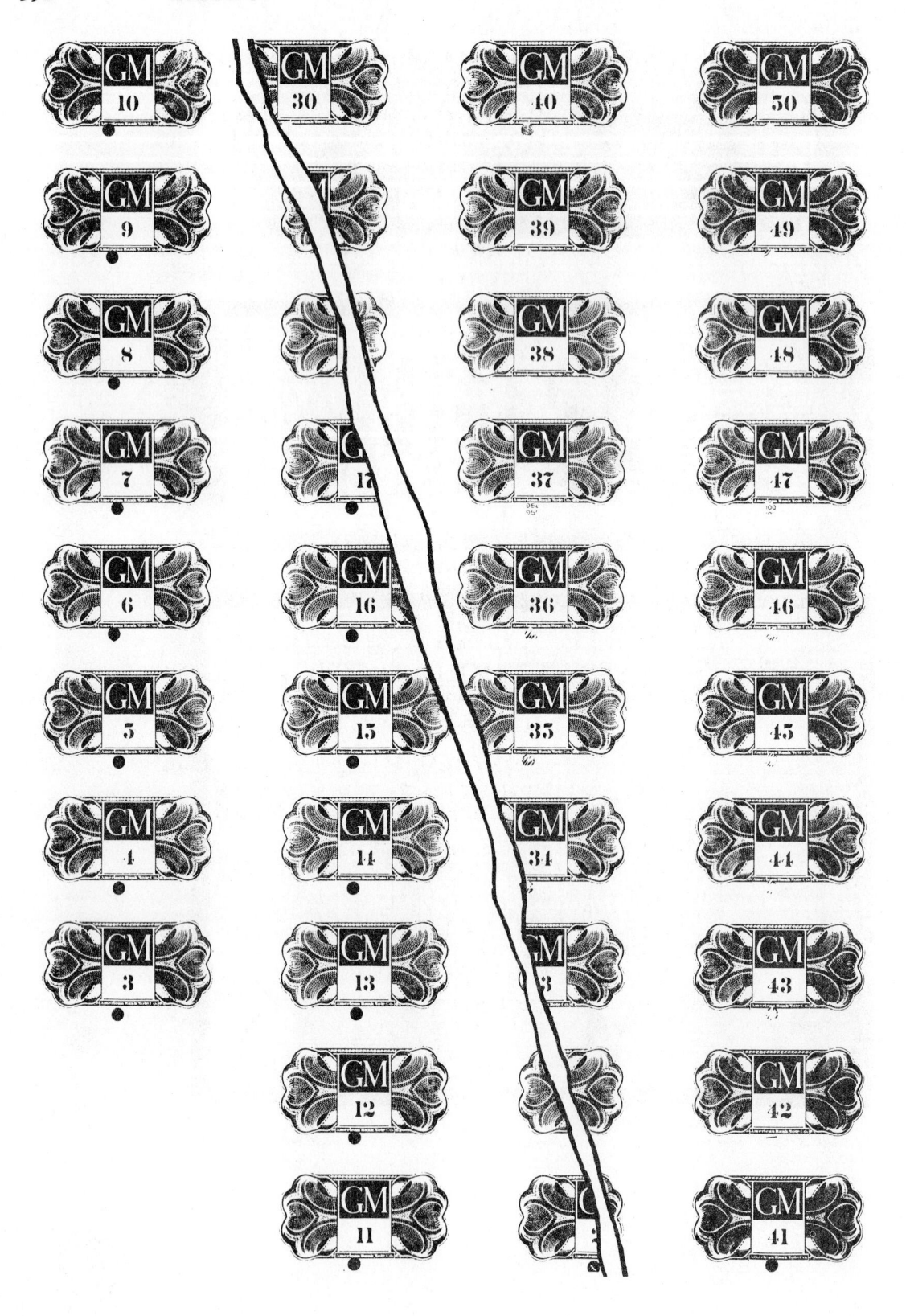

FORMS 593

FORM 7B

STATEMENT OF RESOLUTION ESTABLISHING SERIES FOR SHARES
(PENNSYLVANIA)

APPLICANT'S ACC'T NO

DSCB:BCL—602 (Rev. 8-72)

Filing Fee: $40
AB-2
Statement Affecting Class
or Series of Shares—
Domestic Business Corporation

(Line for numbering)

COMMONWEALTH OF PENNSYLVANIA
DEPARTMENT OF STATE
CORPORATION BUREAU

Filed this _____ day of _____
_____, 19___.
Commonwealth of Pennsylvania
Department of State

Secretary of the Commonwealth

(Box for Certification)

In compliance with the requirements of section 602 of the Business Corporation Law, act of May 5, 1933 (P. L. 364) (15 P. S. §1602), the undersigned corporation, desiring to state the voting rights, designations, preferences, qualifications, privileges, limitations, options, conversion rights, and other special rights, if any, of a class or series of a class of its shares, hereby certifies that:

1. The name of the corporation is:

_____

2. (Check and complete one of the following):

    [ ] The resolution establishing and designating the class or series of shares and fixing and determining the relative rights and preferences thereof, set forth in full, is as follows:

    [ ] The resolution establishing and designating the class or series of shares and fixing and determining the relative rights and preferences thereof is set forth in full in Exhibit A attached hereto and made a part hereof.

3. The aggregate number of shares of such class or series established and designated by (a) such resolution, (b) all prior statements, if any, filed under the Business Corporation Law with respect thereto, and (c) any other provision of the Articles is _____ shares.

4. (Check and complete one of the following):

    [ ] The resolution was adopted by the Board of Directors of the corporation at a duly called meeting held on the _____ _____ day of _____ _____, 19____.

DSCB BCL—602 (Rev. 8-72)-2

☐ The resolution was adopted by a consent or consents in writing dated the _____ day of _____ 19 ___, signed by all of the Directors of the corporation and filed with the Secretary of the corporation.

IN TESTIMONY WHEREOF, the undersigned corporation has caused this statement to be signed by a duly authorized officer and its corporate seal, duly attested by another such officer, to be hereunto affixed this _____ day of _____, 19 ___.

_____
(NAME OF CORPORATION)

By: _____
(SIGNATURE)

_____
(TITLE PRESIDENT, VICE PRESIDENT, ETC.)

Attest:

_____
(SIGNATURE)

_____
(TITLE SECRETARY, ASSISTANT SECRETARY, ETC.)

(CORPORATE SEAL)

FORM 7C

CANCELLATION OF REDEEMABLE SHARES *

Filing fee: $_____.

STATEMENT OF CANCELLATION OF REDEEMABLE SHARES OF

_____

To the Secretary of State
of the State of _____:

Pursuant to the provisions of Section _____ of the _____ Business Corporation Act, the undersigned corporation submits the following statement of cancellation by redemption or purchase of redeemable shares of the corporation:

FIRST: The name of the corporation is _____

SECOND: The number of redeemable shares of the corporation cancelled through redemption or purchase is _____, itemized as follows:

Class	Series	Number of Shares

THIRD: The aggregate number of issued shares of the corporation after giving effect to such cancellation is _____, itemized as follows:

Class	Series	Number of Shares

FOURTH: The amount of the stated capital of the corporation after giving effect to such cancellation is $_____.

FIFTH: the number of shares which the corporation has authority to issue after giving effect to such cancellation is _____, itemized as follows:

Class	Series	Number of Shares

Dated _____, 19___.

_____ (Note 1)

By _____
  Its _____ President
and _____   (Note 2)
  Its _____ Secretary

(Add Verification Form A)

Notes: 1. Exact corporate name of corporation making the statement.
2. Signatures and titles of officers signing for the corporation.

---

* The Model Act has repealed provisions relating to the cancellation of redeemable shares. (See Section 67 of the M.B.C.A.) Nevertheless, this form is used by most states whose statutes are based upon the Model Act.

FORM 7D

SECURITY AGREEMENT UNDER THE UNIFORM COMMERCIAL CODE

Form UCC 1205 —Bradford Publishing Co., 1824-46 Stout Street, Denver, Colorado—5-73

STATE OF COLORADO

UNIFORM COMMERCIAL CODE — SECURITY AGREEMENT

Debtor:

Name: _____

Address: _____
Residence: _____
   No.   Street   City   State

Business: _____
   No.   Street   City   State

Secured Party:

Name: _____

Address: _____
   No.   Street   City   State

Debtor, for consideration, hereby grants to Secured Party a security interest in the following property and any and all additions, accessions and substitutions thereto or therefor (hereinafter called the "COLLATERAL"):

To secure payment of the indebtedness evidenced by _____ certain promissory note _____ of even date herewith, payable to the Secured Party, or order, as follows:

DEBTOR EXPRESSLY WARRANTS AND COVENANTS:

1. That except for the security interest granted hereby Debtor is, or to the extent that this agreement states that the Collateral is to be acquired after the date hereof, will be, the owner of the Collateral free from any adverse lien, security interest or encumbrances; and that Debtor will defend the Collateral against all claims and demands of all persons at anytime claiming the same or any interest therein.

2. The Collateral is used or bought primarily for:
   ☐ Personal, family or household purposes;
   ☐ Use in farming operations;
   ☐ Use in business.

3. That Debtor's residence is as stated above, and the Collateral will be kept at

_____
No. and Street   City   County   State

4. If any of the Collateral is crops, oil, gas, or minerals to be extracted or timber to be cut, or goods which are or are to become fixtures, said Collateral concerns the following described real estate situate in the _____ County of _____ and State of Colorado, to wit:

5. Not to sell, transfer or dispose of the Collateral, and promptly to notify Secured Party of any change in the location of the Collateral within the State of Colorado and not to remove the same from the State of Colorado without the prior written consent of the Secured Party.

6. To pay all taxes and assessments of every nature which may be levied or assessed against the Collateral.

7. Not to permit or allow any adverse lien, security interest or encumbrance whatsoever upon the Collateral and not to permit the same to be attached or replevined.

8. That the Collateral is in good condition, and that he will, at his own expense, keep the same in good condition and from time to time, forthwith, replace and repair all such parts of the Collateral as may be broken, worn out, or damaged without allowing any lien to be created upon the Collateral on account of such replacement or repairs, and that the Secured Party may examine and inspect the Collateral at any time, wherever located.

9. That he will not use the Collateral in violation of any applicable statutes, regulations or ordinances.

UNTIL DEFAULT Debtor may have possession of the Collateral and use it in any lawful manner, and upon default Secured Party shall have the immediate right to the possession of the Collateral.

DEBTOR SHALL BE IN DEFAULT under this agreement upon the happening of any of the following events or conditions:

(a) default in the payment or performancec of any obligation, covenant or liability contained or referred to herein or in any note evidencing the same;

(b) the making or furnishing of any warranty, representation or statement to Secured Party by or on behalf of Debtor which proves to have been false in any material respect when made or furnished;

(c) loss, theft, damage, destruction, sale or encumbrance to or of any of the Collateral, or the making of any levy seizure or attachment thereof or thereon;

(d) death, dissolution, termination of existence, insolvency, business failure, appointment of a receiver of any part of the property of, assignment for the benefit of creditors by, or the commencement of any proceeding under any bankruptcy or insolvency laws of, by or against Debtor or any guarantor or surety for Debtor.

UPON SUCH DEFAULT and at any time thereafter, or if it deems itself insecure, Secured Party may declare all Obligations secured hereby immediately due and payable and shall have the remedies of a secured party under Article 9 of the Colorado Uniform Commercial Code. Secured Party may require Debtor to assemble the Collateral and deliver or make it available to Secured Party at a place to be designated by Secured Party which is reasonably convenient to both parties. Expenses of retaking, holding, preparing for sale, selling or the like shall include Secured Party's reasonable attorney's fees and legal expenses.

No waiver by Secured Party of any default shall operate as a waiver of any other default or of the same default on a future occasion. The taking of this security agreement shall not waive or impair any other security said Secured Party may have or hereafter acquire for the payment of the above indebtedness, nor shall the taking of any such additional security waive or impair this security agreement; but said Secured Party may resort to any security it may have in the order it may deem proper, and notwithstanding any collateral security, Secured Party shall retain its rights of set-off against Debtor.

All rights of Secured Party hereunder shall inure to the benefit of its successors and assigns; and all promises and duties of Debtor shall bind his heirs, executors or administrators or his or its successors or assigns. If there be more than one Debtor, their liabilities hereunder shall be joint and several.

Dated this_____day of_____, 19_____.

Debtor: Secured Party:*

* If this Security Agreement is intended to serve as a financing statement secured party as well as the debtor must sign.

FORM 7E

FINANCING STATEMENT UNDER THE UNIFORM COMMERCIAL CODE

Bradford Publishing Co., 1824-46 Stout Street, Denver, Colorado

STATE OF COLORADO
UNIFORM COMMERCIAL CODE — FINANCING STATEMENT — COLORADO U.C.C.-1 (Rev. 1-78)
IMPORTANT — Read instructions on reverse side before filling out form

This Financing Statement is presented for filing pursuant to the Uniform Commercial Code.

1. Debtor(s) Name and Mailing Address:
2. Secured Party(ies) Name and Address:
3. For Filing Officer (Date, Time, Number, and Filing Office):
4. This Financing Statement covers the following types (or items) of property: (WARNING: If collateral is crops, fixtures, timber, or minerals or other substances to be extracted or accounts resulting from the sale thereof, read instructions on back.)
5. Name and address of Assignee of Secured Party:

Check only if applicable.
☐ This Financing Statement is to be filed for record in the real estate records.
☐ Products of collateral are also covered.

6. This Statement is signed by the Secured Party instead of the Debtor to perfect a security interest in collateral (Please check appropriate box)
   ☐ already subject to a security interest in another jurisdiction when it was brought into this state, or when the debtor's location was changed to this state.
   ☐ which is proceeds of the original collateral described above in which a security interest was perfected;
   ☐ as to which the filing has lapsed; or
   ☐ acquired after a change of name, identity or corporate structure of the debtor.

7. Check only if applicable: ☐ The Debtor is a transmitting utility.

Signature(s) of Debtor(s)

Form approved by the Secretary of State and the County Clerks and Recorders Association
(1) Filing Officer Copy

Signature(s) of Secured Party(ies)

COLORADO FORM U.C.C. 1 (REV. 1-78)
BRADFORD PUBLISHING CO.
DENVER, COLO.

FORM 7F

SKELETON TRUST INDENTURE

THIS INDENTURE, dated _____ _____, 19__, between _____ Corporation, a corporation organized and existing under the laws of the State of _____ (hereinafter called the Corporation), and the _____ Trust Company of _____, a corporation organized and existing under the laws of the State of _____, as Trustee (hereinafter called the Trustee), WITNESSETH:

WHEREAS, the Corporation, in the exercise of its corporate powers and for the purpose of furthering and accomplishing its corporate objects and purposes and pursuant to due corporate action, has determined to create an issue of First Mortgage Bonds, in an aggregate principal amount not exceeding $_____ at any one time outstanding, and to secure the same by this Indenture; and

WHEREAS, the Corporation has determined to create an initial series of Bonds hereunder and to issue forthwith $_____ in principal amount of said initial series of Bonds to be known as "First Mortgage Bonds, _____% Series, due _____ _____, 19__", to contain such provisions as are hereinafter specified; and

WHEREAS, the text of all the First Mortgage Bonds, _____% Series, due _____ _____, 19__, of the coupons for interest to be attached thereto and of the Trustee's certificate to be endorsed thereon, is to be substantially as follows:

[*Here insert full form of bond;*] and

WHEREAS, all the requirements of law relating to the authorization of the Bonds and the execution of this Indenture and the mortgage and pledge hereby evidenced have been complied with; and all things necessary to make the Bonds, when authenticated by the Trustee and issued as in this Indenture provided, the valid and binding obligations of the Corporation, and all things necessary to constitute this Indenture a valid and binding mortgage for the security of said Bonds have been done and performed and the issue of said Bonds subject to the terms hereof and the execution of this Indenture have been in all respects duly authorized;

Now, THEREFORE, In order to secure the payment of the principal and interest of all the Bonds at any time issued and outstanding under this Indenture, according to their tenor, purport and effect, and the performance and observance of all the covenants, agreements and conditions therein and herein contained, and to declare the terms and conditions upon which said Bonds are to be issued, authenticated, secured and held, and for and in consideration of the premises and of the purchase and acceptance of the Bonds by the holders thereof, and of the sum of _____ dollar(s) duly paid by the Trustee to the Corporation at or before the ensealing and delivery of these presents, the receipt whereof is hereby acknowledged, the Corporation has mortgaged, pledged, assigned, transferred, granted, bargained, sold, aliened, remised, released, conveyed, confirmed and set over, unto the Trustee, and its successor or successors, in the trusts hereby created, and its and their assigns, the following described properties:

[*Insert full description of properties. This usually includes all land, plants, offices and other buildings, together with all improvements and fixtures, etc., and a clause providing for after-acquired property. This is followed by the "Habendum clause":*]

To HAVE AND TO HOLD the lands and interest in lands, estates, plants and appurtenances and other property hereby conveyed, mortgages, pledged or transferred unto the Trustee, its successors and assigns forever;

[*There follows a clause excepting any specific property from the mortgage. This is followed by the "Trust" clause:*]

IN TRUST NEVERTHELESS, under and subject to the conditions herein set forth, for the common and equal benefit and security of all the holders of Bonds and coupons issued and to be issued under this Indenture.

[*The remainder of the indenture is divided into articles, as indicated below, each article being further divided into a number of sections and subsections:*]

Article 1: Form, Execution, Delivery and Registration of the Bonds

[Authentication by Trustee; aggregate amount outstanding; recording of indenture.—Date of initial series; interest; place of payment of principal and interest; denominations.—Terms of later series.—Title of initial series; identification of later series; numbering of bonds.—Execution of supplemental indenture upon request for authentication and delivery of later series.—Registration and transfer of bonds.—Signature of bonds; use of facsimile signatures; seal; effect of Trustee's certificate.—Evidence of ownership of bonds.—Issuance of temporary bonds.—Mutilated, lost, destroyed or stolen bonds.]

Article 2: Issue of Bonds

[Authentication and delivery of initial series of bonds.—Use of deposited funds for capital expenditures.—Limitation on amount of bonds authenticated and moneys paid out for capital expenditures.—Sale of bonds reserved for authentication.—Documents required before paying out deposited moneys and authenticating and delivering bonds.—Discharge of prior lien on property.—Trustee not liable for use of bonds or deposited moneys.—Delivery of bonds in exchange for bonds cancelled.—Delivery of bonds upon surrender of bonds about to mature or called for redemption.—Cancellation of bonds converted into stock or retired through sinking fund.]

Article 3: Redemption of Bonds

[Premium paid on redemption.—Notice of redemption.—Cancellation of indenture on redemption of all outstanding bonds.—Cancellation of redeemed or reacquired bonds.]

Article 4: Sinking fund for First Mortgage Bonds, ——% Series, due —————— ————, 19——.

[Amounts to be paid into sinking fund.—Additional sinking fund equal to percentage of net profits.—Fund payments in bonds purchased by Corporation.—Application of fund to redemption of bonds.—Notice of redemption through fund.—Cancellation of bonds redeemed.]

Article 5: Particular Covenants of the Corporation
[Covenants to pay principal and interest—not to extend time for payment of interest—to subject present and after-acquired property to lien of indenture and to execute further instruments of conveyance—not to permit prior lien on property and to discharge liens—to discharge taxes and assessments—not to merge or sell assets unless purchaser assumes payment of bonds—to maintain property—to preserve corporate existence—to keep property insured—to pay expenses of Trustee—to record and file indenture—not to dispose of bonds contrary to indenture provisions—to restrict declaration of dividends, distributions and redemption of stock—to restrict purchase of stock—to maintain office for payment of principal and interest—to deliver to Trustee annual financial statements—to furnish opinion of expert as to fair value of property.]

Article 6: Release of Property Included in the Trust Estate
[Power of Corporation to sell obsolete property.—Power of Corporation to remove property.—Power of Corporation to sell limited amount of property.—Obligations in satisfaction of debt not to be subject to lien of indenture.—Power of Corporation to move, alter or remodel buildings.—Power of Corporation to amend, alter or cancel lease, license or easement.—Power of Corporation to sell or exchange for other property.—Release of trust property taken by eminent domain.—Method of release of mortgaged properties.—Application of moneys received by Trustee.—Powers of Corporation to be exercised by receiver or Trustee.]

Article 7: Events of Default—Remedies of Trust and Bondholders
[Events of default: default in payment of principal, payment of interest or sinking fund payment—involuntary bankruptcy or receivership—voluntary bankruptcy, reorganization, assignment for benefit of creditors—default in performance of covenants.—Acceleration of due date of principal; waiver of default.—Power of Trustee to take possession.—Power of Trustee to sell trust estate.—Notice of sale.—Execution of instruments and transfer to purchaser at sale.—Divesting of Corporation's title upon sale.—Suit by Trustee to enforce payment of bonds; foreclosure.—Power of bondholders to decide on remedy sought.—Payment by Corporation to Trustee for benefit of bondholders on default.—Restrictions on suits by bondholders.—Application of proceeds of sale of trust estate.—Principal of all bonds to become due on sale.—Appointment of receiver upon default.—Covenant of Corporation to waive service of process, enter appearance and consent to entry of judgment.—Waiver of Corporation of benefits of laws for stay or appraisal of trust estate.—Remedies cumulative.—Delay or omission to exercise right not waiver.—Restrictions against rem-

edies which would surrender lien of indenture.—Power of Trustee to restrain compliance with invalid law.]

Article 8: Immunity of Incorporators, Stockholders, Officers and Directors

Article 9: Merger, Consolidation or Sale
[Covenant of Corporation not to merge, consolidate or sell assets unless new company can meet provisions of indenture.—Successor company to assume conditions of bonds and indentures.—Successor company to succeed to rights of Corporation.—Indenture to become lien on improvements by successor company and on after-acquired property.]

Article 10: Concerning the Trustee
[Power of Trustee to employ agents and attorneys.—Limitation on liability of Trustee.—Indemnification of Trustee by bondholders.—Form of request, notice or authorization to Trustee by Corporation.—Compensation of Trustee; lien for payment.—Return of moneys deposited with Trustee.—Advances by Trustee to preserve trust estate.—Conflicting interests of Trustee.—Removal of Trustee.—Appointment of successor Trustee.—Effect of merger or consolidation of Trustee.—Appointment of co-trustee.]

Article 11: Bondholders' Lists and Reports by the Corporation and the Trustee
[Corporation to furnish list of bondholders; Trustee to preserve list.—Application by bondholders for list.—Corporation to file annual and other reports.—Reports by Trustee to bondholders.—Notice by Trustee to bondholders of defaults.]

Article 12: Supplemental Indentures, Bondholders' Acts, Holdings and Apparent Authority
[Purposes for execution of supplemental indenture.—Consent to execution by proportion of bondholders.—Binding effect of supplemental indenture on non-consenting bondholders.—Revocation of consent by bondholders.—Trustee to join in supplemental indenture.—Proof of ownership of registered and bearer bonds.—Supplemental indenture to be considered part of original indenture.]

Article 13: Possession Until Default
[Corporation to retain possession until default, use income and dispose of profits.—Reversion of property to Corporation on payment of principal and interest; discharge of indenture.]

Article 14: Definitions and Miscellaneous Provisions
[Agreements binding on successors and assigns.—Definitions.—Provisions conflicting with Trust Indenture Act of 1939.—Agreements to be for exclusive benefit of parties and bondholders.—Notices to Corporation or Trustee.—Acceptance of trust by Trustee.—Appointment of attorneys for acknowledgement of indenture.]

IN WITNESS WHEREOF, _____ Corporation has caused this instrument to be signed in its corporate name and its corporate seal to be affixed by its President and its Secretary, and its corporate seal to be attested by its Secretary, by order of its Board of Directors, and the _____ Trust Company of _____, in token of its acceptance of the trusts created hereby, has caused this instrument to be signed in its corporate name and its corporate seal to be affixed by its President and its Secretary, and its corporate seal to be attested by its Secretary, by order of the Executive Committee of its Board of Directors, as of the date given at the beginning of this indenture.

_____ Corporation

[Corporate Seal]

by _____ President

Attest:

_____ Secretary   _____ Secretary

The _____ Trust Company of _____, Trustee

[Corporate Seal]

by _____ President

Attest:

_____ Secretary   _____ Secretary [22]

22. Prentice Hall, Corporations, Forms § 60351. Reprinted with the permission of Prentice Hall.

FORM 8A

SPECIAL MEETING OF THE BOARD OF DIRECTORS OF _____, INC.

A Special Meeting of the Board of Directors of _____, Inc., was held at _____, _____, _____ on the ___ day of _____, 19___, at ___ o'clock.

The meeting was called pursuant to section _____ of the _____ Corporation Code [and] [or] Article___ of the Articles of Incorporation of the corporation [and] [or] Section___ of the Bylaws of the corporation.

The following directors were present: _____.
The following directors were absent: _____.

The presence of the foregoing directors constitutes a quorum. The following other persons were also present: _____.

The meeting was held pursuant to notice addressed to each director in accordance with the statute, the Articles of Incorporation, and the Bylaws of the corporation. A copy of the notice, together with the Secretary's certificate that such notice was properly mailed or delivered, is attached to the minutes of the meeting.

[or]

The meeting is held pursuant to Waiver of Notice from each director, a copy of which is attached to the minutes of the meeting.

The minutes of the meeting of the Board of Directors on _____, 19___, were approved as read.

The President stated that the purpose of the meeting was to [here describe purpose in narrative form].

Following full discussion, upon motion duly made, seconded and unanimously adopted it was

RESOLVED, [here describe substance of resolution]

[or]

Following full discussion, upon motion duly made by _____, seconded by _____, the following directors voted in favor: _____; and the following directors voted against: _____; the following resolution:

[names]

[names]

RESOLVED, [here describe substance of resolution]

The Treasurer of the corporation reported on the financial condition of the corporation, a copy of which is attached to these minutes.

The Board of Directors informally discussed [here describe] and no action was taken at this time.

There being no further business, the meeting was adjourned.

_____
Secretary

FORM 8B

SPECIAL MEETING OF THE SHAREHOLDERS OF _____, INC.

A Special Meeting of the Shareholders of _____, Inc., was held at _____, _____, _____ on the day of _____, 19____, at ____ o'clock.

The meeting was called pursuant to section _____ of the _____ Corporation Code [and] [or] Article ____ of the Articles of Incorporation [and] [or] Section ____ of the Bylaws of the corporation, by the [President], [Secretary] [The holders of % of the shares entitled to vote] or [other].

[A copy of the call of the meeting dated _____, 19___, addressed to the Secretary of the corporation and signed by the holders of ___% of the shares entitled to vote is attached to the minutes of this meeting.]

The meeting was held pursuant to notice addressed to each shareholder in accordance with the statute, the Articles of Incorporation, and the Bylaws of the corporation. A copy of the notice, together with the Secretary's certificate that such notice was properly mailed or delivered to each Shareholder, is attached to the minutes of the meeting.

The Board of Directors, by resolution dated _____, 19___, set _____, 19___, as the record date for the determination of the Shareholders entitled to vote at this meeting, and only Shareholders of record on that date are entitled to vote.

[or]

The meeting was held pursuant to Waiver of Notice from each Shareholder, a copy of which is attached to the minutes of this meeting.

Shareholders holding _____ Shares of record were present at the meeting. Shareholders holding _____ Shares of record were represented by proxy at the meeting, and their shares were voted by _____, duly constituted proxy in their names.

The minutes of the Shareholder meeting on _____, 19___, were approved as read.

The President stated that the purpose of the meeting was to [here describe purpose in narrative form].

Following full discussion, upon motion duly made, and seconded, _____ Shares voted in person in favor; _____ Shares voted by proxy in favor; _____ Shares voted in person against; and _____ Shares voted by proxy against the following resolution:

RESOLVED, [here describe substance of resolution]

The Treasurer of the corporation reported on the financial condition of the corporation, a copy of which is attached to these minutes.

Several questions were raised by the Shareholders concerning [here describe informal discussion and questions]. No action was taken on these matters.

There being no further business, the meeting was adjourned.

_____
Secretary

FORM 9A

STATEMENT OF CANCELLATION OF REACQUIRED SHARES
(NEW JERSEY)

Form C-126 7-1-71

STATEMENT OF CANCELLATION

OF REACQUIRED SHARES OF

_____

(For Use by Domestic Corporations Only)

To: The Secretary of State
    State of New Jersey

Pursuant to the provisions of Section 14A:7-18, Corporations, General, of the New Jersey Statutes, the undersigned corporation hereby submits the following Statement of Cancellation of Reaquired Shares:

1. The name of the corporation is _____ .

2. The number of shares cancelled is _____ ; itemized as follows:

Class	Series	No. of Shares

(Omit the following if not applicable.)

3. If cancelled shares were not reacquired out of stated capital or by their conversion into other shares of the corporation, the date of adoption of the resolution of the board of directors cancelling such shares was on the _____ day of _____ , 19_____ .

4. The aggregate number of issued shares of the corporation after giving effect to such cancellation is _____ ; itemized as follows:

Class	Series	No. of Shares

5. The amount of the stated capital of the corporation after giving effect to such cancellation is $ _____ . (Must be set forth in dollars.)

(Use the following if the Certificate of Incorporation, or the Plan of Merger or Consolidation, in the case of shares acquired by the corporation pursuant to Section 14A:11-1 et seq., Corporations, General, of the New Jersey Statutes (regarding rights of dissenting shareholders), provides that the cancelled shares shall not be reissued.)

6. The Certificate of Incorporation is amended pursuant to a resolution of the board of directors decreasing the aggregate number of shares which the corporation is authorized to issue by the number of shares cancelled.

The number of shares which the corporation has authority to issue, after giving effect to such cancellation is _____ ; itemized as follows:

Class	Series	No. of Shares

(Use the following if shareholder approval is required for reduction of stated capital, pursuant to Section 14A:7-18(3), Corporations, General, of the New Jersey Statutes.)

7. The shareholders approved the reduction of stated capital on the _____ day of _____ , 19_____ .

APPENDIX G

The number of shares outstanding at the time of approving such reduction was _____. The number of shares entitled to vote thereon was _____ ; itemized as follows: (If the shares of any class or series are entitled to vote as a class, set forth the number of shares of each such class and series voting for and against the reduction respectively.)

No. of Shares Voting For Reduction   No. of Shares Voting Against Reduction

Dated this _____ day of _____ , 19_____ .

_____
(Corporate Name)

By _____ *
(Signature)

_____
(Type or Print Name and Title)

(*May be executed by the chairman of the board, or the president, or a vice-president of the corporation.)

Fees for filing in Office of the Secretary of State, State House, Trenton, N. J. 08625.

    Filing Fee $25.00

NOTE: No recording fees will be assessed.

TRANSACTION NO.:

FILED BY:

STATEMENT OF CANCELLATION OF REACQUIRED SHARES OF

FOLDER NO.:

Recorder's Initials

RECORDED AND FILED:

FORM 10A
NON-DISCLOSURE AGREEMENT

The Coca-Cola Company

NON-DISCLOSURE AGREEMENT
Covering Inventions, Discoveries, and Confidential Matter

In consideration of my employment, or my continued employment, as the case may be, by The Coca-Cola Company, a Delaware corporation (hereinafter called the Company), I agree with the Company as follows:

So long as I shall remain in the employ of the Company I will devote my whole time and ability to the service of the Company in such capacity as it shall from time to time direct, and I will perform my duties faithfully and diligently.

I will not, during my employment or thereafter, use or disclose to others without the written consent of the Company, any trade secrets, secret "know-how", confidential or secret technical information or other confidential information relative to your business, obtained by me while in the employ of the Company. Upon leaving the employ of the Company I will not take with me any confidential data, drawings, or information obtained by me as the result of my employment, or any reproductions thereof. All such Company property will be surrendered to the Company on termination or at any time on request.

I will disclose to the Company and, upon the Company's request, assign to it, without charge, all my right, title, and interest in and to any and all inventions and discoveries which I may make, solely or jointly with others, while in the employ of the Company which relate to or are useful or may be useful in connection with business of the character carried on or contemplated by the Company, and all my right, title, and interest in and to any and all domestic and foreign applications for patents covering such inventions and discoveries and any and all patents granted for such inventions and any and all reissues and extensions of such patents; and upon request of the Company whether during or subsequent to this employment I will do any and all acts and execute and deliver such instruments as may be deemed by the Company necessary or proper to vest all my right, title, and interest in and to said inventions, applications, and patents in the Company and to secure or maintain such patents, reissues and/or extensions thereof. Any inventions and discoveries relating to the Company's business made by me within one year after termination of my employment with the Company shall be deemed to be within this provision, unless I can prove that the same were conceived and made following said termination. All necessary and proper expenses in connection with the foregoing shall be borne by the Company, and if services in connection therewith are performed at the Company's request after termination of employment, the Company will pay reasonable compensation for such.

Attached hereto is a list of patent applications and unpatented inventions made prior to my employment by the Company, which I agree is a complete list and which I desire to remove from the operation of this agreement.

This agreement shall enure to the benefit of the Company, its subsidiaries, allied companies, successors and assigns or nominees of the Company, and I specifically agree to execute any and all documents considered convenient or necessary to assign, transfer, sustain and maintain inventions, discoveries, applications and patents, both in this and foreign countries.

IN WITNESS WHEREOF, I have hereunto signed my name and affixed my seal, this _____ day of _____, 19___.

Witness: _____   _____(SEAL)

_____   _____(DEPT.)

Distribution: Execute in triplicate — White copy for Department; yellow copy for Employee; and pink copy for Personnel Relations Department.

FORM 761 (1-68)

FORM 11A

VOTING TRUST AGREEMENT

Agreement, made this _____ day of _____, 19___, between _____, _____, _____, _____, and _____, hereinafter designated as Trustees, and the undersigned shareholders of _____ Company, hereinafter designated as the Beneficiaries.

Whereas, the parties do hereby agree and declare that the intent and purpose of this Agreement is to provide a means whereby the parties hereto may initiate or maintain in effect any general policy, plan, or program affecting _____ Company which the parties should determine to be to their joint benefit, interest, and advantage, and to the best interests of all stockholders of _____ Company, and to that end to elect or retain or replace any officer, executive, or employee of said corporation;

Now, therefore, the parties do hereby agree with each other as follows:

1. **Delivery of Shares to Trustees, Term of Trust.** Upon the signing of this agreement the Beneficiaries shall deliver to the Trustees the certificate or certificates representing all the shares of _____ Company now owned or controlled by them, said certificates to be endorsed in blank or accompanied by proper instruments of assignment and transfer thereof in blank. Said shares will be held by the Trustees for a period of ten years from _____, 19___ (unless this trust is sooner terminated, as hereinafter provided) in trust, however, for the Beneficiaries, their heirs, executors, administrators, successors and assigns, and at all times subject to the terms and conditions herein set forth.

2. **Additional Shares.** Any and all certificates for additional shares of _____ Company that shall hereafter during said ten year period be issued to any of the Beneficiaries shall be in like manner endorsed and delivered to the Trustees, to be held by them under the terms hereof.

3. **Voting.** During the term of this Agreement the Trustees or their successors in trust shall have the sole and exclusive voting power of the stock standing in their names as such. They shall have the power to vote the stock at all regular and special meetings of the stockholders and may vote for, do, or assent or consent to any act or proceeding which the shareholders of said corporation might or could vote for, do or assent or consent to and shall have all the powers, rights and privileges of a shareholder of said corporation. The Trustees shall consult and confer with each other, and shall make every effort to agree on how their votes are cast. The Trustees, as soon as this Agreement becomes effective, shall appoint a chairman. In any

case where shareholder action is required, the chairman may, or upon the request of any two Trustees, shall, call a meeting of the Trustees, on reasonable notice, for the purpose of reaching an agreement on the manner of voting the stock held by the Trustees, or for any other purpose deemed to be in the best interests of _____ Company. The vote of the Trustees shall always be exercised as a unit, as any four of said Trustees shall direct and determine. If any four Trustees fail to agree on any matter on which a vote of the stockholders is called for, then the question in disagreement shall be submitted for arbitration to some disinterested person (i. e., one having no financial interest in _____ Company) chosen by the affirmative vote of four of the Trustees, as sole arbitrator. If four of the Trustees are unable to agree on an arbitrator, then each of the Trustees shall nominate a similarly disinterested person as a candidate and the arbitrator shall be selected by the affirmative vote of four of the Trustees from the panel of such candidates. If any candidate receives the affirmative vote of four of the Trustees he shall be elected sole arbitrator. If no candidate receives the affirmative vote of four of the Trustees, then the candidate receiving the lowest number of votes shall be eliminated from the panel (or if there should be a tie among the low candidates, or among all the candidates, if more than two, one of such candidates shall be eliminated by lot) and the Trustees shall continue the process of voting among those remaining on the panel until one has been selected by the affirmative vote of four of the Trustees. If the voting continues to the point where no candidate receives the vote of four of the Trustees, then those two candidates receiving the highest number of votes respectively from those who voted with the majority and those who voted with the minority on the issue to be submitted to arbitration (ties among the majority and minority candidates to be decided by lot) shall be appointed arbitrators and these two shall appoint a third disinterested person as arbitrator. The decision of the arbitrator or, if more than one, a majority thereof, shall be binding upon the parties hereto and the vote of all the stock in trust shall be cast in accordance with such decision. The Beneficiaries may by unanimous written agreement designate any person as sole arbitrator who shall act during the life of this agreement.

4. **Proxies.** Any Trustee may vote in person or by proxy and a proxy in writing signed by any four of the Trustees shall be sufficient authority to the person named therein to vote all the stock held by the Trustees hereunder at any meeting, regular or special, of the stockholders of _____ Company. If at any such meeting less than four Trustees shall be present either in person or by proxy, then all of the stock held by the Trustees may be voted in accordance with the unanimous decision of those Trustees present in person or by proxy.

5. **Appointment of Successor Trustees.** In the event of the death, resignation, removal or incapacity of any of the Trustees his successor shall be named by an instrument in writing signed by a majority of the remaining Trustees. All Successor Trustees shall be clothed with all the rights, privileges, duties and powers herein conferred upon the Trustees herein named.

6. **Voting Trust Certificates.** Upon the delivery to the Trustees of said certificates representing the shares of _____ Company, the Trustees will cause the same to be transferred on the books of the corporation to themselves as Trustees and will deliver to each of the Beneficiaries a Trustees' Certificate for the number of shares delivered to said Trustees, substantially in the form hereinafter set out. Upon receipt of certificates for additional shares of _____ Company issued to any of the Beneficiaries, and upon receipt of certificates for such shares issued to other persons and which may be issued to future subscribers for shares of _____ Company, and upon compliance with the terms of this agreement by the owners of such shares, the Trustees will cause said shares to be transferred on the books of said corporation to their names as trustees, and shall deliver to each of the persons so depositing said certificates a Trustees' Certificate for the number of shares so deposited by said person.

The Trustees' Certificate shall be substantially in the following form:

Trustees' Certificate

This is to certify that the undersigned Trustees have received a certificate or certificates issued in the name of _____, evidencing the ownership of _____ shares of _____ Company, a _____ corporation, and that said shares are held subject to all the terms and conditions of that certain agreement, dated _____, 19__, by and between _____, _____, _____, _____, and _____, as Trustees, and certain shareholders of _____ Company. During the period of ten years from and after _____, 19__, the said Trustees, or their successors, shall, as provided in said agreement, possess and be entitled to exercise the right to vote and otherwise represent all of said shares for all purposes, it being agreed that no voting right shall pass to the holder hereof by virtue of the ownership of this certificate.

This certificate is assignable with the right of issuance of a new certificate of like tenor only upon the surrender to the undersigned or their successors of this certificate properly endorsed. Upon the termination of said Trust this certificate shall be surrendered to the Trustees by the holder hereof upon delivery to such holder of a stock certificate representing a like number of said shares.

In witness whereof, the undersigned Trustees have executed this Certificate this _____ day of _____, 19__.

_____
_____
_____
_____
_____
Trustees

Said Trustees' Certificate, subject to the conditions hereof, may be transferred by endorsement by the person to whom issued, or by his attorney in fact, or by the administrator, executor or guardian of his estate, and delivery of the same to said Trustees; but said transfer shall not be evidence to or be binding upon said Trustees until the certificate is surrendered to them and the transfer is so entered upon their "Trustees' Certificate Book", which shall be kept by them to show the names of the parties by whom and to whom transferred, the numbers of the certificates, the number of shares and the date of transfer. No new Trustees' Certificate shall be issued until the former Trustees' Certificate for the shares represented thereby shall have been surrendered to and cancelled by said Trustees, and they shall preserve the certificates so cancelled as vouchers. In case any Trustees' Certificate shall be claimed to be lost or destroyed, a new Trustees' Certificate may be issued in lieu thereof, upon such proof of loss and such security as may be required by said Trustees.

7. **Restrictions on Transfer of Voting Trust Certificates.** Each of the Beneficiaries agrees that during the term of this agreement said Trustees' Certificates will not be sold or transferred except in accordance with Paragraph _____ of the Organization Agreement of _____ Company, dated _____, 19__, relating to the sale of shares of _____ Company, so long as said Organization Agreement remains in effect. Said Trustees' Certificates shall be regarded as stock of the _____ Company within the meaning of any provision of the Bylaws of said corporation imposing conditions or restrictions upon the sale of stock of said corporation.

8. **Dividends.** Before declaring any dividend the Board of Directors of _____ Company shall request the Trustees to certify to the Board the names of all persons who are the owners and holders of Trustees' Certificates, and the number of shares to which each of such persons is or may then be entitled as shown by the books of the Trustees and no dividend shall be declared and paid by said corporation until reasonable opportunity has been given the Trustees to submit such certificate. Said corporation is hereby irrevocably authorized and directed (a) to accept such certificate of the Trustees as true; and (b) to pay any and all dividends upon the shares enumerated in such certificate directly to the holders of the Trustees' Certificates.

In the event that any dividend paid in capital stock of the Company shall be received by the Trustees, the respective holders of Trustees' Certificates issued hereunder shall be entitled to the delivery of new or additional Trustees' Certificates to the amount of the stock received by the Trustees as such dividend upon the number of such shares of the Company represented by their respective Trustees' Certificates theretofore outstanding.

9. **Termination.** Except as herein otherwise provided the trust hereby created shall not be revoked and the powers herein delegated to the Trustees shall be irrevocable during said period of ten years from and after _____, 19__. This trust, however, shall terminate upon the vote of any four of the Trustees and their declaration in writing that said trust is terminated. Unless the Trustees by unanimous vote otherwise determine, this trust shall also terminate if and when less than 50% of the outstanding shares of _____ Company remain subject to this Trust Agreement. Upon the termination of said trust the certificates representing all of the shares so held under this agreement and then remaining in the hands of the Trustees or their successors shall be assigned to the parties then entitled thereto as shown by Trustees' Certificates then outstanding, upon surrender to the Trustees of the Trustees' Certificates representing said shares.

10. **Compensation of Trustees.** The Beneficiaries may pay a reasonable compensation to the Trustees for their service hereunder and all expenses and costs incurred by them in executing said trusts, and the Beneficiaries do agree to save and hold harmless said Trustees from any and all liability arising out of the holding by them of any of the shares of said _____ Company hereunder.

11. **Exculpatory Clause.** The Trustees shall not be liable or incur any responsibility by reason of their acts of omission or commission in the premises except for wilful misconduct or gross negligence in the execution of the trusts hereby created.

12. **Extension of Term.** At any time within one year prior to the time of expiration of this agreement, one or more Beneficiaries hereunder may, by agreement in writing and with the written consent of all of the Trustees, extend the duration of this agreement for an additional period not exceeding ten years; provided, however, that no such extension agreement shall affect the rights or obligations of persons not parties thereto.

13. **Counterparts.** This agreement may be executed in several counterparts, each of which so executed shall be deemed to be the original, and such counterparts shall together constitute one and the same instrument.

In witness whereof, the parties have hereunto set their hands or have caused their corporate names to be hereunto affixed by their officers thereunto duly authorized, the day and year first above written.

```
                                    _____
                                    _____
                                    _____
                                    _____
                                    _____
                                          Trustees
```

_____ holding _____ shares
_____ holding _____ shares
_____ holding _____ shares
_____ holding _____ shares
_____ holding _____ shares
_____ holding _____ shares

                        Stockholders of _____ Company
                                    Beneficiaries [25]

    25. West's Modern Legal Forms § 3012.-
      1.

FORM 12A

APPLICATION FOR CERTIFICATE OF AUTHORITY (MISSISSIPPI)

File in Duplicate Originals

APPLICATION FOR CERTIFICATE OF
AUTHORITY OF

_____
(EXACT CORPORATE NAME)

To the Secretary of State
of the State of Mississippi

    Pursuant to the provisions of Section 110 of the Mississippi Business Corporation Act, the undersigned corporation hereby applies for a Certificate of Authority to transact business in your State, and for that purpose submits the following statement:

    FIRST: The name of the corporation is_____

_____

    SECOND: The name which it elects to use in Mississippi is_____

_____,_____(Note 1)

    THIRD: It is incorporated under the laws of_____

    FOURTH: The date of its incorporation is_____and the period of its duration is

_____

    FIFTH: The address of its principal office in the state or country under the laws of which it is incorporated is_____

    SIXTH: The address of its proposed registered office in Mississippi is_____

_____and the name of its proposed registered agent in Mississippi at that address is_____

    SEVENTH: The purpose or purposes which it proposes to pursue in the transaction of business in Mississippi are_____

    EIGHTH: The names and respective addresses of its directors and officers are:

Name	Office	ADDRESS
	Director	
	Director	
	Director	
	President	
	Vice President	
	Secretary	
	Treasurer	

    NINTH: The aggregate number of shares which it has authority to issue, itemized by classes, par value of shares, shares without par value, and series, if any within a class, is:

Number of Shares	Class	Series	Par Value per Share or Statement that Shares are without Par Value

TENTH: The aggregate number of its issued shares, itemized by classes, par value of shares, shares without par value, and series, if any, within a class, is:

Number of Shares	Class	Series	Par Value per Share or Statement that Shares are without Par Value

ELEVENTH: The amount of its stated capital is $_____ (Note 2)

TWELFTH: An estimate of the value of all property to be owned by it for the following year, wherever located, is $_____.

THIRTEENTH: An estimate of the value of its property to be located within Mississippi during such year is $_____.

FOURTEENTH: An estimate of the gross amount of business to be transacted by it during such year is $_____.

FIFTEENTH: An estimate of the gross amount of business to be transacted by it at or from places of business in Mississippi during such year is $_____

SIXTEENTH: This Application is accompanied by a copy of its articles of incorporation and all amendments thereto, duly authenticated by the proper officer of the state or country under the laws of which it in incorporated.

Dated_____, 19____.

_____
EXACT CORPORATE NAME

By _____
    Its_____President

By _____
    Its_____Secretary

STATE OF _____
COUNTY OF _____ } SS.

I, _____, a notary public, do hereby certify that on this _____ day of _____, 19____, personally appeared before me _____ _____, who, being by me first duly sworn, declared that he is the _____ of _____, that he executed the foregoing document as _____ of the corporation, and that the statements therein contained are true.

_____
Notary Public

My commission expires _____.
(NOTARIAL SEAL)

Notes: 1. If the name of the corporation does not contain the word "corporation", "company", "incorporated", or "limited" or an abbreviation of one of such words, insert the name of the corporation with the word or abbreviation which it elects to add thereto for use in this State.

2. "Stated capital" means, at any particular time, the sum of (1) the par value of all shares of the corporation having a par value that have been issued, (2) the amount of the consideration received by the corporation for all shares of the corporation without par value that have been issued, except such part of the consideration therefor as may have been allocated to capital surplus in a manner permitted by law, and (3) such amounts not included in clauses (1) and (2) of this paragraph as have been transferred to stated capital of the corporation, whether upon the issue of shares as a share dividend or otherwise, minus all reductions from such sum as have been effected in a manner permitted by law.

STATE OF _____
COUNTY OF _____ } SS.

I, _____, a notary public, do hereby certify that on this _____ day of _____, 19____, personally appeared before me _____ _____, who, being by me first duly sworn, declared that he is the _____ of _____, that he executed the foregoing document as _____ of the corporation, and that the statements therein contained are true.

_____
Notary Public

My commission expires _____.
(NOTARIAL SEAL)

FORM 12B

STATEMENT OF CHANGE OF REGISTERED OFFICE OR AGENT
(SOUTH DAKOTA)

STATEMENT OF CHANGE OF REGISTERED OFFICE
OR REGISTERED AGENT, OR BOTH,
OF

....

To the Secretary of State
of the State of South Dakota:

Pursuant to the provisions of the South Dakota Corporation Acts, the undersigned corporation, organized under the laws of the State of .... submits the following statement for the purpose of changing its registered office or its registered agent, or both, in the State of South Dakota:

FIRST: The name of the corporation is ....
....

SECOND: The address of its previous registered office was ....
....

THIRD: The address to which its registered office is to be changed is ....
....

FOURTH: The name of its previous registered agent is ....
....

FIFTH: The name of its successor registered agent is ....
....

SIXTH: The address of its registered office and the address of the business office of its registered agent, as changed, will be identical. The address of its place of business in South Dakota is ....
....

SEVENTH: This change has been authorized by resolution duly adopted by the board of directors.

Dated ...., 19 ....

               .... (Note 1)

              By .... (Note 2)

                Its .... President

STATE OF ....)
) ss.
COUNTY OF ....)

Before me, ..., a Notary Public in and for the said County and State, personally appeared .... who acknowledged before me that ...he is the (President) (Vice-President) of.... ...., that ...he signed the foregoing, and that the statements contained therein are true.

In witness whereof I have hereunto set my hand and seal this .... day of ...., A.D., 19 ....

               ....
                    Notary Public

My commission expires ....
(Notarial Seal)

Notes: 1. Exact corporate name of corporation making the statement.
     2. Signature and title of officer signing for the corporation — must be a President or a Vice-President.

Filing fee $5.00
Submit one copy.

FORM 12C

CERTIFICATE OF AUTHORITY
(MODEL ACT)

STATE OF ―――
OFFICE OF THE SECRETARY OF STATE

**CERTIFICATE OF AUTHORITY
OF**

_____

The undersigned, as Secretary of State of the State of _____, hereby certifies that duplicate originals of an Application of _____ _____ for a Certificate of Authority to transact business in this State, duly signed and verified pursuant to the provisions of the _____ Business Corporation Act, have been received in this office and are found to conform to law.

ACCORDINGLY the undersigned, as such Secretary of State, and by virtue of the authority vested in him by law, hereby issues this Certificate of Authority to _____
to transact business in this State under the name of _____
_____ and attaches hereto a duplicate original of the Application for such Certificate.

Dated _____, 19___.

_____
Secretary of State

FORM 12D

APPLICATION FOR AMENDED CERTIFICATE OF AUTHORITY (SOUTH CAROLINA)

APPLICATION FOR AMENDED CERTIFICATE OF AUTHORITY

STATE OF SOUTH CAROLINA
SECRETARY OF STATE

For Use by The Secretary of State	file this form in duplicate	This Space For Use by The Secretary of State
File No. _____ Fee Paid $_____ Date _____ C. B. _____		

Pursuant to Section 13.8 of the South Carolina Business Corporation Act of 1962, the undersigned corporation hereby applies for an amended certificate of authority to transact business in the State of South Carolina, and for that purpose submits the following statement: (Section 12-23.8 of the 1962 supplement)

First: The name of the corporation is _____
_____.

Second: The registered office of the Corporation in the State of South Carolina is _____ in the City of _____.

Third: It is incorporated under the laws of the State of _____.

Fourth: The corporation was domesticated in the State of South Carolina on the _____ day of _____, 19___.

Fifth: The proposed amendment to its application of authority is:

Sixth: Attached to this application is a duly authenticated copy of the amendment authorizing the change.

Date _____

_____
Name of Corporation

By _____   By _____
   (Secretary or Assistant)   (President or Vice President)

APPENDIX G

STATE OF _____
COUNTY OF _____ } SS:

The undersigned _____ and _____ do hereby certify that they are the duly elected and acting _____ and _____, respectively, of _____ corporation and are authorized to execute this verification; that each of the undersigned for himself does hereby further certify that he has read the foregoing document, understands the meaning and purport of the statements therein contained and the same are true to the best of his information and belief.

Dated at _____, this _____ day of _____, 19___.

_____
(President or Vice President)

_____
(Secretary or Assistant Secretary)

NOTE: This certificate has been prepared for execution by the president (or vice president) and secretary (or assistant secretary). It may be executed by any of the persons enumerated in section 1.4 (Section 12-11.4 Supplement 1962 Code) of the South Carolina Business Corporation Act under the circumstances indicated. If anyone other than the president (or vice president) and secretary (or assistant secretary) executes the form, the wording of this verification should be changed accordingly.

Filing fees:
For amendment of Certificate of Authority $40.00
For recording application _____   5.00
Total fee _____ $45.00

FORM 12E

AMENDED CERTIFICATE OF AUTHORITY
(MODEL ACT)

STATE OF ———
OFFICE OF THE SECRETARY OF STATE

**AMENDED CERTIFICATE OF AUTHORITY
OF**

_____

The undersigned, as Secretary of State of the State of ———, hereby certifies that duplicate originals of an Application of ——— ——————————— for an Amended Certificate of Authority to transact business in this State, duly signed and verified pursuant to the provisions of the ——— Business Corporation Act, have been received in this office and are found to conform to law.

ACCORDINGLY the undersigned, as such Secretary of State, and by virtue of the authority vested in him by law, hereby issues this Amended Certificate of Authority to ——————————— ——————— to transact business in this State under the name of ——————————————— and attaches hereto a duplicate original of the Application for such Amended Certificate.

Dated ———, 19—.

_____
Secretary of State

FORM 12F

APPLICATION FOR CERTIFICATE OF WITHDRAWAL
(TEXAS)

APPLICATION FOR
CERTIFICATE OF WITHDRAWAL
OF

_____

To the Secretary of State
of the State of Texas

Pursuant to the provisions of Article 8.14 of the Texas Business Corporation Act, the undersigned corporation hereby applies for a Certificate of withdrawal from the State of Texas, and for that purpose submits the following statement:

1. The name of the Corporation is _____

2. It is incorporated under the laws of _____

3. It is not transacting business in the State of Texas.

4. It hereby surrenders its authority to transact business in said state.

5. It revokes the authority of its registered agent in the State of Texas to accept service of process and consents that service of process in any action, suit or proceeding based upon any cause of action arising in the State of Texas during the time it was authorized to transact business therein may thereafter be made on it by service thereof on the Secretary of State of State of Texas.

6. The post office address to which the Secretary of State may mail a copy of any process against the corporation that may be served on him is _____

7. All sums due or accrued by this corporation to the State of Texas have been paid.

8. All known creditors or claimants have been paid or provided for and the corporation is not involved in or threatened with litigation in any court in the State of Texas.

_____

By _____

Its _____ President

and _____

Its _____ Secretary

STATE OF _____

COUNTY OF _____

I, _____ , a notary public, do hereby certify

that on this _____ day of _____ , 19____ ,

personally appeared before me _____ , who

being by me first duly sworn, declared that he is the _____

of _____

that he signed the foregoing document as _____

of the corporation, and that the statements therein contained are true.

_____
Notary Public

FORM 12G

CERTIFICATE OF WITHDRAWAL

STATE OF ———
OFFICE OF THE SECRETARY OF STATE

**CERTIFICATE OF WITHDRAWAL
OF**

_____

The undersigned, as Secretary of State of the State of _____, hereby certifies that duplicate originals of an Application of _____ for a Certificate of Withdrawal from this State, duly signed and verified pursuant to the provisions of the _____ Business Corporation Act, have been received in this office and are found to conform to law.

ACCORDINGLY the undersigned, as such Secretary of State, and by virtue of the authority vested in him by law, hereby issues this Certificate of Withdrawal to _____ _____, and attaches hereto a duplicate original of the Application for such Certificate.

Dated _____, 19__.

_____
Secretary of State

FORM 12H

CERTIFICATE OF REVOCATION OF AUTHORITY

STATE OF ———
OFFICE OF THE SECRETARY OF STATE

**CERTIFICATE OF REVOCATION OF
CERTIFICATE OF AUTHORITY
OF**

_____

The undersigned, as Secretary of State of the State of _____, and by virtue of the authority vested in him by Section 122 of the _____ Business Corporation Act, hereby revokes the Certificate of

Authority of _____ to transact business in this State, for the following reasons: _____
_____
_____

Dated _____, 19___.

_____
Secretary of State

FORM 13A

ARTICLES OF AMENDMENT
(PENNSYLVANIA)

APPLICANT'S ACC'T NO.

DSCB: BCL-806 (Rev. 8-72)

Filing Fee: $40
AB-2

**Articles of Amendment—
Domestic Business Corporation**

(Line for numbering)

COMMONWEALTH OF PENNSYLVANIA
DEPARTMENT OF STATE
CORPORATION BUREAU

Filed this _____ day of _____, 19___.
Commonwealth of Pennsylvania
Department of State

_____
Secretary of the Commonwealth

(Box for Certification)

In compliance with the requirements of section 806 of the Business Corporation Law, act of May 5, 1933 (P. L. 364) (15 P. S. §1806), the undersigned corporation, desiring to amend its Articles, does hereby certify that:

1. The name of the corporation is:
_____

2. The location of its registered office in this Commonwealth is (the Department of State is hereby authorized to correct the following statement to conform to the records of the Department):

_____ _____
(NUMBER)   (STREET)

_____ Pennsylvania _____
(CITY)   (ZIP CODE)

3. The statute by or under which it was incorporated is:
_____

4. The date of its incorporation is: _____

5. (Check, and if appropriate, complete one of the following):

☐ The meeting of the shareholders of the corporation at which the amendment was adopted was held at the time and place and pursuant to the kind and period of notice herein stated.

Time: The _____ day of _____, 19___.

Place: _____

Kind and period of notice _____
_____

☐ The amendment was adopted by a consent in writing, setting forth the action so taken, signed by all of the shareholders entitled to vote thereon and filed with the Secretary of the corporation.

6. At the time of the action of shareholders:

(a) The total number of shares outstanding was:
_____

(b) The number of shares entitled to vote was:
_____

DSCB:BCL—806 (Rev. 8-72)-2

7. In the action taken by the shareholders:

   (a) The number of shares voted in favor of the amendment was:

_____

   (b) The number of shares voted against the amendment was:

_____

8. The amendment adopted by the shareholders, set forth in full, is as follows:

      IN TESTIMONY WHEREOF, the undersigned corporation has caused these Articles of Amendment to be signed by a duly authorized officer and its corporate seal, duly attested by another such officer, to be hereunto affixed this _____ day of _____, 19____.

Attest:
                                                           (NAME OF CORPORATION)

_____ By: _____
      (SIGNATURE)   (SIGNATURE)

(TITLE SECRETARY, ASSISTANT SECRETARY, ETC.)   (TITLE PRESIDENT, VICE PRESIDENT, ETC.)

(CORPORATE SEAL)

INSTRUCTIONS FOR COMPLETION OF FORM

    A. Any necessary copies of Form DSCB:17.2 (Consent to Appropriation of Name) or Form DSCB:17.3 (Consent to Use of Similar Name) shall accompany Articles of Amendment effecting a change of name.

    B. Any necessary governmental approvals shall accompany this form.

    C. Where action is taken by partial written consent pursuant to the Articles, the second alternate of Paragraph 5 should be modified accordingly.

    D. If the shares of any class were entitled to vote as a class, the number of shares of each class so entitled and the number of shares of all other classes entitled to vote should be set forth in Paragraph 6(b).

    E. If the shares of any class were entitled to vote as a class, the number of shares of such class and the number of shares of all other classes voted for and against such amendment respectively should be set forth in Paragraphs 7(a) and 7(b).

    F. BCL §807 (15 P. S. §1807) requires that the corporation shall advertise its intention to file or the filing of Articles of Amendment. Proofs of publication of such advertising should not be delivered to the Department, but should be filed with the minutes of the corporation.

FORM 13B
CERTIFICATE OF AMENDMENT
(NORTH DAKOTA)

Certificate No._____

State of North Dakota

CERTIFICATE OF AMENDMENT

OF

_____

The undersigned, as Secretary of State of the State of North Dakota, hereby certifies that duplicate originals of Articles of Amendment to the Articles of Incorporation of _____

duly signed and verified pursuant to the provisions of the North Dakota _____ Corporation Act have been received in this office and are found to conform to law.

ACCORDINGLY the undersigned, as such Secretary of State, and by virtue of the authority vested in him by law, hereby issues this Certificate of Amendment to the Articles of Incorporation of _____
_____
_____

and attaches hereto a duplicate original of the Articles of Amendment.

IN TESTIMONY WHEREOF, I have hereunto set my hand and affixed the Great Seal of the State at the Capitol in the City of Bismarck, this _____ day of _____ A.D., 19___.

_____
Secretary of State.

File No._____
ORIGINAL

By _____, Deputy.

"Buy North Dakota Products"

FORM 13C

RESTATED ARTICLES OF INCORPORATION (NEW JERSEY)

Form C-100a 1-1-69

RESTATED CERTIFICATE OF INCORPORATION

OF

_____

To: The Secretary of State

State of New Jersey

Pursuant to the provisions of Section 14A:9-5, Corporations, General, of the New Jersey Statutes, the undersigned corporation hereby executes the following Restated Certificate of Incorporation:

FIRST: The name of the corporation is ....

SECOND: The purpose or purposes for which the corporation is organized are:

(Use the following if the shares are to consist of one class only.)

THIRD: The aggregate number of shares which the corporation shall have authority to issue is .... of the par value of .... Dollars ($............) each (or without par value.)

(Use the following if the shares are divided into classes, or into classes and series.)

FOURTH: The aggregate number of shares which the corporation shall have authority to issue is ...., itemized by classes, par value of shares, shares without par value, and series, if any, within a class, is:

Class	Series (if any)	Number of Shares	Par value per share or statement that shares are without par value

The relative rights, preferences and limitations of the shares of each class and series (if any), are as follows:

(If, the shares are, or are to be divided into classes, or into classes and series, insert a statement of any authority vested in the board of directors to divide the shares into classes or series, or both, and to determine or change for any class or series its designation, number or shares, relative rights, preferences and limitations.)

FIFTH: The address* of the corporation's current registered office is: ....
(*Include zip code)

................................, and the name of its current registered agent at such address is:

....

SIXTH: The number of directors constituting the current board of directors is ....

The names and addresses of the directors are as follows:

Names	Addresses (including zip code)
....	....
....	....
....	....
....	....

SEVENTH: The duration of the corporation, if other than perpetual, is ....

(Use the following only if an effective date, not later than 30 days subsequent to the date of filing is desired.)

EIGHTH: The effective date of this Certificate shall be ....

Dated this .... day of ...., 19......

....
(Corporate Name)

By ....*

....
(Type or Print Name and Title)

(*May be executed by the chairman of the board, *or* the president, *or* a vice-president.)

CERTIFICATE REQUIRED TO BE FILED WITH THE
RESTATED CERTIFICATE OF INCORPORATION
OF

_____

Pursuant to the provisions of Section 14A:9-5 (5), Corporations, General, of the New Jersey Statutes, the undersigned corporation hereby executes the following certificate:

FIRST: The name of the corporation is ....

SECOND: The Restated Certificate of Incorporation was adopted on the .... day of ...., 19......

(Use the following clause if the Restated Certificate was adopted by the shareholders.)

THIRD: At the time of the adoption of the Restated Certificate of Incorporation, the number of shares outstanding was .... The total of such shares entitled to vote thereon, and the vote of such shares was:

Total Number of Shares Entitled to Vote	Number of Shares Voted
	For Against

At the time of the adoption of the Restated Certificate of Incorporation, the number of outstanding shares of each class or series entitled to vote thereon as a class and the vote of such shares, was: (if inapplicable, insert "none".)

Class or Series	Number of Shares Entitled to Vote	Number of Shares Voted
		For Against

(Use the following if the Restated Certificate does not amend the Certificate of Incorporation.)

FOURTH: This Restated Certificate of Incorporation only restates and integrates and does not further amend the provisions of the Certificate of Incorporation of this corporation as heretofore amended or supplemented and there is no discrepancy between those provisions and the provisions of this Restated Certificate of Incorporation.

(Use the following if the Restated Certificate further amends the Certificate of Incorporation.)

FIFTH: This Restated Certificate of Incorporation restates and integrates and further amends the Certificate of Incorporation of this corporation by: *

(*Insert amendment or amendments adopted. If such amendment is intended to provide for an exchange, reclassification or cancellation of issued shares, insert a statement of the manner in which the same shall be effected.)

(Use the following only if an effective date, not later than 30 days subsequent to the date of filing is is desired.)

SIXTH: The effective date of this amendment shall be ....

Dated this .... day of ...., 19......

....
(Corporate Name)

By ....*

....
(Type or Print Name and Title)

(*May be executed by the chairman of the board, _or_ the president, _or_ a vice-president.)

FORM 13D
CERTIFICATE OF RESTATED ARTICLES OF INCORPORATION
(NORTH DAKOTA)

No. _____

Certificate No: _____

State of North Dakota

RESTATED CERTIFICATE OF INCORPORATION

OF

_____

The undersigned, as Secretary of State of the State of North Dakota, hereby certifies that duplicate originals of Restated Articles of Incorporation of

_____

duly signed and verified pursuant to the provisions of the North Dakota _____ _____ Act, have been received in this office and are found to conform to law.

ACCORDINGLY the undersigned, as such Secretary of State and by virtue of the authority vested in him by law hereby issues this Restated Certificate of Incorporation to

_____

and attaches hereto a duplicate original of the Restated Articles of Incorporation.

IN TESTIMONY WHEREOF, I have hereunto set my hand and affixed the Great Seal of the State at the Capitol in the City of Bismarck, this _____ day of _____ A.D., 19____

_____
Secretary of State

By _____
Deputy

File No. _____

"Buy North Dakota Products"

APPENDIX G

FORM 13E

ARTICLES OF MERGER
(PENNSYLVANIA)

APPLICANT'S ACC'T NO.

DSCB:BCL—903 (Rev. 8-72)

Filing Fee: $80 plus $20 for each party corporation in excess of two
AM8-0

Articles of Merger—
Business Corporation

(Line for numbering)

COMMONWEALTH OF PENNSYLVANIA
DEPARTMENT OF STATE
CORPORATION BUREAU

Filed this _____ day of _____
_____, 19___.
Commonwealth of Pennsylvania
Department of State

Secretary of the Commonwealth

(Box for Certification)

In compliance with the requirements of section 903 of the Business Corporation Law, act of May 5, 1933 (P. L. 364) (15 P. S. §1903), the undersigned corporations, desiring to effect a merger, hereby certify that:

1. The name of the corporation surviving the merger is:

_____

2. (Check and complete one of the following):

☐ The surviving corporation is a domestic corporation and the location of its registered office in this Commonwealth is (the Department of State is hereby authorized to correct the following statement to conform to the records of the Department):

_____   _____
(NUMBER)   (STREET)

_____   Pennsylvania   _____
(CITY)   (ZIP CODE)

☐ The surviving corporation is a foreign corporation incorporated under the laws of _____
(NAME OF JURISDICTION)
_____ and the location of its office registered with such domiciliary jurisdiction is:

_____   _____
(NUMBER)   (STREET)

_____   _____   _____
(CITY)   (STATE)   (ZIP CODE)

3. The name and the location of the registered office of each other domestic business corporation and qualified foreign business corporation which is a party to the plan of merger are as follows:

M. BURR KEIM COMPANY, PHILADELPHIA

Page 1 of 4 pages

DSCB:BCL—903 (Rev. 8-72)-2

4. (Check, and if appropriate, complete one of the following):

☐ The plan of merger shall be effective upon filing these Articles of Merger in the Department of State.

☐ The plan of merger shall be effective on _____ at _____
  (DATE)   (HOUR)

5. The manner in which the plan of merger was adopted by each domestic corporation is as follows:

NAME OF CORPORATION	MANNER OF ADOPTION

6. (Strike out this paragraph if no foreign corporation is party to the merger.) The plan was authorized, adopted or approved, as the case may be, by the foreign corporation (or each of the foreign corporations) in accordance with the laws of the jurisdiction in which it was formed.

7. The plan of merger is set forth in Exhibit A, attached hereto and made a part hereof.

8. (Strike out this paragraph if the surviving corporation is a domestic corporation.) The Secretary of the Commonwealth and his successor in office is hereby designated as the true and lawful attorney of the surviving corporation upon whom may be served all lawful process in any action or proceeding against it for enforcement against it of any obligation of any constituent domestic corporation or any obligation arising from the merger proceedings or any action or proceeding to determine and enforce the rights of any shareholder under the provisions of section 908 of the Business Corporation Law. The surviving corporation hereby agrees that the service of process upon the Secretary of the Commonwealth shall be of the same legal force and validity as if served on the corporation and that the authority for such service of process shall continue in force as long as any of the aforesaid obligations and rights remain outstanding in this Commonwealth.

APPENDIX G

DSCB:BCL—903 (Rev. 8-72)-3

IN TESTIMONY WHEREOF, each undersigned corporation has caused these Articles of Merger to be signed by a duly authorized officer and its corporate seal, duly attested by another such officer, to be hereunto affixed this _____ day of _____, 19____.

_____
(NAME OF CORPORATION)

By: _____
(SIGNATURE)

_____
(TITLE: PRESIDENT, VICE PRESIDENT, ETC.)

Attest:

_____
(SIGNATURE)

_____
(TITLE: SECRETARY, ASSISTANT SECRETARY, ETC.)

(CORPORATE SEAL)

_____
(NAME OF CORPORATION)

By: _____
(SIGNATURE)

_____
(TITLE: PRESIDENT, VICE PRESIDENT, ETC.)

Attest:

_____
(SIGNATURE)

_____
(TITLE: SECRETARY, ASSISTANT SECRETARY, ETC.)

(CORPORATE SEAL)

DSCB:BCL—903 (Rev. 8-72)-4

INSTRUCTIONS FOR COMPLETION OF FORM:

A. If a new corporation results from the transaction the form should be rewritten as Articles of Consolidation and modified accordingly.

B. A foreign business corporation may be a party to a merger notwithstanding the fact that it has not received a certificate of authority to do business in Pennsylvania. However, if the surviving corporation is a foreign corporation which is not the holder of a Certificate of Authority under the Business Corporation Law on the effective date of the merger, there must be submitted with this form tax clearance certificates from the Department of Revenue and the Bureau of Employment Security of the Department of Labor and Industry with respect to each domestic corporation and qualified foreign corporation evidencing payment of all taxes and charges payable to the Commonwealth.

C. Any necessary copies of Form DSCB: 17.2 (Consent to Appropriation of Name) or Form DSCB: 17.3 (Consent to Use of Similar Name) shall accompany Articles of Merger effecting a change of name.

D. Any necessary governmental approvals shall accompany this form.

E. One of the following statements or the equivalent should be used in the second column of Paragraph 5 to set forth the manner of adoption:

"Adopted by action of the board of directors pursuant to section 902.1 of the Business Corporation Law."

"Approved by the affirmative vote of the shareholders entitled to vote thereon at a meeting called after at least ten days written notice to all shareholders of record, whether or not entitled to vote thereon, setting forth such purpose."

"Approved by a consent or consents in writing, setting forth the action so taken, signed by all of the shareholders entitled to vote thereon, and filed with the secretary of the corporation" (where action is taken by partial written consent pursuant to the Articles, this paragraph should be modified accordingly).

F. Where more than two corporations are parties to the merger appropriate additional corporate signatures should be added. All parties to the merger shall execute the Articles of Merger, including a nonqualified corporation which is not a surviving corporation and which is not otherwise mentioned in the body of the Articles of Merger.

FORM 13F
CERTIFICATE OF MERGER
(PENNSYLVANIA)

DSCB-56 B

Commonwealth of Pennsylvania
Department of State

TO ALL TO WHOM THESE PRESENTS SHALL COME, GREETING:

WHEREAS, Under the terms of the Business Corporation Law, approved May 5, 1933, P. L. 364, as amended, the Department of State is authorized and required to issue a

CERTIFICATE OF MERGER

evidencing the merger of one or more corporations into one of such corporations under the provisions of that law:

AND WHEREAS, The stipulations and conditions of that law relating to the merger of such corporations have been fully complied with by

THEREFORE, KNOW YE, That subject to the Constitution of this Commonwealth, and under the authority of the Business Corporation Law, approved May 5, 1933, P. L. 364, as amended, I DO BY THESE PRESENTS, which I have caused to be sealed with the Great Seal of the Commonwealth, merge the above named

which shall continue to be invested with and have and enjoy all the powers, privileges and franchises incident to a domestic business corporation, and be subject to all the duties, requirements and restrictions specified and enjoined in and by the Business Corporation Law and all other applicable laws of this Commonwealth.

GIVEN under my Hand and the Great Seal of the Commonwealth, at the City of Harrisburg, this   day of
in the year of our Lord one thousand nine hundred and
and of the Commonwealth the one hundred and

_____
Secretary of the Commonwealth

FORM 13G

ARTICLES OF CONSOLIDATION

Filing fee: $ _____

ARTICLES OF CONSOLIDATION OF DOMESTIC CORPORATIONS INTO

_____

Pursuant to the provisions of Section 74 of the _____ Business Corporation Act, the undersigned corporations adopt the following Articles of Consolidation for the purpose of consolidating them into a new corporation:

FIRST: The following Plan of Consolidation was approved by the shareholders of each of the undersigned corporations in the manner prescribed by the _____ Business Corporation Act:

(Insert Plan of Consolidation)

SECOND: As to each of the undersigned corporations, the number of shares outstanding, and the designation and number of outstanding shares of each class entitled to vote as a class on such Plan, are as follows:

Name of Corporation	Number of Shares Outstanding	Entitled to Vote as a Class	
		Designation of Class	Number of Shares

THIRD: As to each of the undersigned corporations, the total number of shares voted for and against such Plan, respectively, and, as to each class entitled to vote thereon as a class, the number of shares of such class voted for and against such Plan, respectively, are as follows:

Name of Corporation	Number of Shares			
	Total Voted For	Total Voted Against	Entitled to Vote as a Class		
			Class	Voted For	Voted Against

Dated _____, 19___

_____ (Note 1)

By _____
    Its _____ President
and _____   } (Note 2)
    Its _____ Secretary

_____ (Note 1)

By _____
    Its _____ President
and _____   } (Note 2)
    Its _____ Secretary

(Add Verification Form A for each corporation)

Notes: 1. Exact corporate names of respective corporations executing the Articles.
2. Signatures and titles of officers signing for the respective corporations.

FORM 13H

CERTIFICATE OF CONSOLIDATION

STATE OF _____
OFFICE OF THE SECRETARY OF STATE

**CERTIFICATE OF CONSOLIDATION
OF DOMESTIC CORPORATIONS
INTO**

_____

The undersigned, as Secretary of State of the State of _____, hereby certifies that duplicate originals of Articles of Consolidation of _____ _____ and _____ _____, domestic corporations, into _____, duly signed and verified pursuant to the provisions of the _____ Business Corporation Act, have been received in this office and are found to conform to law.

ACCORDINGLY the undersigned, as such Secretary of State, and by virtue of the authority vested in him by law, hereby issues

this Certificate of Consolidation of _____
_____ and _____
into _____,
and attaches hereto a duplicate original of the Articles of Consolidation.

Dated _____, 19__.

_____
Secretary of State

FORM 13I

ARTICLES OF MERGER FOR A SHORT MERGER

Filing Fee: $_____

**ARTICLES OF MERGER
OF DOMESTIC SUBSIDIARY CORPORATION
INTO
DOMESTIC PARENT CORPORATION**

Pursuant to the provisions of Section 75 of the _____ Business Corporation Act, the undersigned corporation adopts the following Articles of Merger for the purpose of merging a subsidiary corporation into the undersigned as the surviving corporation:

FIRST: The following Plan of Merger was approved by the Board of Directors of the undersigned, as the surviving corporation, in the manner prescribed by the _____ Business Corporation Act:

(Insert Plan of Merger)

SECOND: The number of outstanding shares of each class of the subsidiary corporation and the number of such shares of each class owned by the surviving corporation are as follows:

Name of Subsidiary	Number of Shares Outstanding	Designation of Class	Number of Shares Owned by Surviving Corporation

THIRD: A copy of the Plan of Merger set forth in Article First was mailed on _____ to each shareholder of the subsidiary corporation of record on _____ (Note 1).

Dated: _____, 19___.

_____ (Note 2)

By _____
    Its _____ President
and _____
    Its _____ Secretary
} (Note 3)

(Add Verification Form A)

Notes: 1. Insert date plan mailed to each shareholder of subsidiary and record date for mailing. If all shareholders waived such mailing, insert statement to this effect and date of waiver.
2. Exact name of parent corporation executing Articles.
3. Signatures and titles of officers signing for the corporation.

FORM 13J

NOTICE TO CREDITORS—BULK TRANSFER ACT (COLORADO)

No. 577A. Rev. '67.—Bradford Publishing Company, 1824-46 Stout Street, Denver, Colorado—7-73

NOTICE OF BULK TRANSFER
(Section 155-6-107 Colorado Revised Statutes 1963)
(UCC—Bulk Transfers)

Notice is given that a Bulk Transfer is about to be made from the transferor to the transferee named below.

The name of the transferee is:

The business address of the transferee is:

The name of the transferor is:

The business address of the transferor is:

All other business names and addresses used by the transferor within three (3) years last past so far as known to the transferee are:

*All debts of the transferor are to be paid in full as they fall due as a result of the transaction. The address to which creditors should send their bills is:

*The debts of the transferor are not to be paid in full as they fall due or the transferee is in doubt on that point.

The property to be transferred is located at and consists of

The estimated total of the transferor's debts is $

The address where the schedule of property and list of creditors (Section 155-6-104 C.R.S. 1963) may be inspected is:

**The transfer is to pay existing debts and the amount of such debts and to whom owing are as follows:

Name	Amount
....	....
....	....
....	....

**The transfer is not to pay existing debts.

‡The transfer is for new consideration in the amount of $

The time of payment is:

The place of payment is:

Signed by:

....
Transferee

....

* Strike one or the other according to fact.
** Strike one or the other according to fact.
‡ If there is no new consideration, state 'none'.

FORM 13K

AFFIDAVIT OF SELLER—BULK TRANSFER ACT (COLORADO)

No. 577. Rev. '66. Bradford Publishing Company, 1824-46 Stout Street, Denver, Colorado—6-73

STATE OF COLORADO
_____ County of _____ } ss.

AFFIDAVIT UNDER
155-6-104 C.R.S. 1963
(UCC—Bulk Transfers)

_____, Transferor, makes this affidavit pursuant to Section 155-6-104 Colorado Revised Statutes 1963 in connection with proposed transfer in bulk and being first duly sworn according to law on oath deposes and says:

Exhibit A, annexed to and by reference made a part of this affidavit is a full, accurate and complete list of the names and addresses of all existing creditors of transferor with the amounts when known and also the names of all persons known to the transferor to assert claims against the transferor which are disputed by transferor.

_____
Transferor

Subscribed and sworn to before me this _____ day of _____, 19____

My commission expires

Witness my hand and official seal.

_____
Notary Public

FORM 13L

STATEMENT OF INTENT TO DISSOLVE (SHAREHOLDERS)

Filing Fee $_____

STATEMENT OF INTENT TO DISSOLVE

BY WRITTEN CONSENT OF SHAREHOLDERS

To the Secretary of State
of the State of _____:

Pursuant to the provisions of Section 83 of the _____ Business Corporation Act, the undersigned corporation submits the following statement of intent to dissolve the corporation upon written consent of all of its shareholders:

FIRST: The name of the corporation is _____

SECOND: The names and respective addresses of its officers are:

Name	Office	Address
_____	_____	_____
_____	_____	_____
_____	_____	_____
_____	_____	_____

THIRD: The names and respective addresses of its directors are:

Name	Address
_____	_____
_____	_____
_____	_____

FOURTH: The following written consent to dissolution of the corporation has been signed by all of the shareholders of the corporation, or signed in their names by their respective attorneys thereunto duly authorized:

(Insert copy of Consent)

Dated _____, 19___.

_____ (Note 1)

By _____
   Its _____ President
and _____ } (Note 2)
   Its _____ Secretary

(Add Verification Form A)

Notes: 1. Exact corporate name of corporation making the statement.
        2. Signatures and titles of officers signing for the corporation.

FORM 13M

STATEMENT OF INTENT TO DISSOLVE (CORPORATION)

Filing fee: $_____

STATEMENT OF INTENT TO DISSOLVE
_____

BY ACT OF THE CORPORATION

To the Secretary of State
   of the State of _____:

Pursuant to the provisions of Section 84 of the _____ Business Corporation Act, the undersigned corporation submits the following statement of intent to dissolve the corporation by act of the corporation.

FIRST: The name of the corporation is _____
_____

SECOND: The names and respective addresses of its officers are:

Name	Office	Address
_____	_____	_____
_____	_____	_____
_____	_____	_____
_____	_____	_____

THIRD: The names and respective addresses of its directors are:

Name	Address
_____	_____
_____	_____
_____	_____

FOURTH: The following resolution to dissolve the corporation was adopted by the shareholders of the corporation on _____, 19__:

(Insert copy of Resolution)

FIFTH: The number of shares of the corporation outstanding at the time of such adoption was _____; and the number of shares entitled to vote thereon was:

Class	Number of Shares

(Note 1)

SIXTH: The number of shares voted for such resolution was _____; and the number of shares voted against such resolution was _____.

SEVENTH: The number of shares of each class entitled to vote thereon as a class voted for and against such resolution, respectively, was:

	Number of Shares Voted	
Class	For	Against

(Note 1)

Dated _____, 19__.

_____ (Note 2)

By _____
   Its _____ President
and _____
   Its _____ Secretary
} (Note 3)

(Add Verification Form A)

Notes: 1. If inapplicable, insert "None."
2. Exact corporate name of corporation making the statement.
3. Signatures and titles of officers signing for the corporation.

FORM 13N

STATEMENT OF REVOCATION OF VOLUNTARY DISSOLUTION PROCEEDINGS (SHAREHOLDERS)

Filing fee: $ _____

STATEMENT OF REVOCATION
OF
VOLUNTARY DISSOLUTION PROCEEDINGS
OF

_____

BY WRITTEN CONSENT OF THE SHAREHOLDERS

To the Secretary of State
   of the State of _____:

Pursuant to the provisions of Section 88 of the _____ Business Corporation Act, the undersigned corporation submits the following statement of revocation of voluntary dissolution proceedings heretofore taken upon the written consent of all of its shareholders:

FIRST: The name of the corporation is _____
_____

SECOND: The names and respective addresses of its officers are:

Name	Office	Address

THIRD: The names and respective addresses of its directors are:

Name	Address

FOURTH: The following written consent signed by all the shareholders of the corporation revoking its voluntary dissolution proceedings has been signed by all of the shareholders of the corporation, or signed in their names by their respective attorneys thereunto duly authorized:

(Insert copy of Consent)

Dated _____, 19___

_____ (Note 1)

By _____
    Its _____ President
and _____
    Its _____ Secretary ⎱ (Note 2)

(Add Verification Form A)

Notes: 1. Exact corporate name of corporation making the statement.
       2. Signatures and titles of officers signing for the corporation.

FORM 130

STATEMENT OF REVOCATION OF VOLUNTARY DISSOLUTION PROCEEDINGS (CORPORATION)

Filing fee: $_____

**STATEMENT OF REVOCATION
OF
VOLUNTARY DISSOLUTION PROCEEDINGS
OF**

_____

BY ACT OF THE CORPORATION

To the Secretary of State
  of the State of _____:

Pursuant to the provisions of Section 89 of the _____ Business Corporation Act, the undersigned corporation submits the following statement of revocation of voluntary dissolution proceedings heretofore taken by act of the corporation:

FIRST: The name of the corporation is _____

SECOND: The names and respective addresses of its officers are:

Name	Office	Address

THIRD: The names and respective addresses of its directors are:

Name	Address

FOURTH: The resolution adopted by the shareholders of the corporation revoking its voluntary dissolution proceedings is as follows:

(Insert copy of Resolution)

FIFTH: The number of shares of the corporation outstanding at the time of such adoption was _____

SIXTH: The number of shares voted for such resolution was _____; and the number of shares voted against such resolution was _____.

Dated _____, 19___.

_____ (Note 1)

By _____
    Its _____ President
and _____
    Its _____ Secretary
} (Note 2)

(Add Verification Form A)

Notes: 1. Exact corporate name of corporation making the statement.
        2. Signatures and titles of officers signing for the corporation.

FORM 13P

ARTICLES OF DISSOLUTION BY INCORPORATORS

Filing fee: $_____

**ARTICLES OF DISSOLUTION
BY INCORPORATOR(S)
OF**

_____

Pursuant to the provisions of Section 82 of the _____ Business Corporation Act, the undersigned of the corporation hereinafter named, adopt the following Articles of Dissolution:

FIRST: The name of the corporation is _____

SECOND: The date of issuance of its certificate of incorporation was _____

THIRD: None of its shares has been issued.

FOURTH: The corporation has not commenced business.

FIFTH: The amount, if any, actually paid in on subscriptions for its shares, less any part thereof disposed of for necessary expenses, has been returned to those entitled thereto.

SIXTH: No debts of the corporation remain unpaid.

SEVENTH: The sole incorporator or a majority of the incorporators elects that the corporation be dissolved.

Dated _____, 19___.

_____
_____
_____
Incorporator(s) (Note 1)

(Add Verification Form B)

Note: 1. The sole incorporator or, if more than one, a majority, must execute and verify these Articles.

FORM 13Q
ARTICLES OF DISSOLUTION
(MASSACHUSETTS)

Form CD-100. 10M-4-71-049198

The Commonwealth of Massachusetts

JOHN F. X. DAVOREN
Secretary of the Commonwealth
STATE HOUSE, BOSTON, MASS.

ARTICLES OF DISSOLUTION

General Laws, Chapter 156B, Section 100

The fee for filing articles of dissolution is $25.00. Make checks payable to the Commonwealth of Massachusetts

---

We, ..., President/Vice President, and

...., Clerk/Assistant Clerk of

....
(Name of Corporation)

located at ....

do hereby certify as follows:-

1. The name of the corporation and the post office address of its principal office in the Commonwealth are as set forth above.

2. The names and post office addresses of each of the directors and officers of the corporation are as follows:

Name	Post Office Address	Title

3. On ...., 19......, the dissolution of the corporation was duly authorized in the manner required by Section 100 of Chapter 156B of the General Laws, and notice of the proposed dissolution was duly given in the manner required by said Section.

4. The effective date of the dissolution is (1) the date of filing these articles; or (2) _____, 19___ [Strike out subparagraph (1) if a specific date is desired.]

*5. Other provisions deemed necessary by the corporation for its dissolution.

IN WITNESS WHEREOF AND UNDER THE PENALTIES OF PERJURY, we have hereto signed our names this _____ day of _____, 19___

.... President/Vice President

.... Clerk/Assistant Clerk

*If there are no such provisions, state "None". Provisions for which the space provided above is not sufficient should be set out on continuation sheets to be numbered 2A, 2B, etc. Continuation sheets shall be on 8½" wide x 11" high paper and must have a left-hand margin of 1 inch for binding. Only one side should be used.

NOTE: These articles of dissolution must be accompanied by a certificate of the Commissioner of Corporations and Taxation that all taxes due and payable by the corporation to the Commonwealth have been paid or provided for. COPIES OF NEWSPAPER PUBLICATIONS MUST ALSO ACCOMPANY THIS CERTIFICATE.

APPENDIX G

THE COMMONWEALTH OF MASSACHUSETTS

ARTICLES OF DISSOLUTION

(General Laws, Chapter 156B, Section 100)

I hereby aprove the within articles of dissolution and, the filing fee in the amount of $

having been paid, said articles are deemed to have been filed with me this

day of   , 19

John F. X. Davoren

JOHN F. X. DAVOREN

Secretary of the Commonwealth
State House, Boston, Mass.

TO BE FILLED IN BY CORPORATION

PHOTO COPY OF ARTICLES OF DISSOLUTION TO BE SENT

TO:

....

....

....

Copy Mailed

FORM 13R

CERTIFICATE OF DISSOLUTION BY INCORPORATORS

STATE OF ―――――――
OFFICE OF THE SECRETARY OF STATE

**CERTIFICATE OF DISSOLUTION
BY INCORPORATOR(S)
OF**

―――――――――――――――――

The undersigned, as Secretary of State of the State of ――――― ―――――, hereby certifies that duplicate originals of Articles of Dissolution by the Incorporator(s) of ――――――――――― ―――――――――――――――, duly signed and verified pursuant to the provisions of the .... Business Corporation Act, have been received in this office and are found to conform to law.

ACCORDINGLY, the undersigned, as such Secretary of State, and by virtue of the authority vested in him by law hereby issues this Certificate of Dissolution of ――――――――― ―――――――――――――, and attaches hereto a duplicate original of the Articles of Dissolution.

Dated ――――――――, 19――.

―――――――――――――――
Secretary of State

FORM 13S
CERTIFICATE OF DISSOLUTION
(TEXAS)

In the name and by the authority of
The State of Texas

OFFICE OF THE SECRETARY OF STATE

CERTIFICATE OF DISSOLUTION

OF

....

The undersigned, as Secretary of State of the State of Texas, hereby certifies that duplicate originals of Articles of Dissolution of the above Corporation, duly signed and verified pursuant to the provisions of the Texas Business Corporation Act, have been received in this office and are found to conform to law.

ACCORDINGLY the undersigned, as such Secretary of State, and by virtue of the authority vested in him by law, hereby issues this **Certificate of Dissolution** and attaches hereto a duplicate original of the Articles of Dissolution.

Dated.., 19..........

Mark W. White Jr.
Secretary of State

INDEX

Accumulated Earnings Tax
See Taxation, Corporations

Affidavit
Corporations,
  Assumed name, 116
  Minimum paid-in capital, 134
Trade name, 4, 463–464, 469

Agents
Generally, 247
Authority,
    Generally, 251–252
  Actual, 251
  Apparent, 251
  Ratification, 251
Care, duty of, 250
Corporate, 253–254
Detour, 253
Duties of, 250
Frolic, 253
Loyalty, duty of, 250
Partners, 5, 10
Scope of employment, 252
Sole Proprietorship, 2
Torts by, 252–253
Types,
  Generally, 248–250
  General Agent, 248
  Independent contractor, 249
  Servant, 249
  Special agent, 249
  Subagent, 249

Agreements
Corporations,
  Authority for executing, 146
  Closed corporations, 98
  Dissolution of, 101
  Distributions from, 101
  Promoter's liability, 109
  Share subscriptions, 110–112
  Shareholder management, 100
Employment agreements, see Employment Agreements
Limited partnership, 55–58
Non-disclosure, 609
Partnership,
  Generally, 7, 24–43
  Accounting methods, 30
  Advances, 27
  Assumptions of debts, 19
  Audit, 31
  Authority, limitations, 11, 35–36
  Bank accounts, 31
  Bankruptcy of partner, 39
  Capital gains and losses, 22
  Competition, 20
  Continuation of business, 20, 41
  Contributions of profits, 27
  Contributions, 26
  Death of partner, 39–40
  Depreciation, 14, 22
  Disputes, 35
  Dissolution, 16–20, 37–41
  Duration, 25
  Duties, 12–33
  Equal vote of partners, 10
  Expense accounts, 12, 28
  Expulsion, 38
  Fiscal year, 30
  Interest on contributions, 27
  Limitations on authority, 11
  Liquidation, 20, 42
  Meetings, 32
  Name, 24
  Notice of dissolution, 20
  Place of business, 25
  Profits and losses, 6, 12–15, 27, 28, 29
  Prohibited activities, 35–36

Property, 7
Property contribution, 7
Property owned by partner, 37
Purchase of interest, 42
Purposes, 25
Recitals, 24
Reports to partners, 31
Restriction on partners, 35–36
Restriction on purposes, 25
Salaries, 12, 28
Title to property, 6, 37
Valuing interest, 41–42
Withdrawal of contributions, 27
Preincorporation, 109, 199
Promoters, 109, 533–535
Shareholder,
    Generally, 100–101
  Buy out,
      Generally, 303–325
    Death, 309
    Funding, 322–325
    Price, 312–319
    Purpose of, 304–305
    Restrictions on transfer distinguished, 307
    Security for payment, 320
    Terms of payment, 320
  Concentration of voting power, 299–303
  Director representation, 303
  Organizing close corporation, 100–101, 513–516
  Pooling,
    Generally, 215, 301–303
    Arbitration, 302
    Deadlock, 302
    Duration, 302
    Enforcement of, 301
    Restriction on transfer, 301
    Statutory regulation, 301
  Restrictions on transfer,
    Generally, 304–308
    Price provisions, 312–319
    Security for payment, 321–322
    Terms of payment, 320
  Sell out,
    Generally, 303–325
    Employment termination, 311
    Price, 312–319
    Security for payment, 321–322
    Terms of payment, 320
  Statutory authority for, 298, 299
  Voting trust,
    Generally, 300–301
    Authority of trustee, 300–301
    Contents, 300
    Duration, 300
    Form, 610–615
    Statutory authority, 300
    Voting trust certificates, 300

Annual Reports
Contents of, 337
Domestic corporation, 337
Foreign corporations, 337

Arbitration
Partnerships, 35
Shareholder buy-out agreements, 319
Stock Voting Agreement, 302

Articles of Agreement
See Articles of Incorporation

Articles of Amendment
  See also Articles of Incorporation
  Generally, 345

Articles of Association
See Articles of Incorporation

See Articles of Consolidation
  See also Consolidation
Form, 639–640

Articles of Dissolution
  See also Dissolution
  Generally, 363

Articles of Incorporation
  Generally, 116–134
Action without meeting, 131, 223–225
Amendment,
    Generally, 70–71, 116, 342–346
  Adoption of, 343
  Articles of amendment, 345, 626–627
  Certificates of, form, 628
  Class voting, 344
  Director action, 81, 343
  Foreign corporation, 337–338
  Increasing number of directors, 77
  Merger, 349
  Notice of, 344
  Power to amend, 343–346
  Prior to issuance of shares, 345
  Procedure, 344–345
  Share dividend, requirement for, 237
  Shareholder approval, 85, 221–222
  Shareholder's right to dissent, 357
  Stock split, 240
  Types of amendments, 344–345

INDEX 659

Voting by classes, 170, 345
Bonds, 183
By laws compared, 116, 131–132
Checklist for, 556–558
Close corporations, 98–101
Consideration of shares, 130
Consolidated corporation, 350
Content, 116–134
Conversion privilege, 174–175
Corporate powers, 70–74, 122
Corporate purposes, 122–123
Cumulative voting, 84, 124, 217–221
Delaware, form, 558–563
Directors,
    Classification of, 76, 133
    Compensation of, 133
    Conflict of interest, 79, 133
    Delegation of authority, 79–80
    Election of, 76
    Effect on power of, 78
    Indemnification of, 125, 130
    Interested, 79, 133
    Number of, 77
    Powers, 78
    Qualification of, 77, 125
    Restrictions on Authority, 76, 126
Dividends,
    Generally, 132, 167–168
    Depletion reserves, 235
    Preferences, 167–168
    Restrictions upon, 233–235
Duration, 121
Effect on statutory rules, 70
Filing, 134
Incorporators, 75, 117
Indemnification of personnel, 125–130
Initial directors, 76, 121
Liquidation,
    Distributions, 244–246
    Preferences, 168–169, 245
Medical corporation, form, 517–521
Name, 117
North Dakota, form, 564–566
Optional provisions, 124–134
Permissive provisions, 121–124, 124–134
Perpetual duration, effect on, 72, 121
Power to,
    Borrow, 71
    Conduct interstate business, 71, 72
    Deal in property, 72
    Donate, 73
    Engage in Transactions in Aid of Government Policy, 73
    Establish pension plans, 74
    Exist perpetually, 72, 121
    Lend money, 73
    Own property, 72
    Partnership, 73
Preemptive rights, 86, 123–124
Preferred stock, statements of variations, 166–174
Presentation at meeting, 192
Purchase of corporate shares, 129–130, 241–244
Qualifications of directors, 76–77, 133
Quorum and vote, 131
Redemption provisions, 171–174
Registered agent, 120
Registered office, 120
Regulation of internal affairs, 124
Restated,
    Generally, 345–346
    Certificate of, 633
    Form, 629–632
Restrictions on transfer of shares, 304
Share dividends, 237–239
Shareholder approval, 343
Shareholders,
    Approval of compensation, 80
    Authority to fix consideration for shares, 130, 156–157
    Control over, 221–222
    Election of officers, 80
    Management power, 76
    Removal of directors, 77
Shares,
    Generally, 118–120
    Authority to purchase, 123–124
    Classes, 118–119, 159–165
    Description of, 118–119
    Restrictions upon purchase, 129–130, 241–243
    Series, 161–163
    Special features, 120, 159–165
Signing, 134
Sinking fund, 172–174
Statutory requirements, 116–117
Stock rights and options, 130
Voting rights, 165–166, 169–171, 183, 215–216
Weighted voting, 215–216

Articles of Merger
See also Merger
Form, 634–637
Short form, 641–642

Assignment
Limited partnership, limited partner's interest, 50, 56, 497

Partnership,
    Interest in partnership, 9–10, 22, 471
    Property, 9
Share subscriptions, 110, 194
Stock options, 287

Assumed Name
    See also Trade Name
Abandonment of, California, 470
Affidavit, 463–464
Authority to use, 201
Business certificate, New York, 469
Corporations, 116, 465–466, 555
Foreign corporation, 333–334
Publication of, California, 467–468
Statement, California, 465–466

Bank Accounts
Corporations,
    Authority for, 147
    Resolution establishing, 199
Partnership, 31

Blue Sky Laws
    Generally, 154

Board of Directors
See Directors

Bonds
    Generally, 178–183
Articles of incorporation, 118
Conversion, generally, 182–183
Debenture
    Defined, 154
    Form, 178–179
Debt securities, generally, 154
Debt to equity ratio, 186
Discount, 154
Features, of, 181–183
Financing statement, form, 598
Forms, 579–592
Indenture,
    Defined, 154
    Form, Trust, 598–603
    Trust Indenture Act of 1939, 181
    Trustee for, 181
Mortgage Bonds, defined, 154
Premium, 154
Priority, 183
Provisions of, 177–180
Redemption,
    Generally, 181–182
    Discretion of directors, 181

Notice, 182
Price, 182
Secured,
    Generally, 180
    Agreement for, 180
    Collateral for, 180
    Financing statement, 180, 598
Security agreement, form, 596–597
Senior securities, 184–186
Subordination, 183
Taxation, 186
Thin incorporation, 186
Trust indenture, 181, 598–603
Voting rights, 154, 183

Books
See Records

Bulk Transfer
Affidavit, 356, 644
Notice to creditors, 643
Sale of corporate assets, 356
Schedule of property, 356

Business Purposes
    See also Corporate Purposes
Partnerships, 25

Buy Out Agreements
See Shareholders, Agreements between

By-Laws
Action without a meeting, 223–225
Adoption of, 80
Amendment,
    Generally, 80
    Procedure, 149
Annual meetings, 137
Approval, of, 193
Articles of incorporation compared, 116, 125, 136
Authority to adopt, 136
Certificates for shares, 147
Closing of transfer books, 138
Content, 137–149
Contracts, authority for executing, 147
Cumulative voting, 140
Delaware, form, 567–578
Directors,
    Generally, 140–143
    Classification of, 141
    Compensation, 142
    Conduct of meetings, 78
    Delegation of authority of, 79
    Informal action by, 142

Manner of acting, 142
Meetings, 141
Notice for meeting, 141
Number, 81, 141
Presumption of assent, 143
Qualifications, 141
Quorum, 142
Removal, 142
Vacancies, 142
Dividends, 148
Effect on statutory rules, 69–70
Emergency, 149
Executive committee,
   Action without a meeting, 144
   Appointment, 143
   Authority, 143
   Meetings, 143–144
   Procedure, 144
   Qualifications, 143
   Quorum, 144
   Removal, 144
   Vacancies, 144
Fiscal year, 148
Fixing of record date, 138
Form, 567–578
Informal action by shareholders, 140
Initial, 136–137
Meetings,
   Date of, 205
   Special, 137–138, 141
Notice of meeting, 138–141
Officers,
   Assistant secretary, 146
   Assistant treasurer, 146
   Election, 145
   Number, 144–145
   President, 146
   Removal, 145
   Responsibilities, 145–146
   Salary, 146
   Secretary, 146
   Term of office, 145
   Treasurer, 146
   Vacancies, 145
   Vice-president, 145–146
Offices, 137
Place of meeting, 137–138
Power to make, 70
Powers of directors, 140
Proxies, 139
Repeal of, 80–81
Restriction on transfer of shares, 304
Rules for internal management, 136
Seal, 149
Shareholder control of, 131–217
Shareholders,
   Generally, 130–217
   Election of officers, 80
   Quorum, 139
   Right to inspect books, 85
Shares, authority to transfer, 147–148
Transfer agent, 148
Transfer of shares, 148
Voting lists, 139
Voting of shares, 139–140

Capital
Certificate of paid-in, New Jersey, 536–537
Corporations,
   Generally, 153–155
   Affidavit of minimum paid-in capital, 134
   Debt and equity compared, 184–186
   Minimum paid-in, 110–112
   Partnerships, see Contributions and Partnership
   Share subscriptions, see Share Subscriptions
   Sole proprietorship,
     Generally, 2
     Dependent upon proprietor's resources, 2
     Limits, 2
     Personal loans, 2

Capital Surplus
Consideration for shares, effect on, 157–158
Defined, 234
Effect on shares, 119–120
Purchase of shares by corporation, 120, 241–244

Certificate
Bonds, 587–592
Limited partnership,
   Amendment of, 50, 63–64, 508
   Cancellation of, 64
   Content of, 46, 62–63
   Filing, 63
   Form, 503–506
   Maintenance of, 61–64
   Statement to continue business, 51
Of incorporation, see Articles of Incorporation
Paid-in capital, 536–537
Shares,
   Approval of, 193
   Form, 579–588
Voting trusts, 300

Certificate of Authority
   Generally, 335
   Amended,
     Generally, 337–339

Application for, 621–622
Form, 623
Application for,
    Generally, 331–335
    Articles of incorporation filed, 332
    Certificate of good standing, 332
    Contents, 331–333
    Form, 616–618
    Purpose of, 332
    Verified, 333
Denial of, 331
Revocation of, 340, 625
Withdrawal of, 339–340

Certificate of Dissolution
Effect of, 363–364
Issuance of, 363

Certificate of Incorporation
See also Articles of Incorporation
Close corporation, 99
Corporate existence commencing, 134
North Dakota, form, 566

Common Stock
See Shares

Compensation
    See also Incentive Compensation
        Plans; Pension Plans; Profit Sharing Plans; and
        Salary
Bonus, 258, 261
Commission,
    Generally, 258–261
    Date of payment, 259
    Drawing accounts, 259
    On sale, 259
    Termination during year, 260
Corporations,
    Directors, 80, 133–134, 142
    Officers, 80, 146
Deferred,
    Generally, 273–275
    Amount, 273–274
    Death of employee, 275
    Forfeiture, 275
    Incentive, 273–275
    Payment to spouse, 275
    Purpose of, 273–274
    Retirement, 275
    Tax advantages, 275
Directors, 80, 133–134, 142
Effect on performance, 257–258
Employee, generally, 257–262

Group incentive plans,
    Generally, 272–273
    Administration of, 272
    Committee, 272
    Content of, 272–273
    Modification of, 273
    Participants, 272–273
    Payment of, 273
    Purpose, 272–273
Incentive compensation plans, 257–258, 272–273

Certificate of Merger
See also Merger
Form, 638

Certificate of Withdrawal
Application for, form, 624
Form, 625

Classification of Directors
See Directors

Close Corporation
Generally, 98–102
Agreement between shareholders, 513–516
Defined, 99–100
Dissolution, 102
Fundamental changes, 101
Judicial supervision, 101–102
Liquidation, 102
Management of, 76, 100–101
Partnership compared, 98–99
Share provisions, 100
Shareholder agreements, generally, 297–304
Shareholder control, 100–101, 299
Pension plans, see Pension Plans
Piercing corporate veil, 102
Profit sharing plans, see Profit Sharing Plans
Purchase of shares, 100

Competition
    See also Agreements; Employees;
        Employment Agreements; and Forms
Employees, covenants prohibiting, 268–272

Consolidation
Generally, 346–351
"A" Reorganization, 347
Agreement for, 347–349
Approval of, 85, 222, 349
Articles of consolidation,
    Contents of, 350–351
    Effective date, 351
    Filing, 351

Form, 640–641
    Statutory effect of, 351
Certificate of, form, 640–641
Defined, 222, 346
Directors' duties, 78–79
Dissenting shareholders, 357–358
Effect of, 351
Foreign corporation, 338–339
Hostile, 351–354
Letter of intent, 348
Plan of consolidation, 348
Procedure for, 347–350
Resolution for adoption, 348–349
Shareholder approval, 85, 222, 349

Constituent Corporations
See Merger and Consolidation

Contracts
    See also Agreements
Corporations,
    Authority for executing, 147
    Power to enter into, 70–71

Contributions
Limited partnership,
    Generally, 48–49, 56–57
    Distribution and liquidation, 51, 53
    Limited partners, 48–49, 56–57
    Return of, 57
Partnership,
    Additional capital, 27
    Agreement, 26–27
    Depreciation, 22
    In liquidation, 21
    Interest on, 27
    Pre-contribution gain or loss, 21–22
    Profit, 28
    Property, 9, 26
    Services, 26
    Taxation of, 21–23
    Withdrawal, 27–28
Shareholders, 82

Control Statutes
Affiliated corporations, 353
Control Statutes, 358
Corporate, 353–354
Hostile takeovers, 351

Conversion
Bonds, generally, 182
Shares, generally, 174–175

Corporate Powers
    Generally, 70–74
Articles of incorporation, 122
Borrow money, 71
Business in aid of government, 73–74
Bylaws, 70
Contracts, 70
Corporate purposes distinguished, 72, 122–123
Determined by statute, 70–71
Donations, 70, 73
General powers, 70–71
Guaranties, 70
Implied, 122
Incentive compensation plans,
    to pay, 71
Indemnification, 125–129
Interstate business, 71–72
Litigation, 71
Loans, 71, 73
Partner, to be, 71, 73
Perpetual duration, 70, 72
Promoter, to be, 71
Property, to deal in, 71, 72–73
Restrictions upon, 71–72
Seal, maintenance of, 70
Shares, ownership of, 70

Corporate Purposes
"Any lawful activity", 122
Articles of incorporation, 117, 122–123
Drafting, 122–123
Effect on name, 114
Effect on sale of assets, 354–355
Limitations upon, 122
Powers distinguished, 72, 122–123
Professional corporations, 103–104
Ultra vires act, 123

Corporate Seal
    Generally, 136
By-law provision, 149
Power to maintain, 70

Corporations
Aid government, power to, 73–74
Articles of incorporation,
    Generally, 116–134
    Amendment of, 70, 342–345
By-laws, 131
    Consideration for shares, 130
    Corporate purposes, 117, 122–123
    Cumulative voting, 124
Directors,
    Generally, 125, 133–134

Indemnification of, 125–129
Interested, transactions with, 132–133
Qualifications of, 133–134
Dividends, 132
Duration, 117, 121
Effect on statutory rules, 70
Filing, 134
Incorporators, 120
Indemnification of employees, 125–129
Initial directors, 121
Name, 117
Permissive provisions, 121–124
Preemptive rights, 123–124
Quorum, 131
Registered agent, 120
Registered office, 120
Shares, 118–120
Description of, 118–120
Purchase of, 129–130
Statutory requirements, 116–117
Stock rights and options, 130
Vote, 131
As an entity, 68–70
As partners, 6, 73
Best judgment, 78
Bonds,
    Generally, 177–183
    Features of, 181–183
    Secured, 180–181
    Trust indenture, 181
    Unsecured, 178–180
Books, shareholder right to inspect, 85–86
By-laws,
    Amendment of, 80
    Authority to adopt, 136–137
    Content, 136–149
    Effect on statutory rules, 70
    Initial, 136–137
    Officers, 145–146
Cancellation of shares, 174
Capital,
    Generally, 153–155
    Payment of, 134
Capital surplus, 132, 231
Characteristics of, 68–70
Close, generally, 98–102
Compensation, 80
Consolidation,
    Generally, 81, 346–351
    Shareholder approval, 85, 222, 349
Contracts,
    Authority for executing, 147
    Power to enter into, 70

Cumulative voting, 84, 124
De jure, 135
Directors
    As fiduciaries, 78–79
    Classification of, 76, 125, 133
    Compensation of: 80, 125
    Conflict of interest, 78–79
    Delegation of authority, 79–80
    Duties,
        Amendment of articles, 81, 343–344
        By-laws, 80
        Consolidation, 81, 348–349
        Dividends, 81
        Issuance of shares, 81
        Management compensation, 80
        Merger, 81, 348–349
        Sale of assets, 81, 355–356
        Selection of officer, 80
        Supervision of officer, 80
    Election of, 76, 84
    Initial, 121
    Liability, 78–80, 87–89
    Nominal, 191–192
    Number of, 77
    Powers, 75–76
        Qualifications of, 76–77, 125, 133
        Removal of, 77–78
        Vacancies, 77
Dissolution,
    By agreement, 89, 362
    By court, 89, 364–366
    Distributions in, 245–246, 366–368
    Involuntary, 364–366
    Shareholder approval, 83, 222–223
    Voluntary, 89, 361–364
Dividends,
    Generally, 132, 229–230
    Shareholders' rights, 86–87
Domestic, 69, 112–113, 327–328
Donations, power to make, 70, 73
Duration, 70, 72, 89, 121
Executive committee, 79–80, 143–144
Existence, 134–135
Fiscal year, 148
Foreign, defined, 327–328
Franchise fees, 157
Group incentive plans, 272–273
Guarantees, power to make, 70
History of, 68–70
Incentive compensation, 94–95, 272–273
Incorporators,
    Generally, 75, 124
    As subscribers, 75, 110

"Dummy", 75
Function of, 75, 134
Number of, 75
Qualifications of, 75
Indemnification of personnel, 125–129
Insolvent,
    Defined, 232
    Effecting redemption of shares, 74
Insurance, 94–95, 289–290
Insurance benefit plans, 289–290
Interstate business, power to conduct, 71–72
Jurisdiction, selection of, 112–113, 327
Liability,
    Generally, 87, 89
    Limited partnership compared, 46, 87
    Partnership compared, 87
    Sole proprietorship compared, 87
Limited partnership compared, 46, 87
Liquidation,
    Generally, 366–368
    Shareholders' rights, 87
Litigation, power to maintain, 70
Loans,
    Effect on taxation, 91
    Power, 71, 73
Management,
    Limited partnership compared, 75
    Partnership compared, 74
    Sole proprietorship compared, 74
Merger,
    Generally, 85, 346–351
    Shareholder approval, 85, 221–223, 349
Minutes, 225, 226
Name,
    Application for registration, 545–546
    Application for renewal of registered name, 553
    Application for reservation, 547
    Articles of incorporation, 116, 117
    Assumed,
        Domestic, 116
        Foreign, 333–334
        Statement of, 555
    Availability of, 114–115
    Certificate of renewal, 554
    Certificate of reservation, 552
    Certificate of transfer, 550
    Foreign, 333–334
    Notice of transfer, 548–549
    Period of reservation, 115
    Reservation, 115
    Registered, 115, 333–334
    Requirements of, 113
    Selection of, 113–116
    Transfer of, 115
    Unfair competition, 114
Officers,
    Authority, 82
    Delegation of authority to, 82
    Liability, 87–88
    One person holding two offices, 82
    Removal, 82
    Responsibilities of, 145–146
    Selection of, 80
Organizational meetings,
    Generally, 188–205
    Business conducted, 190–205
    Directors, 189–190
    Incorporators, 190
Ownership, 74
Parent, piercing the corporate veil, 88, 102
Partners, power to be, 71, 73
Partnership compared, 68–69
Pension plans, power to pay, 74
"Person", 327
Piercing the corporate veil, 88, 102
Powers,
    Generally, 70–74
    Emergency, 74
    Implied, 123
    Restrictions upon, 72
    To loan to employees, 73
Preemptive rights, 86, 123–124
Preincorporation agreements, 109–110, 197–198
Professional,
    Generally, 102–107
    Directors, 106
    Foreign, 106–107
    Fundamental Changes in, 106
    Liability, 105
    Name, 104
    Officers, 106
    Powers, 103–104
    Prohibited activities, 103–104
    Purposes, 103–104
    Scope, 103
    Statutory authority for, 102–103
    Structural variation, 106
Promoters,
    As organizers, 109
    Duties, 109–110
    Liability on contract, 109
    Power to be, 71
Property, power to deal in, 70, 72
Purchase of shares, generally, 129–130, 241–244
Purposes,
    Articles of incorporation, 122–123

Interpretation, 122–123
Power distinguished, 72
Registered agent, 120
Registered office, 120
Sale of assets,
    Generally, 81, 354–357
    Shareholder approval, 81, 355–356
Seal, power to maintain, 70
Selection of jurisdiction, 112–113, 327, 538–544
Share subscriptions,
    Acceptance of, 111
    Call of, 112
    Forfeiture of, 112
    Irrevocability, 111
    Payment of, 110–111
Shareholders,
    As owners, 82
    Close corporation, 100–101
    Election of directors, 84
    Holder of record, 83
    Liability, 87–89
    Management power, 75–76, 100–101
Shares,
    Articles of incorporation, 118–120
    Authorized, 154
    Certificates for, 158–159
    Classes, 118–120, 159–163
    Consideration for, 163–165
    Corporate purchase of, 129, 241–244
    Fractions, 163
    Issuance of, 83, 153–155
    Outstanding, 154
    Par value, 118, 156–158
    Power to own, 71
    Preincorporation subscriptions, 110–112
    Series, 161–163
    Special features, 118–119
Sole proprietorship compared, 68
Stated capital, 132, 231
Statement of cancellation of shares, 174
Stock transfer ledger, 83
Subsidiary, piercing the corporate veil, 88, 102
Supply kits, 134
Takeovers, 351–354
Taxation,
    Accumulated profits, 91
    Double, 3, 90–91, 236–237
    Franchise tax, 93, 157
    Fringe benefits, 94
    Partnership compared, 89
    Rates, 3, 90–91
    Salaries, 91
    Section 1244 stock, 93–94, 201–202
    Separate entity, 90
    Sole proprietorship compared, 89
    State, 93, 113
    Subchapter S, 91–93, 202–203
    Transfer agent, 176–177

Creditors
Corporation,
    Generally, 87–89
    Bulk transfer violation, 356–357
    Dissolution by, 361
    Notice of dissolution, 363
    Piercing the corporate veil, 88–102
Limited partnership,
    Effect on return of contributions, 48–49
    Rights in liquidation, 52
Partnerships,
    Claims against firm property, 6–9, 15–16
In distribution, 19
Marshaling of assets, 15

Cumulative Voting
    Generally, 217–221
Articles of incorporation, 124
Ballot for, 220–221
Bylaws, 140
Classification of directors, effect on, 219
Provision for, 133
Removal, effect on, 219

Customer List
See Trade Secrets

Debentures
    See also Bonds
    Generally, 178–180
Defined, 153–154
Form for, 178–180

Debt Securities
See Bonds

Deferred Compensation
See Compensation

Depreciation
Partnership contributions, 21–23

Directors
Action without meeting, 142, 223
Amendments to articles, by resolution, 344
As fiduciaries, 79–80
Authority,
    Delegated to officer, 204–205
    To fix series shares, 161–163

To qualify foreign corporations, 328
Best judgment, 78
Bonds, redemption of, 181–182
By-law provisions regarding, 140–144
By-laws,
    Authority to adopt, 131, 136–137
    Authority to amend, 149
Compensation, 80, 125
Conflict of interest, 78–79
Consideration for shares, authority to fix, 156–158, 163–165
Consolidation, resolution for adoption, 348–349
Classification of, 76, 133–134, 141, 219
Close corporations, duties, 100–101
Delegation of authority, 79–80
Dissolution, voluntary, 361–362
Dividends,
    Authority to declare, 229–230, 235–236
    Authority to pay, 148, 154
    Discretion, 229
"Dummy", 189, 191–192
Duties,
    Amendment of articles, 81, 343–344
    By-laws, 80
    Consolidation, 81, 348–349
    Dividends, 81
    Issuance of shares, 81
    Management compensation, 80
    Merger, 81, 348–349
    Sale of assets, 81, 355–356
    Selection of officers, 80
    Supervision of officer, 80
Election of,
    Generally, 76, 84, 191–192
    Agreement to control, 303–304
    Cumulative voting, 86, 217–221
Evaluation of property, 164–165
Indemnification of,
    Generally, 125–129
    Advance payments, 128–129
    Definitions for, 126–127
    Insurance, 129
    Limitations upon, 128
    Mandatory, 127
    Reimbursement of, 129
Informal action by, 131, 142
Initial,
    Generally, 121
    Consent of, 121
    Number of, 121
    Qualifications, 121
Interested, 79, 132–133
Interlocking, 132–133
Liability, 78–80, 87–89

Meetings,
    Action without, 142, 223–225
    Call of, 206
    Consent to action, 142, 223–225
    Manner of acting, 142
    Method of voting, 208
    Minutes, form, 225, 603–604
    Necessity for, 189–190
    Notice, 141, 207–208
    Place of, 206
    Quorum, 131, 142, 205
    Regular, 141, 205–208
    Special, 141, 205–208
    Voting provisions, 208
    Waiver of notice, 208
Merger, resolution for adoption, 347–350
Misconduct, 78–79
Nominal, 189, 191–192
Number, 77, 133, 141
Organizational meeting,
    Generally, 135–136
    Actual directors, 189, 191–192
    Business conducted, 190–205
Powers, 75–76, 140
Presumption of assent, 143
Professional corporations,
    qualifications, 106
Property, valuation of, 195
Qualifications of, 76–77, 125, 133
Quorum, 131, 142, 205
Removal, 77–78, 84, 142, 219
Resignation, 190
Sale of assets, procedure, 355–356
Scrip, authority to create, 163
Section 1244 stock, 93–94, 201–202
Share subscriptions, call of, 112
Shares,
    Authority to issue, 194–195
    Authority to pay by installments, 196
Stock options,
    Administration of plan, 287–289
    Adoption of, 285
Stock split, authority for, 239–241
Subchapter S election, 202–203
Term of office, 217
Transfer agents, duties delegated to, 176–177
Vacancies, 77, 144
Votes, regulated by articles of incorporation, 131

Dissolution
Corporations,
    Articles of dissolution, 363–364, 651–654
    By agreement, 89, 362

By court, 89, 364–366
   Certificate of dissolution
      Generally, 363–364
      Effect of, 364
      Forms, 655, 656
Close corporations, 101–102
Distributions, generally, 245–246, 366–368
Involuntary,
   Generally, 364–366
   By creditor, 366
   By shareholders, 365–366
   By the state, 364–365
Notice to creditors, 363
Shareholder approval, 83, 222–223
Shareholder's right to dissent, 362
Statement of intent to dissolve, 362–363, 645–647
Voluntary,
   Generally, 89, 361–364
   Revocation of, 364
Limited partnership,
   Generally, 51–53
  Acts of general partner, 51–52
  Agreement, 51
  Causes of, 51–52
  Limited partner's request, 51
  Misconduct by limited partner, 51
  Right to continue business, 52
Partnership
   Generally, 6, 16–21, 37–42
  Agreement to continue, 18–20
  At will, 17
  Bankruptcy of partner, 17–18, 39
  By agreement, 17
  By operation of law, 17–18
  Causes of, 16–18, 37–41
  Compared with sole proprietorship, 16
  Continuation of business, 18–20
  Deadlock, 18
  Death of a partner, 17–18, 39–40
  Decree of court, 18
  Disability of a partner, 40–41
  Expulsion of a partner, 17, 38–39
  Life insurance, 20
  Liquidation and winding-up, 20–21, 42–43
  Notice of, 20, 471, 472
  Purchasing interest, 18–19, 41–42
  Unlawful business, 18
  Wrongful, 18
Sole proprietorship,
  Death of a proprietor, 2
  Liquidation upon death, 2
Statement of intent to dissolve,
  Forms, 645–647

Dividends
Articles of incorporation provisions, 132
Authority to pay, by law provision, 148
Cash,
   Generally, 165, 210, 229–230, 233–237, 235–239
  Accounting, 235–236
  Depletion reserves, 235
  Payment, 235–236
  Procedure for declaration, 235–236
  Reports required, 236–237
  Tax ramifications, 236–237
Common stock, 165
Directors' duties, 81
Effect on taxation, 90–91
Equal distribution, 233
Frequency, 230
Legally available funds, 230–232
Preference to, 160–161, 167–168
Preferred,
  Cash, 233
  Cumulative, 167
  Cumulative to the extent earned, 168
  Liquidation, treatment in, 244–246
  Non-cumulative, 167–168
  Participating, 168
  Share dividends, 237–239
Property,
   Generally, 165, 210, 229–230, 233–237
  Accounting, 235–236
  Payment, 235–236
  Procedure for declaration, 235–236
  Reports required, 236–237
  Tax ramifications, 236–237
Purchase of shares, see Shares
Record date, 236
Restriction on payment of, 233–235
Return on investment, 154, 229, 230
Share dividends,
   Generally, 237–239
  Accounting, 238–239
  Capitalization of earnings, 238–239
  Legal restrictions upon, 237–238
  Payment, 238–239
  Procedure for declaration, 238–239
  Sources of, 237–238
  Stock splits compared, 239–240
  Tax ramifications of, 239
Shareholders' rights, 86–87, 233
Shares, 230, 237–239
Source of funds for, 230–232
Stock dividends, see Share dividends, above
Stock splits, see Stock Splits
Treasury shares, 155

Voting trusts, 301
Yield, 229

Donations
Corporations
　Power to make, 71, 73
　Purpose of, 73

Double Taxation
　See Corporations and Taxation

Duration
　See also Dissolution and Termination
Corporations,
　Articles of incorporation, 121
　Perpetual, 70, 72, 89
Employment agreements, 259
Partnerships, agreement, 25
Pooling agreements, 302–303
Stock voting agreements, 302–303
Voting trust, 300

Earned Surplus
Cancellation of shares, 243
Corporations, 157
Defined, 231
Dividends,
　Restriction on payment of, 233–235
　Source of funds for, 231
Restriction on purchase of shares, 242–243
Share dividends, 237–238
Stock splits, effect on, 241
Unreserved and unrestricted, 234

Employees
Agreements, see Employment Agreements
Authority, limitations upon, 255–257
Benefits, see Incentive Compensation, Expense Reimbursement Plans Compensation, 257–261
Competition, common law prohibition, 269
Corporations,
　Effect on taxation, 91
　Loans from, 73
　Officers' contracts, 82
　Stock option plans, preemptive rights, 86
Covenants not to compete, 268–272
Death benefit compensation, 275
Duties, 275–277
Expense reimbursement plans, 290–296
Insurance benefits, 289–290
Pension plans,
　See also Pension Plans
　Requirements for qualifications, 277–280
Profit sharing plans,
　See also Profit Sharing Plans
　Requirements for qualification, 277–280
Sole proprietorship, 1, 4
Stock options,
　See also Stock Options
　Administration of, 287–289
　Adoption of, 285
　Assignability, 287
　Death, 284
　Deceased, 284
　Defined, 282
　Incentive, 282–290
　Limitation on share ownership, 286–287
　Option Period, 286
　Option Price, 286
　Participants, 284
　Qualification of, 283–287
　Termination of employment, 284
　Termination of plan, 285
Termination, effect on covenants not to compete, 269

Employment Agreements
　Generally, 254–255
Authority, limitation on, 255–257
Automatic renewal, 262
Compensation,
　Generally, 257–261
　Bonus, 259–261
　Commission, 258–259
　Current incentive provisions, 259–261
　Deferred,
　　Generally, 273–275
　　Amount, 274
　　Death of employee, 275
　　Incentive, 273–274
　　Tax advantages, 273
　Expense reimbursement, 259
　Group incentive plans,
　　Generally, 272–273
　　Administration of, 272
　　Committee, 272
　　Content of, 272–273
　　Modification of, 273
　　Participants, 272
　　Payment of, 272–273
　Incentive compensation plans, 272–273
　Profits, defined, 258
　Retirement, 274
　Royalties for inventions, 264–267
　Salary, 258

Covenants not to compete,
    Generally, 268–272
  Ambiguities, 269
  Effect of termination, 269
  Enforcement of, 269–270
  Prohibited activities, 270–271
  Time restrictions, 270
  Trade area, 270
Current incentive programs, drafting problems, 259–260
Death benefit compensation, 273–275
Duties, 255–257
Employee work product, generally, 264–267
Enforcement of, 254
Insurance benefit plans, 289–290
Inventions,
    Generally, 264–267
  Common law protection, 264
  Legally protectable, 264
  Negotiation, 264, 266
  Protection of, 264–267
  Royalties, 266–267
  Scope of employment, 264–265
Option to renew, 262
Pension Plans,
    Generally, 276–281
  Age and service rules, 278
  Benefits, 276, 281
  Contributions, 276, 281
  Coverage requirements, 278–280
  Funded, 281
  Qualification, 277–281
  Tax ramifications, 277
  Termination, 277
  Vesting, 281
Profit sharing plans,
    Generally, 276–281
  Age and service rules, 288
  Benefits, 276–277
  Contributions, 276, 281
  Coverage requirements, 278–280
  Funded, 281
  Qualification, 277–281
  Tax ramifications, 277
  Termination, 277
  Vesting, 281
Proprietary covenants, generally, 263–264
Renewal, 262
Restrictive covenants, generally, 263–264
Shares, sell out, 310
Split-dollar insurance, 290
Stock options,
    Generally, 282–289
  Administration of plan, 287–289
  Amendment of, 288
  Assignability, 287
  Date of grant, 282
  Defined, 282
  Duration of, 285
  Exercise, 282
  Incentive factors, 282
  Limitation on share ownership, 286
  Option price, 282, 286
  Qualification of, 283–287
  Registered securities, 289
  Tax ramifications, 283–284, 287
Structure, 254–263
Term, 261–263
Termination,
    Generally, 262–263
  Causes, of, 262
  Deferred compensation, effect on, 274
  Discontinued business, 262
  Effect on covenants not to compete, 271
  Group incentive plans, effect on, 273
  Involuntary, 263
  Notice, 263
  Salary continuation, 263
  Without cause, 263
Trade secrets,
  Common law protection, 267
  Customer list, 268
  Drafting problems, 267
  Liquidated damages for disclosure, 267–268
  Protection of, 267–268
Vacations, 261

Entity Theory
Corporations, 68–70
Partnerships, 5–6

Equity Securities
See Shares

Executive Committee
Action without a meeting, 144
Appointment, 143
Authority, 143
By-law provisions, 143–144
Delegation of authority to, 79–80
Meetings, 143–144
Procedure, 144
Qualifications, 143
Quorum, 144
Removal, 144
Vacancies, 144
Expense reimbursement plans
    Generally, 290–296

Accident plans, 290
Benefits test, 293
Compensation of employees, 291–292
Dependent care assistance programs, 290
Educational assistance plans, 290
Eligibility, 292
Group term life insurance, 290
Health plans, 290
Legal services plans, 290
Life insurance, group term, 290
Plan for,
    Generally, 293–296
    Administration, 293
    Amendment, 296
    Benefits, 294
    Effective date, 293
    Family unit, 295
    Financing benefits, 295
    Information required, 295
    Membership, 294
    Payments, 295
    Purpose, 293
    Rights of employees, 295
    Termination of employee, 296
    Termination of plan, 296

Expulsion of Partner
See Dissolution

Extraordinary Corporate Changes
See Articles of Incorporation; Consolidation;
    Dissolution; Merger and Sale of Assets

Financing
See Capital

Financing Statement
Form, 598

Foreign Corporations
Admission, denial of, 327
Amended certificate of authority, 338
Amendment to articles of incorporation, 337–338
Annual reports, 337, 340
Application for certificate of authority,
    Generally, 331–333
    Contents of, 332–333
    Name, 333–334
    Purpose of, 331
    Registered office, 334–335
    Verified, 333
Application for withdrawal, 339
Articles of incorporation, filed, 332
Articles of merger, 338
Authority,
    To qualify, 200, 328
    Withdrawal of, 339–340
Certificate of authority,
    Amended, 623
    Application for amended, 621
    Denial of, 328
    Effect of, 335
    Form, 620
    Revocation of, 340
Certificate of withdrawal, 341
Consolidation, 338–339
Denial of access to courts, 331
Fees and taxes, 330, 335
Fines, 331
Franchise taxes, 335
Laws of domestic state, 327, 335
Laws of host state, 335
Merger, 338–339
Name,
    Changes in, 338
    Fictitious, 333
    Registration of, 115, 333–334
Name saver subsidiaries, 115
Qualification,
    Generally, 331–337
    Constitutional basis, 327–328
    Effect of, 335–337
Registered agent, 334
Registered office, 334
Restrictions imposed by domestic state, 335
Restrictions imposed by host state, 335
Revocation of authority, certificate of, 625
Sanctions for not qualifying, 331
Secretary of State as agent, 334
Service of process upon, 336
Statement of good standing, 332
Statutory prohibitions, 328–329
Taxes, 336–337
Title to property, 331
Transacting business, 329–330
Validity of contracts, 331
Withdrawal,
    Generally, 339, 625
    Application for certificate of, 624
    Certificate of, 625

Formation
Corporations, 109–149
Limited partnership, 54–65
Partnerships, 23–43
Sole proprietorship, 3–4

INDEX

Forms
Abandonment of fictitious name,
   California, 470
Bulk transfer,
   Affidavit of seller, 644
   Notice to creditors, 643
Business certificate, New York, 469
Corporations,
   Amendment of articles, resolution, 343
   Approval of bylaws, 193
   Application for registration of name, 551
   Approval of minutes, 192–193
   Approval of seal, 193
   Articles of amendment, 626–627
   Articles of consolidation, 640–641
   Articles of incorporation,
      Checklist for, 556–558
      Delaware, 558–563
      Medical corporation, 517–521
      North Dakota, 564–565
   Articles of merger, 634–637
   Articles of merger for a short merger, 641–642
   Bank resolution, 200
   Bonds,
      Certificates, 587–592
      Conversion, 183
      Redemption, 182
      Subordination, 183
   Buy out agreements, death, 309
   By-laws,
      Generally, 567–578
      Action of directors, 142
      Amendment, 149
      Certificates for shares, 147–148
      Classification of directors, 141
      Closing of transfer books, 138–139
      Compensation of directors, 142
      Cumulative voting, 140
   Directors, 140
   Dividends, 148
   Emergency, 149
   Executive committee,
      Action without meeting, 144
      Appointment, 143
      Authority, 143
      Meetings, 143–144
      Procedure, 144
      Qualifications, 143
      Quorum, 144
      Removal, 144
      Vacancies, 144
   Fiscal year, 148
   Fixing of record date, 138–139
   Informal action by shareholders, 140
   Informal action by directors, 142
   Notice of meeting, 138, 141
   Officers,
      Election, 145
      Number, 144
      Removal, 145
      Responsibilities, 145–146
      Salaries, 146
      Term of office, 145
      Vacancies, 145
   Offices, 137
   Place of meeting, 138
   Powers of directors, 140
   Presumption of assent, 143
   Proxies, 139
   Quorum, 139, 142
   Regular meetings, 137, 141
   Removal of directors, 142
   Seal, 149
   Special meeting, 137-38, 141
   Time of meeting, 137
   Transfer agent, 148
   Transfer of shares, 148
   Vacancy of director, 142
   Voting lists, 139
   Voting shares, 139–40
   Call of subscriptions, 112
   Cancellation of shares, 607–608
   Certificate of amendment, 628
   Certificate of consolidation, 640–641
   Certificate of incorporation, North Dakota, 566
   Certificate of limited partnership, 503–506
   Certificate of merger, 638
   Certificate of paid-in capital, 536–537
   Certificate of registration of name, 552
   Certificate of renewal of name, 547
   Certificate of restated articles, 633
   Certificate of transfer of reserved name, 550
   Checklist for selection of jurisdiction, 538–544
   Classification of directors, 133
   Common stock, 118–119
   Consent to action without meeting, 226
   Conversion privilege, 175, 183
   Cumulative voting, 84, 124, 140
   Debenture, 178–180
   Designation of accountant, 200
   Designation of counsel, 200
   Directors,
      Agreement to secure representation, 303
      Conflict of interest, 79, 133
      Delegation of authority, 80, 204–205
      Meetings, 207, 209
      Power to sell assets, 81
      Resignation, 190

Waiver of notice, 189, 208, 212–213
Dissolution,
   Articles of dissolution, 651–654
   Certificate of, 655–656
   Notice to shareholders, 360
   Shareholder resolution, 360
   Statement of intent to dissolve, 645–647
   Statement of revocation of voluntary dissolution, 648–650
   Voluntary, resolution, 360
Dividends,
   Cumulative, 167
   Declaration of, 235–236, 238
   Non-cumulative, 168
   Restrictions on, 132
   Share dividends, declaration of, 238
Election of officers, 198
Election for Subchapter S, 508–510
Expense reimbursement plans, 293–296
Fees, reimbursement of, 197
Foreign corporation, qualification of, 200
Forfeiture of subscription, 112
General powers, 71
Indemnification of personnel, 126–129
Initial directors, 121
Internal Revenue form 2553, 509–510
Liquidation preferences, 168–169
Medical expense plans, 293–296
Meetings,
   Ballots for, 216, 220–221
   Consent to action without, 223–224
   Dates of, 203
   Directors,
      Call of, 206–207
      Notice of, 207
   Minutes, 603–606
   Shareholders,
      Call of, 209
      Notice of, 211
   Merger, resolution, 348–349
   Notice of transfer of reserved name, 548–549
   Partial liquidation, 244–245
   Pooling agreements, 302–303
   Power to borrow money, 71
   Power to conduct interstate business, 71–72
   Power to hold property, 73
   Preemptive rights, 86, 124
   Preincorporation share subscriptions, 110–111
   Preincorporation worksheet, 527–532
   Promissory note, 178
   Promoters, agreement between, 533–535
   Purposes, 122
   Redemption of shares, 171–172
   Registered agent, statement of change of, 619

Removal of directors, 84
Resolution establishing series, 593–594
Restated articles of incorporation, 629–632
Restriction on transfer of shares, 306, 310
Sale of assets, resolution, 356
Sale of shares,
   Price, 313–319
   Bona fide offer, 318
   Book value, 316
   Capitalized earnings, 315
   Firm price, 313
   Terms of payment, 320–321
Section 1244 plan, 201–202, 511–513, 521–523
Series shares, 162
Share certificates, 194, 579–586
Share subscriptions, acceptance of, 195
Shareholder approval of compensation, 80
Shareholders,
   Agreement to secure representation, 303
   Arbitration, 302, 313–314, 319
   Joint action in voting, 302
   Proxy, 213–214
   Right to inspect, 85
   Statement of consent to Subchapter S, 202–203, 508
   Shares,
      Authority to issue, 119, 194, 196
      Call, 196
      Repurchase of, 130
      Restrictions on issuance of, 130
      Restrictions on transfer, 306, 310
      Statement of cancellation, 607–618
Sinking fund, 172–174
Statement of assumed name, 555
Stock splits, resolution for, 243
Subchapter S election, 202–203, 508–510
Transactions with interested directors, 79, 133
Transfer agent, appointment of, 176–177
Trust indenture, 598–603
Vote of directors, 131
Voting rights, 169–170
Voting trust agreement, 610–615
Employment agreements
   Generally, 255–263
   Automatic renewal, 262
   Compensation,
      Bonus plans, 258–259
      Commissions, 258–259
      Deferred, 273–275
      Drawing accounts, 258–259
      Retirement, 275
      Royalties, 266–267
      Salary, 258
      Termination, 274

Covenants not to compete, 270–271
Duties, 255–256, 261
Expenses reimbursement, 259
Inventions,
    Right to inventions, 265–266
    Royalties, 266–267
Limitations on authority, 257
Option to renew, 262
Term, 261
Trade-secret protection, 267–268
Traveling expenses, 259
Vacations, 261
Fictitious name statement,
    California, 465–466
Financing statement, 598
Foreign corporations,
    Application for certificate of authority, 616–618
    Financing statement, 598
    Foreign corporations,
        Application for certificate of authority, 616–618
        Certificate of authority, 620
            Amended, 623
            Application for amended, 621–622
        Certificate of revocation of authority, 625–626
        Certificate of withdrawal, 625
            Application for, 624
    Limited partnership,
        Additional capital, 56–57
        Additional partners, 56
        Admission of partners, 56, 61
        Agreement, 498–502
        Amendment of interest, 497
        Certificate, 56, 503–504
        Consent to substitution, 497
        Limitations on general partner liability, 61
        Limitations of partner loans, 61
        Power of attorney, 60
        Powers of general partner, limitations on, 58
        Removal of general partner, 59
        Rights of general partner, 58
        Rights of limited partner, 59
        Role of limited partner, 57
        Statement of cancellation, 508
        Transfer of limited partner interests, 60–61
        Voting rights of partners, 61
        Withdrawal of capital, 57
Non-disclosure agreement, 609
Partnership,
    Accounting method, 30, 35, 37, 41
    Activities of partners, 34
    Advances of partners, 30, 41
    Agreement, 24–43, 473–498
    Arbitration, 35
    Assignment of interest in firm, 471
    Audit of books, 31–32
    Authority, limitations, 11–12, 34, 35–36
    Bankruptcy, 39
    Bank accounts, 31
    Bond, 35
    Books, location of, 30–31
    Capital contributions, 26
    Cash allocations, 14–15, 30
    Competition of partner, 20
    Continue business after dissolution, 18–19, 42
    Contributions, 7, 26–27
    Death, 39–40
    Debts, limitation on, 36
    Depreciation, 22
    Disability, 40–41
    Disputes, 35
    Dissolution,
        Agreement to terminate, 17, 42
        Contingent, 17
    Distributions on termination, 42–43
    Duration, 25
    Duty, devotion to, 12
    Equal vote of partners, 10, 32
    Expense accounts, 12, 28
    Expulsion, 38
    Fiscal year, 30
    Indemnification, 15
    Interest on contributions, 27
    Loans of property, 7, 37
    Location of records, 30–31, 35
    Management duties, 10, 32
    Managing partner, authority, 10–11, 33–34
    Meetings, 32
    Name, 24
    Nature of business, 25
    Notice of dissolution, 20, 471–472
    Partners' duties, 10–11, 33–34
    Place of business, 25
    Profits and losses, 13–15, 27, 28, 29
    Property, 8, 37
    Property loaned, 7, 37
    Purchase of interest, 19, 36, 42
    Purposes, 25
    Restrictions on partners, 11–12, 34, 35–36
    Reports, 31, 34
    Retirement, 38
    Sale of partner's interest, 36–37
    Salaries, 12, 28
    Services, contribution of, 26
    Sharing of capital gains and losses, 22
    Tax items, allocation, 22
    Withdrawal of contributions, 27–28

Withdrawal of partner, 38
Professional corporation,
    Application for registration of, 522–526
    Articles of incorporation, 517–521
Publication of fictitious name, California, 466–467
Security agreement, 596–597
Stock options,
    Administration, 287
    Adoption resolution, 285
    Allotment of shares, 287
    Amendment, 288–289
    Assignability, 287
    Changes in capitalization adjustment, 288
    Consideration for option, 289
    Death, 284
    Employment termination, 284
    Event of death, 284
    Event of termination, 284
    Identification of shares, 283–284
    Option period, 286
    Option price, 286
    Participants, 284–285
    Payment for stock, 289
    Prior options, 286–287
    Purchase for investment, 289
    Shares subject to plan, 283–284
    Termination, 285
Trade name affidavit, Colorado, 463–464

General Partnership
See Partnerships

Good Will
Valuation in partnership, 42

Guarantees
Corporations, power to make, 70

Holder of Record
    See also Shareholders
Dividends, right to receive, 236
Notice, 209–210

Incentive Compensation Plans
    See also Compensation; Pension Plans; Profit Sharing Plans; Retirement Plans; Stock Option Plans
Corporations,
    Power to pay, 74
    Preemptive rights, 86
    Tax advantages, 94–95

Incorporators
Articles of dissolution by, form, 651
Articles of incorporation, subscribing, 75, 116, 134
Certificate of dissolution by, form, 655
Close corporation, contract to organize, 513–516
Dissolution by, 361
"Dummy", 75, 194
Function, 75
Number of, 75
Organizational meeting,
    Business conducted, 190–205
Procedures, 134, 190
Preincorporation agreements, 197–198
Qualifications of, 75
Services, as consideration for shares, 164–165
Share subscriptions,
    Assignment, 110, 194
    Preincorporation, 110

Indemnification
Corporations, articles of incorporation provisions, 126–129
Partners, 15–16, 38

Indenture
    Generally, 181
Defined, 154
Trust Indenture Act of 1939, 181
Trustee for, 181

Insurance
Corporations,
    Buy-out agreements, funding, 322–324
    Employee benefit plans, 289–290
    Tax plan, 95
    Cross purchase plan, 20, 323
    Death benefit compensation, 289–290
    Employee benefit plans, 289–290
    Entity purchase plan, 20
    Liability,
        Partnerships, 15–16
        Sole proprietorships, 2
    Partnerships,
        Funding of, 20, 40
    Split dollar, 289–90

Interest in Partnership
See Partners

Internal Revenue Code
See Taxation

Interstate Business
Corporations,
    Generally, 112–113, 327
  Permissive jurisdiction, 112–113
  Power to conduct, 71–72
  Partnership, 25

Inventions
Common law protection, 264
Employee work product, generally, 264–267
Protection of, 264–267
Royalties, 266–267

Jurisdiction
Corporations
  Permissive, 112–113
  Selection of, 112–113, 327

Liability
Corporations,
    Generally, 87–89
  Directors, 87, 100, 105
  Officers, 87
  Piercing the corporate veil, 87–89, 102
  Shareholders, 88–89, 100–101, 105
Limited partnership,
  General partners, 48
  Limited partners, 48–49
Partnership,
  Agreements to negate, 15
  Individual assets, 6
  Insurance, 15
  Marshaling of assets, 15
  Partners, 15–16
  Proprietorship contrasted, 15
Professional corporations, 105–106
Sole proprietorship,
  Contrasted with corporation, 2
  Contrasted with partnership, 2
  Control over, 2
  Effect of agreement, 2
  Effect of insurance, 2
  Personal, 2

Licenses
Limited partnerships, 54
Partnership, 23
Sole proprietorship, 4

Limited Partnership
    See also Partnerships
Agreement, 55–61, 498–502
Amendment of certificate, form, 507
Assignment of interest, form, 497
Books, 50
Certificate,
    Generally, 61–62
  Amendments to, 63–64
  Cancellations of, 64
  Content of, 62–63
  Filing, 63
  Form, 503–504
  Maintenance of, 63–64
  Publication of, 63
Consent to substitution, form, 497
Contributions, 48–49, 56–57
Corporation compared, 46
Derivative actions, 65
Dissolution,
  Acts of general partners, 51–52
  By agreement, 51–52
  Causes of, 51–52
  Limited partner's request, 51
  Misconduct by limited partner, 51
  Right to continue business, 52
Distributions from, 52–53
Foreign, 64–65
Formation, 54–64
General partners, 49, 58–59, 61
General partners compared, 49
Liability,
    Generally, 49–50
  Corporation compared, 46
Licenses, 54
Limited partners,
  Admission of, 50, 56
  Assignment of interest, 51, 56
  Defined, 55
  Status, 57
  Substitution of, 50, 60
  Withdrawal of, 50–51
Liquidation, 52–53
Loans, limitations on, 61
Management,
    Generally, 49–50
  Corporation compared, 75
  Limited partners' participation, 49–50
Name, 54–55
Power of attorney, 60
Registered agent, 63
Registered office, 63
Removal of general partner, 59
Statement of cancellation, form, 508
Taxation,
  Corporation compared, 53
  General partnership compared, 53–54

Termination of, 52–53
Transfer of limited partner interests, 60–61
Voting rights, 61
Withdrawal,
   Capital, 57
   General partner, 48, 51–52
   Limited partner, 50–51

Liquidation
Corporations,
   Generally, 366–368
   Common stock, 166
   Distributions, 245–246
   Judicial proceedings, 367–368
   Nonjudicial, 367
   Partial, 244–245
   Preferences, 168–169
   Preferred shares, 168–169, 245–246
   Series shares, 162
   Shareholders' rights, 86–87, 162, 166, 168–169
Limited partnership,
   Generally, 52–53
   Distribution to partners, 52–53
Partial,
   Generally, 244–245
   Defined, 244
   Procedure for, 244–245
   Requirements for, 244
   Tax advantage, 244
Partnership,
   Generally, 20–21, 42–43
   Remaining partners, 18–19
   Taxation of, 22–23

Litigation
Corporations, power to maintain, 70

Loans
Corporations
   Generally, 73
   Authority for creating, 71, 147
   Bonds, 153–154, 177–178
   To employees, 73
Partnership, property, 7, 27

Losses
See also Profits
Partnerships,
   Generally, 6, 12–15
   Additional capital required, 27, 56
   Agreement, 12–15, 29–30
   Definition, 13–14, 17

   Effect of contributions, 13
   Sharing, 12–15

Management
Corporations,
   Close corporations, 100–101
   Directors, 75–76, 78–79
   Officers, 81–82
   Partnership compared, 74–75
   Shareholders, 82–83, 100–101
   Sole proprietorship compared, 74
Limited partnership,
   Generally, 49–50
   Effect on taxation, 55–56
   Limited partners' participation, 49–50
Partnership,
   Generally, 6, 10–12
   Duties, 33–34
   Equal vote of partners, 10, 32
   Limitations on authority, 11–12, 34, 35–36
   Managing partners, 10–11, 33–34
   Meetings, 32
   Method of, 32–33
   Prohibited activities, 34, 35–36
   Services as contributions, 26
Sole proprietorship, 1, 3–4

Meetings
Corporations,
   Generally, 188–226
   Accountants, designated, 200
   Action without, 225–227
   Approval of by-laws, 193
   Approval of minutes, 192–193
   Approval of seal, 193
   Approval of share certificates, 193–194
   Assumed name, authority to use, 200–201
   Bank resolution, 199–200
   By-law provisions, 137–138, 141
   Chairman, 190–191
   Consent to action, 223–224
   Counsel, designated, 200
   Delegation of authority, 203–205
   Directors,
      Authority to qualify foreign corporations, 328
      Informal action, 142, 223–224
      Method of voting, 142, 208
      Necessity for, 189–190
      Notice, 141, 189, 207
      Organizational, 190
      Quorum, 142, 206
      Regular, 141, 206
      Resignation, 190

Special, 141, 206–207
Voting provisions, 206, 208
Waiver of notice, 208
Election of directors, 191–192, 217–221
Executive committee,
　Action without, 144
　Procedure, 144
　Quorum, 144
　Regular, 143–144
Fees, reimbursement of, 197
Foreign corporation,
　qualifications as, 200
Incorporators, 190
Minutes, content, 225–226
Notice, 141, 189, 207, 211–212
Officers, election of, 198
Organizational,
　Generally, 135–136, 188–189
　Business conducted, 135–136, 190–205
　Incorporators, 135, 190
　Necessity for, 135–136, 188–189
　Nominal directors, 189–190
Preincorporation of agreements, 197–198
Presentation of articles of incorporation, 192
Proxies, 213–214
Registered agent, 200
Registered office, 200
Secretary, 190–191
Section 1244 plan, adoption of, 201–202
Shareholders,
　Generally, 208–216
　Annual, 137, 208
　Business, 216–223
　Call of, 209
　Consent to action, 140, 223–225
　Consolidation, approval of, 222
　Cumulative voting, 217–221
　Dissolution, approval of, 222
　Election judges, 216
　Frequency, 208–209
　Location of, 138, 209
　Merger, approval of, 222
　Necessity for, 188
　Notice,
　　Generally, 138, 209–213
　　Content, 210–211
　　Delivery of, 210–212
　　Persons entitled to, 138, 209–210
　　Record date, 138–139, 210
　　Waiver of, 212–213
　Organizational, 135
　Proxies, 139, 213–215
　Quorum, 139, 215
　Regular, 137, 208
　Sale of assets, approval of, 222
　Special, 137–138, 208–209
　Transfer books, closing of, 138–139, 210
　Voting of shares, 139, 215–216
　Weighted voting, 215
Share subscriptions, 194–196
Shares, authority to issue, 196
Subchapter S election, adoption of, 202–203
Partnership, 32

Merger
　Generally, 346–347
"A" Reorganization, 347
Agreement for, 348
Articles of merger,
　Contents of, 350–351
　Effective date, 351
　Filing, 351
　Form, 634–637
　Publication of, 351
Certificate of, form, 638
Defined, 346–347
Directors' duties, 81
Dissenting shareholders, 357–358
Effect of, 351
Foreign corporations, 338–339
Hostile, 351–354
Letter of intent, 348
Plan of merger, 348
Procedure for, 347–349
Resolution for adoption, 348–349
Shareholder approval, 85, 221–223, 349
Short form,
　Articles of merger, 641–642
　Defined, 349–350
Small impact merger, 349

Minutes
Accountant, designation of, 200
Action of previous meeting, approval of, 192–193
Agreements, preincorporation, 197–198
Assumed name, authority to use, 200–201
Bank resolution, 199–200
By-laws, approval of, 193
Content, 225–226
Corporate records, 134
Corporations,
　Approval of, 193
　Organizational meeting, 135–136, 188–189
Counsel, designation of, 200
Date of meetings, 206, 208–209
Delegation of authority, 203–205

Directors,
  Authority to qualify foreign corporation, 328
  Form, 603–604
Fees, reimbursement of, 197
Foreign corporation, qualification of, 200, 328
Informal activity, 225–227
Officers, election of, 198
Registered agent, 200
Registered office, 200
Seal, approval of, 193
Secretary, duties of, 225
Section 1244 plan, adoption of, 201–202, 511–513
Share certificates, approval of, 193–194
Share subscription,
  Acceptance of, 194–196
  Assignment of, 194
Shareholders,
  Form, 605–606
  Right to inspect, 85
Shares,
  Authority to issue, 196
  Call of consideration, 196
Subchapter S election, 202–203

Mortgage Bonds
  See also Bonds
  Generally, 153–155, 177–178
  Agreement, 180
  Collateral for, 180
  Defined, 153–154
  Financing statement, 180, 598

Name
Assumed,
  Abandonment of, California, 470
  Affidavit, 463–464
  Business certificate, New York, 469
  Publication of, California, 467–468
  Statement of California, 465–466
Corporate purposes, 114
Corporations,
  Application for registration, 551
  Application for renewal of registered name, 553
  Articles of incorporation, 117
  Assumed,
    Generally, 116
    Authority to use, 201
    Statement of, 555
  Availability of, 114–115
  Certificate of registration, 552
  Certificate of renewal, 554
  Certificate of reservation, 547
  Certificate of transfer, 550
  Foreign, 333–334, 338
  Notice of transfer, 548–549
  Period of reservation, 115
  Registration of, 115, 334
  Requirements of, 113–114
  Reservation of, 115–116, 334
  Selection of, 113–114
  Unfair competition, 114
Limited partnership, 52, 54–55, 62
Partnership, 23, 24
Professional corporations, 104
Sole proprietorship, 4

Net Assets
Defined, 231

Officers
Assistant secretary, 146
Assistant treasurer, 146
Authority, 82
By-law provisions, 144–146
Chief executive officer, 81
Chief financial officer, 81
Compensation, 146
Delegation of authority to, 81
Election, 145, 198
Liability, 87–89
Number, 144–145
One person holding two offices, 81–82
President, 81, 145
Removal, 82, 145
Responsibilities, 145–146
Salary, 146
Secretary, 81, 146
Selection of, 80
Shares, authority to issue, 196
Supervision by directors, 82
Term of office, 145
Transfer agents, instructions to, 176
Treasurer, 81, 146
Vacancies, 145
Vice-President, 81, 145–146

Parent Corporations
Piercing the corporate veil, 87, 102

Partial Liquidations
See Liquidation

Partners
Advances, 27
As agents, 10
Assignment of interest in firm, 9–10, 471, 497
Authority, limitations, 11–12

Bankruptcy,
   Cause of dissolution, 17–18, 39
   Of partner, 17–18, 39
Compensation, 12
Competition with firm, prohibited, 20
Continuation of business, right, 18–20, 41–42
Contributions,
      Generally, 7–8, 26–28
   Dissolution, 21
   Interest on, 27
   Withdrawal, 27–28
Co-owners, 6, 8
Corporations, power to be, 6, 70, 73
Death, cause of dissolution, 17, 39–40
Disability, cause of dissolution, 17–18, 40–41
Distributions to, 21, 42–43
Dormant, 32
Duties, 12, 32–37
Equal vote, 10, 32
Expense accounts, 12, 28
Expulsion, 17, 38, 473
General,
   Acts effecting limited partnership, 47–48
   Limited partnership, 47–48
   Power to manage in limited partnership, 47
Incapacity, causing dissolution, 18, 40–41
Indemnification, 15, 18–20
Insane, causing dissolution, 18, 40–41
Interest in partnership,
      Generally, 9–10
   Assignability, 9–10
   Capital gain and loss, 21–23
   Determined by capital contribution, 9
   Effective withdrawals, 9
   Heirs, 9
   Intangible, 9
   Purchase in dissolution, 19–20, 41–42
   Sale of, 19–20
Liability,
      Generally, 15–16, 48–49
   Agreements to negate, 15
   Insurance, 15
   Personal, 15, 47
Life insurance, 20, 40
Limitations on authority, 11–12, 34, 35–36
Limited,
   Admission of, 50–51
   Construed as general partner, 49–50
   Incapacity, 51
   Management and control, 49–50
   Misconduct by, 51
   Right to inspect books, 50
   Right to request dissolution, 51
   Substitution of, 50–51
   Withdrawal of, 50–51
   Voting rights, 61–62
Limited partnership, general partners, 47–48, 49
Liquidating, 20–21, 42–43, 52–53, 68
Loans, 27, 61
Management,
   Consent to acts outside of ordinary business, 11
   Duties, 33–34
   Privileges, 6
Managing, 10–11, 33–34
Meetings, 32
Misconduct by, causing dissolution, 17
Natural persons, 6
Ownership rights, 7–8
Profits,
   As contributions, 28
   Preference to, 13
   Sharing of, 12–15, 28–30
Property, 6–9
Property loaned to firm, 7, 27
Purchase of interest in dissolution, 19–20, 41–42
Remuneration, right to, 12
Reports to, 31
Restrictions in agreement, 11–12, 34, 35–36
Retirement, 38
Right to manage, 10–12
Right to property, 6–9
Salaries, 12, 28
Silent, 32
Surname in firm name, 24, 55
Surviving partner's right to property, 8–9
Taxation, 21–23
Withdrawal, 38

Partner's Interest in Partnership
See Partners

Partnerships
Agency, 5–6
Aggregate theory, 5–6
Agreement,
      Generally, 5, 24–43, 55–61, 473–498, 498–502
   Accounting method, 30, 31–32, 37
   Additional capital
     contributions, 28
   Advances, 27
   Assumption of debts, 19
   Audit, 31–32
   Bank accounts, 31
   Bankruptcy of partner, 17–18, 39
   Continuation of business, 18–20, 41–42
   Contribution in services, 26
   Contribution of profit, 28

INDEX 681

Contributions, 7–8, 26–28
Death of partner, 17, 39–40
Disputes, 35
Dissolution, 17, 37–41
Duration, 25–26
Expenses of partners, 12, 28
Expulsion, 17, 38, 473
Fiscal year, 30
Interest on contributions, 27
Liquidation, 20–21, 42–43, 52–53
Location of records, 31–32
Management duties, 11, 33–34
Management method, 33–34
Meetings, 32
Profits and losses, 12–15, 28–30
Prohibited activities, 11–12, 34, 35–36
Property loaned by partner, 7, 27
Purchase of interest, 19–20, 41–42
Purposes, 25
Reports to partners, 31
Restrictions on purposes, 25
Restrictions on partners, 11–12, 34, 35–36
Salaries, 12, 28
Title to property, 6–9
Valuing interest, 41–42
Withdrawal of contributions, 27–28
Arbitration, 35
Assets, distribution of, 20–21
Association of persons, 6
Authority of partners as agents, 10–12
Bank accounts, 31
Characteristics, 5–6
Compensation of partners, 12
Competition with, prohibited, 20
Continuation of business, 18–20, 41–42
Contributions,
 Additional capital, 26–27
 Depreciation, 22
 Interest on, 27
 Of profit, 28
 Property, 6–9
 Withdrawal, 27–28
Co-owners, 6
Corporation compared, 68
Corporations as, 6
Definition, 5–6
Dissolution,
 Generally, 5, 17, 37–41, 52–53
 Agreement to continue, 18–20, 41–42
 At will, 17
 Bankruptcy of partner, 17–18, 39
 By agreement, 17
 By operation of law, 17–18
 Causes of, 16–18, 37–41, 51–52

Compared with sole
 proprietorship, 16
Deadlock, 18
Death of a partner, 17, 39–40
Decree of court, 18
Disability of a partner, 17–18, 40–41
Expulsion of a partner, 17, 38, 473
Life insurance, 20, 40
Notice of, 20, 472
Purchasing partner's interest, 18–20, 41–42
Unlawful business, 18
Wrongful, 18
Duties of partners, 12, 32–37
Entity, 5–6
Equal vote of partners, 10, 32
Expectation of profit, 6
Expense accounts of partners, 12, 28
Formation, 24–43, 55–61
Indemnification of partners, 15, 20
Insurance,
 Cross purchase plan, 20
 Entity plan, 20
 Funding, 20
 Life of partner, 40
Interstate business, 25
Liability,
 Generally, 15–16, 48–49
 Agreements to negate, 15
 Corporation compared, 87–88
 Insurance, 15
 Marshaling of assets, 15
 Partners, 15–16
 Proprietorship contrasted, 15
Licenses, 23
Limited partnership compared, 46
Liquidation, 20–21, 42–43, 52–53
Losses, additional capital required, 26–27
Management,
 Generally, 10–12, 32–37
 Corporation compared, 74–75
 Duties, 10–11, 33–34
 Limitation on authority, 11–12, 34, 35–36
 Method of, 32–37
 Outside ordinary business, 11
 Privileges, 6
Managing partner, 10–11, 33–34
Meetings, 32
Name, 26–27
Natural persons, 6
Notice of dissolution by publication, form, 472
Partner's interest, 9–10
Place of business, 28
Profits and losses,
 Generally, 6, 12–15, 28–30

Preference, 13
Sharing, 12–15, 28–30
Property,
    Generally, 6–9, 37
    Creditors' claims, 8
    Description in agreement, 8, 37
    Division, 7–8
    Firm property, 8
    Identification, 8
    Individual property, 8, 9
    Intention of the parties, 8
    Loaned, 7
    Possession by partner, 8
    Presumptions, 8
    Rights of surviving partners, 8–9
    Sale, 8
    Tenancy in partnership, 8
    Title, 8
Records,
    Fiscal year, 30
    Location of, 31–32
    Method of accounting, 30, 31–32, 37
Rule by majority vote, 10, 33
Sale of goodwill, 11
Services, 26
Sole proprietorship contrasted, 5
Taxation,
    Generally, 21–23
    Capital gains and losses, 21–22
    Corporation compared, 89
    Depreciation, 22
    Distribution in liquidation, 22
    Informational return, 21
    Limited partnerships compared, 53
    Pre-contribution gain or loss, 22
    Sale of partner's interest, 22
    Sole proprietorship compared, 21
    Tax identification number, 23
Termination, 20–21

Patents
See Inventions

Pension Plans
    See also Incentive
        Compensation Plans and Retirement Plans
    Generally, 276–281
Age and service requirements, 278
Average benefits test, 279
Benefits, 276–277
Contribution by employer, 276
Corporations, power to pay, 74
Employer's objectives, 276
Fair Cross section test, 279
Funded, 281
Qualification, requirements for, 277–281
Ratio test, 279
Tax ramifications, generally, 277
Termination, 277
Vesting, 281

Piercing the Corporate Veil
Grounds for, 87–88, 102
Liability of shareholders, 87–88, 102

Poison pills
Generally, 351–352

Pooling Agreement
    See also Stock Voting Agreements and
        Agreements
    Generally, 300–302
Arbitration, 302
Deadlock, 302
Duration, 302
Enforcement of, 301
Issues submitted to vote, 301
Restrictions on transfer, 301
Statutory regulation, 301

Preemptive Rights
    Generally, 86, 123–124
Amendment to articles of incorporation, 344
Articles of incorporation, 123–124
Common stock, 166
Issuance of new shares, 156
Limited, 123–124
Maintenance of control, 86
Provision for, 86, 123–24

Preferred Stock
See Shares

Preincorporation Agreements
See Agreements and Corporations

Preincorporation Share Subscriptions
See Share Subscriptions

Principals
    Agency, generally, 250–251
    Duties,
        Generally, 250–251
        Compensation, 250
        Indemnification, 250
        Means of service, 250
Embarrass agent, not, 250
Interference by, 250–251

Ratification by, 251
Types of,
  Disclosed, 248
  Partially disclosed, 248
  Undisclosed, 248
Vicarious liability of, 252

Professional Corporations
Generally, 102–107
Application for registration of, 522–526
Directors, qualifications, 106
Foreign, 106–107
Fundamental changes, 106
Liability, 105
Name, 104
Professions to which available, 103
Purposes, 103–104
Shareholders, qualifications, 104–105
Structural variations, 106
Taxation, 102, 107

Profit Sharing Plans
See also Incentive Compensation Plans
Generally, 276–281
Age and service requirements, 278
Average benefits test, 279
Benefits, 276–277
Contribution by employers, 276
Corporation, power to pay, 74
Employer's objectives, 276
Fair cross section test, 279
Funded, 281
Qualification, requirements for, 277–281
Ratio test, 279
Tax ramifications, generally, 277
Termination, 277
Vesting, 281

Profits
See also Losses
Corporations, dividends, source of funds for, 232–235
Element of partnership definition, 6
Employment agreements, defined, 258
Partnership,
  Generally, 6, 12–15, 28–30
  Agreement, 6, 12–15, 28–30
  Contributed, 28
  Definition, 13
  Distribution, 12–15, 28–30
  Effect of contribution, 13
  Equal shares, 12–15, 28–30
  Preference, 13

Promoters
See also Incorporators
Agreement between, 109, 533–535
Contracts, liability, 109–110
Corporations, power to be, 73
Duties, 109–110
Organizers of a corporation, 109
Services, consideration for shares, 164–165
Share subscriptions, assignment, 110

Property
Corporations,
  Consideration for shares, 164–165
  Dividends, 233–235
  Good faith rule, 164
  Power to deal in, 70, 72–73
  True value rule, 164
  Valuation of, 164, 195
Limited partnership, contribution, 48–49
Partnership,
  Generally, 6–9, 37
  Contribution of, 30
  Creditors' claims, 8
  Division, 7–8
  Firm property, 8
  Identification, 8
  Individual property, 8, 9
  Intention of the parties, 8
  Loaned, 7–27
  Owners, 8
  Possession by partner, 8
  Presumptions, 8
  Rights of surviving partners, 8–9
  Sale, 8
  Tenancy in partnership, 8
  Title, 8
Sole proprietorship,
  Ownership, 1
  Taxation, 4

Proprietorship
See Sole Proprietorship

Proxy
Generally, 213–214
Coupled with an interest, 214
Defined, 213
Duration, 213–214
Form, 214
Regulation by statute, 213

Purposes
See Business Purposes and Corporate Purposes

Qualification
See Foreign Corporations

Quorum
See Directors; Meetings; and Shareholders

Records
Corporations,
    Shareholder's right to inspect, 85–86
    Transfer books, 136
Limited partnership, limited partner's right to
    inspect, 50
Partnership,
    Accounting method, 30, 31–32, 37
    Audit, 31–32
    Location of, 31–32

Redemption
Bonds,
    Generally, 181–182
    Discretion of directors, 182
    Notice, 182
    Price, 181–182
Shares,
    Generally, 171–174
    Articles of incorporation provision, 171–172
    Cancellation of, 174
    Insolvent corporation, 174
    Limitations upon, 174
    Sinking fund for, 172–173

Reimbursement Plans
See Expense Reimbursement Plans

Registered Agent
Appointment of, 200
Articles of incorporation, 120
Foreign corporation, 334–335
Functions, 120
Requirements for, 120
Responsibility, 120
Statement of change of, 619

Registered Office
Appointment of, 200
Articles of incorporation, 120
Foreign corporation, 334–335
Functions, 120
Requirements for, 120
Statement of change of, 619

Registrar
See Transfer Agent

Removal
    See also Directors and Officers
Directors, 77, 142, 219
Executive committees, 144
Officers, 82, 145

Reorganization
    See also Consolidation; Merger; and Sale of Assets
"A" Reorganization, 347
"B" Reorganization, 347
"C" Reorganization, 347, 354
"D" Reorganization, 354

Restated Articles of Incorporation
See Articles of Incorporation

Restrictions on Transfer
See Shareholders and Shares

Retained Earnings
Dividends, source of funds for, 233

Retirement Plans
    See also Pension Plans and Profit Sharing Plans
Corporations, power to pay, 74

Salary
    See also Compensation
Bonus, coupled with, 261
Continuation agreements, 273–275
Corporations,
    Effect on taxation, 91
    Officers, 146
Partners, 12, 28
Terms of, 257–261

Sale of Assets
Generally, 354–357
Assent by shareholders, 355–357
"B" Reorganization, 347
Bulk transfer,
    Generally, 356–357
    Affidavit, 356, 644
    Notice to creditors, 357, 643
"C" Reorganization, 347, 354
Corporation,
    Directors' duties, 81
    Dissenting shareholders, 357–358
    Shareholder approval, 85, 221–222, 356
"D" Reorganization, 354
Mortgage, 354
Pledge, 354
Procedure for, 355–356

Regular course of business, 354
Schedule of property, 356–357
Shareholder approval of, 225, 356
Statutory regulation, 354

Scrip
See Shares

Seal
See also Corporate Seal
Approval of, 193
By-law provision, 148–149

Section 1244 Stock
Effect of, 93–94
Equity capital, effect on, 94
Plan,
    Adoption of, 201–202
    Length of, 201
Requirements for, 93–94, 201–202
Small business corporation, 94, 201

Securities Act of 1933
Generally, 154

Securities Exchange Act of 1934
    Generally, 154
Capitalization of earnings, 241
Proxy regulation, 214

Security Agreement
Form, 596–597

Sell Out Agreements
See Agreements and Shareholders

Share Subscriptions
Acceptance of, 110–112, 194–196
Assignment of, 110, 194
Call, 112, 196
Default, 112
Forfeiture of, 112
Form, 111
Incorporators, 110
Payment of, 111–112, 135
Preincorporation, 110–112
Written, 110

Shareholders
Agreements between,
    Generally, 298–299
    Buy out,
        Death, 309

        Funding, 322–324
        Legally available funds, 307, 311
        Price,
            Generally, 312–319
            Adjusted stated value, 313
            Agreed, 313, 319
            Appraisal, 318–319
            Arbitration, 313, 319
            Book value, 315–316
            Firm, 313
            Formula, 316–317
            Matching Offer, 317–318
            Multiple of earnings, 314–315
    Purpose of, 304
    Restrictions on transfer
        distinguished, 306
    Security for payment, 320–321
Concentration of voting power, 299–303
Director representation, 303–304
Organizing a close corporation, form, 513–516
Pooling,
    Generally, 301–303
    Arbitration, 302
    Deadlock, 302
    Duration, 303
    Enforcement of, 301
    Issues submitted to vote, 301
    Restriction on transfer, 302
    Statutory regulation, 301
Restriction on transfer of shares,
    Bona fide offer, 305–306
    Drafting, 304–308
    Price,
        Appraisal, 318–319
        Arbitration, 313, 320
        Book value, 315–316
        Firm, 313
        Formula, 316–317
        Matching, 317–318
        Multiple of earnings, 314–315
    Notice, 311–312
    Option to corporation, 306–307
    Options to shareholders, 306–307
    Partial purchase, 308
    Prohibited, 305
    Security for payment, 320–321
    Terms of payment, 320–322
    Validity, 305
Sell out,
    Employment termination, 309–311
    Price,
        Generally, 312–319
        Adjusted stated value, 313

Agreed, 313, 319
Appraisal, 318–319
Arbitration, 313, 319
Book value, 315–316
Firm, 313
Formula, 316–317
Matching, 317–318
Multiple of earnings, 314–315
Security for payment, 320–321
Terms of payment, 320–322
Statutory authority for, 304
Stock Voting Agreement,
Generally, 310–303
Arbitration, 302
Deadlock, 302
Duration, 303
Enforcement of, 301
Issues submitted to vote, 301
Restrictions on transfer, 302
Statutory regulation, 301
Voting trust,
Generally, 300–301
Authority of trustee, 300
Contents, 300
Dividends, 301
Duration, 300
Statutory authority, 300
Voting trust certificates, 300
Amendments to articles of incorporation, approval required, 81, 221–223, 299, 344–345
Appraisal rights,
See also Right to dissent, this heading
Generally, 357–361
Approval required,
Amendments of articles, 81, 85, 221–223, 299, 344–345
Consolidation, 81, 85, 221–223, 348–350
Dissolution, 81, 85, 221–223, 362
Donations, 73
Extraordinary corporate changes, 81, 85, 221–223
Loans to employees, 73
Merger, 81, 85, 221–223, 348–350
Sale of assets, 81, 85, 221–223, 355–356
Share exchange, 81, 85, 221–223, 348–350
Articles of incorporation,
amendments to, 344–345
Authority to fix consideration for shares, 130
By-laws,
Authority to adopt, 131
Meetings, 137–140
Class voting, amendments to articles, 344–345
Close corporations,
Generally, 98–102

Agreements, 100–101
Common,
Advantages from senior securities, 184–186
Dividends, 165
Liquidation rights, 166
Preemptive rights, 166
Voting rights, 165–166
Compensation, approval of, 80
Consent to action, 223–225
Consideration for shares, authority to fix, 130
Consolidation, approval of, 81, 85, 221–223, 348–350
Control, close corporations, 100–101
Control of by-law, 80, 131
Cumulative voting, 84, 217–221
Dissenters' rights, 357–361
Dissolution,
Approval of, 81, 85, 221–223, 360
Distributions to, 245–246
Involuntary, 365–366
Notification of, 362
Statement of intent to dissolve, 645–647
Statement of revocation of proceedings, 648–650
Voluntary, 361–364
Revocation of, 364
Dividends, record date, 236
Election of directors, 84, 217–221
Election of officers, 80
Holder of record, 82–83
Informal action, 140, 223–225
Liability, 87–89
Liquidation, distributions in, 245–246, 366–368
Majority, oppression of minority, 299
Management,
Close corporations, 100–101
Power, 75–76
Meetings,
Generally, 208–216
Action without, 140, 223–225
Amendment to articles of incorporation, 221–223
Annual, 137, 208
Business, 216–223
Call of, 209
Consent of action, 140, 223–225
Consolidation, approval of, 222
Cumulative voting, 217–221
Dissolution, approval of, 222
Election judges, 216
Election of directors, 217–221
Frequency, 208–209
Location of, 138, 209
Merger, approval of, 222
Minutes, form, 605–606
Necessity for, 188
Notice,

Generally, 138, 209–213,
Content, 210–211
Delivery of, 210–212
Persons entitled to, 138, 209–210
Record date, 138–139, 120
Waiver of, 212–213
Proxy,
Coupled with an interest, 214
Duration, 213–214
Quorum, 139, 215
Sales of assets, approval of, 222
Special, 137–138, 208–209
Voting of shares, 139, 215–216
Weighted voting, 215
Merger, approval of, 81, 85, 221–223, 355–356
Minority,
Protection of, 299, 303
Representation on board, 218, 303
Organizational meeting, 134
Ownership rights, 82–83
Pooling agreement, 215, 301–303
Preemptive rights, 86, 123–124
Preferred,
Generally, 166–175
Conversion privilege, 174–175
Dissolution distributions, 245–246
Dividends,
Generally, 166–168
Cumulative, 167
Cumulative to the extent earned, 168
Non-cumulative, 167–168
Treatment in liquidation, 245–246
Liquidation preferences, 168–169
Participating dividends, 168
Participating liquidation preferences, 169
Voting rights, 169–170
Professional corporations,
qualifications, 104–105
Proxies,
Generally, 139, 213–216
Defined, 139, 213
Quorum, 139, 215
Removal of directors, 77–78, 84, 219
Right to dissent,
Generally, 357–361
Dissolution, 362
Exceptions to, 359
Exclusivity, 361
Less than all shares, 358
Procedure for, 358–361
Value of shares, 359
When available, 357–358
Rights,
Dividends, 86–87, 233

Election of directors, 84, 217–221
Inspection of corporate books, 85
Liquidation, 83, 86–87
Preemptive, 86, 123–124
Removal of director, 77–78, 84, 219
Vote, 83
Salaries, 91
Sale of assets, approval of, 81, 85, 221–223, 355–356
Sale of shares to corporation, 241–244
Share exchange, approval of, 81, 85, 221–223, 348–350
Stock options, approval of, 285
Subchapter S election, 205
Voting of shares, 131, 139–140, 298–299
Voting power, concentrated, 299–304
Voting trust, 300–301

Shares
Accounting classifications, 155–56
Appraisal rights, 357–361
Articles of incorporation, 118–120, 159–163
Assessable, 156
Assets, 155
Authority to issue, 194
Authorized, 155
Blank stock, 162
Buy-out agreements, generally, 304–305, 309
Call, 196
Cancellation of,
Generally, 174, 243
Procedure for, 243
Statement of, 594–595, 607–608
Certificates for,
Generally, 158–159
Approval of, 193
By-law provision, 147–148
Contents of, 159
Execution by officers, 82, 158–159
Facsimile signature, 159
Forms, 579–586
Signed by, 82, 158–159
Classes,
Generally, 159–163
Articles of incorporation, 118–120, 159–163
Certificates for, 158
Changes in, 344
Conversion privilege, 174–175
Statement of variations, 161
Statutory authority for, 161
Voting, 169–171, 344–345
Common stock,
Generally, 120–122, 165–166
Advantages of senior securities, 184–186
Liquidation rights, 166

Preemptive rights, 166
Right to dividends, 165
Voting rights, 165–166
Consideration for,
    Generally, 156–158, 163–165
    Authority to fix, 130, 156–157
    Cash, 164, 195
    Future services, 164
    Good faith rule, 164
    Promissory notes, 164
    Property, 164, 195
    Services, 164
    True value rule, 164
Conversion,
    Generally, 174–175
    Articles of incorporation provision, 175
Corporation's power to own, 73
Debt to equity ratio, 186
Diluted, 157
Discount, 156
Dividends, generally, 229–239
Earnings, 155
Fractions,
    Generally, 163
    Authority to issue, 163
    Rights of, 163
    Vote, 215
Franchise fees, 157
Fully paid, 165
Issuance of,
    Generally, 81, 155–156
    Consideration received, 163–165
    Preemptive rights, 156
    Preferred stock, 166–167
No par value,
    Generally, 156–158
    Consideration for, 164
    Decision to issue, 119–120
    Discouraged, 119
    Effect on share dividends, 238
    Stock split, effect on, 240
Options, see Stock Options
Outstanding, 155
Ownership interest, 155
Par value,
    Generally, 156–158
    Consideration for, 164
    Decision to issue, 119–120
    Effect on share dividends, 238
    Stock split, effect on, 240
Preferred,
    Generally, 160–163, 166–175
    Advantages, 160–161
    As senior securities, 184–186
    Conversion privilege, 174–175
    Dividends,
        Generally, 167–168
        Cumulative, 167
        Cumulative to the extent earned, 168
        Non-cumulative, 167
    Liquidation preferences, 168–169
    Non-cumulative dividends, 167
    Participating dividends, 168
    Participating liquidation preferences, 169
    Practical considerations, 160–161
    Statutory authority for, 161
    Voting rights, 161, 169–170
Purchase by corporation,
    Generally, 129–130, 158, 241–244
    Cancellation of, 243
    Designating shareholders, 243
    Legally available funds, 242, 307, 311
    Mandatory buy out, 309–311
    Mandatory sell out, 309–311
    Restrictions upon, 242
Reacquisition of, 171–174
Redemption rights,
    Generally, 171–174
    Articles of incorporation provision, 171–172
    Cancellation of shares, 174
    Insolvent corporation, 174
    Limitations upon, 174
    Sinking fund, 172–173
Repurchase of, 129–130, 158, 241–244
Restrictions on transfer,
    Generally, 304–308
    Drafting, 304–308
    Notice, 311–312
    Option to corporation, 306
    Option to shareholders, 306–307
    Partial purchase, 308
    Pooling agreement, 301–303
    Price,
        Generally, 312–319
        Adjusted stated value, 313
        Appraisal, 318–319
        Arbitration, 313, 319
        Book value, 315–316
        Firm, 313
        Matching, 317–318
        Multiple of earnings, 314–315
    Prohibited, 304
    Security for payment, 320–321
    Terms of payment, 320–322
    Validity, 304
Return on investment, 153–154

Rights and options, 130
Scrip,
    Authority to create, 163
    Exchange of, 163
    Rights of, 163
Sell out agreements, generally, 309–311
Senior securities, 184–186
Series,
    Generally, 161–163
    Compared to classes, 161
    Resolution, 162
    Resolution establishing form, 593–595
    Statement of variations, 162
    Statutory authority for, 162
    Variations in, 162
Special features, description of, 118
Splits, see Stock Splits
Statement of cancellation, 174
Stock transfer ledger, 176
Subscriptions, see Share Subscriptions
Taxation, 164, 186
Thin incorporation, 186
Transfer, authority, 147–148
Transfer agent,
    Generally, 176–177
    By-law provision, 148
    Duties, 176
    Stock transfer ledger, 176
Transfer books, closing of, 210
Treasury,
    Authorized and issued, 156
    Determining a quorum, 156
Value of, 81
Voting, 154, 155, 215–216
Watered, 156

Sinking Fund
Redemption of shares, 172–174

Sole Proprietorship
Agents of, 3–4
Business in other jurisdictions, 4
Corporation compared, 68
Death of proprietor, 2
Employees, 1, 4
Financing, 2
Formation, 3–4
Governmental regulation, 4
Liability,
    Generally, 2
    Control over, 2
    Corporation compared, 2, 68
    Limited by agreement, 2
    Limited by insurance, 2
    Partnership compared, 2, 15
    Personal assets, 2
Licensing, 4
Liquidation upon death, 2
Management,
    Generally, 1
    Ability, 1
    Corporation compared, 74
Personal identity, 1
Property,
    Ownership, 1
    Taxation, 3
Taxation,
    Generally, 3
    Advantages, 3
    Corporation compared, 3, 89
    Individual rates, 3
    Losses offset against income, 4
    Partnership compared, 21
    Planning, 4
    Property, 4

State Statutes
    See also other specific topics
Bonds, regulation of, 177
Close corporations, 98–102
Corporate powers, 70–74
Corporations, taxation, 90
Effect on corporate form, 68–70
Effect on shareholders' ownership rights, 83
Modified by articles of incorporation, 124
Permissive, 69
Professional corporations, 102–107

Stated Capital
Cancellation of shares, 243
Consideration for shares, effect on, 119, 156–158
Defined, 231
Share dividends, 238–239
Stock splits, 240–241

Statement of Intent to Dissolve
    See also Dissolution
Effect of, 362
Filing of, 363

Stock
See Shares

Stock Option Plans
    See also Incentive Compensation Plans
    Generally, 282–289

Adjustment for changes in capitalization, 288
Adoption of, 282–283
Allotment of shares, 288
Consideration for option, 289
Defined, 282
Exercise, 282
Incentive factors, 282
Modification of terms, 288
Option price, 282–283, 286
Payment for stock, 289
Preemptive rights, effect on, 86–87
Qualification of,
    Generally, 283–287
  Deceased employee, 284
  Employees covered, 284
  Event of termination, 284
  Identification of shares, 283
  Limitation of share ownership, 286–287
  Number of shares, 283
  Option price, 286
  Outstanding prior options, 286–287
  Shareholder approval, 285
  Termination, 285
Qualified,
  Administration of plans, 287–289
  Date of grant, 285
  Duration of, 285
  Holding period, 283
  Surtax, 283
  Tax rates, 283
  Tax Reform Act, 283
  Taxable event, 283
Registered securities, 289
Regulated by articles of incorporation, 130
Shareholder approval of, 285
Tax ramifications, 282–283
Transferability, 287

Stock Splits
    Generally, 239–241
Capitalization of earnings, 241
Procedure for, 240–241
Stock dividends compared, 240
Stock options, effect on, 288

Stock Transfer Ledger
Holders of record, 82–83

Stock Voting Agreement
  See also, Agreements; Pooling Agreement; Voting Trust
    Generally, 300–302
  Arbitration, 302

Deadlock, 302
Duration, 302
Enforcement of, 301
Issues submitted to vote, 301
Restrictions on transfer, 301
Statutory regulation, 301

Stockholders
See Shareholders

Subchapter S Election
Adoption, 202–203
Effect of, 91–93
Election, definition of, 202–203
Period for election, 92
Qualifications for, 92, 203
Shareholder consent, 92, 203
Small business corporation, 92, 203
Termination of, 92–93

Subscriptions
See Share Subscriptions

Subsidiary Corporations
Name savers, 115
Piercing the corporate veil, 87–88, 102

Surplus
  See also Capital Surplus and Earned Surplus
Defined, 231

Takeovers
  Generally, 351–354
  Affiliated corporation rules, 353–354
  Control share statutes, 353
  Hostile, 351–354
  People pills, 353
  Poison pills, 352
  Reasons for, 351–352
  Structural defenses, 352

Taxation
"A" Reorganization, 349
"B" Reorganization, 347
"C" Reorganization, 347, 354
"D" Reorganization, 354
Compensation, deferred, 273–274
Corporations,
    Generally, 89–95, 112–113
  Accumulated profits, 91
  Double taxation, 3, 90–91, 237
  Establishment of series shares, 162
  Foreign, 336

Franchise tax, 93, 157
Fringe benefits, 94–95
Organizational tax, 93, 193
Partial liquidation, 244
Professional, 102
Qualified incentive plans, 94–95
Sale of stock, 320
Section 1244 plan, 93–94, 201–202
Separate entity, 89–91
State income tax, 93, 112–113
Subchapter S election, 91–93, 202–203
Dividends,
   Cash, 233
   Property, 233
   Reports required, 235
   Share dividends, 237–239
Limited partnerships,
   Corporation compared, 54
   General partnership compared, 53
   Management scheme, 54
Partial liquidations, 244
Partnership,
     Generally, 21–23
   Capital gains and losses, 22
   Depreciation, 22
   Distribution in liquidation, 23
   Informational return, 21
   Pre-contribution gain or loss, 22
   Property, 7
   Sale of partner's interest, 22
   Sole proprietorship compared, 21
   Tax identification number, 23
Profit sharing plans, qualified, 277
Section 1244 stock, plan for issuance, 93–94, 201–202, 511–513
Sole proprietorship,
     Generally, 3
   Advantages, 3
   Corporation compared, 3, 89
   Individual tax rates, 3
   Losses offset against income, 3
   Partnership compared, 21
   Planning, 3
   Property, 3
Stock options,
     Generally, 282–283
   Holding period, 283
   Qualification of,
     Generally, 283–287
     Rates, 283
     Surtax, 283
     Taxable event, 283
     Tax Reform Act, 283
Subchapter S election, 91–93, 202–203
Thin incorporation, 186

Tenancy in Common
Tenancy in partnership compared, 8

Tenancy in Partnership
   See also Partnerships and Property
Creditors' claims, 8
Possession of property, 8
Sale of property, 8
Surviving partners, 8
Tenancy in common compared, 8

Termination
   See also Dissolution
Limited partnership,
   Acts of general partners, 47, 51
   By agreement, 51–52
   Causes of, 51
   Limited partners' request, 51
   Misconduct by limited partner, 47, 51
   Right to continue business, 52
Partnership,
     Generally, 16–18, 37–41
   Agreement to continue, 18–20, 41–42
   At will, 17
   Bankruptcy of partner, 17–18, 39
   By agreement, 17
   By operation of law, 17–18
   By remaining partners, 17
   Causes of, 16–18, 37–41, 51–52
   Continuation of business, 21–22
   Deadlock, 18
   Death of a partner, 17, 39–40
   Decree of court, 18
   Disability of a partner, 17–18, 40–41
   Expulsion of a partner, 17, 38, 473
   Life insurance, 20, 40
   Liquidation and winding-up, 20–21, 42–43
   Notice of, 20, 472
   Purchasing interest, 18–20, 41–42
   Sole proprietorship compared, 16
   Unlawful business, 18
   Wrongful, 18

Thin Incorporation
Generally, 186

Trade Name
   See also Assumed Name
Abandonment of, California, 470
Affidavits, 4

Business certificate, New York, 469
Filing, 4
Limited partnership, 54–55
No deceptive similarities, 4
Partnership, 23
Publication, 4, 467–468
Sole proprietorship, 4
Statement, California, 465–466

Trade Secrets
Common law protection of, 267
Customer list, 268
Definitions of, 267
Liquidated damages for a disclosure, 268
Non-disclosure agreement, form, 609
Prohibition against divulging, partnerships, 20
Protection of, generally, 267–268

Transacting Business
See Foreign Corporations

Transfer Agent
Generally, 176–177
Authority delegated by directors, 176
By-law provisions, 148
Duties, 176
Instructions from officers, 176
Registrar, duties compared, 176
Stock transfer ledger, 176

Treasury Shares
Authorized and issued, 155
Cancellation of, 129–130, 243
Dividends, 155
Power to purchase, 129, 242
Preemptive rights, 123–124
Purchase of shares by corporation, 241–244
Quorum, effect on, 155
Restrictions on surplus, 242–243
Restrictions upon, 129–130
Share dividends, used as, 238
Vote, 155

Trust Indenture
See also Bonds and Indenture
Form, 598–603

Ultra Vires Act
Corporate purposes effect upon, 122–123

Unfair Competition
Corporations, name, 113–114

Vacancies
See also Directors
Directors, 77, 142
Executive committee, 144
Officers, 82, 145

Voting Trust
Generally, 300–301
Agreement, form, 610–615
Authority of trustee, 300
Contents, 300
Dividends, 300
Function of, 215, 300
Statutory authority, 300
Term, 300
Trustee, 300
Voting trust certificates, 300

Winding-Up
See Liquidation

Work Product
See Employment Agreements and Inventions